The Waite Group®
Windows Programming Primer Plus™

Jim Conger

WAITE GROUP PRESS™
Corte Madera, California

Editorial Director • Scott Calamar
Development Editor • Mitchell Waite
Content Editor • Harry Henderson
Technical Reviewer • David Calhoun
Managing Editor • John Crudo
Design and Production • Barbara Gelfand
Illustrations • Pat Rogondino and Max Seabaugh
Cover Design • Michael Rogondino
Production Manager • Julianne Ososke

© 1992 by The Waite Group, Inc.
Published by Waite Group Press, 200 Tamal Plaza, Corte Madera, CA 94925.

Waite Group Press is distributed to bookstores and book wholesalers by Publishers Group West, Box 8843, Emeryville, CA 94662, 1-800-788-3123 (in California 1-510-658-3453).

All rights reserved. No part of this manual shall be reproduced, stored in a retrieval system, or transmitted by any means, electronic, mechanical, photocopying, desktop publishing, recording, or otherwise, without permission from the publisher. No patent liability is assumed with respect to the use of the information contained herein. While every precaution has been taken in the preparation of this book, the publisher and author assume no responsibility for errors or omissions. Neither is any liability assumed for damages resulting from the use of the information contained herein.

All terms mentioned in this book that are known to be registered trademarks, trademarks or service marks are listed below. All other product names are trademarks and registered trademarks of their respective owners. In addition, terms suspected of being trademarks or service marks have been appropriately capitalized. Waite Group Press cannot attest to the accuracy of this information. Use of a term in this book should not be regarded as affecting the validity of any registered trademark, trademark, or service mark.

The Waite Group and Primer Plus are registered trademarks of The Waite Group, Inc.
Waite Group Press is a trademark of The Waite Group, Inc.
Microsoft and MS-DOS are registered trademarks of Microsoft Corporation.
Windows is a trademark of Microsoft Corporation.
Borland, Borland C++, and Turbo C++ for Windows are registered trademarks of Borland
    International, Inc.
PostScript is a registered trademark of Adobe Systems Incorporated.
HP and LaserJet are registered trademarks of Hewlett-Packard Co.
LaserJet IIP is a trademark of Hewlett-Packard Co.

Printed in the United States of America
92 93 94 95 • 10 9 8 7 6 5 4 3 2 1

Conger, Jim
    Windows programming primer plus / Jim Conger
        p. cm.
    Includes bibliographical references and index.
    ISBN: 1-878739-21-2: $29.95
    1. Windows (Computer programs) I. Title.
QA76.76.W56C672   1992
005.4'3--dc20   92-23486
                                                                 CIP

To Robert and Scott

Acknowledgments

This book was written during a period of rapid evolution of both Microsoft Windows and Windows programming tools. The book was started using Windows 3.0 and command line compilers from Borland and Microsoft. By the time the book was complete, Windows had gone through several beta test releases and evolved into Windows 3.1. Microsoft's QuickC for Windows and Borland's Turbo C++ for Windows were also released, greatly reducing the complexity of writing Windows applications.

Writing a book on programming is always a challenge, but writing while the foundations of Windows were continually being revamped was doubly difficult. I am indebted to a number of people, employees both of Microsoft and Borland, as well as private individuals, who took the time to answer my questions and kept me up-to-date with the latest tools and techniques. David Fang, David Schneider, Paul Yau, David D'Souza, David Flenninken, Joe Wikert, Paul Stafford, Dan Boone, and may other users of the WINBTDEV forum on CompuServe all contributed. I would also like to thank Harry Henderson, who edited the book and provided substantial input as to its content and design. Finally, I would like to thank Mitchell Waite, who proposed the book, suffered through the initial drafts and proposals, and championed the project from start to finish.

Dear Reader:

One glance at most Windows books on the market would have you believe that the learning curve to write Windows programs can be insurmountable. You need to: know internally how Windows is structured, master a programming language such as C or C++, learn various resource compilers, linkers, and tools, understand almost a thousand API's, be comfortable with a state-of-the-art debugger—it's overwhelming. It was clear to us the world needed a Primer on Windows programming.

One of the first mountains a Windows programmer has to climb is what language to program Windows in, C or C++? And what products: Borland or Microsoft? Our feeling was that it was too much to expect a programmer to learn Object Oriented Programming in C++ AND Windows at the same time. Sure C++ is a hot language, but most programmers are still coming up to speed on it. Not a great time to learn a new environment too. But most programmers do know C; so we chose that as the lingua franca for this book. It allows you to focus on the Windows environment, rather than the language. Since we could not be sure what platform you would want, and since they are all good performers, we chose to use almost all of the big ones: Turbo C++, Borland C++, and QuickC for Windows.

Study Windows programming books further and you'll be daunted by the length of the example programs. Most Chapter One "Hello Windows" source code examples are two pages and 100+ lines. So I whined to author Jim Conger about this for days and was later floored when Jim uploaded the most reduced Windows program I'd ever seen. He was able to create a window that displays "Hello World" in only 17 lines of code. And the part of the code that was actual Windows calls was only six lines. Perfect!

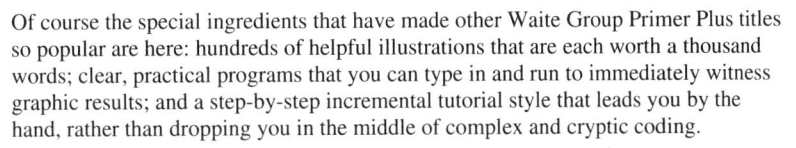

Of course the special ingredients that have made other Waite Group Primer Plus titles so popular are here: hundreds of helpful illustrations that are each worth a thousand words; clear, practical programs that you can type in and run to immediately witness graphic results; and a step-by-step incremental tutorial style that leads you by the hand, rather than dropping you in the middle of complex and cryptic coding.

If you like Jim Conger's *Windows Programming Primer Plus*, you might like to get his *Windows API Bible*, the definitive reference to all Windows API functions. It is the perfect computer-side companion for your programming hours. We publish two Visual Basic books; the *Visual Basic How-To* and the *Visual Basic SuperBible*, if you'd rather program in the more graphic Visual Basic language than in C.

A catalog of our titles can be obtained by filling out our reader response card, found in this book. Thanks again for considering the purchase of this title. If you care to tell me anything you like (or don't like) about the book, please use our reader response card.

Sincerely,

Mitchell Waite

Mitchell Waite
Publisher

WAITE GROUP
PRESS™

200 Tamal Plaza   Corte Madera   California   94925   415-924-2575   Fax 415-924-2576

About the Author

Jim Conger began programming in 1972 while studying Engineering at the University of Southern California. He has been writing programs ever since for a variety of computers. Most of his early work was done on mainframe computer systems using FORTRAN and BASIC for process simulation work. Jim started programming microcomputers in the early 1980s while living in London. These projects were primarily financial models, using BASIC, Pascal, and assembly language. His first C programs were written in 1983 while under the CP/M operating system, and he has continued using C and C++ under MS-DOS and Windows.

Jim's hobby of playing woodwind instruments lead to his interest in computer music. He is the author of two books on the subject, *C Programming for MIDI* (M&T Books, 1988), and *MIDI Sequencing in C* (M&T Book, 1989). His most recent book is *The Waite Group's Windows API Bible* (Waite Group Press, 1992). Jim lives in California with his wife and two children.

Introduction

Microsoft Windows has been around since 1985. This is remarkable because the computer hardware needed to effectively run Windows did not become broadly available until about 1988. Microsoft had the vision to continue the development of Windows, and Windows application programs like Excel, long before the market developed. This vision paid off in 1990, with the tremendous success of Windows 3.0.

At the time of writing, Windows has become "the" programming environment for the PC family of computers. This is great for PC users, but demands a lot from programmers. Besides needing to know how to use a programming language such as C or C++, the novice programmer is confronted with the Windows API (Application Programming Interface) with over 600 functions, 200 messages, and a wide range of unfamiliar terms and concepts. To make matters worse, Windows programs are structured completely differently from conventional programs that run under DOS.

Despite these obstacles, Windows programs are not difficult to create, once the basic principles are understood. The purpose of this book is to provide a painless introduction to Windows programming. This goal has become much easier to realize with the introduction of superb Windows programming tools such as Microsoft's QuickC for Windows, and Borland's Turbo C++ for Windows. These tools automate many of the mundane details, leaving the programmer free to concentrate on the program itself. (You can also use the more conventional command-line compilers provided with Borland C++ 3.0 and Microsoft C++ 7.0. Techniques for using these tools are discussed in Appendix 2.)

Although other languages can be used, Windows development today is done almost exclusively with the C and C++ programming languages. In this book the reader is assumed to be familiar with the C language, but not an expert. Special attention is given to reviewing the parts of the C language that you may not have used before, such as data structures and the compiler pre-processor. Creating the programs in this book will help improve your C language skills because Windows makes full use of the language. Turbo C++, which is also sold as part of Borland C++, and the Microsoft QuickC compilers are shown in the examples. Although the C++ compilers are fully supported, the examples use standard C, without the C++ extensions.

The chapters are arranged in order of difficulty. Chapter 1 provides an overall discussion of how Windows works. This includes the outline of the way Windows is able to run more than one program at a time, and how Windows programs make use of the Windows environment for many tasks. The concept of Windows messages is introduced. The different elements of Windows programs, such as the separation of program instructions and data, are also covered as preparation for compiling the first program.

Chapter 2 concentrates on setting up your computer to write and compile Windows programs. Turbo C++ for Windows and QuickC for Windows are used as examples. The computer setup is tested by writing, compiling, and running a very short Windows program. A common criticism of Windows is that the smallest Windows program requires "over 400 lines of code." This simply is not true. The first Windows program presented in Chapter 2 requires 17 lines of code, of which only five lines are executable statements.

Chapter 3 starts with this simple Windows program, and improves it in three steps to create a complete Windows application. Each step is fully explained, allowing the reader to see what each of the specialized Windows functions accomplishes. This approach is different from most Windows tutorials, which start out with a fairly lengthy "first" program. The stepwise approach, building up to the full program, gives the reader a chance to see clearly how the different parts of a Windows program operate.

Windows' extensive graphics functions are introduced in Chapter 4. The initial examples focus on output of text, followed by painting objects such as rectangles and ellipses. Painting brings up the subject of how Windows programs update the center of each program's window, which is important in an environment where one program's window can be covered up by another program. The last program in Chapter 4 demonstrates animated graphics, producing a ball that continually bounces around inside the program's window.

Windows controls, such as buttons, scroll bars, and list boxes, are discussed in Chapter 5. Controls are the building blocks of most applications. These ready-to-use tools are a big savings in programmer's time when writing for the Windows environment. Each type of control is demonstrated with a separate example program. The examples also introduce exchanging message data between separate parts of a Windows program.

Chapter 6 focuses on the mouse. Many mouse function are built into Windows' default logic for window controls. Sometimes it is necessary to deal more directly with the mouse. Examples that track the mouse and change the mouse cursor shape are provided. The latter is also used to introduce menus that include drop-down (popup) menus with additional items.

Chapter 7 discusses the Windows character set, character fonts, and dealing with the keyboard. Windows uses a different character set than DOS, so the distinction between the two character sets is important, particularly if you are writing programs that may be translated into different languages. Several techniques for dealing with character fonts are covered, again using example programs.

Child and popup windows are discussed in Chapter 8. They are small windows that can be used for utility functions within a program. Creating child and popup windows provides insight into how the Windows environment manages the screen and separates activities between different running programs. The examples in Chapter 8 also demonstrate the important programming technique of sending messages between different window elements of the same program.

Chapters 9 through 11 focus on different types of resource data that Windows programs use to store information. Chapter 9 covers menus, including menus with multiple levels of "popup" menus, and menu items consisting of bitmap pictures. Chapter 10 discusses dialog boxes. Windows provides partial automation in creating dialog box windows using dialog box editors. Both the Microsoft and Borland versions of the dialog box editor are discussed, with step-by-step examples. Several versions of each dialog box function are used in examples, showing the advantages of new features in the

3.0 and 3.1 versions of Windows that are often overlooked. Chapter 11 covers the remaining resource types, such as storing character strings and other data in the program's resource data.

Chapter 12 covers Windows' memory management functions. Windows includes sophisticated memory management functions, which can be used to allocate blocks of memory for use by the application. The chapter discusses how to use fixed, moveable, and discardable memory blocks. Chapter 13 looks at Windows' graphics functions in more detail, focusing on the role of the "device context" settings in controlling the size and position of the finished output. This leads to the discussion of using the printer in Chapter 14. The examples using the printer show how to allow the user to set up the printer and to cancel a printer job while it is in progress.

Disk file operations are discussed in Chapter 15. Windows takes advantage of the DOS file system for disk file access, so many of these functions will be familiar if the reader has programmed under DOS. This chapter includes an example editor and a file selection dialog box, which is used several times in later chapters.

Chapter 16 covers bitmaps, which are one of Windows' techniques for storing graphical data. The examples demonstrate displaying bitmaps, stretching and shrinking bitmap images, using various binary operations when copying a bitmap to the screen, and drawing on the bitmap image in memory. The latter is a technique used in animating drawings, which is demonstrated with an example which animates an image using two different drawing techniques.

The Windows clipboard is discussed in Chapter 17. The clipboard allows different Windows applications to exchange data, usually via cut and paste operations. Examples are given using the clipboard to exchange text, graphics, and user-defined data. The simple text editor developed in Chapter 15 is also expanded to include cut, copy, and paste operations.

Chapter 18 concludes the book with a discussion of dynamic link libraries (DLLs). DLLs provide the Windows programmer with the ability to store frequently used functions in libraries, which can be accessed by more than one program during a single Windows session. Besides being a useful programming tool, creating a DLL provides insights into how Windows works internally, as most of the Windows environment consists of functions residing in DLLs.

You will find that a reference book that explains the syntax of all of the Windows functions and messages is useful, particularly as you approach the end of this book. Either the *Microsoft Windows Software Development Kit Reference* or the *Waite Group's Windows API Bible* will do nicely. The latter includes example programs that document all of the functions and messages common to Windows versions 3.0 and 3.1. After completing this text, you will have experience with the elements of Windows that are used in most applications. You will have created programs with animated graphics and written your own simple word processor. The examples should provide starting points for a wide variety of programs.

Good luck with your Windows projects!

Jim Conger

Contents

Acknowledgments		x
Introduction		xi
Chapter 1	*How Windows Works*	1-22
Chapter 2	*Setting Up Your System*	23-42
Chapter 3	*First Programming Experiments*	43-82
Chapter 4	*Text And Graphics Output*	83-122
Chapter 5	*Window Controls*	123-182
Chapter 6	*Taming The Mouse*	183-212
Chapter 7	*Character Sets, Fonts, and the Keyboard*	213-252
Chapter 8	*Child And Popup Windows*	253-282
Chapter 9	*Menus*	283-322
Chapter 10	*Dialog Boxes*	323-374
Chapter 11	*Other Resources*	375-400
Chapter 12	*Managing Memory*	401-442
Chapter 13	*The Device Context*	443-472
Chapter 14	*Printing*	473-522
Chapter 15	*Disk File Access*	523-560
Chapter 16	*Bitmaps*	561-598
Chapter 17	*The Clipboard*	599-642
Chapter 18	*Dynamic Link Libraries*	643-680
Conclusion		682
Appendix A	*Virtual Key Codes*	683-685
Appendix B	*Using Command Line Compilers and the MAKE Utility*	686-689
Appendix C	*Glossary*	690-695
Appendix D	*Bibliography*	696-697
Index		698-714

Contents

Acknowledgments x

Introduction xi

Chapter 1: How Windows Works 1
    What Is Microsoft Windows? 1
    The Advantages of Windows 3
    How Windows Programs Work 3
    Running Several Programs Simultaneously 5
    Messages 7
    An Analogy 10
    The Structure of a Windows Program 10
    Code and Resources 12
    Program Instances 13
    Compiling a Windows Program 14
    Windows Memory Management 16
        Memory Options 17
        Stacks and Heaps 18
        An Example Module Definition File 20
    Summary 21
    Questions 22
    Answers to Questions 22

Chapter 2: Setting Up Your System 23
    What You Will Need 24
        Hardware: 24
        Software: 24
        Installing Turbo C++ For Windows 26
        Setup Options for Turbo C++ 27
        Installing Microsoft QuickC for Windows 31
        Microsoft QuickC Setup 32
    Creating The World's Shortest Windows Program 33
        Creating a Project File 36
        Compiling and Running MINIMAL 37
    Common Problems in Compiling and Their Solutions 38
        Typos in the C Program 38
        Typos in the Module Definition File 40
        Setup Problems 40
        Other Errors 41
    Summary 41
    Questions 42
    Answers 42

Chapter 3: First Programming Experiments 43
The WINDOWS.H 44
The WinMain() Functions 46
Hungarian Notation 48
WinMain() Parameters 50
Creating The Program's Window 51
Messages 54
Adding a Message Loop 54
Creating a New Windows Class 61
    Separate Message Processing 62
    Creating a New Window Class 64
    The Style Member of WNDCLASS 64
    Extra Memory Blocks for Windows 65
    Icon, Cursor, and Background Brush 65
    The Menu Name and Class Name 65
    Registering the Window Class 66
    Exporting the WndProc Function Name 66
Message Processing Function—WndProc() 67
    Compiling MINIMAL3 69
Adding Custom Resource Data 70
    Header Files 71
    Creating a Program Icon 71
    Defining a Menu 72
Compiling the Resource Data 73
    Remaining MINIMAL4 Program Files 74
    Passing a Command Line Argument 77
Summary 78
Questions 79
Exercises 80
Answers to Questions 80
Solutions to Exercises 81

Chapter 4: Text and Graphics Output 83
Character Mode Versus Graphics Mode 84
The Device Context 85
Windows GDI 85
Text Output 86
The WM_PAINT Message 90
Changing the Device Context 95
Device Context Settings 100
Graphics Output 101
Animated Graphics 107
The Peek Message() Loop 108

Summary 115
Questions 115
Exercises 116
Answers to Questions 117
Solutions to Exercises 117

Chapter 5: Window Controls 123
What Is a Window? 124
Types of Window Controls 125
The CreateWindow() Function 126
Static Controls 130
Sending a Message to a Control 136
C Language Casts 138
Button Controls 139
Processing Button Control Messages 145
Button Notification Codes 148
List Boxes 149
Combo Boxes 156
Scroll Bars 161
Scroll Bars Attached To A Window 168
Edit Controls 172
Summary 178
Questions 179
Exercises 179
Answers to Questions 180
Solutions to Exercises 180

Chapter 6: Taming The Mouse 183
The WM_MOUSEMOVE 184
Notification Codes with WM_MOUSEMOVE 185
Mouse Button Messages 187
The MOUSE1 Program 189
The Input Focus 193
Nonclient Mouse Messages 194
Capturing the Mouse 195
Changing the Mouse Cursor Shape 200
The Caret 203
Experimenting With Cursor Shapes and the Caret 204
Summary 208
Questions 210
Exercises 210
Answers to Questions 211
Solutions to Exercises 211

xiii

Chapter 7: Character Sets, Fonts, and the Keyboard 213
The ANSI Character Set 215
Trying the Character Functions 217
Keyboard Message Processing 221
The WM_CHAR Message 223
System Key Messages and Dead Characters 224
Implementing a Simple Keyboard Interface 228
Selecting a Stock Font 229
Using Logical Fonts 230
Text Metrics 234
Putting Fonts To Work 235
Keyboard Accelerators 240
The FONT2 Program 242
Summary 248
Questions 250
Exercises 250
Answers to Questions 251
Solutions to Exercises 251

Chapter 8: Child and Popup Windows 253
Creating a Child Window 254
Sending Messages to Child Windows 259
Fixed Child Windows 266
Popup Windows 273
The Big Picture 277
Summary 278
Questions 279
Exercises 279
Answers to Questions 280
Solutions to Exercises 280

Chapter 9: Menus 283
Creating Menus 285
Menus Defined as Resource Data 285
    Menu Loading and Memory Options 287
    Menu Items 288
    Popup Menus 289
    Menu Item Options 290
Creating a Menu Using the Borland Resource Workshop 292
An Example with a Complex Menu 296
    Menu Functions 299
    Other Files for MENU1 301
    Determining Menu Item Status 301
Creating a Menu as the Program Operates 302

The MENU2 Program 304
    Creating a Menu Containing Bitmaps 305
    Other MENU2 Files 306
The System Menu 311
    An Example That Changes the System Menu 313
    Setting a Timer 313
    SYSMENU Program Files 315
Summary 319
Questions 320
Exercises 320
Answers to Questions 321
Solutions to Exercises 321

Chapter 10: Dialog Boxes 323
What Is A Dialog Box 324
How Dialog Boxes Work 325
    Dialog Base Units 327
    Compiling a Dialog Box 327
Designing a Dialog Box 327
    Using the Microsoft Dialog Editor 328
    Using the Borland Resource Workshop Dialog Editor 331
Using the Dialog Box 335
    DIALG1.C 336
    The Dialog Box Function 339
Exchanging Data with a Dialog Box—Global Variable Method 341
    Creating the DIALG2 Dialog Box 341
    Creating the DIALG2.C Program 342
    Working with Controls in a Dialog Box Function 346
    Other Files for the DIALG2 Program 347
Problems with Using Global Variables 348
Exchanging Data with a Dialog Box—Pointer Method 349
Modal, Modeless, and System Modal Dialog Boxes 357
Creating a Modeless Dialog Box 359
    Defining the Modeless Dialog Box 360
    Calling the Modeless Dialog Box 362
Summary 367
Questions 369
Exercises 369
Answers to Questions 370
Solutions to Exercises 370

Chapter 11: Other Resources 375
String Tables 376
    Defining String Tables 377

    Conditional Compilation of Resources 377
    Using the String Data 378
    A String Table Example 379
    The STRTAB.C Program 380
User-Defined Resources 380
    Resource Data in a Separate File 384
    Locating and Loading a Custom Resource 386
    The RESOR1 Program 387
    Exercising DrawText() 390
    Other Program Files for RESOR1 390
The RCDATA Statement 391
    The RCDATA Example Program 393
Summary 397
Questions 398
Exercises 398
Answers to Questions 398
Solutions to Exercises 399

Chapter 12: Managing Memory 401
Local Versus Global Memory 402
Local Memory Blocks 405
    The Lock Count 407
    Passing Handles to Functions 407
    Storing Other Types of Data 408
Using Fixed Memory Blocks 418
An Example Allocating Local Memory 410
Changing the Size of a Memory Block 413
An Example Using LocalReAlloc() 414
Discardable Memory Blocks 418
    Using Discardable Blocks 419
    An Example Using Discardable Blocks 420
    The MEM3 Program 422
Global Memory Allocation 427
    Allocating Global Memory Blocks 429
    The GMEM1 Program 430
What Windows Is Actually Doing with Memory 435
System Memory and System Resources 436
Summary 437
Questions 438
Exercises 438
Answers to Questions 439
Solutions to Exercises 439

Chapter 13: The Device Context 443
Private Device Contexts 444
Creating a Private Device Context 445
Using a Private Device Context 446
An Example with a Private Device Context 447
OWNDC.C 448
Mapping Modes 449
Text and Mapping Modes 454
Moving the Origin 455
An Example Program That Changes the Origin and Mapping Mode 456
MAPMODE Program Listings 458
Scaleable Mapping Modes 462
Text and Scaleable Mapping Modes 464
An MM_ANISOTROPIC Example 464
Summary 468
Questions 469
Exercises 469
Answers to Questions 470
Solutions to Exercises 470

Chapter 14: Printing 473
How Windows Supports Printers 474
Printer Device Contexts 476
Sending Special Commands to a Printer 477
A Simple Printing Example 478
Problems with PRINT1 482
Scaling the Printer Output 483
Allowing Interruption of a Print Job 488
The PRINT3 Program 491
Getting Information About A Device 497
Using GetDeviceCaps() 498
An Example Using GetDeviceCaps() 499
Calling Functions in the Printer Driver 504
Accessing the Printer Driver's Functions 505
The DeviceCapabilities() Function 508
A Printer Driver Access Example 510
Summary 516
Questions 518
Exercises 518
Answers to Questions 519
Solutions to Exercises 519

Chapter 15: Disk File Access 523
How Windows Programs Access Disk Files 524
Opening a Disk File 525
Reading and Writing Data 527
Closing a File 530
A File Access Example 531
How FILE1 Works 531
FILE1 Program Listings 533
Creating a File Selection Dialog Box 538
The DlgDirList() Function 539
The DlgDirSelect() Function 540
Creating a File Selection Dialog Box 540
The File Selection Dialog Box Function 543
Creating A Text Editor 547
Creating the Edit Control 548
Using the File Selection Dialog Box 549
Summary 557
Questions 558
Exercises 558
Answers to Questions 559
Solutions to Exercises 559

Chapter 16: Bitmaps 561
How Bitmaps Store Images 562
Loading a Bitmap File 563
Displaying a Bitmap 564
An Example Program Using BitBlt() 566
Stretching and Compressing a Bitmap 570
Using Stretch Blt() 571
Raster Operation Codes 575
An Example Using Raster Operation Codes 576
The BITMAP3 Program 577
Drawing on a Memory Bitmap 583
Memory Bitmaps and Animation 583
Coding the BITMAP4 Program 584
BITMAP4 Program Listings 586
BITMAP Data Format 590
The DIB Format 591
Summary 594
Questions 596
Exercises 596
Answers to Questions 597
Solutions to Exercises 597

Chapter 17: The Clipboard ... 599
How the Clipboard Works ... 600
Basic Clipboard Functions ... 602
Clipboard Formats ... 603
Clipboard Limitations ... 605
A Simple Clipboard Example ... 605
CLIPBRD1 Listings ... 606
Multiple Clipboard Formats ... 610
An Example Using Multiple Clipboard Formats ... 612
Delayed Rendering of Clipboard Data ... 618
WM_RENDERALLFORMATS and WM_DESTROYCLIPBOARD ... 620
A Delayed Rendering Example ... 620
DELREND Listings ... 623
Using the Clipboard With an Edit Control ... 627
Adding Clipboard Functionality to a Simple Editor ... 628
Summary ... 635
Questions ... 637
Exercises ... 637
Answers to Questions ... 638
Solutions to Exercises ... 638

Chapter 18: Dynamic Link Libraries ... 643
Compiler Runtime Libraries ... 644
Dynamic Link Libraries ... 645
How DLLs Work ... 646
Problems with Static Variables in DLLs ... 647
Writing a DLL ... 648
An Example DLL ... 649
Module Definition File for a DLL ... 652
Header File for a DLL ... 653
Compiling REVSTR to Make a DLL ... 653
Creating a DLL with Turbo C++ ... 653
Creating a DLL with QuickC ... 654
Using the DLL ... 655
Alternate Ways to Reference DLL Functions ... 659
Import Libraries ... 660
Creating an Import Library ... 661
Using an Import Library ... 661
Turbo C++ Import Libraries ... 662
QuickC Import Libraries ... 662
The Big Picture on Import Libraries ... 662
Programming Considerations for DLLs ... 663
An Example DLL That Fails ... 664

xix

Avoiding Memory Problems in DLLs	666
A More Complete DLL Example	666
Converting FILEDLG to a DLL	666
Other Files for FILESEL.DLL	672
Using FILESEL.DLL	674
Summary	678
Questions	679
Exercises	679
Answers To Questions	680
Solutions to Exercises	680

Conclusion ... 682

Appendix A: Virtual Key Codes ... 683

Appendix B: Using Command Line Compilers and The MAKE Utility ... 686

Appendix C: Glossary ... 690

Appendix D: Bibliography ... 696

Index ... 698

CHAPTER 1

How Windows Works

This chapter provides an overview of how Microsoft Windows works internally and the different elements that make up a Windows program. We will look at the differences between Windows and DOS programs and examine how the Windows environment appears to run more than one program at one time. Some of the unique aspects of creating Windows programs are also discussed, such as processing Windows messages and using resources to store the program's data.

Windows' built-in memory management functions are vital to Windows' ability to run many applications at the same time. As a programmer, you will be able to control how different portions of a program are managed in memory. This control is specified in parts of a Windows program that do not have equivalents when compiling a DOS program, such as the Windows module definition file and a Windows resource script file. These files are explained in this chapter as preparation for compiling your first Windows program in Chapter 2, Setting Up Your System.

Concepts Covered

How Windows Programs Work
Messages
Resource Data
Structure of a Windows Application Program
Compiling and Linking
Program Instances
Windows Messages

Controls
Resources
Client Area
Static Data
Local Heap
Module Definition Files

Keywords Covered

GUI
PRELOAD
LOADONCALL
MOVEABLE

FIXED
MULTIPLE
SINGLE

What Is Microsoft Windows?

If you have been using Microsoft Windows for some time, you probably take its ease of use for granted. You do not need to understand how Windows works internally to use it or run complex Windows programs. In fact, the Windows environment does an excellent job of shielding the user from the underlying workings. The situation is different when you decide to write your own Windows programs. You will need to look "under the hood" and see how Windows works.

When you get down to fundamentals, Microsoft Windows is a DOS program that has the ability to run other programs written in a special way. That probably sounds odd, as Windows looks different on the screen than most DOS programs. When you think

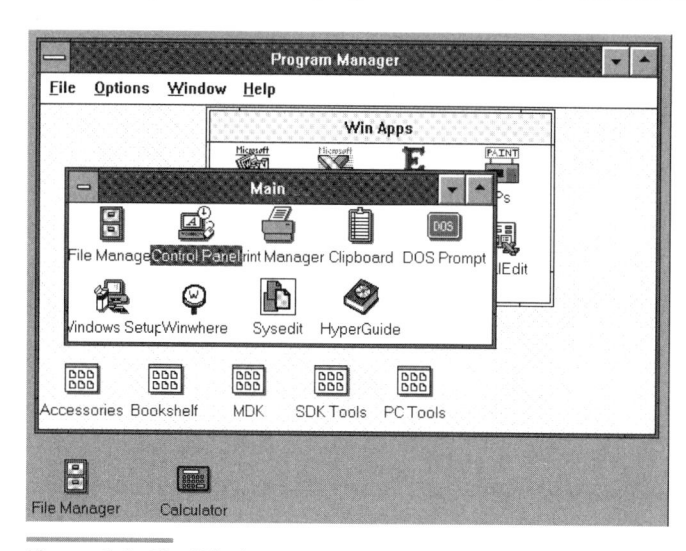

Figure 1-1 The Windows Graphical Environment

about it, Windows is started from DOS like any DOS program. To start Windows you type WIN (Enter) from the DOS prompt. What you are doing is running the DOS program WIN.COM, which is the core of Windows. WIN.COM loads several other files into memory, displays the Windows logo, and gets the Windows Program Manager application running. At that point, you are in the "Windows Graphical Environment," as shown in Figure 1-1. It is called "graphical" because Windows uses graphics to organize the workspace and present the user with intuitive ways to accomplish tasks. It is called an "environment" because you can run other programs from within Windows. Environments like Windows are sometimes called "GUI" for "Graphical User Interface."

When Windows is running, you can run Windows programs like Excel and Write. A number of these programs can be run at the same time and share the screen. The Windows environment takes care of making sure that each program gets its own portion of the screen, that the programs do not interfere with each other, and that each receives a slice of the computer's time.

The Advantages of Windows

As mentioned, Windows itself is just a big DOS program. The programs that you run from within Windows, like Paintbrush and Excel, are definitely *not* DOS programs. These applications will only run within Windows. Why is that?

The answer lies in the internal structure of Windows. Windows includes all sorts of built-in functions and data. For example, Windows includes functions with the ability to draw text in different sizes and styles using font data. Windows has a broad range of graphical functions for drawing lines and geometric shapes in color. Windows programs (like Excel) make use of these built-in functions and do not need to supply the program logic to do these tasks. Excel uses these functions by requesting them from Windows.

Because programs like Excel use Windows' built-in functions, the programs end up smaller than they would be if each program had to include all of that logic. There are a number of advantages to this approach:

- Windows programs (called "applications programs" or just "applications") take up less disk space, and less room in memory, when Windows is already running.
- Windows applications all tend to have the same "look and feel" because they are using the same built-in logic to draw text, display menus, etc.
- As soon as the user sets up his or her system to run Windows, every Windows application can take advantage of the configuration. If a printer works for one Windows application, it will work for every other Windows application because every program will take advantage of Windows' built-in printing functions instead of creating them from scratch. This eliminates the complex installation programs of many DOS programs that must have their own printer installation, memory configuration program, font data, etc.

These advantages are in addition to the fundamental advantage that Windows allows many programs to operate at the same time.

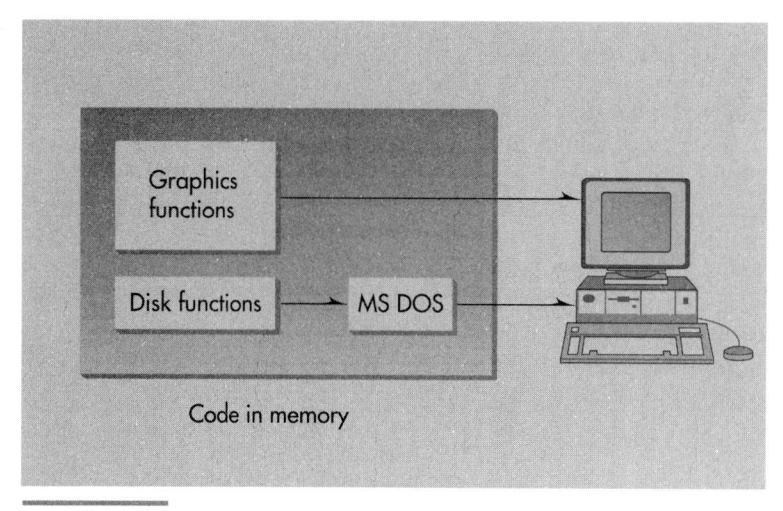

Figure 1-2 How a DOS Program Works

How Windows Programs Work

All programs function by telling the computer's hardware what to do. The difference between a Windows application and a DOS program lies in how direct a connection there is between the running program and the actual hardware. Most DOS programs have a structure like the one shown in Figure 1-2. Besides the program logic (do this first, that second, etc.), DOS programs deal directly with the computer's hardware to access the screen, read the keyboard, and so on. The main support the DOS operating system provides is for disk file access.

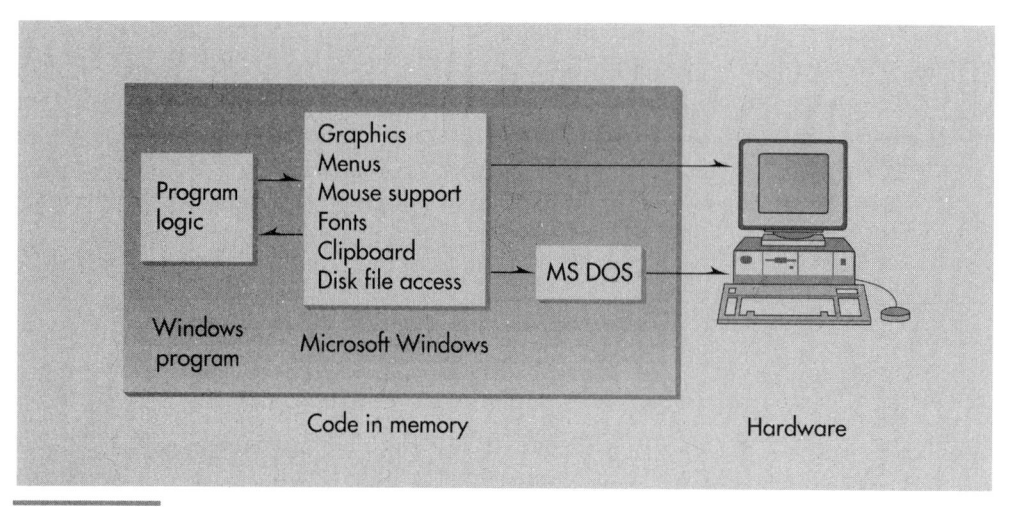

Figure 1-3 How a Windows Program Works

Windows Programming Primer Plus®

Figure 1-2 is a bit simplified. There are some limited functions within DOS for dealing with the screen and communications devices. Most DOS programs do not use these features because it is usually faster to deal directly with the computer's hardware.

Figure 1-3 illustrates how a Windows program operates. Windows applications interact with the Windows environment, not directly with the hardware. If an application decides to write on the screen, it calls a function within Windows. Internally, Windows decodes the function call and translates it into hardware commands. If Windows was installed specifying a VGA video system, VGA hardware commands are sent out. If an IBM 8514 video adapter was specified when Windows was installed, IBM 8514 video hardware commands are sent out. The application program does not necessarily know or care what type of hardware the user has installed. The Windows environment takes care of the hardware for the program.

Note in Figure 1-3 that disk file commands are still done via DOS. Because Windows is a DOS program, DOS is always running before Windows is started. All of the DOS file support functions are available to Windows, just like they are available to any DOS program. Windows designers took advantage of DOS to do what it does best — disk file access. Files created by Windows programs are really DOS files. This means that you can save a text file created by the Windows Notepad application on a floppy disk and hand it to a coworker who uses a DOS word processor. The DOS word processor will have no trouble reading the file, even though it was created by a Windows program. Using the DOS file functions has the disadvantage of limiting file names to eight characters, plus a three character extension, like "ANEWFILE.TXT."

Running Several Programs Simultaneously

Windows allows you to run many application programs at the same time. "Running" means that the program is loaded into memory. It does not mean that the program is necessarily doing anything. Most of the time Windows applications just sit in memory. They only do something when requested to by the Windows environment. A well designed Windows program constantly tries to finish what it is doing and give control back to Windows. Think of Windows programs as being incredibly polite. They only act when commanded to do so by Windows, and then they promptly give control back to their host, the Windows environment.

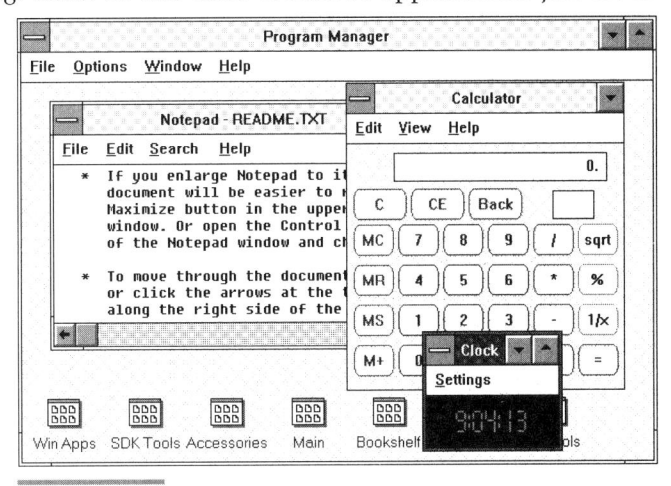

Figure 1-4 Windows Session with Several Programs Running

To understand why Windows applications must be so polite, consider a situation where you have several applications running at the same time. Figure 1-4 shows a typical Windows screen image with several programs running. The Program Manager, Notepad, Clock, and Calculator are all visible. This means that these four applications are loaded into memory. We will see later that Windows has the ability to load just parts of a program to conserve memory space. Any running program will be at least partly loaded into memory.

Note that each of the running applications in Figure 1-4 occupies its own rectangular area on the screen. These areas are said to be the program's "window." The Windows' environment gets its name from the concept of these program windows. Each program window is an independent entity. Each program can only write on its own window area, not on another program's window. You can think of each window's border as being a fence that restricts output from the program to a limited area.

Two Meanings of "Window"

The word "window" has two meanings in this book. When the first letter is capitalized ("Windows"), it means the complete Microsoft Windows environment. This environment includes the Program Manager, File Manager, and all of the Windows API (Application Programming Interface) functions. In small letters ("a window"), it refers to an individual program window on the screen.

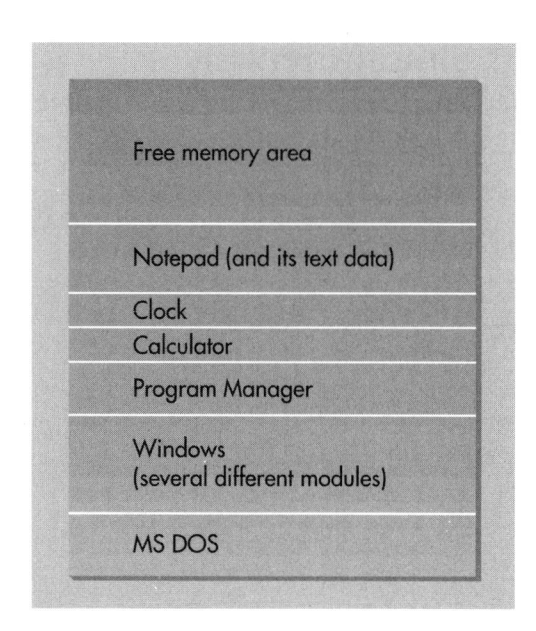

Figure 1-5 Memory Organization for a Windows Session

If you could look into the memory chips of the computer that is displaying the screen depicted in Figure 1-4, you would find things organized roughly as shown in Figure 1-5. DOS is loaded from the disk drive when the computer is turned on and stays in memory while Windows operates. Windows is loaded into memory when the user types WIN (Enter). Windows consists of several files, each called a "program module." Starting Windows also automatically loads the Program Manager program into memory. Finally, Windows applications that the user starts are loaded into memory along with the data that each application uses, such as the text file that Notepad may be editing.

At any one time, the computer CPU will be executing instructions residing in one of these memory areas. The program with "control" of the system is the one whose code currently is being executed. Those instructions are in the memory block occupied by the program. If the user does not do anything, the Windows environment has "control" of the "system." "System" is just another word for a running computer, including all of the programs that are currently active. When a program is processing instructions, the program is said to have "control of the system." When Windows has control, instructions in Windows' portion of memory are being executed. Windows just keeps checking to see if any key was pressed, if the mouse was used, etc.

Messages

Now imagine that the user moves the mouse cursor (the little arrow that moves when you move the mouse) over to the Calculator program's window area and clicks the left mouse button. Windows contains the logic for decoding the hardware signals sent from the mouse. The functions containing this hardware decoding logic are in the block of memory occupied by Windows. When the hardware information from the mouse is decoded, Windows must figure out which program the user selected with the mouse cursor. Windows does this by comparing where the mouse cursor is located to the location of the program windows on the screen. The top-most window under the mouse cursor must be the one that the user wants to activate. Again, the logic for figuring out which application the user has selected is built into the Windows environment and is always ready to run.

Next, Windows must tell the Calculator program what has happened, so that the Calculator can do something, such as display a new digit. Windows does this by sending the Calculator application a "message." The message tells Calculator something like "The user has clicked the right mouse button over point X,Y on your (the Calculator application's) window. Do whatever is appropriate, then return control back to Windows."

Of course, computers do not really have internal message systems like telephones and telexes. Computers just execute instructions in memory. To pass the message data to a running program, Windows writes some data into a memory block, and then lets the program receiving the message data start running. The program reads the memory block, does whatever is required, and then returns control to Windows.

To pass the message data to a program, Windows writes the information into a memory area set aside for each running program. The message data is in the format shown in Table 1-1. Each message occupies 18 bytes of memory space.

ELEMENT	MEANING
Window ID (2 bytes)	ID number of the program's window sending the message (called the "window's handle"). Windows maintains a list of these ID values internally to keep track of which program window is active, etc.
Message ID (2 bytes)	ID number of the message. About 200 code numbers exist for things like "the mouse moved" or "a key was pressed." We will see in Chapter 3 that these codes are given names, like WM_MOUSEMOVE, to clarify programs.

(continued)

Table 1-1 (cont'd)

Data Word (2 bytes)	Data passed with the message. "Word" means two bytes of data. The data's meaning will depend on the message being passed. For example, if a key was pressed, these two bytes would encode which key was pressed.
Data Double Word (4 bytes)	Additional data passed with the message. "Double Word" means four bytes of data. The data's meaning will depend on the message being passed. For example, if the mouse is moved, the four bytes would encode the new X,Y position of the mouse cursor on the screen.
Message Time (4 bytes)	The time the message was sent. This is in milliseconds from the time that the Windows session was started. This is usually ignored.
Mouse Position (4 bytes)	The X,Y position on the screen of the mouse cursor when the message was sent.

Table 1-1 Windows Message Data Format

As soon as Windows has written the message data into memory, Windows allows the program that is receiving the message to execute its instructions. The program reads the message data from the memory block, decodes all of the data bytes, decides what to

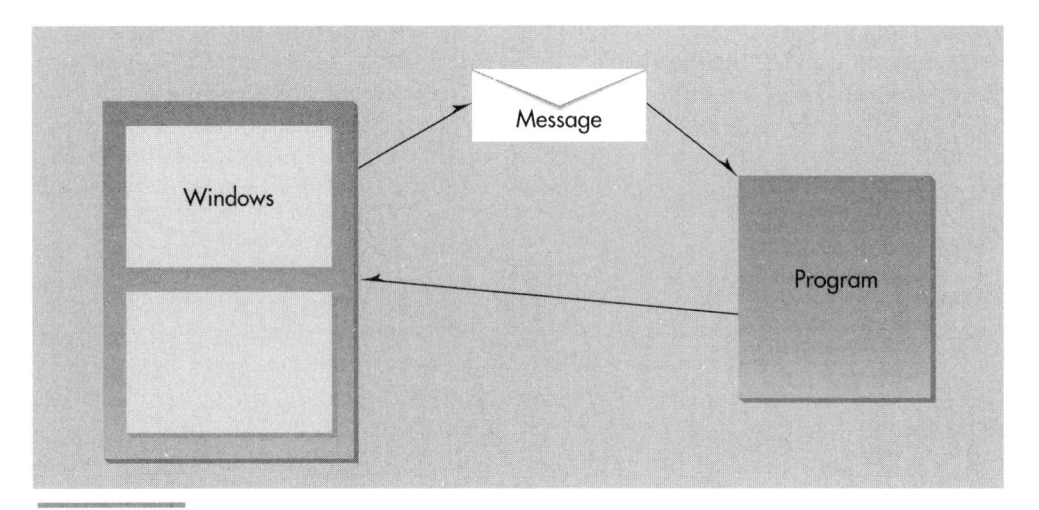

Figure 1-6 The Message Cycle

Windows Programming Primer Plus®

do, and then returns control back to Windows.

This message cycle, shown in Figure 1-6, allows Windows to send messages to any number of programs in memory. If the user moves the mouse cursor over one program's window and clicks a mouse button, that program will receive messages. The messages will be information from Windows like "the mouse moved," "the left mouse button was depressed," or "the left mouse button was released." If the user then moves the mouse over another window on the screen and clicks a mouse button, that program will start receiving the messages from Windows.

The channeling of message data to different applications is the secret of Windows' ability to appear to run more than one application at the same time. The computers that Windows runs on can really only execute one instruction at a time. Either Windows itself is executing instructions (has control) or one of the programs in memory is executing its instructions. Windows can rapidly switch which program is getting the messages in order to reflect which application the user has selected with a mouse action or keystroke. The switching of messages from one program to the next is the sleight of hand that Windows uses to make it appear that all of the programs are running at once. Figure 1-7 shows two applications receiving different messages from Windows. Keep in mind that each message is sent at a different time and that only one program can process a message at any one time.

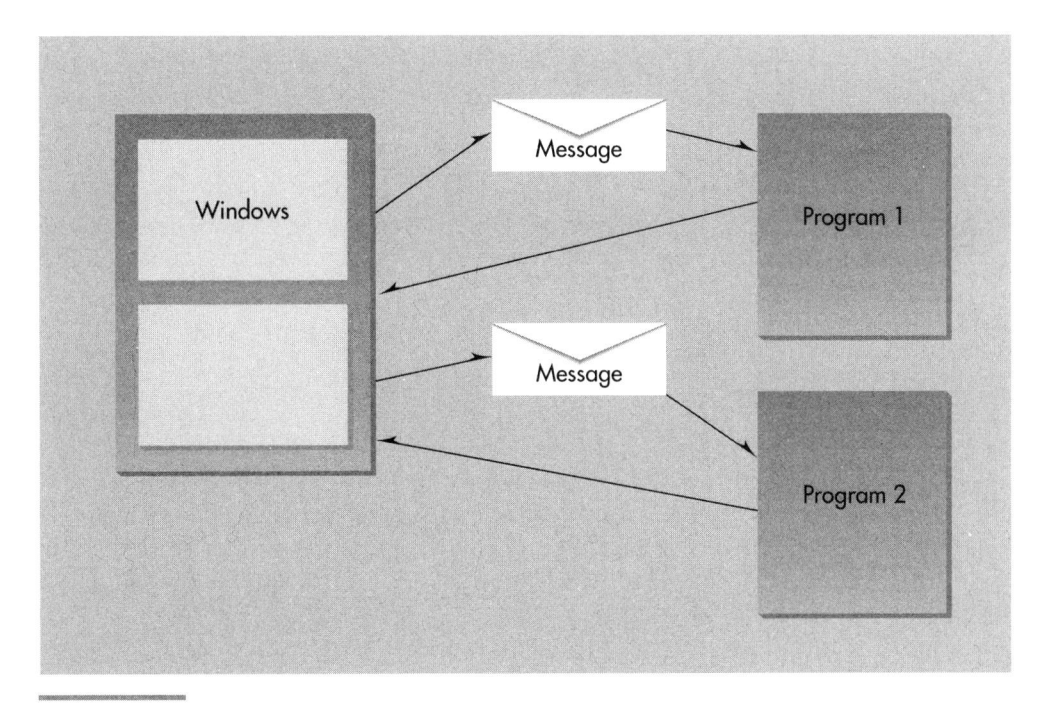

Figure 1-7 Two Application Programs Receiving Messages

An Analogy

If you want to draw an analogy at this point, think of Windows as the boss and the running programs as workers. Each program worker sits behind a desk with an "In" box. To begin with, the Windows boss is active, but all of the program workers are frozen in place. The boss determines which worker needs to do a task, writes the message on a piece of paper and puts it in the worker's "In" box. The boss goes back to his desk and stops moving. The worker begins moving, reads the message, and does whatever is required. Unlike a normal office, none of the other workers or the boss can move while another worker processes a message. When the worker is done, the boss becomes active again and all of the workers are frozen.

You may be wondering if the workers (programs) have both "In" and "Out" boxes. Absolutely! Windows programs can both send and receive messages. We will use the ability to send messages to allow a program to communicate with other windows, such as editing windows and list boxes. Independent application programs can also exchange data with each other by sending messages. This is called "Dynamic Data Exchange" or DDE.

The office analogy points out the importance of writing Windows programs correctly. You can write a Windows program that includes CPU instructions that directly access the computer's hardware, takes over the entire screen, keeps other programs from running, and generally behaves like a wild dog. A poorly written Windows program can act like a very slow worker in an otherwise efficient office — no other workers can get any work done while they wait for the slow worker to finish his or her task. Windows does not stop the programmer from doing things wrong. It is up to the programmer to write a well-behaved program that will coexist with other running programs in memory.

This all sounds intimidating. You may be thinking "If I write my program wrong, I could make all the other programs running under Windows fail." This is basically true, and every Windows programmer has the responsibility of writing "well-behaved" programs. However, writing well-behaved Windows programs is not difficult. We will see in the next chapter that a program with only five instructions to execute can be a perfectly acceptable and well-mannered Windows program. This book will guide you through the process of designing programs that will coexist with any other Windows application.

The bottom line is: Windows applications are written to coexist with other running programs. This is a basic design consideration that will impact every Windows application you write. The reward for this effort is that the incredible built-in power of the Windows environment will be available to every program. Once you know how to use Windows, you will be able to create impressive applications in a fraction of the time it would take to create a comparable application using a conventional programming environment like DOS.

The Structure of a Windows Program

Windows programs basically do two things:

- Initial activities when the program is first loaded into memory. These activities consist of creating the program's own window and any startup activities, such setting aside some memory space.
- Processing messages from Windows.

The key item in the first step is creating the program's window, which is the piece of the screen that the program will control. Application programs only write inside their own window, not in other program's windows or on the background of the screen. Restricting output to the program's window is one of the keys to having several programs coexist on the same screen. Program windows are always rectangular and will contain different elements, such as menus and captions, depending on what the program does. Figure 1-8 shows a typical program window with the elements labeled.

Windows uses a standard set of names to describe the various parts of a program's window area. The *client area* of the window is the central portion in which the program can draw graphics and text. If a program tries to write outside of the client area, nothing shows up on the screen. This is how Windows keeps programs from interfering with each other on the screen. If the window has a thick border (like the border in Figure 1-8), the window size can be changed by positioning the mouse cursor over a corner, depressing the left mouse button, dragging the corner to a new location, and releasing the mouse button. Changing the window's size changes the size of the client area. If the client area is increased in size, the program will be able to write on all of the area, but not outside of the client area.

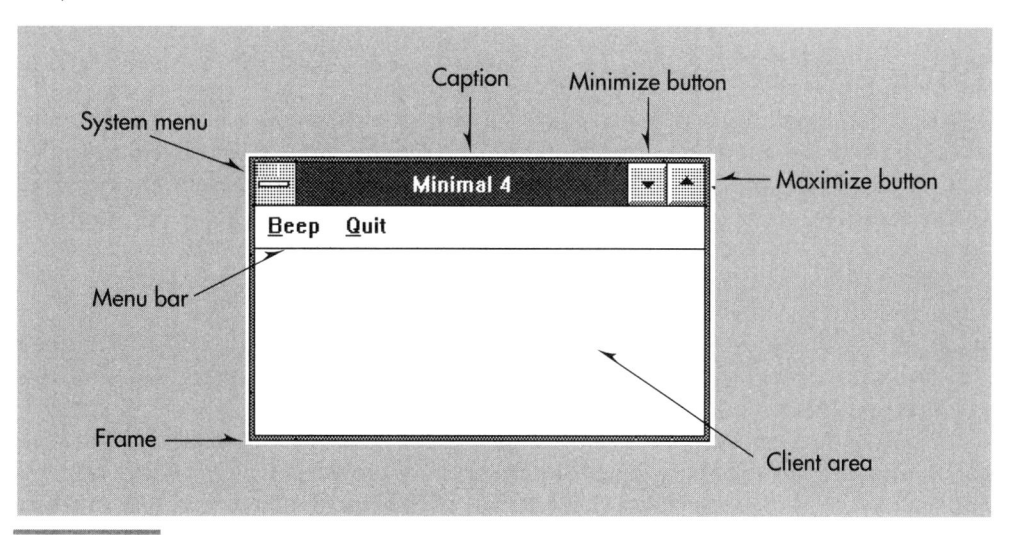

Figure 1-8 Program Window Elements

When a program's window is visible, it will just wait until Windows sends the program a message. The waiting is accomplished by a program loop, called the "message loop." Listing 1-1 shows the structure of a Windows program. This listing is not in a specific computer language, just an outline. Program outlines like Listing 1-1 are usually called "pseudocode" listings and are an excellent way to diagram the structure of any programming project without getting lost in the specifics of the computer language being used.

Listing 1-1 Pseudocode Outline of a Windows Program

```
Create the program's Window
Do any initialization of variables or memory space
Loop
      Fetch any message sent from Windows to this program
      Is the message QUIT?
            If the message is QUIT
                  Terminate program, return control to Windows
            If it is another message
                  Do any appropriate actions based on the message
      Return control to Windows
End Loop
```

Once you have the initial step of creating code that makes the program's window, the remainder of the program is a matter of thinking through how the program should respond to various messages that Windows can send. Listing 1-1 shows that Windows programs just loop until they get a message. Waiting for a message is the key to the polite behavior of correctly written Windows programs.

Code and Resources

Most programmers think of a program as a series of instructions that the computer executes. Actually, programs consist of both instructions and *static data*. Static data is any portion of the program this is not executed as a machine instruction and which does not change as the program executes. Examples of static data are character strings for messages to the user, menu definitions, and character data to create fonts.

Static data is different from *dynamic data*. Dynamic data changes as the program runs. Usually, dynamic data is stored in separate files and is the data which the program reads and writes. For example, Microsoft Excel stores the (dynamic) worksheet data in .XLS spreadsheet files, but has static data defining its menu structure as part of the Excel program.

The designers of Windows wisely decided that static data should be handled separately from the program code. The Windows term for static data is "resource data," or just "resources." Resource data can include any of the items listed in Table 1-2. By separating static data from the program code, the creators of Windows were able to use a standard C compiler to create the code portion of the finished Windows program, and they only had to write a "resource compiler" to create the specialized resources that Windows programs use. Separating the code from the resource data has other advantages in reducing memory demands and making programs more portable. It also means that a programmer can work on the program's logic, while a designer works on how the program looks.

DATA TYPE	MEANING
Accelerators	Definition of keyboard shortcuts for executing menu items, or other commands using the keyboard instead of the mouse.
Bitmaps	Picture data defining larger images. Bitmaps can be used to display many types of images in a program, including graphical menu items (for selecting pens, brushes, etc.), pictorial information in the program's client area, etc.
Cursors	Picture (bitmap) data defining the types of mouse cursor shapes.
Dialog Box Definitions	Defines the layout of dialog boxes. Dialog boxes are small windows that a program "pops up" to display information or ask for specific input. A typical example is a dialog box to request the user type a word before starting a search operation in a word processor.
Fonts	Data defining characters.
Icons	Picture (bitmap) data defining small images. Icons are most often used for displaying a small image when the program is minimized.
Menu	Defines the menu structure for the program. This structure includes the top menu bar (shown in Figure 1-8) and all drop-down menus.
String Tables	Tables of character strings that are used for messages and other static character data used within the program.
User-defined Resources	Any static data that the programmer may need in the application, such as tables of numbers.

Table 1-2 Resource Data

Program Instances

Windows allows you to run more than one copy of a program at a time. This is handy for cutting and pasting between two copies of Notepad or when running more than one terminal session with a terminal emulator program. Each running copy of a program is called a "program instance."

An interesting memory optimization trick that Windows performs is to share a single copy of the program's code between all running instances. For example, if you get three instances of Notepad running, there will only be one copy of Notepad's code in memory. All three instances share the same code, but will have separate memory areas to hold the text data being edited. The difference between the handling of the code and data is logical, as each instance of Notepad will be able to edit a different file, so the data must be unique to each instance. The program logic to edit the files is the same for every instance, so there is no reason a single copy of Notepad's code cannot be shared.

Compiling a Windows Program

Because Windows programs store resource data in separate files, the process of putting together a complete Windows program is a little more involved than compiling a DOS program. Figure 1-9 shows how a C program written to run under DOS is compiled and linked to create a finished program. The C compiler converts the source code file into an objective file. A linker converts the objective file into the finished executable program.

Figure 1-10 shows a flow diagram for the creation of a Windows program. The compilation of the source code files to make objective files is the same in both the DOS and Windows case. In creating a Windows program, the linker gets some additional information from a small file called the "module definition file" with the file name extension ".DEF." This file tells the linker how to assemble the program. We will examine the module definition file later in this chapter. The linker combines the module definition file information and the object files to make an unfinished .EXE file. The unfinished .EXE file lacks the resource data.

The biggest difference Windows programs have compared to compiling DOS programs is in the compilation of the resource data. The resource data is compiled by the resource compiler to make a resource data file with the extension ".RES." The resource data is added to the unfinished .EXE file to create the finished executable program. The resource data is basically stuck onto the end of the program's code and becomes part of the program file. In addition to adding the resource data, the resource compiler writes the Windows version number into the program file. This version data is how Windows tells if a program was compiled for the 2.0 version of Windows or under a more recent version. If you try to run a Windows 2.0 program under Windows 3.0 or 3.1, you will get a warning message telling you that the program needs to be updated.

One of the many advantages of using a Windows development environment such as Turbo C++ or QuickC is that most of the individual steps in compiling and linking a program are done automatically by the development tools. Both Turbo C++ and

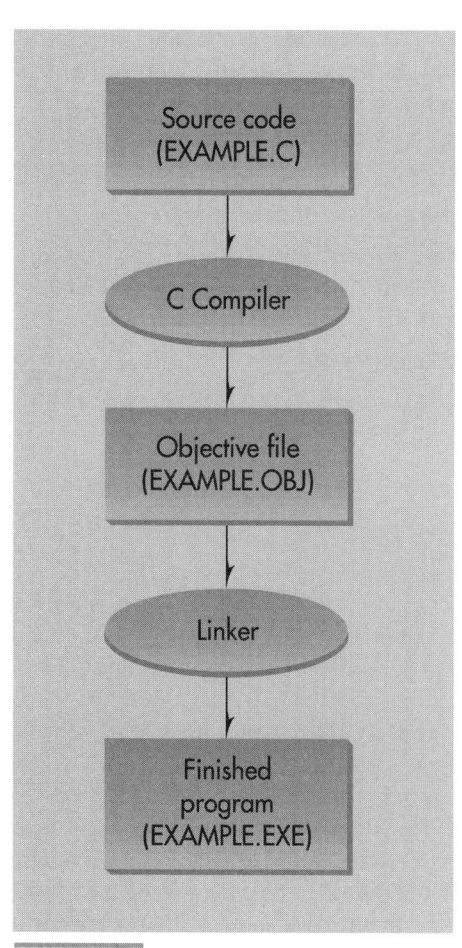

Figure 1-9 Steps in Creating a DOS Program

QuickC automatically call the compiler and linker, with all of the necessary settings and in the right order. This is a big improvement from the "old days" of Windows programming, when you needed to control each step in the compile/link process manually.

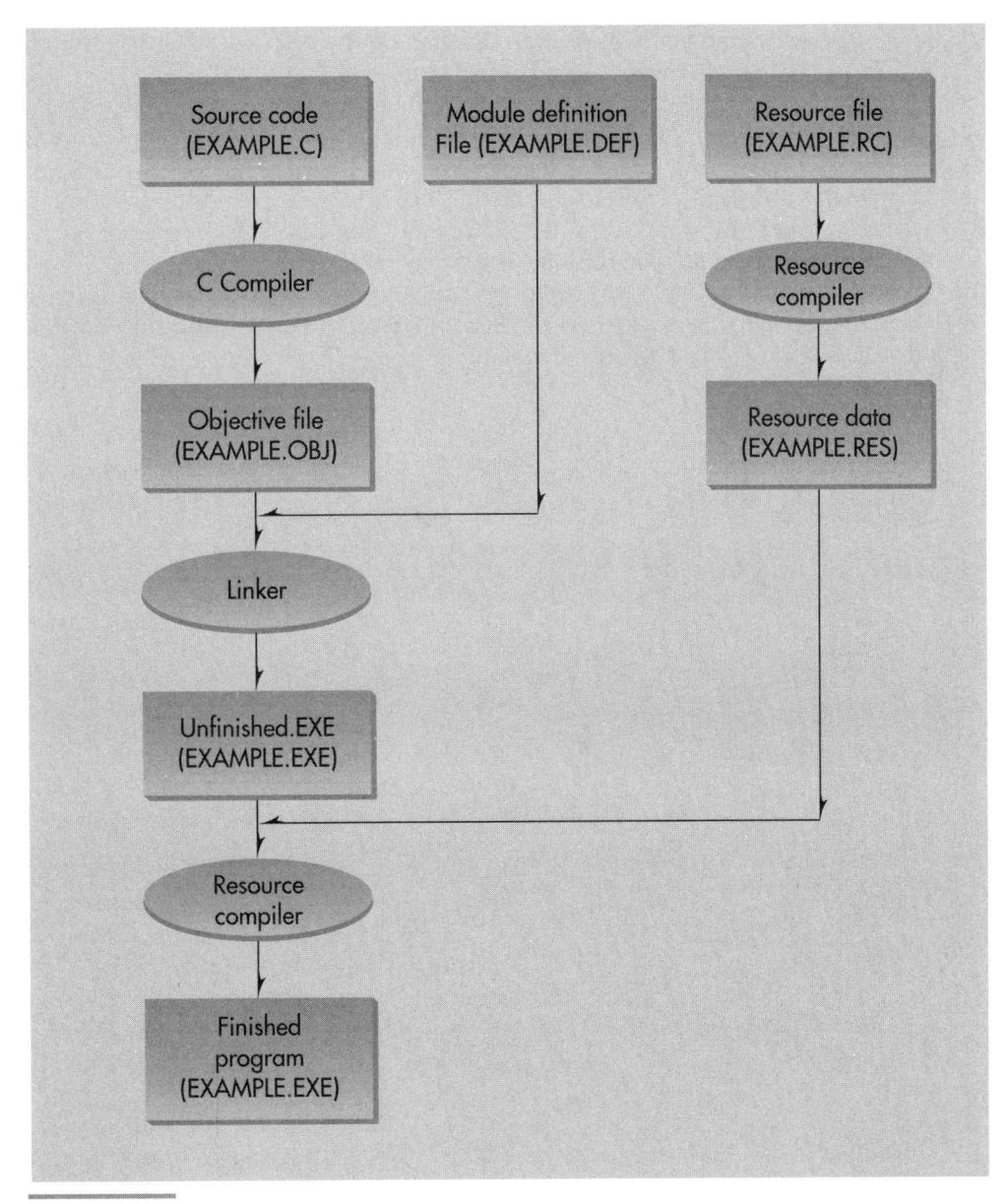

Figure 1-10 Steps in Creating a Windows Program

Windows Memory Management

A computer's memory is like money — you can never have too much. No matter how much memory you install on your computer, sooner or later you will run out. Windows goes to a lot of trouble to make the best possible use of whatever amount of memory is installed. For the most part, these memory management functions are automatic. As a programmer, you will need to understand the basics of what Windows is doing, so that you can properly design the program.

The first thing you need to know about Windows' memory management is that almost everything in memory can be moved. Windows moves objects (code and data) automatically to make room for new programs and data. To understand why this is necessary, consider the example in Figure 1-11. To begin with, there are three programs loaded into memory. If the user stops (terminates) program 2, its block of memory is free for use. The total free memory on the system ends up fragmented into two sections. If the user decides to load another large program, the largest available single block of memory may not be big enough. To make room for program 4, Windows moves program 3 down in memory. This makes a larger section of memory available for program 4 to load.

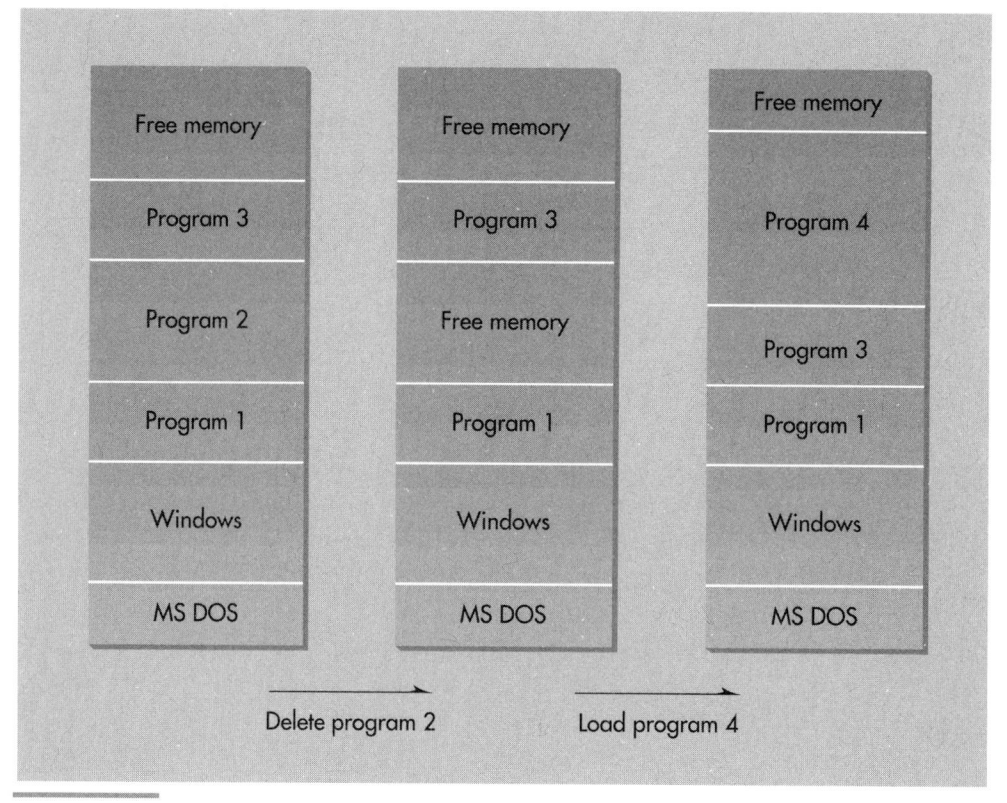

Figure 1-11 Programs Being Moved in Memory

Memory shifts like the one shown in Figure 1-11 happen all of the time as you run Windows application programs. This is the reason that programs take longer to start running if you already have several other Windows applications running. Windows has to make room for the next program, which frequently involves shifting things around in memory.

For simplicity, Figure 1-11 showed the programs as single big blocks. In reality, Windows handles program files in a much more sophisticated manner. If you compile a big Windows program consisting of many C program files, each of the C program files ends up turned into a separate piece of the final program, called a "segment." Windows can load and remove each segment of a program to and from memory separately. If you had five C program files, there will be five program segments. At any one time, Windows may have between one and five of these segments loaded in memory. If a function is called in a segment that is not already loaded, Windows will automatically load the segment before it tries to execute the function.

Windows manages data with a similar degree of sophistication. Each piece of data in the program's resource data will be separately managed. For example, if you define a series of small windows (called "dialog boxes") to get information from the user as the program runs, the dialog box data can be set to not be loaded into memory until it is needed. Each dialog box can be separately loaded and unloaded from memory as it is needed.

Memory Options

As a programmer, you can control how program code and data is managed in memory by specifying options in the program's module definition file (.DEF file) and in the program's resource script file (.RC file). Table 1-3 shows some of the memory management options. For example, most small windows programs have their code set up as PRELOAD and MOVEABLE. This loads all of the code into memory when the program first starts, but then allows the code to be moved in memory to make room for other objects. Program resources, such as the definitions for dialog box windows, are usually LOADONCALL, MOVEABLE, and DISCARDABLE. This means that the data is not loaded until needed, can be moved in memory, and can be erased from memory to make room for other objects if the data is not being used.

OPTION	MEANING
PRELOAD	The code or data is loaded into memory when the program first starts.
LOADONCALL	The code or data is not loaded into memory until it is needed.
MOVEABLE	The code or data can be moved in memory. This is the most common option.
FIXED	The code or memory remains at a fixed address in memory. This restricts Windows' ability to manage memory, so the FIXED option is only used in rare situations such as interrupt driven interfaces with hardware devices.

(continued)

Table 1-3 (cont'd)

DISCARDABLE	The code or memory can be temporarily removed from memory to make room for other objects. The code or data will then be reloaded if it is needed.
MULTIPLE	Applies only to program data. MULTIPLE means that if the same program is started several times (several instances), each will have a different set of data.
SINGLE	Applies only to program data. SINGLE means that all instances share the same data.

Table 1-3 Memory Management Options in Windows

You cannot use certain memory options together. For example, it would not be logical to have a block marked both FIXED and MOVEABLE at the same time. To be DISCARDABLE, a block must also be marked as MOVEABLE. DISCARDABLE is the ultimate form of MOVEABLE — moving the block right out of memory. This means that the block will have to be reloaded if that portion of the program is again needed. This takes a little time, but gives Windows the maximum flexibility to optimize memory. DISCARDABLE blocks are not removed from memory unless simply moving blocks does not make enough room. FIXED memory blocks are to be avoided. A few FIXED blocks scattered about in memory will make it impossible for Windows to properly optimize memory.

One final bit of optimization that Windows does is only possible in "enhanced" mode. Windows starts up in enhanced mode automatically if you are running on a 80386 or 80486 based computer. With these advanced CPU chips, Windows is capable of using the hard disk to store data and code if Windows runs out of RAM memory room. This is called "virtual memory management." All of this is done automatically by Windows. If you are running a lot of applications at the same time, you may notice the hard disk running periodically. That is Windows reading and writing memory blocks to and from the hard disk.

Stacks and Heaps

If you have been programming with the C language, you are probably familiar with automatic, static, and global variables. Listing 1-2 shows a simple C program with all three types of variables defined. The function CountByTen() just adds ten to the static variable *nKeep* ten times. This is trivial, but it does demonstrate the three variable types. Automatic variables (*n* in Listing 1-2) are defined inside a function, but only retain their values while the function's code is being executed. If you call the function a second time, the automatic variable's last value is forgotten. Static variables (*nKeep* and *cBuf[]* in Listing 1-2) are defined inside of a function, but with the prefix "static." These values are stored in a permanent memory block and are not forgotten each time the function exits. Global variables are defined outside of any function (*nGlobal* in Listing 1-2). Global variables are known to every function in the program, and they retain their values as functions during program execution.

Listing 1-2 Automatic, Static, and Global Variables

```
int nGlobal = 10 ;       /* a global variable */

int CountByTen ()        /* start a function */
{
    int    n ;           /* an automatic variable */
    static int nKeep ;   /* a static integer */
    char   cBuf [] = "This is static text."

    for (n = 0 ; n < nGlobal ; n++)
        nKeep += 10 ;
    return (nKeep) ;
}
```

You can use automatic, static, and global variables in a Windows program. Physically, automatic variables are stored in a memory area called the "stack." Global and static variables are stored in a memory area called the "local heap." Each Windows program has its own memory area to hold its stack and local heap. The combined size of the stack and local heap is limited to 64K, as they are physically stored in a single memory "segment." This 64K limit is due to the limitations of the 80286 processors, with a maximum segment size of 64K. The 80386 and 80486 processors do not have this limit, but Windows maintains compatibility with the older CPUs.

Figure 1-12 shows how a Windows program exists in memory. The program's code is in one or more segments. A separate segment holds the stack and local heap. The stack is used by every function that uses automatic variables. Each time a new function executes, the stack holds that function's automatic variables, writing over the values from the previous function. In contrast, the static and global variables in the local heap occupy fixed positions within the segment. These variables do not get written over when a new function is called.

Windows programs can also request blocks of memory as the program runs. This is similar to a C program running under

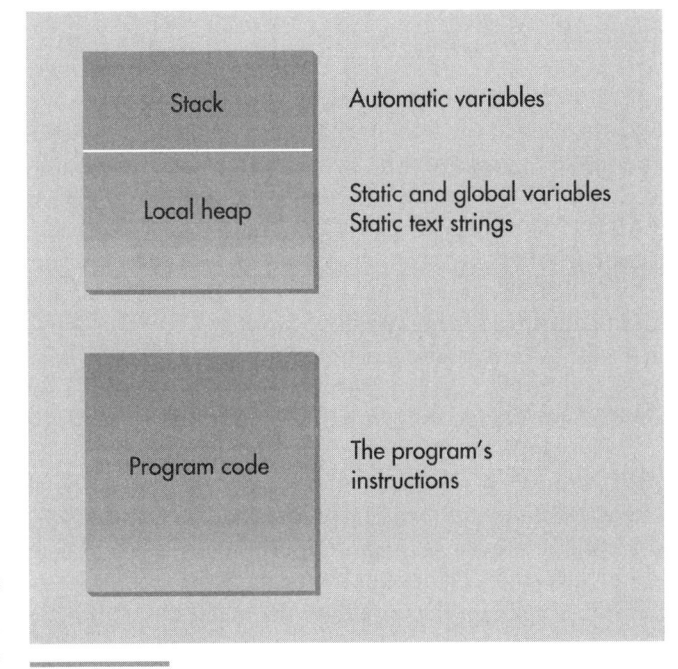

Figure 1-12 A Windows' Program in Memory

Chapter 1 • How Windows Works

DOS calling the alloc() function. Windows programs call similar functions to request memory blocks either in the local memory heap or outside of the local heap in main memory called the "global heap." You can request blocks that are fixed, moveable, or discardable as the program runs. Most of the time, Windows applications set aside memory blocks that are movable, so that Windows can continue to optimize memory space by moving things around. We will discuss allocating memory blocks in Chapter 12, *Managing Memory*.

An Example Module Definition File

Listing 1-3 shows a typical module definition file for a Windows program. Remember that the module definition file is used by the linker during the compilation step. There is no equivalent to a module definition file when compiling a DOS program. The data in the module definition file controls memory options that are specific to Windows.

Listing 1-3 Example Module Definition File (MINIMAL1.DEF)

```
NAME            MINIMAL1
DESCRIPTION     'Basic Windows application'
EXETYPE         WINDOWS
STUB            'WINSTUB.EXE'
CODE            PRELOAD MOVEABLE
DATA            PRELOAD MOVEABLE MULTIPLE
HEAPSIZE        1024
STACKSIZE       5120
EXPORTS         WndProc
```

The NAME statement just gives the name of the file. This is optional, but it makes it easier to read the listing. DESCRIPTION adds a text string to the beginning of the file (about 760 bytes from the start). This is handy for embedding copyright notices in the code. EXETYPE marks the program as a Windows 3.0 or later program. Without EXETYPE specified as WINDOWS, the program will be a Windows 2.0 version and will generate a nasty warning message if a user runs it under Windows 3.0 or later.

The STUB statement provides the name of a small DOS program that is added to the beginning of the Windows application. The purpose of the stub is to print the message "The program requires Microsoft Windows." if the user attempts to run the program from DOS. The WINSTUB.EXE program is provided with the Turbo C++ and QuickC for Windows compilers.

The CODE statement controls the memory options for the program's instructions. In MINIMAL1.DEF, the code will be loaded into memory when the program starts and will be moveable in memory. The program's data segment will also be preloaded into memory and will be moveable. If more than one instance of the program is started at the same time, each copy will have its own data (MULTIPLE statement). The module definition file also sets the size of the program's data segment with the HEAPSIZE and STACKSIZE statements. The minimum stack size for a windows program is 5,120 bytes. The HEAPSIZE statement sets the starting size of the local memory heap. The heap will be expanded automatically if the program stores more data in the local memory area as it runs.

The last line in the MINIMAL1.DEF module definition file is the EXPORTS statement. This lists the functions in the program that will be accessed directly by Windows as the program runs, or which may be called by another application running at the same time. In MINIMAL1.DEF, only the function named WndProc() is listed. The EXPORTS section is important, because Windows will track the functions listed under EXPORTS as the program's code is moved in memory.

Summary

Windows applications are designed to allow many running programs to coexist in memory at the same time. Windows is able to switch between applications by sending message data to the program when the program needs to do something. Each Windows program waits to receive a message, acts on messages it receives, and returns control back to Windows as soon as possible.

Windows programs are compiled differently than DOS programs. Both DOS and Windows programs use a C compiler to convert the source code files into object files. In addition to the source code files, Windows programs have separate resource files that contain static data, such as menus and bitmaps. Resource data is compiled by a separate compiler, called the resource compiler. The compiled resource data is combined with the objective files to create the finished Windows program.

Each program will have access to a data segment containing both the stack and the local heap. Windows uses the stack for automatic variables and the local heap to store static and global variables. Windows can move program code and data in memory to make room for new objects. The program's module definition file (.DEF file) sets the memory options used for code and data.

QUESTIONS

1. What is the minimum number of files needed to create a DOS program? How many for a Windows program? Count only the files the programmer writes, not the output of compilers and linkers.
2. What does a Windows program do when it is done processing a message?
3. Draw a picture of a program window. Show the location of the client area, frame, caption, system menu, menu bar, minimize button, and maximize button.
4. If a Windows program's client area is 100 pixels wide and 200 pixels high and the program outputs graphics commands to draw a 200 by 300 rectangle, what size and shape ends up drawn? Where does the rest of the rectangle show up?
5. The DISCARDABLE memory option is always used with the _____ option.
6. If more than one copy of a Windows application is running, each is said to be a separate _____ of the application.
7. The _____ combines the object files to build an unfinished .EXE program file.
8. When more than one application is running in the same Windows session, two or more applications can be processing separate messages at the same time. (True/False)
9. Each application will have its own local data segment containing a) the application's stack; b) the application's local data heap; c) resource data; d) a and b.

ANSWERS

1. A DOS program needs only one program file, a .C source code file. A Windows program needs a minimum of <u>two</u> files: a .C source code file and a .DEF module definition file. Almost all Windows programs also have an .RC resource script file containing resource data, so <u>three</u> is also a correct answer.
2. Windows programs return control back to Windows when they have processed a message.
3. The picture should look roughly as shown in Figure 1-13.
4. Only the portion of the rectangle within the client area will be visible. The portions of the rectangle to extend beyond the client area do not show up at all.
5. MOVEABLE
6. instance.
7. linker.
8. False. At any one time, only one application can have code that is being executed by the computer's CPU.
9. d.

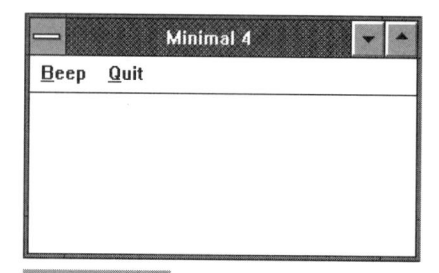

Figure 1-13

Windows Programming Primer Plus®

CHAPTER 2

Setting Up Your System

Starting to program in the Windows environment is a litlle like learning to ride a bike. Getting started is a bit difficult; but once you get the knack, it becomes second nature. No amount of reading or attending lectures will teach you how to ride a bike. You have to get on the bike and fall off a few times before you can learn to ride. Programming is the same way. You have to do it to understand it.

For the best results, prop this book up next to your computer and turn on the machine. Try out every example. You can take advantage of our source code disks to save some typing, but typing the programs is even better. It is amazing how much you will discover during the simple process of copying examples from this book to the computer screen that you would otherwise miss. The examples build on previous ones. You will be able to copy parts from one example to the next without retyping. The changes to the C program from one example to the next will be highlighted to make this easier.

Before you can create the Windows programs in this book, you must install a C compiler with Windows development tools on your computer. This chapter discusses how to set up your system and tests the configuration by creating a simple Windows program. The logic behind how the program works will be explained in the next chapter. Both the Microsoft QuickC and Borland Turbo C++ compilers for Windows will be used in the examples. The end of the chapter covers common problems that may occur when you set up your system and provides their solutions.

Concepts Covered
Hardware and Software Requirements	Small and Medium Memory Models
Program Files	Module Definition Files
Compiling and Linking	Objective Files
Segments	Project Files
Offsets	

Keywords Covered
DEF	NEAR
OBJ	FAR

What You Will Need

Programming in Windows requires that both the hardware (your computer) and the software (the programs) be set up to run correctly. This section describes how to set your system up as a Windows programming environment.

Hardware

To develop Windows programs, you need a computer that will run Windows. The minimum system is an 80286 based PC with 2 megabytes of memory, a hard disk, and an EGA or VGA video screen. Faster computers with more memory speed things up, but they are not a necessity. A mouse *is* a necessity to use several of the programming tools.

Software

A copy of Windows 3.0 or 3.1 should be installed on your machine. For programming, you will need a C compiler that supports Windows and a Windows resource compiler. In the past, this meant buying a DOS-based C compiler and a Windows resource toolkit separately. Both Borland and Microsoft now sell the compiler and resource tools as single packages, including Windows-based development tools. These new tools are ideal for learning to program Windows, as many of the low-level details are handled automatically by the programming tools, freeing you to concentrate on creating programs.

Borland and Microsoft both sell "beginning" and "advanced" versions of their development tools. The beginning version of the Borland compiler is *Turbo C++ for Windows*, which is one of the two compilers this book uses in the examples. This package includes a Windows-based programming environment with an editor, C++ compiler and linker, a Windows-based debugger, an excellent resource editor, and a few other tools. The more advanced version is called Borland C++, which includes all of the Turbo C++ tools, plus a DOS-based C++ command line compiler with more optimization options, and a large collection of advanced programming tools. If you have the Borland C++ package, you can follow the Turbo C++ examples in this book without change by just using the Turbo C++ tools that come in the Borland C++ package. Later, if you are interested in using the command line compiler, look at Appendix B, *Using Command Line Compilers*, for a discussion of automating the compilation steps. For simplicity, the Borland compiler is referred to as just "Turbo C++" throughout the book. Keep in mind that this is the Windows version of the product, not the DOS version.

The beginning version of the Microsoft C compiler is called *Microsoft QuickC for Windows*, which is referred to simply as "QuickC" throughout this book. This package also contains a Windows-based programming environment with an editor, C compiler, linker, simple debugger, and resource editing tools. QuickC is also used in examples in this book. Microsoft sells the advanced programming tools as a separate *Microsoft C++ Compiler version 7.0*, which includes the *Microsoft Windows Software Development Kit* (SDK). The compiler/SDK combination is suited for advanced users who need precise control of the compilers optimization options. Appendix B, *Using Command Line Compilers*, discusses how to use these tools to compile the examples in this book.

An inevitable question at this point is "Which is the best C compiler?" The C compiler market has been competitive for a number of years and there are many excellent C compilers available. Both the Turbo C++ and QuickC packages are excellent tools for Windows development. The Turbo C++ package has the advantage (at the time of writing) of supporting C++, although the examples in this book stick to the basic C language, without the C++ extension. QuickC has the advantage of better documentation of Windows functions. With either compiler you will probably need to buy a reference book (such as *The Waite Group's Windows API Bible*). Other manufacturers, such as Zortech, offer specialized support for specific hardware, such as 32-bit processing, as well as Windows support and C++ extensions. Most large programming houses will use several compilers, favoring one in development and another in the final stages.

Your choice of Windows development tools will not affect the coding of Windows programs. All of the examples in this book will compile properly under QuickC, Turbo C++, Borland C++, and Microsoft C. However, the process of installing the development tools is different for each compiler. This chapter provides separate discussions for how to install the Turbo C++ and QuickC programming tools, and then tests your installation by creating a simple Windows program.

Installing Turbo C++ for Windows

Turbo C++ also has its own Windows-based installation program, which is called INSTALL.EXE. To install Turbo C++ on your hard disk, put the first installation disk in your floppy drive and start the INSTALL program from within Windows. You can either double-click the INSTALL.EXE file name from the Windows File manager application, or select the "File/Run..." menu item in the Windows Program Manager menu and run INSTALL.EXE.

The INSTALL program will display a color bitmap, and then give you a number of options for customizing the installation. The simplest thing to do is to accept all of the defaults, and let INSTALL copy everything to your hard disk. If you are short of space on your hard disk, you can leave out the Object Windows and source code examples. This book does not use either of these tools, although you will probably want to look at them later, when you are done with this book.

When the INSTALL program is done, your Windows Program Manager window will contain a new group titled "Turbo C++." Figure 2-1 shows the appearance of this group. The Turbo C++ icon is the C compiler, including the Windows-based editor. "Import Library" is a specialized tool that we will not use until Chapter 18, *Dynamic Link Libraries*. "Workshop" is the Borland Resource Workshop, which will be used throughout the book to create menus, bitmaps, icons, dialog boxes, and other resources. "TDW" is the Turbo Debugger for Windows. The programs in this book have already been debugged, so you probably will not use the debugger while working through the book. However, the debugger is an excellent tool and will come in handy once you begin writing your own applications. The "FConvert" program is a utility for converting text files between the OEM and ANSI character sets. Chapter 7, *Character Sets, Fonts, and the Keyboard* discusses the differences between these two character sets.

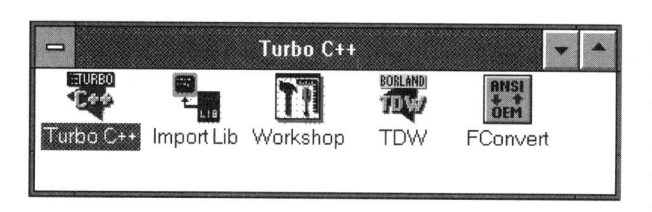

Figure 2-1 The Turbo C++ Group

The Turbo C++ INSTALL program allows you to change the names of subdirectories that INSTALL creates to store all of the Turbo C++ files. If you stick with the default subdirectory names (normally the best choice), your disk file will include the subdirectories shown in Figure 2-2.

One additional subdirectory you may want to create is a "work" subdirectory. This is just a place to put files for the project you are currently working on. Figure 2-2 shows a "work" subdirectory added on to the TCWIN directory chain. New subdirectories can be created within the Windows File Manager application using the "File/Create Directory..." menu item. You can position the "work" subdirectory anywhere in the directory chain you like, but putting in the TCWIN directory chain makes it easy to keep track of what type of data is stored in that portion of the hard disk.

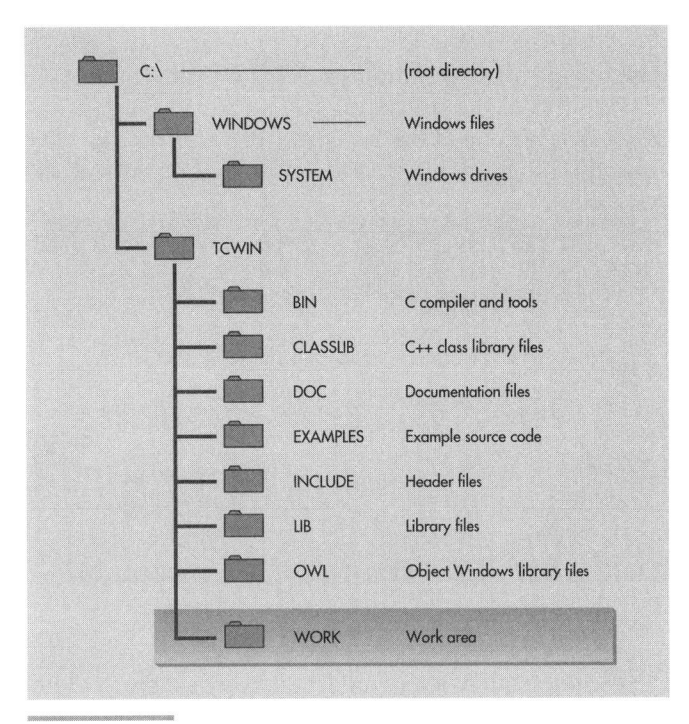

Figure 2-2 Subdirectory Structure with Turbo C++

Setup Options for Turbo C++

Before you can create a Windows application with Turbo C++, you will need to make a few selections from the Turbo C++ menus, to set up your working environment. To start Turbo C++, double-click the "Turbo C++" icon in the "Turbo C++" program group (shown on the left side of Figure 2-1). The application's window will appear, and look like Figure 2-3.

You will need to tell Turbo C++ which subdirectories to use on your hard disk, and the compiler options you intend to use. To specify the directory names, use the "Options/Directories..." menu item. A dialog box will appear displaying the current subdirectory settings, as shown in Figure 2-4. You can enter more than one subdirectory path by separating the path names with a semicolon. This is important for the "Include Directories" entry, where you will want to give the name of both the Turbo C++ include

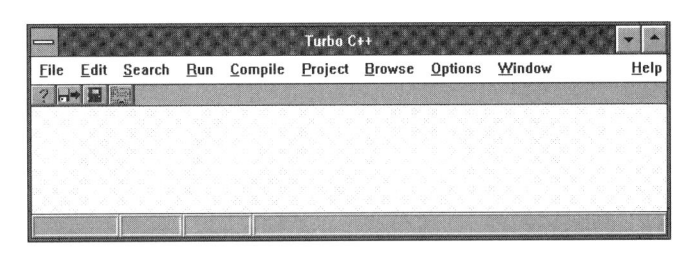

Figure 2-3 Turbo C++

Chapter 2 • Setting Up Your System   27

directory (C:\TCWIN\INCLUDE by default) and the name of the working directory where your own working files will be kept. Figure 2-4 shows the working directory C:\TCWIN\WORK, following the suggested placement of the WORK subdirectory. Be sure to specify the "work" subdirectory name as the "Output Directory," or all of your compiled programs will end up in the same subdirectory with the Turbo C++ compiler.

The other selections tell Turbo C++ what type of memory options and assumptions to make when compiling the program. Select the "Options/Compiler/Code Generation..." menu item, and select the "Small Memory Model." The small memory model is ideal for programs where all of the program's code fit within 64K when compiled. All of the programs in this book are that small, so you

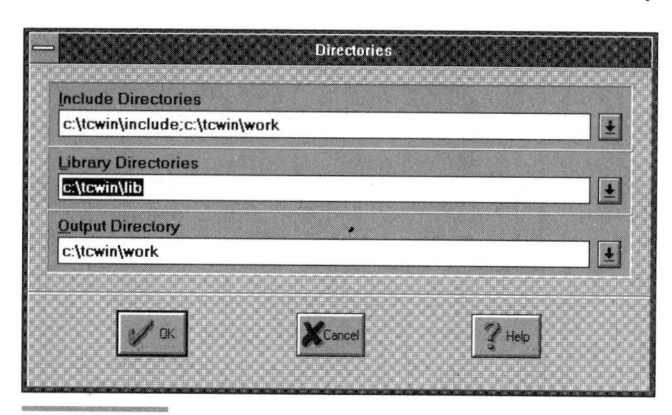

Figure 2-4 Entering Subdirectory Names in Turbo C++

can use the small memory model for every example. More on this subject in the info box *Segments, Offsets, and Memory Models*.

The last selection you will need to make is to pick the "Options/Compiler/Entry/Exit Code..." menu item and select "Windows explicit functions exported." This selection tells Turbo C++ than you will be including a module definition file in your project, which includes the names of all of the functions that will be called from outside of Windows. If you do not select this option, Turbo C++ will create a default module definition file for you, and it will add extra code to the beginning and ending of every function in the compiled program. If you do not select "Windows explicit functions exported," but include a module definition file in the project, the compiler will generate error messages when you compile a program, because it will have duplicate entries for exported functions.

(There is an intermittent bug in Turbo C++ Version 3.0 that sometimes ignores the EXPORT section of the module definition file. If your program compiles, but does not run properly, try selecting the "Windows all functions exportable" option from the "Options/Compiler/Entry/Exit Code..." menu item, and then recompiling. One of the people that tested the examples in this book found that this change was necessary for a number of examples on his system. An alternative is to use the _export key word before the function names of exported functions. This is demonstrated in Chapter 18, *Dynamic Link Libraries*.)

To make sure that Turbo C++ is properly configured, select the "Options/Application..." menu item. The dialog box that appears should look like the one shown in Figure 2-5. If it does, you are ready to compile your first Windows program. If not, go back and

Windows Programming Primer Plus®

check the menu selections for the "Options/Compiler/Code Generation…" and "Options/Compiler/Entry/Exit Code…" menu items.

By default, Turbo C++ includes debugging information in the program files it creates, so that you can run the Turbo Debugger for Windows. All of the programs on the source code disks were created with debugging information included. Later, when you are ready to ship a fin-

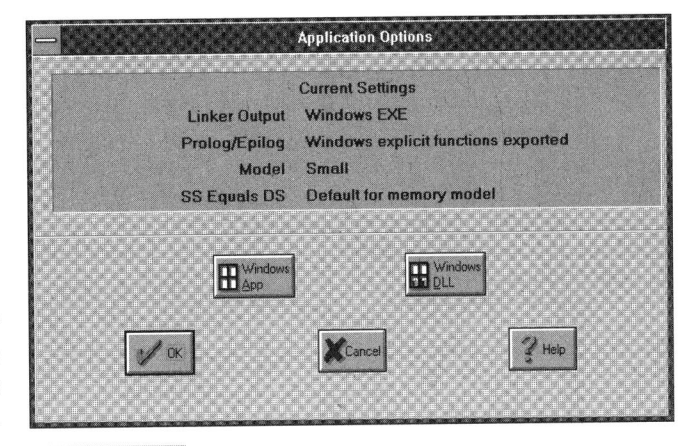

Figure 2-5 Turbo C++ "Options/Application…" Dialog Box

ished Windows program, you can turn off the debugging options to reduce the size of the finished program. The "Options/Advanced Code Generation…" menu item activates the dialog box that allows debugging options to be turned on and off.

Segments, Offsets, and Memory Models

C compilers for DOS and Windows programs come with all sorts of options. A number of the possibilities revolve around the "memory model" the compiler will use. To understand memory models requires an understanding of how the computer's CPU (central processing unit) deals with memory.

The Intel 80x86 family of CPU chips uses what is called the "segmented" memory model. The idea is that any location in memory is described by two addresses, the segment and the offset. The segment describes a portion of the memory on the computer system. The offset specifies an individual location within the segment. As shown in Figure 2-6, the full address is the combination of the segment and the offset. This is similar to describing a person's address in terms of a street and an address number. The name of the street localizes the address to a given street, and the address number provides the location (offset) from the beginning of the street.

The advantage of the segmented memory model is that you

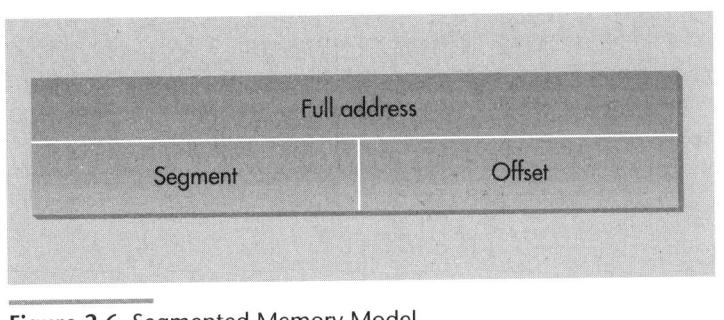

Figure 2-6 Segmented Memory Model

(continued)

Chapter 2 • Setting Up Your System

Segments, Offsets, and Memory Models (cont'd)

can describe an address within a single segment by just specifying the offset. This is faster than specifying the full segment + offset for every address, as long as the addresses are all within the same segment. Again, this is just like specifying a street number once you know the street name. There is no need to keep repeating the street name, as long as you know a group of addresses are all on the same street.

Your C compiler can take advantage of the segmented memory model to make the program more efficient. For small programs, all of the program's code can be put in a single segment. This is called the "small memory model." By using a small memory model, all of the function addresses can just use the offset value, as the segment will always be the same. Windows limits the maximum size of a segment to 64K because Windows maintains compatibility with the older 80286 CPU chips which could not handle segments larger than 64K. The largest small memory model program has 64K of compiled code.

The other option is to break up the program's code into multiple segments. If you compile with the "medium memory model," each C program file will end up compiled into a separate segment. This means that the function addresses must be the full offset + segment values. Figure 2-7 shows a comparison of the two memory models. Although the medium memory model makes the program a little larger and a tiny bit slower, there is an advantage. Windows can move each segment of the program in memory individually. This allows much greater freedom for memory optimization. If your program is over 15K in size, use the medium memory model, as the benefits of Windows' memory management far outweigh the slight increase in program size.

In the C language, "pointers" are memory locations used to hold the numeric value of another memory address. Because of the difference in size between an address that just contains an offset and a full address that contains both the segment and offset, you will need to specify what type of pointer you want to use. This is done with two compiler key words, NEAR and FAR. NEAR pointers just contain the offset portion of the address. FAR pointers contain both the seg-

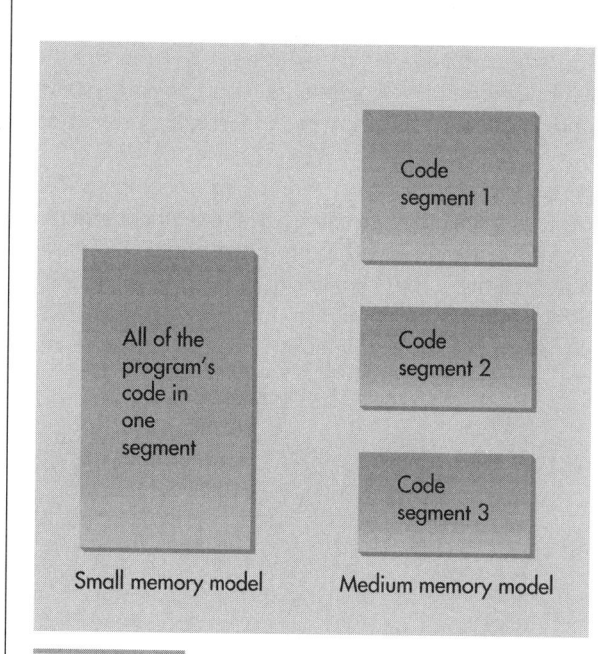

Figure 2-7 Small and Medium Memory Model Programs

(continued)

> **Segments, Offsets, and Memory Models (cont'd)**
>
> ment and the offset. For example, to declare a near pointer to an integer and a far pointer to a character, you would use the following statements:
>
> ```
> int  NEAR    *n ;     /* near pointer to an address containing an integer */
> char FAR     *c ;     /* far pointer to an address containing a character */
> ```
>
> If you study the C compiler's documentation, you will also find references to other memory models such as "large," "huge," and "tiny." These models control how the program handles data in one or more segments of memory. These memory models are important to DOS programs, but are of less value to a Windows programmer. Windows has its own memory management functions, which are much more sophisticated than the DOS models. We will examine storing data in memory using Windows functions in Chapter 12, *Managing Memory*.

Installing Microsoft QuickC for Windows

QuickC has its own Windows-based installation program, which is called INSTALL.EXE. To install QuickC on your hard disk, put the first installation disk in your floppy drive, and start the INSTALL program from within Windows. You can either double-click the INSTALL.EXE file name in the Windows File manager application, or select the "File/Run..." menu item from the Windows Program Manager menu and run INSTALL.EXE.

The INSTALL program will give you several options for customizing the installation. The simplest thing to do is to accept all of the defaults and let INSTALL copy everything to your hard disk. If you are short of space on your hard disk, you can leave out the "Quick Case:W" and the source code examples. The examples in this book do not use these tools, although you will probably want to look at them when you are done with the book. You can run INSTALL again later and just add these files to your hard disk.

The INSTALL program will add a new group named "Microsoft QC/Win" to your Program Manager window. Figure 2-8 shows the contents of that group. The "QC/Win" icon is the QuickC programming environment. "QuickCase:W" is a program generation tool that we will not use in this book, but which you may find useful when you have completed the book and are looking for ways to speed up program development. The "Dialog Editor" and "Image Editor" are tools that we will use later in the book to create dialog box definitions and bitmap images for cursors, icons, and bitmap pictures.

The QuickC INSTALL program allows you to change the names of subdirectories that INSTALL creates to store all of the QuickC files. If you

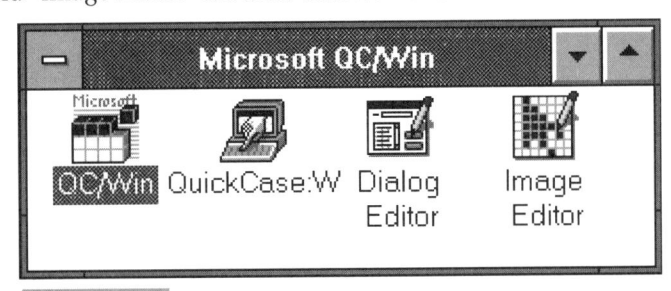

Figure 2-8 The QuickC Program Group

stick with the default directory names, your disk file will include the directories shown in Figure 2-9.

One additional subdirectory you may want to create is a "work" subdirectory. This is just a place to put files for the project you are currently working on. Figure 2-9 shows a "work" subdirectory added on to the QCWIN directory chain. New subdirectories can be created within the Windows File Manager application using the "File/Create Directory..." menu item. You can position the "work" subdirectory anywhere in the directory chain you like, but putting it in the QCWIN directory chain makes it easy to keep track of what type of data is stored in that portion of the hard disk.

Microsoft QuickC Setup

The default options for Microsoft QuickC are exactly what you will need to compile the examples in this book, so no additional work is needed before you start work on your first Windows program. If you would like to verify that the compiler is set up correctly, select the "Options/Project..." menu item. A dialog box like the one shown in Figure 2-10 will appear. The default options create a Windows EXE program and include debugging information. Later, when you want to create a finished Windows program,

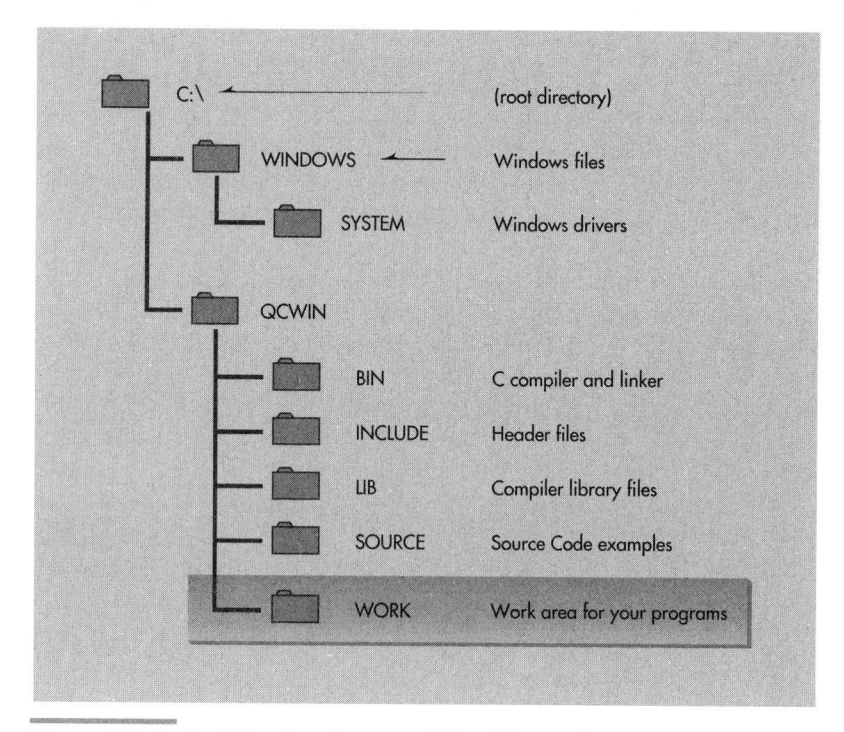

Figure 2-9 Typical Directory Structure Using Microsoft QuickC

Windows Programming Primer Plus®

select the "Release" option under "Build Mode" to eliminate debug information from the final program.

If you select the "Compiler" button from the Project dialog box, you will get another dialog box, as shown in Figure 2-11. By default, QuickC uses the compiler "small" memory model. This is ideal for the example programs in this book, where the compiled program's code occupies less than 64 K. Later, when you are working on your own larger projects, you will want to switch to the "medium" memory model.

The QuickC compiler keeps track of the directory you are using to save the program files you create. The compiler's output will automatically be placed in the same directory with your source code files.

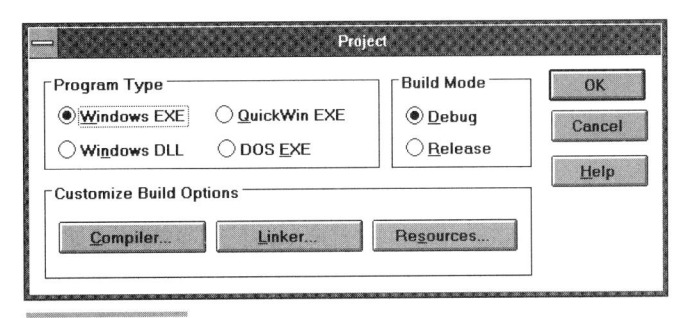

Figure 2-10 The QuickC Options/Project... Dialog Box

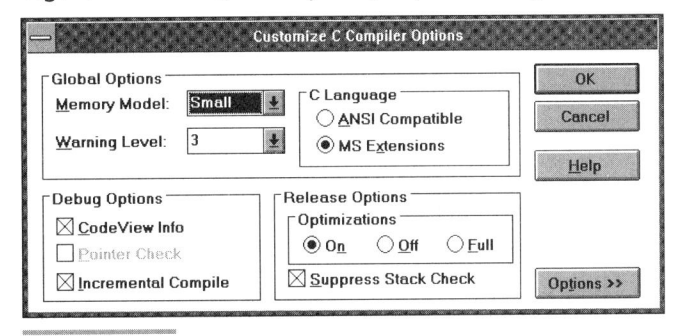

Figure 2-11 The QuickC Compiler Dialog Box

Creating the World's Shortest Windows Program

Now for the acid test: compiling your first Windows program called "MINIMAL1." This program will appear as shown in Figure 2-12 when started. The program is very shy, as even touching an edge of the MINIMAL1 window with the mouse cursor will result in the window vanishing from the screen.

Creating MINIMAL1 requires that you create three small files: MINIMAL1.C, MINIMAL1.DEF, and a project file. The project file will be called MINIMAL1.PRJ for the Turbo C++ compiler, or MINIMAL1.MAK for QuickC. Project files are used to tell the compiler which files to use in creating the finished program. For MINIMAL1, the project will consist of just MINIMAL1.C and MINIMAL1.DEF. Figure 2-13 shows how these files are used to create the intermediate objective file MINIMAL1.OBJ and then combined to make the finished program, MINIMAL1.EXE.

Figure 2-12 The MINIMAL1 program

Chapter 2 • Setting Up Your System 33

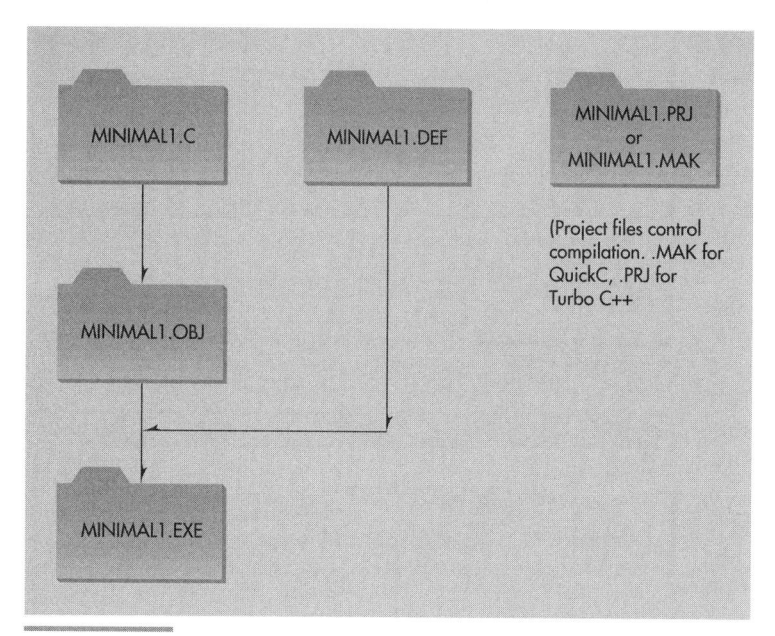

Figure 2-13 Files Used to Create the MINIMAL1.EXE Program

Object Files

C compilers do not produce ready-to-run programs in one step. Instead, the C compiler outputs an intermediate file called an "object" file. With small programs like MINIMAL1.C, the object file seems like an unnecessary step. Why doesn't the compiler go ahead and create the .EXE file right away?

The reason for object files has to do with compiling larger programs that have more than one C source code file. Each of the files will contain references to functions that are defined in another source code file. The C compiler does not know exactly where functions in other program files will ultimately be located, so the compiler cannot determine their addresses. Instead, the compiler produces the object file with the file extension ".OBJ." The object file has all of the C language instructions converted into CPU instructions, but leaves spaces for addresses. If the program uses the small memory model, the object file will have space only for the offset portion of the address. If the program is compiled with the medium memory model, the compiler will leave room for both the segment and the offset for each function address.

When all of the object files are created, the addresses of each of the functions can be determined by putting together all of the object files and finding out where each function ends up being located. This is the job of the linker. Linker programs literally link together a series of object files, and insert the function addresses where needed. The Turbo C++ and QuickC compilers automatically start the linker when the compiler is done, so that it appears that only a single activity is taking place. Keep in mind that both the compiler and linker are being run when you compile a program from source code files.

The first file to create is MINIMAL1.C, the source code file. The complete program is shown in Listing 2-1. It is about as short as a Windows program can be. In this chapter, we will focus on the mechanics of compiling the MINIMAL1 program. The function of each of the lines in MINIMAL1.C will be explained in the next chapter.

Listing 2-1 MINIMAL1.C Program File

```
/* minimal1.c   minimal1 windows application */

#include <windows.h>              /* window's header file - always included */

int PASCAL WinMain (HANDLE hInstance, HANDLE hPrevInstance, LPSTR lpszCmdLine,
                    int nCmdShow)
{
    HWND   hWnd ;
                             /* create the program window */
    hWnd = CreateWindow ("BUTTON," "Hello World.," BS_PUSHBUTTON,
        10, 10, 100, 100, NULL, NULL, hInstance, NULL) ;
    ShowWindow (hWnd, nCmdShow) ;    /* display the window */
    WaitMessage () ;                 /* wait for ANY message */
    return (0) ;                     /* quit */
}
```

You can either create the MINIMAL1.C program by typing the code or take advantage of the files on the source code disks. At this point, typing the code is an excellent idea, as it will allow you to try out the editing features of your compiler. Follow the steps in Table 2-1 to type the MINIMAL1.C program.

TURBO C++	QUICKC
Select the "File/New" menu item.	Select the "File/New" menu item.
An empty edit window will appear, initially titled "noname00."	An empty edit window will appear, initially titled "Untitled 1."
Type in the MINIMAL1.C program, copying the code in Listing 2-1.	Type in the MINIMAL1.C program, copying the code in Listing 2-1.
Select the "File/Save As..." menu item.	Select the "File/Save As..." menu item.
Change the file name to MINIMAL1.C, and save the file in your work directory.	Change the file name to MINIMAL1.C, and save the file in your work directory.

Table 2-1 Creating the MINIMAL1.C File

The module definition file for MINIMAL1 is similar to the example we looked at in the last chapter. MINIMAL1.DEF (Listing 2-2) sets the standard memory options that most Windows programs use. The program's code will be loaded when the

MINIMAL1.EXE is started (PRELOAD), and the code can be moved in memory by the Windows environment (MOVEABLE). The program's data is also marked PRELOAD MOVEABLE. In addition the data is marked MULTIPLE, meaning that if more than one copy of the program is running, each copy will have its own data segment. The HEAPSIZE sets 1,024 bytes of memory for the "local heap," a memory area programs can use to store relatively small amounts of data. STACKSIZE sets the size of the program's stack to 5,120 bytes, the smallest allowable stack size for a Windows 3.x program. MINIMAL1 is so simple that there is no resource data.

Listing 2-2 MINIMAL1.DEF Module Definition File

```
EXETYPE     WINDOWS
STUB        'WINSTUB.EXE'
CODE        PRELOAD MOVEABLE
DATA        PRELOAD MOVEABLE MULTIPLE
HEAPSIZE    1024
STACKSIZE   5120
```

Create the MINIMAL1.DEF file exactly as you created the MINIMAL1.C file, and save the file in your work directory. The only thing left to do is to define the project file for the program so that the compiler knows that MINIMAL1.C and MINIMAL1.DEF should be used to create the finished program.

Creating a Project File

Creating a project file for a program is remarkably easy. All you do is open a new project file with the same name as your program, and add each of the source code files to the project list. The project file for MINIMAL1 is called MINIMAL1.PRJ with Turbo C++, and MINIMAL1.MAK for QuickC. Table 2-2 summarizes the steps needed to create this simple project file.

TURBO C++	QUICKC
Select the "Project/Open Project..." menu item.	Select the "Project/Open Project..." menu item.
Select your working directory.	Select your working directory.
Enter the file name MINIMAL1.PRJ in the edit control labeled "File Name," and then click the "OK" button. A project window will appear at the bottom of the Turbo C++ edit area.	Enter the file name MINIMAL1.MAK in the edit control labeled "File Name," and then click the "OK" button. A small message box will appear, "MINIMAL1.MAK does not exist. Would you like to create it?". Select the "OK" button. A dialog box labeled "Edit - MINIMAL.MAK" will appear.

Type or select the file name MINIMAL1.C, and then select the "Add" button. The MINIMAL1.C file appears in the project window.	Type or select the file name MINIMAL1.C, and then select the "Add" button. The MINIMAL1.C file appears in the project window.
Type or select the file name MINIMAL1.DEF, and then select the "Add" button. The file MINIMAL1.DEF appears in the project window.	Type or select the file name MINIMAL1.DEF, and then select the "Add" button. The file MINIMAL1.DEF appears in the project window.
Select the "Done" button. Your project file is now complete.	Select the "OK" button. Your project file is now now complete.

Table 2-2 Creating a Project File

Before attempting to compile MINIMAL1, use the Windows File Manager application to check that the files MINIMAL1.C, MINIMAL1.DEF, and MINIMAL1.PRJ (Turbo C++) or MINIMAL1.MAK (QuickC) are in your work subdirectory. If not, you probably saved the files in some other directory, so find them and move them to the correct subdirectory before proceeding.

Compiling and Running MINIMAL1

Once you have the project file defined, you can compile the program by just selecting a menu item. Assuming that there are no mistakes in the files, the compiler will both compile and link the files to create the MINIMAL1.EXE program. Table 2-3 summarizes the steps needed to compile and run MINIMAL1.

TURBO C++	QUICKC
Select the "Compile/Make" menu item. This will selectively rebuild any portions of the program that have been updated.	Select the "Project/Build" menu item. This will selectively rebuild any portions of the program that have been updated.
The compiler and linker will run, with each step displayed in a dialog box as it is performed. Assuming that there are no errors, the message "Success" will be shown in on the dialog box window. Select the "OK" button.	The compiler and linker will run, with each step displayed in a dialog box as it is performed. Assuming that there are no errors, the message "MINIMAL1.EXE - 0 errors, 0 warnings" will appear at the bottom of the QuickC window.
Compiler errors and warnings will be listed in a "Messages" window at the bottom of the editing area. MINIMAL1.C will generate two warning messages, even if there are no errors. Figure 2-14 shows the message window.	Unless there was a typo, QuickC will not detect errors or warnings in MINIMAL1.

(continued)

Table 2-3 (cont'd)

Select the "Run/Run" menu item. Turbo C++ will check that the file is up-to-date, and will then run MINIMAL1.EXE. The MINIMAL1 window will appear at the upper left corner of the screen, but will vanish as soon as it is touched with the mouse cursor.	Select the "Run/Go" menu item. QuickC will run the MINIMAL1.EXE program. The MINIMAL1 window will appear at the upper left corner of the screen, but will vanish as soon as it is touched with the mouse cursor.

Table 2-3 Compiling and Running MINIMAL1

Although both Turbo C++ and QuickC produce an equivalent MINIMAL1.EXE program, there are differences between the compilers. One difference is that Turbo C++ checks to make sure that every parameter passed to a function is used. If some are not used, Turbo C++ prints out warning messages. In MINIMAL1.C, the *hPrevInstance* and *lpszCmdLine* parameters passed to the WinMain() function are never used. This is deliberate, and not an error. MINIMAL1.C does not need the information passed in these two parameters (their meaning will be explained in the next chapter). Turbo C++ issues two warning messages, as shown in Figure 2-14. These warnings are just information and do not stop the compilation from making a finished program. QuickC ignores the unused parameters and does not issue any warnings.

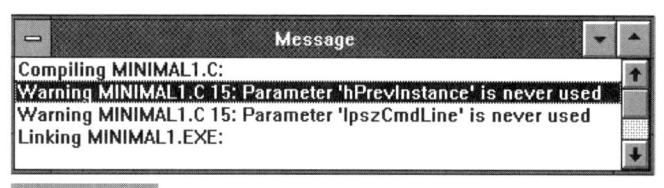

Figure 2-14 Turbo C++ Messages for MINIMAL1 Compilation

If you were able to compile and run MINIMAL1 without any trouble, congratulations! Do not expect this to happen every time, as there are lots of little things that can go wrong when creating a program, and more often than not you will need to fiddle a bit to get everything working. The next section describes several common problems and their solutions.

Common Problems in Compiling and Their Solutions

The author has frequently suspected that he has already made every possible error, only to invent a new one on the next program. The reader will probably discover some new ones that the author has not stumbled into. Nevertheless, the most common errors are predictable and worth discussing before you have a chance to find them for yourself.

Typos in the C Program

Perhaps the most likely type of error is simply when you do not type the program code exactly right. In most cases, these errors are easy to find, as the compiler will tell you the line number the error occurred on and highlight the offending line in the edit window if the source code file is visible. Because the examples in this book all compile without error (but sometimes give warning messages), you should be able to find the error by quickly comparing the line you typed to that in this book.

There are a few cases where the error will slip through the compiler and not show up until the linking step. For example, assume that the function name "ShowWindow()" was typed in without the first letter "o." Listing 2-3 shows the MINIMAL1.C program Listing with this error. The program line still reflects valid C language syntax. There just happens to be no such function.

Listing 2-3 MINIMAL1.C with a Typographical Error

```
/* minimal1.c   minimal1 windows application */

#include <windows.h>          /* window's header file - always included */

int PASCAL WinMain (HANDLE hInstance, HANDLE hPrevInstance, LPSTR lpszCmdLine,
    int nCmdShow)
{
    HWND   hWnd ;

    hWnd = CreateWindow ("BUTTON," "Hello World.," BS_PUSHBUTTON,
       10, 10, 100, 100, NULL, NULL, hInstance, NULL) ;
    ShwWindow (hWnd, nCmdShow) ; /* display the window   <- typo here !!! */
    WaitMessage () ;             /* sit there */
    return 0 ;                   /* quit */
}
```

The type of error in Listing 2-3 is difficult to spot. The compiler will assume that you are going to define the ShwWindow() function in some other source code file, so the compiler does not show any new errors or warnings. The problem does not surface until the linker tries to figure out the address of ShwWindow() and finds that it does not know where to find that function. Figure 2-15 shows the result for both compilers.

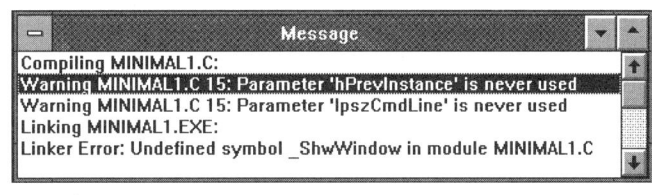

a) Turbo C++

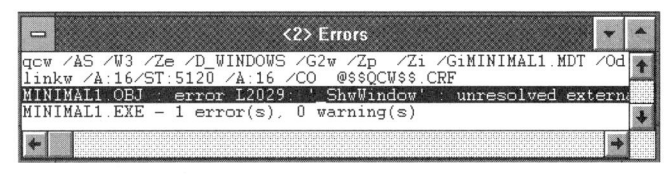

b) QuickC

Figure 2-15 Incorrect Function Name in MINIMAL1

Error messages like "Undefined symbol" and "Unresolved external reference" are not easy for a new programmer to interpret. The best approach is to use the compiler's editor to search for the offending word, "ShwWindow" in this case. When you have located the line in the source code file, you should be able to figure out what is wrong. In the example, simply putting the "o" back into ShowWindow() solves the problem. The file must be recompiled to create the finished MINIMAL1.EXE program.

Typos in the Module Definition File

There are only two source code files in MINIMAL1, so the only other place you can make a typo is in MINIMAL1.DEF. Listing 2-4 shows an example error, with an "S" added to the end of the EXETYPE statement, making "EXETYPES."

Listing 2-4 Error in MINIMAL1.DEF

```
EXETYPES        WINDOWS
STUB            'WINSTUB.EXE'
CODE            PRELOAD MOVEABLE
DATA            PRELOAD MOVEABLE MULTIPLE
HEAPSIZE        1024
STACKSIZE       5120
```

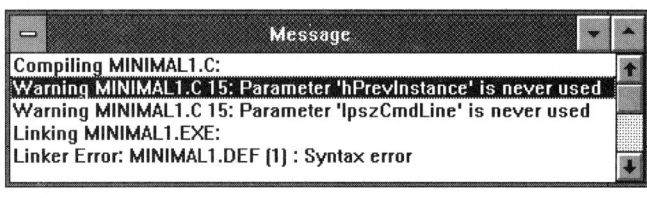

```
                        Message
Compiling MINIMAL1.C:
Warning MINIMAL1.C 15: Parameter 'hPrevInstance' is never used
Warning MINIMAL1.C 15: Parameter 'lpszCmdLine' is never used
Linking MINIMAL1.EXE:
Linker Error: MINIMAL1.DEF (1) : Syntax error
```

a) Turbo C++

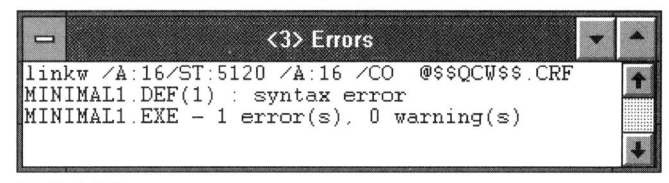

```
                        <3> Errors
linkw /A:16/ST:5120 /A:16 /CO  @$$QCW$$.CRF
MINIMAL1.DEF(1) : syntax error
MINIMAL1.EXE - 1 error(s), 0 warning(s)
```

b) QuickC

Figure 2-16 Errors in the Module Definition File

The MINIMAL1.DEF file is not used until the linking step, so the compiler cannot jump to the offending line in the source code. Instead, an error message is printed in the message window, as shown in Figure 2-16.

Both compilers give the cryptic message "syntax error," following the file name MINIMAL1.DEF. The line number of the offending line is given in parentheses: (1). You must go to that line number in the MINIMAL1.DEF file and figure out what is wrong with the statements. Fortunately, module definition files are short, so it is usually easy to find the error.

Setup Problems

Although the INSTALL programs work well, there is still the potential that you do not have your compiler set up properly. Figure 2-17 shows typical error messages. The compiler could not find the WINDOWS.H header file. This means that the subdirectory names that you specified for the compiler are not correct.

To change the compiler's subdirectory names, select the "Options/Directories..." menu item in Turbo C++ or QuickC. The default directory names shown in the previous illustrations in the discussion of installing your compiler. If these do not work, use the Windows File Manager application to look at the subdirectory names on your hard

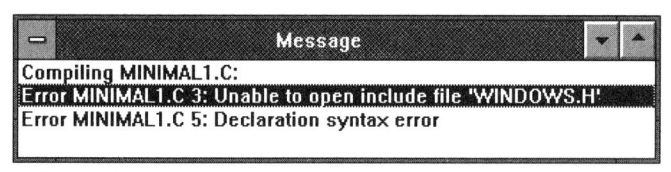

```
┌─────────────────── Message ───────────────▼─▲──┐
│ Compiling MINIMAL1.C:                          │
│ Error MINIMAL1.C 3: Unable to open include file 'WINDOWS.H' │
│ Error MINIMAL1.C 5: Declaration syntax error   │
└────────────────────────────────────────────────┘
```

a) Turbo C++

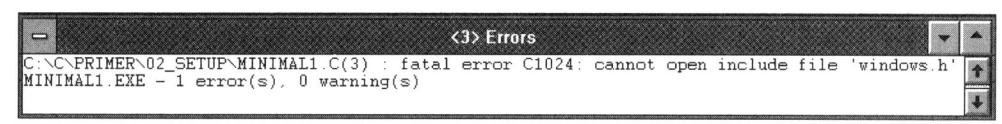

```
┌─────────────────── <3> Errors ────────────▼─▲──┐
│ C:\C\PRIMER\02_SETUP\MINIMAL1.C(3) : fatal error C1024: cannot open include file 'windows.h' │
│ MINIMAL1.EXE - 1 error(s), 0 warning(s)        │
└────────────────────────────────────────────────┘
```

b) QuickC

Figure 2-17 Turbo C++ and Quick C Configuration Errors

disk. The "include" subdirectory should contain a number of header files, including WINDOWS.H. The library subdirectory should contain a number of .OBJ and .LIB files, including CWS.LIB for Turbo C++ and QWIN.LIB for QuickC.

Other Errors

There are certainly many other possible errors that you may run into. The key to success is perseverance. If the error message does not make sense to you, look it up in your compiler's manual. Sometimes the description in the manual will give you an idea of where to look. If you are really stuck, try to go back to a previous situation where you did not run into the error, and then add one change at a time until the error pops up. Most important—don't give up! Computers are stupid machines. You just can't let them get the upper hand.

Summary

This chapter focused on setting up your system to compile Windows programs. Both Turbo C++ and QuickC for Windows have easy-to-use installation programs that take most of the guesswork out of installing the compiler. There are a few settings for each compiler that you will need to check, and potentially change. With Turbo C++, make sure that the subdirectory names that the compiler uses match your hard disk's organization. All of the programs in this book will use the compiler's small memory model. The small model puts all of the program's code in a single segment. This limits the size of the code to 64K, the maximum size of segment. Larger Windows programs use the medium memory model.

The compiler's setup was tested by creating a simple Windows application program named MINIMAL1. Windows programs are made up of more files than DOS programs. Even our simple MINIMAL1 program required three files, MINIMAL1.C, MINIMAL1.DEF and a project file. The compiler processes these files, creating an intermediate objective file and the finished .EXE program, ready to run. In the next chapter, we will build on MINIMAL1 to create a more complete Windows application.

QUESTIONS

1. In a small memory model program, the program's code is located in several small segments. (True/False).
2. The module definition file (.DEF file) is used by the compiler to set memory options. (True/False).
3. Under Windows, the largest size of a single segment in memory is ___ .
4. Explain what the word "PRELOAD" means in a module definition file.
5. The full (FAR) address of a location in memory is given by the combination of a _____ and _____ .

ANSWERS

1. False. Small memory model programs have all of their code in one segment.
2. False. The module definition file is used by the linker.
3. 64 K.
4. PRELOAD means that the code or data is loaded into memory when the program starts running, not later when the specific code or data is needed.
5. segment, offset.

CHAPTER 3

First Programming Experiments

This chapter explains the coding behind the MINIMAL1 program from the previous chapter and then expands the program in three steps. Each addition to the program will explain more of the fundamentals behind Windows programming. The message processing logic will be improved and a new "class" of windows created. By the end of the chapter, you will have a complete Windows application with its own icon and menu. This program will serve as an excellent starting point for other programming projects, including other programs in this book.

Besides improving the MINIMAL1 application, the additions will introduce two new types of files that will be used in all of the remaining example programs. The first is a header file, which will store definitions of constants and function declarations. The second is a resource file, containing the program's menu definition and icon image. Many other uses for resource data will be explored in subsequent chapters.

Concepts Covered

WINDOWS.H	Binary Flags
WinMain() Function	Message Loop
Hungarian Notation	Message Structure
Creating the Program's Window	Creating a Window Class
Window Styles	Adding Icons and Menus

Keywords Covered

PASCAL	LPSTR
HANDLE	EXPORTS
WORD	ICON
PSTR	MENUITEM

Functions Covered

CreateWindow()	WndProc()
ShowWindow()	DispatchMessage()
RegisterClass()	PostQuitMessage()
GetMessage()	TranslateMessage()
DefWindowProc()	MessageBeep()

Messages Covered

WM_LBUTTONDOWN	WM_DESTROY
WM_COMMAND	WM_QUIT

The WINDOWS.H File

The last chapter focused on getting the MINIMAL1 program compiled and ready to run. Let's take another look at MINIMAL1.C and examine what each line of code does. The complete program is shown in Listing 3-1.

Listing 3-1 MINIMAL1.C

```
/* minimal1.c   minimal1 windows application */

#include <windows.h>            /* window's header file - always included */

int PASCAL WinMain (HANDLE hInstance, HANDLE hPrevInstance, LPSTR lpszCmdLine,
    int nCmdShow)
{
    HWND    hWnd ;
```

```
    hWnd = CreateWindow ("BUTTON","Hello World.", BS_PUSHBUTTON,
       10, 10, 100, 100, NULL, NULL, hInstance, NULL) ;
    ShowWindow (hWnd, nCmdShow) ;    /* display the window */
    WaitMessage () ;                 /* sit there */
    return (0) ;                     /* quit */
}
```

The top line in Listing 3-1 is just a comment and has no effect on the final program. The first line that does anything is #include <windows.h>. This statement inserts the entire Windows header file WINDOWS.H at this location in the program. WINDOWS.H comes with Turbo C++, Borland C++, Microsoft C++, and QuickC for Windows. WINDOWS.H is a big header file, too big to load into the Windows NOTEPAD application to view. If you have not already done so, take a look at the WINDOWS.H file using your compiler's editor, or print it out for future reference. WINDOWS.H is about 30 pages long. In it you will find all sorts of definitions. Listing 3-2 shows a few examples which show the definition of some of the special data types used in Windows programs.

Listing 3-2 WINDOWS.H Excerpt

```
typedef int                BOOL;
typedef unsigned char      BYTE;
typedef unsigned int       WORD;
typedef unsigned long      DWORD;
typedef char near          *PSTR;
typedef char near          *NPSTR;
typedef char far           *LPSTR;
typedef BYTE near          *PBYTE;
typedef BYTE far           *LPBYTE;
typedef int near           *PINT;
typedef int far            *LPINT;
typedef WORD near          *PWORD;
typedef WORD far           *LPWORD;
typedef long near          *PLONG;
typedef long far           *LPLONG;
typedef DWORD near         *PDWORD;
typedef DWORD far          *LPDWORD;
typedef void far           *LPVOID;

typedef WORD               HANDLE;
typedef HANDLE             HWND;
```

WINDOWS.H makes good use of the C language typedef statement. For example, the new type WORD is not defined in the C language, but is defined in WINDOWS.H as an unsigned integer (0 to 65,535). This means that in a Windows program, you can use "WORD" anywhere that you would otherwise have to type out "unsigned int." At the end of Listing 3-2 you will see that WORD is then used to create two other data types: HANDLE and HWND (handle of a window). The result is that WORD, HANDLE, and HWND are all unsigned integers, even though each has a different purpose. These new names will make declarations of variable types more obvious than would be by using the declaration "unsigned int." We will see examples of this in a moment.

Browse through WINDOWS.H. You will see all sorts of define statements, giving names to numeric values. You will include WINDOWS.H in essentially every Windows program that you compile. (A Windows programmer lost on a desert island, who could only keep one listing, would make sure that it was a listing of WINDOWS.H!)

Turbo C++ Hint—Pre-Compiled Header Files

WINDOWS.H is a big header file, over 120K. For small programs, the compiler takes more time reading and converting WINDOWS.H into a form the compiler can use (called a "symbol table") than it does reading and compiling the program's code.

Turbo C++ provides a shortcut to this process: pre-compiled header files. The idea is to save the compiled version of the header file(s) information as a disk file. The next time the compiler needs the header information, it just reads the pre-compiled header file, rather than parsing it again. Compilation of small Windows programs becomes almost instantaneous using this feature.

To use pre-compiled header files, select the "Options\Compiler\Code Generation..." menu item and click the "Use pre-compiled headers" button. Save this selection by selecting the "Options\Save..." menu item. The next time you compile the same program, the header symbol table will be written to the file TCDEF.SYM in the compiler's subdirectory. As long as the same header files are listed in the same order in each file that you compile, the symbol table will be read without modification. If you compile a new list of header files, the first compilation will update TCDEF.SYM. Subsequent compilations will read the new symbol table.

The Borland C++ 3.0 and Microsoft C++ 7.0 compilers have similar features. This option is not available with the QuickC version 1.0 release.

The WinMain() Function

Now that you have seen a portion of WINDOWS.H, you can begin to make sense out of the rest of MINIMAL1.C. The next line is the WinMain() function call:

```
int PASCAL WinMain (HANDLE hInstance, HANDLE hPrevInstance, LPSTR lpszCmdLine,
    int nCmdShow)
```

The function WinMain() is declared to be "int PASCAL." The "int" means that the function returns an integer when it is finished. "PASCAL" is a compiler key word. PASCAL tells the C compiler to use the function calling conventions of the Pascal language, rather than the C language. This seems a bit odd, as we are using C and not Pascal. The reason for using the PASCAL function calling convention is that this produces a bit less computer code when compiled into machine instructions. This is because the PASCAL calling convention puts the parameters passed by a function on the stack in the order that they are listed in the function's declaration (see Figure 3-1), rather than in reverse order, which is the C language convention. The compiler always knows that the first argument is on top of the stack with the PASCAL convention, while with the C

```
                    C function              Pascal function
    ┌────────┐    ┌──────────────┐        ┌──────────────┐
    │ Top of │    │              │        │              │
    │ stack  │    │   nCmdShow   │        │   hInstance  │
    └────────┘    │              │        │              │
                  ├──────────────┤        ├──────────────┤
                  │              │        │              │
                  │  lpszCmdLine │        │ hPrevInstance│
                  │              │        │              │
                  ├──────────────┤        ├──────────────┤
                  │              │        │              │
                  │hPrevInstance │        │  lpszCmdLine │
                  │              │        │              │
                  ├──────────────┤        ├──────────────┤
                  │              │        │              │
                  │   hInstance  │        │   nCmdShow   │
                  │              │        │              │
                  └──────────────┘        └──────────────┘

         int WinMain (HANDLE hInstance, HANDLE hPrevInstance,
                  LPSTR lpszCmdLine, int nCmdShow)
```

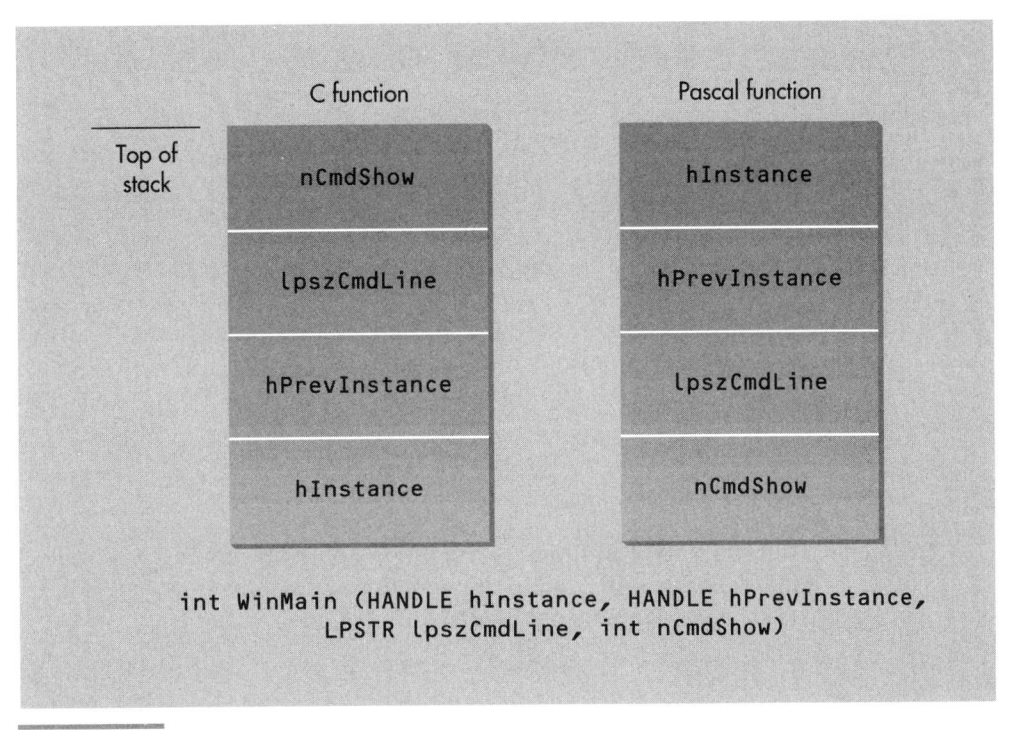

Figure 3-1 Stack Order for C and Pascal Function Calling Conventions

convention, the compiler must determine the location of the first argument by working down the stack. When converted into the CPU instructions, the C calling convention results in some extra instructions each time any function is called. The trade-off is that the PASCAL calling convention does not allow functions to have a variable number of arguments. Functions like the C library printf() function can have any number of arguments between the parentheses. Windows uses the PASCAL function calling convention whenever possible to make the programs smaller and faster. With the one exception of the wsprintf() function, Windows functions always use a fixed number of arguments, so the limitation of the PASCAL calling convention is not a problem.

WinMain() is the Windows equivalent of the normal C language main() function, and every Windows program must have a WinMain() function. When a Windows application starts, it is the WinMain() function that begins execution. When a Windows application terminates (exits, quits operating), it is WinMain() that returns an exit code to Windows. The exit code is an integer value because WinMain() is declared as an "int PASCAL" function, so it returns an integer. At present, Windows 3.1 does not do anything with this integer value.

Within the parentheses are the four parameters that Windows passes to WinMain() when the program starts. We can figure out the underlying data types of the parameters by looking up the types HANDLE and LPSTR in WINDOWS.H. Listing 3-3 shows the key lines, extracted from the WINDOWS.H file.

Chapter 3 • First Programming Experiments

Listing 3-3 Definition of HANDLE and LPSTR in WINDOWS.H

```
typedef unsigned int   WORD;
...
typedef WORD           HANDLE;
...
typedef char far       *LPSTR;
```

So a HANDLE is an unsigned int, and LPSTR is a far pointer to a char (a pointer to a character location, or memory byte). Recall from Chapter 2, *Setting Up Your System*, that a far pointer consists of a segment value plus an offset, and far pointers can address any location in memory, not just values within one segment. If we did not have the WINDOWS.H file definitions, the WinMain() function declaration would have been written:

```
int PASCAL WinMain (unsigned int hInstance, unsigned int hPrevInstance,
     char far *lpszCmdLine, int nCmdShow)
```

The "spelled out" version of WinMain() is perfectly acceptable from the compiler's point of view, and it will result in exactly the same final program. However, it is less clear what each of the data elements represents.

Hungarian Notation

To make it even clearer what type of data elements are being used, Windows programmers use a naming convention called "Hungarian Notation" in honor of its inventor, Charles Simonyi. The idea is to precede variable names with key letters that describe what type of data the variable represents. Table 3-1 shows the basic system of prefixes.

PREFIX	DATA TYPE
b	BOOL (int, use only TRUE and FALSE values, 1 and 0)
by	BYTE (unsigned char)
c	char
dw	DWORD (double word, a four byte unsigned long integer)
fn	function
h	handle. This is an ID value that Windows uses internally to keep track of memory blocks, window ID values, etc.
i	int (two byte signed integer)
l	long
n	short (int) or near pointer
p	pointer

s	character string
sz	character string terminated by zero
w	word (two bytes)

Table 3-1 Variable Name Prefix Codes Used in Hungarian Notation

Figure 3-2 shows an example using Hungarian notation. The variable *lpszBigName* is a long pointer to a zero terminated string (l = long, p = pointer, sz = zero terminated string). Also note the use of capital letters in the name to make the word breaks obvious without wasting space.

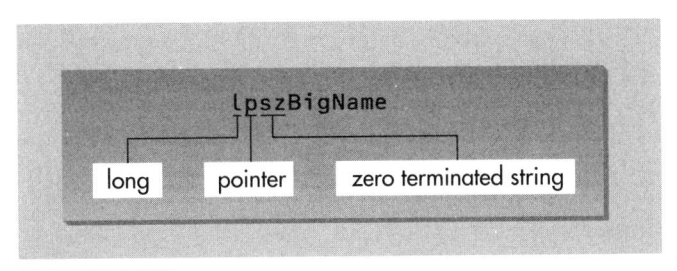

Figure 3-2 Hungarian Notation Example

Listing 3-4 shows some additional examples of variables named using Hungarian notation. The bottom two declarations show pointers to strings. Pointers to character strings are used so frequently that WINDOWS.H includes typdef statements for PSTR (char *), a near pointer to a string, and LPSTR (char FAR *), a far pointer to a string. These definitions just save a bit of typing.

Listing 3-4 Hungarian Notation Used in Declaring Variable Types

```
int          nMyValue ;           /* an integer */
int          *pnPointerOne ;      /* near pointer to an integer */
int     FAR  *fpnPointerTwo ;     /* far pointer to an integer */
WORD         wOtherValue ;        /* WORD = unsigned integer */
WORD    FAR  *fpwPointerThree ;   /* far pointer to a word */
CHAR    FAR  *fpChar ;            /* far pointer to a character */
PSTR         pszNearString ;      /* near pointer to a null terminated string */
LPSTR        lpszFarString ;      /* far pointer to a null terminated string */
```

The one unusual data type in the list of variable name prefixes is HANDLE. Handles are unsigned integers that Windows uses internally to keep track of objects in memory. For example, every window on the screen has a unique window handle. Handles are also used to keep track of running applications, of allocated memory blocks, and a host of other objects.

We will use handles frequently while programming in Windows to keep track of various objects in memory. You can think of handles as being similar to the "handle" (nickname) that truck drivers call themselves when using the CB radio. If you use the radio you contact another driver using his or her handle. When you get a response, you will not know where that driver is located, unless you specifically ask. The location of the driver is not important to getting the information, but the handle is. You will get the information from Windows by using Windows function calls (instead of a CB radio) and by using the handle of the object you want to contact.

Internally, a portion of Windows called the "Kernel" maintains tables that allow Windows to convert from handles to physical memory addresses. A handle is actually a pointer to a pointer to a memory location. The reason for this complexity is that Windows moves objects (memory blocks, programs, etc.) in memory to make room. Figure 3-3 shows the relationship between a handle used in a Windows program and a physical memory location. If Windows moves the object in memory, the handle table is updated. The handle used by the program does not need to change, as it always gets correctly translated to the right physical address by the Windows Kernel no matter where the object is moved in memory. As a Windows programmer, you will not need to be concerned with the internal workings of Window's memory management functions. Windows keeps the handles valid, and the handle is all that you will need to locate and access any object in memory.

WinMain() Parameters

We are now ready to figure out what those four parameters in the WinMain() function declaration mean:

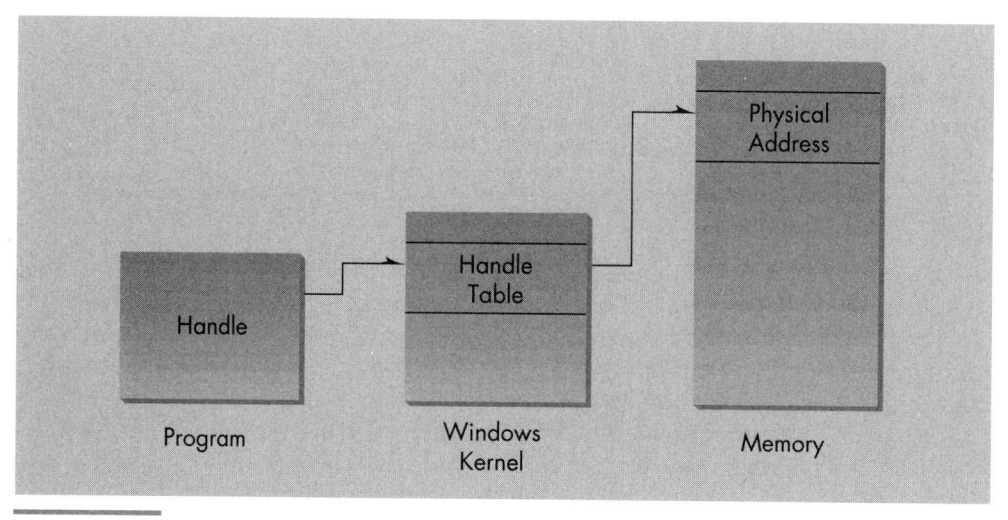

```
int PASCAL WinMain (HANDLE hInstance, HANDLE hPrevInstance, LPSTR lpszCmdLine,
    int nCmdShow)
```

Figure 3-3 How Handles Point to Memory

hInstance   This is the "instance handle" for this running application. Windows creates this unique ID number when the application starts. If you start more than one instance of a program, each will have a unique instance handle. We will use this value in many Windows functions to identify an application's data. Physically, *hInstance* is the memory handle to the application's default data segment. This low-level meaning is not important to you as a Windows programmer, and you can consider *hInstance* to be an arbitrary number that identifies the running application's data.

hPrevInstance   More than one copy of the same Windows application can run at the same time. If another copy is started, *hPrevInstance* will contain the *hInstance* value for the last copy started. If this is the only instance of the application running, *hPrevInstance* will be zero. Zero values of handles are referred to as NULL values (NULL is defined as zero in WINDOWS.H), so *hPrevInstance* would be equal to NULL in our example.

lpszCmdLin   A pointer (memory address) to a character string containing the command line arguments passed to the program. This is similar to the *argv*, *argc* parameters passed to main() in a DOS program. We will examine several ways to pass a command line string to a program in the last example in this chapter.

                    Note how the Hungarian notation used for *lpszCmdLine* helps us remember what this parameter represents. It is a long pointer (*lp*) to a null terminated character string (*sz*) containing the command line arguments (*CmdLine*).

nCmdShow   An integer value that is passed to the ShowWindow() function. This is how Windows tells the program whether to appear minimized, as an icon, normal, or maximized when first displayed.

In the simple MINIMAL1 program, only *hInstance* and *nCmdShow* are used. The Turbo C++ compiler will detect that *hPrevInstance* and *lpszCmdLine* were not used, and it will issue two warning messages. The QuickC compiler just lets this pass and gives no warning messages. As long as you have no intention of using the two parameters, there is nothing wrong with getting the two warning messages.

Creating the Program's Window

The next couple of lines in MINIMAL1.C create the program's window, the window frame, caption bar, center area (called the "client area"), and the words "Hello World."

```
HWND    hWnd ;

hWnd = CreateWindow ("BUTTON", "Hello World.", BS_PUSHBUTTON,
    10, 10, 100, 100, NULL, NULL, hInstance, NULL) ;
```

The variable *hWnd* is declared to be a HWND, a handle to a window. We saw the HWND variable type defined in the WINDOWS.H excerpt at the beginning of this chapter. The function CreateWindow() creates the program's window. CreateWindow() returns a unique ID value for the window created, which is actually an unsigned integer. We will call it a HWND to make the meaning clear. Note that the variable name *hWnd* starts with a letter "h" to tag the variable type as a handle.

When a window is created, its properties are based on some starting information. This information includes what color to paint the background, what type of cursor shape to display if the mouse pointer is over the window, etc. This data is used to define a *class* of windows. MINIMAL1.C uses the predefined class of windows called "BUTTON." Windows maintains the class data for a BUTTON at all times because buttons are common to so many programs. Buttons have a gray background with black text in the center. The class defines the cursor shape to be the normal Windows arrow cursor.

MINIMAL1 takes advantage of this predefined window type BUTTON to place a button in the center (or "client area") of the program's window. The button is given the text "Hello World." Because the button is also the main program window, "Hello World" automatically becomes the program's caption, shown at the top of the program window. Inserting the name of the program's main window in the caption bar is an automatic feature that Windows does for every program. In fact, the caption itself was created automatically—we did not do anything special in MINIMAL1.C to create a caption bar. Figure 3-4 shows the appearance of MINIMAL1, showing both the top caption bar and the center client area filled with the button. The button's text and the caption's text are automatically centered, and Windows uses the default system font for the lettering of the button and caption bar. The dotted lines around the button's text are also automatic.

The CreateWindow() function call also specifies window "style" information. In this case, the style parameter is BS_PUSHBUTTON. BS_PUSHBUTTON is an integer defined in WINDOWS.H. CreateWindow() uses this value to modify the window display properties. In this case, we are specifying a normal button, using the standard system font for the letters in the center, with a gray client area and black lettering.

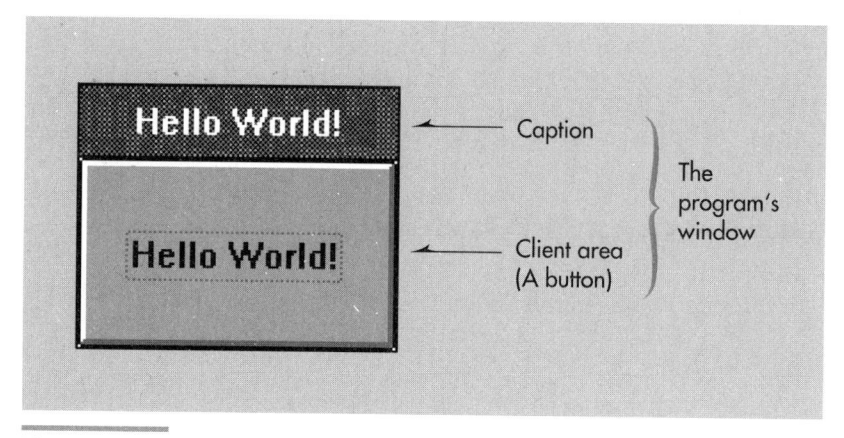

Figure 3-4 MINIMAL1 Button Text and Caption

The numbers following BS_PUSHBUTTON in the CreateWindow() function call specify the size and location of the window when it is created. By default, Windows uses pixels to measure vertical and horizontal distance. A pixel is one dot on the screen. The upper left corner of the screen is the origin (0,0 point). X values increase to the right, and Y values increase downward. Using these "screen coordinates," the upper left corner of the MINIMAL1 program's window (caption bar, plus client area, plus borders) will be at a location 10 pixels left and 10 pixels down from the top left corner of the screen. The bottom right corner of the window will be at 100,100. This makes the window a fixed 90 by 90 pixel square. This size was arbitrarily picked to have enough room to show the text "Hello World." in the button's center and caption bar.

The remaining parameters passed to the CreateWindow() function (the NULLs and *hInstance*) tell Windows the program's instance handle that this is a top-level window (not part of another program), with no menu and no extra data stored with the window's definition. We will not cover these parameters used in CreateWindow() in any further detail until Chapter 5, *Window Controls*. The remainder of MINIMAL1.C's code is shown highlighted in Listing 3-5.

Listing 3-5 MINIMAL1.C Revisited

```
/* minimal1.c   minimal1 windows application */

#include <windows.h>          /* window's header file - always included */

int PASCAL WinMain (HANDLE hInstance, HANDLE hPrevInstance, LPSTR lpszCmdLine,
    int nCmdShow)
{
    HWND    hWnd ;

    hWnd = CreateWindow ("BUTTON","Hello World.", BS_PUSHBUTTON,
        10, 10, 100, 100, NULL, NULL, hInstance, NULL) ;
    ShowWindow (hWnd, nCmdShow) ; /* display the window */
    WaitMessage () ;              /* sit there */
    return (0) ;                  /* quit */
}
```

ShowWindow() is another Windows function that makes the window we created with CreateWindow() visible on the screen. It can also be used to hide a window. Note that the *nCmdShow* parameter is one of the parameters passed to the WinMain() function, and is passed on unchanged to ShowWindow(). The *nCmdShow* value will tell ShowWindow() whether to display MINIMAL1 as a normal, minimized, or maximized window. *nCmdShow* is set by the Windows environment when the MINIMAL1 program is started. Windows will usually start programs with a normal (not minimized or maximized) window size. You can override this by starting a program from the Windows Program Manager "File/Run" menu item, selecting the "Run minimized" option, or by automatically loading a program when Windows starts by adding the program's name to the "[load]" section of the WIN.INI file.

Chapter 3 • First Programming Experiments

Messages

The last function in MINIMAL1.C is WaitMessage(). This function causes the program to just sit there, waiting for a message from Windows. WaitMessage() was used in MINIMAL1.C instead of a more complex function to make the program as small as possible. Any message sent to the window causes WaitMessage() to return. Moving the mouse cursor to within the edge of the MINIMAL1 window causes MINIMAL1 to start getting mouse messages from Windows, so WaitMessage() returns. Pressing any key has the same effect.

When WaitMessage() gets a message from Windows and returns, control passes to the last line in the program, return (0). This exits the WinMain() function, terminating the program. The Windows environment gets the zero value, which is ignored. Windows automatically destroys the program's window, erasing it from the screen, and removes the program code and data from memory. References to the program's data, such as entries in Window's Kernel section for handles to memory objects, are also removed. MINIMAL1 still exists as a disk file, but it has to be started again to load it back into memory.

Adding a Message Loop

MINIMAL1 has the advantage of being small, but it does not behave like most Windows programs. It would be better to have the MINIMAL1 Window remain on the screen, and only disappear when the central button is clicked. To do this, MINIMAL1.C must be modified to wait for a *specific* Windows message. Figure 3-5 shows what the MINIMAL2 program looks like when running.

As mentioned in Chapter 1, messages are small packets of data that Windows sends to running programs to let the program know that something has happened. Typical messages are:

The mouse cursor moved to *X,Y* on the screen (WM_MOUSEMOVE).

The left mouse button was depressed (WM_LBUTTONDOWN).

A key was pressed (WM_KEYDOWN).

The minimize button on the window was clicked (WM_SIZE).

Figure 3-5 MINIMAL2

Each message has a unique integer ID value, which is given a name in WINDOWS.H like WM_MOUSEMOVE. You can find a complete description of each message in Chapter 9 of the *Waite Group's Windows API Bible*, and in the QuickC *Windows Programming Reference*.

Windows applications cooperate with the Windows environment by continually checking whether there are any incoming messages. This is done by writing a small program loop called a *message loop*. The message loop will use either the GetMessage() or

PeekMessage() function to read messages sent to the program. WaitMessage() also checks for messages, but it is not used in a message loop, because WaitMessage() just waits for any message. WaitMessage() does not retrieve the actual message data from Windows, it just notices that a message has been sent. We used WaitMessage() in MINIMAL1.C for simplicity, but most Windows programs use either GetMessage() or PeekMessage(). Figure 3-6 illustrates the interactions between the Windows environment and an application program containing a message loop.

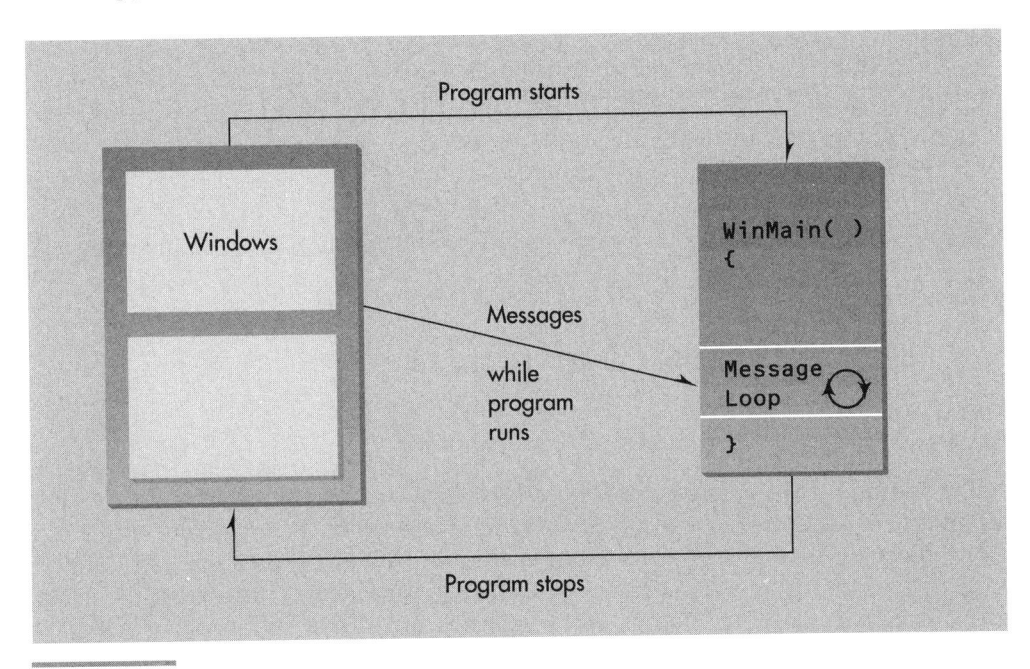

Figure 3-6 The Message Loop

Let's improve on MINIMAL1 by making a new program, MINIMAL2. You can copy the files MINIMAL1.C and MINIMAL1.DEF to make new files named MINIMAL2.C and MINIMAL2.DEF, or just use the copies of the MINIMAL2 files on the source code disks. Use your editor to modify MINIMAL2.C so that it looks like Listing 3-6.

Listing 3-6 MINIMAL2.C Adding a Message Loop

```
/* minimal2.c   minimal windows application - add message loop */

#include <windows.h>

int PASCAL WinMain (HANDLE hInstance, HANDLE hPrevInstance, LPSTR lpszCmdLine,
   int nCmdShow)
```

Chapter 3 • First Programming Experiments

```
{
    HWND    hWnd ;      /* the window's "handle" */
    MSG     msg ;       /* a message structure */

    hWnd = CreateWindow ("BUTTON","Press Me!", BS_PUSHBUTTON,
        10, 10, 100, 100, NULL, NULL, hInstance, NULL) ;
    ShowWindow (hWnd, nCmdShow) ;    /* display the window */

    while (GetMessage (&msg, NULL, NULL, NULL))   /* message loop */
    {
        if (msg.message == WM_LBUTTONDOWN)    /* if left mouse button, */
            break ;    /* exit loop/program */
        else           /* otherwise default actions */
            DefWindowProc (msg.hwnd, msg.message, msg.wParam,
                            msg.lParam) ;
    }
    return (0) ;    /* quit */
}
```

You will also need to create a new project file for MINIMAL2, as shown in Listing 3-7.

Listing 3-7 Contents of MINIMAL2 Project File

```
MINIMAL2.C
MINIMAL2.DEF
```

Let's examine the changes made to MINIMAL1.C to make MINIMAL2.C. The first modification is to add a new local variable *msg* at the top of the WinMain() function. *msg* is declared to be of the type MSG. If you go into WINDOWS.H, you can find the MSG data structure defined, as shown in Listing 3-8. If you are a little rusty on C language structures, read the info box "C Language Structures."

Listing 3-8 MSG Structure Definition In WINDOWS.H

```
/* Message structure */
typedef struct tagMSG
  {
    HWND    hwnd;          /* the window's handle */
    WORD    message;       /* the message ID value, like WM_LBUTTONDOWN */
    WORD    wParam;        /* one WORD of data passed with the message */
    LONG    lParam;        /* LONG data passed with the message */
    DWORD   time;          /* time the message was sent (milliseconds) */
    POINT   pt;            /* mouse cursor X,Y location when sent */
  } MSG;
typedef MSG         *PMSG;       /* pointer to a MSG */
typedef MSG NEAR    *NPMSG;      /* near pointer to a MSG */
typedef MSG FAR     *LPMSG;      /* far pointer to a MSG */
```

Review: C Language Structures

Windows uses a lot of data structures, so it is important to be comfortable with how the C language creates and uses structures. The idea of a structure is simple: Combine a group of related data elements into one object so that they are easier to work with.

As an example, let's create a custom data structure to hold the *X,Y* locations of both ends of a straight line. In C, this would be done as follows:

```
typedef struct
{
    int    nFirstX;
    int    nFirstY;
    int    nSecondX;
    int    nSecondY;
} StraightLine ;
```

This tells the C compiler that a variable declared as a "StraightLine" requires that the compiler set aside room for four integers in memory. Each of the items in the structure is called a "member" of the structure. To access a specific one of the four integers, we call it by name. The member's name is combined with the structure's name using a period:

```
StraightLine        StLn;          /* declare StLn to be of type StraightLine */

StLn.nFirstX = 20 ;                /* assign some values to members */
StLn.nFirstY = 30 ;
/* etc. */
```

Here we have created a variable *StLn* that is of the newly defined type *StraightLine*. The first two members of the data structure have their values set to 20 and 30. This example is equivalent to the following code using array notation:

```
int    nStLn [4];                  /* an array of four integers */

nStLn[0] = 20 ;                    /* assign some values to members */
nStLn[1] = 30 ;
```

The array notation accomplishes the same thing, but it is not clear what the meaning of the elements of the array represent.

Another common use for structures is to pass a bunch of data to another function. This is done by passing a pointer to the structure. The pointer is just the address of the first member in the structure. For example:

```
typedef struct tagPoint    /* define the structure */
{
   int     nX ;
   int     nY ;
} POINT ;

void DoPoint (POINT *p)    /* define a function that receives a pointer */
```

(continued)

Chapter 3 • First Programming Experiments

Review: C Language Structures (cont'd)

```
{                          /* as a parameter passed to the function */
  int X, Y ;

  X = p->nX ;              /* access the data in the structure using the */
  Y = p->nY ;              /* pointer to the structure in memory */
}

main ()
{
  POINT    p ;             /* declare p to be a POINT structure */

  p.nX = 5 ;               /* set the values for both members */
  p.nY = 10 ;

  DoPoint (&p) ;           /* pass a pointer to p to the DoPoint() function */
}
```

The new data type POINT is defined as a structure containing two integers. The function DoPoint() receives a pointer to a POINT structure as the parameter *p*. This allows DoPoint() to obtain both the *X* and *Y* values of the point, even though only one parameter (a pointer) was passed to the function. The C language operator -> comes in handy. It obtains the value of a member of the structure, given a pointer to the structure and the member's name.

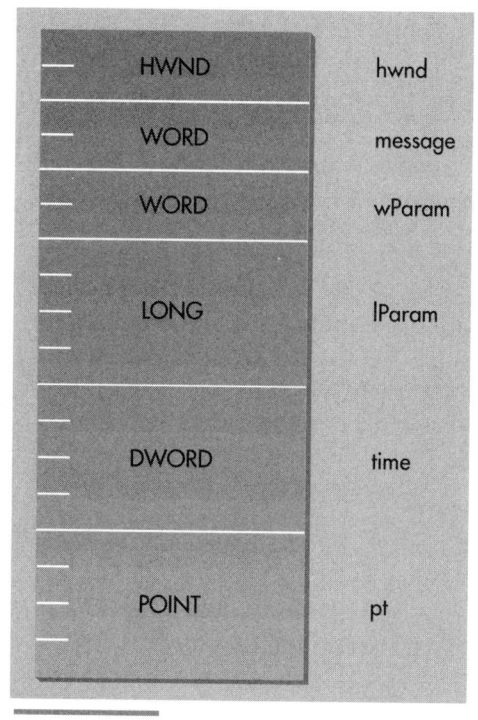

Figure 3-7 An MSG Structure in Memory

You can visualize a message as being a block of memory, divided into the six different types of data defined in the MSG data structure. Figure 3-7 shows how the MSG structure is organized in memory. The HWND and WORD data types occupy two bytes of memory each. The LONG, DWORD, and POINT data types all occupy four bytes. This sums to 18 bytes of memory space required per message.

When Windows sends a message to a running application, Windows fills in the data in a MSG data structure and stores the data in a memory block that the application can read. The actual memory that holds the message is managed by the Kernel portion of Windows. Our program does not need to concern itself with where the message is physically located in memory. The program calls either the GetMessage() or PeekMessage() function to read the message data. WaitMessage() will detect an incoming message, but it will not fill in the MSG data structure.

To make MINIMAL2 always check for incoming messages, we created a program loop, called a "message loop." Listing 3-9 shows the message loop for MINIMAL2.C.

Listing 3-9 A Message Loop in MINIMAL2.C

```
while (GetMessage (&msg, NULL, NULL, NULL))  /* message loop */
{
        if (msg.message == WM_LBUTTONDOWN)   /* if left mouse button, */
            break ;                          /* exit loop/program */
        else                                 /* otherwise default actions */
            DefWindowProc (msg.hwnd, msg.message, msg.wParam,
                msg.lParam) ;
}
```

MINIMAL2.C uses GetMessage() to fetch the message data from Windows. If Windows has sent a message to the program, GetMessage() puts all of the message data into a message structure named *msg*. The first parameter passed to the GetMessage() function is a pointer to a message structure. GetMessage() copies the message data into this structure so that the program can use it. The other three parameters passed to GetMessage() are all NULLs. They are set to NULL as a default value, meaning that we want to receive every message. GetMessage() has the ability to only read a range of messages (such as just mouse messages, or just keyboard messages), but this is rarely used.

An interesting aspect of the GetMessage() function is that it cooperates with the Windows environment. When a program executes GetMessage(), the Windows environment checks whether there are any messages waiting for the program. If there are none, Windows does not allow the GetMessage() program loop to return. Instead, Windows retains control of the system and goes about doing other things until a message to the program is generated. Only then does the GetMessage() function return, allowing the program to start operating (gain control). GetMessage() is one of the keys to Windows' ability to run several programs at the same time.

If you think back to the analogy made in Chapter 1, *How Windows Works*, that compared Windows to an office, GetMessage() is the function that takes work from a worker's "In" box and places it on the worker's desk. GetMessage() does not do anything unless there is something (a message) in the "In" box. The worker only does work if there is a message to process. Otherwise, either the boss (Windows) or another worker (another application program) is doing work.

MINIMAL2 uses GetMessage() to check whether there are any messages from Windows. If there is a message, MINIMAL2 checks whether the message is notification that the user has depressed the left mouse button. Windows sends a WM_LBUTTONDOWN message to the program if the mouse cursor is over the window when the left button is depressed. WM_LBUTTONDOWN is defined in WINDOWS.H as the value 0x201 hexadecimal.

The WM_LBUTTONDOWN value (0x201) will be stored in the *message* member of the MSG data structure. That sounds a little confusing, so let's break it down into pieces. Look at Listing 3-8. The second member of the structure is named *message*. That is where the value 0x201 will be stored after GetMessage() returns, assuming that the left mouse button was depressed. To get at the message number, we need to access this member of the MSG structure. Recall that the C language uses a period as the operator to reference one member of a structure. For example, the following code checks whether the message is equal to WM_LBUTTONDOWN.

```
if (msg.message == WM_LBUTTONDOWN)
      /* do something if the message is: left mouse button down */
```

This statement says, "Does the *message* member of the *msg* data structure equal the value defined by WM_LBUTTONDOWN?" We could also access the other members of the MSG structure such as *hwnd, wParam, lParam* using the period operator, but MINIMAL2.C has no need for these values. If a message is received, the message ID value is compared to WM_LBUTTONDOWN. If the message ID value equals WM_LBUTTONDOWN, the user must have depressed the left mouse button over the MINIMAL2 window. In this case, the program executes a return(0), terminating the program and returning the zero value to Windows.

If the message ID value does not equal WM_LBUTTONDOWN, some other message was sent to the application. For example, if the user clicked the right mouse button, the WM_RBUTTONDOWN message is sent. For all messages except WM_LBUTTONDOWN, we want the default actions for a window to occur. The DefWindowProc() function carries out all of the default (built-in) actions for a window. For example, MINIMAL2 can be moved around on the screen by depressing the left mouse button while the cursor is over the window's caption bar and dragging the window to a new location. The outlining of the window, movement, and repainting is all handled by the DefWindowProc() function.

DefWindowProc() handles all sorts of default actions, such as minimizing and maximizing windows, displaying their icons when minimized, resizing windows when they are restored from being an icon, etc. DefWindowProc() greatly simplifies writing Windows programs, as most of the time the default action for a window is just what the program needs. If the default action is not appropriate, it is simply a matter of trapping a specific message and coding in the action desired. In MINIMAL2, the default action for receiving a WM_LBUTTONDOWN message is being superseded by the program's code, which causes the program to terminate when this message is received. Otherwise, the MINIMAL2 button would be briefly highlighted (gray color changes quickly), which is the default action for a button receiving a WM_LBUTTONDOWN message.

The Importance of the Message Loop

A running application program will only receive mouse and keyboard messages from Windows if the user has activated that program. For example, if you have several programs running and click one with the mouse cursor, only the window under the mouse cursor will receive the WM_LBUTTONDOWN message.

> **The Importance of the Message Loop (cont'd)**
>
> An important aspect of GetMessage() is that if there are no messages waiting for the application, GetMessage() gives control back to the Windows environment so that other programs can run. This is how Windows allows the user to switch between applications. For example, if the user has been using one program, but moves the mouse over to a second program's window and clicks a mouse button, the second program will start getting messages from Windows. The application that starts getting the messages becomes the active program, and all other programs are inactive.
>
> Every Windows application will have a message loop. The loop will contain either the GetMessage() function (most common), or a function called "PeekMessage()," for programs that operate in the background or which show animated graphics. You can write a Windows program without a message loop. Unless it terminates immediately (MINIMAL1 is an example), a Windows program without a message loop will take over all of the system's processing time and the user will not be able to switch to another program. All of the remaining examples in this book will contain a message loop.

MINIMAL2.C is an acceptable Windows application. It does not take over the system, and it limits its activities to the bounds of its own window. From a programming point of view, MINIMAL2.C is rather odd. The program takes advantage of the predefined BUTTON window class to keep things simple, but this makes the entire client area look like a big button. Also, MINIMAL2.C processes messages within the message loop. The normal practice is to process messages in a separate function, usually called the WndProc() function. We will make both of these additions in the next example.

Creating a New Class of Windows

If you have been using Windows for any length of time, you have become accustomed to buttons, scroll bars, list boxes, and program main windows. It turns out that all of these objects are "classes of windows." In other words, the scroll bar itself is a long, narrow window, each list box is a window, and even the small arrow buttons at the ends of scroll bars are windows. The Windows environment supports the concept of creating new types of windows from a "class" of windows. Individual windows created from a class have the same background color when repainted, use the same cursor shape, and pass Windows messages to the same function. MINIMAL1 and MINIMAL2 both used the predefined window class BUTTON for the application's main window. This time we will define our own class of window, rather than using a predefined window class.

New window classes are created using the RegisterClass() function. RegisterClass() only takes one parameter, a pointer to a WNDCLASS structure. As usual for Windows structures, the WNDCLASS structure is defined in WINDOWS.H, as shown in Listing 3-10. To use RegisterClass(), we first fill in all of the members of the WNDCLASS structure, and then pass a pointer to RegisterClass(). Our new program, MINIMAL3.C will use RegisterClass() to create a new window class.

Listing 3-10 WNDCLASS Structure Definition from WINDOWS.H

```
typedef struct tagWNDCLASS
   {
   WORD     style;                      /* binary flags specify the window's style */
   LONG     (FAR PASCAL *lpfnWndProc)();  /* pointer to the message function */
   int      cbClsExtra;                 /* extra bytes with class (can be 0) */
   int      cbWndExtra;                 /* extra bytes with each window (can be 0)*/
   HANDLE   hInstance;                  /* the creating program's instance handle */
   HICON    hIcon;                      /* the window icon */
   HCURSOR  hCursor;                    /* the window cursor shape */
   HBRUSH   hbrBackground;              /* the brush to use in painting background */
   LPSTR    lpszMenuName;               /* the class menu name */
   LPSTR    lpszClassName;              /* the name of the class once registered */
   } WNDCLASS;
typedef WNDCLASS              *PWNDCLASS;
typedef WNDCLASS NEAR         *NPWNDCLASS;
typedef WNDCLASS FAR          *LPWNDCLASS;
```

Separate Message Processing

The other change to MINIMAL2.C to make MINIMAL3.C is to take the message processing logic out of the message loop and put it into a separate function. This keeps the size of the WinMain() function from getting too big and makes the message processing logic clearer. Windows programs use the convention that the message processing function is called WndProc(). You can name it anything you like, but most programmers stick with WndProc().

MINIMAL3.C is shown in Listing 3-11. Several changes are apparent from our last program. In WinMain() you will see the WNDCLASS window class structure defined, and all of the member values filled in. The RegisterClass() function is used to register the new class with Windows. The other changes to the program are a simplified message loop that uses DispatchMessage() and a custom function called WndProc() at the end of the listing. There is also a prototype for the WndProc() function at the top of Listing 3-11 so that the compiler will know the data types the function uses in advance, and will not generate warning messages. We will examine each of these changes in more detail below.

Listing 3-11 MINIMAL3.C

```
/* minimal3.c   Creating a new window class */

#include <windows.h>

long FAR PASCAL WndProc (HWND, WORD, WORD, LONG) ;  /* declaration */

int PASCAL WinMain (HANDLE hInstance, HANDLE hPrevInstance, LPSTR lpszCmdLine,
    int nCmdShow)
   {
   HWND    hWnd ;                /* the window's "handle" */
   MSG     msg ;                 /* a message structure */
```

```
    WNDCLASS    wndclass ;      /* window class structure */
                                /* fill in class data for new class */
if (!hPrevInstance)
  {
      wndclass.style          = CS_HREDRAW | CS_VREDRAW ;
      wndclass.lpfnWndProc    = WndProc ;
      wndclass.cbClsExtra     = 0 ;
      wndclass.cbWndExtra     = 0 ;
      wndclass.hInstance      = hInstance ;
      wndclass.hIcon          = LoadIcon (NULL, IDI_APPLICATION) ;
      wndclass.hCursor        = LoadCursor (NULL, IDC_ARROW) ;
      wndclass.hbrBackground  = GetStockObject (WHITE_BRUSH) ;
      wndclass.lpszMenuName   = NULL ;
      wndclass.lpszClassName  = "MyClass" ;
                                /* register the new window class */
      if (!RegisterClass (&wndclass))
            return (0) ;        /* quit if can't register class */
  }

  hWnd = CreateWindow ("MyClass", "Minimal 3", WS_OVERLAPPEDWINDOW,
      10, 10, 200, 100, NULL, NULL, hInstance, NULL) ;
  ShowWindow (hWnd, nCmdShow) ; /* display the window */

  while (GetMessage (&msg, NULL, NULL, NULL))  /* message loop */
  {
      DispatchMessage (&msg) ; /* send message to WndProc() */
  }
  return (msg.wParam) ;        /* quit */
}

/* WndProc() is a custom function for processing messages from Windows */

long FAR PASCAL WndProc (HWND hWnd, WORD wMessage, WORD wParam, LONG lParam)
{
    switch (wMessage)            /* process windows messages */
    {
      case WM_DESTROY:           /* stop application */
          PostQuitMessage (0) ;  /* this will exit message loop */
          break ;
      default:                   /* default windows message processing */
          return DefWindowProc (hWnd, wMessage, wParam, lParam) ;
    }
    return (0L) ;
}
```

The WinMain() function has the interesting line:

```
if (!hPrevInstance)       /* no need if program is already running */
```

This line checks whether *hPrevInstance* parameter passed to WinMain() is nonzero. Remember that Windows assigns each running program a unique ID value called the *program instance*. If this is the first time the program has been started, then there will not be a previous instance of the program, so *hPrevInstance* will be NULL. If a copy of the program is already running and the user starts another copy, the *hPrevInstance* will be the instance value of the last copy running. If the same application is already running, then the window class "MyClass" has already been registered with the Windows

Chapter 3 • First Programming Experiments

environment. There is no need to do this more than once, so MINIMAL3.C skips the RegisterClass() section if *hPrevInstance* is nonzero. This is typically the only use you will make of the *hPrevInstance* parameter passed to WinMain().

Creating a New Window Class

While MINIMAL1.C and MINIMAL2.C took the shortcut of using the predefined "BUTTON" window class for the program's main window, MINIMAL3.C creates a new class of windows, which gives us more control of what the program's window will look like. The RegisterClass() function, which does the work of creating a new window class, is well named, as the new class of windows is "registered" with the Windows environment. Windows will remember the class definition until the Windows session is terminated. RegisterClass() just uses one parameter, a pointer to a WNDCLASS data structure. The values for all of the WNDCLASS structure members are filled in before RegisterClass() is called, and RegisterClass() passes the data to Windows. Once the class is registered, any number of windows can be created using CreateWindow() based on the new class.

Listing 3-12 shows the creation of the window class "MyClass" in MINIMAL3.C. This is a typical example and will apply to most Windows programs. The only unusual aspect of the "MyClass" definition is that this program's window does not have a menu, so the *lpszMenuName* member of the WNDCLASS structure is set to NULL. We will add a menu to the class definition in the last example program in this chapter.

Listing 3-12 Creating a New Window Class in MINIMAL3.C

```
WNDCLASS        wndclass ;          /* window class structure */
wndclass.style                  = CS_HREDRAW | CS_VREDRAW ;
wndclass.lpfnWndProc            = WndProc ;
wndclass.cbClsExtra             = 0 ;
wndclass.cbWndExtra             = 0 ;
wndclass.hInstance              = hInstance ;
wndclass.hIcon                  = LoadIcon (NULL, IDI_APPLICATION) ;
wndclass.hCursor                = LoadCursor (NULL, IDC_ARROW) ;
wndclass.hbrBackground          = GetStockObject (WHITE_BRUSH) ;
wndclass.lpszMenuName           = NULL ;   /* note - no menu */
wndclass.lpszClassName          = "MyClass" ;
                                /* register the new window class */
if (!RegisterClass (&wndclass))
    return (0) ; /* quit if can't register class */
```

Note that the program's instance handle *hInstance* is passed on to RegisterClass() as a member of the WNDCLASS structure. Windows uses this handle as a unique identification value for the application calling RegisterClass().

The Style Member of WNDCLASS

The *style* member of the WNDCLASS structure is set to CS_HREDRAW | CS_VREDRAW. They are two numbers defined in WINDOWS.H that specify that windows of this class should be redrawn if either the horizontal or vertical size changes. The two values are combined using the C language binary OR operator "|." If you look in WINDOWS.H, you will find that CS_VREDRAW is equal to 1, and CS_HREDRAW is equal to 2. These two values end up being combined as shown in Table 3-2.

	DECIMAL	BINARY
CS_HREDRAW	2	00000010
CS_VREDRAW	1	00000001
Combined via "|" OR Operator	3	00000011

Table 3-2 Combining Binary Flags

Because the values for CS_HREDRAW and CS_VREDRAW are powers of two, the values do not overlap when combined using the binary OR operator. These values are called "binary flags." Windows uses binary flags in many functions. All of the binary flags are defined in WINDOWS.H.

Extra Memory Blocks for Windows

The *cbClsExtra* and *cbWndExtra* members of the WNDCLASS structure allow you to set aside a memory block for each class or window of a class. This is a way to store data with a class or window, providing a direct means of increasing the "object oriented" nature of a Windows program. "Object oriented" means that the complete window, including any related program logic and data, is considered to be a single entity. MINIMAL3.C does not need to store data, so the *cbClsExtra* and *cbWndExtra* values are set to zero.

Icon, Cursor, and Background Brush

The *hIcon, hCursor,* and *hbrBackground* members of the WNDCLASS structure contain the handle (ID value) for the class icon, cursor, and background color brush. To keep the example simple, our new window class takes advantage of several predefined objects. Windows keeps predefined icons, cursor shapes, and brushes available for the most common objects, such as the objects that Windows itself uses frequently. LoadIcon() loads the IDI_APPLICATION icon, and returns the handle value for the icon's data in memory. LoadCursor() loads the standard arrow cursor shape, again returning a handle to the cursor's data in memory. The background color for the window class is a predefined white brush, loaded with GetStockObject(). The data for all of these predefined objects is always stored with the Windows environment. We will look at creating our own icons and brushes later in the book.

The Menu Name and Class Name

MINIMAL3 does not have a menu, so *lpszMenuName* is set to NULL. The *lpszClassName* member of WNDCLASS is set to the string "MyClass," and becomes the class name for the new window class we are about to register. We will use the class name when creating the program's window with CreateWindow(). The *lpfnWndProc* member of the WNDCLASS structure specifies the name of the function that will receive Windows messages. This is a programming convenience, as the WinMain() function will get too large if we try to deal with all of the message logic within the message loop as we did in MINIMAL2.C. In MINIMAL3.C, the messages will be passed to the WndProc() function, shown at the bottom of Listing 3-12.

Registering the Window Class

With all of the WNDCLASS members filled in, we can register the window class. RegisterClass() is called, passing the address of the WNDCLASS structure (the & operator obtains the address of a variable in the C language). If the class is successfully registered, RegisterClass() returns a nonzero value, and the program continues. Otherwise, an error occurred and MINIMAL3 terminates, returning a zero value to Windows.

With the window class registered, we can create the program's window based on the class "MyClass." This is the first parameter passed to CreateWindow().

```
hWnd = CreateWindow ("MyClass", "Minimal 3," WS_OVERLAPPEDWINDOW,
    10, 10, 200, 100, NULL, NULL, hInstance, NULL) ;
ShowWindow (hWnd, nCmdShow) ;   /* display the window */
```

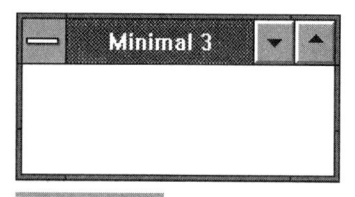

Figure 3-8 MINIMAL3

The window title is changed to "Minimal 3." The window style is set to WS_OVERLAPPEDWINDOW, which is the standard window style for a program's main window. This includes the specification of a thick border, minimize and maximize buttons, and a caption bar. The window will start with its upper left corner at location 10,10 on the screen, and will have a width of 200 pixels and a height of 100 pixels. The *hWndParent*, *hMenu*, and *lpParam* parameters passed to CreateWindow() are all set to NULL. We will discuss the *hWndParent* and *lpParam* parameters in Chapter 5, *Window Controls*.

The appearance of MINIMAL3 is shown in Figure 3-8. This is a more normal looking window than those of MINIMAL1 and MINIMAL2, as we have defined a "plain vanilla" window class for the program's main window, instead of using the BUTTON class. The WS_OVERLAPPEDWINDOW style adds the minimize and maximize buttons, as well as the system menu box on the upper left corner, and a thick window frame that can be used to resize the window.

Exporting the WndProc Function Name

The Windows environment will send message data from windows constructed from the new "MyClass" window class directly to the WndProc() function in MINIMAL3. To make this work, we need to make the address of the WndProc() function available to Windows when the program is running. This is done by adding the EXPORTS line to the program's module definition file. Listing 3-13 shows MINIMAL3.DEF. This definition file also includes the NAME statement. This is optional, but makes it easier to figure out which .DEF file goes with a given program.

Listing 3-13 MINIMAL3.DEF Module Definition File with EXPORTS Section

```
NAME        MINIMAL3
EXETYPE     WINDOWS
STUB        'WINSTUB.EXE'
CODE        PRELOAD MOVEABLE
DATA        PRELOAD MOVEABLE MULTIPLE
HEAPSIZE    1024
STACKSIZE   5120
EXPORTS     WndProc
```

The physical effect of adding a function name to the EXPORTS section of the program's module definition file is to notify Windows that the location of the function must be tracked as it is moved in memory. Windows tracks the function's location by maintaining two internal tables called the "Task Database" and the "Module Database." Windows keeps these tables up-to-date as the program is moved. This is all automatic, so the only action the programmer needs to do to make sure that Windows can call a function is to add a function name to the EXPORTS section of the module definition file. This is easy to forget, so get in the habit of adding the EXPORTS section as soon as you create a message processing function, or any other function that will be called from outside of the program. The one exception to this rule is the WinMain() function. Windows knows how to call WinMain() without adding its name to the EXPORTS section.

Message Processing Function—WndProc()

In MINIMAL2.C, the message decoding was done right in the message loop at the bottom of the WinMain() function. Normally, the message data is passed to another function, usually named WndProc(), which figures out which actions to take depending on the message received. We must modify the program's message loop to allow processing of messages in a separate function. Listing 3-14 shows just the message loop from MINIMAL3.C.

Listing 3-14 Message Loop From MINIMAL3.C

```
while (GetMessage (&msg, NULL, NULL, NULL))    /* message loop */
{
        DispatchMessage (&msg) ;        /* send message to WndProc() */
}
```

The key to passing the message data on to the WndProc() function is the DispatchMessage() function. This DispatchMessage() sends the message data to the function specified in the window's class definition (*lpfnWndProc* member of the WNDCLASS structure). The message data was copied into the MSG data structure *msg* by GetMessage(), so DispatchMessage() can use the same message data to send the message on. In MINIMAL3.C, "WndProc" is specified as the window procedure name, so the message data is sent to that function each time DispatchMessage() is called.

The last section of MINIMAL3.C is the code for the WndProc() function, shown again in Listing 3-15. There is also a function prototype at the top of MINIMAL3.C for the WndProc() function so that the compiler will know the data types of each of the WndProc() parameters. WndProc() functions (sometimes called "window functions" or "message functions") will always have the same four parameter types passed as the function arguments and are always declared "long FAR PASCAL." If you compare the MSG data structure (Listing 3-8) to the parameter list for WndProc(), you will realize that the first four members of the MSG structure are being passed as parameters to WndProc(). The *time* and *pt* members of the MSG structure are not passed directly to WndProc(), as they are seldom used. If you need those values, Windows provides the GetMessageTime() and GetMessagePos() functions to fetch them.

Listing 3-15 WndProc() Function from MINIMAL3.C

```
long FAR PASCAL WndProc (HWND hWnd, WORD wMessage, WORD wParam, LONG lParam)
{
    switch (wMessage)            /* process windows messages */
    {
      case WM_DESTROY:           /* stop application */
          PostQuitMessage (0) ;  /* this will exit message loop */
          break ;
      default:                   /* default windows message processing */
          return DefWindowProc (hWnd, wMessage, wParam, lParam) ;
    }
    return (0L) ;
}
```

The WndProc() function in MINIMAL3.C does not do much. If the WM_DESTROY message is received, the application is being terminated. WM_DESTROY is sent to the application when the user double-clicks the system menu button at the top left corner of the program's window, or selects "Close" from the system menu, or presses the Ctrl F4 key combination. The program exits by calling PostQuitMessage(). Otherwise, the message data is passed on to DefWindowProc() for default processing, just like we did in MINIMAL2.

PostQuitMessage() is a specialized function, designed to make terminating a Windows program simple. PostQuitMessage() is always used in response to the program receiving a WM_DESTROY message, and this should be the only PostQuitMessage() in a Windows program. Although PostQuitMessage() is simple to use, the sequence of events that happen after the function is called are fairly complex. When PostQuitMessage() is called, Windows sends a WM_QUIT message to the program's message loop. The message loop is designed to continue to loop as long as GetMessage() returns a nonzero value (see Listing 3-13). This will be the case for every message except WM_QUIT, as GetMessage() is designed so that it returns zero *only* when it receives a WM_QUIT message. The WM_QUIT message is the only way to break out of the message loop. The program line immediately after the message loop is:

```
return(msg.wParam)
```

    Calling *return( )* from WinMain( ) terminates the application and returns control to Windows. Figure 3-9 shows the whole sequence of events, starting with the PostQuitMessage() function call. The PostQuitMessage() function is usually called with a parameter value (in parentheses) of zero. This value ends up as the *wParam* value passed with the WM_QUIT message, which in turn ends up returned to Windows as the program terminates. Windows does not currently do anything with the returned value. However, the Microsoft documentation suggests following this procedure for possible compatibility with future releases of Windows.

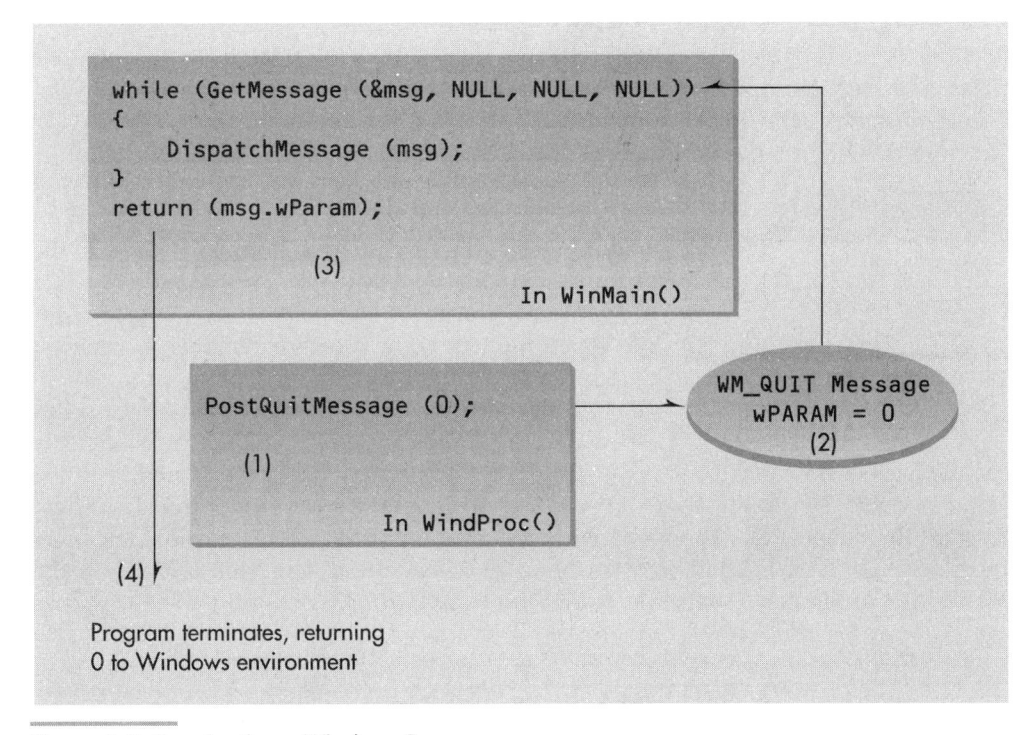

Figure 3-9 Terminating a Windows Program

Compiling MINIMAL3

You will also need to create a project file for MINIMAL3, as shown in Listing 3-16. Go ahead and build the MINIMAL3.EXE program, using Turbo C++ or QuickC.

Listing 3-16 Project File Contents for MINIMAL3

```
MINIMAL3.C
MINIMAL3.DEF
```

If you get MINIMAL3 running on your machine, you will note that you can change the size of the main window using the window's border, move the window by dragging the caption bar, minimize and maximize the window using the buttons on the top right of the caption, and terminate the program by double clicking the button at the top left corner. When minimized, the program will show a white box icon, the IDI_APPLICATION predefined icon we specified in the class definition. All of these activities are handled by the built-in logic we access with the DefWindowProc() function at the bottom of the MINIMAL3.C WndProc() function.

Adding Custom Resource Data

To close out this chapter, we will do one more improvement to MINIMAL. After this, we will not be able to call the program "minimal" any more, as it will be a complete Windows application. This final example is called MINIMAL4 and is shown in Figure 3-10. Note that MINIMAL4 has a menu bar containing two menu items, "Beep" and "Quit."

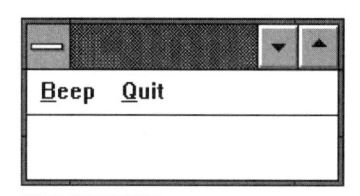

Figure 3-10 The MINIMAL4 Program

The main additions to our new MINIMAL4 program are a menu and an icon which is displayed when MINIMAL4 is minimized. These items are defined in the resource script file MINIMAL4.RC. As we saw in Chapter 1, *How Windows Works*, the data in the resource script file gets compiled by the resource compiler to make an .RES resource data file. The linker combines the data in the .RES file with the rest of the program to make a finished Windows application. Resources allow static data (data that does not change as the program runs) to be separately maintained from the program code. You can change the wording of the menu items, even translate them into another language, without changing the program code. We will explore resources in more detail later in the book. For now, let's just add an icon and a menu to the MINIMAL4 program's resource script file, shown in Listing 3-17.

Listing 3-17 MINIMAL4.RC Resource Script File

```
/* minimal4.rc resource file */

#include "minimal4.h"

MyIcon        ICON    minimal4.ico

MyMenu        MENU
BEGIN
   MENUITEM "&Beep,"              IDM_BEEP
   MENUITEM "&Quit,"              IDM_QUIT
END
```

MINIMAL4.RC introduces the three most common elements in resource script files. The first is a header file (named MINIMAL4.H) included at the top of the file.

There is also an icon and the definition of a simple menu. Each of these elements is discussed in the following sections.

Header Files

The header file MINIMAL4.H is included at the top of the resource script file MINIMAL4.RC, and in the C program file MINIMAL4.C, to provide definitions of constants. Each menu item must have an ID number so that the program can determine which menu item was selected. Rather than just use integer values in the program files, the menu item IDs are given names. IDM_BEEP is the ID for the "Beep" menu item, and "IDM_QUIT" is the ID for the "Quit" menu item. The names make the program files easier to read and reduce the chance of using the wrong ID value for a menu item. The function declaration for the WndProc() function has also been moved to the header file. You can leave it at the top of the C program if you like, but adding it to the header file makes the C listing more readable. The header file MINIMAL4.H (shown in Listing 3-18) is included at the top of both the .RC and .C programs so that the same ID values are known to both the C compiler and the resource compiler.

Listing 3-18 MINIMAL4.H Header File

```
/* minimal4.h header file */

#define IDM_BEEP   1
#define IDM_QUIT   10

long FAR PASCAL WndProc (HWND, WORD, WORD, LONG) ;
```

Creating a Program Icon

The icon named "MyIcon" in the MINIMAL4.RC file is loaded from the file MINIMAL4.ICO. The icon will be used to display a small image when the program is minimized. Before the icon can be included in the resource data, the MINIMAL4.ICO file must be created using either the Image Editor application (QuickC) or WORKSHOP (Turbo C++). Figure 3-11 shows the example icon supplied with the source code disks. Creating an icon image like Figure 3-11 is delightfully simple with both the WORKSHOP and Image Editor applications. The individual steps are described in Table 3-3.

Figure 3-11 MINIMAL4.ICO Icon Image

RESOURCE WORKSHOP (TURBO C++)	IMAGE EDITOR (QUICKC)
Select the "File/New Project..." menu item, and then select ".ICO" from the dialog box.	Select the "File/New..." menu item. A dialog box will appear giving you a choice of editing a bitmap, cursor, or icon. Select icon, and click the "OK" button.

(continued)

Table 3-3 (cont'd)

A dialog box giving you a choice of icon size and colors will appear. Select the 32 by 32 pixel size and 16 colors (the defaults), and click the "OK" button. The icon editor will appear in the WORKSHOP work area.	A dialog box giving you a choice of the icon size and colors will appear. Select the default "4-Plane 16 COLORS 32x32 Pixels," and click the "OK" button. A blank editing area and the editing tools will appear in the work area.
Use the drawing tools and color palette to draw an icon image. This works just like other "paint" programs.	Use the drawing tools and color palette to draw an icon image. This works just like other "paint" programs.
When you are done, select the "File/Save File As..." menu item. A dialog box will appear. Make sure that the directory name matches the "work" area where you are saving your program files. Enter the file name MINIMAL4.ICO, and then	When you are done, select the "File/Save File As..." menu item. A dialog box will appear. Make sure that the directory name matches the "work" area where you are saving your program files. Enter the file name MINIMAL4.ICO, and then click the "OK" but click the "OK" button.
The MINIMAL4.ICO icon file will be saved on your hard disk, ready to be included in the program's resource data.	The MINIMAL4.ICO icon file will be saved on your hard disk, ready to be included in the program's resource data.

Table 3-3 Creating an Icon File

Defining a Menu

Menus are defined in the .RC file with a few lines of text. MINIMAL4 defines a menu called "MyMenu" that contains two menu items (see Listing 3-19). The first item is "Beep" and the second is "Quit." Note that the ID values (IDM_BEEP and IDM_QUIT) defined in the MINIMAL4.H header file are assigned to each menu item. These menu ID values are used to determine which menu item has been selected in the body of the C program.

Listing 3-19 The Menu Definition

```
MyMenu      MENU
BEGIN
    MENUITEM "&Beep,"              IDM_BEEP
    MENUITEM "&Quit,"              IDM_QUIT
END
```

The menu character strings that will be displayed on the menu bar are both preceded by ampersand characters. This results in the first letter of each menu item being underlined. Pressing (Alt)-(B) will result in the "Beep" menu item being activated, while pressing (Alt)-(Q) will result in the "Quit" menu item being activated. This a quick way to provide keyboard alternatives for menu item selections.

Compiling the Resource Data

The resource script file MINIMAL4.RC cannot be compiled by the C compiler—it is not a C language file. Instead, a separate compiler called a "resource compiler" is used to convert the raw data in MINIMAL4.RC into a form that Windows will be able to use. Physically, the resource compiler reads the MINIMAL4.RC file and creates the compiled resource data file MINIMAL4.RES, which is added to the final Windows program MINIMAL4.EXE.

The exact steps you will take to compile the MINIMAL4.RC file will depend on the programming tools you are using. The QuickC compiler automatically compiles the MINIMAL4.RC file if it is included in the project file. The Turbo C++ compiler requires that the resource data be already compiled using WORKSHOP before Turbo C++ is used to build the finished program. This basic difference in approach is discussed in more detail in the info box *The Borland Resource Workshop vs. Microsoft QuickC*.

The Borland Resource Workshop vs. Microsoft QuickC

The Turbo C++ and Borland C++ compilers come with the Resource Workshop (WORKSHOP) for creating Windows resource files. This is an excellent application and greatly simplifies creating and editing resource data. The WORKSHOP integrates the editors for all types of resource data in one Windows application and allows the resource data to be compiled directly. WORKSHOP will also allow you to change resource data in *finished* programs without recompiling the data, including resource data in programs written by other people where you do not have access to the source code.

There is a significant difference in the approach taken by the Microsoft QuickC compiler and the Borland WORKSHOP application. With QuickC you write the resource script file (such as MINIMAL4.RC) using the QuickC editor, much like writing the C program. If there are icons, cursors, bitmaps, or dialog boxes to define, they are created as separate files using the Image Editor and Dialog Box Editor applications. You include the resource script file in the program's project file, and let QuickC compile the resource data along with the C program. QuickC builds the entire program for you.

Turbo C++ and Borland C++ take a different approach. The WORKSHOP application expects you to do all of your editing of resource data using WORKSHOP. WORKSHOP outputs the compiled resource data (MINIMAL4.RES). You then include the resource data (MINIMAL4.RES), not the raw .RC resource script file, in the project file. Turbo C++ just links the .RES data with the compiled code to build the finished application. Turbo C++ does not compile the resource data, so you must switch back to WORKSHOP anytime you want to edit the resource data.

There are two ways to use WORKSHOP when working with the examples in this book. The first is to type in the resource script files, such as MINIMAL4.RC in Listing 3-16, using the Turbo C++ editor. You then create separate files for bitmaps, icons, and cursors using the WORKSHOP tools. When you have all of the bits and pieces created, you can compile the program's resources by loading the resource script file (MINIMAL4.RC), and then using the "File/Save As..." menu item to save the file in the compiled resource form (MINIMAL4.RES).

The other way to use WORKSHOP is to build all of the resources from scratch within the WORKSHOP application, without concern for the .RC resource script file. The tools provided

(continued)

> **The Borland Resource Workshop vs. Microsoft QuickC (cont'd)**
>
> with WORKSHOP cover every possible type of resource, so there is no reason to leave WORKSHOP to edit the .RC file. This is probably how you will use WORKSHOP when you become accustomed to all of the tools. Unfortunately, this technique is difficult to document in a book, as essentially every action is performed via mouse actions. This book will stick to the resource script file approach for the examples.
>
> As an example of using WORKSHOP to compile a resource script file, go ahead and create the MINIMAL4.RC file (Listing 3-17), and the MINIMAL4.ICO icon image (Figure 3-11) as described above. Now start the WORKSHOP application, and select the "File/Open Project..." menu item. A dialog box will appear, allowing you to select a file. Select the file type "RC - resource script," select the MINIMAL4.RC file, and then click the "OK" button. WORKSHOP will read in the resource script file and compile all of the data, including the icon. The project will be summarized in a project window at the right side of the editing area, as shown in Figure 3-12.
>
> **Figure 3-12** Resource Workshop Editing MINIMAL4.RC
>
> To save the compiled resource data, select the "File/Save File As..." menu item. From the dialog box that appears, select the "RES - resource object" file type and enter the file name MINIMAL4.RES. Check that the subdirectory name matches the subdirectory that you are using for your programs, and then click the "OK" button. WORKSHOP will write the compiled MINIMAL4.RES file to your hard disk. You are all set to add this file to your project file in Turbo C++ and build the finished MINIMAL4.EXE program.

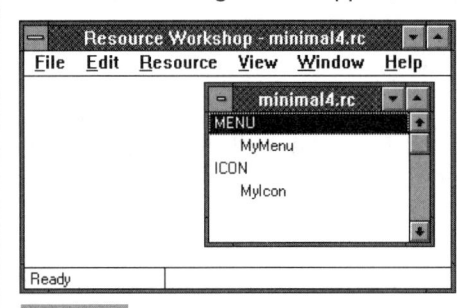

Remaining MINIMAL4 Program Files

Like all Windows programs, MINIMAL4 needs a module definition file, which is shown in Listing 3-20. There is nothing new here.

Listing 3-20 MINIMAL4. DEF

```
NAME          MINIMAL4
DESCRIPTION   'Basic Windows application'
EXETYPE       WINDOWS
STUB          'WINSTUB.EXE'
CODE          PRELOAD MOVEABLE DISCARDABLE
DATA          PRELOAD MOVEABLE MULTIPLE
HEAPSIZE      1024
STACKSIZE     5120
EXPORTS       WndProc
```

You will also need to create a project file for the program. The project files for Turbo C++ (Listing 3-21) and QuickC (Listing 3-22) are slightly different, as QuickC will compile the raw resource script file as part of its normal compilation activities, while Turbo C++ requires that you have already compiled the .RC data to a .RES file before compiling the finished program.

Listing 3-21 Turbo C++ Project File for MINIMAL4

```
minimal4.c
minimal4.def
minimal4.res
```

Listing 3-22 QuickC Project File for MINIMAL4

```
minimal4.c
minimal4.def
minimal4.rc
```

Finally, the program itself must be created. As before, copy MINIMAL3.C to a new file called MINIMAL4.C, and add the new code shown in bold face in Listing 3-23. Note that the menu name "MyMenu" is specified for the window class. All windows created from this class will use the same menu.

The TranslateMessage() function was added to the message loop. This function creates WM_CHAR messages when WM_KEYDOWN messages are detected. WM_CHAR messages are used by DefWindowProc() to provide the keyboard alternative to selecting menu items with a mouse by using (Alt)-*letter* key combinations. TranslateMessage() is included in almost all message loops in commercial Windows programs, so this is the first "normal" looking message loop in the book. We will use this form of message loop from now on in the example programs. Chapter 7, *Character Sets, Fonts, and the Keyboard,* explores the WM_CHAR message in more detail.

Listing 3-23 MINIMAL4.C

```
/* minimal4.c   generic Windows program with a menu */

#include <windows.h>
#include "minimal4.h"

int PASCAL WinMain (HANDLE hInstance, HANDLE hPrevInstance, LPSTR lpszCmdLine,
    int nCmdShow)
{
    HWND       hWnd ;           /* the window's "handle" */
    MSG        msg ;            /* a message structure */
    WNDCLASS   wndclass ;       /* window class structure */

    if (!hPrevInstance)
    {
       wndclass.style          = CS_HREDRAW | CS_VREDRAW ;
       wndclass.lpfnWndProc    = WndProc ;
       wndclass.cbClsExtra     = 0 ;
       wndclass.cbWndExtra     = 0 ;
       wndclass.hInstance      = hInstance ;
       wndclass.hIcon          = LoadIcon (hInstance, "MyIcon") ;
```

```
        wndclass.hCursor        = LoadCursor (NULL, IDC_ARROW) ;
        wndclass.hbrBackground  = GetStockObject (WHITE_BRUSH) ;
        wndclass.lpszMenuName   = "MyMenu" ;
        wndclass.lpszClassName  = "MyClass" ;
                                /* register the window class */
        if (!RegisterClass (&wndclass))
              return 0 ;
    }

    hWnd = CreateWindow ("MyClass," lpszCmdLine, WS_OVERLAPPEDWINDOW,
       10, 10, 200, 100, NULL, NULL, hInstance, NULL) ;
    ShowWindow (hWnd, nCmdShow) ;   /* display the window */

    while (GetMessage (&msg, NULL, NULL, NULL))      /* message loop */
    {
       TranslateMessage (&msg) ;    /* translate keyboard messages */
       DispatchMessage (&msg) ;     /* send message to WndProc() */
    }
    return (msg.wParam) ;
}

long FAR PASCAL WndProc (HWND hWnd, WORD wMessage, WORD wParam, LONG lParam)
{
    switch (wMessage)                  /* process windows messages */
    {
       case WM_COMMAND:
           switch (wParam)
           {
           case IDM_BEEP:              /* menu items */
               MessageBeep (0) ;       /* just beep */
               break ;
           case IDM_QUIT:              /* Quit menu item */
               DestroyWindow (hWnd) ;  /* destroy window, */
               break ;                 /* terminating application */
           }
           break ;
       case WM_DESTROY:                /* stop application */
           PostQuitMessage (0) ;
           break ;
       default:                        /* default windows message processing */
           return (DefWindowProc (hWnd, wMessage, wParam, lParam)) ;
    }
    return (0L) ;
}
```

The WndProc() function in MINIMAL4 has been expanded to interpret menu items. When a menu item is selected with either the mouse, or the keyboard alternative, Windows sends the application a WM_COMMAND message. The *wParam* parameter that is sent as part of the message data contains the ID number of the menu item selected. In MINIMAL4.C, the IDM_BEEP menu item results in MessageBeep() being called. This just beeps the computer's speaker or sound device. The IDM_QUIT menu item causes DestroyWindow() to be called. Destroying the program's Window is the best way to terminate a program. Windows sends the WM_DESTROY message to the program after DestroyWindow() is called. This results in the same shutdown sequence being followed if the "Quit" menu item is selected, or if the program is terminated by double clicking the system button at the top left corner of the program.

Passing a Command Line Argument

Another change in MINIMAL4 is to change the window's title from a fixed character string to the *lpszCmdLine* parameter passed to WinMain(). The CreateWindow() function call now looks like:

```
hWnd = CreateWindow ("MyClass," lpszCmdLine, WS_OVERLAPPEDWINDOW,
    10, 10, 200, 100, NULL, NULL, hInstance, NULL) ;
```

The *lpszCmdLine* string is passed to the WinMain() function by Windows when the program is started. There are a couple of ways to establish a command line string when starting a program. One is to select the "File/Run" menu item from the Windows Program Manager. You will be presented with a dialog box similar to Figure 3-13. Enter the full path name where the MINIMAL4.EXE program is stored, followed by the command line string. In Figure 3-13 the string "Hi There" is passed with the function name.

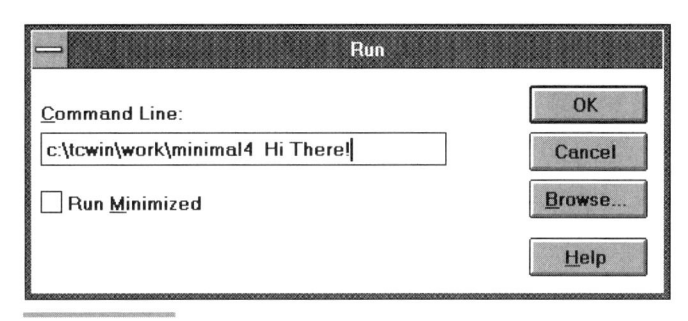

Figure 3-13 The Program Manager "File/Run" Menu Dialog Box

Any characters following the file name in the "File/Run" dialog box are passed to MINIMAL4.EXE as the lpsz*CmdLine* string. This string is then used to create the MINIMAL4 window title, as shown in Figure 3-14. This is a trivial use for the command line string. Normally, the command line string is used to pass a file name to the program so that the program can load the file on startup. All of the applications bundled with Windows, such as NOTEPAD and WRITE, support this feature.

Figure 3-14 MINIMAL4 after Receiving the "Hi There!" Command Line

Another way to pass a command line string to a program is by associating the command line with a program icon. To do this, open one of the groups in the Program Manager application, such as the Accessories group, and select the "File/New" menu item from the Program Manager menu. A dialog box will appear, similar to that shown in Figure 3-15, allowing you to enter the program's description (which will appear under the icon in the Program Manager group window), the command line string includ-

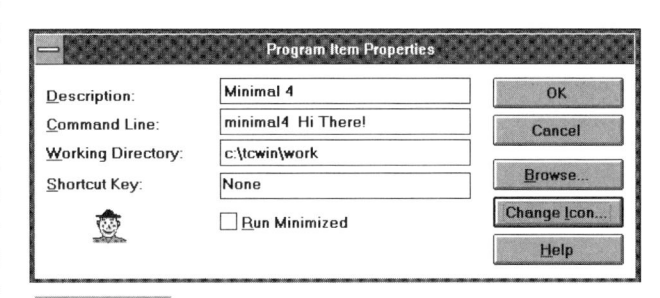

Figure 3-15 Adding a Program Icon to a Program Manager Group

Chapter 3 • First Programming Experiments

ing the program name, and the working directory. You can also select either the program's icon, or another of the stock icon images supplied with Windows. When you select the "OK" button, the program will appear iconized in the Program Manager group window. Double clicking the icon image will start the program, again passing the command line string on as the *lpszCmdLine* parameter in WinMain() when the program starts.

One last way to pass a command line argument to a Windows program is to do it while starting Windows. For example, if you start Windows with the following line, Windows will start running and start the MINIMAL4.EXE program at the beginning of the Windows session. The MINIMAL4 program will receive the command line string "Hi There!" as the *lpszCmdLine* parameter passed to the WinMain() function.

```
win c:\msc\work\minimal4 Hi There!
```

Summary

This chapter improved the MINIMAL1 program in three steps to build a complete Windows application. First we added a message loop so that the window would stay on the screen until the central button was clicked with the mouse. Then we created a new window class to make a more normal looking program window. We also moved the message processing logic out of the message loop and into the WndProc() function. Finally, we added an icon and a simple menu to the program's resource data.

The final version, MINIMAL4, does nothing special except beep the computer's sound device. However, it has all of the elements of a normal Windows program. It creates its own window class, processes several messages, and makes use of data in a header file and a resource file. MINIMAL4 is an ideal starting point for many Windows projects.

In the course of improving MINIMAL1, a number of new functions and messages were introduced. RegisterClass() is used to create a new window class. GetMessage() fetches messages in message loops, while DispatchMessage() sends them on to the WndProc() function for processing. Messages not processed in the WndProc() logic are passed on to the DefWindowProc() function, which carries out the default actions for all messages. DestroyWindow() is used to initiate termination of the program by destroying the main window. TranslateMessage() was inserted into the MINIMAL4.C message loop to allow the user to select menu items using (Alt)-(Key) combinations.

Several messages were also demonstrated. WM_COMMAND messages are generated by the user selecting a menu item. These messages are processed in MINIMAL4 to cause actions when the menu is used. WM_DESTROY messages are sent to the application to terminate the program. The usual response is to call the PostQuitMessage() function, which sends the WM_QUIT message to the program's message loop, terminating the application. WM_LBUTTONDOWN was used in MINIMAL2 to detect the left mouse button being depressed.

QUESTIONS

1. Write in standard C notation the following Windows types:
   a. WORD
   b. LPSTR
   c. PINT
   d. BOOL

2. Add a Hungarian notation prefix to each of the following variable names to reflect its type. For example, if the variable "MyInt" is an integer, it would be labeled "nMyInt."
   a. Name, a near pointer to a null-terminated character string.
   b. Toggle, an unsigned integer that is either zero or one.
   c. Window, a handle of a window.

3. If you are starting a program for the first time in a Windows session, what value does the hPrevInstance parameter passed to WinMain() have?

4. The nCmdShow parameter passed to the WinMain() function when a Windows program starts is used as a parameter in what other function? Why?

5. Which Windows message does WaitMessage() wait for?

6. While the program's message loop is "looping," no other Windows program can gain control. (True/False).

7. The DispatchMessage() function only takes one parameter, a pointer to a MSG data structure. How does DispatchMessage() know which function should receive the message data?

8. The MINIMAL4 program can be minimized to an icon. Where is the program logic that handles this action? How is the action initiated?

9. What change would you make to MINIMAL4 to have the client area of the window painted black?

10. Besides adding the DispatchMessage() function to a program's message loop, what other change do we need to have messages from Windows sent to the WndProc() function? (Hint: the change is in another file.)

11. What function should be called when a WM_DESTROY message is received from Windows? What message does that function generate?

12. List two of the three ways that a program will receive a character string as the lpszCmdLine parameter passed to the WinMain() function when a Windows program first starts.

EXERCISES

1. Change the cursor shape in the MINIMAL4 class definition to IDC_CROSS, and change the icon shape to IDI_ASTERISK. What changes do you observe when the program is running? (Hint: set the first parameter to NULL when loading predefined icons with LoadIcon().)

2. Run your MINIMAL4 application from within the debugger. Set a break point on the line containing GetMessage() and within the WndProc() function on the line containing the switch statement. At what point in the message loop is the WndProc() function called?

3. Add a third menu item to the resource file. Give it a unique ID value in the header file, and define it in the resource file. In MINIMAL4.C, execute the command:

   ```
   SetWindowText (hWnd, "Hi There Sport!") ;
   ```

   when the new menu item is activated. What happens to MINIMAL4 when your new menu item is clicked? (Hint: Do not forget the break statement after your menu item selection in the WndProc() function.)

ANSWERS TO QUESTIONS

1. a) unsigned int; 1b) char FAR *; 1c) int *; 1d) int.
2. a) pszName; 2b) bToggle; 2c) hWindow.
3. NULL (zero), as there is no previous instance of the program.
4. nCmdShow is passed to the ShowWindow() function as the second parameter so that ShowWindow knows whether to start the window minimized, maximized, or normally sized.
5. WaitMessage() waits for *any* message, and then returns.
6. False. The GetMessage() function returns control back to Windows if there are no pending messages.
7. The message processing function is defined in the window's class. DispatchMessage() determines the window from the *hwnd* element of the MSG data structure and determines the message processing function based on that window's class definition.
8. The logic for minimizing a window to an icon resides in Windows, not in the MINIMAL4 program. MINIMAL4 calls the DefWindowProc() function to take advantage of the built-in logic.
9. Change the main window's class definition to load a black brush. This would be done with the line:

   ```
   wndclass.hbrBackground = GetStockObject (BLACK_BRUSH) ;
   ```

10. Add WndProc to the EXPORTS section of the program's module definition file.

ANSWERS TO QUESTIONS (cont'd)

11. PostQuitMessage(), WM_QUIT.
12. The three ways are: 1) Use the "File/Run" menu item in the Program Manager; 2) Associate a command line with a program icon using the Program Manager "New/Program Item" or "Properties" menu items; 3) Start Windows, specifying a program name and command line string at the MS DOS command line like:

    ```
    win filename command line string here
    ```

SOLUTIONS TO EXERCISES

1. The only changes are to the initialization of the window class definition in the WinMain() function. Listing 3-24 shows the changed lines:

Listing 3-24 Changes to the Windows Class Definition

```
wndclass.style          = CS_HREDRAW | CS_VREDRAW ;
wndclass.lpfnWndProc    = WndProc ;
wndclass.cbClsExtra     = 0 ;
wndclass.cbWndExtra     = 0 ;
wndclass.hInstance      = hInstance ;
wndclass.hIcon          = LoadIcon (NULL, IDI_ASTERISK) ;
wndclass.hCursor        = LoadCursor (NULL, IDC_CROSS) ;
wndclass.hbrBackground  = GetStockObject (WHITE_BRUSH) ;
wndclass.lpszMenuName   = "MyMenu" ;
wndclass.lpszClassName  = "MyClass" ;
            /* register the window class */
if (!RegisterClass (&wndclass))
    return 0 ;
```

When these changes are made and the program is recompiled, the cursor will change into a cross shape any time the cursor is within the program's window area. The program will minimize to an icon with a letter "i" in a blue background (the predefined IDI_ASTERISK icon). The complete solution is under the file name C03EXER1 on the source code disks.

2. You may be surprised to find out that a number of messages are sent to the WndProc() function before a message reaches the program's message loop. Windows sends about 20 messages directly to WndProc(), bypassing the message loop, when the program first starts. These messages, like WM_CREATE and WM_NCCREATE are passed on to the DefWindowProc() function, which does the default actions. Basically, the default actions create the window. Only when all of the startup messages have been sent does Windows begin sending messages to the program's message loop.

3. Adding a new menu item requires modifications to several files. First the ID number for the new menu item must be added to the program's header file:

Chapter 3 • First Programming Experiments

SOLUTIONS TO EXERCISES (cont'd)

```
/* c03exer3.h header file */

#define IDM_BEEP    1
#define IDM_SHOW    2
#define IDM_QUIT   10

long FAR PASCAL WndProc (HWND, WORD, WORD, LONG) ;
```

The new menu item must be added to the program's resource data:

```
/* c03exer3.rc resource file */

#include "c03exer3.h"

MyIcon     ICON    c03exer3.ico

MyMenu MENU
BEGIN
   MENUITEM "&Beep",      IDM_BEEP
   MENUITEM "&Show",      IDM_SHOW
   MENUITEM "&Quit",      IDM_QUIT
END
```

Finally, the WndProc() function's logic must be modified to process the WM_COMMAND message from the new menu item:

```
long FAR PASCAL WndProc (HWND hWnd, WORD wMessage, WORD wParam, LONG lParam)
{
   switch (wMessage)            /* process windows messages */
   {
      case WM_COMMAND:
         switch (wParam)
         {
            case IDM_BEEP:    /* menu items */
               MessageBeep (0) ;      /* just beep */
               break ;
            case IDM_SHOW:
               SetWindowText (hWnd, "Hi There Sport!") ;
               break ;
            case IDM_QUIT:    /* Quit menu item */
               DestroyWindow (hWnd) ;   /* destroy window, */
               break ;        /* terminating application */
            default:          /* otherwise, let Windows process it */
               return (DefWindowProc (hWnd, wMessage, wParam, lParam));
         }
         break ;
      case WM_DESTROY:         /* stop application */
         PostQuitMessage (0) ;
         break ;
      default:    /* default windows message processing */
         return (DefWindowProc (hWnd, wMessage, wParam, lParam)) ;
   }
   return (0L) ;
}
```

The effect of these changes is that the program's caption changes to "Hi There Sport!" when the "Show" menu item is selected. The complete program files are given under the file name C03exer3 on the optional source code disks.

CHAPTER 4

Text and Graphics Output

This chapter explains how to output text and graphics using the rich collection of graphics functions that Windows provides. Windows allows programmers to write programs without concern over the specifics of the video hardware. A Windows program that works on a VGA display will work without modification on an EGA, Super VGA, IBM 8514, or any other video display that Windows supports. The key to this "device independence" is Windows use of a "device context." We will explore how the device context can be used for both text and graphics output, and how using the device context keeps our programs from interfering with each other on the screen. The last example program demonstrates animated graphics by creating a ball that bounces around inside the program's window.

Concepts Covered

Device Independence
Device Context
Invalid Rectangle
Paint Cycle
Changing Device Context Settings

RGB Color Model
Freeing Graphics Objects from Memory
Local Versus Global Variables
Animation

Keywords Covered

HDC
Pixel
GDI

PAINTSTRUCT
RECT
COLORREF

Functions Covered

GetDC()
ReleaseDC()
BeginPaint()
EndPaint()
TextOut()
PeekMessage()
SetTextColor()
SetBkColor()

SelectObject()
CreatePen()
CreateSolidBrush()
CreateHatchBrush()
Ellipse()
Rectangle()
HIWORD()
LOWORD()

Messages Covered

WM_CREATE
WM_PAINT

WM_SIZE

Character Mode Versus Graphics Mode

When you start a program under MS-DOS, the computer's screen is in character mode. The dot pattern for each character shown on the screen is stored in the video board's memory chips. The usual display configuration allows 80 characters across each row, and 25 lines of characters. Each character occupies a fixed position on the screen. The characters always have the same font (character shapes), although the color of each letter and its background can be changed.

Character mode displays have the advantage of being relatively fast. However, character mode displays limit what you can show on the screen. There is no good way to show different character fonts, such as italics and bold face letters of different sizes, with a character mode display. There is also no way to show pictures, unless the pictures are crudely formed from colored characters and character-sized symbols.

To get around the limitations of character mode displays, all modern video boards also support one or more graphics modes. In graphics modes, everything is drawn one dot (pixel) at a time. A typical VGA display will show 640 pixels horizontally by 480 pixels vertically. Each pixel can be any of 16 colors. Less expensive displays, such as the older CGA and EGA types, display fewer pixels and have fewer simultaneous colors. More expensive displays, such as Super VGA boards, typically show 1,028 by 760 pixels with 256 simultaneous colors. Even higher resolutions are available at a price.

Many DOS programs switch to a graphics mode to show charts and graphs. This setup is more flexible, but requires that the DOS program use different commands if the output is to a CGA, EGA, VGA, Super VGA, printer, plotter, or some other graphics device. MS-DOS programs must be continually updated to keep up with the evolution of computer hardware. It also means that if you have five MS-DOS programs on your computer that support graphics, each of the programs will have its own program logic for supporting the different types of displays. This adds up to a lot of duplicate code.

Windows always runs in a graphics mode. This is slower than using a character mode display, but much more flexible. Because everything (even letters and numbers) is drawn one pixel at a time, any shape or size is possible. Windows has no trouble displaying characters in different sizes, with italics, and bold face letters. Windows is also free to draw any desired shape or color on the screen at any location. The designers of Windows 3.0 had the flexibility to come up with attractive "three dimensional" shapes for buttons and scroll bars, and attractive color combinations for the window elements.

The Device Context

During the original design of Windows, one of the goals was to provide "device independence." Device independence means that the same program should be able to work using different screens, keyboards, and printers without modification to the program. Windows takes care of the hardware, allowing the programmer to concentrate on the program itself. If you have ever had to update the code of an MS-DOS program for the latest printer, plotter, video display, or keyboard, you will recognize device independence as a huge advantage for the developer.

Windows programs do not send data directly to the screen or printer. Instead, the program obtains a handle (ID value) for the screen or printer's *device context*. The output data is sent to the device context (DC), and then Windows takes care of sending it to the real hardware. The advantage of using the DC is that the graphics and text commands you send to the DC are always the same, regardless of whether the physical output is showing up on a VGA screen, IBM 8514 video device, printer, etc.

Windows GDI

The part of Windows that converts the Windows graphics function calls to the actual commands sent to the hardware is the GDI, or Graphics Device Interface. The GDI is a program file called GDI.EXE that is stored in the Windows System directory. The Windows environment will load GDI.EXE into memory when it is needed for graphical output. Windows will also load a "device driver" program if the hardware conversions are

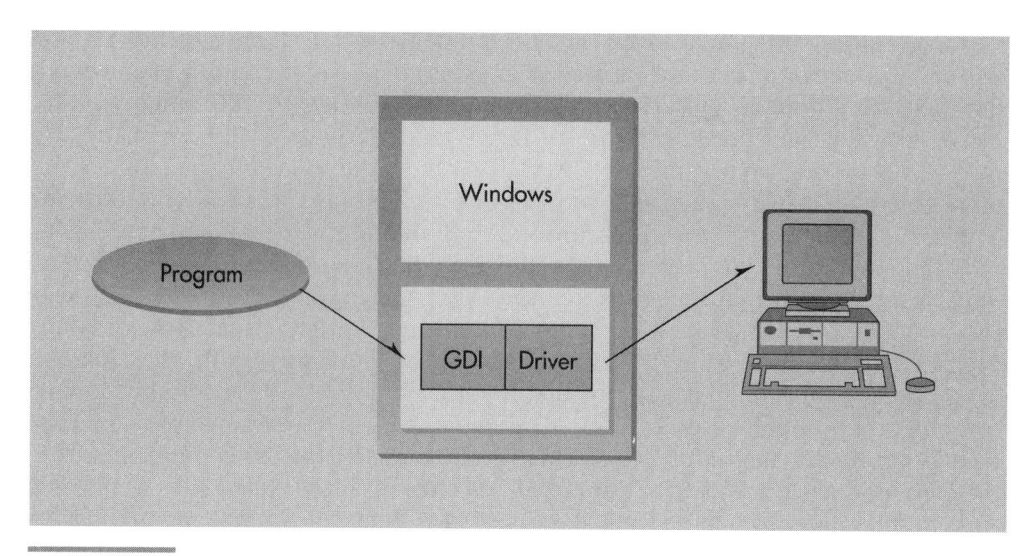

Figure 4-1 Output to a Device by a Windows Program

not part of GDI.EXE. Common examples are VGA.DRV for a VGA video screen and HPPLC.DRV for the HP Laserjet printer. Drivers are just programs that assist the GDI in converting Windows graphics commands to hardware commands. Figure 4-1 shows the relationship between the program and the physical hardware for a Windows application.

Text Output

To get started, we will output some text to the screen. The program called TEXT1 is similar to MINIMAL4.C. When the "Show Text" menu item is clicked, the string "First Menu Item Pressed!" is displayed below the menu bar. Figure 4-2 shows the result.

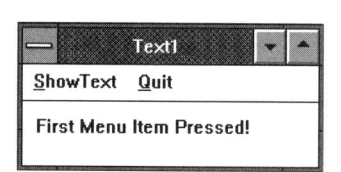

Figure 4-2 TEXT1 Program

If you want to create the TEXT1 program from scratch, you can start by copying the MINIMAL4 files to new names starting with TEXT1 (MINIMAL4.C copied to TEXT1.C, and so on). The header file TEXT1.H (Listing 4-1) uses a different name for the menu item ID. Otherwise it is identical to MINIMAL4.H.

Listing 4-1 TEXT1.H Header File

```
/* text1.h header file */

#define IDM_SHOW   1
#define IDM_QUIT   10

long FAR PASCAL WndProc (HWND, WORD, WORD, LONG) ;
```

The module definition file is shown in Listing 4-2. This is identical to the module definition file for MINIMAL4, except that the program name has been changed.

Listing 4-2 TEXT1.DEF Module Definition File

```
NAME        text1
EXETYPE     WINDOWS
STUB        'WINSTUB.EXE'
CODE        PRELOAD MOVEABLE
DATA        PRELOAD MOVEABLE MULTIPLE
HEAPSIZE    1024
STACKSIZE   5120
EXPORTS     WndProc
```

The resource script file TEXT1.RC in Listing 4-3 just defines the program icon name and the menu. You can create a new icon using your icon editor (Resource Workshop or Image Editor). The source code disks include an icon file that looks like Figure 4-3.

Listing 4-3 TEXT1.RC Resource Script File

```
/* text1.rc resource file */

#include "text1.h"

MyIcon      ICON    text1.ico

MyMenu      MENU
BEGIN
   MENUITEM "&ShowText"    IDM_SHOW
   MENUITEM "&Quit",       IDM_QUIT
END
```

The C program TEXT1.C in Listing 4-4 is also very close to MINIMAL4.C. The main change is to replace the MessageBeep() function with three lines that get the device context, output a line of text, and release the device context. These lines are in the WndProc() function under the IDM_SHOW menu item.

Figure 4-3
TEXT1.ICO Icon

Listing 4-4 TEXT1.C

```
/* text1.c  Demonstrates painting text on the screen */

#include <windows.h>
#include "text1.h"

int PASCAL WinMain (HANDLE hInstance, HANDLE hPrevInstance, LPSTR lpszCmdLine,
   int nCmdShow)
{
```

Chapter 4 • Text and Graphics Output

```
    HWND        hWnd ;              /* the window's "handle" */
    MSG         msg ;               /* a message structure */
    WNDCLASS    wndclass ;          /* window class structure */

    if (!hPrevInstance)
    {
        wndclass.style          = CS_HREDRAW | CS_VREDRAW ;
        wndclass.lpfnWndProc    = WndProc ;
        wndclass.cbClsExtra     = 0 ;
        wndclass.cbWndExtra     = 0 ;
        wndclass.hInstance      = hInstance ;
        wndclass.hIcon          = LoadIcon (hInstance, "MyIcon") ;
        wndclass.hCursor        = LoadCursor (NULL, IDC_ARROW) ;
        wndclass.hbrBackground  = GetStockObject (WHITE_BRUSH) ;
        wndclass.lpszMenuName   = "MyMenu" ;
        wndclass.lpszClassName  = "MyClass" ;
                                /* register the window class */
        if (!RegisterClass (&wndclass))
            return 0 ;
    }

    hWnd = CreateWindow ("MyClass","Text1", WS_OVERLAPPEDWINDOW,
        CW_USEDEFAULT, CW_USEDEFAULT, CW_USEDEFAULT, CW_USEDEFAULT,
        NULL, NULL, hInstance, NULL) ;
    ShowWindow (hWnd, nCmdShow) ;   /* display the window */

    while (GetMessage (&msg, NULL, NULL, NULL))     /* message loop */
    {
        TranslateMessage (&msg) ;   /* translate keyboard messages */
        DispatchMessage (&msg) ;    /* send message to WndProc() */
    }
    return (msg.wParam) ;
}

long FAR PASCAL WndProc (HWND hWnd, WORD wMessage, WORD wParam, LONG lParam)
{
    HDC hDC ;                       /* the device context handle */

    switch (wMessage)               /* process windows messages */
    {
        case WM_COMMAND:
            switch (wParam)
            {
                case IDM_SHOW:                  /* menu items */
                    hDC = GetDC (hWnd) ;        /* get DC */
                    TextOut (hDC, 10, 10,       /* output text */
                        "First Menu Item Pressed!", 24) ;
                    ReleaseDC (hWnd, hDC) ;     /* release DC */
                    break ;
                case IDM_QUIT:
                    DestroyWindow (hWnd) ;      /* destroy window, */
                    break ;                     /* terminating application */
            }
            break ;
        case WM_DESTROY:                        /* stop application */
            PostQuitMessage (0) ;
            break ;
        default:                                /* default windows message processing */
```

```
                return DefWindowProc (hWnd, wMessage, wParam, lParam) ;
        }
        return (0L) ;
}
```

To automate the compile/link cycle, you will need to create a project file. Listings 4-5 and 4-6 show the files which should be included.

Listing 4-5 Turbo C++ Project File for TEXT1

```
text1.c
text1.def
text1.res
```

Listing 4-6 QuickC Project File for TEXT1

```
text1.c
text1.def
text1.rc
```

The key part of TEXT1.C to notice is the part of WndProc() that is activated when the user selects the "Show Text" menu item. Selecting the menu item results in the WM_COMMAND message being sent to the WndProc() function with *wParam* set to the menu item ID value of IDM_SHOW. Listing 4-7 shows just this portion.

Listing 4-7 Output of Text in TEXT1.C

```
        case IDM_SHOW:              /* menu items */
            hDC = GetDC (hWnd) ;    /* get DC */
            TextOut (hDC, 10, 10,   /* output text */
                "First Menu Item Pressed!", 24) ;
            ReleaseDC (hWnd, hDC) ; /* release DC */
            break ;
```

The GetDC() function retrieves a device context handle (HDC) for the client area of the application's window. The TextOut() function then outputs text to this device context starting at a point 10 pixels down and 10 pixels to the right of the upper left corner of the client area. Finally, ReleaseDC() is used to free the memory associated with the device context.

There are a few subtle things going on here. As GetDC() returned the device context for just the window's client area, this is the only part of the screen that can be painted using this device context. If you tried to output the text at location -20, -20, the TextOut() function would execute, but the text would not be visible. The location -20, -20 is somewhere up in the window's caption area and is not part of the client area. The device context's built-in limits for output are the mechanisms that Windows uses to keep applications from writing outside of their own window's area.

When GetDC() is called, Windows retrieves about 800 bytes of information about the device and stores this data in memory. Windows will store a maximum of five device contexts in memory. Only one device context can be created for a window at one time. These considerations are why ReleaseDC() is called as soon as the text output is done. Forgetting to release the device context is a common error, and it will cause your program to fail when it attempts to create a second device context for the same device or window.

The device context internal structure is not defined in WINDOWS.H, or anywhere else in the Windows documentation. This omission is because you will never make use of the internal data in the device context. All you need is the handle to the device context in memory. Windows keeps the inner workings of the device context a secret. This is just as well. After all, one of the advantages of programming Windows applications is that Windows takes care of the hardware for us. No matter what type of video equipment the user has on his or her computer, you will be able to get a device context handle and output text to the device.

When the device context handle is first retrieved from Windows with GetDC(), the device context is set with default values. For example, the origin (0,0 point) is set to the top left corner of the window's client area. The default units are pixels. Positive horizontal distances are measured in pixels from the left side, while vertical distances are measured in pixels downward from the top of the client area (*Y* values increase going down). The default text color is black, with a default background color of white. All of these values can be changed as desired, but for now the default values are convenient.

Compile TEXT1 and give it a try. Note that the text appears when you click the "Show Text" menu item, but it is not repainted if you resize the window, minimize it and then restore it, or cover TEXT1's window with another program's window and then uncover it. These are all comonplace activities for a Windows application, so the text needs to be made more permanent.

The WM_PAINT Message

The reason that the text painted in the client area (center) of the TEXT1 window keeps disappearing is that Windows repaints the window every time it is uncovered or changed in size. This automatic repainting logic is what keeps your window from vanishing from the screen when it is covered up by another application.

When Windows is about to repaint the client area of an application program's window, Windows sends the application a WM_PAINT message. In TEXT1 this message is read by GetMessage() and sent to the WndProc() function by TransmitMessage(). As the WM_PAINT message is not processed by the program logic in TEXT1.C, it just gets passed on to the DefWindowProc() function. The default processing just repaints the client area with the window's class brush, which has the effect of recreating a blank client area.

To avoid having the text disappear, we can intercept the WM_PAINT message and repaint the text. The text lines will be redrawn right after the client area is painted with the window's class brush. Listing 4-8 shows TEXT2.C, which is very similar to TEXT1.C (the changes are highlighted).

Listing 4-8 TEXT2.C

```c
/* text2.c   Demonstrates WM_PAINT cycle */

#include <windows.h>
#include "text2.h"

int PASCAL WinMain (HANDLE hInstance, HANDLE hPrevInstance, LPSTR lpszCmdLine,
    int nCmdShow)
{
    HWND       hWnd ;          /* the window's "handle" */
    MSG        msg ;           /* a message structure */
    WNDCLASS   wndclass ;      /* window class structure */

    if (!hPrevInstance)
    {
        wndclass.style         = CS_HREDRAW | CS_VREDRAW ;
        wndclass.lpfnWndProc   = WndProc ;
        wndclass.cbClsExtra    = 0 ;
        wndclass.cbWndExtra    = 0 ;
        wndclass.hInstance     = hInstance ;
        wndclass.hIcon         = LoadIcon (hInstance, "MyIcon") ;
        wndclass.hCursor       = LoadCursor (NULL, IDC_ARROW) ;
        wndclass.hbrBackground = GetStockObject (WHITE_BRUSH) ;
        wndclass.lpszMenuName  = "MyMenu" ;
        wndclass.lpszClassName = "MyClass" ;
                               /* register the window class */
        if (!RegisterClass (&wndclass))
            return 0 ;
    }

    hWnd = CreateWindow ("MyClass","text2", WS_OVERLAPPEDWINDOW,
        CW_USEDEFAULT, CW_USEDEFAULT, CW_USEDEFAULT, CW_USEDEFAULT,
        NULL, NULL, hInstance, NULL) ;
    ShowWindow (hWnd, nCmdShow) ;   /* display the window */

    while (GetMessage (&msg, NULL, NULL, NULL))   /* message loop */
    {
        TranslateMessage (&msg) ; /* translate keyboard messages */
        DispatchMessage (&msg) ;  /* send message to WndProc() */
    }
    return (msg.wParam) ;
}

long FAR PASCAL WndProc (HWND hWnd, WORD wMessage, WORD wParam, LONG lParam)
{
    PAINTSTRUCT   ps ;
    HDC           hDC ;

    switch (wMessage)      /* process windows messages */
    {
        case WM_COMMAND:
            switch (wParam)
            {
                case IDM_SHOW:       /* menu items */
                    hDC = GetDC (hWnd) ;
                    TextOut (hDC, 10, 10, "First Menu Item Pressed!", 24) ;
```

```
                        ReleaseDC (hWnd, hDC) ;
                        break ;
                case IDM_QUIT:
                        DestroyWindow (hWnd) ;    /* destory window, */
                        break ;       /* terminating application */
            }
            break ;
      case WM_PAINT:      /* window's client area needs repainting */
            hDC = BeginPaint (hWnd, &ps) ;
            TextOut (hDC, 10, 40,
                "This text output when WM_PAINT received.", 40) ;
            EndPaint (hWnd, &ps) ;
            break ;
      case WM_DESTROY:     /* stop application */
            PostQuitMessage (0) ;
            break ;
      default:             /* default windows message processing */
            return DefWindowProc (hWnd, wMessage, wParam, lParam) ;
   }
   return (0L) ;
}
```

In TEXT1.C we used GetDC() to obtain the window's client area device context handle, and ReleaseDC() to release the DC. These two functions work everywhere *except* when processing WM_PAINT messages. When processing WM_PAINT, the specialized BeginPaint() and EndPaint() functions are used to obtain and release the client area device context.

Note in Listing 4-8 that a new variable *ps* of type PAINTSTRUCT has been declared. The PAINTSTRUCT data structure is defined in WINDOWS.H. This data type is needed to call BeginPaint() and EndPaint(). If you look in WINDOWS.H, you will find the definition for this structure, which is also shown in Listing 4-9.

Listing 4-9 PAINTSTRUCT Definition in WINDOWS.H

```
typedef struct tagPAINTSTRUCT
  {
   HDC       hdc;                /* the device context handle */
   BOOL      fErase;             /* background redrawn? TRUE/FALSE */
   RECT      rcPaint;            /* the rectangular area to update */
   BOOL      fRestore;           /* reserved */
   BOOL      fIncUpdate;         /* reserved */
   BYTE      rgbReserved[16];    /* reserved */
  } PAINTSTRUCT;
```

The PAINTSTRUCT data gets filled in when you call BeginPaint(). The *hdc* element is the device context handle for the window's client area. BeginPaint() also returns the device context handle as the function's returned value. You can either use the returned value as shown in Listing 4-10 or use the PAINTSTRUCT member *hdc*. The advantage of using the PAINTSTRUCT member is that you do not need to declare a separate variable to hold the device context handle. For example, Listing 4-10 shows the WM_PAINT logic using the *hdc* member of the PAINTSTRUCT for the device context handle.

Listing 4-10 Alternative Method of Getting the Device Context Handle in Processing WM_PAINT Messages

```
case WM_PAINT:              /* window's client area needs repainting */
    BeginPaint (hWnd, &ps) ;
    TextOut (ps.hdc, 10, 40,
        "This text output when WM_PAINT received.", 40) ;
    EndPaint (hWnd, &ps) ;
    break ;
```

The *fErase* member of the PAINTSTRUCT will be TRUE if the background has been redrawn, FALSE if not. The most interesting member of the PAINTSTRUCT structure is *rcPaint*. This member is defined as a RECT. Elsewhere in WINDOWS.H you can find the RECT definition as shown in Listing 4-11. The RECT structure defines a rectangle by its upper left and lower right corners.

Listing 4-11 RECT Definition in WINDOWS.H

```
typedef struct tagRECT
  {
    int left;
    int top;
    int right;
    int bottom;
  } RECT;
```

In the PAINTSTRUCT structure, the *rcPaint* RECT defines the smallest rectangle in the client area that includes all of the area that needs to be repainted. For example, if another program's window only covers up a corner of TEXT2's client area, then only that corner will need to be repainted. This area is called the "invalid rectangle" of the client area, and will be reflected in the *rcPaint* data. Complex applications sometimes check the invalid rectangle and only repaint the parts of the client area that fall inside *rcPaint*. Most simple applications, such as TEXT2, just repaint the whole client area every time a WM_PAINT message is received.

Figure 4-4 shows TEXT2 in action. The text line "This text output when WM_PAINT received." is repainted when-

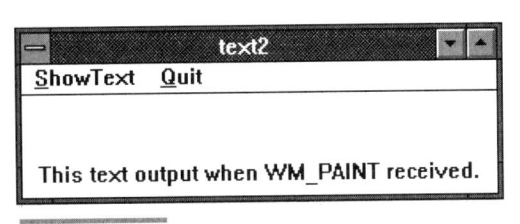

Figure 4-4 TEXT2 Updated by Processing WM_PAINT Messages

ever Windows sends a WM_PAINT message. This gives the illusion of the text being permanently on the TEXT2 client area. Clicking the "Show Text" menu item on TEXT2 outputs the string "First Menu Item Pressed!" on the client area, but this string is not automatically repainted when the window is resized.

Chapter 4 • Text and Graphics Output

Listings 4-12 to 4-16 show the TEXT2 header, resource script, module definition, and project files. They are identical to the TEXT1 example, except that the program name has been changed. The icon image is shown in Figure 4-5.

Listing 4-12 TEXT2.H Header File

```
/* text2.h  header file */

#define IDM_SHOW   1
#define IDM_QUIT   10

long FAR PASCAL WndProc (HWND, WORD, WORD, LONG) ;
```

Listing 4-13 TEXT2.RC Resource Script File

```
/* text2.rc   resource file */

#include "text2.h"

MyIcon      ICON    text2.ico

MyMenu      MENU
BEGIN
    MENUITEM "&ShowText"   IDM_SHOW
    MENUITEM "&Quit",      IDM_QUIT
END
```

Listing 4-14 TEXT2.DEF Module Definition File

```
NAME        text2
EXETYPE     WINDOWS
STUB        'WINSTUB.EXE'
CODE        PRELOAD MOVEABLE
DATA        PRELOAD MOVEABLE MULTIPLE
HEAPSIZE    1024
STACKSIZE   5120
EXPORTS     WndProc
```

Listing 4-15 Turbo C++ Project File for TEXT2

```
text2.c
text2.def
text2.res
```

94 Windows Programming Primer Plus®

Listing 4-16 QuickC Project File for TEXT2

```
text2.c
text2.def
text2.rc
```

Although it is a simple example, TEXT2 gives you an outline of the structure of any Windows application program that needs to keep the client area painted. You repaint the client area every time a WM_PAINT message is received. Windows detects when the client area needs to be repainted and sends WM_PAINT messages to the application. Windows also calculates the minimum-sized invalid rectangle that needs to be repainted. It is up to the programmer to decide whether to put in logic to only paint the parts of the screen that need to be repainted, or to just go ahead and repaint the whole client area. For simplicity, most programs repaint the entire client area every time a WM_PAINT message is sent, like our TEXT2 example.

Figure 4-5
TEXT2.ICO Icon Image

Changing The Device Context

So far we have used just the TextOut() function to output character strings to the client area of a window. The default settings for a device context are to show the characters in black and white, using the system character font. We can change the color and character font by selecting new values into the device context before the characters are output. TEXT3.C in Listing 4-17 shows two examples of this being done, both within the WM_PAINT logic, and in response to a menu selection. Listing 4-18 to 4-22 show the support files. Figure 4-6 shows the icon image.

Figure 4-6
TEXT3.ICO Icon Image

Listing 4-17 TEXT3.C

```
/* text3.c   Demonstrates changine the device context attributes */

#include <windows.h>
#include "text3.h"

int PASCAL WinMain (HANDLE hInstance, HANDLE hPrevInstance, LPSTR lpszCmdLine,
    int nCmdShow)
{
    HWND       hWnd ;            /* the window's "handle" */
    MSG        msg ;             /* a message structure */
    WNDCLASS   wndclass ;        /* window class structure */

    if (!hPrevInstance)
    {
```

```c
        wndclass.style          = CS_HREDRAW | CS_VREDRAW ;
        wndclass.lpfnWndProc    = WndProc ;
        wndclass.cbClsExtra     = 0 ;
        wndclass.cbWndExtra     = 0 ;
        wndclass.hInstance      = hInstance ;
        wndclass.hIcon          = LoadIcon (hInstance, "MyIcon") ;
        wndclass.hCursor        = LoadCursor (NULL, IDC_ARROW) ;
        wndclass.hbrBackground  = GetStockObject (WHITE_BRUSH) ;
        wndclass.lpszMenuName   = "MyMenu" ;
        wndclass.lpszClassName  = "MyClass" ;
                        /* register the window class */
        if (!RegisterClass (&wndclass))
            return 0 ;
    }

    hWnd = CreateWindow ("MyClass", "Text 3", WS_OVERLAPPEDWINDOW,
        CW_USEDEFAULT, CW_USEDEFAULT, CW_USEDEFAULT, CW_USEDEFAULT,
        NULL, NULL, hInstance, NULL) ;
    ShowWindow (hWnd, nCmdShow) ;   /* display the window */

    while (GetMessage (&msg, NULL, NULL, NULL))   /* message loop */
    {
        TranslateMessage (&msg) ;   /* translate keyboard messages */
        DispatchMessage (&msg) ;    /* send message to WndProc() */
    }
    return (msg.wParam) ;
}
long FAR PASCAL WndProc (HWND hWnd, WORD wMessage, WORD wParam, LONG lParam)
{
    PAINTSTRUCT  ps ;
    HDC          hDC ;

    switch (wMessage)          /* process windows messages */
    {
        case WM_COMMAND:
            switch (wParam)
            {
                case IDM_SHOW:                   /* menu items */
                    hDC = GetDC (hWnd) ;
                    SelectObject (hDC, GetStockObject (ANSI_VAR_FONT)) ;
                    TextOut (hDC, 10, 10, "First Menu Item Pressed!", 24) ;
                    ReleaseDC (hWnd, hDC) ;
                    break ;
                case IDM_QUIT:
                    DestroyWindow (hWnd) ;       /* destory window, */
                    break ;      /* terminating application */
            }
            break ;
        case WM_PAINT:     /* window's client area needs repainting */
            hDC = BeginPaint (hWnd, &ps) ;
            SetTextColor (hDC, RGB (255, 0, 0)) ;
            SetBkMode (hDC, OPAQUE) ;
            SetBkColor (hDC, RGB (0, 0, 255)) ;
            TextOut (hDC, 10, 40,
          "This text output when WM_PAINT received.", 40) ;
            EndPaint (hWnd, &ps) ;
            break ;
        case WM_DESTROY:                     /* stop application */
```

```
            PostQuitMessage (0) ;
            break ;
    default:                     /* default windows message processing */
            return DefWindowProc (hWnd, wMessage, wParam, lParam) ;
    }
    return (0L) ;
}
```

Listing 4-18 TEXT3.H Header File

```
/* text3.h  header file */

#define IDM_SHOW    1
#define IDM_QUIT    10

long FAR PASCAL WndProc (HWND, WORD, WORD, LONG) ;
```

Listing 4-19 TEXT3.RC Resource Script File

```
/* text3.rc  resource file */

#include "text3.h"

MyIcon      ICON    text3.ico

MyMenu      MENU
BEGIN
    MENUITEM "&ShowText"  IDM_SHOW
    MENUITEM "&Quit",     IDM_QUIT
END
```

Listing 4-20 TEXT3.DEF Module Definition File

```
NAME        text3
EXETYPE     WINDOWS
STUB        'WINSTUB.EXE'
CODE        PRELOAD MOVEABLE
DATA        PRELOAD MOVEABLE MULTIPLE
HEAPSIZE    1024
STACKSIZE   5120
EXPORTS     WndProc
```

Listing 4-21 Turbo C++ Project File for TEXT3

```
text3.c
text3.def
text3.res
```

Listing 4-22 QuickC Project File for TEXT3

```
text3.c
text3.def
text3.rc
```

Windows RGB Color Model

Windows uses 32-bit (four byte) numbers to represent colors. This data type is called COLORREF, a DWORD value declared in WINDOWS.H.

```
typedef DWORD           COLORREF;
```

Only the least significant three bytes are used to store color data. The most significant byte is used to distinguish between the Windows RGB color model and color palettes for devices that support more than 16 simultaneous pure colors. For now, we can assume that the most significant byte is zero and that the user is using a video device showing only 16 simultaneous pure colors, such as VGA.

The basic color data is three values that represent the intensity of the red, green, and blue contributions to color. Each value can vary from 0 to 255. This provides 256*256*256 = 16,777,216 possible colors. The storage format is shown in Figure 4-7.

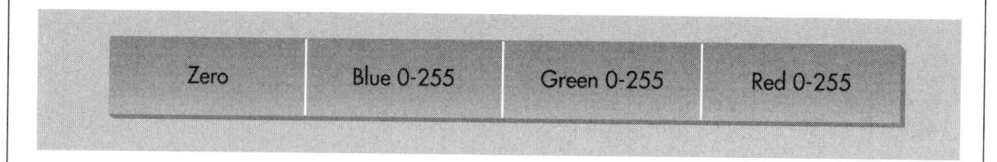

| Zero | Blue 0-255 | Green 0-255 | Red 0-255 |

Figure 4-7 RGB Color Data Format

To create a color value and set it to pure blue, use the code shown in Listing 4-23.

Listing 4-23 Declaring and Initializing a COLORREF Value

```
COLORREF    cr ;
cr = RGB (0, 0, 255) ;
```

RGB() is a macro defined in WINDOWS.H that puts the red, green, and blue intensity values in the correct byte positions. RGB (0, 0, 0) encodes black, as black is created by using zero intensity for all three color elements. RGB (255, 255, 255) encodes white, which is the combination of equal amounts of red, green, and blue colors. Note that the RGB macro follows the convention of having the red value on the left, even though the actual byte value is stored on the right (least significant) end of the COLORREF block in memory.

> ### Windows RGB Color Model (cont'd)
>
> In many cases, you can skip declaring a COLORREF value and use the RGB macro right inside a function call. For example, to create a red pen, Listing 4-24 uses RGB() in a call to the CreatePen() function. The value returned by CreatePen() is the handle (ID value) of the pen created.
>
> #### Listing 4-24 Creating a Red Pen Three Pixels Wide
>
> ```
> HPEN       hPen ;
> hPen = CreatePen (PS_SOLID, 3, RGB (255, 0, 0)) ;
> ```
>
> With the default color model, Windows assumes that the device (such as a video screen) is limited to 20 "system" colors. If fewer than 20 are available, some of the 20 will be identical. This is the case for most VGA systems, which have only 16 simultaneous colors. If a color value is specified with RGB() that does not match one of the system colors, Windows will approximate the requested color by "dithering." Dithering puts pixels of available colors in a pattern to create the illusion of a color between the two colors being mixed. The dithering logic in Windows is very fast and does not slow down painting operations appreciably.
>
> With Windows 3.0, support for devices with more than 20 colors was added via color palette control. The same RGB color encoding is used, but the high-order byte contains a code for either an index into a palette or a color value. The subject of color palettes is beyond the scope of this book. See Chapter 12 in the *Windows API Bible* if you need to use these advanced features.

The result of these changes is shown in Figure 4-8. The upper line, which is displayed when the "Show Text!" menu item is clicked, now uses the small ANSI_VAR_FONT character font. This is a stock font that is always available within Windows. The second line, painted each time a WM_PAINT message is processed, uses the standard font, but shows the text with red letters on a blue background. SetTextColor() changes the color of the text characters, but not their background. SetBkColor() changes the color of the background around each color. SetBkMode() changes the background painting mode. There are only two possibilities, OPAQUE and TRANSPARENT. By default, the TRANSPARENT mode is used, which allows any color or pattern already on the device context to "show through" around the characters. The OPAQUE mode causes the entire rectangle around the character to be repainted with the current background color. SetBkColor() is usually used with SetBkMode() to color the background around each character.

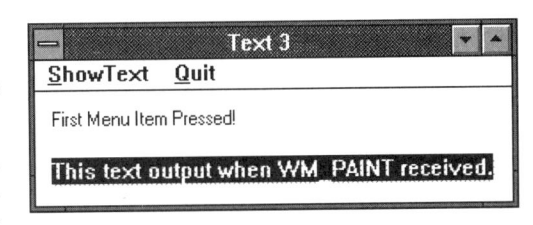

Figure 4-8 The TEXT3 Program

Device Context Settings

In TEXT3, both of the changes to the device context were made *before* the text was output. You can think of the device context as "remembering" the current settings for the character font, character color, background color, etc. Table 4-1 shows the range of objects and settings that can be selected into a device context. In the case of fonts, pens, brushes, and palettes, the device context is changed by "selecting an object into the device context." This just means that the data for the pen, brush, etc. is made available to the device context for immediate use. The SelectObject() function does this for the graphics objects. The other changes are just changes to data settings that the device context keeps track of internally.

SETTING	SELECTED BY FUNCTION	MEANING
Character font	SelectObject()	Sets the font used by TextOut() and related text output functions.
Character color	SetTextColor()	Sets the color of the text.
Character background	SetBkColor()	Sets the background color that surrounds each character.
Background Mode	SetBkMode()	Sets if the paint of text and graphics covers everything underneath (OPAQUE) or if the white areas are transparent (TRANSPARENT).
Text Alignment	SetTextAlign()	Sets how characters are aligned when output. The default alignment is based on the upper left corner of the character.
Text Spacing	SetTextCharacterExtra()	Sets the amount of extra space between each character.
Text Justification	SetTextJustification()	Justifies a string prior to output by TextOut(). Used with GetTextExtent() to determine the amount of space needed to make a character string exactly fill a space.
Pen	SelectObject()	The pen used to draw lines and outlines of objects. CreatePen() is used to create new pens.
Brush	SelectObject()	The pattern used to fill the interior of objects. Use CreateSolidBrush() and CreatePatternBrush() to create the brushes prior to calling SelectObject().

Origin	SetWindowOrg() and SetViewportOrg()	Moves the logical origin (0,0 point).
Mapping Mode	SetMapMode()	Changes the scaling of the device context. Scaling can be used to expand or shrink images or make the system of units based on inches or millimeters rather than pixels.
Raster Drawing Mode	SetROP2()	Determines how the existing pixels on the device (screen) are combined with the new pixels in drawing lines.
Polygon Filling Mode	SetPolyFillMode()	Determines how polygons are filled. This only changes the image if the polygon lines cross.
Clipping Region	SelectClipRgn()	Limits the area within which output will be displayed. Regions are created with CreateRectRgn(), CreateEllipticRgn(), etc.
Color Palette	SelectPalette()	The color palette to use if the output device supports more than the default 20 colors (such as Super VGA).

Table 4-1 Device Context Settings

We will explore selecting pens and brushes into the device context in the next section. Logical origins, mapping modes, raster modes, and regions are discussed in Chapter 13, *The Device Context*.

Graphics Output

So far the example programs have only displayed text. The next example program will output graphics images. The process is similar to output of text (remember that Windows does all output to the screen in graphics mode, so text and graphics operations are very similar).

1. Get the device context handle with either GetDC() or BeginPaint(). BeginPaint() is only used when processing WM_PAINT messages.
2. Select any pens or brushes into the device context.
3. Draw the lines, ellipses, rectangles, arcs, chords, pies, etc. using the Windows graphics functions.

4. Delete any pens or brushes created after displacing them from the device context. Graphics objects should not be deleted if they are currently selected into the device context (see the info box *Deleting Objects in a Device Context*).

5. Release the device context with either ReleaseDC() or EndPaint(). EndPaint() is only used at the end of the code for processing WM_PAINT messages.

Listing 4-25 shows GRAPHIC1.C. The first changes to the WndProc() function are to add declarations for two handles to pens and two handles to brushes. All handles are just unsigned integers, but it is clearer to use the HPEN and HBRUSH declarations.

Listing 4-25 GRAPHIC1.C

```
/* graphic1.c   Demonstrates painting functions */

#include <windows.h>
#include "graphic1.h"

int PASCAL WinMain (HANDLE hInstance, HANDLE hPrevInstance, LPSTR lpszCmdLine,
    int nCmdShow)
{
    HWND       hWnd ;           /* the window's "handle" */
    MSG        msg ;            /* a message structure */
    WNDCLASS   wndclass ;       /* window class structure */

    if (!hPrevInstance)
    {
        wndclass.style         = CS_HREDRAW | CS_VREDRAW ;
        wndclass.lpfnWndProc   = WndProc ;
        wndclass.cbClsExtra    = 0 ;
        wndclass.cbWndExtra    = 0 ;
        wndclass.hInstance     = hInstance ;
        wndclass.hIcon         = LoadIcon (hInstance, "MyIcon") ;
        wndclass.hCursor       = LoadCursor (NULL, IDC_ARROW) ;
        wndclass.hbrBackground = GetStockObject (WHITE_BRUSH) ;
        wndclass.lpszMenuName  = "MyMenu" ;
        wndclass.lpszClassName = "MyClass" ;
                                /* register the window class */
        if (!RegisterClass (&wndclass))
            return 0 ;
    }

    hWnd = CreateWindow ("MyClass","graphic1", WS_OVERLAPPEDWINDOW,
        CW_USEDEFAULT, CW_USEDEFAULT, CW_USEDEFAULT, CW_USEDEFAULT,
        NULL, NULL, hInstance, NULL) ;
    ShowWindow (hWnd, nCmdShow) ;     /* display the window */

    while (GetMessage (&msg, NULL, NULL, NULL))   /* message loop */
    {
        TranslateMessage (&msg) ;     /* translate keyboard messages */
        DispatchMessage (&msg) ;      /* send message to WndProc() */
    }
    return (msg.wParam) ;
}
long FAR PASCAL WndProc (HWND hWnd, WORD wMessage, WORD wParam, LONG lParam)
{
```

```
       HDC           hDC ;      /* the device context handle */
       PAINTSTRUCT   ps ;       /* paint structure */
       HPEN          hPen, hOldPen ;
       HBRUSH        hBrush, hOldBrush ;

       switch (wMessage)        /* process windows messages */
       {
           case WM_COMMAND:
               switch (wParam)
               {
                   case IDM_QUIT:
                       DestroyWindow (hWnd) ; /* destroy window, */
                       break ;                /* terminating application */
               }
               break ;
           case WM_PAINT:
               hDC = BeginPaint (hWnd, &ps) ;
                                        /* create new pen and brush */
               hPen = CreatePen (PS_SOLID, 3, RGB (255, 16, 16)) ;
               hBrush = CreateSolidBrush (RGB (0, 128, 128)) ;
               hOldPen = SelectObject (hDC, hPen) ;
               hOldBrush = SelectObject (hDC, hBrush) ;
                                        /* use to draw rectangle */
               Rectangle (hDC, 10, 10, 80, 60) ;
                                        /* delete the new brush after */
                                        /* putting old one back */
               hBrush = SelectObject (hDC, hOldBrush) ;
               DeleteObject (hBrush) ;
                                        /* create a hatched brush */
               hBrush = CreateHatchBrush (HS_DIAGCROSS, RGB (0, 0, 255)) ;
               hOldBrush = SelectObject (hDC, hBrush) ;
                                        /* use pen and brush to draw */
                                        /* an ellipse */
               Ellipse (hDC, 100, 30, 180, 90) ;
                                        /* delete pen and brush after */
                                        /* putting old ones back */
               hBrush = SelectObject (hDC, hOldBrush) ;
               DeleteObject (hBrush) ;
               hPen = SelectObject (hDC, hOldPen) ;
               DeleteObject (hPen) ;
                                        /* release the DC */
               EndPaint (hWnd, &ps) ;
               break ;
           case WM_DESTROY:    /* stop application */
               PostQuitMessage (0) ;
               break ;
           default:            /* default windows message processing */
               return DefWindowProc (hWnd, wMessage, wParam, lParam) ;
       }
       return (0L) ;
}
```

All of the logic to paint the window's client area is in the processing of the WM_PAINT message. Before the rectangle is drawn, a red pen and a green brush are created using CreatePen() and CreateSolidBrush(). They are selected into the device context. The Rectangle() function is then used to draw a rectangle. The red pen is automatically used to draw the border, while the green brush ends up filling the inside of the rectangle.

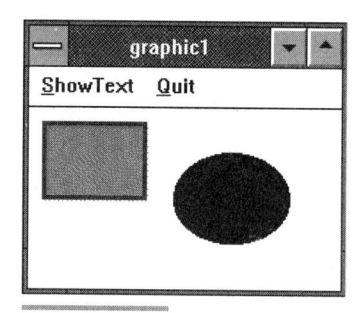

Figure 4-9 The GRAPHIC1 Program

Next the old brush is deleted, and a new one created. This time CreateHatchBrush() is used to create a blue pattern brush. This brush is selected into the device context. When Ellipse() is called, the red pen is used for the border and the pattern brush is used for filling the interior.

With the painting done, it is time to delete the pen and brush and to free the device context. The pen and brush cannot be deleted until they are removed from the DC. This is done by selecting the old pen and brush back into the DC, displacing the new ones. DeleteObject() frees the memory associated with the pen and brush. EndPaint() frees the device context. The result is shown in Figure 4-9. Because they are redrawn with every WM_PAINT message, the ellipse and rectangle reappear if the window is covered up, and then uncovered.

Listings 4-26 to 4-30 show the support files for GRAPHIC1. Figure 4-10 shows the icon image.

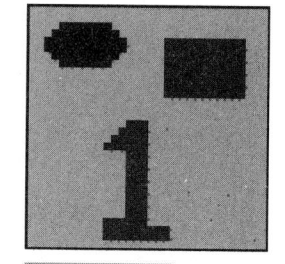

Figure 4-10 GRAPHIC1.ICO Icon Image

Listing 4-26 GRAPHIC1.H Header File

```
/* graphic1.h header file */

#define IDM_QUIT    1

long FAR PASCAL WndProc (HWND, WORD, WORD, LONG) ;
```

Listing 4-27 GRAPHIC1.RC Resource Script File

```
/* graphic1.rc resource file */

#include "graphic1.h"

MyIcon      ICON    graphic1.ico

MyMenu      MENU
BEGIN
    MENUITEM "&Quit",       IDM_QUIT
END
```

Listing 4-28 GRAPHIC1.DEF Module Definition File

```
NAME        graphic1
EXETYPE     WINDOWS
```

Windows Programming Primer Plus®

```
STUB        'WINSTUB.EXE'
CODE        PRELOAD MOVEABLE
DATA        PRELOAD MOVEABLE MULTIPLE
HEAPSIZE    1024
STACKSIZE   5120
EXPORTS     WndProc
```

Listing 4-29 GRAPHIC1.PRJ Turbo C++ Project File Contents

```
graphic1.c
graphic1.def
graphic1.res
```

Listing 4-30 GRAPHIC1.MAK QuickC Project File Contents

```
graphic1.c
graphic1.def
graphic1.rc
```

Deleting Objects in a Device Context

Probably the most confusing part of Windows graphics operations is keeping track of when it is safe to delete objects such as pens and brushes. They must be deleted, as otherwise they will continue to take up memory after the program that created them has terminated. However, if you delete an object that is still selected into the device context, Windows may crash. Before a graphics object (such as a pen or brush) can be safely deleted, it must be displaced out of the device context. The key to making this work is to understand that a device context can hold only one pen at a time, one brush at a time, one font, etc. Anytime you select a new object, the old one is displaced from the DC, but not from memory.

SelectObject() has the handy property of returning a handle to the last object the device context had of the same type. For example, if SelectObject() selects a pen into the DC, the value returned by SelectObject() is the handle of the last pen the DC stored. Listing 4-31 shows a typical creation of a pen and selection into the DC.

Listing 4-31 Getting the Handle to the Previously Selected Pen

```
HPEN    hOldPen, hNewPen ;
HDC     hDC ;

hDC      = GetDC (hWnd) ;
hNewPen  = CreatePen (PS_SOLID, 3, RGB (23, 128, 9)) ;
hOldPen  = SelectObject (hDC, hNewPen) ;
```
[Other program lines]

We can select the old pen back into the DC to displace the one we created. That makes it safe to delete the pen we created, freeing it from memory. This is shown in Listing 4-32

continued

> **Deleting Objects in a Device Context (cont'd)**
>
> **Listing 4-32** Safely Deleting a Pen
>
> ```
> SelectObject (hDC, hOldPen) ;
> DeleteObject (hNewPen) ;
> ReleaseDC (hWnd, hDC) ;
> ```
>
> The other way to displace an object out of the device context so that it can be deleted is to select one of the "stock" Windows objects into the DC. GetStockObject() returns a handle to a stock object. Listing 4-33 shows using this method to delete a pen.
>
> **Listing 4-33** Deleting a Pen Using a Stock Pen to Displace the New Pen
>
> ```
> SelectObject (hDC, GetStockObject (BLACK_PEN)) ;
> DeleteObject (hNewPen) ;
> ReleaseDC (hWnd, hDC) ;
> ```
>
> Never attempt to delete a stock object. They are maintained by Windows.

Frequently, you will be able to take advantage of the stock objects that Windows always has available. The default objects are a black line one pixel wide, a solid white brush, and black text on a white background using the variable pitch system font. GetStockObject() is used to retrieve a handle to one of the other stock objects, so that it can be selected into the device context. Table 4-2 shows the complete list of stock objects.

OBJECT TYPE	CHOICES
Pen	BLACK_PEN, WHITE_PEN (both one pixel wide), NULL_PEN
Brush	DKGRAY_BRUSH, GRAY_BRUSH, BLACK_BRUSH, LTGRAY_BRUSH, NULL_BRUSH, WHITE_BRUSH.
Font	ANSI_FIXED_FONT, ANSI_VAR_FONT, DEVICE_DEFAULT_FONT, OEM_FIXED_FONT, SYSTEM_FIXED_FONT, SYSTEM_FONT.

Table 4-2 Stock Objects that Can Be Obtained with GetStockObject()

The NULL pen and NULL brush are handy for modifying graphics function behavior. The most common use is to select the NULL_BRUSH and a custom pen. The drawing function will then draw only the outline. Selecting the NULL_PEN and a custom brush allows the center of the object to be filled without drawing a border. Of the stock character fonts, the default SYSTEM_FONT serves well for most purposes. You may want to select a fixed font, such as ANSI_FIXED_FONT, if you have tables of characters that need to line up vertically. The ANSI_VAR_FONT is handy if space is limited, as it is the smallest of the stock fonts.

Table 4-3 provides a summary of the graphics functions supported by Windows. All of these functions use the currently selected pen and brush. Objects such as lines and arcs are not closed, and, therefore, are not filled with the currently selected brush.

FUNCTION	EXAMPLE	COMMENTS
Arc()		Draws portions of an ellipse.
Chord()		Draws the filled portion of an ellipse, bounded by the ellipse border and a line.
Ellipse()		Draws an ellipse.
MoveTo(), LineTo()		MoveTo() establishes a position to start the line. LineTo() draws a line from the starting point to a second point.
Pie()		Draws a filled ellipse. The cut-out portion is defined by the interception of two points and the center of the ellipse.
Polygon()		Paints one or more closed polygons. The example uses a white brush for painting the interior.
Polyline()		Paints a series of one or more connected lines. This is equivalent to a call to MoveTo() for the first point, followed by a series of one or more LineTo() function calls.
PolyPolygon()		Paints one or more polygons. The polygons are filled based on the current polygon filling mode, using the selected brush of the DC.
Rectangle()		Paints a rectangular region based on the location of the upper left and lower right corners.
RoundRect()		Paints a rectangular region with rounded corners.

Table 4-3 Windows Graphics Functions

Animated Graphics

The next example uses what you have learned about selecting objects into a device context and drawing shapes. Rather than just draw a fixed picture, the program will create a moving graphics image of a ball bouncing around inside of the program's window. Figure 4-11 shows the GRAPHIC2 program in action.

The illusion of a moving ball is created by continually redrawing the ball at new locations. The ball is drawn using the Ellipse() function. The Ellipse() function uses the currently selected brush to fill the center, and the currently selected pen to draw the

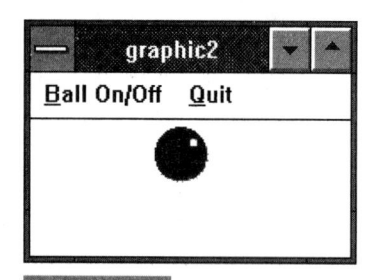

Figure 4-11 GRAPHIC2
Bouncing Ball Program

ellipse outline. A solid red brush is selected prior to calling Ellipse(), so the ball ends up painted red on the interior. A thick white brush is selected into the device context to draw the ellipse outline. The thick white border erases the "old" part of the ball's image as the ball is moved in the window's client area.

A small rectangle is also drawn on the upper right portion of the ball to simulate a point of reflected light from a three dimensional ball. This could be further enhanced by using the Arc() function to shade the bottom left of the ball with a darker shade of red.

The interesting part of programming an animated graphic under Windows is the problem of how to make the program repeatedly draw the ball at new locations without taking over the Windows environment. In a DOS application, we would probably program this as shown in Listing 4-34.

Listing 4-34 Program Loop in a DOS Application

```
while (TRUE)
{
        /* quit the loop if a key is pressed */
        /* erase the old ball image */
        /* draw the ball at the new location */
}
```

You can write a loop like this in a Windows program. The result will be that no other program will be able to run while the loop is executing. Windows programs must keep giving control back to the Windows environment to allow other programs to operate.

The PeekMessage() Loop

The key to animation and other repeating actions under Windows is the PeekMessage() function. PeekMessage() is similar to GetMessage() that we have been using in the program message loops, but with an important difference. PeekMessage() will return control to the program if there are no active messages in the system. GetMessage() only returns control if there is a message for the program that called it. By using PeekMessage(), we can let our program take advantage of the "dead time" when no other program is doing work.

PeekMessage() requires a different construction of the program's message loop. The difference is because we will want to take an action if PeekMessage() does *not* find a pending message. Unlike GetMessage(), PeekMessage() does not return zero if a WM_QUIT message is processed, so the logic must specifically check for the WM_QUIT message to exit the program. Listing 4-35 shows the message loop for the GRAPHIC2.C program that displays the bouncing ball.

Listing 4-35 PeekMessage() in a Windows Message Loop

```
while (TRUE)              /* peek message loop */
{
    if (PeekMessage (&msg, NULL, 0, 0, PM_REMOVE))
    }
        if (msg.message == WM_QUIT)   /* if WM_QUIT, quit! */
            return msg.wParam ;
        else                          /* else, process message */
        {
            TranslateMessage (&msg) ;
            DispatchMessage (&msg) ;
        }
    }   /* no message waiting, so paint the ball if drawing enabled */
    else if (_bDrawOn)
        DrawBall (hWnd, _nXSize, _nYSize) ;
}
```

Like GetMessage(), PeekMessage() fills in a MSG message data structure. We can check the *message* member of the structure to see if the message is WM_QUIT. If it is, the application should terminate. Otherwise, the message is passed on to the TranslateMessage() and DispatchMessage() functions, just like in a GetMessage() message loop.

If there are no messages waiting for any application, PeekMessage() will return a zero. In this case, we know that the system is idle, so we can go ahead and draw the ball at a new location. As we will see in a moment, the DrawBall() function is part of GRAPHIC2.C and does the work of redrawing the ball as it moves across the window's client area. The module definition file GRAPHIC2.DEF is shown in Listing 4-36.

Listing 4-36 GRAPHIC2.DEF

```
NAME        graphic2
EXETYPE     WINDOWS
STUB        'WINSTUB.EXE'
CODE        PRELOAD MOVEABLE
DATA        PRELOAD MOVEABLE MULTIPLE
HEAPSIZE    1024
STACKSIZE   5120
EXPORTS     WndProc
```

The header file GRAPHIC2.H in Listing 4-37 includes the declaration of the function DrawBall(). This will keep the compiler happy when it runs into a call to DrawBall() before it finds DrawBall() in the source code. Without the declaration, the compiler would not know how many parameters DrawBall() uses, the parameter data types, or the returned data type for the function. Also note the definition of three constants, VELOCITY, BALLRAD, and MINRAD, in the header file. They are used throughout the C program and make it easier to change a value uniformly throughout the code in a future edit of the program.

Listing 4-37 GRAPHIC2.H

```
/* graphic2.h  header file */

#define    IDM_SHOW    1    /* menu item ID numbers */
#define    IDM_QUIT   10

#define    VELOCITY    5    /* pixels per move velocity */
#define    BALLRAD    20    /* radius of the ball */
#define    MINRAD     15    /* how close to the wall it can come */

long FAR PASCAL WndProc (HWND, WORD, WORD, LONG) ;
void DrawBall (HWND hWnd, int nXsize, int nYSize) ;
```

The resource script file GRAPHIC2.RC in Listing 4-38 is pretty standard. The first menu item is given the text string "Ball On/Off," and will act as a toggle switch. "Toggle" means that clicking the menu item once will turn the animation on, while clicking it a second time will turn the animation off.

Listing 4-38 GRAPHIC2.RC

```
/* graphic2.rc  resource file */

#include "graphic2.h"

MyIcon     ICON    graphic2.ico

MyMenu     MENU
BEGIN
    MENUITEM "&Ball On/Off"  IDM_SHOW
    MENUITEM "&Quit",        IDM_QUIT
END
```

GRAPHIC2's icon can be created with the Resource Workshop or Image Editor applications. The GRAPHIC2.ICO image is shown in Figure 4-12. You will also need to create a project file for your compiler, as shown in Listings 4-39 and 4-40.

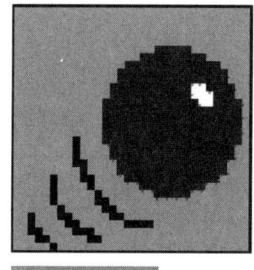

Figure 4-12
GRAPHIC2.ICO Icon Image

Listing 4-39 GRAPHIC2.PRJ Turbo C++ Project File Contents

```
graphic2.c
graphic2.def
graphic2.res
```

Listing 4-40 GRAPHIC2.MAK QuickC Project File Contents

```
graphic2.c
graphic2.def
graphic2.rc
```

The program file GRAPHIC2.C is shown in Listing 4-41. Note that three global variables are declared. In the C language, global variables are created by declaring the variable names outside of the body of any function. Global variables can be accessed by any function in the program file. Global variables differ from local variables that are declared within the body of a function. Local variables are only defined within the function that defines them, and they cannot be referenced by code in another function. In the listings in this book, the global variable names are preceded by an underscore character, so that it is clear later in the program listing which variables are global in scope.

The WndProc() function of GRAPHIC2.C processes several Windows messages. WM_CREATE is sent by Windows when the program starts, but before the program's window is displayed. GRAPHIC2.C just uses WM_CREATE as a convenient place to initialize the global variable _bDrawOn. This is a BOOL (integer) variable that takes only one of two values, TRUE or FALSE. BOOL, TRUE, and FALSE are all defined in WINDOWS.H. The purpose of _bDrawOn is to keep track of whether the ball should be drawn.

WndProc() also processes WM_SIZE. This message is sent by Windows any time the application's window is resized. This occurs before the window is created the first time, when the window is minimized, maximized, or restored, and when the window's thick border is used to change the size of the window. WM_SIZE encodes the vertical and horizontal size of the window's client area in the lParam value passed with the message. lParam is a LONG value, containing four bytes of information. Only two bytes are needed to encode an integer, so the lower (least significant) two bytes are used to encode the horizontal size in pixels, while the higher (most significant) two bytes are used to encode the vertical size in pixels.

WINDOWS.H includes two handy macro definitions for obtaining the two halves of a LONG value. HIWORD() returns the most significant two bytes, while LOWORD() returns the least significant two bytes. GRAPHIC2.C uses these macros to obtain the window's client area size every time a WM_SIZE message is processed. The values are stored in two global variables, _nXSize and _nYSize. Global variables are used so that the values can be used in both the WinMain() function and WndProc() function.

Listing 4-41 GRAPHIC2.C

```
/* graphic2.c   Demonstrates animated drawing */

#include <windows.h>
#include "graphic2.h"

BOOL    _bDrawOn = FALSE ;      /* global to track if drawing is on or off */
int     _nXSize, _nYSize ;      /* window width and height */

int PASCAL WinMain (HANDLE hInstance, HANDLE hPrevInstance, LPSTR lpszCmdLine,
    int nCmdShow)
{
    HWND        hWnd ;              /* the window's "handle" */
    MSG         msg ;               /* a message structure */
    WNDCLASS    wndclass ;          /* window class structure */
```

```c
    if (!hPrevInstance)
    {
        wndclass.style         = CS_HREDRAW | CS_VREDRAW ;
        wndclass.lpfnWndProc   = WndProc ;
        wndclass.cbClsExtra    = 0 ;
        wndclass.cbWndExtra    = 0 ;
        wndclass.hInstance     = hInstance ;
        wndclass.hIcon         = LoadIcon (hInstance, "MyIcon") ;
        wndclass.hCursor       = LoadCursor (NULL, IDC_ARROW) ;
        wndclass.hbrBackground = GetStockObject (WHITE_BRUSH) ;
        wndclass.lpszMenuName  = "MyMenu" ;
        wndclass.lpszClassName = "MyClass" ;
                    /* register the window class */
        if (!RegisterClass (&wndclass))
            return 0 ;
    }

    hWnd = CreateWindow ("MyClass","graphic2", WS_OVERLAPPEDWINDOW,
        CW_USEDEFAULT, CW_USEDEFAULT, CW_USEDEFAULT, CW_USEDEFAULT,
        NULL, NULL, hInstance, NULL) ;
    ShowWindow (hWnd, nCmdShow) ;      /* display the window */

    while (TRUE)                        /* peek message loop */
    {
        if (PeekMessage (&msg, NULL, 0, 0, PM_REMOVE))
        {
        if (msg.message == WM_QUIT) /* if WM_QUIT, quit! */
            return msg.wParam ;
        else                        /* else, process message */
        {
            TranslateMessage (&msg) ;
            DispatchMessage (&msg) ;
        }
        } /* no message waiting, so paint the ball if drawing enabled */
        else if (_bDrawOn)
            DrawBall (hWnd, _nXSize, _nYSize) ;
    }
}

long FAR PASCAL WndProc (HWND hWnd, WORD wMessage, WORD wParam, LONG lParam)
{
    switch (wMessage)      /* process windows messages */
    {
        case WM_CREATE:    /* application starting, turn draw on */
            _bDrawOn = FALSE ;
            break ;
        case WM_SIZE :     /* save the window client area size */
            _nXSize = LOWORD (lParam) ;
            _nYSize = HIWORD (lParam) ;
            break ;
        case WM_COMMAND:   /* menu items */
            switch (wParam)
            {
                case IDM_SHOW:
                    if (_bDrawOn)
                        _bDrawOn = FALSE ; /* toggle drawing on/off */
                    else
                        _bDrawOn = TRUE ;
                    break ;
```

```
                    case IDM_QUIT:
                        DestroyWindow (hWnd) ;   /* destroy window, */
                        break ;    /* terminating application */
            }
            break ;
        case WM_DESTROY:    /* stop application */
            PostQuitMessage (0) ;
            break ;
        default:            /* default windows message processing */
            return DefWindowProc (hWnd, wMessage, wParam, lParam) ;
    }
    return (0L) ;
}

/* DrawBall() draws a red ball on the window hWnd every time the function is called */
/* The ball is BALLRAD in radius. The walls (client area size) are from 0,0 to */
/* nXSize,nYsize. The location is moved each time by VELOCITY units. The signs of */
/* the X and Y velocity terms nVelX,nVelY are reversed each time the ball gets */
/* within MINRAD units of a wall. This causes the ball to appear to bounce off the */
/* wall. Drawing the ball at the new location causes the old ball to be erased, as */
/* the ball is drawn using a white pen for the outline that is 1.5 * VELOCITY in */
/* width. The white pen ends up painting over any portion of the ball that is */
/* otherwise visible from the previous location. */

void DrawBall (HWND hWnd, int nXSize, int nYSize)
{
    HDC     hDC ;
    HPEN    hPen, hOldPen ;
    HBRUSH  hBrush, hOldBrush ;
    static  int    nX = 2 * BALLRAD, nY = 2 * BALLRAD, /* starting X,Y */
            nVelX = VELOCITY, nVelY = VELOCITY;     /* X,Y velocity */

    nX = nX + nVelX ;          /* compute new center X,Y of ball */
    nY = nY + nVelY ;
                               /* check if user moved walls and hid the ball */
    if (nY > nYSize)
      nY = 2 * BALLRAD ;       /* put the ball back at the starting */
    if (nX > nXSize)           /* position if it is not going to be */
      nX = 2 * BALLRAD ;       /* visible with the new window size */
                               /* check if hit wall. if so, change direction */
    if (nY < MINRAD || nYSize - nY < MINRAD)
        nVelY = -1 * nVelY ;
    else if (nX < MINRAD || nXSize - nX < MINRAD)
        nVelX = -1 * nVelX ;
                               /* get the device context handle */
    hDC = GetDC (hWnd) ;
                               /* create a thick white pen and a red brush */
    hPen = CreatePen (PS_SOLID, VELOCITY + VELOCITY / 2, RGB (255, 255, 255)) ;
    hBrush = CreateSolidBrush (RGB (255, 0, 0)) ;
    hOldPen = SelectObject (hDC, hPen) ;   /* select int the DC */
    hOldBrush = SelectObject (hDC, hBrush) ;
                               /* draw the ball in the new location */
                               /* the outline pen deletes behind the ball */
    Ellipse (hDC, nX - BALLRAD, nY - BALLRAD, nX + BALLRAD, nY + BALLRAD) ;
                               /* delete old pen and create a new thin one */
    SelectObject (hDC, hOldPen) ;
    DeleteObject (hPen) ;
    hPen = CreatePen (PS_SOLID, 3, RGB (255, 255, 255)) ;
    hOldPen = SelectObject (hDC, hPen) ;
```

```
                        /* draw a highlight mark on the ball */
    Rectangle (hDC, nX + BALLRAD/3, nY - BALLRAD/3, nX + 2 + BALLRAD/3,
        nY - 2 - BALLRAD/3) ;
                        /* delete all objects and free DC */
    SelectObject (hDC, hOldPen) ;
    DeleteObject (hPen) ;
    SelectObject (hDC, hOldBrush) ;
    DeleteObject (hBrush) ;
    ReleaseDC (hWnd, hDC) ;
}
```

The DrawBall() function in GRAPHIC2.C shows the creation and deletion of two pens and a brush. Initially, a red brush and a thick white pen are created and selected into the device context. When Ellipse() is used to draw the ball, the white pen is used by the function to outline the ball. The white outline is not visible against the white background of the window's client area, but has the desirable effect of erasing the portion of the "old" ball that would be visible after the "new" ball is drawn at the next location.

To make the ball look a bit more three dimensional, a small white highlight is drawn at the upper right of the ball's surface. This requires deleting the thick pen used to draw the ball's outline and creating a thin pen that is three pixels wide. This new pen is selected into the device context before Rectangle() is called to draw a small rectangle for the highlight. Finally, the pen and brush are deleted, and the device context is released.

Note that the old pen and brush are selected into the device context before the new pen and brush are deleted. This ensures that the new pen and brush are no longer selected into the device context when they are deleted. Deleting objects that are selected into a device context will cause the application to crash randomly.

The actual movement of the ball is computed by adding the velocity values to the previous X,Y location of the ball. When the ball gets within MINRAD pixels of a wall (client area border), the velocity value in the direction of the collision is reversed. For example, if the ball hits the bottom wall, the Y velocity value is reversed in sign.

When you get GRAPHIC2 running, you can experiment with moving and resizing the window. If you change the window's size, the ball will bounce off the walls in their new locations. An interesting case is where part of GRAPHIC2 is obscured by another program's window. In this case, the ball will continue to "bounce" underneath the hidden parts of the window, showing up again when it gets out from underneath. Figure 4-13 shows this effect, with the Program Manager window particularly covering GRAPHIC2. The ball is bouncing out from

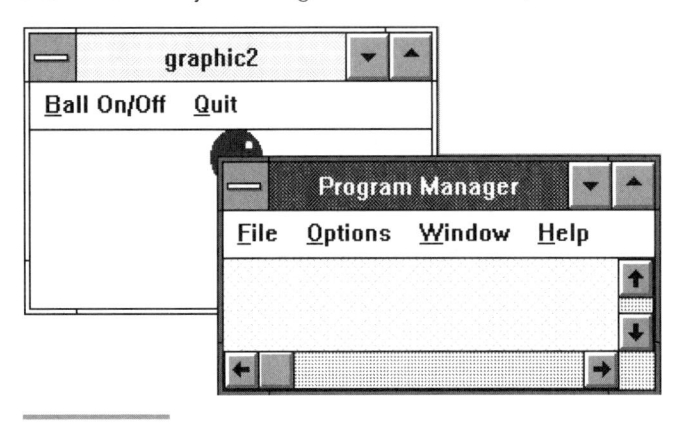

Figure 4-13 GRAPHIC2 Partially Covered by Program Manager

under the corner of Program Manager's window. The calculation of which parts of the GRAPHIC2 window are covered up is all done by Windows. All GRAPHIC2 has to do is to send the output to the device context. Windows takes care of figuring out which portions of the window are visible and which are not.

Summary

Windows does all output to the video display in graphics mode. This means that everything, including text characters, is drawn one pixel at a time. Although slower than character mode output, graphics mode output is completely flexible. Windows can draw characters of any size or shape at any location on the screen. The designers of Windows 3.0 and 3.1 took advantage of the graphics capability to create attractive buttons, window elements, and color combinations.

Windows uses the concept of a device context to insulate Windows applications from the computer's hardware. The application program sends graphics commands to the device context. Windows takes care of translating the device context data into the specific commands used by the hardware. As a software developer, you will not be concerned about the exact type of computer, video, or printer technology that the user may use. Properly written Windows programs will function on any hardware system that Windows supports.

Before a device context can be used, its handle (ID value) must be obtained. GetDC() is used to obtain the handle of a window's client area device context. The only exception is when processing a WM_PAINT message from Windows. In this case, BeginPaint() is used. The device context must be released after use by calling ReleaseDC() or EndPaint().

At any one time, a device context holds a set of values that control the graphics operations. This includes the size and color of the pen used to draw lines and the outlines of shapes, and the brush color and pattern used to fill the interior of shapes. Pens and brushes are selected into the device context before being used and must be displaced out of the device context (by selecting another pen or brush) before being deleted.

In the GRAPHIC2.C example, the message loop was modified to use the PeekMessage() function. This allowed animation of the graphics while still allowing other Windows applications to run. PeekMessage(), along with the GetMessage() and WaitMessage() functions introduced in the previous chapter, are the only functions in Windows that allow control to be passed to another application. One of these three functions will find its way into every properly written Windows application. They are the secret to Windows' ability to run more than one application at the same time, and they allow the user to quickly switch between them.

QUESTIONS

1. When using the Rectangle() function, the center of the rectangle is filled with the currently selected _____, and the border is drawn with the currently selected _____ of the device context.

2. To use a custom pen or a brush, you must first _____ the object and then select it into the _____ _____.

3. The currently selected pen or brush cannot be safely deleted until it is selected out of the device context. (True or false?).

4. How do you remove a pen or a brush from the device context?

5. To change the color of the characters output by TextOut(), use the _____ function. To change the background color of the characters, use the _____ function.

6. The _____ message is sent by Windows when the program is first started. The _____ message is sent when the size of the program window changes.

7. The only time the BeginPaint() message is used to retrieve a device context handle is when processing a _____ message. The _____ function must be called after BeginPaint() to free the device context.

8. Stock pens and brushes can be safely deleted. (True or false?)

EXERCISES

At this point you should spend some time experimenting with the graphics drawing functions summarized in Table 4-3. Be sure to try out a number of pens and brushes in your creations.

1. Modify TEXT1.C to create a graphics image using the Rectangle(), MoveTo(), and LineTo() functions. Fill the rectangle with a green brush, and draw the lines and the rectangle's border with a blue pen.

2. Convert the client area of GRAPHIC2 to a gray color. Modify the DrawBall() function appropriately so that the gray color is not disturbed by the ball's movement. (Hint: The window's client area color is set in the class definition.)

3. Insert the line

   ```
   hWnd = GetDesktopWindow () ;
   ```

   right before the line

   ```
   hDC = GetDC (hWnd) ;
   ```

   in GRAPHIC2.C. What happens? Can you improve on this basic idea to do something useful? (Hint: You may find the GetSystemMetrics() function useful.)

ANSWERS TO QUESTIONS

1. brush, pen.
2. create, device context.
3. True.
4. Selecting another pen or brush into the device context displaces the old object. This makes it safe to delete the displaced object.
5. SetTextColor(), SetBkColor().
6. WM_CREATE, WM_SIZE.
7. WM_PAINT, EndPaint()
8. False. They are maintained by Windows.

SOLUTIONS TO EXERCISES

1. The only changes will be to the WndProc() function. The portions that are modified to display the line and rectangle are shown in Listing 4-42. CreatePen() is used to create a blue pen, while CreateSolidBrush() creates a green brush. These functions are selected into the device context before graphics output begins. MoveTo(), LineTo(), and Rectangle() do the actual output. Note that the old brush and pen are selected back into the device context before they are deleted. This avoids the error of deleting an object (the new pen or brush) while it is still selected into the device context.

Listing 4-42 Changes to TEXT1.C WndProc() Function for Exercise 1

```
long FAR PASCAL WndProc (HWND hWnd, WORD wMessage, WORD wParam, LONG lParam)
{
    HDC     hDC ;                       /* the device context handle */
    HPEN    hPen, hOldPen ;             /* handles for pens */
    HBRUSH  hBrush, hOldBrush ;         /* handles for brushes */

    switch (wMessage)                   /* process windows messages */
    {
        case WM_COMMAND:
            switch (wParam)
            {
                case IDM_SHOW:                  /* menu items */
                    hDC = GetDC (hWnd) ;        /* get DC, create pen/brush */
                    hPen = CreatePen (PS_SOLID, 2, RGB (0, 0, 255)) ;
                    hBrush = CreateSolidBrush (RGB (0, 255, 0)) ;
                                                /* select pen/brush into DC */
                    hOldPen = SelectObject (hDC, hPen) ;
                    hOldBrush = SelectObject (hDC, hBrush) ;
                                                /* draw a line */
```

continued

SOLUTIONS TO EXERCISES (cont'd)

```
            MoveTo (hDC, 10, 10) ;
            LineTo (hDC, 100, 30) ;
                                    /* draw a rectangle */
            Rectangle (hDC, 50, 50, 150, 120) ;
                                    /* displace old objects */
            SelectObject (hDC, hOldPen) ;
            SelectObject (hDC, hOldBrush) ;
                                    /* delete pen and brush */
            DeleteObject (hPen) ;
            DeleteObject (hBrush) ;
            ReleaseDC (hWnd, hDC) ;  /* release DC */
            break ;
```
[Other program lines]

The complete solution is under the file name C4EXER1 on the optional source code disks.

2. The background color of a window is set in the window's class definition. The WinMain() function must be changed to specify a gray brush for the *hbrBackground* member of the WNDCLASS structure. The changes to WinMain() are shown in Listing 4-43. Note that any RGB setting (such as within CreateSolidBrush() in the listing) with all three color elements set to equal values will create a gray brush. The higher the values, the lighter the gray color. Note also that the brush is deleted within the PeekMessage() loop when the program exits.

Listing 4-43 Changes to WinMain() of GRAPHIC2.C for Gray Background

```
int PASCAL WinMain (HANDLE hInstance, HANDLE hPrevInstance, LPSTR lpszCmdLine,
   int nCmdShow)
{
    HWND        hWnd ;           /* the window's "handle" */
    MSG         msg ;            /* a message structure */
    WNDCLASS    wndclass ;       /* window class structure */
    HBRUSH      hBrush ;         /* handle of background brush */

    if (!hPrevInstance)
    {                            /* create a gray brush */
       hBrush = CreateSolidBrush (RGB (200, 200, 200)) ;

       wndclass.style         = CS_HREDRAW | CS_VREDRAW ;
       wndclass.lpfnWndProc   = WndProc ;
       wndclass.cbClsExtra    = 0 ;
       wndclass.cbWndExtra    = 0 ;
       wndclass.hInstance     = hInstance ;
       wndclass.hIcon         = LoadIcon (hInstance, "MyIcon") ;
       wndclass.hCursor       = LoadCursor (NULL, IDC_ARROW) ;
       wndclass.hbrBackground = hBrush ;  /* use gray brush */
       wndclass.lpszMenuName  = "MyMenu" ;
       wndclass.lpszClassName = "MyClass" ;
              /* register the window class */
       if  (!RegisterClass (&wndclass))
```

118   *Windows Programming Primer Plus®*

SOLUTIONS TO EXERCISES (cont'd)

```
            return 0 ;
    }
    hWnd = CreateWindow ("MyClass", "c4exer2", WS_OVERLAPPEDWINDOW,
        CW_USEDEFAULT, CW_USEDEFAULT, CW_USEDEFAULT, CW_USEDEFAULT,
        NULL, NULL, hInstance, NULL) ;
    ShowWindow (hWnd, nCmdShow) ;       /* display the window */

    while (TRUE)                         /* peek message loop */
    {
        if (PeekMessage (&msg, NULL, 0, 0, PM_REMOVE))
        {
            if (msg.message == WM_QUIT)  /* if WM_QUIT, quit! */
            {
                DeleteObject (hBrush) ;  /* delete the grey brush */
                return msg.wParam ;      /* on exit */
            }
            else                         /* else, process message */
            {
                TranslateMessage (&msg) ;
                DispatchMessage (&msg) ;
            }
        }   /* no message waiting, so paint the ball if drawing enabled */
        else if (_bDrawOn)
            DrawBall (hWnd, _nXSize, _nYSize) ;
    }
}
```

The same gray must be specified for the line color used to draw the outside border of the ball. In GRAPHIC2.C, the line was white so that the border would erase the "old" part of the moving ball's image when the ball is drawn in the new location. Change this to the same color used to draw the background by modifying the CreatePen() RGB color settings in the DrawBall function as follows:

`hPen = CreatePen (PS_SOLID, VELOCITY + VELOCITY / 2, RGB (200, 200, 200)) ;`

One interesting consequence of this exercise is that the gray color of the window background will not be a pure color. The gray window area will have some white pixels evenly distributed in the window. This is because Windows approximates the color specified by RGB() by dithering available pure colors. The colors available with the default 16 VGA colors used include two shades of gray. Both of the available pure gray colors are darker than the RGB value specified in this example. Windows, therefore, mixes in a few white colored pixels with the lightest available pure gray color to get the specified average color for the window background.

The complete solution is under the file name C4EXER2 on the source code disks.

3. The GetDesktopWindow() function retrieves the window handle of the "desktop" background on which all windows applications appear. Internally, Windows deals with the desktop background as a window, without a caption or borders. If

SOLUTIONS TO EXERCISES (cont'd)

you modify the DrawBall() function to output on the desktop window rather than the program window, the ball will bounce around on the background of the screen.

You can have fun with this exercise by further improving the program. Instead of limiting the ball to the bounds of the program's window, limit it to the size of the total screen. The GetSystemMetrics() function will retrieve the *X* and *Y* size of the screen (use the SM_CXSCREEN and SM_CYSCREEN index values). The C3EXER03.C program on the optional source code disks has these improvements included. Listing 4-44 shows just the DrawBall() function from C3EXER3.C with the changes highlighted.

Listing 4-44 Modifications to the DrawBall() Function

```
/* This ia a modified version of the DrawBall() function from GRAPHIC2 */
/* The ball is drawn on the Windows desktop. The size of the desktop */
/* is determined using the GetSystemMetrics() function. */
/* GetDesktopWindow() retrieves the window handle of the desktop window. */

void DrawBall (void)
{
   HWND       hWnd ;
   int        nXSize, nYSize ;
   HDC        hDC ;
   HPEN       hPen, hOldPen ;
   HBRUSH     hBrush, hOldBrush ;
   static int nX = 2 * BALLRAD, nY = 2 * BALLRAD,   /* starting X,Y */
              nVelX = VELOCITY, nVelY = VELOCITY;    /* X,Y velocity */

   nXSize = GetSystemMetrics (SM_CXSCREEN) ;         /* desktop window size */
   nYSize = GetSystemMetrics (SM_CYSCREEN) ;

   nX = nX + nVelX ;      /* compute new center X,Y of ball */
   nY = nY + nVelY ;
              /* check if user moved walls and hid the ball */
   if (nY > nYSize)
      nY = 2 * BALLRAD ;  /* put the ball back at the starting */
   if (nX > nXSize)       /* position if it is not going to be */
      nX = 2 * BALLRAD ;  /* visible with the new window size */
              /* check if hit wall. if so, change direction */
   if (nY < MINRAD || nYSize - nY < MINRAD)
      nVelY = -1 * nVelY ;
   else if (nX < MINRAD || nXSize - nX < MINRAD)
      nVelX = -1 * nVelX ;
              /* get the desktop window device context handle */
   hWnd = GetDesktopWindow () ;
   hDC = GetDC (hWnd) ;
              /* create a thick black pen and a red brush */
```

SOLUTIONS TO EXERCISES (cont'd)

```
   hPen = CreatePen (PS_SOLID, VELOCITY + VELOCITY / 2,
      RGB (200, 200, 200)) ;
   hBrush = CreateSolidBrush (RGB (255, 0, 0)) ;

   hOldPen = SelectObject (hDC, hPen) ;              /* select into the DC */
   hOldBrush = SelectObject (hDC, hBrush) ;
            /* draw the ball in the new location */
            /* the outline pen deletes behind the ball */
   Ellipse (hDC, nX - BALLRAD, nY - BALLRAD, nX + BALLRAD, nY + BALLRAD) ;
            /* delete old pen and create a new thin one */
   SelectObject (hDC, hOldPen) ;
   DeleteObject (hPen) ;
   hPen = CreatePen (PS_SOLID, 3, RGB (255, 255, 255)) ;
   hOldPen = SelectObject (hDC, hPen) ;
            /* draw a highlight mark on the ball */
   Rectangle (hDC, nX + BALLRAD/3, nY - BALLRAD/3, nX + 2 + BALLRAD/3,
      nY - 2 - BALLRAD/3) ;
            /* delete all objects and free DC */
   SelectObject (hDC, hOldPen) ;
   DeleteObject (hPen) ;
   SelectObject (hDC, hOldBrush) ;
   DeleteObject (hBrush) ;
   ReleaseDC    (hWnd, hDC) ;
}
```

The complete solution is under the file name C4EXER3 on the optional source code disks.

CHAPTER 5

Window Controls

This chapter describes how to create buttons, scroll bars, and other control windows. Learning to use these elements of the Windows environment is a key to becoming a proficient programmer. Once mastered, window controls will allow you to simplify complex programming tasks by letting Windows do most of the work in painting and updating screen elements, and determining what the user is doing. We will examine each type of control separately.

Concepts Covered

Window Controls
Button Styles
Child and Parent Windows
Sending Messages to Controls
Control ID Values
Notification Codes

Static Text and Icons
Combo Boxes
List Boxes
Scroll Bars
Edit Controls
C Language Casts

Keywords Covered

BUTTON
COMBOBOX
EDIT

LISTBOX
SCROLLBAR
STATIC

all window styles (WS_CHILD...) and all control styles (BS_PUSHBUTTON...).

Functions Covered

CreateWindow()
SetWindowText()
SendMessage()
MessageBox()
wsprintf()
InvalidateRect()

GetWindowWord()
SetScrollPos()
SetScrollRange
ShowScrollBar()
GetScrollPos()
GetScrollRange()

Messages Covered

WM_SETTEXT
BM_SETCHECK
BM_GETCHECK
LB_RESETCONTENT
LB_ADDSTRING
LB_GETCURSEL

LB_GETTEXT
EM_GETLINECOUNT
EM_LINEINDEX
EM_LINELENGTH
EM_GETLINE

What Is a Window?

The word "window" brings to mind the main window of a program. It turns out that the Windows environment uses the same low-level logic to create buttons, scroll bars, list boxes, combo boxes, edit controls, and the screen background. These objects have the following properties in common:

1. The object is rectangular.

2. The area occupied by the object must be repainted when covered and uncovered by another object to maintain the illusion of permanence.
3. The object is a separate entity that can send and receive messages.

The Windows environment generalizes these characteristics into a common group of objects called "windows." The Windows environment manages windows for the program. Once created, the program communicates with the individual window elements by sending and receiving messages.

Using the windowing logic is much more powerful than simply drawing the window using graphics commands. Once created, program windows and specialized windows, such as buttons, are maintained by the Windows environment. This means that the Windows environment will repaint the object when needed, detect when it is selected with the mouse, and provide many ways for the programmer to change the appearance and functioning of the window object during execution of the program.

Windows uses the term "control" to describe predefined classes of windows for common objects such as buttons. In Chapter 3, *First Programming Experiments*, we initially used the predefined BUTTON window class for the MINIMAL1 program's main window. During the chapter, we improved the program by defining our own window class with the RegisterClass() function, and then using the new class for the program's main window. Normally, you will create your own window class for a program's main window. However, there is seldom a need to modify the behavior of the predefined window classes for common objects such as buttons and list boxes. In most cases, these objects can be used "as is," saving you a lot of programming time.

Types of Window Controls

Windows defines six different types of window controls. They are predefined window classes, so you will not have to call the RegisterClass() function to create a window class before creating a control. Table 5-1 summarizes the different classes of windows. Keep in mind that the appearance of each type of control can be modified by using different style parameters when calling CreateWindow(). We will explore these options for each class of control during this chapter.

OBJECT	EXAMPLE IMAGE	DESCRIPTION
Static Text	Static Text	Created from the STATIC window class when calling CreateWindow(). Static controls are usually used for titles and other text that the user does not directly manipulate. Static controls can also be used to paint rectangular areas to improve the appearance of a screen.
Button	Button 1	Created from the BUTTON window class when calling CreateWindow(). Button controls can have many shapes, including check boxes, radio buttons, and group boxes.

continued

Table 5-1 (cont'd)

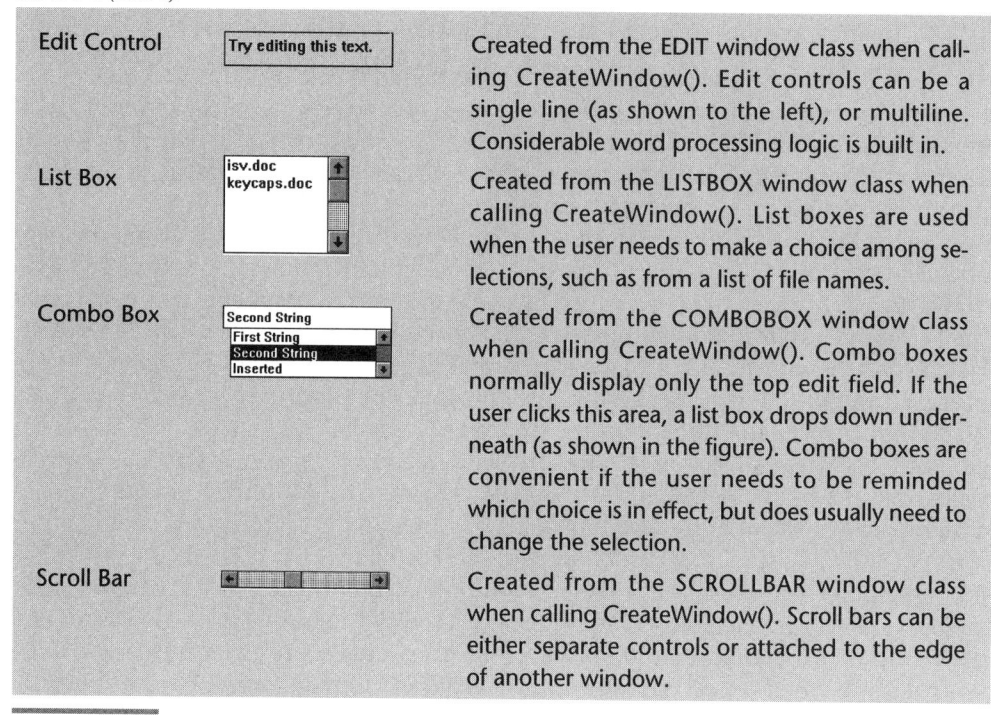

Control		Description
Edit Control	Try editing this text.	Created from the EDIT window class when calling CreateWindow(). Edit controls can be a single line (as shown to the left), or multiline. Considerable word processing logic is built in.
List Box	isv.doc keycaps.doc	Created from the LISTBOX window class when calling CreateWindow(). List boxes are used when the user needs to make a choice among selections, such as from a list of file names.
Combo Box	Second String First String Second String Inserted	Created from the COMBOBOX window class when calling CreateWindow(). Combo boxes normally display only the top edit field. If the user clicks this area, a list box drops down underneath (as shown in the figure). Combo boxes are convenient if the user needs to be reminded which choice is in effect, but does usually need to change the selection.
Scroll Bar		Created from the SCROLLBAR window class when calling CreateWindow(). Scroll bars can be either separate controls or attached to the edge of another window.

Table 5-1 Static Control Types

There is an additional predefined window class, MDICLIENT. This is a programming convenience provided for complex applications, such as the Excel and the Windows File Manager, that use multiple child windows within the bounds of a single parent window. MDI stands for "Multiple Document Interface." MDI programs are not covered in this book. If you are interested, see Chapter 29 of *The Waite Group's Windows API Bible*.

The CreateWindow() Function

All windows, including window controls, are created with the CreateWindow() function. It is one of the more complicated functions in the Windows programming environment because it can create such a wide range of objects. Listing 5-1 shows the syntax for CreateWindow().

Listing 5-1 CreateWindow() Syntax

```
HWND CreateWindow (LPSTR lpClassName, LPSTR lpWindowName, DWORD dwStyle,
    int X, int Y, int nWidth, int nHeight,
    HWND hWndParent, HMENU hMenu, HANDLE hInstance, LPSTR lpParam) ;
```

Table 5-2 describes the meaning of each of the parameters used by the CreateWindow() function. The *dwStyle* parameter has so many options that these values are shown separately in tables for each type of control throughout the chapter.

PARAMETER	MEANING
lpClassName (LPSTR)	The name of the window class that the window will be based on. This is either a new class created with RegisterClass(), or one of the predefined classes: BUTTON, COMBOBOX, EDIT, LISTBOX, MDICLIENT, SCROLLBAR, STATIC.
lpWindowName (LPSTR)	The window's name. This is a pointer to a character string. For windows with a caption bar, this will be the caption. For the BUTTON, EDIT, and STATIC classes, it is the text in the center of the control. For COMBOBOX, LISTBOX, MDICLIENT, and SCROLLBAR classes, the name is ignored (just put in "").
dwStyle (DWORD)	The window's style. This is a series of bit values that tell the Windows environment the properties needed for the window being created. The bit values are defined in WINDOWS.H and can be combined with the C language binary OR operator (|). An example is: WS_VISIBLE	WS_VSCROLL	WS_THICKFRAME
X (int)	Specifies the X position of the upper left corner of the window. For parent windows, this will be the location relative to the upper left corner of the screen (screen coordinates). For child windows and window controls, the location will be relative to the upper left corner of the parent window's client area (client coordinates). Distance is measured in pixels. You can use the CW_USEDEFAULT value for X to let Windows decide where to put the window.
Y (int)	Specifies the Y position of the upper left corner of the window. For parent windows, this will be the location relative to the upper left corner of the screen (screen coordinates). For child windows and window controls, the location will be relative to the upper left corner of the parent window's client area (client coordinates). Distance is measured in pixels. You can use the CW_USEDEFAULT value for Y to let Windows decide where to put the window.
nWidth (int)	Specifies the width of the window in pixels. You can use the CW_USEDEFAULT value for *nWidth* to let Windows decide the window's width.
nHeight (int)	Specifies the height of the window in pixels. You can use the CW_USEDEFAULT value for *nHeight* to let Windows decide the window's height.

continued

Table 5-2 (cont'd)

hWndParent (HWND)	The window handle of the parent window. For top-level windows (the program's main window) set this value to NULL, as there is no parent window. For child windows and child window controls, specify the handle of the parent window.
hMenu (HMENU)	For windows that have menus, this is the handle of the menu to use. Set to NULL to use the menu defined in the class definition. For controls, *hMenu* is used to hold the integer ID value for the control. This is important, as the ID value will be passed with the WM_COMMAND message when the user activates the control. This ID value will be how your program identifies which control was activated.
hInstance (HANDLE)	The instance handle of the program creating the window. You can use the GetWindowWord() function to retrieve this value.
lpParam (LPSTR)	Normally set to NULL. It will be set to NULL in every example in this book. (This parameter is used in advanced applications to pass data with the WM_CREATE message that Windows sends every time a window is created. The *lpParam* value ends up as the *lpCreateParams* member of a CREATESTRUCT data structure. The CREATESTRUCT data is pointed to by the *lParam* value passed with the WM_CREATE message when the window is created. This is most commonly used in MDI applications, where *lpParam* is used to point to data in a specialized CLIENTCREATESTRUCT data structure. See Chapter 29 of *The Waite Group's Windows API Bible* for additional information.)

Table 5-2 CreateWindow() Parameters

Table 5-3 summarizes the values for the *dwStyle* parameter passed to CreateWindow(), just for child, popup, and main program windows. The styles for controls (buttons, list boxes, etc.) are shown later in this chapter, summarized for each type of control. All of these styles are binary flags, defined in WINDOWS.H. For example, to create a window with a thin border, caption bar, minimize and maximize buttons, and a vertical scroll bar, you would combine styles as follows:

```
WS_BORDER | WS_CAPTION | WS_MINIMIZEBOX | WS_VSCROLL
```

Don't be intimidated by the number of window styles given in this chapter. Even the most experienced Windows programmers have to look up flag names occasionally. The tables are included for reference so that you can follow the examples in this chapter and use the data later for your own projects.

WS_BORDER	Specifies a thin border on a window.
WS_CAPTION	Specifies a caption (title) on a window. This cannot be used with the WS_DLGFRAME style.
WS_CHILD	Creates a child window. This cannot be used with the WS_POPUP style.
WS_CHILDWINDOW	Same as WS_CHILD.
WS_CLIPCHILDREN	Used when creating the parent window. Specifies that child windows will not extend past the boundary of the parent.
WS_CLIPSIBLINGS	Use with WS_CHILD style. Keeps child windows from overlapping in painting operations.
WS_DISABLED	Creates a window that is initially disabled (cannot receive the input focus). This style can be used with controls, such as buttons and edit controls.
WS_DLGFRAME	A window with a double border.
WS_GROUP	This style marks a control that the user can reach by using the direction (arrow) keys. Used in dialog boxes.
WS_HSCROLL	A window with a horizontal scroll bar.
WS_ICONIC	A window that is initially shown minimized (iconic). Use with the WS_OVERLAPPED style.
WS_MAXIMIZE	A window that is initially maximized.
WS_MAXIMIZEBOX	A window with a maximize box in the upper right corner.
WS_MINIMIZE	Same as WS_ICONIC.
WS_MINIMIZEBOX	A window with a minimize box in the upper right corner.
WS_OVERLAPPED	A window with a caption and a border.
WS_OVERLAPPEDWINDOW	Combines the WS_OVERLAPPED, WS_CAPTION, WS_SYSMENU and WS_THICKFRAME styles. This is a standard parent window.
WS_POPUP	A popup window. Cannot be used with the WS_CHILD style. The window can be displayed outside of the parent's boundaries.
WS_POPUPWINDOW	Combines the WS_POPUP, WS_BORDER, and WS_SYSMENU styles. This is a standard popup window.
WS_SYSMENU	A window with a system menu. This is the square at the upper left corner of the window. Clicking the system menu reveals menu items for "Restore," "Move," etc.
WS_TABSTOP	Used in dialog boxes to specify which control is stopped at when the tab key is depressed.

continued

Table 5-3 (cont'd)

WS_THICKFRAME	A window with a thick frame. The frame is used to size the window.
WS_VISIBLE	A window that is initially visible. Used with overlapped and popup windows.
WS_VSCROLL	A window with a vertical scroll bar.

Table 5-3 Window Styles (*dwStyle* values for CreateWindow())

Static Controls

The simplest of the controls is the STATIC class. Static controls are used primarily for displaying text, although they can also display icon images and rectangles. The advantage of using a static control over painting on the window's client area is that the static control is automatically redrawn if it is covered by another window and then uncovered. This avoids having to process WM_PAINT messages to keep the window's client area up-to-date.

When the CreateWindow() function is called to create a window with the STATIC class, the *dwStyle* parameter passed to CreateWindow() can take a number of values, which are summarized in Table 5-4. The most common style is SS_LEFT, which is left-justified text. However, static controls can be used to shade and outline areas, using styles like SS_GRAYRECT and SS_BLACKFRAME. You can also display an icon image created with the Resource Workshop or Image Editor, using the SS_ICON style. The first example program demonstrates several static control styles.

SS_BLACKFRAME	A static control with a black frame outline.
SS_BLACKRECT	A static control with the entire center filled with the color used to draw the window frame. This is black with the default Windows color scheme.
SS_CENTER	A static text control with the text centered.
SS_GRAYFRAME	A static control with the frame color equal to the Windows desktop background. This is gray with the default Windows color scheme.
SS_GRAYRECT	A static control with the entire center filled with the color used to draw the Windows desktop background. This is gray with the default Windows color scheme.
SS_ICON	A static control containing an icon. The *lpWindowName* parameter specifies the name of the icon to use.
SS_LEFT	A static text control with the text left aligned.
SS_LEFTNOWORDWRAP	A static text control. Text is flush left and truncated to the size of the control.

SS_NOPREFIX	A static control where it is desirable to display ampersands (&) in the text of the control. Normally, ampersands are used to cause the next character in the static control's text string to be underlined.
SS_RIGHT	A static text control with the text string right aligned.
SS_SIMPLE	A static text control.
SS_USERITEM	A user-defined static control.
SS_WHITEFRAME	A static text control with a frame matching the windows background color (default is white).
SS_WHITERECT	A static control with the entire center filled with the color used to draw the parent window's background. This is white with the default Windows color scheme.

Table 5-4 Static Control Styles

Figure 5-1 shows the STATIC program, designed to demonstrate different types of static controls. Inside the client area you will see some text, an icon image, and a gray rectangle. Each of these is a static window control. The program also has three menu options. We will get to these in a moment.

The STATIC program requires the usual collection of program files. STATIC.C (Listing 5-2) can be created by copying and modifying the MINIMAL4 program from Chapter 3, *First Programming Experiments*. With the exception of changing the program name in several locations, all of the changes are to the WndProc() function.

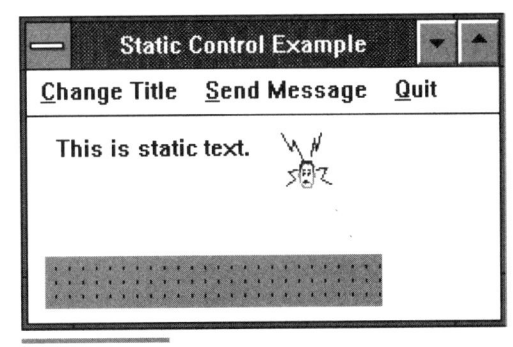

Figure 5-1 The STATIC Program

Listing 5-2 STATIC.C

```
/* static.c   Creating child window controls */

#include <windows.h>
#include "static.h"

int PASCAL WinMain (HANDLE hInstance, HANDLE hPrevInstance, LPSTR lpszCmdLine,
    int nCmdShow)
{
    HWND        hWnd ;         /* the window's "handle" */
    MSG         msg ;          /* a message structure */
    WNDCLASS    wndclass ;     /* window class structure */

    if (!hPrevInstance)
    {
```

```
        wndclass.style         = CS_HREDRAW | CS_VREDRAW ;
        wndclass.lpfnWndProc   = WndProc ;
        wndclass.cbClsExtra    = 0 ;
        wndclass.cbWndExtra    = 0 ;
        wndclass.hInstance     = hInstance ;
        wndclass.hIcon         = LoadIcon (hInstance, "MyIcon") ;
        wndclass.hCursor       = LoadCursor (NULL, IDC_ARROW) ;
        wndclass.hbrBackground = GetStockObject (WHITE_BRUSH) ;
        wndclass.lpszMenuName  = "MyMenu" ;
        wndclass.lpszClassName = "MyClass" ;
                        /* register the window class */
        if (!RegisterClass (&wndclass))
            return 0 ;
    }

    hWnd = CreateWindow ("MyClass", "Static Control Example",
        WS_OVERLAPPEDWINDOW,
        CW_USEDEFAULT, CW_USEDEFAULT, CW_USEDEFAULT, CW_USEDEFAULT,
        NULL, NULL, hInstance, NULL) ;
    ShowWindow (hWnd, nCmdShow) ;  /* display the window */

    while (GetMessage (&msg, NULL, NULL, NULL))   /* message loop */
    {
       TranslateMessage (&msg) ;  /* translate keyboard messages */
       DispatchMessage (&msg) ;   /* send message to WndProc() */
    }
    return (msg.wParam) ;
}

long FAR PASCAL WndProc (HWND hWnd, WORD wMessage, WORD wParam, LONG lParam)
{
    static  BOOL     bFirstTime = TRUE ;
    static  HANDLE   hStaticText, hStaticIcon, hStaticRect ;
    HANDLE           hInstance ;

    switch (wMessage)           /* process windows messages */
    {
        case WM_CREATE:         /* program is just starting */
            if (bFirstTime)     /* only do this once */
            {
                bFirstTime = FALSE ;
                        /* get the instance handle */
                hInstance = GetWindowWord (hWnd, GWW_HINSTANCE) ;
                        /* create three static controls */
                hStaticText = CreateWindow ("STATIC", "This is static text.",
                    WS_CHILD | SS_CENTER,
                    10, 10, 130, 60,
                    hWnd, NULL, hInstance, NULL) ;
                hStaticIcon = CreateWindow ("STATIC", "MyIcon",
                    WS_CHILD | SS_ICON,
                    150, 10, 0, 0,           /* icon height & width used */
                    hWnd, NULL, hInstance, NULL) ;
                hStaticRect = CreateWindow ("STATIC", "",
                    WS_CHILD |  SS_GRAYRECT,
                    10, 80, 200, 30,
                    hWnd, NULL, hInstance, NULL) ;
                        /* display the controls */
                ShowWindow (hStaticText, SW_SHOWNORMAL) ;
```

```
              ShowWindow (hStaticIcon, SW_SHOWNORMAL) ;
              ShowWindow (hStaticRect, SW_SHOWNORMAL) ;
           }
           break ;
      case WM_COMMAND:
           switch (wParam)        /* menu items */
           {
              case IDM_CHANGE:                   /* change static text */
                 SetWindowText (hStaticText,
                   "New Text Via SetWindowText().") ;
                 break ;
              case IDM_SEND:                     /* change static text */
                 SendMessage (hStaticText, WM_SETTEXT, 0,
                   (LONG) (LPSTR) "New Text Via SendMessage().") ;
                 break ;
              case IDM_QUIT:
                 DestroyWindow (hWnd) ;    /* destroy window, */
                 break ;   /* terminating application */
           }
           break ;
      case WM_DESTROY:         /* stop application */
           PostQuitMessage (0) ;
           break ;
      default:                 /* default windows message processing */
           return DefWindowProc (hWnd, wMessage, wParam, lParam) ;
   }
   return (0L) ;
}
```

STATIC also has the usual module definition file, header file, resource file, and make file. They are shown in Listings 5-3 through 5-7. The icon image is shown in Figure 5-2.

Listing 5-3 STATIC.DEF Module Definition File

```
NAME         static
EXETYPE      WINDOWS
STUB         'WINSTUB.EXE'
CODE         PRELOAD MOVEABLE
DATA         PRELOAD MOVEABLE MULTIPLE
HEAPSIZE     1024
STACKSIZE    5120
EXPORTS      WndProc
```

Listing 5-4 STATIC.H Header File

```
/* static.h  header file */

#define IDM_CHANGE  1    /* menu items */
#define IDM_SEND    2
#define IDM_QUIT    10

long FAR PASCAL WndProc (HWND, WORD, WORD, LONG) ;
```

Listing 5-5 STATIC.RC Resource Script File

```
/* static.rc resource file */

#include "static.h"

MyIcon      ICON    static.ico

MyMenu      MENU
BEGIN
    MENUITEM "&Change Title"    IDM_CHANGE
    MENUITEM "&Send Message"    IDM_SEND
    MENUITEM "&Quit",           IDM_QUIT
END
```

Listing 5-6 Turbo C++ Project File Contents for STATIC

```
static.c
static.def
static.res
```

Listing 5-7 QuickC Project File Contents for STATIC

```
static.c
static.def
static.rc
```

Figure 5-2
STATIC.ICO Icon Image

The key parts of the listings to notice are within the WndProc() function of STATIC.C. When the program is just starting and creates the main program window, the Windows environment sends the WM_CREATE message to the program. STATIC.C detects this message and uses it as a good point to create the three static controls. This part of STATIC.C is shown again in Listing 5-8.

We are going to use the CreateWindow() function three times to create the three static controls. These three calls to CreateWindow() will be noted by Windows, which will generate three additional WM_CREATE messages. This would create an infinite loop of messages. Each call to CreateWindow() would generate another WM_CREATE message, which would result in three more calls to CreateWindow() in the program. This type of infinite loop crashes Windows in a hurry. To avoid this problem, STATIC.C uses a static variable *bFirstTime* to decide if this is the first WM_CREATE message processed. If it is the first WM_CREATE, then the three windows controls are created. Any subsequent WM_CREATE messages are ignored. (If you follow the complete listing of STATIC.C in Listing 5-2, you will see that subsequent WM_CREATE messages are passed on to the DefWindowProc() function for default processing.)

Windows Programming Primer Plus®

Listing 5-8 Creating Three Static Controls in STATIC.C

```
    static BOOL    bFirstTime = TRUE ;
```
[Other program lines...]
```
        case WM_CREATE:         /* program is just starting */
            if (bFirstTime)     /* only do this once */
            {
                bFirstTime = FALSE ;
                                /* get the instance handle */
                hInstance = GetWindowWord (hWnd, GWW_HINSTANCE) ;
                                /* create three static controls */
                hStaticText = CreateWindow ("STATIC", "This is static text.",
                    WS_CHILD | SS_CENTER,
                    10, 10, 130, 60,
                    hWnd, NULL, hInstance, NULL) ;
                hStaticIcon = CreateWindow ("STATIC", "MyIcon",
                    WS_CHILD | SS_ICON,
                    150, 10, 0, 0,       /* icon height & width used */
                    hWnd, NULL, hInstance, NULL) ;
                hStaticRect = CreateWindow ("STATIC", "",
                    WS_CHILD | SS_GRAYRECT,
                    10, 80, 200, 30,
                    hWnd, NULL, hInstance, NULL) ;
                                /* display the controls */
                ShowWindow (hStaticText, SW_SHOWNORMAL) ;
                ShowWindow (hStaticIcon, SW_SHOWNORMAL) ;
                ShowWindow (hStaticRect, SW_SHOWNORMAL) ;
            }
```
[Other program lines]

All of the calls to CreateWindow in Listing 5-8 use the WS_CHILD style. This makes the window created a *child* window. Child windows are attached to a parent window, and are only visible if the parent is shown. Child windows can only exist within their parent's client area. In this case, all of the children are attached to the main window. The relationship of child to parent is established by setting the WS_CHILD *dwStyle* parameter and by setting the *hWndParent* parameter to the parent window's handle. This gives the Windows environment the information it needs to figure out which windows have children.

The first static control created in Listing 5-8 is a static text control. This control uses the combination WS_CHILD | SS_CENTER style, creating a child window control with the text centered. We could have used the SS_LEFT or SS_RIGHT styles to have the text left or right-justified. The location and dimensions of the control are set with the upper left corner at 10,10, with a width of 130 pixels and a height of 60 pixels. Note that the *X,Y* location of 10,10 is relative to the parent window's client area upper left corner. This is a child window control, so the control's entire existence is relative to its parent.

The second control created in Listing 5-8 is a static icon. Although static icons are created using the same editing tools used to create program icons, the icon data is used here simply to fill in a static window control. Static icon controls have nothing to do with the program icon which is displayed when an application is minimized. It turns out that the STATIC program uses the same icon data (created with the Resource Workshop or Image Editor) for both the program icon and the static icon control. This does not have to be the case. You can use different icons for the program icon (attached to the window class) and for static icon controls. For the STATIC program, just one icon image file was added to the resource data in the STATIC.RC resource script data and given the name "MyIcon."

```
MyIcon    ICON    static.ico
```

We then use the icon's name "MyIcon" as the *lpWindowName* parameter, so that CreateWindow() can access the icon data. The icon control is created using the WS_CHILD | SS_ICON style. It is positioned at *X,Y* location 150,10 in the parent window's client area. The *nWidth* and *nHeight* parameters in CreateWindow() are set to zero, as the icon's size is determined by the icon data, not by these two parameters (which are ignored).

The last control created in Listing 5-8 is a gray rectangle. This is an area painted using the same color brush that Windows uses to paint the background of the screen (desktop window). The default color is gray, although the user can change this to any color using the Control Panel application. The WS_CHILD | SS_GRAYRECT style will create a rectangle that always matches the background color. Other static control styles use different colors from the Window's system color scheme. Look at the discussion of the SS_BLACKFRAME, SS_BLACKRECT, SS_GRAYFRAME, SS_WHITEFRAME, and SS_WHITERECT control styles in Table 5-4 for more information.

Compile STATIC and get it running. Test out the automatic repainting of the child window controls by covering STATIC with another program's window, and then uncovering it. The controls will be redrawn automatically. The redrawing will also occur if you resize the window, or minimize it and then restore it. The Windows environment takes care of keeping all of the windows current. This is a lot easier than having to process WM_PAINT messages for the text and icons.

It is not always possible to eliminate WM_PAINT message processing logic from your program. Although static controls are handy, they are limited to text, icons, and rectangles. If you want to have more elaborate colored images in the program's client area, you will need to process WM_PAINT messages and repaint each time the WM_PAINT message is received. You can use a combination of static controls and direct painting logic in many applications. Use static controls whenever possible to simplify your program, and just paint the portions which demand the use of graphics functions.

Sending a Message to a Control

The choice of the word "static" to describe static controls is a bit misleading, as you may get the idea that static controls never change. It turns out that you can change static controls while the program runs. The STATIC.C program shows two examples of changing a static text control's character string. If you click the "Change Title" menu item, the static text control will change to the words "New Text Via SetWindowText()." If you click the "Send Message" menu item, the static text control will change to "New Text Via SendMessage()." Figure 5-3 shows the latter case.

Listing 5-9 shows the key parts of STATIC.C that change the words in the static text control.

Listing 5-9 Portion of STATIC.C that Changes the Static Text Control

```
case WM_COMMAND:
    switch (wParam)        /* menu items */
    {
        case IDM_CHANGE:   /* change static text */
            SetWindowText (hStaticText,
                "New Text Via SetWindowText().") ;
            break ;
        case IDM_SEND:     /* change static text */
            SendMessage (hStaticText, WM_SETTEXT, 0,
                (LONG) (LPSTR) "New Text Via SendMessage().") ;
            break ;
```
[Other program lines]

When the user selects a menu item, Windows sends a WM_COMMAND message to the program, with the *wParam* parameter set to the menu item's ID number. In STATIC.C, the IDM_CHANGE menu item ID results in calling the SetWindowText() function. This function changes the text of any window. Remember that our static text control is a window, even though it may not look like one. SetWindowText() changes the text string inside of the control. You can also use SetWindowText() to change the caption on main program windows and the text inside a button control.

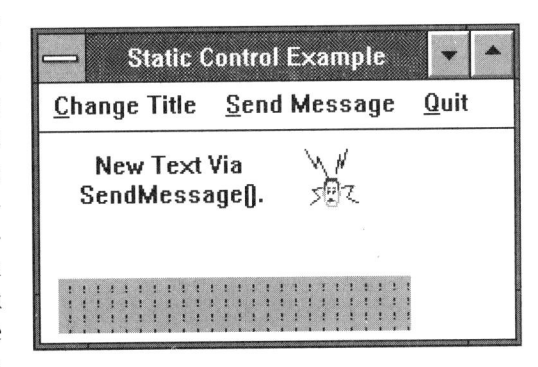

Figure 5-3 STATIC Program After "Send Message" Menu Item Selected

STATIC.C demonstrates another way to change a static control's text, if the IDM_SEND menu item is selected. In this case, STATIC.C sends the WM_SETTEXT message to the static control window. The *lParam* parameter passed with the WM_SETTEXT message is a pointer to the character string "New Text Via SendMessage()." When the static control gets this message, it changes its text string. The result is shown in Figure 5-3.

This is the first example we have seen of a program sending a message to another window. Windows provides two functions for sending messages: SendMessage() and PostMessage(). SendMessage() sends the message directly to the receiving window's WndProc() function. PostMessage() puts the message on the receiving window's message queue. The message queue is the memory area where Windows stores messages that have not yet been processed. Either SendMessage() or PostMessage() could have been used in this case.

C Language Casts

You may have noticed the interesting use of the cast "(LONG)" in the SendMessage() function call in Listing 5-9. This is needed to keep the compiler from complaining about sending a pointer to a string in the call to SendMessage(). If you look in WINDOWS.H, you will find the function prototype for the SendMessage() function.

```
LONG  FAR PASCAL SendMessage(HWND, WORD, WORD, LONG);
```

The compiler reads WINDOWS.H before the rest of the program, as the WINDOWS.H file is included at the top of STATIC.C. After reading WINDOWS.H, the compiler expects the fourth parameter passed to the SendMessage() function to be a LONG value. LONG values are four bytes of numeric information.

In using SendMessage() to send the WM_SETTEXT message, we need the fourth parameter to be a LPSTR, a long pointer to a string. A LPSTR is also four bytes long, but the four bytes refer to the address of a character string, not to a numeric value. The compiler distinguishes between these two data types, even though they both have four bytes. For example, the compiler will detect an error if you attempt to call SendMessage() with the syntax:

```
char   cBuf [] = "New Text Via SendMessage()." ;
SendMessage (hStaticText, WM_SETTEXT, 0, cBuf ) ;       /* will generate warning */
```

In this example, the C compiler will see that *cBuf* is not a LONG value, but rather a pointer to a string. The compiler will generate an error message. To get around this problem, we must tell the compiler that we want to pass the pointer to a string in place of the LONG value. To do this, we use the C language feature of "casting." The example below shows the casting of the character string pointer to a LONG value. This actually takes two casts, a cast to LPSTR to convert the near pointer to a far pointer (32-bit), and a second cast to a LONG value. This makes the compiler happy when it processes the SendMessage() function call, because it was expecting a LONG value based on the function prototype.

```
char   cBuf [] = "New Text Via SendMessage()." ;
SendMessage (hStaticText, WM_SETTEXT, 0, (LONG)(LPSTR) cBuf) ;
```

You can shorten this example by taking advantage of a shortcut. If you put a character string in quotes inside of the SendMessage() function call, the compiler will automatically store the string as a static variable and pass a pointer to the string to the function as a parameter. The casting of the static data is then done directly as follows:

```
SendMessage (hStaticText, WM_SETTEXT, 0,
    (LONG) (LPSTR) "New Text Via SendMessage().") ;
```

You will often see DWORD in place of LONG in Windows program listings. DWORD is defined in WINDOWS.H as an unsigned long int. You will only want to use C language casts with a few Windows functions, such as SendMessage() and PostMessage(). These functions are so versatile that no one variable type will describe all of the data types that the function may want to pass as a parameter. The general guideline about casting is to only do it when necessary. With most functions, only one type of data will be transmitted for each parameter. By avoiding unnecessary casting, your compiler will have the best chance of detecting errors caused by passing the wrong data type to a function.

Button Controls

Windows supports a variety of objects created from the BUTTON class, such as push buttons, radio buttons, check boxes, and group outlines. Our next example demonstrates most of these button styles. Along the way, we will learn some more about using SendMessage(), and we will also use the handy MessageBox() and wsprintf() functions for the first time.

When you call CreateWindow() with the BUTTON window class, the *dwStyle* parameter passed to CreateWindow() can have any of the values shown in Table 5-5. These styles can be combined using the C language OR operator (|). For example, to create a check box control with the text on the left side (the default is the right side), use WS_CHILD | BS_CHECKBOX | BS_LEFTTEXT. Buttons are almost always child windows, so the WS_CHILD style will usually be part of the *dwStyle* definition.

BS_AUTOCHECKBOX	Small rectangular button with text to the right. The rectangle can either be open or checked. This style toggles automatically between checked and open.
BS_AUTORADIOBUTTON	Small circular button with text to the right. The circle can either be filled or open. This style toggles automatically between checked and open.
BS_AUTO3STATE	Small rectangular button with text to the right. The button can either be filled, grayed, or open. This style toggles automatically between checked, grayed, and open.
BS_CHECKBOX	Small rectangular button with text to the right. The rectangle can either be open or checked.
BS_DEFPUSHBUTTON	Button with text in the center and with a defined (dark) border. This should be the button that is pressed when the user presses the (Enter) key. There should be only one DEFPUSHBUTTON on a window.
BS_GROUPBOX	A box outline with text at the upper left. Used to group other controls.
BS_LEFTTEXT	Causes text to be on the left side of the button. Use this with other button styles.
BS_OWNERDRAW	Designates a button that will be drawn by the program. Windows sends messages to request paint, invert, and disable. Use this style for custom button controls.

continued

Table 5-5 (cont'd)

BS_PUSHBUTTON	A rectangular button with text in the center.
BS_RADIOBUTTON	Small circular button with text to the right. The circle can either be filled or open.
BS_3STATE	Small rectangular button with text to the right. The button can either be filled, grayed, or open.

Table 5-5 Button Styles

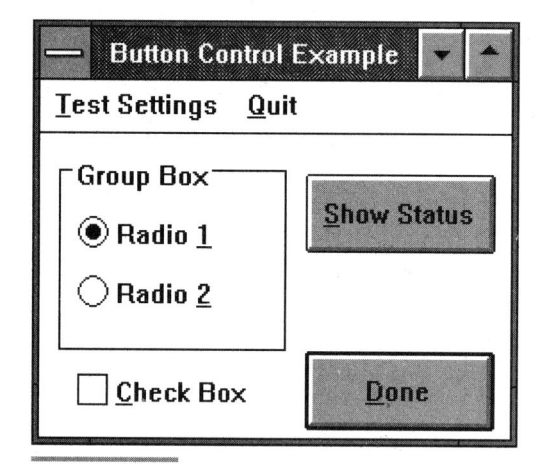

Figure 5-4 BUTTON Program in Operation

The example program for this section is called BUTTON (surprise!). When activated, the program's window appears as shown in Figure 5-4. BUTTON has two radio buttons inside of a group box. Radio buttons and group boxes are forms of buttons. There is also a check box button at the bottom left. Two push buttons are on the right side of the window. All told, there are six buttons inside of the parent window's client area, counting the group box control.

The most obvious type of button is the push button. The BUTTON program has two of these on the right side. Push buttons initiate some action when selected. The other types of buttons allow the user to make selections. Radio buttons are used to make a single selection from a group of possibilities. In the BUTTON program, selecting radio button1 automatically results in de-selecting radio button 2, and vice versa. This is typical of a situation where only one of a group of possibilities can be selected at any one time. It is common to put related radio buttons into groups, so that their relationship is clear. In BUTTON, the group box is sized to hold both radio buttons.

Check boxes are specialized buttons that are used to show an on/off status for a selection. Both check boxes and radio buttons have the ability to show three states: off, checked, and grayed. The grayed state fills in the selection area on the left with a gray color, rather than showing a solid radio button or X for the check box. Graying the selection can be used to allow three different selection states, such as on/off/disabled. Generally, it is best to stick with just two states, off and checked, because users may confuse the grayed and checked states. The BUTTON program implements a three-state check box, so that you can experiment with this option.

BUTTON.C (Listing 5-10) shows many similarities to the STATIC.C program we just finished. All of the button controls are created using the CreateWindow() function. Each is a child window (WS_CHILD style). The second style parameter determines what type of button is created. The BS_GROUPBOX style creates the group box. This is an open rectangle with a title at the upper left corner. The BS_RADIOBUTTON style is used to create the two radio buttons. By default, the selection area (small circle) is on the left side, but you can move it to the right by adding the BS_LEFTTEXT style to the radio button or check box style.

The checkbox uses the BS_AUTO3STATE style. "AUTO" means that the checkbox automatically cycles through the off, checked, and grayed states each time it is selected. "3STATE" means that the off, checked, and grayed states are all available. The BS_AUTOCHECKBOX is the equivalent style with only the off and checked states available. If you do not want the automatic changing of the button's state each time it is selected, use the BS_CHECKBOX (two states) or BS_3STATE (three states) styles.

The two push buttons are created with the BS_PUSHBUTTON and BS_DEFPUSH-BUTTON styles. The only difference is that the BS_DEFPUSHBUTTON style adds a dark outline to the button's outline. This is usually used to highlight the default action that will happen if the user presses the (Enter) key. We have not gotten to keyboard input yet, so this feature is not implemented in BUTTON.C.

Listing 5-10 BUTTON.C

```
/* button.c   Creating button controls */

#include <windows.h>
#include "button.h"

int PASCAL WinMain (HANDLE hInstance, HANDLE hPrevInstance, LPSTR lpszCmdLine,
    int nCmdShow)
{
    HWND        hWnd ;              /* the window's "handle" */
    MSG         msg ;               /* a message structure */
    WNDCLASS    wndclass ;          /* window class structure */

    if (!hPrevInstance)
    {
        wndclass.style          = CS_HREDRAW | CS_VREDRAW ;
        wndclass.lpfnWndProc    = WndProc ;
        wndclass.cbClsExtra     = 0 ;
        wndclass.cbWndExtra     = 0 ;
        wndclass.hInstance      = hInstance ;
        wndclass.hIcon          = LoadIcon (hInstance, "MyIcon") ;
        wndclass.hCursor        = LoadCursor (NULL, IDC_ARROW) ;
        wndclass.hbrBackground  = GetStockObject (WHITE_BRUSH) ;
        wndclass.lpszMenuName   = "MyMenu" ;
        wndclass.lpszClassName  = "MyClass" ;
                /* register the window class */
        if (!RegisterClass (&wndclass))
            return 0 ;
    }

    hWnd = CreateWindow ("MyClass", "Button Control Example",
        WS_OVERLAPPEDWINDOW,
        CW_USEDEFAULT, CW_USEDEFAULT, CW_USEDEFAULT, CW_USEDEFAULT,
        NULL, NULL, hInstance, NULL) ;
    ShowWindow (hWnd, nCmdShow) ;       /* display the window */
```

```c
      while (GetMessage (&msg, NULL, NULL, NULL))   /* message loop */
      {
         TranslateMessage (&msg) ;   /* translate keyboard messages */
         DispatchMessage (&msg) ;    /* send message to WndProc() */
      }
      return (msg.wParam) ;
   }

   long FAR PASCAL WndProc (HWND hWnd, WORD wMessage, WORD wParam, LONG lParam)
   {
      static   BOOL      bFirstTime = TRUE ;
      static   HWND      hGroup, hRad1, hRad2, hCheck, hBut1, hBut2 ;
      HANDLE             hInstance ;
      BOOL               bIsChecked, bTopRadioOn ;
      char               cBuf [128] ;

      switch (wMessage)        /* process windows messages */
      {
         case WM_CREATE:    /* program is just starting */
            if (bFirstTime) /* only do this once */
            {
               bFirstTime = FALSE ;
                       /* get the instance handle */
               hInstance = GetWindowWord (hWnd, GWW_HINSTANCE) ;
                       /* create button controls */
               hGroup = CreateWindow ("BUTTON", "Group Box",
                  WS_CHILD | BS_GROUPBOX,
                  10, 10, 120, 100,
                  hWnd, NULL, hInstance, NULL) ;
               hRad1 = CreateWindow ("BUTTON", "Radio &1",
                  WS_CHILD | BS_RADIOBUTTON,
                  20, 40, 80, 20,
                  hWnd, RADIO1, hInstance, NULL) ;
               hRad2 = CreateWindow ("BUTTON", "Radio &2",
                  WS_CHILD | BS_RADIOBUTTON,
                  20, 70, 80, 20,
                  hWnd, RADIO2, hInstance, NULL) ;
               hCheck = CreateWindow ("BUTTON", "&Check Box",
                  WS_CHILD | BS_AUTO3STATE,
                  20, 120, 100, 20,
                  hWnd, CHECK_BOX, hInstance, NULL) ;
               hBut1 = CreateWindow ("BUTTON", "&Show Status",
                  WS_CHILD | BS_PUSHBUTTON,
                  140, 20, 100, 40,
                  hWnd, STATUS_BUTTON, hInstance, NULL) ;
               hBut2 = CreateWindow ("BUTTON", "&Done",
                  WS_CHILD | BS_DEFPUSHBUTTON,
                  140, 110, 100, 40,
                  hWnd, DONE_BUTTON, hInstance, NULL) ;

                       /* display the buttons */
               ShowWindow (hGroup, SW_SHOWNORMAL) ;
               ShowWindow (hRad1, SW_SHOWNORMAL) ;
               ShowWindow (hRad2, SW_SHOWNORMAL) ;
               ShowWindow (hCheck, SW_SHOWNORMAL) ;
               ShowWindow (hBut1, SW_SHOWNORMAL) ;
               ShowWindow (hBut2, SW_SHOWNORMAL) ;
                       /* start with radio button 1 checked */
               SendMessage (hRad1, BM_SETCHECK, TRUE, 0L) ;
```

```
            }
                break ;
        case WM_COMMAND:
            switch (wParam)        /* control ID's */
            {
                case RADIO1:        /* top radio button clicked */
                    SendMessage (hRad1, BM_SETCHECK, TRUE, 0L) ;
                    SendMessage (hRad2, BM_SETCHECK, FALSE, 0L) ;
                        break ;
                case RADIO2:        /* bottom radio button clicked */
                    SendMessage (hRad1, BM_SETCHECK, FALSE, 0L) ;
                    SendMessage (hRad2, BM_SETCHECK, TRUE, 0L) ;
                        break ;
                case CHECK_BOX:     /* auto check box */
                    break ;        /* no need to process message */
                case STATUS_BUTTON:
                    bIsChecked = (int) SendMessage (hCheck, BM_GETCHECK,
                        0, 0L) ;
                    bTopRadioOn = (int) SendMessage (hRad1, BM_GETCHECK,
                        0, 0L) ;
                    wsprintf (cBuf,
                        "Top Radio Button = %d, Check box = %d",
                        bTopRadioOn, bIsChecked) ;
                    MessageBox (hWnd, cBuf, "Current Button Status", MB_OK) ;
                    break ;
                case DONE_BUTTON:
                    DestroyWindow (hWnd) ; /* terminate application */
                        break ;
                    /* The action taken for the IDM_TEST menu item is the */
                    /* same as that for the STATUS_BUTTON control, so just */
                    /* simulate the same message as if the control had */
                    /* been activated (by sending a WM_COMMAND message). */
                case IDM_TEST:
                    SendMessage (hWnd, WM_COMMAND, STATUS_BUTTON, 0L) ;
                        break ;
                case IDM_QUIT:
                    DestroyWindow (hWnd) ;  /* destroy window */
                    break ;    /* terminating application */
            }
                break ;
        case WM_DESTROY:    /* stop application */
            PostQuitMessage (0) ;
            break ;
        default:         /* default windows message processing */
            return DefWindowProc (hWnd, wMessage, wParam, lParam) ;
    }
    return (0L) ;
}
```

Note in the SendMessage() function calls that the last parameter *lParam* is a LONG value. When this parameter is not used for a particular message, a zero is used as a place holder. In these listings, the shortcut "0L" (zero, letter L) is used to pass a zero to the SendMessage() function.

The BUTTON.H header file is shown in Listing 5-11. Each of the controls is assigned an ID value above 1000. This follows the general practice of assigning number 0-99 for menu items, 100-999 for dialog box items (covered in Chapter 10, *Dialog Boxes*), and 1000 and above for control ID numbers.

The remaining support files for BUTTON are shown in Listings 5-12 to 5-15. Figure 5-5 shows the icon image.

Listing 5-11 BUTTON.H Header File

```
/* button.h header file */

#define IDM_TEST       1       /* menu items ID's */
#define IDM_QUIT       10

#define DONE_BUTTON    1000    /* control ID's */
#define STATUS_BUTTON  1001
#define RADIO1         1002
#define RADIO2         1003
#define CHECK_BOX      1004

long FAR PASCAL WndProc (HWND, WORD, WORD, LONG) ;
```

Figure 5-5
BUTTON.ICON
Icon Image

If you look at the CreateWindow() function calls that create the button controls in the WndProc() function of BUTTON.C (Listing 5-12), you can see that the control ID name is used in each call to CreateWindow() as the *hMenu* parameter. *hMenu* is the third from the last parameter in each CreateWindow() function call. For main program windows, the *hMenu* parameter is used to pass a handle to the menu definition. For window controls, there is no room for a menu, so the *hMenu* parameter is used to pass the control's ID value. This is how Windows finds out the ID value for each control. The group box cannot be selected, so its ID value is just set to NULL (zero).

When a control is selected with the mouse, Windows sends a WM_COMMAND message to the parent window of the control. Windows makes the control's ID value the *wParam* value passed with the WM_COMMAND message. BUTTON.C examines the *wParam* value passed with WM_COMMAND to determine which control was activated. WM_COMMAND is also sent if a menu item is selected. For menu items, the *wParam* value is the menu item's ID value. It is important to have separate numbers for menu items and controls, so that it is a simple matter to determine whether a WM_COMMAND message comes from a menu item or control.

Listing 5-12 BUTTON.DEF Module Definition File

```
NAME        button
EXETYPE     WINDOWS
STUB        'WINSTUB.EXE'
CODE        PRELOAD MOVEABLE
DATA        PRELOAD MOVEABLE MULTIPLE
HEAPSIZE    1024
STACKSIZE   5120
EXPORTS     WndProc
```

Listing 5-13 BUTTON.RC Resource Script File

```
/* button.rc resource file */

#include "button.h"

MyIcon     ICON    button.ico

MyMenu     MENU
BEGIN
   MENUITEM "&Test Settings"    IDM_TEST
   MENUITEM "&Quit",            IDM_QUIT
END
```

Listing 5-14 Turbo C++ Project File Contents for BUTTON

```
button.c
button.def
button.res
```

Listing 5-15 QuickC Project File Contents for BUTTON

```
button.c
button.def
button.rc
```

Processing Button Control Messages

The most interesting portion of BUTTON.C is the processing of the WM_COMMAND message. This portion of BUTTON.C is shown again in Listing 5-16. If either of the radio buttons is selected, BUTTON.C sends a BM_SETCHECK message to each of the radio button windows. SendMessage() is used to transmit the BM_SETCHECK message to the control windows. The BM_SETCHECK message allows the check mark to be set on or off on a radio button or check box. For the radio buttons, only one of the two buttons is allowed to be checked at any one time. If RADIO1 was selected, it is set checked and RADIO2 is set unchecked. If RADIO2 was selected, it is set checked and RADIO1 is set unchecked.

The processing of the radio button WM_COMMAND messages shown in Listing 5-16 is typical of the case where the button control does not have an "AUTO" style. The check box control in BUTTON.C was created with the BS_AUTO3STATE style, so it automatically cycles through the checked, grayed, and unchecked status each time it is clicked with the mouse. No processing of the WM_COMMAND message from this control is necessary.

Listing 5-16 Processing of WM_COMMAND Messages in BUTTON.C

```c
case WM_COMMAND:
    switch (wParam)    /* control ID's */
    {
        case RADIO1:    /* top radio button clicked */
            SendMessage (hRad1, BM_SETCHECK, TRUE, 0L) ;
            SendMessage (hRad2, BM_SETCHECK, FALSE, 0L) ;
            break ;
        case RADIO2:    /* bottom radio button clicked */
            SendMessage (hRad1, BM_SETCHECK, FALSE, 0L) ;
            SendMessage (hRad2, BM_SETCHECK, TRUE, 0L) ;
            break ;
        case CHECK_BOX: /* auto check box */
            break ;    /* no need to process message */
        case STATUS_BUTTON:
            bIsChecked = (int) SendMessage (hCheck, BM_GETCHECK,
                0, 0L) ;
            bTopRadioOn = (int) SendMessage (hRad1, BM_GETCHECK,
                0, 0L) ;
            wsprintf (cBuf,
               "Top Radio Button = %d, Check box = %d",
               bTopRadioOn, bIsChecked) ;
            MessageBox (hWnd, cBuf, "Current Button Status", MB_OK) ;
            break ;
        case DONE_BUTTON:
            DestroyWindow (hWnd) ;  /* terminate application */
            break ;
                    /* menu items */
                    /* The action taken for the IDM_TEST menu item is the */
                    /* same as that for the STATUS_BUTTON control, so just */
                    /* simulate the same message as if the control had */
                    /* been activated (by sending a WM_COMMAND message). */
        case IDM_TEST:
            SendMessage (hWnd, WM_COMMAND, STATUS_BUTTON, 0L) ;
            break ;
        case IDM_QUIT:
        DestroyWindow (hWnd) ; /* destroy window */
        break ;         /* terminating application */
    }
    break ;
```

The other basic activity you will need to do with button controls is to determine their status. The BM_GETCHECK message allows you to determine if a radio button or check box is checked, grayed, or unchecked. If you use SendMessage() to send the BM_GETCHECK message to a button control, SendMessage() will return zero for unchecked, one for checked, and two for grayed. SendMessage() returns a DWORD value. It is common to cast the return value to an integer, as you do not need a full four-byte DWORD to hold a value limited to between zero and two.

When the user clicks the button labeled "Show Status," Windows sends the program a WM_COMMAND message with *wParam* set equal to the button's ID value,

STATUS_BUTTON. If you look in Listing 5-16, you will see that the current status of the top radio button and the check box are determined using the BM_GETCHECK message. It is not necessary to check both radio buttons, as our program logic makes sure that only one is selected at a time.

Once the status of the radio button and check box is determined, the status values are displayed in a small popup window. This introduces two new functions, wsprintf() and MessageBox(). wsprintf() function is the Windows equivalent of the C compiler library function sprintf(). Both of these functions copy a formatted string to a character buffer. You can use wsprintf() in any Windows program, as the function's code is part of Windows. This reduces the size of your finished program, as the sprintf() code would otherwise be added to your Windows program by the compiler/linker.

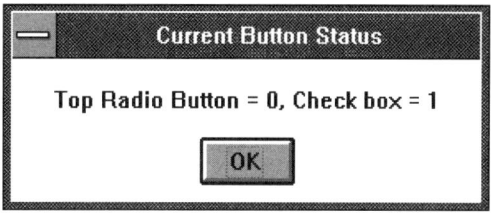

Figure 5-6 The Message Box from the BUTTON Program

MessageBox() is a handy function that allows you to put a small window containing text and a couple of buttons in the center of the screen. When it is activated, MessageBox() displays the window shown in Figure 5-6. The first character string passed to MessageBox() ends up in the center of the window. The second string ends up as the window's caption. The message box window remains on the screen until the user clicks the "OK" button.

There is a sneaky trick in BUTTON.C that deserves an explanation. Selecting either the "Test Settings" menu item or the "Show Status" button has the same effect: displaying the message box. Rather than use the dreaded C language *goto:* statement, BUTTON.C uses SendMessage(). The idea is that you can simulate the user selecting a button by sending a WM_COMMAND message to the WndProc() function when the menu item is selected. When the user selects the "Test Settings" menu item, SendMessage() is used to send a message from a program to itself.

```
SendMessage (hWnd, WM_COMMAND, STATUS_BUTTON, 0L) ;
```

hWnd is the program's own window handle, not the handle of a window control. WM_COMMAND is the same message that would be received if a button control were clicked. STATUS_BUTTON is the ID of the button that we are simulating being selected. The result of calling SendMessage() is that the program gets another WM_COMMAND message and processes it just as if the STATUS_BUTTON button had been selected.

Experienced Windows programmers use messages within a program as an efficient way to control execution. Properly used, transmitting messages within a single program is an efficient way to avoid duplicating code that is common to several parts of the program. Windows even allows you to define your own messages starting with WM_USER, WM_USER+1, WM_USER+2, etc. Don't go overboard with this idea. You can end up with program logic that resembles the wiring behind my desk (very messy indeed).

Button Notification Codes

In the BUTTON program, we only used the *wParam* parameter sent with the WM_COMMAND message. *wParam* holds the button's ID value that was set when the button was created. Windows also fills in the *lParam* parameter sent with WM_COMMAND. *lParam* is a LONG value, so it has four bytes of information. The low-order two bytes will contain the handle of the button control's window. This is convenient, as you can avoid saving the handles of the button controls as they are created by using the handle sent with WM_COMMAND. Listing 5-17 shows an example of this type of logic. The LOWORD macro from WINDOWS.H extracts the low-order two bytes from *lParam*, which are saved temporarily as *hButton*. This handle is then used in the SendMessage() call to set the check mark on with the BM_SETCHECK message.

Listing 5-17 Using the Button Handle Passed with WM_COMMAND

```
long FAR PASCAL WndProc (HWND hWnd, WORD wMessage, WORD wParam, LONG lParam)
{
   HANDLE    hButton ;

   switch (wMessage)
      case WM_COMMAND:
         switch RADIO1: /* button control RADIO1 was selected */
            hButton = LOWORD (lParam) ; /* get button handle */
            SendMessage (hButton, BM_SETCHECK, TRUE, 0L) ;
```
[Other program lines]

The high-order two bytes of the *lParam* value passed with the WM_COMMAND message will contain a *button notification code*. These codes are defined in WINDOWS.H and summarized in Table 5-6. Normally, you will ignore the notification codes. Occasionally, you may find it useful to determine if the user double clicked a button, which will result in the BN_DOUBLECLICKED notification code being sent as the high-order word of *lParam* in the WM_COMMAND message.

NOTIFICATION CODE	PURPOSE
BN_CLICKED	Notification that a button control has been clicked by the mouse or by pressing the space bar when the control has the input focus.
BN_DISABLE	Notification that a button control has been disabled.
BN_DOUBLECLICKED	Notification that a button control has been double clicked with the mouse.
BN_HILITE	Notification that a button control will be highlighted.
BN_PAINT	Notification that a button control is about to be painted.

| BN_UNHILITE | Notification that a button control will loose its highlighting. |

Table 5-6 Button Notification Codes

List Boxes

List boxes and combo boxes are similar, as they both have a list of items that can be selected. The main difference is that the list box is always visible, while the combo box can be "shrunk" to only show the top edit line. Combo boxes take up less space, and they are a better choice if the user normally will not make a selection, but just needs to be reminded of the currently selected value. List boxes are more appropriate if the user usually will make a selection. The term "list box" is used in the discussion that follows to save space. Unless otherwise noted, the comments on list boxes apply to both list boxes and combo boxes.

When you create a list box using CreateWindow() with the LISTBOX window class, the *dwStyle* parameter passed to CreateWindow() can have any of the values in Table 5-7. Don't forget the LBS_NOTIFY style, or the list box will not send messages to the parent window when the listbox is activated by the user. Listboxes are almost always child windows, so a typical set of style values would be WS_CHILD | LBS_NOTIFY | LBS_SORT | LBS_HASSTRINGS. The LBS_HASSTRINGS style tells Windows to store the list box contents in the application's local heap. Windows will delete the list box data when the list box is destroyed.

LBS_DISABLENOSCROLL	The list box control shows a disabled vertical scroll bar when the list box does not contain enough items to fill the list box window. Without this style, the scroll bar disappears when there are not enough items.
LBS_EXTENDEDSEL	List box control where more than one item can be selected by using the mouse and the shift key.
LBS_HASSTRINGS	List box control containing lists of strings. Send the LB_GETTEXT message to retrieve the strings.
LBS_MULTICOLUMN	List box with multiple columns. Can be scrolled horizontally and vertically. Send the LB_SETCOLUMNWIDTH to set the column widths.
LBS_MULTIPLESEL	Any number of strings can be selected within the list box. Selection by mouse clicking, de-selection by double clicking.
LBS_NOINTEGRALHEIGHT	A list box of fixed size. The list box height is not scaled to match an even number of items (the default case).
LBS_NOREDRAW	A list box which is not automatically redrawn. Convert the control back to normal by sending the WM_SETREDRAW message.

continued

Table 5-7 (cont'd)

LBS_NOTIFY	A list box that sends the parent window messages when the user selects one or more items.
LBS_OWNERDRAWFIXED	A list box where the program is responsible for drawing all items. Items are of fixed vertical size.
LBS_OWNERDRAWVARIABLE	A list box where the program is responsible for drawing all items. Items can be of different vertical sizes.
LBS_SORT	A list box where the items are maintained in sort order.
LBS_STANDARD	A list box containing strings, automatically sorted, with messages sent to the parent window when selections are made.
LBS_USETABSTOPS	A list box that recognizes and expands tab characters. By default, tabs are every eight spaces. See the EM_SETTABSTOPS message to change this value.
LBS_WANTKEYBOARDINPUT	The parent window receives WM_VKEYTOITEM and WM_CHARTOITEM messages from the list box when it has the input focus and keys are pressed. Handy for setting up keyboard shortcut combinations.

Table 5-7 List Box Styles

Using list boxes is similar to using button controls. Your program will communicate with the list box by sending it messages. The list box will notify your program if the user makes a selection by sending a WM_COMMAND message to the program. The specific messages and notification codes exchanged are different for list boxes and buttons.

Figure 5-7 shows the LISTBOX example program. When the program is started, the list box is empty and shows up as a rectangle without the scroll bar at the right. If the user selects the "Fill Listbox" menu item, a series of strings are added to the list box. The strings are automatically sorted into ASCII order. If the user selects a string in the list box, the program displays a message box containing the selected string.

Listing 5-18 shows the program file LISTBOX.C. The list box is created using the CreateWindow() function, from the predefined window class LISTBOX. The list box window style is WS_CHILD | LBS_STANDARD. This makes the list box a child window, with standard list box attributes. The standard list box sorts the entries in ASCII sort order and displays a vertical scroll bar on the right side of the list box if all of the entries cannot be seen. As with all controls, the *hMenu* parameter in the CreateWindow() function call (third from the last parameter) is used to set the ID number for the control. The ID value LISTBOX_ID is defined in the header file LISTBOX.H (Listing 5-19).

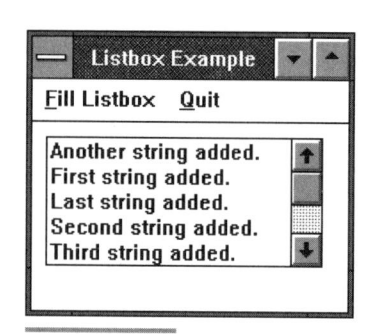

Figure 5-7 The LISTBOX Program

Listing 5-18 LISTBOX.C

```c
/* listbox.c   Creating listbox controls */

#include <windows.h>
#include "listbox.h"

int PASCAL WinMain (HANDLE hInstance, HANDLE hPrevInstance, LPSTR lpszCmdLine,
    int nCmdShow)
{
    HWND        hWnd ;      /* the window's "handle" */
    MSG         msg ;       /* a message structure */
    WNDCLASS    wndclass ;  /* window class structure */

    if (!hPrevInstance)
    {
        wndclass.style         = CS_HREDRAW | CS_VREDRAW ;
        wndclass.lpfnWndProc   = WndProc ;
        wndclass.cbClsExtra    = 0 ;
        wndclass.cbWndExtra    = 0 ;
        wndclass.hInstance     = hInstance ;
        wndclass.hIcon         = LoadIcon (hInstance, "MyIcon") ;
        wndclass.hCursor       = LoadCursor (NULL, IDC_ARROW) ;
        wndclass.hbrBackground = GetStockObject (WHITE_BRUSH) ;
        wndclass.lpszMenuName  = "MyMenu" ;
        wndclass.lpszClassName = "MyClass" ;
                    /* register the window class */
        if (!RegisterClass (&wndclass))
            return 0 ;
    }

    hWnd = CreateWindow ("MyClass", "Listbox Example",
        WS_OVERLAPPEDWINDOW,
        CW_USEDEFAULT, CW_USEDEFAULT, CW_USEDEFAULT, CW_USEDEFAULT,
        NULL, NULL, hInstance, NULL) ;
    ShowWindow (hWnd, nCmdShow) ;   /* display the window */

    while (GetMessage (&msg, NULL, NULL, NULL))  /* message loop */
    {
        TranslateMessage (&msg) ;  /* translate keyboard messages */
        DispatchMessage (&msg) ;   /* send message to WndProc() */
    }
    return (msg.wParam) ;
}

long FAR PASCAL WndProc (HWND hWnd, WORD wMessage, WORD wParam, LONG lParam)
{
    static BOOL   bFirstTime = TRUE ;
    static HWND   hListbox ;
    HANDLE        hInstance ;
    int           nSel ;
    char          cBuf [256], cSelBuf [128] ;

    switch (wMessage)      /* process windows messages */
    {
        case WM_CREATE:    /* program is just starting */
            if (bFirstTime) /* only do this once */
```

```c
          {
              bFirstTime = FALSE ;
                      /* get the instance handle */
              hInstance = GetWindowWord (hWnd, GWW_HINSTANCE) ;
                      /* create listbox control */
              hListbox = CreateWindow ("LISTBOX", "",
                  WS_CHILD | LBS_STANDARD,
                  10, 10, 180, 80,
                  hWnd, LISTBOX_ID, hInstance, NULL) ;
              ShowWindow (hListbox, SW_SHOWNORMAL) ;
          }
              break ;
      case WM_COMMAND:
          switch (wParam)          /* menu item or control ID's */
          {
              case LISTBOX_ID:   /* user did something to listbox */
                 if (HIWORD (lParam) == LBN_SELCHANGE)
                    {            /* if user selected an item */
                            /* get number of selected item */
                  nSel = (int) SendMessage (hListbox, LB_GETCURSEL,
                      0, 0L) ;
                            /* load sel. string into cSelBuf */
                     SendMessage (hListbox, LB_GETTEXT, nSel,
                         (DWORD) (LPSTR) cSelBuf) ;
                            /* build a readable string */
                     wsprintf (cBuf, "The selected item = %s.",
                         (LPSTR) cSelBuf) ;
                            /* show string in a message box */
                     MessageBox (hWnd, cBuf, "Selection", MB_OK) ;\
                   }
                   break ;
              case IDM_FILL:   /* fill listbox with strings */
                    SendMessage (hListbox, LB_RESETCONTENT, 0, 0L) ;
                    SendMessage (hListbox, LB_ADDSTRING, 0,
                       (DWORD) (LPSTR) "First string added.") ;
                    SendMessage (hListbox, LB_ADDSTRING, 0,
                       (DWORD) (LPSTR) "Second string added.") ;
                    SendMessage (hListbox, LB_ADDSTRING, 0,
                       (DWORD) (LPSTR) "Third string added.") ;
                  SendMessage (hListbox, LB_ADDSTRING, 0,
                       (DWORD) (LPSTR) "Another string added.") ;
                  SendMessage (hListbox, LB_ADDSTRING, 0,
                      (DWORD) (LPSTR) "Yet another string added.") ;
                  SendMessage (hListbox, LB_ADDSTRING, 0,
                      (DWORD) (LPSTR) "Last string added.") ;
                  break ;
              case IDM_QUIT:
                 DestroyWindow (hWnd) ; /* destroy window */
                 break ;     /* terminating application */
          }
          break ;
      case WM_DESTROY:   /* stop application */
          PostQuitMessage (0) ;
          break ;
      default:         /* default windows message processing */
          return DefWindowProc (hWnd, wMessage, wParam, lParam) ;
   }
   return (0L) ;
}
```

Listings 5-19 to 5-23 show the support files for LISTBOX. The program's icon is shown in Figure 5-8.

Listing 5-19 LISTBOX.H Header File

```
/* listbox.h header file */

#define    IDM_FILL     1      /* menu items ID's */
#define    IDM_QUIT    10

#define    LISTBOX_ID  1000

long FAR PASCAL WndProc (HWND, WORD, WORD, LONG) ;
```

Figure 5-8
LISTBOX.ICO
Icon Image

Listing 5-20 LISTBOX.RC Resource Script File

```
/* listbox.rc  resource file */

#include "listbox.h"

MyIcon      ICON     listbox.ico

MyMenu      MENU
BEGIN
   MENUITEM "&Fill Listbox",     IDM_FILL
   MENUITEM "&Quit",             IDM_QUIT
END
```

Listing 5-21 LISTBOX.DEF Module Definition File

```
NAME          listbox
EXETYPE       WINDOWS
STUB          'WINSTUB.EXE'
CODE          PRELOAD MOVEABLE
DATA          PRELOAD MOVEABLE MULTIPLE
HEAPSIZE      1024
STACKSIZE     5120
EXPORTS       WndProc
```

Listing 5-22 Turbo C++ Project File Contents for LISTBOX

```
listbox.c
listbox.def
listbox.res
```

Listing 5-23 QuickC Project File Contents for LISTBOX

```
listbox.c
listbox.def
listbox.rc
```

The interesting parts of the LISTBOX program are where it fills the list box with new entries and detects when the user selects an item. The list box is filled when the user selects the "Fill Listbox" menu item, which has the menu ID value IDM_FILL. Windows sends a WM_COMMAND message with the *wParam* value set to IDM_FILL when this menu item is selected. The code to fill the list box is shown again in Listing 5-24.

Listing 5-24 Filling the List Box in LISTBOX.C

```
    case IDM_FILL:      /* fill listbox with strings */
      SendMessage (hListbox, LB_RESETCONTENT, 0, 0L) ;
      SendMessage (hListbox, LB_ADDSTRING, 0,
        (DWORD) (LPSTR) "First string added.") ;
      SendMessage (hListbox, LB_ADDSTRING, 0,
        (DWORD) (LPSTR) "Second string added.") ;
      SendMessage (hListbox, LB_ADDSTRING, 0,
        (DWORD) (LPSTR) "Third string added.") ;
      SendMessage (hListbox, LB_ADDSTRING, 0,
        (DWORD) (LPSTR) "Another string added.") ;
      SendMessage (hListbox, LB_ADDSTRING, 0,
        (DWORD) (LPSTR) "Yet another string added.") ;
      SendMessage (hListbox, LB_ADDSTRING, 0,
        (DWORD) (LPSTR) "Last string added.") ;
      break ;
```
[Other program lines]

Filling the list box involves sending the list box control two types of message. The LB_RESETCONTENT message empties the list box of any data already stored. The *wParam* and *lParam* values sent with this message are both ignored, so they are just set to zero. To add a string, the LB_ADDSTRING message is sent to the listbox control, once for each string added. A pointer string is passed as the *lParam* parameter with the LB_ADDSTRING message. As SendMessage() expects *lParam* to be a LONG value, not a pointer to a string, the string must be cast to a LONG type to keep the compiler happy. Listing 5-24 shows the normal Windows convention of using DWORD for the cast, rather than LONG (DWORD is defined in WINDOWS.H as an unsigned LONG value).

If the user clicks any part of the list box with the mouse cursor, Windows sends the program a WM_COMMAND message. The list box control's ID number will be the *wParam* value passed with WM_COMMAND. Just getting a WM_COMMAND message from a list box does not mean that the user made a selection. The user may simply have used the scroll bar to view the hidden portion of the list.

To make sure that the user made a selection from the list box, we need to check the list box notification code transmitted with WM_COMMAND. Like buttons, list box controls encode the control's handle and the notification code in the *lParam* data passed with WM_COMMAND. The list box handle will be in the low-order word of *lParam*, and the list box notification code will be in the high-order word. Table 5-8 summarizes the list box notification codes. Each of these values is defined in WINDOWS.H.

NOTIFICATION CODE	MEANING
LBN_DBLCLK	Notification that the user double clicked an item in a list box.
LBN_KILLFOCUS	Notification that a list box has lost the input focus.
LBN_SELCHANGE	Notification that the user has selected or deselected an item in a list box.
LBN_SETFOCUS	Notification that a list box has received the input focus.

Table 5-8 List Box Notification Code Summary

Listing 5-25 shows the portion of LISTBOX.C that deals with the user selecting an item from the list box. If the notification code in the *lParam* value passed with the WM_COMMAND message is equal to the LBN_SELCHANGE notification code, then the user has made a selection from the list box. The current selection is determined by sending a LB_GETCURSEL message to the list box control. SendMessage() will return the item number of the current selection, zero for the first item, one for the second, etc.

With the selected item's number known, the string at that item number can be extracted by sending LB_GETTEXT message to the list box control. Windows will copy the string into the character buffer pointed to by the *lParam* parameter sent with the LB_GETTEXT message. In LISTBOX.C, the character buffer is named *cSelBuf*. As usual, the character buffer pointer must be cast to a DWORD to satisfy the compiler's type checking.

Listing 5-25 Selection of a List Box Item in LISTBOX.C

```
case WM_COMMAND:
   switch (wParam)        /* menu item or control ID's */
   {
      case LISTBOX_ID:    /* user did something to listbox */
         if (HIWORD (lParam) == LBN_SELCHANGE)
            {             /* if user selected an item */
                          /* get number of selected item */
               nSel = (int) SendMessage (hListbox, LB_GETCURSEL,
                   0, 0L) ;
                          /* load sel. string into cSelBuf */
               SendMessage (hListbox, LB_GETTEXT, nSel,
                  (DWORD) (LPSTR) cSelBuf) ;
                          /* build a readable string */
               wsprintf (cBuf, "The selected item = %s.",
                  (LPSTR) cSelBuf) ;
                          /* show string in a message box */
```

```
            MessageBox (hWnd, cBuf, "Selection", MB_OK) ;
         }
```
[Other program lines]

Note another example of the double cast (DWORD)(LPSTR) in Listing 5-25 for one SendMessage() function call. The cast (LPSTR) converts the pointer *cSelBuf* from a near pointer to a far pointer. Far pointers take four bytes of room, which is the same size as a DWORD value that SendMessage() expects as the last parameter. However, DWORD and LPSTR are two different data types, so the compiler will issue a warning message if you only cast the *cSelBuf* pointer to a LPSTR. By casting the value a second time to a DWORD, the compiler is satisfied that a DWORD value is being passed to the SendMessage() function. The actual value of the bytes being passed is not affected by converting the LPSTR to a DWORD value, it just stops the compiler from complaining.

Once the current selection's character string is copied into the *cSelBuf* character buffer, LISTBOX.C formats a complete sentence using the wsprintf() function and displays it in a message box. The result is shown in Figure 5-9.

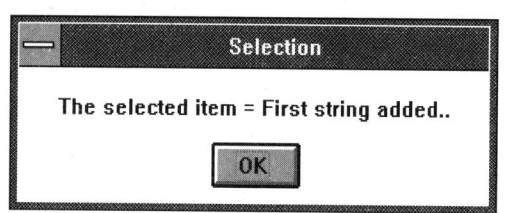

Figure 5-9 Message Box for Display of Selected Item in LISTBOX

Combo Boxes

Combo boxes are created using the CreateWindow() function, using the COMBOBOX window class. The *dwStyle* parameter passed to CreateWindow() can have any of the values specified in Table 5-8. Normally, the list box (under the edit control of the combo box) is only visible if the user clicks the edit control with the mouse. The list box can be made visible at all times by adding the CBS_SIMPLE style. The list box contents will not be sorted unless the CBS_SORT style is included. The CBS_OWNERDRAWFIXED and CBS_OWNERDRAWVARIABLE styles allow the combo box elements to be drawn by the program creating the combo box. This is an advanced technique, and it is useful if you need to display lists of colors or bitmaps in the combo box. See Chapter 9 of *The Waite Group's Windows API Bible* if you need to use owner-drawn elements.

CBS_AUTOHSCROLL	Combo box control. This is a list box with an edit control at the top to display the current selection. With the CBS_AUTOHSCROLL style, the edit area at the top automatically scrolls when typing fills the edit box.
CBS_DISABLENOSCROLL	The list box of the combo box control shows a disabled vertical scroll bar when the list box does not contain enough items to fill the list box window. Without this style, the scroll bar disappears when there are not enough items.

CBS_DROPDOWN	Combo box control with a drop-down scroll area. This reduces the space taken by the combo box when the list is not needed.
CBS_DROPDOWNLIST	Combo box control with a drop-down scroll area. The edit area at top is a static text item which only displays the current selection in the list box.
CBS_HASSTRINGS	The combo box control maintains the list box strings in memory. Fetch them by sending a CB_GETLBTEXT message.
CBS_OEMCONVERT	Combo box edit text is converted to OEM character set and then back to ANSI. Useful for lists of file names.
CBS_OWNERDRAWFIXED	An owner-drawn combo box. The combo box items are of fixed height.
CBS_OWNERDRAWVARIABLE	An owner-drawn combo box. The combo box items can be of different heights.
CBS_SIMPLE	The combo box has a list box that is displayed at all times.
CBS_SORT	The combo box items are automatically sorted.

Table 5-8 Combo Box Styles

Combo boxes are so similar to list boxes that you can switch between them in your program code quickly. The differences boil down to:

1. List boxes are created from the LISTBOX window class. Combo boxes are created from the COMBOBOX class.
2. Combo boxes have their own window style values that start with CBS_.
3. Combo boxes send WM_COMMAND messages in the same format as list boxes. The combo box notification codes start with CBN_, rather than the LBN_ notification codes for list boxes.
4. The messages sent to a combo box start with CB_, rather than LB_ messages sent to list boxes. The messages are otherwise similar.
5. Combo boxes have an extra object—an edit field at the top of the combo box. You normally will not deal with this edit field directly, although it is possible. (Windows includes specialized messages for manipulating the edit field. See Chapter 9 of *The Waite Group Windows API Bible* for more details on this subject.)

Listing 5-26 shows COMBO.C, which is similar to LISTBOX.C. The combo box window style is make up of four flags: WS_CHILD | CBS_SIMPLE | CBS_SORT | WS_VSCROLL. WS_CHILD makes the combo box a child of the program's window. The CBS_SIMPLE flag creates a combo box where the list box underneath is always visible. CBS_SORT keeps the contents of the list box sorted in ASCII order. The WS_VSCROLL adds a scroll bar to the right side of the list box. The list box underneath a combo box does not automatically generate a vertical scroll bar when there are more entries than can be shown.

Listing 5-26 COMBO.C

```c
/* combo.c   Creating combo controls */

#include <windows.h>
#include "combo.h"

int PASCAL WinMain (HANDLE hInstance, HANDLE hPrevInstance, LPSTR lpszCmdLine,
    int nCmdShow)
{
    HWND      hWnd ;         /* the window's "handle" */
    MSG       msg ;          /* a message structure */
    WNDCLASS  wndclass ;     /* window class structure */

    if (!hPrevInstance)
    {
        wndclass.style         = CS_HREDRAW | CS_VREDRAW ;
        wndclass.lpfnWndProc   = WndProc ;
        wndclass.cbClsExtra    = 0 ;
        wndclass.cbWndExtra    = 0 ;
        wndclass.hInstance     = hInstance ;
        wndclass.hIcon         = LoadIcon (hInstance, "MyIcon") ;
        wndclass.hCursor       = LoadCursor (NULL, IDC_ARROW) ;
        wndclass.hbrBackground = GetStockObject (WHITE_BRUSH) ;
        wndclass.lpszMenuName  = "MyMenu" ;
        wndclass.lpszClassName = "MyClass" ;
                    /* register the window class */
        if (!RegisterClass (&wndclass))
            return 0 ;
    }

    hWnd = CreateWindow ("MyClass", "Combo Box Example",
        WS_OVERLAPPEDWINDOW,
        CW_USEDEFAULT, CW_USEDEFAULT, CW_USEDEFAULT, CW_USEDEFAULT,
        NULL, NULL, hInstance, NULL) ;
    ShowWindow (hWnd, nCmdShow) ;   /* display the window */

    while (GetMessage (&msg, NULL, NULL, NULL))   /* message loop */
    {
        TranslateMessage (&msg) ;   /* translate keyboard messages */
        DispatchMessage (&msg) ;    /* send message to WndProc() */
    }
    return (msg.wParam) ;
}

long FAR PASCAL WndProc (HWND hWnd, WORD wMessage, WORD wParam, LONG lParam)
{
    static BOOL   bFirstTime = TRUE ;
    static HWND   hCombo ;
    HANDLE        hInstance ;
    int           nSel ;
    char          cBuf [256], cSelBuf [128] ;
```

```c
switch (wMessage)       /* process windows messages */
{
   case WM_CREATE:      /* program is just starting */
      if (bFirstTime) /* only do this once */
      {
         bFirstTime = FALSE ;
                /* get the instance handle */
         hInstance = GetWindowWord (hWnd, GWW_HINSTANCE) ;
                /* create combo box control */
         hCombo = CreateWindow ("COMBOBOX", "",
             WS_CHILD | CBS_SIMPLE | CBS_SORT | WS_VSCROLL,
             10, 10, 180, 80,
             hWnd, COMBO_ID, hInstance, NULL) ;
         ShowWindow (hCombo, SW_SHOWNORMAL) ;
      }
      break ;
   case WM_COMMAND:
      switch (wParam)          /* menu item or control ID's */
      {
         case COMBO_ID:  /* user did something to combo */
            if (HIWORD (lParam) == CBN_SELCHANGE)
            {             /* if user selected an item */
                          /* get number of selected item */
               nSel = (int) SendMessage (hCombo, CB_GETCURSEL,
                   0, 0L) ;
                          /* load sel. string into cSelBuf */
               SendMessage (hCombo, CB_GETLBTEXT, nSel,
                  (DWORD) (LPSTR) cSelBuf) ;
                          /* build a readable string */
               wsprintf (cBuf, "The selected item = %s.",
                  (LPSTR) cSelBuf) ;
                          /* show string in a message box */
               MessageBox (hWnd, cBuf, "Selection", MB_OK) ;
            }
                break ;
         case IDM_FILL:     /* fill combo with strings */
            SendMessage (hCombo, CB_RESETCONTENT, 0, 0L) ;
            SendMessage (hCombo, CB_ADDSTRING, 0,
               (DWORD) (LPSTR) "First string added.") ;
            SendMessage (hCombo, CB_ADDSTRING, 0,
               (DWORD) (LPSTR) "Second string added.") ;
            SendMessage (hCombo, CB_ADDSTRING, 0,
               (DWORD) (LPSTR) "Third string added.") ;
            SendMessage (hCombo, CB_ADDSTRING, 0,
               (DWORD) (LPSTR) "Another string added.") ;
            SendMessage (hCombo, CB_ADDSTRING, 0,
               (DWORD) (LPSTR) "Yet another string added.") ;
            SendMessage (hCombo, CB_ADDSTRING, 0,
               (DWORD) (LPSTR) "Last string added.") ;
                    /* start with first item selected */
            SendMessage (hCombo, CB_SETCURSEL, 0, 0L) ;
                break ;
         case IDM_QUIT:
            DestroyWindow (hWnd) ;  /* destroy window */
            break ;    /* terminating application */
      }
         break ;
   case WM_DESTROY:     /* stop application */
```

```
            PostQuitMessage (0) ;
            break ;
        default:        /* default windows message processing */
            return DefWindowProc (hWnd, wMessage, wParam, lParam) ;
    }
    return (0L) ;
}
```

Character strings are added to the combo box when the user selects the "Fill Combo Box" menu item. The strings are added by sending the CB_ADDSTRING message to the combo box control. In addition, the CB_SETCURSEL message is sent to the combo box after all the strings have been added to start the combo box with the first item selected. The selected item automatically shows up in the top edit control of the combo box. If another item is selected from the list box area, that item's string shows up in the combo box. Figure 5-10 shows the COMBO program after the user has selected the last item. Listings 5-27 to 5-31 show the support files for COMBO. The program's icon is shown in Figure 5-11.

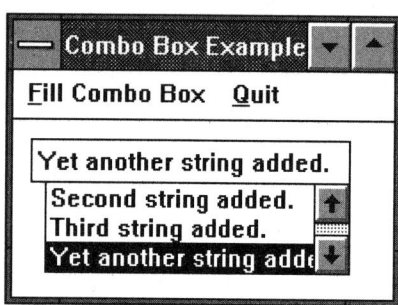

Figure 5-10 COMBO Program After the Last Item Was Selected

Listing 5-27 COMBO.H Header File

```
/* combo.h  header file */

#define IDM_FILL    1    /* menu items ID's */
#define IDM_QUIT    10

#define COMBO_ID    1000

long FAR PASCAL WndProc (HWND, WORD, WORD, LONG) ;
```

Listing 5-28 COMBO.RC Resource Script File

```
/* combo.rc  resource file */

#include "combo.h"

MyIcon      ICON      combo.ico

MyMenu      MENU
BEGIN
    MENUITEM "&Fill Combo Box", IDM_FILL
    MENUITEM "&Quit",           IDM_QUIT
END
```

Listing 5-29 COMBO.DEF Module Definition File

```
NAME        combo
EXETYPE     WINDOWS
STUB        'WINSTUB.EXE'
CODE        PRELOAD MOVEABLE
DATA        PRELOAD MOVEABLE MULTIPLE
HEAPSIZE    1024
STACKSIZE   5120
EXPORTS     WndProc
```

Figure 5-11
COMBO.ICO
Icon Image

Listing 5-30 Turbo C++ Project File Contents for COMBO

```
combo.c
combo.def
combo.res
```

Listing 5-31 QuickC Project File Contents for COMBO

```
combo.c
combo.def
combo.rc
```

If you want to have only the top edit control of the combo box normally visible, use the CBS_DROPDOWN or CBS_DROPDOWNLIST styles in place of CBS_SIMPLE. The list box will only be visible beneath the combo box edit area if the user clicks the button on the right side of the combo box control. This style saves space on the screen, and it is ideal for situations where the user needs to be reminded of the current selection, but does not change the selected item frequently.

Scroll Bars

There are two types of scroll bar controls in the Windows' interface. The most common type is attached to the edge of a parent window. These scroll bars are used to scroll the image in the window's client area. The second type of scroll bar is a stand-alone control. These controls are child window controls, and they are typically used to allow the user to enter an integer value by moving the scroll bar thumb (the thumb is the central button on the scroll bar that moves). We will look at two example programs, one for each type of scroll bar.

Both types of scroll bars send messages to the program when the user moves the scroll bar thumb. The messages sent are WM_HSCROLL if a horizontal scroll bar is being used, and WM_VSCROLL if a vertical scroll bar is being used. For both messages, the window handle of the scroll bar control will be in the high-order word of the

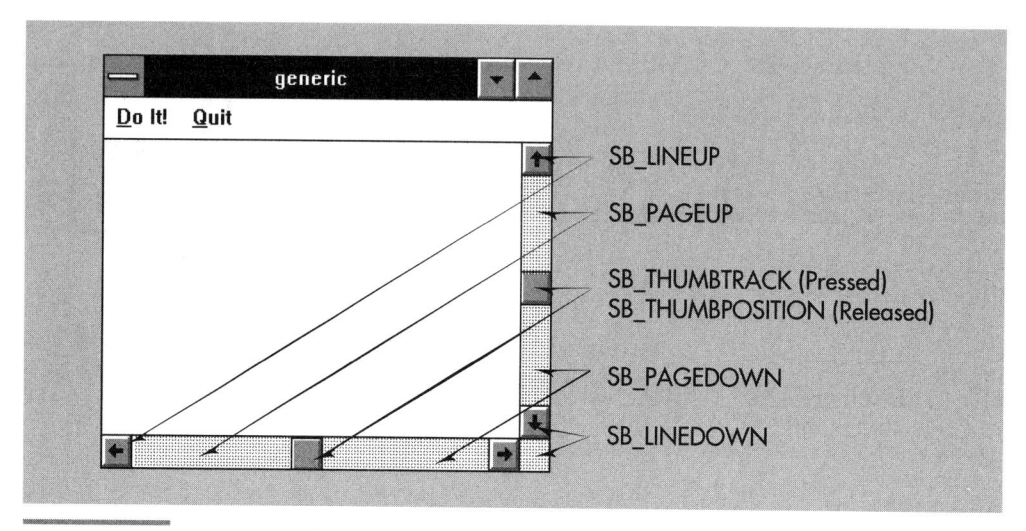

Figure 5-12 Scroll Bar Codes Transmitted as *wParam* with WM_HSCROLL and WM_VSCROLL Messages

lParam parameter passed with the message. The *wParam* parameter will contain a code number describing what action the user has taken. These code numbers are given names starting with "SB_" in WINDOWS.H. Figure 5-12 shows the codes that are transmitted when the user clicks different areas of the scroll bar. Note that names like "SB_LINEUP" are used with horizontal scroll bars, as well as vertical ones. Up is always to the left, and down is to the right.

When using the CreateWindow() function to create a scroll bar (using the SCROLLBAR window class), the *dwStyle* parameter passed to CreateWindow() can have any of the values shown in Table 5-9. The default alignment attaches scroll bars to the right side and bottom of a window, but the SBS_LEFTALIGN and SBS_TOPALIGN can be used with the SBS_VERT and SBS_HORZ styles to attach scroll bars to the top and left edges of a window if desired. For example, the combination SBS_LEFTALIGN | SBS_VERT would specify a vertical scroll bar on the left side of a window. The SBS_SIZEBOX is seldom used. This is a small box with four arrows that the user can grab with the mouse to size an object. Windows uses thick borders for these operations, so the sizebox style has become obsolete.

SBS_BOTTOMALIGN	A scroll bar control, aligned with the bottom edge of the rectangle specified by the *X*, *Y*, *nWidth*, and *nHeight* parameters used in calling CreateWindow() for the parent window. The default scroll bar height is used.
SBS_HORZ	A horizontal scroll bar control.

Windows Programming Primer Plus®

SBS_LEFTALIGN	A scroll bar control, aligned with the left edge of the rectangle specified by the *X, Y, nWidth,* and *nHeight* parameters used in calling CreateWindow() for the parent window. The default scroll bar width is used.
SBS_RIGHTALIGN	A scroll bar control, aligned with the right edge of the rectangle specified by the *X, Y, nWidth,* and *nHeight* parameters used in calling CreateWindow() for the parent window. The default scroll bar width is used.
SBS_SIZEBOX	A scroll bar size box control. This is a small box that allows sizing of a window from one location.
SBS_SIZEBOXBOTTOMRIGHTALIGN	Used with the SBS_SIZEBOX style. A size box control, aligned with the lower right edge of the rectangle specified by the *X, Y, nWidth,* and *nHeight* parameters used in calling CreateWindow() for the parent window. The default size box size is used.
SBS_SIZEBOXTOPLEFTALIGN	Used with the SBS_SIZEBOX style. A size box control, aligned with the top left edge of the rectangle specified by the *X, Y, nWidth,* and *nHeight* parameters used in calling CreateWindow() for the parent window. The default size box size is used.
SBS_TOPALIGN	Used with the SBS_HORZ style. Puts the scrollbar at the top of the parent window's client area.
SBS_VERT	A vertical scroll bar control.

Table 5-9 Scroll Bar Styles

A Windows program can move the scroll bar's thumb, change the range of values represented by the scroll bar, and determine its current position by using specialized Windows functions. Table 5-10 summarizes these functions.

FUNCTION	PURPOSE
GetScrollPos()	Retrieve the current position of the scroll bar's thumb.
GetScrollRange()	Retrieve the minimum and maximum value range of a scroll bar.
SetScrollPos()	Set the position of the scroll bar thumb.
SetScrollRange()	Set the minimum and maximum values of a scroll bar.
ShowScrollBar()	Display the scroll bar, optionally attaching it to the window's border.

Table 5-10 Scroll Bar Function Summary

To show how these functions are used, let's create a program with a single scroll bar control in the center of the client area. The scroll bar control will allow the user to enter an integer value within a range of zero to 50. Figure 5-13 shows the SCROLL1 program in operation. The integer value is displayed in a static control to the left of the scroll bar. The scroll bar is horizontal and is not attached to the window's frame. The scroll bar is a stand-alone child window control.

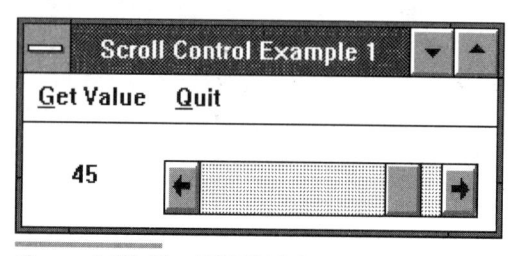

Figure 5-13 The SCROLL1 Program

Listing 5-32 shows the SCROLL1.C program. The scroll bar control and static control are both created when the program processes a WM_CREATE message on startup. The scroll bar is created as a child window (WS_CHILD style flag) from the predefined window class SCROLLBAR. This process is similar to creating a button or listbox control from their respective window classes. After the scroll bar is created, its upper and lower numeric ranges are set with the SetScrollRange() function. The constant MAXSCROLL is defined as being equal to 50 in SCROLL1.H. The scroll bar range is set from zero to 50. A static text control is also created to display the current value represented by the scroll bar. This small control is positioned to the left of the scroll bar control.

A static integer *nScrollPos* is used to keep track of the current scroll bar position. The *nScrollPos* variable is declared at the top of WndProc(). This variable must be declared "static," as we do not want the WndProc() function to "forget" the value of *nScrollPos* during periods where some other function is being called. The scroll bar is initially set in the middle of its range, an *nScrollPos* value of 25.

The interesting part of SCROLL1.C is the processing of the WM_HSCROLL message. This message is sent if the user clicks any part of the scroll bar with the mouse. The notification code passed in the *wParam* parameter sent with the WM_HSCROLL message specifies what part of the scroll bar was clicked. If the thumb was dragged to a new position, the SB_THUMBPOSITION code is sent in *wParam*. With the SB_THUMBPOSITION code, the current position of the thumb is sent as the low-order WORD of the *lParam* parameter passed with the WM_HSCROLL message. This makes it easy to set the new value for *nScrollPos* using the LOWORD() macro.

For the remaining codes sent with WM_HSCROLL, Windows does not encode the new thumb position in the *lParam* value. This is because Windows allows the program to specify how much to move the thumb for each of these codes. In SCROLL1.C we will move the thumb one unit for the SB_LINEDOWN and SB_LINEUP codes, and ten units for the SB_PAGEUP and SB_PAGEDOWN codes. As the program's code determines the amount of movement, it is also up to the program to make sure that the resultant value is within range. This is done separately for each of the SB_ codes in SCROLL1.C.

With the SB_LINEUP, SB_LINEDOWN, SB_PAGEUP, and SB_PAGEDOWN codes, the scroll bar thumb must be explicitly repositioned, using a call to the SetScrollPos()

function. This is done at the end of the message processing logic for the WM_HSCROLL message. The current *nScrollPos* value is also displayed in the static text control by calling the SetWindowText() function.

Listing 5-32 SCROLL1.C

```
/* scroll1.c   Creating a child window scroll bar control */

#include <windows.h>
#include "scroll1.h"

int PASCAL WinMain (HANDLE hInstance, HANDLE hPrevInstance, LPSTR lpszCmdLine,
    int nCmdShow)
{
    HWND        hWnd ;           /* the window's "handle" */
    MSG         msg ;            /* a message structure */
    WNDCLASS    wndclass ;       /* window class structure */

    if (!hPrevInstance)
    {
        wndclass.style          = CS_HREDRAW | CS_VREDRAW ;
        wndclass.lpfnWndProc    = WndProc ;
        wndclass.cbClsExtra     = 0 ;
        wndclass.cbWndExtra     = 0 ;
        wndclass.hInstance      = hInstance ;
        wndclass.hIcon          = LoadIcon (hInstance, "MyIcon") ;
        wndclass.hCursor        = LoadCursor (NULL, IDC_ARROW) ;
        wndclass.hbrBackground  = GetStockObject (WHITE_BRUSH) ;
        wndclass.lpszMenuName   = "MyMenu" ;
        wndclass.lpszClassName  = "MyClass" ;
                    /* register the window class */
        if (!RegisterClass (&wndclass))
            return 0 ;
    }

    hWnd = CreateWindow ("MyClass", "Scroll Control Example 1",
        WS_OVERLAPPEDWINDOW,
        CW_USEDEFAULT, CW_USEDEFAULT, CW_USEDEFAULT, CW_USEDEFAULT,
        NULL, NULL, hInstance, NULL) ;
    ShowWindow (hWnd, nCmdShow) ;   /* display the window */

    while (GetMessage (&msg, NULL, NULL, NULL))   /* message loop */
    {
        TranslateMessage (&msg) ;   /* translate keyboard messages */
        DispatchMessage (&msg) ;    /* send message to WndProc() */
    }
    return (msg.wParam) ;
}

long FAR PASCAL WndProc (HWND hWnd, WORD wMessage, WORD wParam, LONG lParam)
{
    static BOOL     bFirstTime = TRUE ;
    static HANDLE   hScroll, hStatic ;
    HANDLE          hInstance ;
```

```
        static int     nScrollPos ;
        char           cBuf [256], cStaticBuf [128] ;

        switch (wMessage)      /* process windows messages */
        {
           case WM_CREATE:    /* application just starting up */
              if (bFirstTime)            /* only do this once */
              {
                 bFirstTime = FALSE ;
                 hInstance = GetWindowWord (hWnd, GWW_HINSTANCE) ;
                    /* create the scroll bar control */
                 hScroll = CreateWindow ("SCROLLBAR", "",
                    WS_CHILD | WS_VISIBLE,
                    80, 20, 180, 30,
                    hWnd, SCROLL_ID, hInstance, NULL) ;
                    /* initialize scroll bar and display */
                 SetScrollRange (hScroll, SB_CTL, 0, MAXSCROLL, FALSE) ;
                 nScrollPos = MAXSCROLL / 2 ;
                 SetScrollPos (hScroll, SB_CTL, nScrollPos, FALSE) ;
                 ShowScrollBar (hScroll, SB_CTL, SW_SHOW) ;
                    /* create static control to display int value */
                 hStatic = CreateWindow ("STATIC", "",
                    WS_CHILD | SS_CENTER,
                    10, 20, 50, 40,
                    hWnd, STATIC_ID, hInstance, NULL) ;
                 wsprintf (cBuf, |%d", nScrollPos) ;
                 SetWindowText (hStatic, cBuf) ;
                 ShowWindow (hStatic, SW_SHOWNORMAL) ;
              }
              break ;
           case WM_HSCROLL:    /* scroll bar was activated */
              switch (wParam) /* check what part was pressed */
              {
                 case SB_THUMBPOSITION: /* user movded scroll thumb */
                    nScrollPos = LOWORD (lParam) ;
                    break ;
                 case SB_LINEDOWN:       /* user clicked bottom arrow */
                    nScrollPos++ ;
                    nScrollPos = nScrollPos > MAXSCROLL ? MAXSCROLL :
                       nScrollPos ;
                    break ;
                 case SB_LINEUP:         /* user clicked top arrow */
                    nScrollPos-- ;
                    nScrollPos = nScrollPos < 0 ? 0 : nScrollPos ;
                    break ;
                 case SB_PAGEDOWN:       /* user clicked bottom area */
                    nScrollPos += 10 ;
                    nScrollPos = nScrollPos > MAXSCROLL ? MAXSCROLL :
                       nScrollPos ;
                    break ;
                 case SB_PAGEUP:         /* user clicked upper area */
                    nScrollPos -= 10 ;
                    nScrollPos = nScrollPos < 0 ? 0 : nScrollPos ;
                    break ;
              }
                                  /* move thumb, change static text */
              SetScrollPos (hScroll, SB_CTL, nScrollPos, TRUE) ;
              wsprintf (cBuf, "%d", nScrollPos) ;
              SetWindowText (hStatic, cBuf) ;
```

```
            break ;
    case WM_COMMAND:              /* menu item or control selected */
        switch (wParam)
        {
           case IDM_GET:          /* show the static control's text */
               GetWindowText (hStatic, cStaticBuf, 128) ;
               wsprintf (cBuf, "The static control contains: %s.",
                   (LPSTR) cStaticBuf) ;
               MessageBox (hWnd, cBuf, "Message",
                   MB_ICONINFORMATION | MB_OK) ;
               break ;
           case IDM_QUIT:
               DestroyWindow (hWnd) ; /* destroy window, */
               break ;           /* terminating application */
        }
        break ;
    case WM_DESTROY:              /* stop application */
        PostQuitMessage (0) ;
        break ;
    default:                      /* default windows message processing */
        return DefWindowProc (hWnd, wMessage, wParam, lParam) ;
    }
    return (0L) ;
}
```

Listings 5-33 to 5-37 show the support files for SCROLL1. The program's icon is shown in Figure 5-14

Listing 5-33 SCROLL1.H Header File

```
/* scroll1.h header file */

#define IDM_GET     1    /* menu items */
#define IDM_QUIT    10

#define SCROLL_ID   1000   /* child window control ID's */
#define STATIC_ID   1001

#define MAXSCROLL   50

long FAR PASCAL WndProc (HWND, WORD, WORD, LONG) ;
```

Figure 5-14
SCROLL1.ICO Icon Image

Listing 5-34 SCROLL1.RC Resource Script File

```
/* scroll1.rc resource file */

#include "scroll1.h"

MyIcon ICON    scroll1.ico

MyMenu MENU
BEGIN
    MENUITEM "&Get Value"        IDM_GET
    MENUITEM "&Quit"             IDM_QUIT
END
```

Listing 5-35 SCROLL1.DEF Module Definition File

```
NAME            scroll1
EXETYPE         WINDOWS
STUB            'WINSTUB.EXE'
CODE            PRELOAD MOVEABLE
DATA            PRELOAD MOVEABLE MULTIPLE
HEAPSIZE        1024
STACKSIZE       5120
EXPORTS         WndProc
```

Listing 5-36 Turbo C++ Project File for SCROLL1

```
scroll1.c
scroll1.def
scroll1.res
```

Listing 5-37 QuickC Project File for SCROLL1

```
scroll1.c
scroll1.def
scroll1.rc
```

Scroll Bars Attached to a Window

The most common use of scroll bar controls is to scroll the central area of a main program window. Word processing programs frequently use both horizontal and vertical scroll bars on the edges of the window. The vertical scroll bar is used to move to new locations in the text. The horizontal scroll bar is used to move the far right edge of the text area into view.

The easy way to add scroll bars to the edge of a window is to add a scroll bar style to the window's style when calling CreateWindow. The WS_HSCROLL style adds a horizontal scroll bar, and the WS_VSCROLL style adds a vertical scroll bar. Here is a typical CreateWindow() call, creating a main program window with both vertical and horizontal scroll bars attached to the edges.

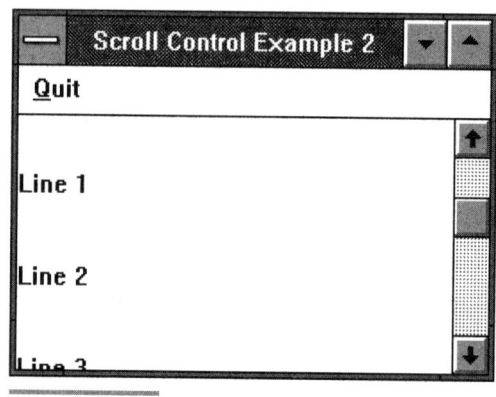

Figure 5-15 The SCROLL2 Program

```
hWnd = CreateWindow ("MyClass", "Window Caption",
        WS_OVERLAPPEDWINDOW | WS_VSCROLL | WS_HSCROLL,
        CW_USEDEFAULT, CW_USEDEFAULT, CW_USEDEFAULT, CW_USEDEFAULT,
        NULL, NULL, hInstance, NULL) ;
```

You can add and subtract attached scroll bars from the windows edge while the program is running with the ShowScrollBar() function. In most cases, the scroll bar will be attached at all times, so ShowScrollBar() is not needed.

Figure 5-15 shows the SCROLL2 program window. SCROLL2 writes three lines of text on the window's client area. The window has a vertical scroll bar, allowing the client area to be scrolled up and down. Figure 5-15 shows the window after the window's client area has been scrolled down to the point that the third line of text is partially obscured.

Listing 5-38 shows SCROLL2.C. The listing is similar to the previous example SCROLL1.C using a scroll bar control. The differences boil down to:

- The scroll bar is created by adding the WS_HSCROLL style to the CreateWindow() call for the main program window, rather than by creating a separate child window scroll bar control.
- The scroll bar's position is again stored in a static variable, *nScrollPos*. The position is used in positioning the text lines. The higher the *nScrollPos* value, the lower in the window's client area the text is painted. The painting logic is all in the WM_PAINT message processing section of SCROLL2.C.

Once the scroll bar is moved, the client area needs to be repainted so that the text lines show up in the new positions. To do this, we need to convince Windows to send the program a WM_PAINT message for repainting the entire client area. This is done by calling the InvalidateRect() function. InvalidateRect() "invalidates" the entire client area if the second parameter is set to NULL. Windows detects that the client area is invalid and sends a WM_PAINT message to the program. Windows also erases the client area by painting it again with the window's class brush. SCROLL2 gets the WM_PAINT message and paints the text lines at the new locations. The illusion is that the text lines moved down, but actually they were erased and redrawn in a new location.

Listing 5-38 SCROLL2.C

```
/* scroll2.c   scroll bar attached to a window */

#include <windows.h>
#include "scroll2.h"

int PASCAL WinMain (HANDLE hInstance, HANDLE hPrevInstance, LPSTR lpszCmdLine,
   int nCmdShow)
{
   HWND       hWnd ;           /* the window's "handle" */
   MSG        msg ;            /* a message structure */
   WNDCLASS   wndclass ;       /* window class structure */

   if (!hPrevInstance)
   {
      wndclass.style          = CS_HREDRAW | CS_VREDRAW ;
      wndclass.lpfnWndProc    = WndProc ;
      wndclass.cbClsExtra     = 0 ;
      wndclass.cbWndExtra     = 0 ;
      wndclass.hInstance      = hInstance ;
      wndclass.hIcon          = LoadIcon (hInstance, "MyIcon") ;
```

```c
        wndclass.hCursor        = LoadCursor (NULL, IDC_ARROW) ;
        wndclass.hbrBackground  = GetStockObject (WHITE_BRUSH) ;
        wndclass.lpszMenuName   = "MyMenu" ;
        wndclass.lpszClassName  = "MyClass" ;
                        /* register the window class */
        if (!RegisterClass (&wndclass))
            return 0 ;
    }

    hWnd = CreateWindow ("MyClass", "Scroll Control Example 2",
        WS_OVERLAPPEDWINDOW | WS_VSCROLL,
        CW_USEDEFAULT, CW_USEDEFAULT, CW_USEDEFAULT, CW_USEDEFAULT,
        NULL, NULL, hInstance, NULL) ;
    ShowWindow (hWnd, nCmdShow) ;      /* display the window */

    while (GetMessage (&msg, NULL, NULL, NULL))   /* message loop */
    {
        TranslateMessage (&msg) ;      /* translate keyboard messages */
        DispatchMessage (&msg) ;       /* send message to WndProc() */
    }
    return (msg.wParam) ;
}

long FAR PASCAL WndProc (HWND hWnd, WORD wMessage, WORD wParam, LONG lParam)
{
    static   int    nScrollPos = 0, nOldScroll = 0 ;
    HDC             hDC ;
    PAINTSTRUCT     ps ;

    switch (wMessage)                  /* process windows messages */
    {
      case WM_CREATE:
            SetScrollRange (hWnd, SB_VERT, 0, MAXSCROLL, FALSE) ;
            SetScrollPos (hWnd, SB_VERT, 0, TRUE) ;
            break ;
      case WM_VSCROLL:                 /* scroll bar was activated */
            switch (wParam)            /* check what part was pressed */
            {
              case SB_THUMBPOSITION:   /* user moved scroll thumb */
                  nScrollPos = LOWORD (lParam) ;
                  break ;
              case SB_LINEDOWN:        /* user clicked bottom arrow */
                  nScrollPos++ ;
                  nScrollPos = nScrollPos > MAXSCROLL ? MAXSCROLL :
                    nScrollPos ;
                  break ;
              case SB_LINEUP:          /* user clicked top arrow */
                  nScrollPos-- ;
                  nScrollPos = nScrollPos < 0 ? 0 : nScrollPos ;
                  break ;
              case SB_PAGEDOWN:        /* user clicked bottom area */
                  nScrollPos += 10 ;
                  nScrollPos = nScrollPos > MAXSCROLL ? MAXSCROLL :
                      nScrollPos ;
                  break ;
              case SB_PAGEUP:          /* user clicked upper area */
                  nScrollPos -= 10 ;
                  nScrollPos = nScrollPos < 0 ? 0 : nScrollPos ;
                  break ;
```

```
            }
            InvalidateRect (hWnd, NULL, TRUE) ; /* for WM_PAINT */
            nOldScroll = nScrollPos ;
                    /* move thumb, change static text */
            SetScrollPos (hWnd, SB_VERT, nScrollPos, TRUE) ;
            break ;
        case WM_PAINT:
            hDC = BeginPaint (hWnd, &ps) ;
            TextOut (hDC, 0, nScrollPos, "Line 1", 6) ;
            TextOut (hDC, 0, 50 + nScrollPos, "Line 2", 6) ;
            TextOut (hDC, 0, 100 + nScrollPos, "Line 3", 6) ;
            EndPaint (hWnd, &ps) ;
            break ;
        case WM_COMMAND:                        /* menu item selected */
            switch (wParam)
            {
                case IDM_QUIT:
                    DestroyWindow (hWnd) ;  /* destroy window, */
                    break ;                 /* terminating application */
            }
            break ;
        case WM_DESTROY:   /* stop application */
            PostQuitMessage (0) ;
            break ;
        default:       /* default windows message processing */
            return DefWindowProc (hWnd, wMessage, wParam, lParam) ;
    }
    return (0L) ;
}
```

Listings 5-39 to 5-43 show the support files for SCROLL2. The program's icon is shown in Figure 5-16.

Listing 5-39 SCROLL2.H Header File

```
/* scroll2.h header file */

#define IDM_QUIT    1

#define MAXSCROLL   100

long FAR PASCAL WndProc (HWND, WORD, WORD, LONG) ;
```

Figure 5-16
SCROLL2.ICO
Icon Image

Listing 5-40 SCROLL2.RC Resource Script File

```
/* scroll2.rc resource file */

#include "scroll2.h"

MyIcon      ICON    scroll2.ico

MyMenu      MENU
BEGIN
    MENUITEM "&Quit",       IDM_QUIT
END
```

Listing 5-41 SCROLL2.DEF Module Definition File

```
NAME       scroll2
EXETYPE    WINDOWS
STUB       'WINSTUB.EXE'
CODE       PRELOAD MOVEABLE
DATA       PRELOAD MOVEABLE MULTIPLE
HEAPSIZE   1024
STACKSIZE  5120
EXPORTS    WndProc
```

Listing 5-42 Turbo C++ Project File for SCROLL2.

```
scroll2.c
scroll2.def
scroll2.res
```

Listing 5-43 QuickC Project File for SCROLL2

```
scroll2.c
scroll2.def
scroll2.rc
```

Edit Controls

The last window control style we have to examine is the edit control. Edit controls can range from a small rectangle for entering a single word or number, up to a window that occupies the parent window's entire client area. Edit controls come with many word processing features built in. The key features are:

- When you type text, the edit control automatically recognizes the [Backspace] key to delete the previous character, the [Delete] key to delete the next character, and the arrow keys for movement inside the edit control. The current location in the edit control is marked by a small vertical line, called the "caret."

- Blocks of text can be marked for selection using the mouse. Marked blocks of text can be deleted and/or copied to the Clipboard for pasting somewhere else (including pasting the text into another application). Cut and paste operations are explained in Chapter 17, *The Clipboard*.

- Simply adding the scroll bar styles (WS_HSCROLL and WS_VSCROLL) during the CreateWindow() function call that creates the control will add the ability to scroll the text within the edit control. You do not need to code in the repainting logic as we did in the SCROLL2 example if all of the text is within an edit control.

This is enough functionality for most applications' text editing needs. Edit controls do not have the ability to format text with different fonts and character styles. Complete word processors generally create their own editing logic, painting the formatted text directly on the screen. Even if you are planning to add text formatting to your program, you may find that the edit control provides an excellent prototyping tool during the early stages of building a program.

When you create an edit control with the CreateWindow() function using the EDIT window class, the *dwStyle* parameter passed to CreateWindow() can have any of the values shown in Table 5-11. Unless the ES_MULTILINE style is included, the edit control will only have a single line of text. Multiline edit controls are usually combined with scroll bar controls, as we will see in the example.

ES_AUTOHSCROLL	Edit control with automatic horizontal scrolling if the text will not fit within the edit box.
ES_AUTOVSCROLL	Automatic vertical scrolling for an edit control. Used with ES_MULTILINE.
ES_CENTER	Text is centered within the edit control.
ES_LEFT	Text is left aligned within the edit control.
ES_LOWERCASE	All characters within the edit control are converted to lowercase as they are entered.
ES_MULTILINE	Allows multiple lines of input within an edit control. This type of control provides basic text processing functions.
ES_NOHIDESEL	Edit control where the text is left unchanged when the control loses the input focus.
ES_OEMCONVERT	Edit control text is converted to OEM character set and then back to ANSI. Useful for file names.
ES_PASSWORD	Displays letters as "*" characters as the letters are typed in. The actual letters typed are stored by the edit control.
ES_READONLY	The edit text can be viewed, but not changed by the user.
ES_RIGHT	Right aligned letters within the edit control.
ES_UPPERCASE	All characters within the edit control are converted to uppercase as they are entered.

Table 5-11 Edit Control Styles

To explore edit controls, we will create a small example called EDIT1. Figure 5-17 shows EDIT1 in action, after the user has typed in a few lines of text. The edit control has a vertical scroll bar, but not a horizontal one. The text automatically wraps words to form new lines if the last word will not fit on a line. When the user selects the "Get Text" menu item, the text inside the edit control is displayed in the parent window's client area, below the edit control.

Listing 5-44 shows the listing of EDIT1.C, which demonstrates creating and using a multiline edit control. As with the other control styles, edit controls are created using the CreateWindow() function using a predefined control class: EDIT. The specific attributes of the control are specified using window style flags in the CreateWindow() function call. In the case of EDIT1.C, the edit control's style flags are:

WS_CHILD | ES_MULTILINE | WS_VSCROLL | WS_VISIBLE | ES_AUTOVSCROLL | WS_BORDER,

Those flags add up to a child window control that has multiple lines and a vertical scroll bar attached to the right side, that is created visible, that automatically scrolls vertically when text exceeds the limits of the edit control's size, and that has a visible border. Note in Listing 5-44 that the edit control was not given a title string (null string "") for the second parameter in CreateWindow(). If a title string is added, this text will be visible inside the edit control when it is created. In EDIT1, we want an empty edit control to begin with, so the null string is used as a place holder for the second parameter.

Once the edit control is created, the program communicates with it by sending and receiving messages. To understand how these messages work, you need to know how edit controls store the text you type. Basically, all of the text is stored as one long character string. If you type in a carriage return to end a line, the string will contain the CR LF character pair (0x0D, 0x0A hexadecimal). If the line wraps because the next word will not fit on the same line, the edit control will insert the characters CR CR LF (0x0D, 0x0D, 0x0A hexadecimal). You will not find a null character until the end of the last line's text.

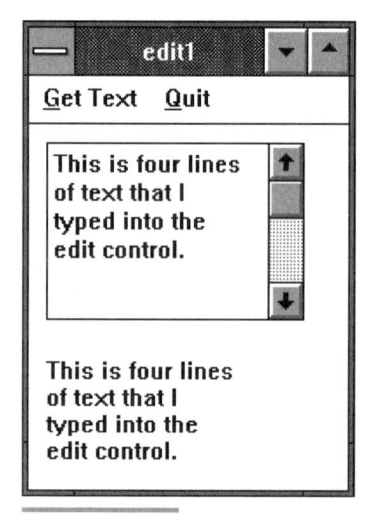

Figure 5-17 EDIT1 Program After Text Input by User

The lack of null characters to mark the end of the lines makes getting the edit control's contents a bit tricky. The easiest way to get the complete text string is to extract each line separately. To do this, you will send the edit control several messages. EM_GETLINECOUNT is sent to determine the total number of lines of text in the control. EM_LINEINDEX is sent to determine the character position (number of bytes from the start of the memory area that contains all of the lines in the edit control) for the start of a given line. EM_LINELENGTH is sent to determine the length of one line of text. EM_GETLINE is sent to copy one line of text into a text buffer.

In EDIT1.C, the text in the edit control is extracted if the "Get Text" menu item is selected. Selecting that menu item generates a WM_COMMAND message with *wParam* set equal to the menu item's ID value, IDM_GET. If you look in the WndProc() function of EDIT1.C, you will see the logic of extracting each line of text from the edit control so that it can be displayed below the edit control using the TextOut() function.

Listing 5-44 EDIT1.C

```
/* edit1.c   demonstrate edit control */

#include <windows.h>
#include "edit1.h"
```

```
int PASCAL WinMain (HANDLE hInstance, HANDLE hPrevInstance, LPSTR lpszCmdLine,
   int nCmdShow)
{
   HWND        hWnd ;                /* a handle to a message */
   MSG         msg ;                 /* a message */
   WNDCLASS    wndclass ;            /* the window class */

   if (!hPrevInstance)
   {
      wndclass.style           = CS_HREDRAW | CS_VREDRAW ;
      wndclass.lpfnWndProc     = WndProc ;
      wndclass.cbClsExtra      = 0 ;
      wndclass.cbWndExtra      = 0 ;
      wndclass.hInstance       = hInstance ;
      wndclass.hIcon           = LoadIcon (hInstance, "MyIcon") ;
      wndclass.hCursor         = LoadCursor (NULL, IDC_ARROW) ;
      wndclass.hbrBackground   = GetStockObject (WHITE_BRUSH) ;
      wndclass.lpszMenuName    = "MyMenu" ;
      wndclass.lpszClassName   = "edit1" ;
                  /* register the window class */
      if (!RegisterClass (&wndclass))
          return FALSE ;
   }

   hWnd = CreateWindow ("edit1", "Edit 1", WS_OVERLAPPEDWINDOW,
     CW_USEDEFAULT, CW_USEDEFAULT, CW_USEDEFAULT, CW_USEDEFAULT,
     NULL, NULL, hInstance, NULL) ;

   ShowWindow (hWnd, nCmdShow) ;
   UpdateWindow (hWnd) ;

   while (GetMessage (&msg, NULL, NULL, NULL))     /* the message loop */
   {
     TranslateMessage (&msg) ;
     DispatchMessage (&msg) ;
   }
   return (msg.wParam) ;
}

long FAR PASCAL WndProc (HWND hWnd, WORD wMessage, WORD wParam, LONG lParam)
{
   static   HWND    hEdit ;
   static   BOOL    bFirstTime = TRUE ;
   HANDLE           hInstance ;
   char             cBuf [256] ;
   int              i, nLines, nLineIndex, nLineLong ;
   HDC              hDC ;

   switch (wMessage)           /* process windows messages */
   {
      case WM_CREATE:          /* make edit control here */
          if (bFirstTime)      /* only do this once - avoids infinite loop */
          {
              hInstance = GetWindowWord (hWnd, GWW_HINSTANCE) ;
              hEdit = CreateWindow ("EDIT", "",
                  WS_CHILD | ES_MULTILINE | WS_VSCROLL | WS_VISIBLE |
                  ES_AUTOVSCROLL | WS_BORDER,
                  10, 10, 150, 100, hWnd, 100, hInstance, NULL) ;
```

```
                    bFirstTime = FALSE ;
                }
                break ;
        case WM_COMMAND:            /* menu item or control selected */
            switch (wParam)
            {
                case IDM_GET:    /* show the edit control's text */
                                 /* find out the number of lines */
                    nLines = (int) SendMessage (hEdit, EM_GETLINECOUNT, 0, 0L) ;
                    hDC = GetDC (hWnd) ;
                    for (i = 0 ; i < nLines ; i++)  /* for each line */
                    {
                                    /* copy line of text to cBuf[] */
                        SendMessage (hEdit, EM_GETLINE, i,
                            (DWORD) (LPSTR) cBuf) ;
                                    /* get the char pos of start of line */
                        nLineIndex = (int) SendMessage (hEdit, EM_LINEINDEX,
                            i, 0L);
                                    /* get the length of the line */
                        nLineLong = (int) SendMessage (hEdit, EM_LINELENGTH,
                            nLineIndex, 0L) ;
                                    /* display the line below edit cntl */
                        TextOut (hDC, 10, 130 + (15 * i), cBuf,
                            nLineLong) ;
                    }
                    ReleaseDC (hWnd, hDC) ;
                    break ;
                case IDM_QUIT:
                    DestroyWindow (hWnd) ;   /* destroy window, */
                    break ;                  /* terminating application */
            }
            break ;
        case WM_DESTROY:    /* stop application */
            PostQuitMessage (0) ;
            break ;
        default:            /* default windows message processing */
            return DefWindowProc (hWnd, wMessage, wParam, lParam) ;
    }
    return (0L) ;
}
```

Listings 5-45 to 5-49 show the support files for EDIT1. The program's icon is shown in Figure 5-18.

Listing 5-45 EDIT1.H Header File

```
/* edit1.h */

#define IDM_GET    1    /* menu item ID values */
#define IDM_QUIT   10

long FAR PASCAL WndProc (HWND, WORD, WORD, LONG) ;
```

Listing 5-46 EDIT1.RC Resource Script File

```
/* edit1.rc */

#include "edit1.h"

MyIcon      ICON    edit1.ico

MyMenu      MENU
BEGIN
    MENUITEM "&Get Text",       IDM_GET
    MENUITEM "&Quit",           IDM_QUIT
END
```

Figure 5-18
EDIT1.ICO
Icon Image

Listing 5-47 EDIT1.DEF Module Definition File

```
NAME            edit1
DESCRIPTION     'edit1 windows program'
EXETYPE         WINDOWS
STUB            'WINSTUB.EXE'
CODE            PRELOAD MOVEABLE
DATA            PRELOAD MOVEABLE MULTIPLE
HEAPSIZE        1024
STACKSIZE       5120
EXPORTS         WndProc
```

Listing 5-48 Turbo C++ Project File for EDIT1

```
edit1.c
edit1.def
edit1.res
```

Listing 5-49 QuickC Project File for EDIT1

```
edit1.c
edit1.def
edit1.rc
```

EDIT1.C does not process WM_COMMAND messages from the edit control. Edit controls tend to be self-contained units, unlike the processing necessary for controls such as scroll bars. In most applications, you will just extract the text from the edit control using the messages demonstrated in EDIT1.C, and you do not need to bother with notification codes sent with WM_COMMAND messages generated when the user selects the edit control.

Summary

Windows comes equipped with six predefined windows classes for common objects: static controls, buttons, list boxes, combo boxes, scroll bars, and edit controls. These objects are called "window controls." Because the window classes for these objects are always defined, you do not have to create the class with RegisterClass() prior to creating a control using CreateWindow().

All six of the controls are types of windows. The Windows environment will automatically repaint the control if it is covered up and later uncovered. Controls are almost always created as child windows, using the WS_CHILD style when calling the CreateWindow() function. Child windows are attached to their parents, and they are only visible if the parent window is visible on the screen. Child window controls always have an ID number, which is set when the control is created, using the *hMenu* parameter passed to CreateWindow(). The ID number is important, as it will end up being sent as the *wParam* value with any WM_COMMAND message from the control. Your program will determine which control was activated by examining the ID values.

Static controls are used for displaying text, icons, and rectangles. Normally, static text is used for titles and fixed character data that does not change as the program runs. The text in a static text control can be changed while the program runs by sending the control a WM_SETTEXT message, or by calling the SetWindowText() function.

Button controls can take a variety of shapes, including push buttons, radio buttons, check boxes, and group boxes. Managing button controls requires that the notification codes passed with the WM_COMMAND message be processed within your program.

List boxes and combo boxes are similar. Both display a list of items, allowing the user to make selections. Items are added and subtracted from the list by sending the control messages. WM_COMMAND messages from the control are also processed to determine when the user has selected an item from the list.

Scroll bar controls are unique in that they can be either stand-alone controls or attached to the parent window's border by creating the parent with the WS_VSCROLL and/or WS_HSCROLL style. Scroll bar controls generate either WM_VSCROLL or WM_HSCROLL messages, depending on whether the control is a vertical or horizontal scroll bar. The data passed in the *wParam* and *lParam* parameters sent with the WM_VSCROLL and WM_HSCROLL messages is used to determine what action the user took with the scroll bar control.

Edit controls are the most sophisticated of the control styles. Edit controls can be thought of as miniature word processor windows. All of the basic logic for entering and editing text is built into the control. Edit controls can be either a single line, or multiline, and can have scroll bars attached. Determining what text is inside of the control requires using several windows messages and is generally done by extracting each line of text separately.

QUESTIONS

1. BUTTON, LISTBOX, and EDIT are all examples of predefined window _____.
2. In creating a button control, the *lpWindowName* parameter passed to CreateWindow() specifies what aspect of the button control's appearance?
3. For all types of controls, the control's ID value is passed as the _____ parameter passed to the CreateWindow() function. When the user selects a control with the mouse, Windows sends a _____ message to the program, with the control's ID value as the _____ value passed with the message.
4. Attaching a scroll bar to the program's main window will automatically allow scrolling of the program's window client area. (True/False).
5. In creating child window controls, the *X, Y* locations passed to CreateWindow() are relative to the upper left corner of the parent window, not relative to the upper left corner of the screen. (True/False).
6. If you click the left arrow on a horizontal scroll bar, the _____ message is sent. a) SB_LINEDOWN; b) SB_LINEUP; c) WM_HSCROLL; d) None of the above.
7. If there is more than one vertical scroll bar control, how would you determine which resulted in a WM_VSCROLL message?
8. If the user normally will make a selection from a list, which type of control is preferable, a list box or a combo box?
9. What window style would you use to color a part of the parent window's client area black? (Hint: More than one style must be combined.)
10. What window style would you use to create a radio button with the text on the right side?

EXERCISES

1. Modify the BUTTON1.C program with the following changes:
    - Use the IDC_CROSS stock cursor shape for the parent window's class definition in WinMain().
    - Use the LTGRAY_BRUSH stock brush for the parent window's class definition in WinMain().
    - Left justify the text in the radio buttons and check box by adding the BS_LEFTTEXT style to their respective CreateWindow() function calls.

   What do you notice about the background color of the controls? What happens to the cursor shape as it passes over controls and the parent window background? Can you explain?

2. Modify the EDIT1.C program so that the edit control takes up the entire client area of the parent window. (Hint: You will need to process the WM_SIZE message and use the MoveWindow() function to resize the edit control every time the parent's size is changed.)

ANSWERS TO QUESTIONS

1. Classes.
2. The *lpWindowName* specifies the text string that appears in the center of the button control's client area.
3. *hMenu*, WM_COMMAND, *wParam*.
4. False. You must add the scrolling logic to the program.
5. True.
6. C.
7. The high-order word of the *lParam* value sent with the WM_VSCROLL message contains the scroll bar's window handle.
8. A list box is preferable, as the list is always visible. This saves the user the step of selecting the combo box to make the list box visible. A CBS_SIMPLE combo box is also a possibility, as the list box is always visible with this style.
9. WS_CHILD | SS_BLACKRECT.
10. WS_CHILD | BS_RADIOBUTTON.

SOLUTIONS TO EXERCISES

1. The changes to the parent window's class definition are as follows:

```
wndclass.hCursor        = LoadCursor (NULL, IDC_CROSS) ;
wndclass.hbrBackground  = GetStockObject (LTGRAY_BRUSH) ;
```

The CreateWindow() function calls for the radio buttons and check box become:

```
hRad1 = CreateWindow ("BUTTON", "Radio &1",
    WS_CHILD | BS_RADIOBUTTON | BS_LEFTTEXT,
    20, 40, 80, 20,
    hWnd, RADIO1, hInstance, NULL) ;
hRad2 = CreateWindow ("BUTTON", "Radio &2",
    WS_CHILD | BS_RADIOBUTTON | BS_LEFTTEXT,
    20, 70, 80, 20,
    hWnd, RADIO2, hInstance, NULL) ;
hCheck = CreateWindow ("BUTTON", "&Check Box",
    WS_CHILD | BS_AUTO3STATE | BS_LEFTTEXT,
    20, 120, 100, 20,
    hWnd, CHECK_BOX, hInstance, NULL) ;
```

Changing the parent window's background brush color causes the parent window's client area to be painted gray. As shown in Figure 5-19, the areas covered by the button controls are not affected because the buttons are based on the predefined BUTTON window class, not the parent's class definition. This means that the background of the text in the radio buttons, check box, and group box are painted with a white brush.

SOLUTIONS TO EXERCISES (cont'd)

The cursor shape will be a cross when the cursor is over the parent window's client area. The cross will change back to the normal arrow shape when the cursor moves over any of the button controls. This is because the controls are based on the BUTTON class, not the parent window's class. The button class defines the cursor shape to be an arrow.

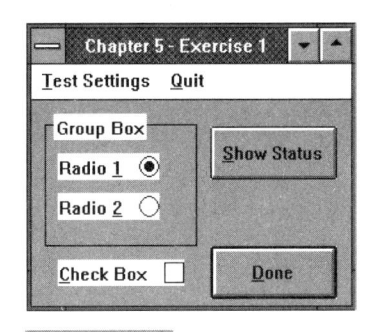

Figure 5-19 Solution to Exercise 5-1

2. The key to having the edit control exactly fit into the center of the parent window's client area is to process the WM_SIZE message. The *lParam* value sent with the WM_SIZE message encodes the X and Y dimensions of the parent window's client area as the low-order and high-order words, respectively. (The WM_SIZE message was discussed in Chapter 4, *Text and Graphics Output*.) These values are then passed to the MoveWindow() function, which "moves" the edit control to fit into the client area of the parent. The upper left corner of the editcontrol is "moved" to the 0,0 point (upper left corner) of the parent's client area. The horizontal and vertical size of the edit control are set to match the size of the parent's client area. These changes are shown in Listing 5-50.

Listing 5-50 Changes to EDIT1.C to Have the Edit Control Exactly Fill the Parent Window's Client Area

```
int    nXSize, nYSize ;

switch (wMessage)           /* process windows messages */
{
    case WM_CREATE:         /* make edit control here */
        if (bFirstTime)     /* only do this once - avoids infinite loop */
        {
            hInstance = GetWindowWord (hWnd, GWW_HINSTANCE) ;
                            /* create edit control, size not important */
            hEdit = CreateWindow ("EDIT", "",
                WS_CHILD | ES_MULTILINE | WS_VSCROLL | WS_VISIBLE |
                ES_AUTOVSCROLL | WS_BORDER,
                0, 0, 1, 1, hWnd, 100, hInstance, NULL) ;
            bFirstTime = FALSE ;
        }
        break ;
    case WM_SIZE:           /* fit edit control to parent's client area */
        nXSize = LOWORD (lParam) ;
        nYSize = HIWORD (lParam) ;
        MoveWindow (hEdit, 0, 0, nXSize, nYSize, TRUE) ;
        break ;
```

SOLUTIONS TO EXERCISES (cont'd)

The results of these changes are shown in Figure 5-20. The beauty of using the WM_SIZE message to resize the edit control is that it will be resized automatically anytime that the parent window's size changes. An interesting side effect of this exercise can be noticed if you select the "Get Text" menu item. The program extracts the text from the edit control and displays it on the parent window's client area. The parent window's client area is now completely covered by the edit control. The text still ends up visible, as the edit control's client area is transparent. Text painted on the underlying client area ends up "showing through" the edit control.

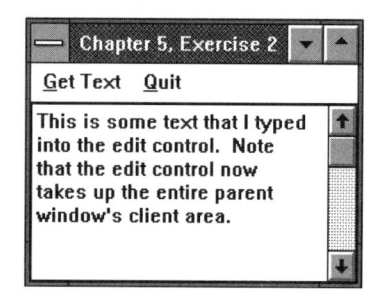

Figure 5-20 Solution to Exercise 5-2

Windows Programming Primer Plus®

CHAPTER 6

Taming the Mouse

If you have been programming under MS-DOS or a mainframe computer system, you may not have had to support a mouse in your programs. Getting away without supporting a mouse is not possible under Windows. Although it is possible to *use* Windows applications without the mouse, as a programmer you must support mouse operations when you create new Windows applications.

Every example program so far has used the mouse to some extent. Even the lowly MINIMAL1 program introduced in Chapters 2 and 3 responded to being touched by the mouse cursor by vanishing from the screen. All of the programs with menu items and child window controls have responded to mouse selections. They are examples of Window's built-in support for the mouse. In most cases, you do not have to do anything special to support the mouse as a pointing device. Mouse support is built into many Windows objects.

There are a few situations where your program will need to deal more directly with the mouse. Examples include painting programs where you will use the mouse to position lines and objects on the screen, and word processing programs that use the mouse to position the input point. In these situations, you will need to determine where the mouse cursor is located, and when the user depresses and releases the mouse buttons. You may also find it useful to change the mouse cursor's shape from the normal arrow to something more appropriate for the task, such as a pen or brush.

Closely tied to the mouse cursor is the caret. Carets are normally thin vertical lines used to show a position in an edit control or in the window's client area. Word processors use the caret to show the location at which the next character will appear. The last example in this chapter explores using the caret with an application that also changes the cursor shape.

Concepts Covered

Mouse Messages
Client Coordinates
Screen Coordinates
Binary Flags
Focus Window

Cursor Hot Spot
Nonclient Mouse Messages
Stock Cursors
Popup Menus

Keywords Covered

CS_DBLCLKS
CURSOR

POPUP

Functions Covered

SetCapture()
ReleaseCapture()
GetSystemMetrics()
LoadCursor()
SetCursor()

CreateCaret()
DestroyCaret()
ShowCaret()
HideCaret()
SetCaretPos()

Messages Covered

WM_MOUSEMOVE
WM_LBUTTONDOWN
WM_RBUTTONDOWN
WM_SETFOCUS

WM_KILLFOCUS
WM_NCMOUSEMOVE
WM_SETCURSOR

The WM_MOUSEMOVE Message

When you use the mouse, Windows automatically moves the mouse cursor on the screen. The updating of the cursor position on the screen is done by low-level logic within Windows, and it is something that you will not need to concern yourself with when programming. To keep programs informed as to the location of the mouse cursor, Windows sends WM_MOUSEMOVE messages as the mouse moves. The WM_MOUSEMOVE messages are sent to the program whose window is under the mouse cursor, not to every running application at once. The *lParam* data passed with WM_MOUSEMOVE contains the mouse cursor's position in the client area. The low-order word contains the *X* position, and the high-order word contains the *Y* position. You will find the HIWORD() and LOWORD() macros defined in WINDOWS.H useful to extract the *X* and *Y* positions. Listing 6-1 shows a typical code fragment from a WndProc() function processing WM_MOUSEMOVE messages.

Listing 6-1

```
long FAR PASCAL WndProc (HWND hWnd, WORD wMessage, WORD wParam, LONG lParam)
{
    int nXpos, nYpos ;

    switch (wMessage)                    /* process windows messages */
    {
        case WM_MOUSEMOVE:               /* mouse movement in client area */
            nXpos = LOWORD (lParam) ;    /* X position */
            nYpos = HIWORD (lParam) ;    /* Y position */
```
[Other program lines]

Both the *X* and *Y* positions passed with the WM_MOUSEMOVE message use "client coordinates." They represent the position of the mouse relative to the upper left corner of the program window's client area. Client coordinates are different from screen coordinates, which are relative to the upper left corner of the screen. Figure 6-1 shows a diagram of the two sets of units. Note that *Y* values increase downward in both systems of units.

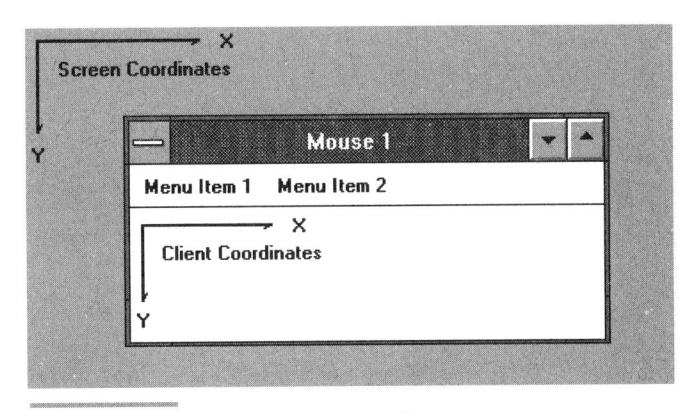

Figure 6-1 Client and Screen Coordinates

Notification Codes with WM_MOUSEMOVE

The *wParam* value that is passed with the WM_MOUSEMOVE message is used to indicate whether one of the mouse buttons, the (Shift) key, or the (Control) key was depressed when the WM_MOUSEMOVE message was sent. Some applications use combinations of the (Shift) or (Control) key and the mouse to allow selections of multiple items, or to perform special drawing functions. You can determine what combination of keys and buttons were depressed by comparing the *wParam* value sent with WM_MOUSEMOVE to the mouse notification codes defined in WINDOWS.H. Table 6-1 summarizes the mouse notification codes.

BINARY NOTIFICATION FLAG	MEANING
MK_CONTROL	The (Control) key was down when the message was sent.
MK_LBUTTON	The left mouse button was down when the message was sent.
MK_MBUTTON	The center mouse button was down when the message was sent.
MK_RBUTTON	The right mouse button was down when the message was sent.
MK_SHIFT	The (Shift) key was down when the message was sent.

Table 6-1 Mouse Notification Codes—Combined to Form *wParam* Value

A typical WinProc() example of processing WM_MOUSEMOVE messages, which checks the notification codes in *wParam*, is shown in Listing 6-2.

Listing 6-2 Processing the *wParam* Flags Sent with WM_MOUSEMOVE

```
long FAR PASCAL WndProc (HWND hWnd, WORD wMessage, WORD wParam, LONG lParam)
{
    int nXpos, nYpos ;

    switch (wMessage)                      /* process windows messages */
    {
        case WM_MOUSEMOVE:                 /* mouse movement in client area */
            nXpos = LOWORD (lParam) ;      /* X position */
            nYpos = HIWORD (lParam) ;      /* Y position */
            if (wParam & MK_SHIFT)
                /* shift key was down */
            else if (wParam & MK_CONTROL)
                /* control key was down */
```
[Other program lines]

Note that the MK values shown in Table 6-1 are binary flags, so more than one of these values can be set at one time. You need to combine the *wParam* value with a flag using the C language binary AND operator (&) to find out if a particular flag was set. For example, if both the (Shift) key and (Control) key were depressed at the time the WM_MOUSEMOVE message was sent, the *wParam* value would be as follows:

	Hexadecimal Value (From WINDOWS.H)	**Binary Value**
MK_SHIFT	0x04	00000100
MK_CONTROL	0x08	00001000
Combined	0x0C	00001100

Because the binary flags are combined to make the *wParam* value, you cannot use simple code like:

```
case WM_MOUSEMOVE:
     if (wParam == MK_SHIFT)                    /* wrong!!! */
```

This would be true only if the shift key was depressed by itself, not the shift key plus another key or button. To find out if the shift key was depressed, independent of any other key or button, combine the *wParam* value with the flag value for the condition you are testing, using the AND operator (&). Here is an example:

```
case WM_MOUSEMOVE:
     if (wParam & MK_SHIFT)                     /* correct */
          /* shift key was depressed */
     if (wParam & MK_CONTROL)                   /* correct */
          /* control key was depressed */
```

Using a binary flag and the C language AND operator (&) is sometimes called using a "mask" because combining the *wParam* value with the flag eliminates any bits that do not match the flag. This is like using masking tape to cover up (mask) the areas that you do not want painted before turning on the paint sprayer. Here is an example of what happens at the binary level if the *wParam* value sent with WM_MOUSEMOVE reflects both the Shift and Control keys being depressed, and the program compares the *wParam* value with the MK_SHIFT flag.

	Hexadecimal Value (From WINDOWS.H)	Binary Value
wParam value sent	0x0C	00001100
MK_SHIFT	0x04	00000100
Combined With &	0x04	00000100

In this case, (*wParam* & MK_SHIFT) will be TRUE (nonzero), so the shift key was depressed when the WM_MOUSEMOVE message was sent.

Mouse Button Messages

Although the *wParam* values sent with the WM_MOUSEMOVE message will be encoded if one of the mouse buttons was depressed, this information is normally not used. Windows sends additional specific messages when a mouse button is depressed or released. Table 6-2 shows the messages that the program will receive if a mouse button is depressed and released over the client area of a program. (Remember that the client area is the central portion of the program's window, excluding the borders, menu bar, and caption bar.) The mouse button messages also pass the client coordinates of the mouse cursor as the *lParam* value, just as with WM_MOUSEMOVE. These messages use the same binary flags listed in Table 6-2 in *wParam* to pass if one of the other mouse buttons, the Shift key, or the Control key was depressed when the message was sent.

	BUTTON DEPRESSED	BUTTON RELEASED
Left Mouse Button	WM_LBUTTONDOWN	WM_LBUTTONUP
Center Mouse Button	WM_MBUTTONDOWN	WM_MBUTTONUP
Right Mouse Button	WM_RBUTTONDOWN	WM_RBUTTONUP

Table 6-2 Client Area Mouse Button Messages

Windows does not provide a means of determining if the user is using a one-, two-, or three-button mouse. Most programs assume the conservative case, and only use the left mouse button. This means that you will usually only deal with two of the button messages, WM_LBUTTONDOWN and WM_LBUTTONUP.

If the program's main window that receives the messages was created with a window class style containing the CS_DBLCLKS style, Windows will also send double-click messages if the user clicks a mouse button twice rapidly. The CS_DBLCLKS style parameter is added to the class data before calling RegisterClass(). Listing 6-3 shows an excerpt from a WinMain() function, registering a window class called "MyClass" that contains the CS_DBLCLKS style.

Listing 6-3 Adding the CS_DBLCLKS Style to a Window Class Definition

```
WNDCLASS wndclass ;

wndclass.style             = CS_HREDRAW | CS_VREDRAW | CS_DBLCLKS ;
wndclass.lpfnWndProc       = WndProc ;
wndclass.cbClsExtra        = 0 ;
wndclass.cbWndExtra        = 0 ;
wndclass.hInstance         = hInstance ;
wndclass.hIcon             = LoadIcon (hInstance, "MyIcon") ;
wndclass.hCursor           = LoadCursor (NULL, IDC_ARROW) ;
wndclass.hbrBackground     = GetStockObject (WHITE_BRUSH) ;
wndclass.lpszMenuName      = "MyMenu" ;
wndclass.lpszClassName     = "MyClass" ;
              /* register the window class */
if (!RegisterClass (&wndclass))
    return 0 ;
```

Windows created from window classes that do not use the CS_DBLCLKS style will not receive these messages. Table 6-3 summarizes the double-click messages. You cannot double-click the mouse without first single clicking it, so double-click messages are always preceded by an UP and DOWN message for the same button.

	BUTTON DOUBLE CLICKED
Left Mouse Button	WM_LBUTTONDBLCLK
Center Mouse Button	WM_MBUTTONDBLCLK
Right Mouse Button	WM_RBUTTONDBLCLK

Table 6-3 Client Area Mouse Double-Click Messages

As with the other mouse messages, the mouse cursor location when the double-click message was sent is encoded in the *lParam* value. The low-order word contains the X position, and the high-order word contains the Y position. Client coordinates are used. The *wParam* value encodes the binary flags shown in Table 6-1 for the combination of other mouse buttons, (Shift) and (Control) keys that were depressed when the message was sent.

The MOUSE1 Program

With the preliminaries out of the way, it's time to look at some working code. The MOUSE1 program is designed to give you a feel for how rapidly the WM_MOUSEMOVE messages are sent from Windows and to let you practice using this and the button messages. Figure 6-2 shows MOUSE1 in action. If the "Show Mouse Tracks" menu item is selected, the mouse cursor will leave behind a small line on the window's client area every time a WM_MOUSEMOVE message is received. If the left mouse button is clicked, the letter "L" is painted. "R" is painted for the right button, and a "D" is painted if the left button is double clicked. Notice in Figure 6-2 that the WM_MOUSEMOVE messages are *not* sent every time the cursor moves from one pixel to the next on the screen. If the cursor is moving rapidly (rapid mouse movement), the WM_MOUSEMOVE message only will be sent every 10 to 20 pixels. The exact distance between WM_MOUSEMOVE messages depends on the mouse speed, and on the speed of the computer running Windows.

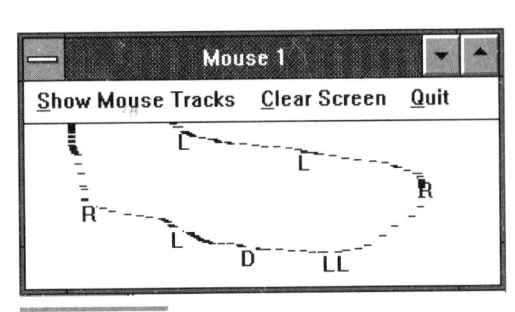

Figure 6-2 The MOUSE1 Program

Listing 6-4 shows MOUSE1.C. The CS_DBLCLKS style is added to the class definition for the parent window in the WinMain() function. This allows MOUSE1 to get the mouse button double-click messages. The processing of the mouse messages is done in the WndProc() function. Clicking the "Show Mouse Tracks" menu item toggles the static variable *bShowMouse* on and off. This variable controls whether the mouse "tracks" are shown. The mouse tracks are just horizontal lines drawn with the MoveTo() and LineTo() functions every time a WM_MOUSEMOVE message is received. The letters "L," "R," and "D" for left, right, and double click, are written on the screen using the TextOut() function.

Note in Listing 6-4 that the processing of all of the mouse message in the WndProc() function is similar. In each case, the mouse cursor location is extracted from the *lParam* value passed with the message using the HIWORD() and LOWORD() macros. The *X* location is always in the low-order word, and the *Y* location is always in the high-order word. Like most Windows programs, MOUSE1 ignores the mouse notification code information passed in the *wParam* parameter with each mouse message.

Listing 6-4 MOUSE1.C

```c
/* mouse1.c   show mouse movement */

#include <windows.h>
#include "mouse1.h"

int PASCAL WinMain (HANDLE hInstance, HANDLE hPrevInstance, LPSTR lpszCmdLine,
   int nCmdShow)
{
   HWND        hWnd ;           /* the window's "handle" */
   MSG         msg ;            /* a message structure */
   WNDCLASS    wndclass ;       /* window class structure */

   if (!hPrevInstance)
   {
      wndclass.style         = CS_HREDRAW | CS_VREDRAW | CS_DBLCLKS ;
      wndclass.lpfnWndProc   = WndProc ;
      wndclass.cbClsExtra    = 0 ;
      wndclass.cbWndExtra    = 0 ;
      wndclass.hInstance     = hInstance ;
      wndclass.hIcon         = LoadIcon (hInstance, "MyIcon") ;
      wndclass.hCursor       = LoadCursor (NULL, IDC_ARROW) ;
      wndclass.hbrBackground = GetStockObject (WHITE_BRUSH) ;
      wndclass.lpszMenuName  = "MyMenu" ;
      wndclass.lpszClassName = "MyClass" ;
            /* register the window class */
      if (!RegisterClass (&wndclass))
         return 0 ;
   }

   hWnd = CreateWindow ("MyClass","Mouse 1", WS_OVERLAPPEDWINDOW,
      CW_USEDEFAULT, CW_USEDEFAULT, CW_USEDEFAULT, CW_USEDEFAULT,
      NULL, NULL, hInstance, NULL) ;
   ShowWindow (hWnd, nCmdShow) ; /* display the window */

   while (GetMessage (&msg, NULL, NULL, NULL))   /* message loop */
   {
      TranslateMessage (&msg) ; /* translate keyboard messages */
      DispatchMessage (&msg) ;  /* send message to WndProc() */
   }
   return (msg.wParam) ;
}
```

```c
long FAR PASCAL WndProc (HWND hWnd, WORD wMessage, WORD wParam, LONG lParam)
{
    static BOOL bShowMouse = FALSE ;
    int        nXpos, nYpos ;
    HDC        hDC ;

    switch (wMessage)              /* process windows messages */
    {
       case WM_COMMAND:
           switch (wParam)         /* menu items */
           {
               case IDM_SHOW:      /* toggle mouse tracks on/off */
                   bShowMouse = bShowMouse ? FALSE : TRUE ;
                   break ;
               case IDM_CLEAR:     /* clear screen */
                   InvalidateRect (hWnd, NULL, TRUE) ;
                   break ;
               case IDM_QUIT:
                   DestroyWindow (hWnd) ; /* destroy window, */
                   break ;         /* terminating application */
           }
           break ;
       case WM_MOUSEMOVE:          /* mouse movement in client area */
           if (bShowMouse)
           {
               nXpos = LOWORD (lParam) ;    /* draw a small line to mark */
               nYpos = HIWORD (lParam) ;    /* where the mouse was when */
               hDC = GetDC (hWnd) ;         /* the WM_MOUSEMOVE message */
               MoveTo (hDC, nXpos, nYpos) ; /* was received. */
               LineTo (hDC, nXpos + 4, nYpos) ;
               ReleaseDC (hWnd, hDC) ;
           }
           break ;
       case WM_LBUTTONDOWN:        /* left mouse button depressed */
           nXpos = LOWORD (lParam) ;    /* in window's client area. */
           nYpos = HIWORD (lParam) ;    /* draw an L at spot */
           hDC = GetDC (hWnd) ;
           TextOut (hDC, nXpos, nYpos, "L", 1) ;
           ReleaseDC (hWnd, hDC) ;
           break ;
       case WM_RBUTTONDOWN:        /* right mouse button depressed */
           nXpos = LOWORD (lParam) ;    /* in window's client area. */
           nYpos = HIWORD (lParam) ;    /* draw an R at spot */
           hDC = GetDC (hWnd) ;
           TextOut (hDC, nXpos, nYpos, "R", 1) ;
           ReleaseDC (hWnd, hDC) ;
           break ;
       case WM_LBUTTONDBLCLK:      /* left mouse button double clicked */
           nXpos = LOWORD (lParam) ;    /* in window's client area. */
           nYpos = HIWORD (lParam) ;    /* draw an R at spot */
           hDC = GetDC (hWnd) ;
           TextOut (hDC, nXpos, nYpos, "D", 1) ;
           ReleaseDC (hWnd, hDC) ;
           break ;
       case WM_DESTROY:            /* stop application */
           PostQuitMessage (0) ;
           break ;
       default:                    /* default windows message processing */
           return DefWindowProc (hWnd, wMessage, wParam, lParam) ;
```

```
        }
        return (0L);
}
```

Listings 6-5 to 6-9 show the support files for MOUSE1. The icon is shown in Figure 6-3.

Listing 6-5 MOUSE1.H Header File

```
/* mouse1.h  header file */

#define IDM_SHOW    1
#define IDM_CLEAR   2
#define IDM_QUIT    10

long FAR PASCAL WndProc (HWND, WORD, WORD, LONG) ;
```

Figure 6-3
MOUSE1.ICO
Icon Image

Listing 6-6 MOUSE1.RC Resource Script File

```
/* mouse1.rc  resource file */

#include "mouse1.h"

MyIcon     ICON    mouse1.ico

MyMenu     MENU
BEGIN
   MENUITEM "&Show Mouse Tracks",   IDM_SHOW
   MENUITEM "&Clear Screen",        IDM_CLEAR
   MENUITEM "&Quit",                IDM_QUIT
END
```

Listing 6-7 MOUSE1.DEF Module Definition File

```
NAME           mouse1
EXETYPE        WINDOWS
STUB           'WINSTUB.EXE'
CODE           PRELOAD MOVEABLE
DATA           PRELOAD MOVEABLE MULTIPLE
HEAPSIZE       1024
STACKSIZE      5120
EXPORTS        WndProc
```

Listing 6-8 Turbo C++ Project File for MOUSE1

```
mouse1.c
mouse1.def
mouse1.res
```

Listing 6-9 QuickC Project File for MOUSE1

```
mouse1.c
mouse1.def
mouse1.rc
```

The Input Focus

An interesting experiment with MOUSE1 is to get two copies running at the same time. You can do this from the Windows file manager window by double clicking the MOUSE1.EXE file name, resizing the program window to make the first copy smaller, and then double clicking the MOUSE1.EXE file name again. Each of the running copies is called an "instance" of the program. With both instances of MOUSE1 visible, select the "Show Mouse Tracks" menu item in each copy. You will notice that the mouse tracks show up in both windows as you move the mouse cursor over their respective client areas. Figure 6-4 shows two instances of MOUSE1 overlapping, with a mouse track extending from one into the next.

One of the two instances of MOUSE1 will have a dark (highlighted) top caption line. The other instance will have a lighter colored caption. The exact color will depend on the selections you made with the colors option in the Windows Control Panel application. The window with the highlighted caption is said to have the "input focus." This is the window that will receive any keyboard input.

You can prove to yourself that only the window with the input focus gets the keyboard input by trying out the keyboard shortcut for the "Clear Screen" menu item. In MOUSE1.RC (Listing 6-6), we put an ampersand (&) in front of the first letter in the menu caption. This makes the "C" underlined in the MOUSE1 menu and makes the Alt-C key combination a keyboard shortcut for that menu item. (Alt)-(C) activates the menu item, clearing the window's client area. Only the instance of MOUSE1 that has the input focus is affected. You can switch the focus to another running application by pressing a mouse key over any part of that program's window. Try switching the focus to the second copy of MOUSE1, and then use the (Alt)-(C) keyboard shortcut to clear that window's screen.

You can see from this discussion that having the input focus is significant for keyboard input, but not significant for mouse actions. The mouse tracks show up in the MOUSE1 client area even if that instance does not have the focus. It makes sense that mouse messages are pro-

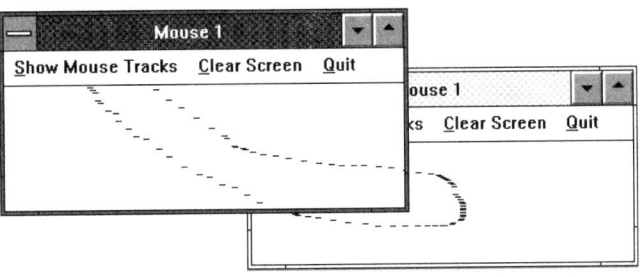

Figure 6-4 Two Instances of MOUSE1. The instance on the left has the input focus

cessed by windows that do not have the focus. After all, you will normally use the mouse to pick which window is active (has the focus). If mouse messages were ignored by inactive windows, the inactive windows would never be able to gain the input focus.

When a window gains the input focus, Windows sends a WM_SETFOCUS message. When the window loses the input focus, Windows sends a WM_KILLFOCUS message. Common actions include highlighting an edit area when the window has focus, or doing some other action that is only necessary when the window may receive keyboard input. One of the exercises at the end of this chapter modifies MOUSE1 to change the window caption when the program gains or loses the input focus.

Normally, you will let the user pick which window has the input focus with the mouse. Occasionally, you may want to explicitly give a window or a window control the focus. For example, you might want an edit control to have the input focus when the program's main window was first displayed. You may also want to allow the user to pick which control has the input focus by using the tab or arrow keys. The SetFocus() function allows you to explicitly give a window or window control the input focus. A typical call to SetFocus() would be:

```
SetFocus (hEdit) ;
```

In this case, *hEdit* is the window handle of an edit control. Different styles of windows respond differently to gaining the input focus. Windows with caption bars have their caption bars highlighted. Edit controls start showing a blinking vertical line (the caret) at the point where keyboard input will start. Button controls show a highlighted outline. List boxes show a highlighted selection item. Combo boxes will either display their list box or highlight a list box item if the listbox is already displayed.

Nonclient Mouse Messages

The common mouse messages like WM_MOUSEMOVE and WM_LBUTTONDOWN, are sent to an application when the mouse cursor is over the window's client area. These messages are not sent when the mouse cursor is over the window's caption bar or menu. Instead, Windows sends nonclient mouse messages. The "nonclient area" of a window is everything except the client area. It includes the window's borders, menu bar, caption bar, system menu button in the upper left corner, and the minimize and maximize buttons in the upper right corner. Figure 6-5 shows a diagram of which parts of the window are in the nonclient portion.

When the mouse is moved in the nonclient area, Windows sends a WM_NCMOUSEMOVE message to the window. There are also nonclient equivalents for all of the mouse-button-click and double-click messages.

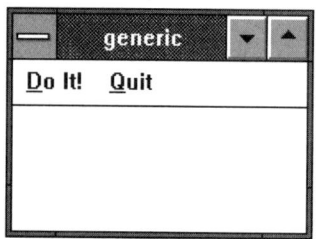

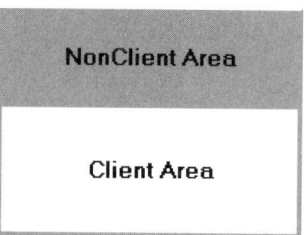

Figure 6-5 Nonclient Parts of a Program Window

These messages are summarized in Tables 6-4 and 6-5. With all of these messages, the *lParam* value sent with the messages contains the mouse position, while *wParam* contains the mouse notification codes (summarized in Table 6-1). One difference between the client and nonclient messages is that the nonclient messages encode the mouse position in *lParam* using screen coordinates, not client coordinates.

	BUTTON DEPRESSED	BUTTON RELEASED
Left Mouse Button	WM_NCLBUTTONDOWN	WM_NCLBUTTONUP
Center Mouse Button	WM_NCMBUTTONDOWN	WM_NCMBUTTONUP
Right Mouse Button	WM_NCRBUTTONDOWN	WM_NCRBUTTONUP

Table 6-4 Nonclient Area Mouse Button Messages

	BUTTON DOUBLE CLICKED
Left Mouse Button	WM_NCLBUTTONDBLCLK
Center Mouse Button	WM_NCMBUTTONDBLCLK
Right Mouse Button	WM_NCRBUTTONDBLCLK

Table 6-5 Nonclient Area Mouse Double-Click Messages

It is unusual for a program to process the nonclient mouse messages. Normally, you will take advantage of Window's built-in logic that converts low-level messages, such as WM_NCLBUTTONDOWN, over a menu item into a WM_COMMAND message encoding the menu item selected. It is much easier to figure out which menu item was picked by processing the WM_COMMAND message (the menu item ID number is in the *wParam* parameter) than by using the coordinates of the cursor sent with WM_NCLBUTTONDOWN.

Capturing the Mouse

If you get two instances of MOUSE1 running, you can switch between them by clicking one with the mouse. The one you click will get the input focus, darken its caption bar, and start responding to keyboard input. The instance losing the focus will lighten its caption bar and stop responding to keyboard input. This is the way most Windows programs operate. The mouse is used to select which of the running applications is to have the focus.

There are a few occasions when you will want to limit the mouse to interaction with only one program. This can be useful in screen capture programs and utility programs that replace the program manager application. An application that takes complete control of the mouse is said to have "captured" the mouse. The application that captures the mouse will be the only one that receives messages like WM_MOUSEMOVE and WM_LBUTTONDOWN.

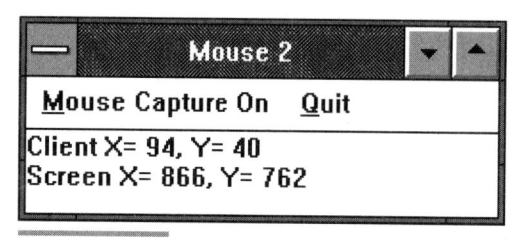

Figure 6-6 The MOUSE2 Program

The MOUSE2 program is designed to demonstrate capturing the mouse. The mouse is captured to demonstrate the difference between screen and client coordinates. When you start MOUSE2 running, it will appear in the lower right corner of the screen, looking roughly like Figure 6-6. Initially, MOUSE2 only receives mouse messages if the mouse cursor is inside the window's client area. The mouse position is displayed using both screen and client coordinates.

When the "Mouse Capture On" menu item is selected, MOUSE2 captures the mouse. With the mouse captured, the screen and client coordinates are updated if the mouse cursor is moved anywhere on the screen. This is because only MOUSE2 is getting the mouse messages. Clicking the left mouse button over another program's window will not switch the focus to that application. MOUSE2 continues to hog the mouse until the right mouse button is clicked. At that point, MOUSE2 releases the mouse and things go back to normal.

You can do an interesting experiment by running both MOUSE1 and MOUSE2 at the same time. Before the mouse is captured, MOUSE1 will show mouse tracks in its client area if its "Show Mouse Tracks" menu item has been selected. This is true whether or not MOUSE1 has the focus, as WM_MOUSEMOVE messages are received with or without the focus. However, if MOUSE2 captures the mouse, mouse tracks will not be visible inside MOUSE1's client area as the mouse cursor moves over the MOUSE1 window. This is because only MOUSE2, the application that captured the mouse, is getting the mouse messages.

Listing 6-10 shows the MOUSE2.C program. There are a few items worth noting in both the WinMain() and WndProc() functions. In WinMain(), the program's window is created with a location and size that fit into the lower right corner of the screen. To do this, we need to know how big the screen is. This is not obvious because Windows can run on systems ranging from a CGA resolution monitor to high-end graphics workstations. We need to determine what resolution screen the system is running while MOUSE2 is running.

Windows provides the GetSystemMetrics() function to retrieve information about the system. In MOUSE2, GetSystemMetrics() is used to find the size of the screen and the height of a program's menu bar. The program's window is made four times the height of a menu bar to make room for the caption, menu bar, and two lines of text. The MOUSE2's window horizontal size is made equal to one fourth of the screen width. CreateWindow() is then called with the correct X,Y position for the window to exactly fit into the corner of the screen.

The actual capturing of the mouse boils down to just one function call: SetCapture(). SetCapture() is called if the "Mouse Capture On" menu item is selected. The window's caption is also changed to "R. Button Releases" at this point as a reminder of how to free the mouse. SetWindowText() changes the window's caption.

Once SetCapture() is called, all the mouse messages go to the application until ReleaseCapture() is called. To make things simple, the WM_RBUTTONDOWN message (right mouse button depressed) is used in the MOUSE2 program as the point at which to call the ReleaseCapture() function. When the user clicks the right mouse button, Windows sends the WM_RBUTTONDOWN message MOUSE2 which calls Release-Capture() to free the mouse. The WM_RBUTTONDOWN message is received whether or not MOUSE2 has captured the mouse. Calling ReleaseCapture() when the mouse is not captured does no harm.

Listing 6-10 MOUSE2.C

```c
/* mouse2.c   show mouse position on screen */

#include <windows.h>
#include "mouse2.h"

int PASCAL WinMain (HANDLE hInstance, HANDLE hPrevInstance, LPSTR lpszCmdLine,
   int nCmdShow)
{
    HWND       hWnd ;          /* the window's "handle" */
    MSG        msg ;           /* a message structure */
    WNDCLASS   wndclass ;      /* window class structure */
    int        nScreenX, nScreenY, nMenuY ;

    if (!hPrevInstance)
    {
      wndclass.style          = CS_HREDRAW | CS_VREDRAW ;
      wndclass.lpfnWndProc    = WndProc ;
      wndclass.cbClsExtra     = 0 ;
      wndclass.cbWndExtra     = 0 ;
      wndclass.hInstance      = hInstance ;
      wndclass.hIcon          = LoadIcon (hInstance, "MyIcon") ;
      wndclass.hCursor        = LoadCursor (NULL, IDC_ARROW) ;
      wndclass.hbrBackground  = GetStockObject (WHITE_BRUSH) ;
      wndclass.lpszMenuName   = "MyMenu" ;
      wndclass.lpszClassName  = "MyClass" ;
                /* register the window class */
      if (!RegisterClass (&wndclass))
            return 0 ;
    }

    nScreenX = GetSystemMetrics (SM_CXSCREEN) ;   /* use screen dimensions */
    nScreenY = GetSystemMetrics (SM_CYSCREEN) ;   /* to provide basis for */
    nMenuY = GetSystemMetrics (SM_CYMENU) ;       /* sizing the window */

    hWnd = CreateWindow ("MyClass","Mouse 2", WS_OVERLAPPEDWINDOW,
         (nScreenX * 3)/4, nScreenY - (4 * nMenuY), nScreenX/4, 4 * nMenuY,
         NULL, NULL, hInstance, NULL) ;
    ShowWindow (hWnd, nCmdShow) ; /* display the window */

    while (GetMessage (&msg, NULL, NULL, NULL))   /* message loop */
    {
        TranslateMessage (&msg) ;  /* translate keyboard messages */
```

```
            DispatchMessage (&msg) ;    /* send message to WndProc() */
    }
    return (msg.wParam) ;
}

long FAR PASCAL WndProc (HWND hWnd, WORD wMessage, WORD wParam, LONG lParam)
{
    POINT       pClient, pScreen ;
    HDC         hDC ;
    char        cBuf [64] ;

    switch (wMessage)                   /* process windows messages */
    {
        case WM_COMMAND:
            switch (wParam)             /* menu items */
            {
                case IDM_CAPTURE:       /* toggle mouse capture on/off */
                    SetCapture (hWnd) ;
                    SetWindowText (hWnd, "R. Button Releases") ;
                    break ;
                case IDM_QUIT:
                    DestroyWindow (hWnd) ;  /* destroy window, */
                    break ;                 /* terminating application */
            }
            break ;
        case WM_RBUTTONDOWN:            /* or right mouse button */
            ReleaseCapture () ;         /* release mouse */
            SetWindowText (hWnd, "Mouse 2") ;
            break ;
        case WM_MOUSEMOVE:              /* mouse movement detected */
            /* copy mouse X,Y to point structure */
            pClient = MAKEPOINT (lParam) ;

            /* convert from client coordinates to screen coord. */
            pScreen = pClient ;
            ClientToScreen (hWnd, &pScreen) ;

            /* display the mouse coordinates */
            hDC = GetDC (hWnd) ;

            wsprintf (cBuf, |Client X= %d, Y= %d    |,
                pClient.x, pClient.y) ;
            TextOut (hDC, 0, 0, cBuf, lstrlen (cBuf)) ;

            wsprintf (cBuf, |Screen X= %d, Y= %d    |,
                pScreen.x, pScreen.y) ;
            TextOut (hDC, 0, 15, cBuf, lstrlen (cBuf)) ;

            ReleaseDC (hWnd, hDC) ;
            break ;
        case WM_DESTROY:                /* stop application */
            PostQuitMessage (0) ;
            break ;
        default:                        /* default windows message processing */
            return DefWindowProc (hWnd, wMessage, wParam, lParam) ;
    }
    return (0L) ;
}
```

Listings 6-11 to 6-15 show the support files for MOUSE2. The program's icon is shown in Figure 6-7.

Listing 6-11 MOUSE2.H Header File

```
/* mouse2.h header file */

#define IDM_CAPTURE   1
#define IDM_QUIT     10

long FAR PASCAL WndProc (HWND, WORD, WORD, LONG) ;
```

Figure 6-7
MOUSE2.ICO
Icon Image

Listing 6-12 MOUSE2.RC Resource Script File

```
/* mouse2.rc resource file */

#include "mouse2.h"

MyIcon    ICON    mouse2.ico

MyMenu    MENU
BEGIN
    MENUITEM "&Show Mouse Tracks",  IDM_SHOW
    MENUITEM "&Clear Screen",       IDM_CLEAR
    MENUITEM "&Quit",               IDM_QUIT
END
```

Listing 6-13 MOUSE2.DEF Module Definition File

```
NAME        mouse2
EXETYPE     WINDOWS
STUB        'WINSTUB.EXE'
CODE        PRELOAD MOVEABLE
DATA        PRELOAD MOVEABLE MULTIPLE
HEAPSIZE    1024
STACKSIZE   5120
EXPORTS     WndProc
```

Listing 6-14 Turbo C++ Project File for MOUSE2

```
mouse2.c
mouse2.def
mouse2.res
```

Listing 6-15 QuickC Project File for MOUSE2

```
mouse2.c
mouse2.def
mouse2.rc
```

Chapter 6 • Taming the Mouse

There are some interesting side effects to capturing the mouse. When MOUSE2 has captured the mouse, you will not be able to select a menu item in MOUSE2 with the left mouse button. This seems a bit odd, as it is MOUSE2 that is getting the mouse messages. Why doesn't it respond to menu selections until the mouse is released?

The problem is that the menu bar is actually another small window. Menus are specialized window controls that have built-in logic for highlighting selections and generating WM_COMMAND messages when an item is selected. Windows will not switch the focus to the menu window (so that it can act like a menu) when MOUSE2 has the mouse captured. The result with the mouse captured is that the WM_MOUSEMOVE and WM_LBUTTONDOWN messages get sent to MOUSE2 when the menu bar is clicked, but the menu bar does not get the messages and generate the WM_COMMAND message that we expect from a menu item when it is selected. The result is that the menu does not function when the mouse is captured.

Changing the Mouse Cursor Shape

For our last experiment on the mouse (sounds sinister doesn't it?), we will switch from the usual arrow cursor shape to some more interesting shapes. We will also try out a related Windows tool, the blinking caret.

The easiest way to create new cursor shapes is to draw them with either the Microsoft Image Editor application or with the Resource Toolkit that comes with the Turbo C++ and Borland C++ compilers. Figure 6-8 shows two cursor shapes created for the MOUSE3 program. They are actually small bitmap images. Each pixel can be either black, white, inverse video, or transparent.

When you create cursors, the editor programs allow you to select a "hot spot." This is the point on the cursor bitmap that is exactly at the cursor's X,Y position. The hot spot should be located at the "point" of the cursor where the user can be expected to visualize the cursor to be "pointing." For MOUSE.ICO this is at the upper left corner, right on the mouse's nose. For HAND.ICO, it is at the tip of the extended index finger.

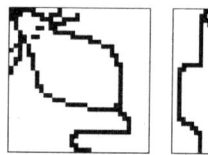

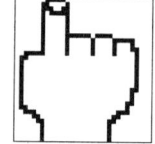

Figure 6-8 Mouse Cursor Shapes Created with SDK Paint

Once you have created the cursor files, you can add them to a program's resource data. The syntax is:

    CursorName   CURSOR   FileName

CURSOR is a reserved word used in resource script files. The file name of the cursor image file is to the right of the word CURSOR. The name given to the resource data within the program is to the left of the word CURSOR. The cursor's name can be anything you want. Listing 6-16 shows two cursor files being added to a program's resource data. Inside of the program, the cursor data will be named "Mouse" and "Hand."

Listing 6-16 Adding Cursor Data to a Resource Script File

```
Mouse   CURSOR mouse.cur    /* two cursor files */
Hand    CURSOR hand.cur
```

With the cursor files referenced in the resource script file, the cursor data will be added to the finished program. We can then change the cursor shape using the SetCursor() function. This is normally done when processing a WM_SETCURSOR message from Windows. Windows sends this message when it is about to display a cursor shape. Listing 6-17 shows a typical example of processing the WM_SETCURSOR message.

Listing 6-17 Setting a Mouse Cursor Shape

```
long FAR PASCAL WndProc (HWND hWnd, WORD wMessage, WORD wParam, LONG lParam)
{
    HCURSOR hCursor ;
    HANDLE  hInstance ;

    switch (wMessage)            /* process windows messages */
    {
        case WM_SETCURSOR:       /* change the cursor shape */
            hInstance = GetWindowWord (hWnd, GWW_HINSTANCE) ;
            hCursor = LoadCursor (hInstance, "Mouse") ;
            SetCursor (hCursor) ;
            break ;
```
[Other program lines]

The LoadCursor() function gets a handle to the cursor data. LoadCursor() needs the instance handle of the parent window as a parameter which is obtained by GetWindowWord(). When the handle to the cursor's data is obtained with LoadCursor(), the cursor shape is changed with SetCursor(). This cursor shape only applies within the client area of the window that changed the cursor shape. The cursor will change back to the default arrow shape if it is moved outside of the bounds of the window.

Changing the cursor shape as the program runs (Listing 6-17) works best if the window's class definition does not contain a cursor handle. You just put a value of NULL in the class definition for the *hCursor* member before calling RegisterClass().

```
wndclass.hCursor = NULL ;
```

If you assign a cursor shape in the window's class definition, the class definition will look like:

```
wndclass.hCursor = LoadCursor (hInstance, "Hand") ;
```

This makes the "Hand" cursor shape appear anytime the cursor is located within the window area (client plus nonclient area). That is perfect if you always want the

"Hand" cursor shape. If you define a class cursor and then use the WM_SETCURSOR logic shown in Listing 6-17 to change the cursor shape, the cursor image will flicker as it is moved. That is because the cursor shape is switching between the class cursor shape and the shape specified by SetCursor() in processing the WM_SETCURSOR message. Avoid the flicker by using a NULL cursor in the class definition if you are going to change the cursor shape by processing WM_SETCURSOR messages.

You will not always need to add cursor data files to your program's resources. Windows always has several *stock cursor* shapes loaded. You get a handle to one of these by specifying NULL for the instance handle when calling LoadCursor(). A typical example of processing a WM_SETCURSOR message and loading a stock cursor is shown in Listing 6-18. In this case, the cursor is switched to a cross hair shape.

Listing 6-18 Loading a Stock Cursor

```
long FAR PASCAL WndProc (HWND hWnd, WORD wMessage, WORD wParam, LONG lParam)
{
    HCURSOR  hCursor ;

    switch (wMessage)          /* process windows messages */
    {
        case WM_SETCURSOR:     /* change the cursor shape */
        hCursor = LoadCursor (NULL, IDC_CROSS) ;
            SetCursor (hCursor) ;
            break ;
```
[Other program lines]

Table 6-6 gives a list of the stock cursor shapes available at all times. We have been taking advantage of stock cursors in many of the program examples, by using a stock cursor for the window's class cursor.

```
wndclass.hCursor = LoadCursor (NULL, IDC_ARROW) ;
```

Most programs just use the stock IDC_ARROW cursor all of the time. However, changing the cursor shape is an excellent way to improve an application in cases where the cursor is going to act on another object. The scientific name for changing the cursor shape to match the task at hand is "tool metaphor." The user visualizes the cursor as a "tool" in performing a task. Paint programs frequently change the cursor to a brush shape when painting and to an eraser when deleting.

VALUE	MEANING
IDC_ARROW	The standard arrow shape.
IDC_CROSS	A thin cross hair cursor.
IDC_IBEAM	An I-beam cursor. Used for positioning text.
IDC_ICON	An empty icon.
IDC_SIZE	A square with a smaller square in the lower right corner. Looks like a window being reduced in size.

IDC_SIZENESW	The double headed arrow Windows uses when adjusting the upper left and lower right sizing borders. Points "NE by SW."
IDC_SIZENS	The double headed arrow Windows uses when adjusting the top and bottom sizing borders. Points "North/South."
IDC_SIZENWSE	The double headed arrow Windows uses when adjusting the upper right and lower left sizing borders. Points "NW by SE."
IDC_SIZEWE	The double headed arrow Windows uses when adjusting the right or left sizing borders. Points "West/East."
IDC_UPARROW	An arrow pointing up.
IDC_WAIT	The hourglass cursor shape.

Table 6-6 Stock Cursor Shapes

The Caret

The caret is a small blinking line that is used in applications like word processors to mark a location on the screen. The caret marks the point at which the next typed letter will show up. Carets appear automatically in edit controls for this purpose.

The caret is interesting from a programming point of view because it is shared by all running application programs. There will never be more than one caret visible on the screen at one time. This is logical, as otherwise the user would not be able to tell where the next typed letter will show up. The caret is closely tied to the concept of input focus. The caret should be visible when a window has the focus and should vanish when the window loses the focus.

The WM_SETFOCUS and WM_KILLFOCUS messages provide an ideal point to create and remove the caret. A typical source code excerpt is shown in Listing 6-20. The caret is created when the WM_SETFOCUS message is received by calling the Create-Caret() function. In Listing 6-20, a caret 2 pixels wide by 10 pixels high is created. The caret is made visible by calling ShowCaret(). There is also a HideCaret() function to temporarily hide the caret shape. This is now used in Listing 6-20. The caret continues to be visible on the window's client area until a WM_KILLFOCUS message is received. DestroyCaret() removes the caret from the screen.

Listing 6-20 Creating and Removing the Caret

```
long FAR PASCAL WndProc (HWND hWnd, WORD wMessage, WORD wParam, LONG lParam)
{
    static int    nXpos = 0, nYpos = 0 ;

    switch (wMessage)            /* process windows messages */
    {
        case WM_SETFOCUS:        /* window gaining input focus */
            CreateCaret (hWnd, NULL, 2, 10) ;
```

```
                              /* put caret back at last X,Y location */
             SetCaretPos (nXpos, nYpos) ;
             ShowCaret (hWnd) ;    /* show caret */
             break ;
     case WM_KILLFOCUS:           /* window losing input focus */
             DestroyCaret () ;    /* destroy caret for now */
             break ;
     case WM_LBUTTONDOWN:         /* move caret to new position */
             nXpos = LOWORD (lParam) ;   /* save X,Y position */
             nYpos = HIWORD (lParam) ;
             SetCaretPos (nXpos, nYpos) ;
             break ;
```
[Other program lines]

Once a caret has been created, it is positioned on the window's client area using the SetCaretPos() function. Listing 6-20 shows a typical case where the mouse position when the left mouse button is depressed (WM_LBUTTONDOWN message received) is used to set the caret's position. The location is saved in two static integers *nXpos, nYpos* so that the caret can be correctly positioned when the window gains the input focus.

Experimenting with Cursor Shapes and the Caret

The last example program in this chapter is MOUSE3. MOUSE3 demonstrates changing the cursor's shape and positioning the caret in the window's client area. We will also learn how to create menus with drop-down (popup) menus attached.

Listing 6-21 shows the resource script file for MOUSE3. Note that an icon file and two cursor files have been added to the resource data. The icon will be used for the main window's class icon, which will be displayed when the window is minimized. The cursor shapes will be used for alternatives to the usual arrow cursor.

Listing 6-21   MOUSE3.RC   Resource Script File

```
/* mouse3.rc  resource file */

#include "mouse3.h"

MyIcon   ICON     mouse3.ico   /* icon file */
Mouse    CURSOR   mouse.cur    /* two cursor files */
Hand     CURSOR   hand.cur

MyMenu      MENU
BEGIN
    POPUP    "&Cursor Shape"
    BEGIN
        MENUITEM "&Arrow",        IDM_ARROW
        MENUITEM "&Cross",        IDM_CROSS
        MENUITEM "&Hand",         IDM_HAND
        MENUITEM "&Mouse",        IDM_MOUSE
    END

    MENUITEM "&Quit",             IDM_QUIT
END
```

Note that the menu definition in MOUSE3.RC includes a line titled "POPUP." This starts the definition of a popup menu. The top menu bar will contain the selection choice "Cursor Shape." When this top item is selected, a popup menu will appear under the menu bar with four selections: Arrow, Cross, Hand, and Mouse. Figure 6-9 shows the appearance of the MOUSE3 window after the "Cursor Shape" menu item has been selected.

The popup menu allows the choice of one of four cursor shapes. Selecting an item in the popup menu results in a WM_COMMAND message being sent to the MOUSE3 program, with *wParam* set to the menu item's ID number. Note in Listing 6-21 that the POPUP menu line with the string "Cursor Shape" does not have an ID number. Selecting the top element of a popup menu does not result in a WM_COMMAND message, so no ID number is needed. Only the items within the POPUP menu (MENUITEM's between the BEGIN and END statement following the POPUP statement) have ID values.

As you may have guessed, the *Arrow* and *Cross* menu items in MOUSE3 take advantage of stock cursor shapes. The *Hand* and *Mouse* menu items select the custom cursor shapes loaded into the MOUSE3 resource data. Listing 6-22 shows the MOUSE3.C program file. Note that the window's class definition in WinMain() has NULL for the class cursor. This is to avoid flicker when we pick a different cursor shape. The cursor shapes are loaded when the menu items are selected (WM_COMMAND message processed) by calling LoadCursor(). The cursor shape is made visible by calling SetCursor() when a WM_SETCURSOR message is processed in WndProc().

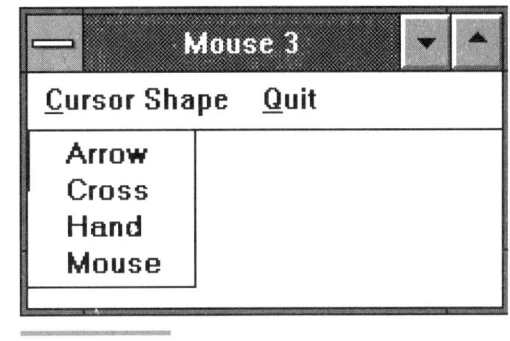

Figure 6-9 MOUSE3 Popup Menu

Listing 6-22 MOUSE3.C

```
/* mouse3.c   change mouse cursor shape and move the caret */

#include <windows.h>
#include "mouse3.h"

int PASCAL WinMain (HANDLE hInstance, HANDLE hPrevInstance, LPSTR lpszCmdLine,
   int nCmdShow)
{
    HWND       hWnd ;       /* the window's "handle" */
    MSG        msg ;        /* a message structure */
    WNDCLASS   wndclass ;   /* window class structure */

    if (!hPrevInstance)
    {
       wndclass.style          = CS_HREDRAW | CS_VREDRAW ;
       wndclass.lpfnWndProc    = WndProc ;
       wndclass.cbClsExtra     = 0 ;
       wndclass.cbWndExtra     = 0 ;
       wndclass.hInstance      = hInstance ;
```

Chapter 6 • Taming the Mouse   **205**

```
        wndclass.hIcon          = LoadIcon (hInstance, "MyIcon") ;
                /* note that no cursor is defined for the class */
        wndclass.hCursor        = NULL ;
        wndclass.hbrBackground  = GetStockObject (WHITE_BRUSH) ;
        wndclass.lpszMenuName   = "MyMenu" ;
        wndclass.lpszClassName  = "MyClass" ;
                /* register the window class */
        if (!RegisterClass (&wndclass))
            return 0 ;
    }

    hWnd = CreateWindow ("MyClass","Mouse 3", WS_OVERLAPPEDWINDOW,
        CW_USEDEFAULT, CW_USEDEFAULT, CW_USEDEFAULT, CW_USEDEFAULT,
        NULL, NULL, hInstance, NULL) ;
    ShowWindow (hWnd, nCmdShow) ;   /* display the window */

    while (GetMessage (&msg, NULL, NULL, NULL))   /* message loop */
    {
        TranslateMessage (&msg) ; /* translate keyboard messages */
        DispatchMessage (&msg) ;   /* send message to WndProc() */
    }
    return (msg.wParam) ;
}

long FAR PASCAL WndProc (HWND hWnd, WORD wMessage, WORD wParam, LONG lParam)
{
    static  HCURSOR     hCursor ;
    HANDLE              hInstance ;
    int                 nBorderWide, nCaptionTall ;
    static  int         nXpos = 0, nYpos = 0 ;

    switch (wMessage)  /* process windows messages */
    {
        case WM_CREATE:  /* program just starting */
                    /* start with the arrow cursor shape */
            hCursor = LoadCursor (NULL, IDC_ARROW) ;
            break ;
        case WM_COMMAND:
            switch (wParam)       /* menu items */
            {                     /* load selected cursor shape */
                case IDM_ARROW:
                    hCursor = LoadCursor (NULL, IDC_ARROW) ;
                    break ;
                case IDM_CROSS:
                    hCursor = LoadCursor (NULL, IDC_CROSS) ;
                    break ;
                case IDM_HAND:
                    hInstance = GetWindowWord (hWnd, GWW_HINSTANCE) ;
                    hCursor = LoadCursor (hInstance, "Hand") ;
                    break ;
                case IDM_MOUSE:
                    hInstance = GetWindowWord (hWnd, GWW_HINSTANCE) ;
                    hCursor = LoadCursor (hInstance, "Mouse") ;
                    break ;
                case IDM_QUIT:
                    DestroyWindow (hWnd) ; /* destroy window, */
```

```
                break ;         /* terminating application */
            }
            break ;
        case WM_SETCURSOR:      /* change the cursor shape */
            SetCursor (hCursor) ;       /* to the last one loaded */
            break ;
        case WM_LBUTTONDOWN:    /* move caret to new position */
            nXpos = LOWORD (lParam) ;   /* save X,Y position */
            nYpos = HIWORD (lParam) ;
            SetCaretPos (nXpos, nYpos) ;
            break ;
        case WM_SETFOCUS:       /* window gaining input focus */
                                /* create the window's caret */
                                /* base caret width on window border width */
            nBorderWide = GetSystemMetrics (SM_CXBORDER) ;
                                /* base caret height on caption height */
            nCaptionTall = GetSystemMetrics (SM_CYCAPTION) ;
            CreateCaret (hWnd, NULL, nBorderWide, nCaptionTall) ;
                                /* put caret back at last X,Y location */
            SetCaretPos (nXpos, nYpos) ;
            ShowCaret (hWnd) ;  /* show caret */
            break ;
        case WM_KILLFOCUS:      /* window losing input focus */
            DestroyCaret () ;   /* destroy caret for now */
            break ;
        case WM_DESTROY:        /* stop application */
            PostQuitMessage (0) ;
            break ;
        default:        /* default windows message processing */
            return DefWindowProc (hWnd, wMessage, wParam, lParam) ;
    }
    return (0L) ;
}
```

Notice in the processing of the WM_SETFOCUS message that MOUSE3 uses GetSystemMetrics() to find the width of the window border and the height of the caption bar. These values are used to size the caret created with CreateCaret(). Using a value based on GetSystemMetrics() assures that the caret will be reasonably sized, regardless of the type of video equipment used.

The header file, module definition file, and make file(s) for MOUSE3 (Listings 6-23 to 6-26) are pretty standard. Note that the menu items in the popup menu are given ID values in the header file. Otherwise, these files are copies of the basic MINIMAL4 program from Chapter 3, *First Programming Experiments*. Figure 6-10 shows the program's icon.

Figure 6-10
MOUSE3.ICO
Icon Image

Listing 6-23   MOUSE3.H Header File

```
/* mouse3.h header file */
```

```
#define IDM_ARROW   1
#define IDM_CROSS   2
#define IDM_HAND    3
#define IDM_MOUSE   4
#define IDM_QUIT   10

long FAR PASCAL WndProc (HWND, WORD, WORD, LONG);
```

Listing 6-24 MOUSE3.DEF Module Definition File

```
NAME        mouse3
EXETYPE     WINDOWS
STUB        'WINSTUB.EXE'
CODE        PRELOAD MOVEABLE
DATA        PRELOAD MOVEABLE MULTIPLE
HEAPSIZE    1024
STACKSIZE   5120
EXPORTS     WndProc
```

Listing 6-25 Turbo C++ Project File for MOUSE3

```
mouse3.c
mouse3.def
mouse3.res
```

Listing 6-26 QuickC Project File for MOUSE3

```
mouse3.c
mouse3.def
mouse3.rc
```

MOUSE3 starts with the caret blinking in the upper left corner of the window's client area. As with most text editing programs, you can move the caret by clicking the left mouse button at another location in the client area. The caret vanishes if another window gains the input focus and reappears when MOUSE3 regains the focus.

The different cursor shapes loaded by menu selections in MOUSE3 remain in effect as long as the cursor is within the window's area. This includes both the client and nonclient parts of the window. As soon as the cursor is moved past the edge of MOUSE3's window, the cursor shape reverts to the default arrow.

Summary

Windows lets your program know what the mouse is doing by sending messages to the program. You can use the WM_MOUSEMOVE message to detect mouse movement and find the current mouse cursor position. Messages like WM_LBUTTONDOWN are used to tell the program that one of the mouse buttons has been depressed. Normally, a program will receive mouse messages only if the mouse is over a part of the program's window. Programs can capture the mouse by calling the SetCapture() function. Once the mouse is captured, all mouse messages are sent to the program that captured the mouse. This continues until the mouse is freed with the ReleaseCapture() function.

The mouse is used to select which window has the input focus. The window with the input focus will have its caption highlighted and will be the window to receive any keyboard input. Windows sends a WM_SETFOCUS message to the program when it receives the input focus and WM_KILLFOCUS when the focus is lost.

You can change cursor shapes by calling the SetCursor() function. The cursor shapes can either be stock cursors or custom cursor images that you create with a bitmap editor, such as the Image Editor or Resource Workshop. Cursor data files are added to the program's resource data, and then accessed with the LoadCursor() function prior to calling SetCursor.

Some applications use a caret to mark a location in the client area where text will be inserted. Only one caret is visible on the screen at any one time. Carets are created when the window receives the input focus (WM_SETFOCUS message received), and destroyed when the window loses the input focus (WM_KILLFOCUS message received.) The caret can also be made temporarily visible and hidden by using ShowCaret() and HideCaret().

QUESTIONS

1. If an edit control shows the caret, you know that the edit control has the _____ _____.

2. In order to receive double-click messages, a window must be created with the _____ window style.

3. If the right mouse button is depressed in the client area of a window, the window's message function will receive a _____ message. If the right mouse button is depressed in the nonclient area, the _____ message will be received.

4. If there are two edit controls in the client area of a window, both child windows of the parent, both of the edit controls can have the caret showing at the same time. (True/False)

5. Carets are created when processing the _____ message and destroyed when processing the _____ message.

6. Use the _____ function to determine the size of window elements, such as the border width and caption height, while the program runs.

7. To use a custom cursor shape in a program, you must add the cursor to the program's _____ _____ file.

EXERCISES

1. Modify the MOUSE1 program so that the window's caption bar shows "I have the focus" when the program's window gets the input focus, and shows "I lost the focus" when the program's window loses the focus.

2. Get two copies of the modified MOUSE1 program running from exercise one. How do you get both of the windows to display the "I lost the focus" caption? How do you get both to display the "I have the focus" caption?

3. Create a program that displays a button control on the program's client area at the location where the user clicks the left mouse button. The button should be destroyed and recreated at the cursor location every time the left mouse button is clicked. Is it possible to get WM_COMMAND messages from this control?

ANSWERS TO QUESTIONS

1. Input focus.
2. CS_DBLCLKS.
3. WM_RBUTTONDOWN, WM_NCRBUTTONDOWN.
4. False. Only one caret will ever be visible on the screen at any one time.
5. WM_SETFOCUS, WM_KILLFOCUS.
6. GetSystemMetrics().
7. Resource script.

SOLUTIONS TO EXERCISES

1. The WndProc() function will need to process WM_SETFOCUS and WM_KILLFOCUS messages, and use SetWindowText() to change the caption string. Listing 6-27 shows the top part of the WndProc() function after these changes. The full program is called C6EXER01 on the source code disks.

Listing 6-27 Modifications to MOUSE1.C
To Change the Window Caption When the Window Gains and Loses the Input Focus

```
long FAR PASCAL WndProc (HWND hWnd, WORD wMessage, WORD wParam, LONG lParam)
{
   static BOOL bShowMouse = FALSE ;
   int        nXpos, nYpos ;
   HDC        hDC ;

   switch (wMessage)          /* process windows messages */
   {
     case WM_SETFOCUS:
         SetWindowText (hWnd, "I have the focus.") ;
         break ;
     case WM_KILLFOCUS:
         SetWindowText (hWnd, "I lost the focus.") ;
         break ;
```
[Other program lines]

2. You can get both instances of the modified MOUSE1 program to show "I lost the focus" by selecting some other program's window. It is not possible to have both instances display "I have the focus," as only one window can gain the focus at one time.

3. Listing 6-28 shows the WndProc() function for a program that repositions a button control every time the left mouse button is depressed over the program window's client area. The full program is called C6EXER03 on the source code disks.

Chapter 6 • Taming The Mouse **211**

SOLUTIONS TO EXERCISES (cont'd)

Listing 6-28 WndProc() Function Which Repositions a Button Control

```
long FAR PASCAL WndProc (HWND hWnd, WORD wMessage, WORD wParam, LONG lParam)
{
    int     nXpos, nYpos ;
    static HANDLE hControl = NULL ;
    HANDLE          hInstance ;
switch (wMessage)                       /* process windows messages */
    {
case WM_COMMAND:
            switch (wParam)             /* menu items */
            {
case IDM_QUIT:
            DestroyWindow (hWnd) ;      /* destroy window, */
            break ;                     /* the new window was activated */
            MessageBox (hWnd, "Got WM_COMMAND from button.", "Message", MB_OK) ;
            break ;
        }
        break ;
    case WM_LBUTTONDOWN:                /* left mouse button depressed */
        nXpos = LOWORD (lParam) ;       /* in window's client area. */
        nYpos = HIWORD (lParam) ;
        if (hControl)
            DestroyWindow (hControl) ;
        hInstance = GetWindowWord (hWnd, GWW_HINSTANCE) ;
        hControl = CreateWindow ("BUTTON", "Hi There!",
            WS_CHILD | BS_PUSHBUTTON,
            nXpos, nYpos, 150, 50, hWnd, 100, hInstance, NULL) ;
        ShowWindow (hControl, SW_SHOWNORMAL) ;
        break ;
    case WM_DESTROY:                    /* stop application */
        PostQuitMessage (0) ;
        break ;
    default:        /* default windows message processing */
        return DefWindowProc (hWnd, wMessage, wParam, lParam) ;
    }
    return (0L) ;
}
```

The button control is destroyed and recreated every time the WM_LBUTTONDOWN message is received. The control is given an ID value of 100. The control does generate WM_COMMAND messages if the mouse is clicked inside the button control's client area. This is demonstrated in this example by showing a message box when the button is clicked.

CHAPTER 7

Character Sets, Fonts, and the Keyboard

Most people think of Windows as a mouse-driven environment. Certainly, the mouse is important in Windows, and it is used more frequently than in most MS-DOS programs. But the keyboard can offer shortcuts (called "keyboard accelerators") that are alternatives to the mouse for menu selections and special functions. Touch typists frequently prefer using keyboard actions so that they don't need to take one hand off the keyboard to use the mouse. The keyboard is also the primary means for the user to enter text and numbers.

Windows allows programs to display text and digits using character fonts with different styles, sizes, and colors. Several fonts are always available under Windows, and others can be added by installing fonts from the Windows Control Panel application. Windows also provides the powerful CreateFont() function, which allows you to interpolate new font sizes and styles based on the currently installed fonts. Windows does not use the same IBM PC character set that is used by MS-DOS. Windows uses the more international ANSI character set. Working with the ANSI set can be a bit tricky because many C compiler runtime library functions assume that the IBM PC or ASCII character sets are in use. Windows has its own specialized functions for working with the ANSI character set and converting between ANSI and IBM PC character codes.

Although Windows tools, such as edit controls, take care of many of the nitty-gritty details of dealing with the keyboard for you, there are situations where you will need to work more directly with the keyboard hardware. Word processing programs make heavy use of the keyboard and do not function well with the limitations imposed by edit controls, such as having only one font. In these cases, you will need to process the messages that Windows generates when keys are depressed and released. You can also take advantage of another time saver in Windows—keyboard accelerators. Accelerators provide a simple way to add keyboard shortcuts to your program. They are often used to provide alternatives to selecting menu items and clicking button controls.

Concepts Covered

ANSI Character Set
Keyboard Messages
Virtual Keys

Variable Pitch Fonts
Logical Fonts
Keyboard Accelerators

Keywords Covered

HFONT

ACCELERATOR

Functions Covered

lstrcpy()
lstrcat()
lstrlen()
lstrcmp()
lstrcmpi()
AnsiLower()
AnsiUpperBuff()
AnsiLowerBuff()
AnsiNext()
AnsiPrev()
AnsiToOem()
AnsiToOemBuff()
AnsiUpper()

IsCharAlpha()
IsCharAlphaNumeric()
IsCharLower()
IsCharEUpper()
OemToAnsi()
OemToAnsiBuff()
ToAscii()
TranslateMessage()
CreateFont()
GetTextMetrics()
GetTextExtent()
LoadAccelerators()
TranslateAccelerator()

Messages Covered

WM_KEYDOWN
WM_KEYUP
WM_CHAR
WM_SYSKEYDOWN

WM_SYSCHAR
WM_SYSKEYUP
WM_DEADCHAR

The ANSI Character Set

Computers store and transmit letters and digits using coding systems. Each character is given a number code. A collection of characters, all given number codes, is called a "character set." Over time, the number of character sets has grown. The most common set is the ASCII character set, which uses code numbers between 0 and 127 to encode the letters, numbers, and common keyboard symbols. When the IBM PC was designed, the builders of the hardware and software added additional graphic and special symbol characters to the ASCII character set to come up with the IBM PC character set. This character set is shown in Figure 7-1, encoding all of the symbols with numbers between 0 and 255 (0x0 to 0xFF hexadecimal). Within Windows, the IBM PC character set is called the "OEM" character set, for Original Equipment Manufacturer.

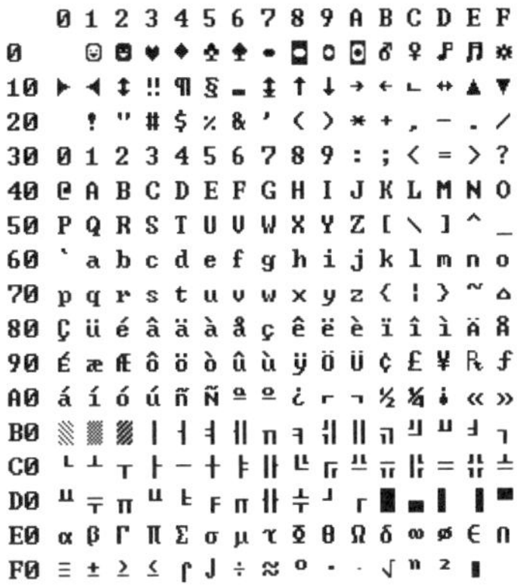

The problem with the OEM character set is that it uses up most of the character positions for graphic symbols, and it does not have a complete collection of accented characters for other languages. The graphic symbols are of little value in an environment where the entire screen is drawn one pixel at a time. The designers of Windows decided to use a more international character coding system, the ANSI character set. This system is shown in Figure 7-2. The ANSI set has fewer graphic symbols, but a more complete collection of accented characters and international symbols. Some of the characters in the ANSI character set are used for control commands, such as tabs and line feeds, which are shown as vertical lines in Figure 7-2.

Normally, you will not need to concern yourself with the exact coding of the characters. A letter "A" is a letter "A." There are a few situations in which the differences are important. Windows programs are expected to work in any language, so care needs to be taken to ensure that accented characters are correctly processed. For example, the following code example works correctly for the unaccented A-Z characters, but completely ignores accented characters.

Figure 7-1 OEM Character Set

Figure 7-2 ANSI Character Set
Add the hexadecimal numbers on the left column and top row to find the code number for a character.

```
char c ;

if (c >= 'A' && c <= 'Z' || c >= 'a' && c <= 'z')   /* wrong !! */
    /* do something assuming c is a character */
```

Chapter 7 • Character Sets, Fonts, and the Keyboard

More difficult to spot are hidden assumptions in standard C compiler library functions like ischar(), toupper(), tolower(), etc. These functions assume the ASCII character set and typically ignore accented characters completely. The problem will not show up until you give your program to a French person to test, and you hear "Il ne march pas!" (It does not work!). It is not possible to spell in French, Spanish, German, or most other languages properly without accented characters.

To get around these problems, Windows provides its own set of functions for doing character conversions. Table 7-1 provides a summary of the character functions.

FUNCTION	PURPOSE
AnsiLower()	Convert a null-terminated character string to lowercase.
AnsiLowerBuff()	Convert a character string to lowercase. Does not have to be null-terminated.
AnsiNext()	Move to the next character in a string.
AnsiPrev()	Move to the previous character in a string.
AnsiToOem()	Convert a string from the ANSI character set to the OEM character set.
AnsiToOemBuff()	Convert a character string from the ANSI to the OEM character set.
AnsiUpper()	Convert a null-terminated character string to uppercase.
AnsiUpperBuff()	Convert a character string to uppercase. The string does not have to be null-terminated.
IsCharAlpha()	Determine if an ANSI character is an alphabetical character.
IsCharAlphaNumeric()	Determine if an ANSI character is an alphabetical or numeric character.
IsCharLower()	Determine if an ANSI character is lowercase.
IsCharUpper()	Determine if an ANSI character is a uppercase letter.
OemToAnsi()	Convert a character string from the OEM character set to the ANSI character set.
OemToAnsiBuff()	Convert a character string from the OEM character set to the ANSI character set. The string does not have to be null-terminated.
ToAscii()	Conversion from virtual key/scan code data to a ANSI character.

Table 7-1 Windows Character Set Functions

There are two reasons to use the Windows character functions in Table 7-1, rather than the C compiler library functions. One is so that the Windows version correctly deals with the ANSI character set, including accented characters. The other reason to use the Windows versions is because they are part of Windows, not part of your program. If you use the C compiler functions, the function's code is added to your program. If you use the Windows versions, the function code remains part of Windows, so your program can be that much smaller. The corrected code, using the Windows function IsCharAlpha(), is shown here.

```
char c ;

if (IsCharAlpha (c))                            /* correct */
   /* do something assuming c is a character */
```

You will note in Table 7-1 that several of the functions allow conversion between the ANSI and OEM character sets. These functions are useful if the text is being exchanged between Windows programs and non-Windows (DOS) programs. Within the Windows environment, you will use the ANSI character set for everything except disk file names. Windows uses MS-DOS to do file input and output, and DOS uses the OEM character set. We will see in Chapter 15, *Disk File Access*, that the file names are converted automatically by the OpenFile() function. However, the file's contents may need to be converted if it is text written using the OEM character set.

Another reason why you may need to go between the ANSI and OEM character sets is if you support different fonts in your program. Suppliers of printer fonts frequently support both Windows and MS-DOS programs. As a result, the fonts may use the OEM character set. This can be very confusing for users of languages other than English (which does not use accented characters). You may need to convert between the two character sets depending on the font in use.

While we are discussing Windows character functions, it is worth noting that Windows includes five functions for copying and comparing strings, which are shown in Table 7-2. Again, the function's code remains part of Windows, not your program, when you make use of these functions. These functions all start with the letter "l," reflecting that they all can handle both long (far) pointers to character strings and near pointers. The functions are indifferent to the character set being used, and they will process both ANSI and OEM character strings.

lstrcat()	Add one character string to the end of another string.
lstrcmp()	Compare two character strings.
lstrcmpi()	Compare two character strings, ignoring the difference between uppercase and lowercase letters.
lstrcpy()	Copy a character string to a memory buffer.
lstrlen()	Determine the length of a character string.

Table 7-2 Windows Functions for Copying and Comparing Character Strings

Trying Out the Character Functions

The first example program in this chapter is called CHAR1. It demonstrates several of the character functions, and it also shows the effects of incorrectly using a C compiler library function. Figure 7-3 shows CHAR1 as displayed on the screen. The first line of text in the client area is the original string. The last word is "Aîné," meaning "aged" in French. This word has two accented characters. The second line shows the effect of using AnsiUpperBuff() to convert the string to the right of the function name to uppercase.

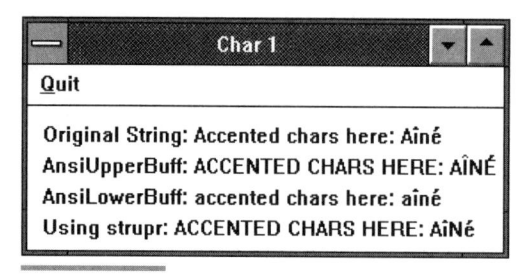

```
┌─────────────────────────────────────┐
│─           Char 1              ▼ ▲ │
│Quit                                 │
├─────────────────────────────────────┤
│ Original String: Accented chars here: Aîné │
│ AnsiUpperBuff: ACCENTED CHARS HERE: AÎNÉ   │
│ AnsiLowerBuff: accented chars here: aîné   │
│ Using strupr: ACCENTED CHARS HERE: AîNé    │
└─────────────────────────────────────┘
```

Figure 7-3 The CHAR1 Program Window

Note that the accented characters are correctly converted. AnsiLowerBuff() is then called to convert the string to entirely lowercase.

The last line in Figure 7-3 shows a programming error. In this case, the C compiler runtime library function strupr() (string uppercase) is used to convert the string back to uppercase. Note that the two accented characters are not converted. The function strupr() assumes that the two accented characters must be graphic symbols, as their codes do not fall in the A-Z, a-z range. The bottom line is: Do not use the C compiler string conversion functions in a Windows program!

Listing 7-1 shows the CHAR1.C program file. All of the character conversion functions are used in processing the WM_PAINT messages to repaint the screen. To begin with, the character string is broken into two pieces. *cStart[]* contains the string "Accented chars here: ," and *cFrench[]* contains "Aîné." The latter string is spelled out letter-by-letter using the hexadecimal code for each character in the ANSI character set. You can compare these values to those shown in Figure 7-2.

The combined string is constructed using the lstrcpy() and lstrcat() functions. lstrcpy() copies *cStart[]* to the beginning of *cTemp[]*. After that, lstrcat() is used to concatenate (add to the end) the *cFrench[]* string to the end of *cTemp[]*. lstrcpy() and lstrcat() are frequently used together to combine strings, such as when adding a file name to the end of a directory path name.

The character conversions to uppercase and lowercase are done using the AnsiUpperBuff() and AnsiLowerBuff() functions. Note that the Windows lstrlen() function is used to determine the length of the string, so that the character conversion functions know how many characters to change. lstrlen() works by finding the first null character (zero) in the string, so the strings must be null-terminated for lstrlen() to work properly. The *cFrench[]* string is explicitly ended with a null character, 0x0 hexadecimal. The *cStart[]* string has an implied null character, as any string enclosed in double quotes will have a null character added to the end by the C compiler. The strings remain null-terminated after the calls to lstrcpy() and lstrcat().

The strings are output to the CHAR1 client area with the TextOut() function. The TextOut() function calls use a common shortcut of combining the wsprintf() function with TextOut().

```
TextOut (ps.hdc, 10, 10, cBuf, wsprintf (cBuf,
    "Original String: %s", (LPSTR) cTemp)) ;
```

The wsprintf() function formats the output string into the character buffer *cBuf[]*. wsprintf() is inside of the parentheses of the TextOut() function, so wsprintf() is executed before TextOut(). wsprintf() puts the string *cTemp[]* into the location marked by "%s" in the wsprintf() format string. wsprintf() copies the combined string into *cBuf[]* ready for output. wsprintf() has the convenient feature of returning the length of the final output string as an integer. This is just what TextOut() needs as its last parameter, so no call to lstrlen() is needed to find the length of the final output string.

Note that in calling wsprintf(), the string *cTemp[]* is cast to a LPSTR (long pointer to a string). This is important, as otherwise wsprintf() will assume the wrong address for the *cTemp[]* string and bomb the program. wsprintf() is one of the few functions in Windows that will cause the program to terminate if the function is called with an improper pointer to the character string.

Listing 7-1 CHAR1.C

```
/* char1.c   demonstrate character conversions */

#include <windows.h>
#include <string.h>      /* included just to demonstrate a programming error */
#include "char1.h"

int PASCAL WinMain (HANDLE hInstance, HANDLE hPrevInstance, LPSTR lpszCmdLine,
   int nCmdShow)
{
    HWND       hWnd ;          /* the window's "handle" */
    MSG        msg ;           /* a message structure */
    WNDCLASS   wndclass ;      /* window class structure */

    if (!hPrevInstance)
    {
       wndclass.style         = CS_HREDRAW | CS_VREDRAW | CS_DBLCLKS ;
       wndclass.lpfnWndProc   = WndProc ;
       wndclass.cbClsExtra    = 0 ;
       wndclass.cbWndExtra    = 0 ;
       wndclass.hInstance     = hInstance ;
       wndclass.hIcon         = LoadIcon (hInstance, "MyIcon") ;
       wndclass.hCursor       = LoadCursor (NULL, IDC_ARROW) ;
       wndclass.hbrBackground = GetStockObject (WHITE_BRUSH) ;
       wndclass.lpszMenuName  = "MyMenu" ;
       wndclass.lpszClassName = "MyClass" ;
                  /* register the window class */
       if (!RegisterClass (&wndclass))
             return 0 ;
    }

    hWnd = CreateWindow ("MyClass","Char 1", WS_OVERLAPPEDWINDOW,
       CW_USEDEFAULT, CW_USEDEFAULT, CW_USEDEFAULT, CW_USEDEFAULT,
       NULL, NULL, hInstance, NULL) ;
    ShowWindow (hWnd, nCmdShow) ;            /* display the window */

    while (GetMessage (&msg, NULL, NULL, NULL)) /* message loop */
    {
       TranslateMessage (&msg) ;             /* translate keyboard messages */
       DispatchMessage (&msg) ;              /* send message to WndProc() */
    }
    return (msg.wParam) ;
}
```

```
long FAR PASCAL WndProc (HWND hWnd, WORD wMessage, WORD wParam, LONG lParam)
{
    PAINTSTRUCT    ps ;
    char           cBuf [128], cTemp [64] ;
    static char    cStart [30] = {|Accented chars here: |} ;
    static char    cFrench [] = {0x41, 0xee, 0x6e, 0xe9, 0x0} ;

    switch (wMessage)                    /* process windows messages */
    {
        case WM_PAINT:
            BeginPaint (hWnd, &ps) ;     /* get device context handle */
            lstrcpy (cTemp, cStart) ;    /* copy cStart[] into cTemp[] */
            lstrcat (cTemp, cFrench) ;   /* add cTemp[] to end of cTemp[] */
            TextOut (ps.hdc, 10, 10, cBuf, wsprintf (cBuf,
                "Original String: %s", (LPSTR) cTemp)) ;
                                         /* convert to upper case */
            AnsiUpperBuff (cTemp, lstrlen (cTemp)) ;
            TextOut (ps.hdc, 10, 30, cBuf, wsprintf (cBuf,
                "AnsiUpperBuff: %s", (LPSTR) cTemp)) ;
                                         /* convert to lower case */
            AnsiLowerBuff (cTemp, lstrlen (cTemp)) ;
            TextOut (ps.hdc, 10, 50, cBuf, wsprintf (cBuf,
                "AnsiLowerBuff: %s", (LPSTR) cTemp)) ;
                                         /* try C compiler library function */
            strupr (cTemp) ;             /* wrong !!! */
            TextOut (ps.hdc, 10, 70, cBuf, wsprintf (cBuf,
                "Using strupr: %s", (LPSTR) cTemp)) ;
                                         /* release the device context */
            EndPaint (hWnd, &ps) ;
            break ;
        case WM_COMMAND:                 /* menu item selected */
            switch (wParam)
            {
                case IDM_QUIT:
                    DestroyWindow (hWnd) ;
                    break ;
            }
            break ;
        case WM_DESTROY:                 /* stop application */
            PostQuitMessage (0) ;
            break ;
        default:                         /* default windows message processing */
            return DefWindowProc (hWnd, wMessage, wParam, lParam) ;
    }
    return (0L) ;
}
```

Listings 7-2 to 7-6 show the support files for CHAR1. The program's icon is shown in Figure 7-4.

Listing 7-2 CHAR1.H Header File

```
/* char1.h header file */

#define IDM_QUIT    10      /* menu item id number */

long FAR PASCAL WndProc (HWND, WORD, WORD, LONG) ;
```

Listing 7-3 CHAR1.RC Resource Script File

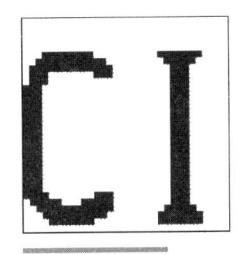

```
/* char1.rc resource file */

#include "char1.h"

MyIcon      ICON    char1.ico

MyMenu      MENU
BEGIN
   MENUITEM "&Quit",        IDM_QUIT
END
```

Figure 7-4
CHAR1.ICO
Icon Image

Listing 7-4 CHAR1.DEF Module Definition File

```
NAME        char1
EXETYPE     WINDOWS
STUB        'WINSTUB.EXE'
CODE        PRELOAD MOVEABLE
DATA        PRELOAD MOVEABLE MULTIPLE
HEAPSIZE    1024
STACKSIZE   5120
EXPORTS     WndProc
```

Listing 7-5 Turbo C++ Project File for CHAR1

```
char1.c
char1.def
char1.res
```

Listing 7-6 QuickC Project File for CHAR1

```
char1.c
char1.def
char1.rc
```

Keyboard Message Processing

Windows was designed to support different types of keyboards for different languages, with different locations on the keyboard for normal and accented characters. When you install Windows, you pick a language. The Windows installation program then takes a keyboard translation table from the installation disks and copies the file to your Windows subdirectory with the name OEMANSI.BIN. This is where the logic table for converting from keypress actions to key codes is stored. Your program can find out which language was installed using the GetKBCodePage() function.

When you depress a key, Windows sends a WM_KEYDOWN message to the window with the input focus. Recall that the window with the input focus is the window with the highlighted caption bar. When the key is released, Windows sends a WM_KEYUP message. Your program can determine which key was pressed by examining the *wParam* parameter that is sent with the keyboard messages. *wParam* will encode the "virtual key code" for the key pressed and released.

Virtual key codes are one of the ways Windows makes sure that a program written for one type of computer keyboard will function properly on another type. The idea is that no matter what type of hardware is being used, the virtual key code for the (A) will have the same value. The virtual codes are all defined in WINDOWS.H and summarized in Appendix A, *Virtual Key Codes*.

The virtual key codes for the letter keys and the numbers at the top of the keyboard have the same value as the ANSI character set. You can use just the letter code (for example 'A' or 'b') for these virtual keys. The other keys have names like VK_F1 for the (F1) function key, VK_TAB for the (Tab) key, VK_CONTROL for the (Cntl) key, and so on. The numeric keypad keys have virtual codes that differ from those of the corresponding number keys at the top of the keyboard. VK_NUMPAD0 is the code for the zero key on the numeric keypad key, while '0' is the code for the zero key at the top of the main keyboard group. The only key which does not have a virtual key code is (Alt). The status of the (Alt) key is passed with the *lParam* value in a WM_KEYDOWN or WM_KEYUP message. This will be explained in a moment.

Using the virtual key codes, you can figure out what the user is doing with the keyboard. Listing 7-7 shows a typical example that checks for the letter (A) key, the (Tab) key, and the (Shift) key. If a WM_KEYDOWN message is sent with *wParam* equal to VK_SHIFT, one of the two shift keys is being depressed. Windows sends a WM_KEYUP message with *wParam* equal to VK_SHIFT. In Listing 7-7, a static variable *bShiftDown* is used to keep track of whether a shift key is currently up or down. This is one way to tell if the user intends to send an uppercase or lowercase A, as in either case the WM_KEYDOWN message will have *wParam* set to the same value ('A' or 0x41 hexadecimal).

Listing 7-7 Processing WM_KEYDOWN Messages

```
long FAR PASCAL WndProc (HWND hWnd, WORD wMessage, WORD wParam, LONG lParam)
{
   static BOOL bShiftDown = FALSE ;

   switch (wMessage)                  /* process windows messages */
   {
     case WM_KEYDOWN:
         switch (wParam)
         {
             case 'A':                /* letter A key */
                 /* do something */
                 break ;
             case VK_TAB:             /* tab key */
```

```
                /* do something */
                break ;
        case VK_SHIFT:          /* shift key depressed */
                bShiftDown = TRUE ;
                break ;
    }
    break ;
case WM_KEYUP:
    switch (wParam)
    {
        case VK_SHIFT:          /* shift key released */
                bShiftDown = FALSE ;
                break ;
```
[Other program lines]

The WM_KEYDOWN and WM_KEYUP messages also put data into the *lParam* parameter sent with the message. Table 7-3 summarizes the data format. Normally, you will use only the *lParam* value to determine if the (Alt) key was depressed. Another use is when you need to distinguish between the right and left (Shift) keys. The OEM scan code for the two keys is different, although Windows gives them both the same VK_SHIFT virtual key code. The standard OEM scan code for the left shift key is 0x2A hexadecimal, and 0x36 hexadecimal for the right shift key.

BITS	MEANING
0-15 (low-order word)	The repeat count. This is the number of times the character was repeated because the user held down a key.
16-23	The keyboard OEM scan code.
24	1 if an extended key, such as a function key or a key on the numeric keypad.
25-28	Reserved.
29	1 if the (Alt) key was held down when the key was pressed, 0 if not.
30	1 if the key was down before the message was sent, 0 if not.
31	1 if the key is being released, 0 if the key is being pressed.

Table 7-3 The *lParam* 32 Bit Data for WM_KEYUP, WM_KEYDOWN Messages

The WM_CHAR Message

The WM_KEYDOWN and WM_KEYUP messages have a limitation. The virtual key code for the letter (A) key is the same whether the user is typing an uppercase or lowercase letter. As mentioned earlier, you can figure out what the user is doing by tracking whether the shift keys are depressed or up, but Windows provides an easier way. The TranslateMessage() function converts the current combination of letter and shift keys to the equivalent ANSI character code. TranslateMessage() is put into the program's message loop in the WinMain() function. Listing 7-8 shows a typical message loop, including the TranslateMessage() function. As usual, GetMessage() is used to fetch the message data from Windows, and DispatchMessage() is used to send the message to the WndProc() function.

Listing 7-8 Typical Message Loop with TranslateMessage()

```
while (GetMessage (&msg, NULL, NULL, NULL))   /* message loop */
{
   TranslateMessage (&msg) ;  /* translate keyboard messages */
   DispatchMessage (&msg) ;   /* send message to WndProc() */
}
```

When TranslateMessage() detects a keyboard action that translates to an ANSI character, it generates a WM_CHAR message. The *wParam* parameter sent with the message is the ANSI character code. This is handy, as the ANSI code is almost always what you will want to display. Function keys and other keys that do not have an ANSI character equivalent do not generate the WM_CHAR message. You will pick those up with the WM_KEYDOWN or WM_KEYUP message using the virtual key code. WM_CHAR uses the same coding of the *lParam* data used by WM_KEYDOWN or WM_KEYUP (Table 7-3). You probably will not find *lParam* very useful with this message.

If your program's message loop contains the TranslateMessage() function, the following messages will be sent when a key is depressed:

WM_KEYDOWN	=	The key is depressed.
WM_CHAR	=	The ANSI character (if there is one).
WM_KEYUP	=	The key is released.

Most of the time you will ignore the WM_KEYUP messages. WM_KEYDOWN is processed for the function keys, the (Cntl) key, and other virtual keys that do not have ANSI equivalents. WM_CHAR is used for the ANSI characters.

System Key Messages and Dead Characters

There are situations when a different series of messages is sent for keyboard actions. One occurs when the user has the (Alt) key down, or when no window on the system has the input focus. In these cases, the system key messages are sent. They are just like the normal character messages and use the same coding of the *wParam* and *lParam* values. The sequence of messages is:

WM_SYSKEYDOWN	=	The key is depressed with (Alt) down.
WM_SYSCHAR	=	The ANSI character (if there is one).
WM_SYSKEYUP	=	The key is released.

224   Windows PROGRAMMING Primer Plus®

With the (Alt) key down, the keystroke signals some special function. Usually, you will use only the WM_SYSKEYDOWN message to determine which virtual key is depressed and ignore the WM_SYSCHAR and WM_SYSKEYUP messages. Note that the (Cntl) key does *not* generate WM_SYSKEYDOWN and WM_SYSKEYUP messages.

One last message is worth noting: WM_DEADCHAR. If the user installed any language other than English, the keyboard logic will include special combinations to generate accent characters. For example, the French accent circumflex (^) is obtained by pressing (Cntl)-([), and then pressing the letter key. This key combination will work only if French was chosen as the default language when Windows was installed. Windows will then send the following series of messages:

WM_KEYDOWN	-	Depressed the accent key.
WM_DEADCHAR	-	The character message for the accent.
WM_KEYUP	-	Released the accent key.
WM_KEYDOWN	-	Depressed the letter key.
WM_CHAR	-	The character code for the accented letter.
WM_KEYUP	-	Released the letter key.

The phrase "dead character" brings all sorts of gruesome images to mind, but all it means is that the keystroke does not result in a visible character. The "dead character" just modifies the next character typed, to add an accent. You usually can ignore the WM_DEADCHAR message. TranslateMessage() automatically will pick the right ANSI character including the accent, and send it with the WM_CHAR message as the *wParam* parameter. Impossible accents for the language, such as an accent circumflex over a consonant, do not have ANSI character codes. There is even a WM_SYSDEADCHAR message for accent keys depressed with the (Alt) key down.

Implementing a Simple Keyboard Interface

Let's put our knowledge of keyboard messages to work with a simple program that allows you to type a line of text. Figure 7-5 shows the KEYBD1 program in action. When the user types at the keyboard, blue characters appear in the client area. The only editing feature is the (Backspace) key. Pressing this key erases the last letter typed.

Listing 7-9 shows the KEYBD1.C program. There are a few subtle things in the WndProc() function. When a WM_CHAR message is processed, the character is added to a static character buffer called *cBuf[ ]*. This buffer is just a character array set aside in the program's local memory heap to hold the ANSI codes for the characters typed. Each character is added to the end of *cBuf[ ]* if:

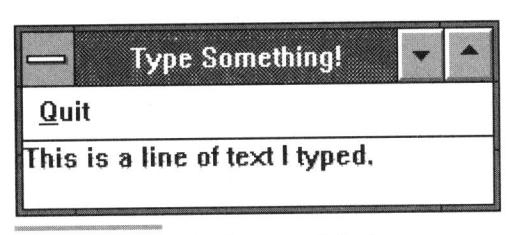

Figure 7-5 KEYBD1 Program Window

Chapter 7 • Character Sets, Fonts, and the Keyboard

1. The end of the *cBuf[]* memory space has not been reached.
2. The character is alphanumeric (as determined by the IsCharAlphaNumeric() function).
3. The character is ANSI punctuation. The function IsAnsiPunc() is defined at the bottom of Listing 7-9. This function checks a character code to see if it falls in the range of codes that are printable but are not characters. We will look more closely at IsAnsiPunc() in a moment.

If all of these conditions are met, the character is added to the end of the *cBuf[]* buffer. The static integer *nCurPos* is used to keep track of the current end of the buffer. Note that a null character (zero) is always added after the last character typed in order to keep the character string null-terminated.

At this point, the character typed has not appeared on the screen. To make the character visible, the InvalidateRect() function is called. This makes the entire client area invalid (needing repainting), which causes a WM_PAINT message to be sent to the WndProc() function. The logic for displaying the typed characters is in the processing of WM_PAINT.

When a WM_PAINT message is received, the character string in *cBuf[]* is output to the window's client area using TextOut(). The only thing special here is that the text color is changed to pure blue, using the SetTextColor() function we learned about in Chapter 4, *Text and Graphic Output*. The reason for waiting to display the string until a WM_PAINT message appears is that the string will be repainted automatically when the window is resized or uncovered. If we output each character as it is typed, without the WM_PAINT logic, the string will disappear when a WM_PAINT message is processed.

The other reason for doing the output of the character string while processing WM_PAINT is to make it easy to erase the last character typed using the backspace key. The backspace key does not have an ANSI character equivalent, so we cannot use the WM_CHAR message to identify it. Instead, KEYBD1.C processes the WM_KEYDOWN message, looking for the virtual key code for the backspace key, VK_BACK. When this key code is received, KEYBD1.C writes over the last character in the *cBuf[]* buffer with a null character (zero). This shortens the string by one character. InvalidateRect() is again called to force a WM_PAINT message. The client area is redrawn, erasing the old characters, and repainted using the new shorter version of *cBuf[]*. The last character in the string is erased.

Listing 7-9 KEYBD1.C

```
/* keybd1.c   simple keyboard interface */

#include <windows.h>
#include "keybd1.h"

int PASCAL WinMain (HANDLE hInstance, HANDLE hPrevInstance, LPSTR lpszCmdLine,
    int nCmdShow)
{
    HWND    hWnd ;          /* the window's "handle" */
    MSG     msg ;           /* a message structure */
```

```c
    WNDCLASS    wndclass ;      /* window class structure */

    if (!hPrevInstance)
    {
       wndclass.style         = CS_HREDRAW | CS_VREDRAW | CS_DBLCLKS ;
       wndclass.lpfnWndProc   = WndProc ;
       wndclass.cbClsExtra    = 0 ;
       wndclass.cbWndExtra    = 0 ;
       wndclass.hInstance     = hInstance ;
       wndclass.hIcon         = LoadIcon (hInstance, "MyIcon") ;
       wndclass.hCursor       = LoadCursor (NULL, IDC_ARROW) ;
       wndclass.hbrBackground = GetStockObject (WHITE_BRUSH) ;
       wndclass.lpszMenuName  = "MyMenu" ;
       wndclass.lpszClassName = "MyClass" ;
                  /* register the window class */
       if (!RegisterClass (&wndclass))
           return 0 ;
    }

    hWnd = CreateWindow ("MyClass","Type Something!", WS_OVERLAPPEDWINDOW,
        CW_USEDEFAULT, CW_USEDEFAULT, CW_USEDEFAULT, CW_USEDEFAULT,
        NULL, NULL, hInstance, NULL) ;
    ShowWindow (hWnd, nCmdShow) ;   /* display the window */

    while (GetMessage (&msg, NULL, NULL, NULL))   /* message loop */
    {
       TranslateMessage (&msg) ;   /* translate keyboard messages */
       DispatchMessage (&msg) ;    /* send message to WndProc() */
    }
    return (msg.wParam) ;
}
long FAR PASCAL WndProc (HWND hWnd, WORD wMessage, WORD wParam, LONG lParam)
{
    static    char     cBuf [LINELONG] ;
    static    int      nCurPos = 0 ;
    PAINTSTRUCT        ps ;
    HDC                hDC ;

    switch (wMessage)                           /* process windows messages */
    {
       case WM_COMMAND:
           switch (wParam)    /* menu items */
           {
              case IDM_QUIT:
                  DestroyWindow (hWnd) ;    /* destroy window, */
                  break ;    /* terminating application */
           }
           break ;
       case WM_PAINT:
           hDC = BeginPaint (hWnd, &ps) ;
           SetTextColor (hDC, RGB (0, 0, 255)) ;    /* blue letters */
           TextOut (hDC, 0, 0, cBuf, lstrlen (cBuf)) ;
           EndPaint (hWnd, &ps) ;
           break ;
       case WM_CHAR:                             /* char input */
           if (nCurPos < LINELONG - 1 &&         /* or punctuation */
              (IsCharAlphaNumeric ((char) wParam) || IsAnsiPunc ((char) wParam)))
           {
```

```
                cBuf [nCurPos++] = (char) wParam ;      /* add new letter */
                cBuf [nCurPos] = 0 ;                    /* null term. string */
                InvalidateRect (hWnd, NULL, TRUE) ;     /* force WM_PAINT */
            }
            break ;
        case WM_KEYDOWN:                                /* non ANSI key input */
            switch (wParam)
            {
                case VK_BACK:                           /* backspace key */
                    if (nCurPos > 0)
                    {
                        nCurPosñ ;                      /* back up one char */
                        cBuf [nCurPos] = 0 ;            /* replace with null */
                        InvalidateRect (hWnd, NULL, TRUE) ;
                    }
            }
            break ;
        case WM_DESTROY:                                /* stop application */
            PostQuitMessage (0) ;
            break ;
        default:         /* default windows message processing */
            return DefWindowProc (hWnd, wMessage, wParam, lParam) ;
    }
    return (0L) ;
}

BOOL IsAnsiPunc (WORD wChar)    /* returns true if wChar is punctuation char */
{
    if ((wChar >= _ _ && wChar <= _@ ) || (wChar >= _[_ && wChar <= _' ) ||
        (wChar >= _{_ && wChar <= _~ ) || (wChar >= 0xA0 && wChar <= 0xBF))
        return (TRUE) ;
    else
        return (FALSE) ;
}
```

KEYBD1.C is the first program we have written that defines an additional function beyond the normal WinMain() and WndProc() functions. IsAnsiPunc() is defined at the bottom of Listing 7-9. A function prototype is also included in the KEYBD1.H header file in Listing 7-10. The function prototype lets the compiler know that IsAnsiPunc() takes one parameter, a WORD value, and returns a value of type BOOL. BOOL is defined as an integer in WINDOWS.H, but used in place of "int" in situations where the value is either TRUE (nonzero) or FALSE (zero). TRUE and FALSE are also defined in WINDOWS.H.

IsAnsiPunc() does not need to be declared in the EXPORTS section of the KEYBD1.DEF module definition file (Listing 7-12), because the function is only called from within KEYBD1, not by Windows or some other program. In other words, IsAnsiPunc() is just like any C language function that you might declare in a DOS program.

Listing 7-10 KEYBD1.H Header File

```
/* keybd1.h header file */

#define IDM_QUIT    10       /* menu item id number */
#define LINELONG    128      /* maximum length of a line */
```

```
long FAR PASCAL WndProc (HWND, WORD, WORD, LONG) ;
BOOL IsAnsiPunc (WORD wChar) ;
```

The remaining support files for KEYBO1. are shown in Listings 7-11 to 7-14. The program icon is shown in Figure 7-6.

Listing 7-11 KEYBD1.RC Resource Script File

```
/* keybd1.rc resource file */

#include "keybd1.h"

MyIcon      ICON    keybd1.ico

MyMenu      MENU
BEGIN
    MENUITEM "&Quit",       IDM_QUIT
END
```

Figure 7-6
KEYBD1.ICO
Icon Image

Listing 7-12 KEYBD1.DEF Module Definition File

```
NAME        keybd1
EXETYPE     WINDOWS
STUB        'WINSTUB.EXE'
CODE        PRELOAD MOVEABLE
DATA        PRELOAD MOVEABLE MULTIPLE
HEAPSIZE    1024
STACKSIZE   5120
EXPORTS     WndProc
```

Listing 7-13 Turbo C++ Project File for KEYBD1

```
keybd1.c
keybd1.def
keybd1.res
```

Listing 7-14 QuickC Project File for KEYBD1

```
keybd1.c
keybd1.def
keybd1.rc
```

Selecting a Stock Font

KEYBD1.C provides a good outline for how a Windows program handles text input. We can build on this example to explore other aspects of processing text, including changing the character fonts and managing the caret to help guide our editing. These

```
Font = ANSI_FIXED_FONT
Font = ANSI_VAR_FONT
Font = DEVICE_DEFAULT_FONT
Font = OEM_FIXED_FONT
Font = SYSTEM_FONT
Font = SYSTEM_FIXED_FONT
```

Figure 7-7 Windows Stock Fonts

improvements will be added in two steps. The next program, FONT1, will add new fonts to our KEYBD1 example. The chapter closes with FONT2, which adds control of the caret to the example.

There are two basic kinds of fonts that you can use in developing a Windows program. The simplest to use are the stock fonts, which are always available within Windows. The stock fonts are shown in Figure 7-7. Like stock pens and brushes, stock fonts are accessed with the GetStockObject() function. GetStockObject() returns a handle (HFONT) to the stock object's data. This is the handle needed by SelectObject() to select the object into a device context.

```
HDC         hDC ;
HFONT       hFont ;

hDC = GetDC (hWnd) ;
hFont = GetStockObject (ANSI_VAR_FONT) ;
SelectObject (hDC, hFont) ;
```
[Other program lines]

You can save a little space by using GetStockObject() and SelectObject() in the same line. There is no need to save the handle to the stock font, as stock objects cannot be deleted.

```
HDC         hDC ;

hDC = GetDC (hWnd) ;
SelectObject (hDC, GetStockObject (ANSI_VAR_FONT)) ;
```
[Other program lines]

In the KEYBD1 program, we did not select a font, so the default font for the device context was used for character output. The default font for a video device context is the system font. This is a variable-pitch font, meaning that the characters are not all the same width. For example, with variable-pitch fonts the letter "I" takes up less room horizontally than the letter "M." Fixed-pitch fonts use the same spacing between characters regardless of the letter being output. Variable fonts are easier to read and take up less space.

Using Logical Fonts

Besides the stock fonts, Windows also comes with separate font files that define the characteristics of characters written in a number of different styles and sizes. You can find the font files in your Windows system directory, usually C:\WINDOW\SYSTEM. Font files have the extension .FON, or .FOT for TrueType fonts introduced with Windows 3.1. These files contain detailed descriptions of each character. You can install new fonts using the Windows Control Panel application.

To use font data in a program, you need to obtain a handle to the font data and select it into the device context. This is just like using a stock font, except we will load the font data from a separate file, not from Windows using GetStockObject(). The CreateFont() function is used in place of GetStockObject(), to load the font and to return a handle to the font data.

CreateFont() does more than just load font data into memory. CreateFont() can create new fonts, by interpolating from the data in a font file. CreateFont() will create new font sizes, create bold and underlined styles, and let you rotate and distort the font's characters. These interpolated fonts are called "logical fonts" because they come from Window's font logic, not just from a font data file.

Listing 7-15 shows a typical programming sequence that creates a logical font, and uses it to draw some text on the device context. In this case, a Roman font is created and used to output the text string "Output string" to the device context. After the font is used, it is deleted. Note that the font is deleted after the device context is deleted to avoid deleting a selected object. You can also select a stock object into the device context to displace the logical font, prior to deleting it. Only one font can be selected into a device context at one time.

Listing 7-15 Creating a Logical Font

```
HFONT      hFont ;
HDC        hDC ;

hFont = CreateFont (36, 0, 0, 0, FW_NORMAL, 0, 0, 0, ANSI_CHARSET,
    OUT_DEFAULT_PRECIS, CLIP_DEFAULT_PRECIS, DEFAULT_QUALITY,
    VARIABLE_PITCH | FF_ROMAN, "Roman") ;
hDC = GetDC (hWnd) ;
SelectObject (hDC, hFont) ;
TextOut (hDC, 0, 0, "Output string.", 14) ;
ReleaseDC (hWnd, hDC) ;
DeleteObject (hFont) ;
```

The font created by the CreateFont() function call in Listing 7-15 is shown in Figure 7-8. The characters are interpolated to a size of 36 pixels high, based on the Roman font that is supplied with Windows. This results in a variable-pitched font, based on the ANSI character set.

The characters are measured in both height and width in *logical units*. With the default units of a device context, logical units are equal to pixels. We will see in Chapter 13, *The Device Context*, that other systems of units can be used. This diversity will allow you to size fonts and other graphical objects in inches, millimeters, or printers units. For now we will just use pixels. The vertical measurements of a font are shown in Figure 7-9.

Figure 7-8 A Logical Roman Font

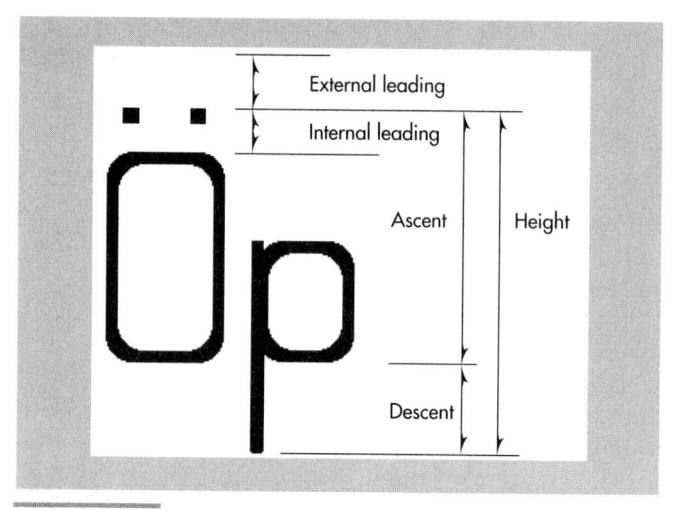

Figure 7-9 Font Measurements

The CreateFont() function is passed fourteen parameters. The example in Listing 7-15 is typical in that many of the options are set to default values, usually zero. Using the defaults causes the adjustments from the font data to be minimal. You can go wild with CreateFont() and make fonts with characters lying on their sides, going upward on the device context instead of left-to-right, etc. These changes are done using the parameters passed to CreateFont(). The full syntax of the CreateFont() function is as follows:

HFONT **CreateFont**(int *nHeight*, int *nWidth*, int *nEscapement*, int *nOrientation*, int *nWeight*, BYTE *cItalic*, BYTE *cUnderline*, BYTE *cStrikeOut*, BYTE *cCharSet*, BYTE *cOutputPrecision*, BYTE *cClipPrecision*, BYTE *cQuality*, BYTE *cPitchAndFamily*, LPSTR *lpFacename*);

nHeight	int: The desired height of the characters, including internal leading, excluding external leading, in logical units. Set equal to zero for the default size. To set the ascent size, rather than the total height, make this value negative. The absolute value will then be used to set the ascent size.
nWidth	int: The desired width of the characters in logical units. Normally, set to 0, which allows Windows to match the width to the height. Positive values force a width, changing the character's aspect ratio.
nEscapement	int: Specifies the orientation of the next character output relative to the previous one in tenths of a degree. Normally set to 0. Set to 900 to have all the characters go upward from the first character, 1800 to write backwards, or 2700 to write each character from the top down. See Figure 7-10.

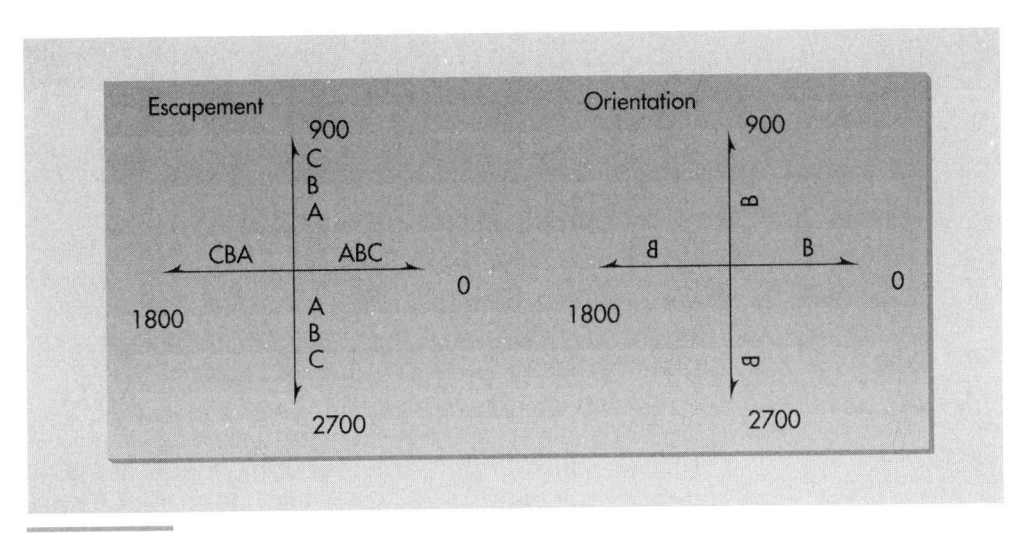

Figure 7-10 Character Orientation and Escapement

nOrientation	int: Specifies how much the character should be rotated when output in tenths of a degree. Set to 900 to have all the characters lying on their backs, 1800 for upside-down writing, etc. See Figure 7-10.
nWeight	int: Sets how thickly to print the lines of each character. The units are arbitrary, with the values of FW_NORMAL (400) for normal characters and FW_BOLD (700) for bold face defined in WINDOWS.H. WINDOW.H has eight other sizes defined, but they are rounded to either the normal or boldface weight.
cItalic	BYTE: TRUE to specify italic characters, FALSE (zero) for normal.
cUnderline	BYTE: TRUE to specify underlined characters, FALSE (zero) for normal.
cStrikeOut	BYTE: TRUE to specify characters with a line through the center, FALSE (zero) for normal.
cCharSet	BYTE: The character set of the font. This can be either ANSI_CHARSET, SYMBOL_CHARSET, OEM_CHARSET or (with Japanese versions of Windows) SHIFTJIS_CHARSET.
cOutputPrecision	BYTE: Set equal to OUT_DEFAULT_PRECIS (zero). This parameter does not do anything.
cClipPrecision	BYTE: Set equal to CLIP_DEFAULT_PRECIS.
cQuality	BYTE: Can be either DRAFT_QUALITY, PROOF_QUALITY, or DEFAULT_QUALITY (the most common choice).

	PROOF_QUALITY forces the closest match to the loaded font data, which may change the font size if the specified size is not available.
cPitchAndFamily	BYTE: Two values combined with the C language binary OR operator "|." The two low-order bits specify the font pitch. This can be either : DEFAULT_PITCH, FIXED_PITCH or VARIABLE_PITCH. The four high-order bits specify the font family. This can be any of the following: FF_DECORATIVE, FF_DONTCARE, FF_MODERN, FF_ROMAN, FF_SCRIPT, or FF_SWISS. For example, use the combination DEFAULT_PITCH	FF_ROMAN to create a Roman style typeface, using the character pitch of the nearest matching font installed on the system. This will be a variable pitch font, if the normal Windows Times Roman typeface is installed.
lpFacename	LPSTR: A pointer to a null-terminated string that specifies the name of the font data. The maximum length of the name is LF_FACESIZE which is defined in WINDOWS.H as 32.

Text Metrics

Because of the way the CreateFont() function generates a logical font using stored font data, modified by the CreateFont() parameters, you will not know all of the dimensions of a font after you create it. Windows provides the GetTextMetrics() function to find out details about a font. GetTextMetrics() determines the characteristics of the font currently selected into the device context, and copies the data into a data structure called TEXTMETRIC. The TEXTMETRIC structure is defined in WINDOWS.H as follows:

```
typedef struct tagTEXTMETRIC
{
    int     tmHeight;              /* character height */
    int     tmAscent;              /* ascent height */
    int     tmDescent;             /* descent height */
    int     tmInternalLeading;     /* internal leading height */
    int     tmExternalLeading;     /* external leading height */
    int     tmAveCharWidth;        /* average width of a character */
    int     tmMaxCharWidth;        /* widest character width */
    int     tmWeight;              /* weight (thickness) of the font */
    BYTE    tmItalic;              /* nonzero for italics */
    BYTE    tmUnderlined;          /* nonzero for underlined */
    BYTE    tmStruckOut;           /* nonzero for strike through characters */
    BYTE    tmFirstChar;           /* code value for first character defined */
    BYTE    tmLastChar;            /* code value for last character defined */
    BYTE    tmDefaultChar;         /* char to substitute for those missing */
    BYTE    tmBreakChar;           /* word break character - usually a space */
    BYTE    tmPitchAndFamily;      /* pitch and family code - see CreateFont() */
    BYTE    tmCharSet;             /* either ANSI_CHARSET, SYMBOL_CHARSET, */
                                   /* SHIFTJIS_CHARSET or OEM_CHARSET */
```

```
    int     tmOverhang;              /* extra width allowed for bold, etc */
    int     tmDigitizedAspectX;      /* ratio of the X and Y digitalized aspects */
    int     tmDigitizedAspectY;      /* is the aspect ratio for which the font */
                                     /* was originally designed */
} TEXTMETRIC;
```

That is probably more information about a font than you will ever need. The most common reason to call GetTextMetrics() is to find out the height of the font's characters. The height can be used to set line spacing, size the caret, or proportion other objects such as buttons. A typical call to GetTextMetrics() is shown in Listing 7-16. In this case, the spacing between lines is determined by adding the character height and the external leading height.

Listing 7-16 Using the GetTextMetrics() Function to Find Line Spacing

```
TEXTMETRIC      tm ;
HDC             hDC ;
int             nLineSpacing ;

hDC = GetDC (hWnd) ;
SelectObject (hDC, GetStockObject (ANSI_VAR_FONT)) ;
GetTextMetrics (hDC, &tm) ;
nLineSpacing = tm.tmHeight + tm.tmExternalLeading ;
```
[Other program lines]

Putting Fonts to Work

Our next program, FONT1, improves on KEYBD1 by allowing a choice of three fonts for output of the text that the user types. Figure 7-11a shows output using the stock ANSI variable font. Figure 7-11b shows the same text string using a logical font created based on the ROMAN.FON data.

Listing 7-17 shows the FONT1.C program file. The logic for processing the character messages is identical to the KEYBD1.C program. FONT1.C creates a logical font when processing the WM_CREATE message as the program starts running. The font is given a logical size of 36 and is built from the FF_ROMAN family of fonts. The handle to the font data is stored in the static variable *hFont*. This is a handle to a font, or HFONT data type.

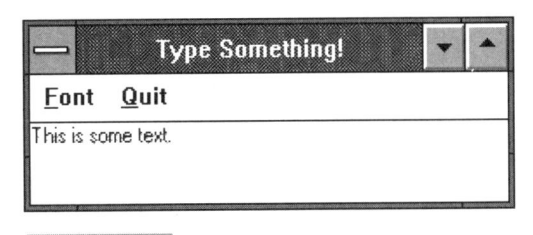

Figure 7-11a FONT1 Program with Stock ANSI Variable Font

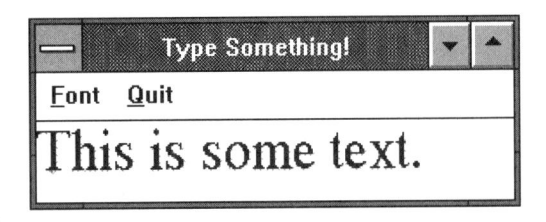

Figure 7-11b FONT1 Program with a Logical 36 Unit Roman Font

Chapter 7 • Character Sets, Fonts, and the Keyboard

When the user selects a font type using the FONT1 menu, the selected font is stored in the static variable *nFontChoice*. The menu item ID number is used as a convenient code to keep track of the selected font in *nFontChoice*. Selecting a new font also results in calling InvalidateRect(), which causes the client area to be repainted and a WM_PAINT message to be sent to the WndProc() function.

The actual output of the character string is done in processing the WM_PAINT message. The currently selected font is selected into the device context before calling TextOut() to output the string. In the case of the stock fonts, the font data is accessed with GetStockObject(). If the Roman font has been selected, the *hFont* handle is used to allow SelectObject() to select the logical font into the device context. In this case, the character string will show up with large Roman characters, as shown in Figure 7-11b.

Listing 7-17 FONT1.C

```c
/* font1.c   Use a new font in client area */

#include <windows.h>
#include "font1.h"

int PASCAL WinMain (HANDLE hInstance, HANDLE hPrevInstance, LPSTR lpszCmdLine,
    int nCmdShow)
{
    HWND       hWnd ;         /* the window's "handle" */
    MSG        msg ;          /* a message structure */
    WNDCLASS   wndclass ;     /* window class structure */

    if (!hPrevInstance)
    {
        wndclass.style         = CS_HREDRAW | CS_VREDRAW | CS_DBLCLKS ;
        wndclass.lpfnWndProc   = WndProc ;
        wndclass.cbClsExtra    = 0 ;
        wndclass.cbWndExtra    = 0 ;
        wndclass.hInstance     = hInstance ;
        wndclass.hIcon         = LoadIcon (hInstance, "MyIcon") ;
        wndclass.hCursor       = LoadCursor (NULL, IDC_ARROW) ;
        wndclass.hbrBackground = GetStockObject (WHITE_BRUSH) ;
        wndclass.lpszMenuName  = "MyMenu" ;
        wndclass.lpszClassName = "MyClass" ;
                /* register the window class */
        if (!RegisterClass (&wndclass))
            return 0 ;
    }

    hWnd = CreateWindow ("MyClass","Type Something!", WS_OVERLAPPEDWINDOW,
        CW_USEDEFAULT, CW_USEDEFAULT, CW_USEDEFAULT, CW_USEDEFAULT,
        NULL, NULL, hInstance, NULL) ;
    ShowWindow (hWnd, nCmdShow) ;   /* display the window */

    while (GetMessage (&msg, NULL, NULL, NULL))   /* message loop */
    {
      TranslateMessage (&msg) ;   /* translate keyboard messages */
      DispatchMessage (&msg) ;    /* send message to WndProc() */
    }
```

```
        return (msg.wParam) ;
}

long FAR PASCAL WndProc (HWND hWnd, WORD wMessage, WORD wParam, LONG lParam)
{
    static char     cBuf [LINELONG] ;
    static int      nCurPos = 0 ;
    PAINTSTRUCT     ps ;
    HDC             hDC ;
    static HFONT    hFont ;
    static int      nFontChoice = IDM_ROMAN ;

    switch (wMessage)                       /* process windows messages */
    {
      case WM_CREATE:
         hFont = CreateFont (36, 0, 0, 0, FW_NORMAL, 0, 0, 0, ANSI_CHARSET,
                OUT_DEFAULT_PRECIS, CLIP_DEFAULT_PRECIS, DEFAULT_QUALITY,
                VARIABLE_PITCH | FF_ROMAN, "Roman") ;
         break ;
      case WM_COMMAND:
         switch (wParam)                    /* menu items */
         {
           case IDM_ANSI:                   /* remember font choice */
              nFontChoice = IDM_ANSI ;
              InvalidateRect (hWnd, NULL, TRUE) ;  /* force WM_PAINT */
              break ;
           case IDM_OEM:
              nFontChoice = IDM_OEM ;
              InvalidateRect (hWnd, NULL, TRUE) ;  /* force WM_PAINT */
              break ;
           case IDM_ROMAN:
              nFontChoice = IDM_ROMAN ;
              InvalidateRect (hWnd, NULL, TRUE) ;  /* force WM_PAINT */
              break ;
           case IDM_QUIT:
              DestroyWindow (hWnd) ;        /* destroy window, */
              break ;                       /* terminating application */
         }
         break ;
      case WM_PAINT:
         hDC = BeginPaint (hWnd, &ps) ;
         SetTextColor (hDC, RGB (0, 0, 255)) ;   /* blue letters */
         switch (nFontChoice)
         {                                  /* select a font into DC */
           case IDM_ANSI:
              SelectObject (hDC, GetStockObject (ANSI_VAR_FONT)) ;
              break ;
           case IDM_OEM:
              SelectObject (hDC, GetStockObject (OEM_FIXED_FONT)) ;
              break ;
           case IDM_ROMAN:
              SelectObject (hDC, hFont) ;
              break ;
         }
         TextOut (hDC, 0, 0, cBuf, lstrlen (cBuf)) ;
         EndPaint (hWnd, &ps) ;
         break ;
      case WM_CHAR:                                 /* char input */
         if (nCurPos < LINELONG &&                  /* or punctuation */
```

```
                (IsCharAlphaNumeric ((char) wParam) || IsAnsiPunc ((char) wParam)))
                {
                    cBuf [nCurPos++] = (char) wParam ;    /* add new letter */
                    cBuf [nCurPos] = 0 ;                  /* null term. string */
                    InvalidateRect (hWnd, NULL, TRUE) ;   /* force WM_PAINT */
                }
                break ;
            case WM_KEYDOWN:                              /* non ANSI key input */
                switch (wParam)
                {
                    case VK_BACK:                         /* backspace key */
                        if (nCurPos > 0)
                        {
                            nCurPosñ ;                    /* back up one char */
                            cBuf [nCurPos] = 0 ;          /* replace with null */
                            InvalidateRect (hWnd, NULL, TRUE) ;
                        }
                }
                break ;
            case WM_DESTROY:                              /* stop application */
                DeleteObject (hFont) ;                    /* remove font from memory */
                PostQuitMessage (0) ;
                break ;
            default:              /* default windows message processing */
                return DefWindowProc (hWnd, wMessage, wParam, lParam) ;
    }
    return (0L) ;
}

BOOL IsAnsiPunc (WORD wChar)   /* returns true if wChar is punctuation char */
{
    if ((wChar >= ' ' && wChar <= '@') || (wChar >= '[' && wChar <= '`') ||
        (wChar >= '{' && wChar <= '~') || (wChar >= 0xA0 && wChar <= 0xBF))
        return (TRUE) ;
    else
        return (FALSE) ;
}
```

The FONT1.H header file in Listing 7-18 defines the menu item ID numbers for the font selections. The constant LINELONG is used to set the maximum length of the character buffer used to store the typed letters. Again note that the IsAnsiPunc() function declaration is in the header file.

Listing 7-18 FONT1.H Header File

```
/* font1.h  header file */
                            /* menu item id number */
#define IDM_ANSI    1       /* ansi variable font menu selection */
#define IDM_OEM     2       /* oem fixed font menu selection */
#define IDM_ROMAN   3       /* roman font menu selection */
#define IDM_QUIT    10
#define LINELONG    128     /* maximum length of a line */

long FAR PASCAL WndProc (HWND, WORD, WORD, LONG) ;
BOOL IsAnsiPunc (WORD wChar) ;
```

The FONT1.RC resource script file (Listing 7-19) defines the popup menu for selecting one of the fonts. The remaining support files are shown in Listing 7-20 to 7-22. The program's icon is shown in Figure 7-12.

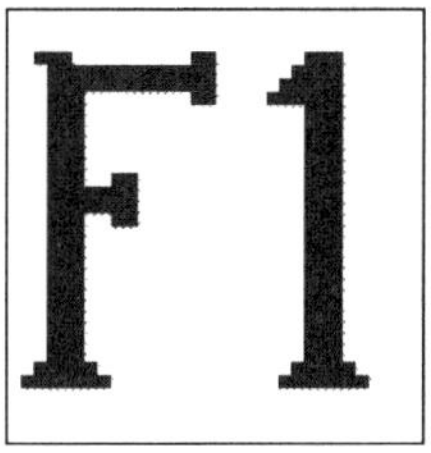

Listing 7-19 FONT1.RC Resource Script File

```
/* font1.rc resource file */

#include "font1.h"

MyIcon     ICON    font1.ico

MyMenu     MENU
BEGIN
    POPUP  "&Font"
    BEGIN
        MENUITEM "ANSI Variable Font",   IDM_ANSI
        MENUITEM "OEM Fixed Font",       IDM_OEM
        MENUITEM "Roman Font",           IDM_ROMAN
    END
    MENUITEM "&Quit",                    IDM_QUIT
END
```

Figure 7-12
FONT1.ICO
Icon Image

Listing 7-20 FONT1.DEF Module Definition File

```
NAME          font1
EXETYPE       WINDOWS
STUB          'WINSTUB.EXE'
CODE          PRELOAD MOVEABLE
DATA          PRELOAD MOVEABLE MULTIPLE
HEAPSIZE      1024
STACKSIZE     5120
EXPORTS       WndProc
```

Listing 7-21 Turbo C++ Project File for FONT1

```
font1.c
font1.def
font1.res
```

Listing 7-22 QuickC Project File for FONT1

```
font1.c
font1.def
font1.rc
```

Chapter 7 • *Character Sets, Fonts, and the Keyboard*

Keyboard Accelerators

Keyboard alternatives to mouse actions are always a good idea. They give the user a choice regarding the most convenient way to select an item in a menu. The simplest keyboard alternatives are provided by simply preceding the menu item's title string with an ampersand character. For example, the menu definition below will produce a menu that responds to (Alt)-(P) for Paint, (Alt)-(C) for Clear, and (Alt)-(Q) for Quit.

```
MyMenu      MENU
BEGIN
   MENUITEM "&Paint",        IDM_PAINT
   MENUITEM "&Clear",        IDM_CLEAR
   MENUITEM "&Quit",         IDM_QUIT
END
```

The letters following the ampersand characters are underlined in the menu bar when they are displayed. The ampersand characters are not visible. Using the ampersand approach is fine for a single menu bar, but it becomes cumbersome if there are popup menus. The user must select the (Alt)-(Key) combination for the top menu item, and then select (Alt)-(Key) for the item in the popup menu. A better keyboard shortcut would require only one keyboard combination to execute the command, no matter where it was in the menu structure.

You can create keyboard shortcuts by processing WM_KEYDOWN and WM_CHAR messages, and directing the program logic accordingly. However, Windows provides a much simpler alternative in the form of keyboard accelerators. The basic idea is that you define the key combinations in the resource script file. Each key combination that is defined ends up sending a WM_COMMAND message to the program. The WM_COMMAND messages imitate menu selections.

Listing 7-23 shows part of a the resource script file. The ACCELERATORS key word at the bottom starts the definition of the keyboard accelerators. Each line between the BEGIN and END statements after ACCELERATORS defines a keyboard combination. For example, the (F1) corresponds to the virtual key code VK_F1. The accelerator table defines that this keyboard combination will send a WM_COMMAND message with *wParam* set equal to IDM_ANSI. This is the same as the WM_COMMAND message sent if the user selects the popup menu item with the caption "ANSI Variable Font," so the (F1) key will result in the same actions as if the user had selected the menu item.

Listing 7-23 The Accelerator Table from FONT2.RC

```
MyAccel     ACCELERATORS
BEGIN
   VK_F1,      IDM_ANSI,       VIRTKEY
   VK_F2,      IDM_OEM,        VIRTKEY, CONTROL
   VK_F3,      IDM_ROMAN,      VIRTKEY, ALT
   "A",        IDM_NOMENU,     VIRTKEY, ALT
END
```

The syntax for an accelerator table is shown in Listing 7-24. The accelerator table is given a name, followed by the key word ACCELERATORS in uppercase letters. We will use the accelerator table name in a moment to load the accelerator data. The keystroke for each key combination is called the "event." There are three ways to specify a key. One is to just put the letter of the key in double quotes, such as "A" for the letter A key. The second way to specify the event is to use an integer representing the ANSI code for the key. This works fine for the letters and digits at the top of the keyboard (not the numeric keypad). The third way is to use the virtual key code for the key, like VK_TAB or VK_NUMPAD1. The virtual key codes for the letter and digit keys are the same as their ANSI equivalent, so you can just put the letter in double quotes for these events.

Listing 7-24 Accelerator Table Syntax

```
TableName   ACCELERATORS
BEGIN
    event,   ID Value,    [VIRTKEY][NOINVERT][ALT][SHIFT][CONTROL]
END
```

After the event is a comma, and then the ID value. This is the integer value that will be sent as the *wParam* value with a WM_COMMAND message when the key combination is pressed. Following the ID value is another comma, and then zero or more flags specifying the type of accelerator. If there are no flags, then the event must be a letter in double quotes. If the event type is labeled VIRTKEY, the event is interpreted as a virtual key code. You can also put the ALT, SHIFT and CONTROL key words, separated by commas, in any combination. For example, if you want the (Cntl)-(Shift)-(Z) key combination to send a WM_COMMAND message with the number 36 for *wParam*, code the accelerator as shown in Listing 7-25.

Listing 7-25 Accelerator Table Syntax

```
TableName   ACCELERATORS
BEGIN
    "Z",    36,    SHIFT,CONTROL
END
```

One additional key word that can be used with an accelerator is NOINVERT. This stops the corresponding menu item (if any) from flashing when the accelerator is activated. Normally, the top menu bar selection corresponding to the accelerator is switched quickly to reverse video and back again to simulate a mouse click. NOINVERT stops this default action.

Besides defining the accelerators in the resource script file, you will also need to make two changes to the WinMain() function of the program to make the accelerators active. The LoadAccelerators() and TranslateAccelerator() functions are used in WinMain() to load and process the accelerator messages. Listing 7-26 shows a typical message loop, using TranslateAccelerator().

Listing 7-26 Message Loop Processing Keyboard Accelerators

```
HANDLE     hAccel ;

hAccel = LoadAccelerators (hInstance, "TableName") ;  /* load accel. table */

while (GetMessage (&msg, NULL, NULL, NULL))           /* message loop */
{
   if (!TranslateAccelerator (hWnd, hAccel, &msg))    /* translate accel. */
   {
        TranslateMessage (&msg) ;   /* translate keyboard messages */
        DispatchMessage (&msg) ;    /* send message to WndProc() */
   }
}
```
[Other program lines]

Listing 7-26 loads the accelerator table named "TableName" from the resource data using LoadAccelerators(). LoadAccelerators() returns a handle to the accelerator table in memory. This handle is passed to the TranslateAccelerator() function in the program's message loop. TranslateAccelerator() returns a nonzero value if a match is found between the keyboard message and the accelerator table. In this case, we do not want the keyboard message sent on to WndProc(), so the TranslateMessage() and DispatchMessage() functions are bypassed if TranslateAccelerator() returns a nonzero value. TranslateAccelerator() sends the WM_COMMAND message directly to WndProc(), with *wParam* set to the accelerator's ID value. The WndProc() function sees the WM_COMMAND message, just as if it had been generated by a menu item selection.

You can define more than one accelerator table in the resource script file, and then load different ones at different times using LoadAccelerators(). Most programs just have one accelerator table. Although accelerators are usually used to activate menu items, they can be used to send WM_COMMAND messages that do not have menu equivalents. The WM_COMMAND message will be sent with the accelerator's ID value as the *wParam* parameter. Typical examples include providing keyboard alternatives for selecting buttons or other controls. Our next example program will demonstrate an accelerator without a menu item equivalent.

The FONT2 Program

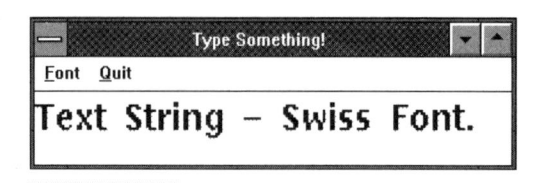

Figure 7-13 The FONT2 Program

Our last example in this chapter is called FONT2. Figure 7-13 shows FONT2 in action, displaying some typed text. FONT2 uses a Swiss font, along with two stock fonts. The Swiss font is shown in the figure. FONT2 improves on our previous example FONT1 in two ways:

1. Keyboard accelerators are provided as alternatives to menu selections.
2. The current editing point is marked by the blinking caret.

The accelerator table is defined in the FONT2.RC resource script file (Listing 7-27). The program has a popup menu, allowing selection of three different fonts. Note how the menu strings show the keyboard shortcut on the left side. This is a good practice because it helps the user remember the accelerator key combinations.

The accelerator table is defined at the bottom of FONT2.RC. The table is named "MyAccel." This is the name we will pass to LoadAccelerators() in the WinMain() function of FONT2.C. Note that two keyboard shortcuts are provided for the IDM_OEM shortcut. Both (F2) and (Cntl)-(F2) will generate the same keyboard shortcut. You can have as many shortcuts for one action as you like, but one is usually enough.

The last accelerator defined in FONT2.RC is for the (Cntl)-(A) combination. In this case, a WM_COMMAND message will be sent that does not correspond to a menu item. We will processe this WM_COMMAND message in the WndProc() function of FONT2.C as a demonstration of accelerators which do not have menu item equivalents.

Listing 7-27 FONT2.RC Resource Script File

```
/* font2.rc resource file */

#include "windows.h"
#include "font2.h"

MyIcon      ICON    font2.ico

MyMenu      MENU
BEGIN
    POPUP   "&Font"
    BEGIN
        MENUITEM "ANSI Variable Font (F1)",     IDM_ANSI
        MENUITEM "OEM Fixed Font (Cntl-F2)",    IDM_OEM
        MENUITEM "Swiss Font (Alt-F3)"          IDM_SWISS
    END
    MENUITEM "&Quit",                           IDM_QUIT
END

MyAccel     ACCELERATORS
BEGIN
    VK_F1,      IDM_ANSI,       VIRTKEY
    VK_F2,      IDM_OEM,        VIRTKEY, CONTROL
    VK_F2,      IDM_OEM,        VIRTKEY
    VK_F3,      IDM_SWISS,      VIRTKEY, ALT
    "A",        IDM_NOMENU,     VIRTKEY, ALT
END
```

Listing 7-28 shows FONT2.C. Note in the WinMain() function that the "MyAccel" accelerator table is loaded into memory before the start of the message loop. The message loop has been modified to include the TranslateAccelerator() function.

In the WndProc() function, note the processing of the WM_COMMAND message with *wParam* set equal to IDM_NOMENU. This is the accelerator without a menu item equivalent. In this case, the WM_COMMAND message just puts a message box on the screen, demonstrating that the command was received.

Listing 7-28 FONT2.C

```c
/* font2.c   Use a new font and add edit caret */

#include <windows.h>
#include "font2.h"

int PASCAL WinMain (HANDLE hInstance, HANDLE hPrevInstance, LPSTR lpszCmdLine,
   int nCmdShow)
{
    HWND       hWnd ;         /* the window's "handle" */
    MSG        msg ;          /* a message structure */
    WNDCLASS   wndclass ;     /* window class structure */
    HANDLE     hAccel ;       /* handle to the accelerator table */

    if (!hPrevInstance)
    {
       wndclass.style         = CS_HREDRAW | CS_VREDRAW | CS_DBLCLKS ;
       wndclass.lpfnWndProc   = WndProc ;
       wndclass.cbClsExtra    = 0 ;
       wndclass.cbWndExtra    = 0 ;
       wndclass.hInstance     = hInstance ;
       wndclass.hIcon         = LoadIcon (hInstance, "MyIcon") ;
       wndclass.hCursor       = LoadCursor (NULL, IDC_ARROW) ;
       wndclass.hbrBackground = GetStockObject (WHITE_BRUSH) ;
       wndclass.lpszMenuName  = "MyMenu" ;
       wndclass.lpszClassName = "MyClass" ;
                 /* register the window class */
       if (!RegisterClass (&wndclass))
            return 0 ;
    }

    hWnd = CreateWindow ("MyClass","Type Something!", WS_OVERLAPPEDWINDOW,
        CW_USEDEFAULT, CW_USEDEFAULT, CW_USEDEFAULT, CW_USEDEFAULT,
        NULL, NULL, hInstance, NULL) ;
    ShowWindow (hWnd, nCmdShow) ;   /* display the window */

    hAccel = LoadAccelerators (hInstance, "MyAccel") ; /* load accel. table */

    while (GetMessage (&msg, NULL, NULL, NULL))   /* message loop */
    {
        if (!TranslateAccelerator (hWnd, hAccel, &msg)) /* translate accel. */
        {
            TranslateMessage (&msg) ;   /* translate keyboard messages */
            DispatchMessage (&msg) ;    /* send message to WndProc() */
        }
    }
    return (msg.wParam) ;
}

long FAR PASCAL WndProc (HWND hWnd, WORD wMessage, WORD wParam, LONG lParam)
{
    static char     cBuf [LINELONG] ;
    static int      nCurPos = 0 ;
    PAINTSTRUCT     ps ;
    HDC             hDC ;
    static HFONT    hFont ;
```

```c
     static int      nFontChoice = IDM_SWISS, nXCaret = 0, nYCaret = 0,
                     nCaretTall, nCaretWide, nClientWide ;
     TEXTMETRIC      tm ;

switch (wMessage)                       /* process windows messages */
    {
    case WM_CREATE:
        hFont = CreateFont (36, 0, 0, 0, FW_NORMAL, 0, 0, 0, ANSI_CHARSET,
            OUT_DEFAULT_PRECIS, CLIP_DEFAULT_PRECIS, DEFAULT_QUALITY,
            VARIABLE_PITCH | FF_SWISS, "Swiss") ;
        break ;
    case WM_SIZE:                       /* remember client area width */
        nClientWide = LOWORD (lParam) ;
        break ;
    case WM_COMMAND:
        switch (wParam)                 /* menu items and/or accelerators */
            {
            case IDM_NOMENU:    /* keyboard accelerator, not menu item */
                MessageBox (hWnd, "Got IDM_NOMENU WM_COMMAND message.",
                        "Accelerator Only", MB_OK) ;
                break ;
            case IDM_ANSI:      /* remember font choice */
                nFontChoice = IDM_ANSI ;
                InvalidateRect (hWnd, NULL, TRUE) ; /* force WM_PAINT */
                break ;
            case IDM_OEM:
                nFontChoice = IDM_OEM ;
                InvalidateRect (hWnd, NULL, TRUE) ; /* force WM_PAINT */
                break ;
            case IDM_SWISS:
                nFontChoice = IDM_SWISS ;
                InvalidateRect (hWnd, NULL, TRUE) ; /* force WM_PAINT */
                break ;
            case IDM_QUIT:
                DestroyWindow (hWnd) ;      /* destroy window, */
                break ;                     /* terminating application */
            }
        break ;
    case WM_PAINT:
        hDC = BeginPaint (hWnd, &ps) ;
        SetTextColor (hDC, RGB (0, 0, 255)) ;   /* blue letters */
        switch (nFontChoice)
            {                                   /* select a font into DC */
            case IDM_ANSI:
                SelectObject (hDC, GetStockObject (ANSI_VAR_FONT)) ;
                break ;
            case IDM_OEM:
                SelectObject (hDC, GetStockObject (OEM_FIXED_FONT)) ;
                break ;
            case IDM_SWISS:
                SelectObject (hDC, hFont) ;
                break ;
            }
        GetTextMetrics (hDC, &tm) ;    /* get font height to size caret */
        nCaretTall = tm.tmHeight + tm.tmExternalLeading ;
                        /* window border width * 2 = caret width */
        nCaretWide = 2 * GetSystemMetrics (SM_CXBORDER) ;
        DestroyCaret () ;
        CreateCaret (hWnd, NULL, nCaretWide, nCaretTall) ;
```

Chapter 7 • Character Sets, Fonts, and the Keyboard

```
                            /* get width of string to position caret */
            nXCaret = LOWORD(GetTextExtent (hDC, cBuf, lstrlen (cBuf))) ;
            SetCaretPos (nXCaret, nYCaret) ;
            TextOut (hDC, 0, 0, cBuf, lstrlen (cBuf)) ;
            EndPaint (hWnd, &ps) ;
            break ;
        case WM_CHAR:                              /* char input */
            if (nCurPos < LINELONG &&              /* or punctuation */
               (IsCharAlphaNumeric ((char) wParam) || IsAnsiPunc ((char) wParam)))
            {
                cBuf [nCurPos++] = (char) wParam ;    /* add new letter */
                cBuf [nCurPos] = 0 ;                  /* null term. string */
                InvalidateRect (hWnd, NULL, TRUE) ;   /* force WM_PAINT */
            }
            break ;
        case WM_KEYDOWN:                           /* non ANSI key input */
            switch (wParam)
            {
                case VK_BACK:                      /* backspace key */
                    if (nCurPos > 0)
                    {
                        nCurPos-- ;                /* back up one char */
                        cBuf [nCurPos] = 0 ;       /* replace with null */
                        InvalidateRect (hWnd, NULL, TRUE) ;
                    }
            }
            break ;
        case WM_SETFOCUS:                          /* window gained focus */
            CreateCaret (hWnd, NULL, nCaretWide, nCaretTall) ;
            SetCaretPos (nXCaret, nYCaret) ;
            break ;
        case WM_KILLFOCUS:                         /* window lost focus */
            DestroyCaret () ;
            break ;
        case WM_DESTROY:                           /* stop application */
            DeleteObject (hFont) ;                 /* remove font from memory */
            PostQuitMessage (0) ;
            break ;
        default:       /* default windows message processing */
            return DefWindowProc (hWnd, wMessage, wParam, lParam) ;
    }
    return (0L) ;
}

BOOL IsAnsiPunc (WORD wChar)    /* returns true if wChar is punctuation char */
{
    if ((wChar >= ' ' && wChar <= '@') || (wChar >= '[' && wChar <= '`') ||
        (wChar >= '{' && wChar <= '~') || (wChar >= 0xA0 && wChar <= 0xBF))
        return (TRUE) ;
    else
        return (FALSE) ;
}
```

Although the WndProc() function in FONT2 is similar to that in FONT1, there are some differences. Note that WM_SETFOCUS and WM_KILLFOCUS messages are processed to show and hide the caret. This is the same procedure we discussed in Chapter

6, *Taming the Mouse*. In FONT2, we want the caret to be located at the end of the text string, marking the point where the next character typed will show up. The location and size of the caret are determined while processing the WM_PAINT message.

Listing 7-29 shows an excerpt from FONT2.C showing the function calls that determine the size and location of the caret. To look right, the caret needs to be the same size as the font's characters. GetTextMetrics() is used to determine the height of a character with whatever font is currently selected into the device context. The caret's height is set equal to the character height plus the external leading space. The caret's width is set equal to twice the thickness of a window border line, obtained by GetSystemMetrics(). This assures that the caret will be a reasonable width, regardless of the video equipment in use. Using GetTextMetrics() and GetSystemMetrics() to determine the size of objects while the program is running is a good programming practice, as the program is sure to look right regardless of what new equipment the manufacturers dream up in the future.

Listing 7-29 Excerpt from FONT2.C Showing Caret Sizing and Positioning

```
GetTextMetrics (hDC, &tm) ; /* get font height to size caret */
nCaretTall = tm.tmHeight + tm.tmExternalLeading ;
                            /* window border width * 2 = caret width */
nCaretWide = 2 * GetSystemMetrics (SM_CXBORDER) ;
DestroyCaret () ;
CreateCaret (hWnd, NULL, nCaretWide, nCaretTall) ;
                            /* get width of string to position caret */
nXCaret = LOWORD(GetTextExtent (hDC, cBuf, lstrlen (cBuf))) ;
SetCaretPos (nXCaret, nYCaret) ;
TextOut (hDC, 0, 0, cBuf, lstrlen (cBuf)) ;
```

Positioning the caret at the end of the character string is a bit more complex than you might expect. The width of the characters in a variable-pitch font varies depending on the character. The letter "I" is much narrower than the letter "M." You cannot simply multiply the average character width by the length of the character string to find the string's length.

Windows provides the GetTextExtent() function to determine the size of a character string. The size will reflect the font currently in the device context. GetTextExtent() returns a DWORD (32 bit) value. The high-order WORD (16 bit) contains the vertical height of the string. The low-order WORD contains the width of the string. FONT2 uses the width to place the caret right at the end of the string.

GetTextExtent() is used frequently in programs that manipulate text. It is the only reliable way to determine how long a character string will be, even if the string is made up of digits. Ones are narrower than twos! Listings 7-30 to 7-37 show the remaining support files for FONT2. The program's icon is shown in Figure 7-14.

Figure 7-14
FONT2.ICO
Icon Image

Listing 7-30 FONT2.H Header File

```
/* font2.h header file */
                        /* menu item id number */
#define IDM_ANSI    1   /* ansi variable font menu selection */
#define IDM_OEM     2   /* oem fixed font menu selection */
#define IDM_SWISS   3   /* roman font menu selection */
#define IDM_NOMENU  4   /* not a menu item, just kybd accelerator */
#define IDM_QUIT    10  /* menu item - quit */

#define LINELONG   128  /* maximum length of a line */

long FAR PASCAL WndProc (HWND, WORD, WORD, LONG) ;
BOOL IsAnsiPunc (WORD wChar) ;
```

Listing 7-31 FONT2.DEF Module Definition File

```
NAME        font2
EXETYPE     WINDOWS
STUB        'WINSTUB.EXE'
CODE        PRELOAD MOVEABLE
DATA        PRELOAD MOVEABLE MULTIPLE
HEAPSIZE    1024
STACKSIZE   5120
EXPORTS     WndProc
```

Listing 7-32 Turbo C++ Project File for FONT2

```
font2.c
font2.def
font2.res
```

Listing 7-33 QuickC Project File for FONT2

```
font2.c
font2.def
font2.rc
```

Summary

Windows uses the ANSI character set to encode each letter, digit, and symbol. This character set is more suitable for international use than the OEM character set used by MS-DOS because it includes a more complete set of the accented characters used in many European languages. Windows also provides a number of functions for manipulating character strings that correctly process accented characters. Always use the Windows functions, such as AnsiLower() and AnsiUpper(), rather than C compiler library functions so that your program will work properly regardless of the language used. It is also better to use the Windows string copying and comparison functions (lstrcpy(), lstrlen(), etc) rather than C compiler library functions, as the Windows functions do not add extra code to your program. The logic for Windows functions remains in Windows itself and is shared by every application that calls those functions.

Windows send WM_KEYDOWN and WM_KEYUP messages when a key is depressed and released. The keys are coded using "virtual key" codes, defined in WINDOWS.H. If the TranslateMessage() function is used in the program's message loop, the program will also get WM_CHAR messages when a printable character key is depressed. WM_CHAR messages encode the ANSI character code as the *wParam* parameter when sent. WM_CHAR messages are usually used for the printable character keys, while WM_KEYDOWN is used for the nonprintable keys, such as function keys.

If the user has the (Alt) key depressed when another key is depressed, Windows will send WM_SYSKEYDOWN, WM_SYSCHAR, and WM_SYSKEYUP messages. If Windows is installed with a language other than English, accented characters will be defined. Windows will send WM_DEADCHAR when the user selects an accent key. The WM_CHAR message sent will transmit the ANSI code for the accented version of the letter.

Windows provides a quick way to add keyboard shortcuts to a program. Keyboard accelerators are defined in the program's resource script file and are loaded into memory using LoadAccelerators(). The program's message loop will need to contain the TranslateAccelerator() function to use the accelerator data. Once installed, accelerator combinations generate WM_COMMAND messages, just as if a menu item had been selected with the mouse.

You can change fonts in a program by either selecting one of the stock fonts or by using a logical font created with CreateFont(). Logical fonts are based on font data in font files. CreateFont() can approximate bold, italics, and other font sizes by interpolating from the existing font data. Once you have selected a new font into the device context, you can find all of its characteristics (size, width, etc.) using the GetTextMetrics() function. You can find the height and width of a character string drawn with the selected font using the GetTextExtent() function.

QUESTIONS

1. The unaccented characters and digits in the OEM and ANSI character sets have the same code values. (True/False).
2. Use the _____ function to convert a character string to uppercase.
   Use the _____ function to copy a string into a character buffer.
3. Both WM_KEYDOWN and WM_CHAR send the ANSI character code for the key depressed as the *wParam* parameter sent with the message (True/False).
4. How would you detect the (Tab) key being depressed in a program?
5. How are WM_CHAR messages generated?
6. If the (Alt) key is down when another key is pressed, which messages will be sent to the window with the input focus?
7. To obtain a handle to a stock font, use the _____ function. To obtain a handle to a logical font, use the _____ function. In both cases you must use the _____ function to select the font into the device context.
8. Once a font is selected into a device context, you can find the dimensions and attributes of the font using the _____ function. Use the _____ function to determine the length of a character string, which returns the length of the string in the _____ order WORD of the DWORD value returned.
9. The three steps needed to use keyboard accelerators in a program are: 1) Add an _____ table to the resource script file; 2) Use the _____ function to load the accelerator data into memory; 3) Add the _____ function to the program's message loop.
10. The following line in an accelerator table will generate a WM_COMMAND message with *wParam* set equal to _____ when the _____ _____ key combination is selected.

    ```
    TableName ACCELERATORS
    BEGIN
       VK_F10,   19,    VIRTKEY,CONTROL
    END
    ```

EXERCISES

1. Modify the FONT2.C program to create a 36 logical-unit-high font using the Modern style, based on the OEM character set. Setup the logical font so that the characters appear vertically downward. How do you determine the location of the end of the string when it is aligned vertically?

2. Modify the FONT2.C program to create a 24 logical-unit-high font using the Modern style, based on the OEM character set. Make the characters lie on their backs, but use the normal alignment of left to right.

EXERCISES (cont'd)

3. Modify the keyboard accelerators for FONT2 so that the three font selections can be made with the (Alt)-(1) (digit one, not function key one), (Cntl)-(2), and (Shift)-(3) key combinations.

ANSWERS TO QUESTIONS

1. True.
2. AnsiUpper() or AnsiUpperBuff(), lstrcpy().
3. False. WM_CHAR does send the ANSI character code. WM_KEYDOWN and WM_KEYUP send the virtual key code for the key as *wParam*. The virtual key code only equals the ANSI code for the unaccented uppercase letters and the digits.
4. Process WM_KEYDOWN messages and look for when *wParam* == VK_TAB.
5. WM_CHAR messages are generated by the TranslateMessage() function in the program's message loop.
6. WM_SYSKEYDOWN, WM_SYSCHAR, WM_SYSKEYUP.
7. GetStockObject(), CreateFont(), SelectObject().
8. GetTextMetrics(), GetTextExtent(), low order WORD.
9. Accelerator table; LoadAccelerators(); TranslateAccelerator().
10. 19, (Cntl)-(F10).

SOLUTIONS TO EXERCISES

1. The solution is under the file name C7EXER01 on the source code disks. The CreateFont() function is modified as follows:

   ```
   hFont = CreateFont (36, 0, 2700, 0, FW_NORMAL, 0, 0, 0, OEM_CHARSET,
       OUT_DEFAULT_PRECIS, CLIP_DEFAULT_PRECIS, DEFAULT_QUALITY,
       DEFAULT_PITCH | FF_MODERN, "Modern") ;
   ```

   Setting the *nEscapement* parameter (third parameter) to 2700 causes the characters to appear 270 degrees offset from the right. This is straight down. Due to a minor bug in the CreateFont() function, the OEM_CHARSET must be selected for this example to work.

   The GetTextExtent() continues to provide the vertical and horizontal size of a string output using the font, even if the font's characters are rotated or appear at an angle to the horizontal. You can do a rough placement of the caret using both the *X* and *Y* values returned by GetTextExtent() as follows:

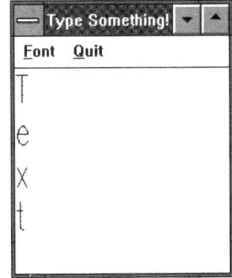

   Figure 7-15 Chapter 7, Exercise 1 Solution

SOLUTIONS TO EXERCISES (cont'd)

```
nXCaret = LOWORD(GetTextExtent (hDC, cBuf, lstrlen (cBuf))) ;
nYCaret = HIWORD(GetTextExtent (hDC, cBuf, lstrlen (cBuf))) ;
```

The result of these changes is shown in Figure 7-15.

2. The solution is under the file name C7EXER02 on the source code disks. The CreateFont() function should be modified as follows:

```
hFont = CreateFont (24, 0, 0, 900, FW_NORMAL, 0, 0, 0, OEM_CHARSET,
    OUT_DEFAULT_PRECIS, CLIP_DEFAULT_PRECIS, DEFAULT_QUALITY,
    DEFAULT_PITCH | FF_MODERN, "Modern") ;
```

The result is shown in Figure 7-16. Note that the horizontal spacing is correctly increased to properly space the characters, even though they are rotated 90 degrees. Due to a minor bug in the CreateFont() function, the OEM_CHARSET must be selected for this example to work.

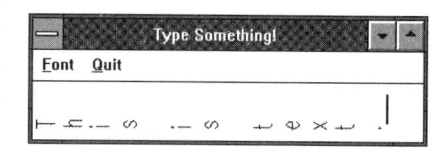

Figure 7-16 Chapter 7, Exercise 2 Solution

3. The solution is under the file name C7EXER03 on the source code disks. The resource script file should be modified as shown in Listing 7-34. Note that the menu strings have been changed to reflect the new accelerators.

Listing 7-34 C7EXER03.RC Resource Script File

```
/* c7exer03.rc resource file */

#include "windows.h"
#include "c7exer03.h"

MyIcon              ICON      c7exer03.ico

MyMenu              MENU
BEGIN

POPUP   "&Font"
   BEGIN
      MENUITEM "ANSI Variable Font (Alt-1)",   IDM_ANSI
      MENUITEM "OEM Fixed Font (Cntl-2)",      IDM_OEM

      MENUITEM "Swiss Font (Shift-3)" IDM_SWISS
   END
   MENUITEM "&Quit",          IDM_QUIT
END

MyAccel    ACCELERATORS
BEGIN
   "1",    IDM_ANSI,      VIRTKEY, ALT
   "2",    IDM_OEM,       VIRTKEY, CONTROL
   "3",    IDM_SWISS,     VIRTKEY, SHIFT
END
```

CHAPTER 8

Child and Popup Windows

So far we have created main program windows and used predefined window controls such as buttons and static text. Window controls are convenient if you can take advantage of the exact features provided. If you need other features, you can create your own specialized windows. The most common type of "custom" windows are child windows, which are attached to a parent window at all times. Child windows are only visible if they are within the client area of their parent. Child windows can be used to deal with a specific task, such as getting input from the user. Child windows are also useful as a programming tool to break up a large screen area into smaller portions, each with its own message processing function.

Popup windows are another useful tool. Popups are not physically attached to a parent window and can be positioned anywhere on the screen. However, popup windows disappear the instant their parent window is destroyed. Popups are handy for items that the user may want to reposition on the screen. We will look at several examples in this chapter with both child windows and popup windows.

Concepts Covered
Child Windows
Separate Class Definitions
and Window Functions
Stock Icons

Popup Windows
Custom Messages Sent Between Windows

Keywords Covered
WS_CHILD
WS_POPUP
WS_MINIMIZEBOX

WS_BORDER
WS_VISIBLE
IDI_APPLICATION

Functions Covered
CreateSolidBrush()
MoveWindow()

GetParent()

Messages Covered
WM_USER
WM_SIZE

WM_SETTEXT

Creating a Child Window

The first example program in this chapter creates a single child window that can be moved in the center of the parent's client area. Figure 8-1 shows the CHILD1 program in action. When the "Create" menu item is selected, a child window appears displaying a caption bar and a gray client area of its own. The child window's client area contains the string "Text in Child Window."

Because CHILD1's child window has a caption bar, the child window can be moved in the client area of the parent window by using the mouse. The child window is only visible within the bounds of the parent's client area. If you move it to an edge of the parent window's border, the child window is clipped. Figure 8-1 shows the left side of the child window being clipped by the parent window. The child window is clipped automatically by the same built-in logic that the Windows environment uses to show portions of program windows on the screen when they overlap.

Creating a child window requires the following steps:

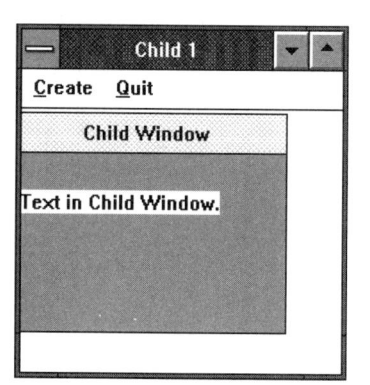

Figure 8-1 The CHILD1 Program

1. Register a new window class for the child window with the RegisterClass() function.
2. Create the child window using the CreateWindow() function with the WS_CHILD window style.
3. Write a separate window message processing function for the child window, similar to WndProc() for the main program window.
4. Declare the child window's message processing function in the EXPORTS section of the program's module definition file.

Listing 8-1 shows the CHILD1.C program. The window classes for the parent window and for the child window are registered in the WinMain() function when the program starts running. It is convenient to register new window classes in WinMain(), as some of the members of the WNDCLASS data structure passed to the RegisterClass() function will be common to more than one window class. In CHILD1.C, the child window's class is created with the following program lines:

```
wndclass.lpfnWndProc    = ChildProc ;
wndclass.hIcon          = NULL ;
wndclass.hCursor        = LoadCursor (NULL, IDC_CROSS) ;
wndclass.hbrBackground  = GetStockObject (LTGRAY_BRUSH) ;
wndclass.lpszMenuName   = NULL ;
wndclass.lpszClassName  = "ChildClass" ;
            /* register the child window class */
if (!RegisterClass (&wndclass))
{
    MessageBox (hWnd, "Could not register child class",
      "Message", MB_OK) ;
    return (0) ;
}
```

The message processing function for this window class is set to "ChildProc." This is the name of a separate function that will process messages for the child window. The ChildProc() function has the same format as WndProc(), but only processes messages sent to child windows created from this new window class. The new window class sets NULL for the class icon handle (no icon is shown if the window is minimized), uses the stock cursor shape IDC_CROSS, uses a light gray brush for the background color, has no class menu, and defines the class name as "ChildClass." These members of the WNDCLASS data structure are all specified before calling RegisterClass() to register the new window class.

When the child window's class is registered, any number of child windows can be created based on this class. CHILD1 creates only one. The child window is created when the user selects the "Create" menu item in the parent's menu. This sends a WM_COMMAND message to the parent's window function [WndProc()], with *wParam* set to the menu item's ID value, IDM_CREATE. The child window is then created with the following calls to CreateWindow() and ShowWindow():

```
hChild = CreateWindow ("ChildClass", "Child Window",
    WS_CHILD | WS_BORDER | WS_CAPTION,
    10, 30, 200, 150, hWnd,
```

```
                    NULL, hInstance, NULL) ;
            ShowWindow (hChild, SW_SHOWNORMAL) ;
```

The key items in creating the child window are specifying the name of the child's window class ("ChildClass") and using the WS_CHILD window style. The class name tells Windows which window function will get messages for the window created, as well as specifying the background brush color, etc. The WS_CHILD style makes the window a child window.

The linkage between the child window and its parent is made in the CreateWindow() function call. The eighth parameter passed to CreateWindow() is the parent window's handle. When the CreateWindow() function is called, Windows stores the linkage between the child window and its parent. If the parent is destroyed, the Windows environment will destory automatically all of the parent's children. In CHILD1, there is only one child window.

Listing 8-1 CHILD1.C

```
/* child1.c   Creating a child window */

#include <windows.h>
#include "child1.h"

int PASCAL WinMain (HANDLE hInstance, HANDLE hPrevInstance, LPSTR lpszCmdLine,
    int nCmdShow)
{
    HWND       hWnd ;             /* the window's "handle" */
    MSG        msg ;              /* a message structure */
    WNDCLASS   wndclass ;         /* window class structure */

    if (!hPrevInstance)
    {                             /* define the parent window class */
        wndclass.style          = CS_HREDRAW | CS_VREDRAW ;
        wndclass.lpfnWndProc    = WndProc ;
        wndclass.cbClsExtra     = 0 ;
        wndclass.cbWndExtra     = 0 ;
        wndclass.hInstance      = hInstance ;
        wndclass.hIcon          = LoadIcon (hInstance, "MyIcon") ;
        wndclass.hCursor        = LoadCursor (NULL, IDC_ARROW) ;
        wndclass.hbrBackground  = GetStockObject (WHITE_BRUSH) ;
        wndclass.lpszMenuName   = "ParentMenu" ;
        wndclass.lpszClassName  = "MyClass" ;
                /* register the parent window class */
        if (!RegisterClass (&wndclass))
            return (0) ;
                /* change the class definition for child */
        wndclass.lpfnWndProc    = ChildProc ;
        wndclass.hIcon          = NULL ;
        wndclass.hCursor        = LoadCursor (NULL, IDC_CROSS) ;
        wndclass.hbrBackground  = GetStockObject (LTGRAY_BRUSH) ;
        wndclass.lpszMenuName   = NULL ;
        wndclass.lpszClassName  = "ChildClass" ;
                /* register the child window class */
```

```c
      if (!RegisterClass (&wndclass))
      {
            MessageBox (hWnd, "Could not register child class", "Message", MB_OK) ;
            return (0) ;
      }
   }

   hWnd = CreateWindow ("MyClass","Child 1", WS_OVERLAPPEDWINDOW,
      CW_USEDEFAULT, CW_USEDEFAULT, CW_USEDEFAULT, CW_USEDEFAULT,
      NULL, NULL, hInstance, NULL) ;
   ShowWindow (hWnd, nCmdShow) ;   /* display the window */

   while (GetMessage (&msg, NULL, NULL, NULL))   /* message loop */
   {
     TranslateMessage (&msg) ;        /* translate keyboard messages */
     DispatchMessage (&msg) ;         /* send message to WndProc() */
   }
   return (msg.wParam) ;
}

long FAR PASCAL WndProc (HWND hWnd, WORD wMessage, WORD wParam, LONG lParam)
{
   static  HWND     hChild = NULL ;
   HANDLE           hInstance ;

   switch (wMessage)                  /* process windows messages */
   {
      case WM_COMMAND:                /* menu items */
         switch (wParam)
         {
            case IDM_CREATE:
            if (hChild == NULL)    /* only create one child */
            {
               hInstance = GetWindowWord (hWnd, GWW_HINSTANCE) ;
                     /* create the child window and display it */
               hChild = CreateWindow ("ChildClass", "Child Window",
                    WS_CHILD | WS_BORDER | WS_CAPTION,
                    10, 30, 200, 150, hWnd,
                    NULL, hInstance, NULL) ;
               ShowWindow (hChild, SW_SHOWNORMAL) ;
            }
            break ;
            case IDM_QUIT:
               DestroyWindow (hWnd) ;    /* destroy window, */
               break ;                   /* terminating application */
         }
         break ;
      case WM_DESTROY:                   /* stop application */
         PostQuitMessage (0) ;
         break ;
      default:      /* default windows message processing */
         return DefWindowProc (hWnd, wMessage, wParam, lParam) ;
   }
   return (0L) ;
}

/* Window procedure for the child window. Note that format is similar to */
/* the WndProc() function for the parent window. */
```

```
long FAR PASCAL ChildProc (HWND hChild, WORD wMessage, WORD wParam, LONG lParam)
{
    PAINTSTRUCT    ps ;

    switch (wMessage)        /* process windows messages */
    {
        case WM_PAINT:
            BeginPaint (hChild, &ps) ;
            TextOut (ps.hdc, 10, 25, "Text in Child Window.", 22) ;
            EndPaint (hChild, &ps) ;
            break ;
        default:              /* default windows message processing */
            return DefWindowProc (hChild, wMessage, wParam, lParam) ;
    }
    return (0L) ;
}
```

The class definition for the child window specified "ChildProc" as the window function for the child window. This function is defined at the bottom of CHILD1.C (Listing 8-1). All window functions are declared "long FAR PASCAL," and they have the same four parameters: the window handle, message ID number, *wParam*, and *lParam* values passed with the message. Child window message processing functions should pass all unprocessed messages to the DefWindowProc() function, just as we have been doing in the WndProc() function. DefWindowProc() takes care of all of the basic window functionality, such as allowing us to move the child window (created with a caption bar) using the mouse.

In CHILD1.C, the ChildProc() function only processes the WM_PAINT message. This is used to output a line of text in the child window's client area. We will do more with the child window's message processing function in our next example, but CHILD1 was designed to be simple.

The Windows environment will call the ChildProc() function every time a message is sent to the child window. Functions that are accessed from outside of the program must be listed in the EXPORTS section of the program's module definition file. This is shown in Listing 8-2. This is an easy thing to forget when creating a program. Your program will terminate unexpectedly if you forget this line.

Listing 8-2 CHILD1.DEF Module Definition File

```
NAME           child1
EXETYPE        WINDOWS
STUB           'WINSTUB.EXE'
CODE           PRELOAD MOVEABLE
DATA           PRELOAD MOVEABLE MULTIPLE
HEAPSIZE       1024
STACKSIZE      5120
EXPORTS        WndProc
               ChildProc
```

In addition, you will need to declare the child window function in the program's header file to satisfy the compiler's type checking. Listing 8-3 shows the CHILD1.H header file.

Listings 8-4 and 8-5 show the project file contents. Figure 8-2 shows the program icon.

Listing 8-3 CHILD1.H Header File

```
/* child1.h header file */

#define IDM_CREATE  1      /* main menu ID values */
#define IDM_QUIT   10

long FAR PASCAL WndProc (HWND, WORD, WORD, LONG) ;
long FAR PASCAL ChildProc (HWND, WORD, WORD, LONG) ;
```

Figure 8-2
CHILD1.ICO
Icon Image

Listing 8-4 Turbo C++ Project File for CHILD1

```
child1.c
child1.def
child1.res
```

Listing 8-5 QuickC Project File for CHILD1

```
child1.c
child1.def
child1.rc
```

Sending Messages to Child Windows

Our next example creates a somewhat more complex child window. Figure 8-3 shows the CHILD2 program in action. The child window in CHILD2 has a caption bar, minimize button, and a thick frame that can be used to change the size of the child window. Inside of the child window's client area is some text and a button control containing the text "Destroy Me." Clicking this button destroys the child window, but does not affect CHILD2's parent window.

One of the interesting things about the CHILD2 program is that the parent window's client area contains both text and a child window. The text string "Text In Parent Client Area" is painted when the parent window processes WM_PAINT messages. The child window itself is painted automatically by the Windows environment, which also sends WM_PAINT messages to the child window's message processing function. The parent window's WM_PAINT message is processed after the child is redrawn by Windows. This results in the text string being painted over the child window

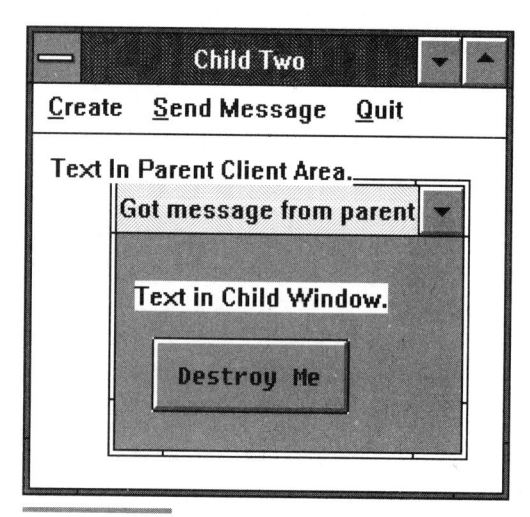

Figure 8-3 CHILD2 Program after Creating Child Window

if they overlap. You can see this effect in Figure 8-3. The top border of the child window is partially erased by the parent window's text string. Windows will properly manage repainting of multiple child windows that overlap, but it has no way of knowing whether you want text to be "above" or "below" a given child window. Because of this, programs that use movable child windows typically do not paint directly on the parent window's client area. If you need to display text in the client area, use a static text control, as described in Chapter 5, *Window Controls*. Windows will then be able to manage the repainting process for you.

The CHILD2 parent window has three menu items. The "Create" menu item creates the child window. The "Send Message" menu item sends a special message to the child window. Custom messages have ID values defined in the program, starting with the values WM_USER, WM_USER +1, etc. When the child window in CHILD2 receives a WM_USER message, its caption is changed to "Got message from parent.," as shown in Figure 8-3. We will explore sending WM_USER messages in a moment. The third menu item 'Quit" simply terminates the program, destroying both the parent and chid windows.

Because the child window has a minimize button, the child window can be minimized. Clicking the child window's minimize button causes the child window to be iconized at the bottom left of the parent window's client area. This is a built-in feature of the Windows environment. Minimized child windows are always constrained to the parent window's client area. Figure 8-4 shows the CHILD2 program window after the child window has been minimized. The minimized child window can be moved in the parent window's client area using the mouse, and it can be restored by double clicking the icon box. The title string shown under the window icon will be the child window's

Figure 8-4 CHILD2 with Child Window Minimized

caption string. This behavior for minimized windows is probably familiar, as this is how the Window Program Manager and File Manager applications behave.

The CHILD2.C program is shown in Listing 8-6. The overall structure of CHILD2.C is similar to CHILD1.C, although a number of additional features have been added. The window class "ChildClass" is registered in the WinMain() function. Note that a class icon is defined, as this child window will have a minimize button, and needs some sort of image to show when it is minimized. The stock icon IDI_APPLICATION is loaded, rather than adding another icon file to the program's resources. The IDI_APPLICATION stock icon is just a rectangular box under Windows 3.0, but appears as a miniature Windows logo under Windows 3.1. This icon is the image that will be shown when a window created from the child window class is minimized (see Figure 8-4).

Loading a Stock Icon

```
wndclass.hIcon = LoadIcon (NULL, IDI_APPLICATION);
```

Note that when you load a stock object with LoadIcon(), the first parameter is set to NULL. This tells Windows that the icon is being loaded from the stock objects stored as part of Windows, rather than from the program's resource data. If you create an icon file with your icon editor and add it to the resource script file, you can use that icon data for the class icon. In this case, the first parameter passed to LoadIcon() will be the *hInstance* instance handle. Windows uses the instance handle to determine which program's resource data contains the requested icon data.

Loading Icon Data Stored in the Program's Resource Data

```
wndclass.hIcon = LoadIcon (hInstance, "MyIcon");
```

The child window is not created until the user selects the "Create" menu item. CreateWindow() is used to create a child window from the "ChildClass" window class. The window styles include WS_CHILD to make a child window, WS_THICKFRAME so that the child window has a thick frame that can be used to size the window, WS_MINIMIZEBOX to add a minimize box, and WS_CAPTION to add a caption bar so that the child window can be moved.

Creating the Child Window

```
hChild = CreateWindow ("ChildClass", "Child Window",
    WS_CHILD | WS_THICKFRAME | WS_MINIMIZEBOX | WS_CAPTION,
    10, 30, 200, 150, hWnd,
    NULL, hInstance, NULL);
```

When the child window is created, the child window's handle *hChild* is stored in a static variable. This handle is used later to send the child window a message. When the user clicks the "Send Message" menu item, CHILD2 executes the following call to SendMessage():

```
if (hChild)
   SendMessage (hChild, WM_USER, 0, 0L) ;
```

This sends the message WM_USER to the window *hChild*. WM_USER is defined in WINDOWS.H as 0x400 hexadecimal. The idea is that this value is above that of any of the predefined Windows messages, so you can have WM_USER mean anything you like. Many programs take advantage of this feature to define a series of internal messages. For example, you can add definitions to the program's header file that define a series of user messages.

```
#define MYWM_KILLCHILD    WM_USER        * tell child window to vanish */
#define MYWM_MAXCHILD     WM_USER + 1    * tell child window to maximize */
#define MYWM_MINCHILD     WM_USER + 2    * tell child window to minimize */
```

In CHILD2.C, we just use a single WM_USER message, so it is not renamed. Renaming user messages in a header file is a good practice, as it makes the meaning of the messages clear.

When the WM_USER message is sent to *hChild*, Windows determines where to send the message based on the class definition of the *hChild* window. We specified that the function ChildProc() was the window procedure when we registered the "ChildClass" window class, so messages sent to the *hChild* window end up being processed by the ChildProc() function. This function is shown at the end of the CHILD2.C listing.

Listing 8-6 CHILD2.C

```
/* child2.c   Sending a message to a child window */

#include <windows.h>
#include "child2.h"

int PASCAL WinMain (HANDLE hInstance, HANDLE hPrevInstance, LPSTR lpszCmdLine,
   int nCmdShow)
{
   HWND        hWnd ;         /* the window's "handle" */
   MSG         msg ;          /* a message structure */
   WNDCLASS    wndclass ;     /* window class structure */

   if (!hPrevInstance)
   {
                              /* define the parent window class */
      wndclass.style          = CS_HREDRAW | CS_VREDRAW ;
      wndclass.lpfnWndProc    = WndProc ;
      wndclass.cbClsExtra     = 0 ;
      wndclass.cbWndExtra     = 0 ;
      wndclass.hInstance      = hInstance ;
      wndclass.hIcon          = LoadIcon (hInstance, "MyIcon") ;
      wndclass.hCursor        = LoadCursor (NULL, IDC_ARROW) ;
      wndclass.hbrBackground  = GetStockObject (WHITE_BRUSH) ;
```

```
            wndclass.lpszMenuName   = "ParentMenu" ;
            wndclass.lpszClassName  = "MyClass" ;
                        /* register the parent window class */
            if (!RegisterClass (&wndclass))
                return (0) ;
                        /* change the class definition for child */
            wndclass.lpfnWndProc    = ChildProc ;
            wndclass.hIcon          = LoadIcon (NULL, IDI_APPLICATION) ;
            wndclass.hCursor        = LoadCursor (NULL, IDC_CROSS) ;
            wndclass.hbrBackground  = GetStockObject (LTGRAY_BRUSH) ;
            wndclass.lpszMenuName   = NULL ;
            wndclass.lpszClassName  = "ChildClass" ;
                        /* register the child window class */
            if (!RegisterClass (&wndclass))
            {
                MessageBox (hWnd, "Could not register class",
                    "Message", MB_OK) ;
                return (0) ;
            }
    }
                                            /* create the parent window */
    hWnd = CreateWindow ("MyClass","Child Two", WS_OVERLAPPEDWINDOW,
        CW_USEDEFAULT, CW_USEDEFAULT, CW_USEDEFAULT, CW_USEDEFAULT,
        NULL, NULL, hInstance, NULL) ;
    ShowWindow (hWnd, nCmdShow) ;       /* display the window */

    while (GetMessage (&msg, NULL, NULL, NULL))   /* message loop */
    {
        TranslateMessage (&msg) ;       /* translate keyboard messages */
        DispatchMessage (&msg) ;        /* send message to WndProc() */
    }
    return (msg.wParam) ;
}

long FAR PASCAL WndProc (HWND hWnd, WORD wMessage, WORD wParam, LONG lParam)
{
    static  HWND    hChild = NULL ;
    PAINTSTRUCT     ps ;
    HANDLE          hInstance ;

    switch (wMessage)                   /* process windows messages */
    {
        case WM_COMMAND:                /* menu items */
            switch (wParam)
            {
                case IDM_CREATE:        /* create another child window */
                    if (!hChild)
                    {
                        hInstance = GetWindowWord (hWnd, GWW_HINSTANCE) ;
                                /* create the child window and display it */
                        hChild = CreateWindow ("ChildClass", "Child Window",
                            WS_CHILD | WS_THICKFRAME | WS_MINIMIZEBOX | WS_CAPTION,
                            10, 30, 200, 150, hWnd,
                            NULL, hInstance, NULL) ;
                        ShowWindow (hChild, SW_SHOWNORMAL) ;
                    }
                    break ;
                case IDM_SEND:                      /* send a custom message to child */
                    if (hChild)
```

Chapter 8 • Child and Popup Windows

```
                    SendMessage (hChild, WM_USER, 0, 0L) ;
                    break ;
                case IDM_QUIT:
                    DestroyWindow (hWnd) ; /* destroy window, */
                    break ;                /* terminating application */
            }
            break ;
        case WM_PAINT:
            BeginPaint (hWnd, &ps) ;
            TextOut (ps.hdc, 10, 10, "Text In Parent Client Area.", 27) ;
            EndPaint (hWnd, &ps) ;
            break ;
        case WM_DESTROY:   /* stop application */
            PostQuitMessage (0) ;
            break ;
        default:       /* default windows message processing */
            return DefWindowProc (hWnd, wMessage, wParam, lParam) ;
    }
    return (0L) ;
}


/* Window procedure for the child window. */

long FAR PASCAL ChildProc (HWND hChild, WORD wMessage, WORD wParam, LONG lParam)
{
    PAINTSTRUCT  ps ;
    HANDLE       hInstance ;

    switch (wMessage)     /* process windows messages */
    {
        case WM_CREATE:    /* child being created - make a button */
            hInstance = GetWindowWord (hChild, hInstance) ;
            CreateWindow ("BUTTON", "Destroy Me",
                WS_CHILD | BS_PUSHBUTTON | WS_VISIBLE,
                20, 55, 110, 40, hChild, 100, hInstance, NULL) ;
            break ;
        case WM_COMMAND:   /* button control is only possible source */
            DestroyWindow (hChild) ;   /* kill whole child window */
            break ;
        case WM_USER:     /* custom message from parent */
            SetWindowText (hChild, "Got message from parent.") ;
            break ;
        case WM_PAINT:
            BeginPaint (hChild, &ps) ;
            TextOut (ps.hdc, 10, 25, "Text in Child Window.", 22) ;
            EndPaint (hChild, &ps) ;
            break ;
        default:       /* default windows message processing */
            return DefWindowProc (hChild, wMessage, wParam, lParam) ;
    }
    return (0L) ;
}
```

The ChildProc() function looks just like a WndProc() function for a parent window's message processing logic. ChildProc() processes the WM_CREATE message when the child window is first created, and it uses this message to prompt creation of a button control. The button control is also a child window, a child of the program's child window. This leads to the following nesting of windows:

Parent Window

Child Window

Button Control

When the button control is clicked, a WM_COMMAND message is sent to its parent, the child window that contains the button (not to the main program window). Because the child window does not have a menu and has no other controls, the button is the only source of WM_COMMAND messages to the child window's ChildProc() function. When the WM_COMMAND message is received, the DestroyWindow() function is called to destroy the child window. This also results in the button control being destroyed, as the button is a child of the child window.

If all this sounds like gobbledygook, just keep in mind the following facts. All child windows are attached to a parent when the CreateWindow() function is called. It does not matter to the child window if the parent happens to be a child of some other higher level parent window.

Listings 8-7 to 8-11 show the support files for CHILD2. The program's icon is shown in Figure 8-5.

Figure 8-5
CHILD2.ICO
Icon Image

Listing 8-7 CHILD2.H Header File

```
/* child2.h header file */

#define IDM_CREATE  1       /* main menu ID values */
#define IDM_SEND    2
#define IDM_QUIT    10

long FAR PASCAL WndProc (HWND, WORD, WORD, LONG) ;
long FAR PASCAL ChildProc (HWND, WORD, WORD, LONG) ;
```

Listing 8-8 CHILD2.RC Resource Script File

```
/* child2.rc resource file */

#include "child2.h"

MyIcon      ICON    child2.ico

ParentMenu  MENU
BEGIN
    MENUITEM "&Create",         IDM_CREATE
    MENUITEM "&Send Message",   IDM_SEND
    MENUITEM "&Quit",           IDM_QUIT
END
```

Listing 8-9 CHILD2.DEF Module Definition File

```
NAME        child2
EXETYPE     WINDOWS
STUB        'WINSTUB.EXE'
CODE        PRELOAD MOVEABLE
DATA        PRELOAD MOVEABLE MULTIPLE
HEAPSIZE    1024
STACKSIZE   5120
EXPORTS     WndProc
            ChildProc
```

Listing 8-10 Turbo C++ Project File for CHILD2

```
child2.c
child2.def
child2.res
```

Listing 8-11 QuickC Project File for CHILD2

```
child2.c
child2.def
child2.rc
```

You may have noticed that the message processing function for the parent and child window of the CHILD2 program are completely independent. When CHILD2 is running, messages for the parent window are processed by the WndProc() function, and messages for the child are processed by the ChildProc() function. This segmentation of the logic for each window into a separate function is a big help in making complex Windows programs manageable. Each window ends up being its own little world. In many cases, you will be able to design utility windows with associated message processing functions that can be used in other applications without change.

Another use of the separation of the program logic for each window is to organize a program that has many objects in the parent window's client area. You can break the parent window's client area up into a series of manageable pieces by covering the client area with separate child windows. Each child window will have its own message processing logic. This helps cut one big programming problem into several smaller sections. We will examine this in our next example program.

Fixed Child Windows

In the CHILD1 and CHILD2 examples, the child windows had caption bars. This allowed the child windows to be moved on the parent window's client area. Sometimes it is useful to have fixed child windows that cannot be moved. Fixed child windows are usually used to break up a larger window into manageable pieces. Our next example, called FIXCHILD, demonstrates fixed child windows by dividing the parent window's client area into two halves. Figure 8-6 shows FIXCHILD in action. The left half of the parent window's client area is covered with a child window that is painted with a red brush, while the right half is covered by a child window painted with a blue brush. The result is that the child windows completely cover the parent window's client area, so the child windows end up getting all of the Windows messages, except for WM_COMMAND messages from the parent's menu, and system messages for the parent such as WM_CREATE and WM_SIZE.

Listing 8-12 shows the FIXCHILD.C program file. The WinMain() function registers three window classes: "MyClass" for the parent window, "Child1Class" for the left child window, and "Child2Class" for the right child window. The two child windows are based on separate window classes so that different message processing functions can be specified, and so that the brush used to paint the child window backgrounds can have a different color. The CreateSolidBrush() function is used to pass a handle of a brush containing a pure color to the class definition.

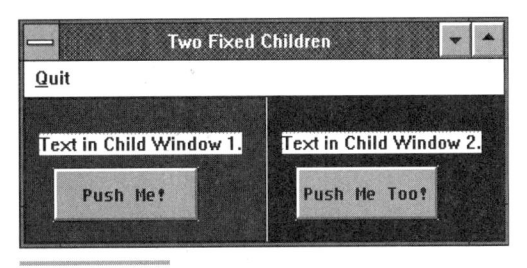

Figure 8-6 The FIXCHILD Program

Registering the First Child Window Class

```
wndclass.lpfnWndProc  = ChildProc1 ;
wndclass.hIcon        = NULL ;
wndclass.hbrBackground = CreateSolidBrush (RGB (255, 0, 0)) ;
wndclass.lpszMenuName = NULL ;
wndclass.lpszClassName = "Child1Class" ;
if (!RegisterClass (&wndclass))
   return (0) ;
```

Note that the child windows set the class icon to NULL, as these child windows will not be minimized. The child window menu names are also set to NULL, as only the parent window has a menu.

With the child window class definitions done in WinMain(), the two child windows can be created while the parent window is processing the WM_CREATE message. Note that each of the child windows uses a separate window class. Both use the WS_CHILD style to become child windows of the parent window *hWnd*. The other window styles are WS_BORDER for a thin window border, and WS_VISIBLE to make the child windows visible automatically without needing to call ShowWindow().

```
hChild1 = CreateWindow ("Child1Class", "Child Window",
   WS_CHILD | WS_BORDER | WS_VISIBLE,
   0, 0, 1, 1, hWnd, NULL, hInstance, NULL) ;
hChild2 = CreateWindow ("Child2Class", "Child Window",
   WS_CHILD | WS_BORDER | WS_VISIBLE,
   0, 0, 1, 1, hWnd, NULL, hInstance, NULL) ;
```

Chapter 8 • Child and Popup Windows

Initially, the windows are arbitrarily sized to be only one pixel square. This size is not important, as we must change the child window sizes to fit the parent window's client area. This is best done when the parent window processes the WM_SIZE message. The WM_SIZE message is sent to the parent window when the program first starts, but before the parent window is displayed. This gives the program a chance to change the window's size before it is shown. The WM_SIZE message is also sent any time the window's size changes. The horizontal size is passed as the low-order word of *lParam*, while the vertical size is the high-order word of *lParam*.

Adjusting the Child Window Sizes as the Parent Processes WM_SIZE

```
case WM_SIZE:        /* use parent size to size children */
    nXsize = LOWORD (lParam) ;
    nYsize = HIWORD (lParam) ;
    MoveWindow (hChild1, 0, 0, nXsize/2, nYsize, TRUE) ;
    MoveWindow (hChild2, 1 + (nXsize/2), 0, nXsize, nYsize, TRUE) ;
    break ;
```

In FIXCHILD, we want to have each of the child windows take up half of the parent window's client area. The MoveWindow() function is used to resize each of the child windows every time the parent window's WndProc() function processes the WM_SIZE message. Child window *hChild1* is positioned to occupy the left half of the parent window's client area, with *hChild2* occupying the right half. This leaves none of the parent window's client area visible, so mouse messages and other messages that would normally go to the parent window end up going to the child window message processing functions instead. The message processing functions for the two child windows are at the end of Listing 8-12 FIXCHILD.C.

Listing 8-12 FIXCHILD.C

```
/* fixchild.c   child windows at fixed locations */

#include <windows.h>
#include "fixchild.h"

int PASCAL WinMain (HANDLE hInstance, HANDLE hPrevInstance, LPSTR lpszCmdLine,
    int nCmdShow)
{
    HWND        hWnd ;          /* the window's "handle" */
    MSG         msg ;           /* a message structure */
    WNDCLASS    wndclass ;      /* window class structure */

    if (!hPrevInstance)
    {
                                /* define the parent window class */
        wndclass.style          = CS_HREDRAW | CS_VREDRAW ;
        wndclass.lpfnWndProc    = WndProc ;
        wndclass.cbClsExtra     = 0 ;
```

```
        wndclass.cbWndExtra       = 0 ;
        wndclass.hInstance        = hInstance ;
        wndclass.hIcon            = LoadIcon (hInstance, "MyIcon") ;
        wndclass.hCursor          = LoadCursor (NULL, IDC_ARROW) ;
        wndclass.hbrBackground    = GetStockObject (WHITE_BRUSH) ;
        wndclass.lpszMenuName     = "ParentMenu" ;
        wndclass.lpszClassName    = "MyClass" ;
                    /* register the parent window class */
        if (!RegisterClass (&wndclass))
            return (0) ;
                    /* create class for first child window */
        wndclass.lpfnWndProc      = ChildProc1 ;
        wndclass.hIcon            = NULL ;
        wndclass.hbrBackground    = CreateSolidBrush (RGB (255, 0, 0)) ;
        wndclass.lpszMenuName     = NULL ;
        wndclass.lpszClassName    = "Child1Class" ;
        if (!RegisterClass (&wndclass))
            return (0) ;
                    /* create class for second child window */
        wndclass.lpfnWndProc      = ChildProc2 ;
        wndclass.hbrBackground    = CreateSolidBrush (RGB (0, 0, 255)) ;
        wndclass.lpszClassName    = "Child2Class" ;
        if (!RegisterClass (&wndclass))
            return (0) ;
    }
                                        /* create the parent window */
    hWnd = CreateWindow ("MyClass","Two Fixed Children", WS_OVERLAPPEDWINDOW,
        CW_USEDEFAULT, CW_USEDEFAULT, CW_USEDEFAULT, CW_USEDEFAULT,
        NULL, NULL, hInstance, NULL) ;
    ShowWindow (hWnd, nCmdShow) ;       /* display the window */

    while (GetMessage (&msg, NULL, NULL, NULL))  /* message loop */
    {
        TranslateMessage (&msg) ;       /* translate keyboard messages */
        DispatchMessage (&msg) ;        /* send message to WndProc() */
    }
    return (msg.wParam) ;
}

long FAR PASCAL WndProc (HWND hWnd, WORD wMessage, WORD wParam, LONG lParam)
{
    static   HWND    hChild1    = NULL, hChild2 = NULL ;
    HANDLE           hInstance ;
    int              nXsize, nYsize ;

    switch (wMessage)              /* process windows messages */
    {
        case WM_CREATE:
            if (!hChild1)                  /* if first time, create children */
            {
            hInstance = GetWindowWord (hWnd, GWW_HINSTANCE) ;
                /* create the child window and display it */
            hChild1 = CreateWindow ("Child1Class", "Child Window",
                WS_CHILD | WS_BORDER | WS_VISIBLE,
                0, 0, 1, 1, hWnd, NULL, hInstance, NULL) ;
            hChild2 = CreateWindow ("Child2Class", "Child Window",
                WS_CHILD | WS_BORDER | WS_VISIBLE,
                0, 0, 1, 1, hWnd, NULL, hInstance, NULL) ;
```

```c
            }
            break ;
        case WM_COMMAND:                /* menu items */
            switch (wParam)
            {
                case IDM_QUIT:
                    DestroyWindow (hWnd) ; /* destroy window, */
                    break ;             /* terminating application */
            }
            break ;
        case WM_SIZE:                   /* use parent size to size children */
            nXsize = LOWORD (lParam) ;
            nYsize = HIWORD (lParam) ;
            MoveWindow (hChild1, 0, 0, nXsize/2, nYsize, TRUE) ;
            MoveWindow (hChild2, 1 + (nXsize/2), 0, nXsize, nYsize, TRUE) ;
            break ;
        case WM_DESTROY:                /* stop application */
            PostQuitMessage (0) ;
            break ;
        default:                        /* default windows message processing */
            return DefWindowProc (hWnd, wMessage, wParam, lParam) ;
    }
    return (0L) ;
}
/* Window procedure for the first child window. */

long FAR PASCAL ChildProc1 (HWND hChild, WORD wMessage, WORD wParam, LONG lParam)
{
    PAINTSTRUCT     ps ;
    HANDLE          hInstance ;
    HWND            hParent ;

    switch (wMessage)           /* process windows messages */
    {
        case WM_CREATE:         /* child being created - make a button */
            hInstance = GetWindowWord (hChild, GWW_HINSTANCE) ;
            CreateWindow ("BUTTON", "Push Me!",
                WS_CHILD | BS_PUSHBUTTON | WS_VISIBLE,
                20, 50, 110, 40, hChild, 100, hInstance, NULL) ;
            break ;
        case WM_COMMAND:    /* button control is only possible source */
            hParent = GetParent (hChild) ;
            SendMessage (hParent, WM_SETTEXT, 0, (DWORD)(LPSTR) "Child1 Button!") ;
            break ;
        case WM_PAINT:
            BeginPaint (hChild, &ps) ;
            TextOut (ps.hdc, 10, 25, "Text in Child Window 1.", 24) ;
            EndPaint (hChild, &ps) ;
            break ;
        default:            /* default windows message processing */
            return DefWindowProc (hChild, wMessage, wParam, lParam) ;
    }
    return (0L) ;
}

/* Window procedure for the second child window. */

long FAR PASCAL ChildProc2 (HWND hChild, WORD wMessage, WORD wParam, LONG lParam)
{
```

```
    PAINTSTRUCT    ps ;
    HANDLE         hInstance ;
    HWND           hParent ;

    switch (wMessage)         /* process windows messages */
    {
        case WM_CREATE:       /* child being created - make a button */
            hInstance = GetWindowWord (hChild, GWW_HINSTANCE) ;
            CreateWindow ("BUTTON", "Push Me Too!",
               WS_CHILD | BS_PUSHBUTTON | WS_VISIBLE,
               20, 50, 110, 40, hChild, 100, hInstance, NULL) ;
            break ;
        case WM_COMMAND:      /* button control is only possible source */
            hParent = GetParent (hChild) ;
            SendMessage (hParent, WM_SETTEXT, 0, (DWORD)(LPSTR) "Child2 Button!") ;
            break ;
        case WM_PAINT:
            BeginPaint (hChild, &ps) ;
            TextOut (ps.hdc, 10, 25, "Text in Child Window 2.", 24) ;
            EndPaint (hChild, &ps) ;
            break ;
        default:       /* default windows message processing */
            return DefWindowProc (hChild, wMessage, wParam, lParam) ;
    }
    return (0L) ;
}
```

Each of the child windows has a separate message processing function, ChildProc1() and ChildProc2(). In both cases, the child window functions create button controls when the child window receives a WM_CREATE message. The button controls are children of the child windows.

Clicking one of the buttons causes a WM_COMMAND message to be sent to the button's parent window—one of the child windows. The child window message processing functions process the WM_COMMAND messages and send the WM_SETTEXT message to its parent window. The handy function GetParent() is used to retrieve the parent window's handle. SendMessage() is used to send the WM_SETTEXT message to the parent window. The WM_SETTEXT message results in the main program window's caption being changed.

```
    case WM_COMMAND:
        hParent = GetParent (hChild) ;
        SendMessage (hParent, WM_SETTEXT, 0, (DWORD)(LPSTR) "Child2 Button!") ;
        break ;
```

With a simple example like FIXCHILD, there is little reason to have the two separate window functions for the right and left side of the parent window's client area. However, with more complex programs, this can be a useful tool in reducing the complexity of the program's WndProc() function. Note that both of the child window message processing functions must be declared in the program's header file and must be listed in the EXPORTS section of the module definition file. The support files for CHILD2 are shown in Listings 8-13 to 8-17. Figure 8-8 shows the program icon.

Listing 8-13 FIXCHILD.H Header File

```
/* fixchild.h header file */

#define IDM_QUIT    10

long FAR PASCAL WndProc (HWND, WORD, WORD, LONG) ;
long FAR PASCAL ChildProc1 (HWND, WORD, WORD, LONG) ;
long FAR PASCAL ChildProc2 (HWND, WORD, WORD, LONG) ;
```

Figure 8-8
FIXCHILD.ICO
Icon Image

Listing 8-14 FIXCHILD.RC Resource Script File

```
/* fixchild.rc resource file */

#include "fixchild.h"

MyIcon    ICON    fixchild.ico

ParentMenu MENU
BEGIN
   MENUITEM "&Quit",       IDM_QUIT
END
```

Listing 8-15 FIXCHILD.DEF Module Definition File

```
NAME         fixchild
EXETYPE      WINDOWS
STUB         'WINSTUB.EXE'
CODE         PRELOAD MOVEABLE
DATA         PRELOAD MOVEABLE MULTIPLE
HEAPSIZE     1024
STACKSIZE    5120
EXPORTS      WndProc
             ChildProc1
             ChildProc2
```

Listing 8-16 Turbo C++ Project File for FIXCHILD

```
fixchild.c
fixchild.def
fixchild.res
```

Listing 8-17 QuickC Project File for FIXCHILD

```
fixchild.c
fixchild.def
fixchild.rc
```

Popup Windows

The last type of window we will explore in this chapter is the popup window. Popups are similar to child windows, in that they are related to a parent window. However, popup windows are not restricted to the parent window's client area. Popups can appear anywhere on the screen, and they can cover up portions of the parent window and other program windows. One interesting aspect of popup windows is that they can never be covered by their parent window. Both the popup and its parent can be covered by other program windows and uncovered, but the parent window will always be "under" the popup window. This is true even if the parent window gains the input focus (dark caption bar).

Figure 8-9 shows our next example program in action. The POPUP program creates a popup window when the "Create" menu item is selected. The popup window has a caption bar, so it can be moved on the screen. In Figure 8-9, the popup window partially covers the parent window. Note that the popup window extends well beyond the bounds of the parent window and can be completely separated from the parent on the screen. This makes popup windows handy for small utility windows, such as windows that show the current cursor X,Y position in painting programs.

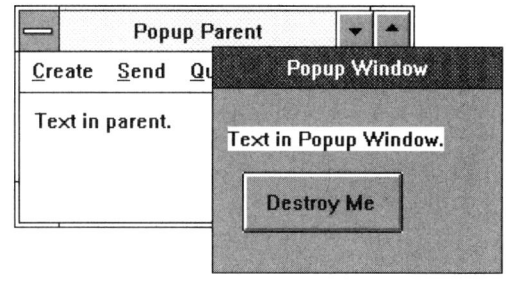

Figure 8-9 The POPUP Program

If the parent window is minimized, the popup window automatically disappears from the screen. When the parent is restored, the popup automatically reappears at its previous screen location. You can think of popup windows as an obedient dog. It is always around its master (the main program window), but not always in the master's lap.

Creating popup windows is just like creating child windows, except the WS_POPUP window style is used in place of WS_CHILD when calling CreateWindow(). You cannot use the WS_CHILD and WS_POPUP styles at the same time to create a window. The two styles are mutually exclusive. Another difference between child and popup windows is that the coordinates passed to CreateWindow() are interpreted as screen coordinates for popup windows, not as client coordinates of the parent window. This makes sense, as popup window can be located anywhere on the screen, while child windows are restricted to the parent window's client area.

Listing 8-18 shows the POPUP.C program. In POPUP.C, only the parent window's class is registered in the WinMain() function. The popup window's class "PopupClass" is registered when processing the WM_CREATE message in the WndProc() function. This is just another convenient place to register new window classes, with no particular advantage or disadvantage compared to registering all of the new window classes in WinMain(), as we did in the previous examples. The "PopupClass" window class uses a function named PopupProc() to process window messages. The PopupProc() function is shown at the end of Listing 8-18.

POPUP.C again uses a WM_USER message to send a message from the parent window to the popup window. In this case, the WM_USER message is processed by PopupProc() and causes the popup window to change its caption to "Got Message!" This seems a little bit magical when you click the "Send" menu item on the parent window and instantly see the caption change on the popup window in a separate location on the screen. Remote control!

If you compare the POPUP.C and CHILD2.C listing, you will note that there are remarkably few differences. You can easily change from popup to child windows and back, if the structure of the window is an independent entity. It would not make sense to use fixed POPUP windows to partition the parent window's client area as we did in the FIXCHILD.C example. Popups are almost always movable.

Listing 8-18 POPUP.C

```
/* popup.c  demonstrate a popup window */

#include <windows.h>
#include "popup.h"

int PASCAL WinMain (HANDLE hInstance, HANDLE hPrevInstance, LPSTR lpszCmdLine,
    int nCmdShow)
{

    HWND            hWnd ;
    MSG             msg ;
    WNDCLASS        wndclass ;

    if (!hPrevInstance)
    {
        wndclass.style          = CS_HREDRAW | CS_VREDRAW ;
        wndclass.lpfnWndProc    = WndProc ;
        wndclass.cbClsExtra     = 0 ;
        wndclass.cbWndExtra     = 0 ;
        wndclass.hInstance      = hInstance ;
        wndclass.hIcon          = LoadIcon (hInstance, "myicon") ;
        wndclass.hCursor        = LoadCursor (NULL, IDC_ARROW) ;
        wndclass.hbrBackground  = GetStockObject (WHITE_BRUSH) ;
        wndclass.lpszMenuName   = "MyMenu" ;
        wndclass.lpszClassName  = "ParentClass" ;
                    /* register the window class */
        if (!RegisterClass (&wndclass))
            return (0) ;
    }

    hWnd = CreateWindow ("ParentClass", "Popup Parent", WS_OVERLAPPEDWINDOW,
        CW_USEDEFAULT, CW_USEDEFAULT, CW_USEDEFAULT, CW_USEDEFAULT,
        NULL, NULL, hInstance, NULL) ;

    ShowWindow (hWnd, nCmdShow) ;
    UpdateWindow (hWnd) ;       /* send first WM_PAINT message */

    while (GetMessage (&msg, NULL, 0, 0))      /* the message loop */
    {
```

```
            TranslateMessage (&msg) ;
            DispatchMessage (&msg) ;
        }
        return (msg.wParam) ;
    }

    long FAR PASCAL WndProc (HWND hWnd, WORD wMessage, WORD wParam, LONG lParam)
    {
        WNDCLASS wndclass ;
        static   HWND   hPopup = NULL ;
        HANDLE          hInstance ;
        PAINTSTRUCT     ps ;

        switch (wMessage)
        {
            case WM_COMMAND:
            switch (wParam)
            {
                case IDM_CREATE:
                    if (hPopup == NULL)    /* only make one popup */
                    {
                        hInstance = GetWindowWord (hWnd, GWW_HINSTANCE) ;

                        wndclass.style         =
                                    CS_HREDRAW | CS_VREDRAW | CS_PARENTDC ;
                        wndclass.lpfnWndProc   = PopupProc ;
                        wndclass.cbClsExtra    = 0 ;
                        wndclass.cbWndExtra    = 0 ;
                        wndclass.hInstance     = hInstance ;
                        wndclass.hIcon         = NULL ;
                        wndclass.hCursor       = LoadCursor (NULL, IDC_ARROW) ;
                        wndclass.hbrBackground = GetStockObject (LTGRAY_BRUSH) ;
                        wndclass.lpszMenuName  = NULL ;
                        wndclass.lpszClassName = "PopupClass" ;
                                        /* register the window class */
                        if(RegisterClass (&wndclass))
                        {
                        hPopup = CreateWindow ("PopupClass", |Popup Window",
                            WS_POPUP | WS_VISIBLE | WS_BORDER | WS_CAPTION,
                            10, 50, 200, 150, hWnd, NULL, hInstance, NULL) ;
                        ShowWindow (hPopup, SW_SHOW) ;
                    }

                break ;
            case IDM_SEND:
                if (hPopup)
                    SendMessage (hPopup, WM_USER, 0, 0L) ;
                break ;
            case IDM_QUIT:
                DestroyWindow (hWnd) ;
                break ;
            }
            break ;
        case WM_PAINT:
            BeginPaint (hWnd, &ps) ;
            TextOut (ps.hdc, 10, 10, "Text in parent.", 15) ;
            EndPaint (hWnd, &ps) ;
            break ;
        case WM_DESTROY:
```

```
            PostQuitMessage (0) ;
            break ;
     default:                          /* default windows message processing */
            return DefWindowProc (hWnd, wMessage, wParam, lParam) ;
    }
    return (0L) ;
}

long FAR PASCAL PopupProc (HWND hPopup, WORD wMessage, WORD wParam, LONG lParam)
{
    PAINTSTRUCT    ps ;
    HANDLE         hInstance ;
    static BOOL    bFirstTime = TRUE ;

    switch (wMessage)                  /* process windows messages */
    {
       case WM_CREATE:
            if (bFirstTime)
            {
            bFirstTime = FALSE ;
            hInstance = GetWindowWord (hPopup, GWW_HINSTANCE) ;
            CreateWindow ("BUTTON", "Destroy Me",
                WS_CHILD | BS_PUSHBUTTON | WS_VISIBLE,
                20, 55, 110, 40, hPopup, 100, hInstance, NULL) ;
            }
            break ;
       case WM_COMMAND:
            DestroyWindow (hPopup) ;
            break ;
       case WM_USER:                   /* user message from parent */
            SetWindowText (hPopup, "Got Message!") ;
            break ;
       case WM_PAINT:
            BeginPaint (hPopup, &ps) ;
            TextOut (ps.hdc, 10, 25, "Text in Popup Window.", 21) ;
            EndPaint (hPopup, &ps) ;
            break ;
       default:                        /* default windows message processing */
            return DefWindowProc (hPopup, wMessage, wParam, lParam) ;
    }
    return (0L) ;
}
```

The support files for POPUP are shown in Listings 8-19 to 8-23. Figure 8-10 shows the program's icon.

Listing 8-19 POPUP.H Header File

```
/* popup.h   */

#define IDM_CREATE   1      /* menu item id values */
#define IDM_SEND     2
#define IDM_QUIT    10

/* function prototypes */
long FAR PASCAL WndProc (HWND, unsigned, WORD, LONG) ;
long FAR PASCAL PopupProc (HWND, unsigned, WORD, LONG) ;
```

Figure 8-10
POPUP.ICO
Icon Image

Listing 8-20 POPUP.RC Resource Script File

```
/* popup.rc    jim conger 1991 */

#include "popup.h"

myicon      ICON    popup.ico

MyMenu      MENU
BEGIN
    MENUITEM "&Create",     IDM_CREATE
    MENUITEM "&Send",       IDM_SEND
    MENUITEM "&Quit",       IDM_QUIT
END
```

Listing 8-21 POPUP.DEF Module Definition File

```
NAME            popup
DESCRIPTION     'create windows example'
EXETYPE         WINDOWS
STUB            'WINSTUB.EXE'
CODE            PRELOAD MOVEABLE
DATA            PRELOAD MOVEABLE MULTIPLE
HEAPSIZE        1024
STACKSIZE       5120
EXPORTS         WndProc
                PopupProc
```

Listing 8-22 Turbo C++ Project File for POPUP

```
popup.c
popup.def
popup.res
```

Listing 8-23 QuickC Project File for POPUP

```
popup.c
popup.def
popup.rc
```

The Big Picture

You may have noticed the similarity between the way child and popup windows behave and the way program windows behave on the Windows desktop (the background screen on which all of the program windows appear). This is not an accident. The Windows desktop is just another window, admittedly a slightly odd one that lacks a caption bar and border. All of the running main program windows behave like children of the desktop window. When you minimize a main program window, it shrinks to an icon on the desktop, just like our child window in CHILD2 shrinks to an icon in the corner of its parent window's client area.

When you write a program with one or more movable child windows (like CHILD2), you end up creating a miniature "little world" in your program's client area. Your program's client area behaves very much like the full Windows desktop. Windows uses the same built-in logic for handling a wide variety of windowing situations, such as minimizing and maximizing windows, moving child windows within a limited area. Using the same code for both main program windows, and for child windows, keeps the size of the Windows system small and gives the environment consistent behavior in a wide variety of situations.

Summary

Child windows are created by registering a new window class, and then using CreateWindow() with the WS_CHILD style. Child windows are restricted to the bounds of the parent window's client area. Child windows normally use separate message processing functions, specified when the child window's class is registered. Messages to the child window are processed by the child window's message function, not by the parent window's WndProc() function. Child windows can be either movable (if they have a caption bar) or fixed at a location in the parent window's client area. Fixed child windows are useful for breaking up the program logic for complex screens into manageable chunks.

Popup windows are like child windows, except that they are free to be located anywhere on the screen. Popup windows are also usually based on a separate window class, and use a separate message processing function. Popup windows are ideal for applications that have multiple independent sections, such as a communications program which supports a number of simultaneous terminal sessions in different popup windows.

User messages are used to communicate between windows with separate message processing functions. Windows defines WM_USER as the first ID value that is above any of the predefined Windows messages. You can use WM_USER and above to define messages for any type of activity. Experienced Windows programmers use user messages and separate message processing functions to break complex programming problems into manageable pieces.

QUESTIONS

1. To create a child window, use the _____ window style when calling CreateWindow(). To create a popup window, use the _____ window style.
2. The message processing function for a child or popup window is specified when you _____ the window _____.
3. The function type and parameters for the message processing functions for parent windows (WndProc() function), child windows, and popup windows are the same (True/False).
4. If a message is not processed by the message processing logic in a message function for a child or popup window, the message should be passed to the _____ function.
5. The location of a popup window is relative to the upper left corner of the _____.
6. In order for a child or popup window to be movable, it must be created with the _____ style (or another style that contains the same binary flag.)

EXERCISES

1. Modify the CHILD1.C program so that the child window contains another child window. This new child window can use the same message processing function, ChildProc(), and should have a caption bar and a border. The result should be roughly as shown in Figure 8-11.

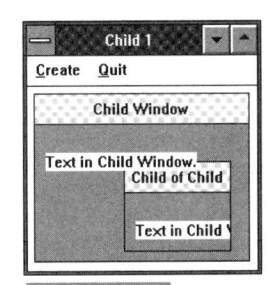

Figure 8-11 Solution to Exercise 8-1

2. Add a menu to the popup window created by the POPUP program. The menu should have only one item, labeled "Enlarge." Modify the popup window's message processing function to process this menu item, enlarging the window to 210 by 210 pixels. Maintain the button control for destroying the popup window. Also add a minimize button to the popup window's caption bar, and add an icon to the popup window's class definition. The popup window should look roughly as shown in Figure 8-12. When the popup window is minimized, does the icon show up in the program's main window client area or at the bottom of the screen? What happens to the popup window when the main program window is destroyed?

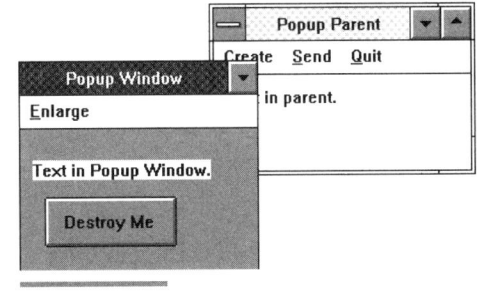

Figure 8-12 Popup Window for Exercise 8-2

Chapter 8 • Child and Popup Windows

ANSWERS TO QUESTIONS

1. WS_CHILD, WS_POPUP.
2. register, class.
3. True.
4. DefWindowProc().
5. screen.
6. WS_CAPTION

SOLUTIONS TO EXERCISES

1. The new child window can take advantage of the same window class used by the first child window. All that is needed to create the second child is a call to CreateWindow(). Note that the parent handle for the second child window is *hChild*, the first child window's handle. The full listings are under the file name C8EXER01 on the source code disks. Listing 8-24 shows the CreateWindow() function call.

Listing 8-24 Solution to Exercise 8-1

```
case IDM_CREATE:
    if (hChild == NULL)    /* only create one child */
    {
            hInstance = GetWindowWord (hWnd, GWW_HINSTANCE) ;
                    /* create the child window and display it */
            hChild = CreateWindow ("ChildClass", "Child Window",
                WS_CHILD | WS_BORDER | WS_CAPTION | WS_VISIBLE,
                10, 30, 200, 150, hWnd,
                NULL, hInstance, NULL) ;
            hChild2 = CreateWindow ("ChildClass", "Child of Child",
                WS_CHILD | WS_BORDER | WS_CAPTION | WS_VISIBLE,
                10, 30, 100, 80, hChild,
                NULL, hInstance, NULL) ;
    }
    break ;
```

2. The resource script file will need to have the new icon and menu items added. Listing 8-25 shows the changes to the POPUP.RC file. The complete listings are under the file name C8EXER02 on the source code disks.

Listing 8-25 Changes to the Resource Script File

```
/* c8exer02.rc */

#include "c8exer02.h"
```

SOLUTIONS TO EXERCISES (cont'd)

```
myicon      ICON    c8exer02.ico
popupicon   ICON    popup.ico           /* new */

MyMenu    MENU
BEGIN
    MENUITEM "&Create",     IDM_CREATE
    MENUITEM "&Send",       IDM_SEND
    MENUITEM "&Quit",       IDM_QUIT
END
PopupMenu  MENU                         /* new */
BEGIN
    MENUITEM "&Enlarge",    IDM_ENLARGE
END
```

You will also need to add define statements to the program's header file for the ID values for both the menu item and the button control, as shown in Listing 8-26. The button control's ID value was not important in the POPUP program, as it was the only source of WM_COMMAND messages. With the addition of the menu, there are two sources of WM_COMMAND messages, so the ID values must be used to determine which has been activated.

Listing 8-26 Changes to the Header File

```
/* c8exer02.h  */

#define IDM_CREATE      1       /* menu item id values */
#define IDM_SEND        2
#define IDM_QUIT        10
#define IDM_ENLARGE     20      /* new - menu item for popup */
#define ID_BUTTON       100     /* new - button control ID value */

/* function prototypes */
long FAR PASCAL WndProc (HWND, unsigned, WORD, LONG) ;
long FAR PASCAL PopupProc (HWND, unsigned, WORD, LONG) ;
```

The class definition for the popup window adds the icon and menu references (Listing 8-27). Also the call to CreateWindow() adds the WS_MINIMIZEBOX style to create a popup window with a minimize box.

Listing 8-27 Changes to the Popup Window Definition

```
wndclass.style          =
    CS_HREDRAW | CS_VREDRAW | CS_PARENTDC ;
wndclass.lpfnWndProc    = PopupProc ;
wndclass.cbClsExtra     = 0 ;
wndclass.cbWndExtra     = 0 ;
wndclass.hInstance      = hInstance ;
wndclass.hIcon          = LoadIcon (hInstance, "popupicon") ;
```

SOLUTIONS TO EXERCISES (cont'd)

```
wndclass.hCursor        = LoadCursor (NULL, IDC_ARROW) ;
wndclass.hbrBackground  = GetStockObject (LTGRAY_BRUSH) ;
wndclass.lpszMenuName   = "PopupMenu" ;
wndclass.lpszClassName  = "PopupClass" ;
            /* register the window class */
if(RegisterClass (&wndclass))
{
    hPopup = CreateWindow ("PopupClass", "Popup Window",
        WS_POPUP | WS_VISIBLE | WS_BORDER | WS_CAPTION |
        WS_MINIMIZEBOX,
        10, 50, 200, 170, hWnd, NULL, hInstance, NULL) ;
}
```

Enlarging the popup window is done with a call to the MoveWindow() function. The logic for processing the WM_COMMAND message in the popup window's message processing function, PopupProc(), should be modified as shown in Listing 8-28.

Listing 8-28 Enlarging the Popup Window when the "Enlarge" Menu Item Is Selected

```
case WM_COMMAND:
    switch (wParam)
    {
        case ID_BUTTON:
            DestroyWindow (hPopup) ;
            break ;
        case IDM_ENLARGE:
            MoveWindow (hPopup, 10, 10, 210, 210, TRUE) ;
            break ;
    }
    break ;
```

When the popup window is minimized, it shows up at the bottom of the screen, not at the bottom of the main program window's client area. When the main program window is destroyed, the popup is destroyed automatically. This is true if the popup is minimized or normally sized.

CHAPTER 9

Menus

This chapter begins a series of three chapters devoted to resources. The most common types of resources are data-defining menus, dialog boxes, and small images (icons and bitmaps). Chapter 7, *Character Sets, Fonts, and the Keyboard*, also introduced keyboard accelerators, which are stored as resource data. This chapter will examine menus, including menus containing graphic objects. Dialog boxes are the subject of Chapter 10, and Chapter 11, *Other Resources*, covers miscellaneous types of data that can be stored in resources.

Up to now the examples in this book have used simple menus, defined as part of the program's resource data. Windows provides tremendous built-in support for more complex menus, including popup menus that appear under the main menu bar, and menu items containing graphic images. Windows also allows a program's menu to be altered as the program operates. This is useful if you want to support beginner and advanced versions of the menus, or if you have a program that operates in more than one state, such as a spreadsheet program that can switch to a graphics mode with a different menu.

This chapter examines a variety of menu types, including complex menus with several levels of submenus, menus that change as the program runs, and menus that include bitmap images. We will also look at how you can use an application's system menu, using a simple program that continually moves its icon around the screen. The system menu example also introduces the Windows timer, which can be used to start actions at fixed time intervals.

Concepts Covered

Main Menus
Popup Menus
Discardable Resource Data
Graying and Checking Menu Items

Creating Menus as the Program Operates
The System Menu
Using Windows Timers

Keywords Covered

MENU
LOADONCAL
MOVEABLE
FIXED
DISCARDABLE
POPUP
BEGIN
END
CHECKED
GRAYED
HELP
INACTIVE
MENUBARBREAK

MENUBREAK
MF_BYCOMMAND
MF_BYPOSITION
MF_ENABLED
MF_GRAYED
MF_DISABLED
SC_CLOSE
SC_MAXIMIZE
SC_MINIMIZE
SC_MOVE
SC_RESTORE
SC_SIZE
SC_TASKLIST

Functions Covered

EnableMenuItem()
CheckMenuItem()
GetMenu()
DestroyMenu()
CreateMenu()
CreatePopupMenu()
SetMenu()
AppendMenu()
InsertMenu()

DeleteMenu()
DestroyMenu()
DrawMenuBar()
GetSystemMenu()
GetMenuState()
GetMenuString()
SetTimer()
KillTimer()

Messages Covered
WM_SYSCOMMAND   WM_TIMER

Creating Menus

There are two different ways to create a menu definition. The most direct way is to write a resource script (.RC) file containing the menu definition using a text editor. This is the assumed method behind all of the simple menus used in the example programs up to this point in the book. You can use either the Borland Resource Workshop or the Microsoft Resource Compiler to compile the resource script file, as explained in Chapter 3, *First Programming Experiments*. The resource data is compiled to make a .RES resource data file, which is added to the finished program during the linking step.

The Borland Resource Workshop (WORKSHOP), which comes with both Turbo C++ and Borland C++, provides an alternative method of creating menus. Menus can be defined without leaving WORKSHOP by using the built-in menu editor. The menu editor automates some of the mundane aspects of creating menus and reduces the opportunities for making an error. Perhaps the biggest advantage of using WORKSHOP's menu editor is that you can define all of a program's resources (menus, icons, bitmaps, etc.) without leaving the WORKSHOP environment.

The actual process of creating a menu is very similar, whether you do it by writing a resource script file or by using the WORKSHOP menu editor. The key words and menu structure are identical in both cases. This chapter introduces menus starting with the resource script technique, as this method applies to both the Borland and Microsoft tools and is the assumed method for all of the example programs in this book. This chapter also includes a section titled *Using the Borland Resource Workshop*, which gives step-by-step instructions on how to use the WORKSHOP menu editor.

Menus Defined as Resource Data

Most programs have a menu that consists only of key words (not graphics) and that does not change as the program operates. Creating this type of menu is almost trivial. You define the menu structure as part of the program's resource script file (.RC file), compile all the resources with the resource compiler, and let Windows take care of all of the details of positioning each item, highlighting items when selected, and sending WM_COMMAND messages when items are selected.

The MINIMAL4 program in Chapter 3, *First Programming Experiments*, provides a good example of a simple menu. Listing 9-1 shows the MINIMAL4.RC resource script file, including the menu definition. MINIMAL4.RC also includes an icon file in the program's resources. The resource compiler (WORKSHOP for the Borland compilers, or RC.EXE or RCW.EXE for Microsoft's compilers) reads the entire .RC file and converts it into the .RES resource data format that Windows can read directly. The .RES data is

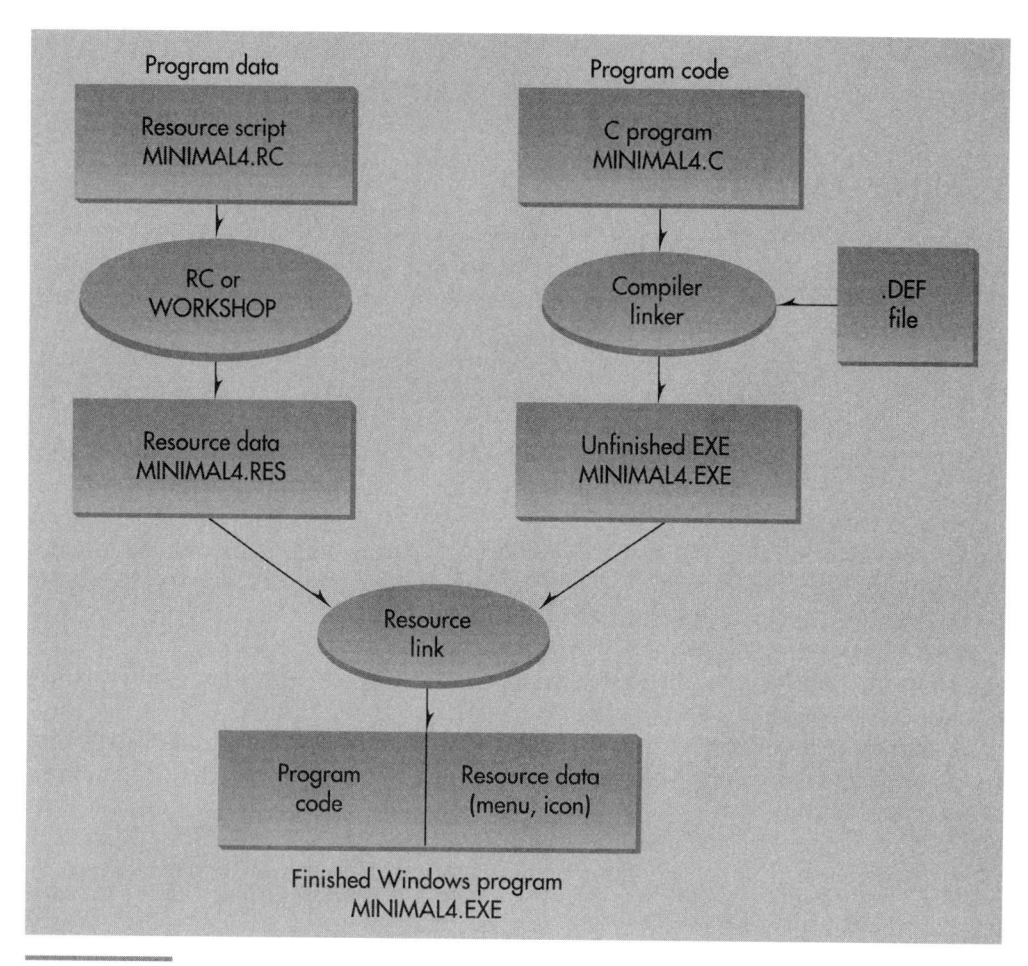

Figure 9-1 How Resource Data Is Added to a Windows Program

added to the end of the program's code to make a finished Windows program. Figure 9-1 shows the sequence of events that lead to a complete Windows program, containing both the program's instructions and the resource data. For the finished MINIMAL4.EXE program, the resource data will contain the icon data and the menu definition in the compiled format Windows uses internally.

Listing 9-1 MINIMAL4.RC Resource Script File

```
/* minimal4.rc  resource file */

#include "minimal4.h"

MyIcon    ICON    minimal4.ico
```

```
MyMenu     MENU
BEGIN
   MENUITEM "&Beep"          IDM_BEEP
   MENUITEM "&Quit",         IDM_QUIT
END
```

"MENU" is a key word that the resource compiler recognizes. The complete syntax of the MENU statement is as follows:

```
MenuName    MENU    [load option] [memory option]
BEGIN
      /* menu definition goes here */
END
```

MenuName is a character string that you use to find the menu data in the program's resources. Even the simple MINIMAL4.RC resource script file has two types of resources, an icon and a menu. More complex programs can have several icons, more than one menu, and all sorts of other data in the resource file. To keep track of all of the resources, the resource data is organized by name. Each resource gets a name, which is saved as part of the resource data. When you load resource data into memory to use it, Windows finds the part of the resource data you have requested using the resource name. Figure 9-2 shows how the resource data is organized in a finished windows program.

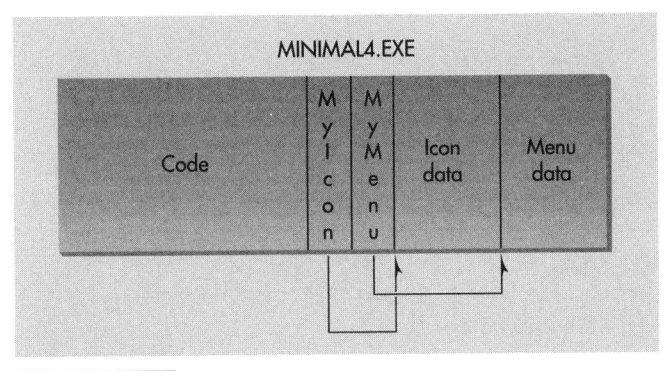

Figure 9-2 How Resource Names Are Used to Locate Resource Data

Menu Loading and Memory Options

There are two load options for menus (and all other types of resources), PRELOAD and LOADONCALL. PRELOAD tells Windows to load the menu data into memory as soon as the program starts running. LOADONCALL tells Windows to wait until the program needs the data to load it into memory. If you do not specify either option, the default value is LOADONCALL. The load option does not make much difference with main program menus, as they are usually needed to create the program's main window as the program starts running.

Once a menu is loaded into memory, it can have different memory options based on the key words FIXED, MOVEABLE, and DISCARDABLE. FIXED means that the data cannot be moved in memory. This is the least desirable option, and it would be silly to use it for a menu because there is no reason to fix the menu data at one address in memory. MOVEABLE means that the resource data can be moved in memory. DISCARDABLE tells Windows that the data can be temporarily removed from memory if the system runs low on memory room. Windows will then reload the menu data when it is again needed. The DISCARDABLE statement is always used with MOVEABLE, and the combination of DISCARDABLE plus MOVEABLE is the default case for resources. The menu in MINIMAL4.RC could have been declared LOADONCALL, MOVEABLE, and DISCARDABLE, as shown in Listing 9-2, to explicitly show the default load and memory options. Normally, you can forget about all of these options, and just use the defaults.

Listing 9-2 Specifying Load and Memory Options (MINIMAL4.RC)

```
MyMenu    MENU    LOADONCALL MOVEABLE DISCARDABLE
BEGIN
    MENUITEM "&Beep"    IDM_BEEP
    MENUITEM "&Quit",   IDM_QUIT
END
```

Menu Items

Following the MENU statement in the program's resource script file is the BEGIN statement. Everything between BEGIN and END is part of the menu definition. There are only two kinds of statements that can be placed between the MENU BEGIN and END statements, MENUITEM and POPUP. We will get to POPUP menus in the next section. MENUITEM statements are used to define individual menu elements, including their character string and ID numbers. Listing 9-2 shows two MENUITEM statements, defining the "Beep" and "Quit" menu items. Note that the menu characters are enclosed in double quotes, and the first letter is preceded by an ampersand character. The ampersand does not show up in the menu when displayed, but it is used to mark which character in the menu item is underlined. Holding the (Alt) key down and depressing the letter key that matches an underlined menu item will cause the menu item to be selected. This keyboard interface will work as long as the program's message loop contains the TranslateMessage() function, as in MINIMAL4.C. Figure 9-3 shows the MINIMAL4 program running, with the menu items underlined. If you want an ampersand in the menu string, put two ampersand's together. For example "&Me&&You" in the menu definition will display "Me&You" on the menu bar.

The menu item's string is followed by a comma, and then the menu item ID number. These ID numbers are important, as they become the *wParam* parameter passed with the WM_COMMAND message when a menu item is selected. *wParam* is used in the program to figure out which menu item was selected. The WM_COMMAND message will be identical whether the mouse or keyboard shortcut is used to select a menu item. Normally, menu item ID numbers are defined in the program's header file, to give each item a readable name. It is convenient to use numbers between 0 and 99 for the menu item IDs, as the dialog box editors start their automatic number of dialog

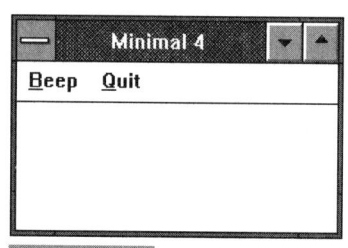

Figure 9-3 The MINIMAL4 Program's Menu

box controls at 100 (the next chapter discusses dialog boxes). If you are using a number of child windows with menus, the menu item ID numbers can overlap, as a window will only receive WM_COMMAND messages when it is the active window and will never get them from another window's menu bar.

Popup Menus

The main menu bar will hold only a few menu items. If you put in more menu items than will fit on a single line, Windows automatically will wrap the menu, creating a two line menu bar. Two line menus are awkward and take up valuable space from the window's client area. It is much better to use popup menus if you need to provide more options. Popup menus (sometimes called "drop-down" or "pull-down" menus) are used to give the user access to more selections, without requiring additional space on the top menu bar. Figure 9-4 shows a typical popup menu, used by the Notepad application. When the user selects "File," a popup menu appears with another group of options. Notepad is typical of most Windows applications, having both a main menu bar and popup menus which drop down from the main menu. You can have popups from popups, with up to eight levels of nesting. The MENU1 example program in this chapter has a menu with a popup menu defined in another popup. Generally, you are better off using dialog boxes in place of many levels of popup menus, because complex menus can be confusing for the user. Dialog boxes are the subject of the next chapter.

Popup menus are defined inside the menu definition, between the BEGIN and END menu statements. Figure 9-5 shows a typical example, with two levels of popup menus. The key word "POPUP" is followed by the title (character string) that will head the popup menu. Note that there is no ID number following the popup's string. This is because popup titles cannot be selected by themselves, and they do not generate WM_COMMAND messages. Popup titles are used to allow the user to select a popup menu that will contain the menu items that can be selected. Only the menu items have ID values and generate WM_COMMAND messages.

Figure 9-5 shows an example with two levels of popup menus. Everything between the BEGIN and END statements that follow the POPUP key word is part of the popup, and will be at a lower level in the menu structure than the popup's title string. Note how the listing on the left side of Figure 9-5 is indented to make the different levels of popup menus clear. The indentation is not necessary and does not affect the resource compiler's conversion of the menu statements into the .RES format, but indentation definitely helps make the resource script file more readable.

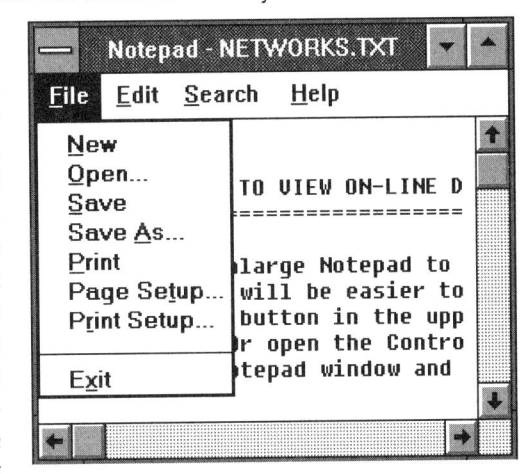

Figure 9-4 The Notepad Application's File Menu

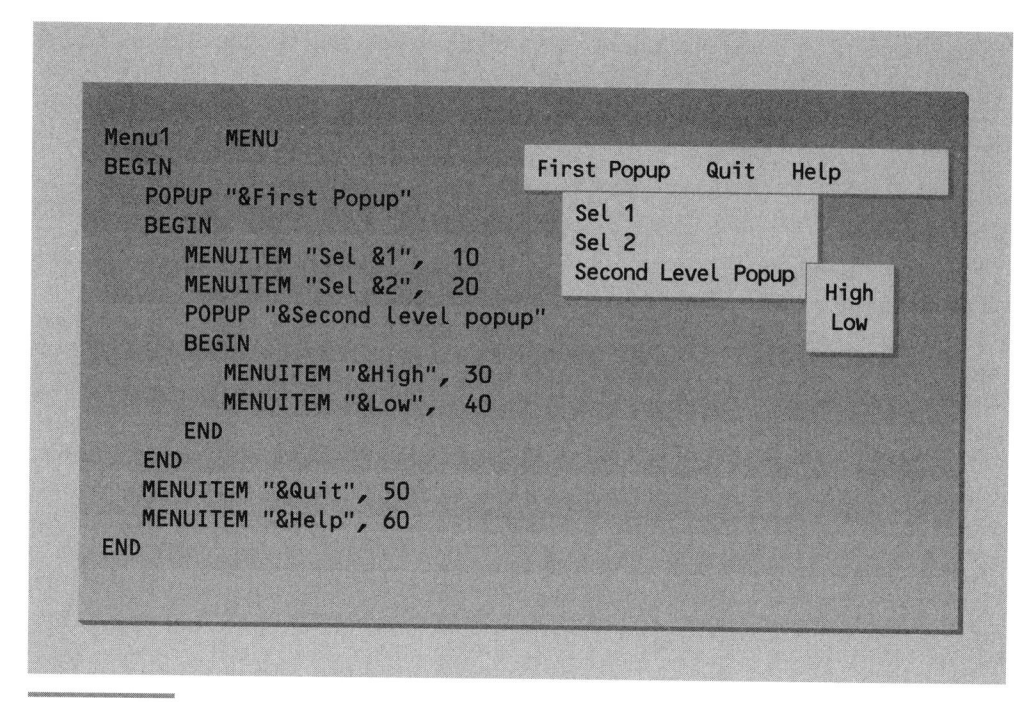

```
Menu1    MENU
BEGIN                        ┌─────────────────────────────┐
    POPUP "&First Popup"     │ First Popup   Quit   Help   │
    BEGIN                    ├──────────────────┐          │
        MENUITEM "Sel &1",  10│ Sel 1           │          │
        MENUITEM "Sel &2",  20│ Sel 2           │          │
        POPUP "&Second level popup"│ Second Level Popup ┌──────┐
        BEGIN                │                    │ High │
            MENUITEM "&High", 30│                 │ Low  │
            MENUITEM "&Low",  40│                 └──────┘
        END
    END
    MENUITEM "&Quit", 50
    MENUITEM "&Help", 60
END
```

Figure 9-5 Defining Popup Menus

Another way to look at the menu definition is to realize that the only two statements that can be put between a BEGIN and END statement for a menu are MENUITEM and POPUP. POPUP is followed by its own BEGIN and END statements. The only thing that can go between *those* BEGIN and END statements are MENUITEM and POPUP.

Menu Item Options

Sometimes you will want to make a menu item inoperative during part of a program's operation. For example, the user should not be able to select a "Paste" menu item if there is nothing to paste. Menu items can be written in gray characters to show that they are inactive. "Grayed" menu items cannot be selected, and they do not generate WM_COMMAND messages. Another handy option is to be able to put a check mark next to the left side of a menu item. This is ideal for situations where there are a few options that are either on or off. If there are more than about four options, menus with check marks become a bit overwhelming, and you are better off using a dialog box with radio buttons for the selection.

You can start a menu with menu items in either a grayed or checked state. This is done by following the menu item's ID number with a menu option key word. Table 9-1 summarizes the various menu item options. You will probably not want to use the INACTIVE key word, as this makes the menu item inactive without graying the menu item's text characters—a confusing combination for the user.

OPTION	MEANING
CHECKED	The item has a check mark next to it.
GRAYED	The item's text is inactive and appears in gray letters.
INACTIVE	The item name is displayed, but cannot be selected. No WM_COMMAND messages are sent from this item until it is enabled. Normally, programs use the GRAYED option in place of INACTIVE to make the inactive status obvious to the user.
MENUBARBREAK	For menus, places the item on a new line, creating a multiline menu. For popups, places the new item on a new column, creating a multicolumn (rectangular) popup menu. A line is used to separate this item from the previous one.
MENUBREAK	Same as MENUBARBREAK, except when used with popup menus. For menus, places the item on a new line, creating a multiline menu. For popups, places the new item on a new column, creating a multicolumn (rectangular) popup menu without a dividing line.

Table 9-1 Menu Item Options—Used to the Right of the Menu Item

The MENUBARBREAK and MENUBREAK options are used to create multiline menus. Although this can be done for the main menu bar, these key words are almost always used with popup menus to form horizontal menus, instead of the default vertical alignment. These options should be used with discretion, as they differ from the usual vertical menu arrangement and can confuse the user. The MENU1 example program in this chapter has a horizontal popup menu to demonstrate this capability.

One additional feature that can be added to menu definitions is to put lines between items in order to break menus into logical groupings. The MENUITEM SEPARATOR statement is used to insert a horizontal line between two menu items. The line does not have an ID value and cannot be selected. Figure 9-6 shows an example, which separates menu items "Selection 1" and "Selection 2" using a SEPARATOR line. Also note the combination of the GRAYED and CHECKED options for the "Selection 3" menu items.

The Menu Definition

```
ExampleMenu MENU
BEGIN
     POPUP "&First Popup"
     BEGIN
          MENUITEM "Selection &1",   IDM_SEL1
          MENUITEM SEPARATOR
          MENUITEM "Selection &2",   IDM_SEL2, CHECKED
          MENUITEM "Selection &3",   IDM_SEL3, GRAYED, CHECKED
     END
     MENUITEM "&Quit",               IDM_QUIT
     MENUITEM "&Help",               IDM_HELP
END
```

The menu appearance:

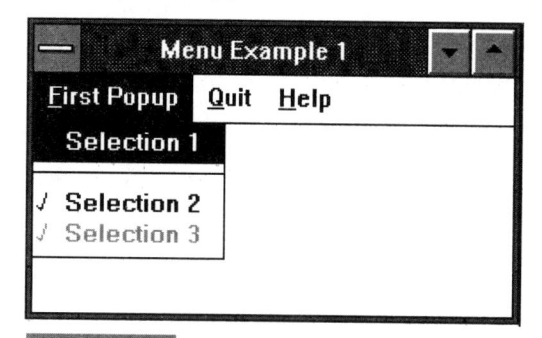

Figure 9-6 Using a MENUITEM SEPARATOR Line

Creating a Menu Using the Borland Resource Workshop

The Borland programing tools give you the choice of writing and compiling resource script files or creating resource data from scratch using the WORKSHOP tools. Creating a menu using WORKSHOP is not that much different from creating one directly by writing the menu definition into the resource script file. The following directions will produce a menu identical to the one shown in Figure 9-6. After trying this example, you can decide for yourself if it is easier to use WORKSHOP, or if you prefer to create the menu by directly writing the resource script file.

1. Before using WORKSHOP, it is convenient if you create a small header file containing the definitions of the menu item ID numbers. You will be able to edit this header file later from within WORKSHOP if you need to create new ID values. Use a text editor, such as the Turbo C++ editor, to create the header file TEST.H, as shown in Listing 9-3, and save it in the same directory that you will use for the other program files.

Listing 9-3 TEST.H Header File

```
/* test.h */

#define IDM_SEL1   1
#define IDM_SEL2   2
#define IDM_SEL3   3
#define IDM_QUIT   4
#define IDM_HELP   5
```

2. Start WORKSHOP and select the "File/New Project..." menu item. Pick the .RC file type and click the "OK" button. This gets WORKSHOP ready to create a new resource script file.

3. Select the "Resource/New…" menu item. From the dialog box that appears, select "Menu" as the resource type, and then click the "OK" button. The WORKSHOP menu editor will appear, as shown in Figure 9-7. The menu editor has three different window areas, which interact. The left half is the editing area where you will enter the text and ID numbers for each menu item. The upper right side shows a demonstration menu, which will continue to reflect the current menu definition as you add and subtract items. The lower right corner shows an outline of the menu definition. You can select any item in the outline using the mouse, in preparation for changing the item or inserting a new item underneath.

4. Select the "Resource/Rename…" menu item, and change the menu's name from the default "MENU_1" to "ExampleMenu." When you click the "OK" button, another dialog box will appear with the message "Create a new identifier ExampleMenu?" Select the "No" button, as there is no reason to create an ID number for the string "ExampleMenu."

5. Select the "File/Add to project…" menu item. From the dialog box that appears, pick the file type "H c header" and select the file TEST.H that you just created. This loads the header file, making WORKSHOP aware of the ID values. You can check that the ID values were properly loaded by selecting the WORKSHOP "Resource/Identifiers…" menu item which causes the WORKSHOP "Identifiers" dia-

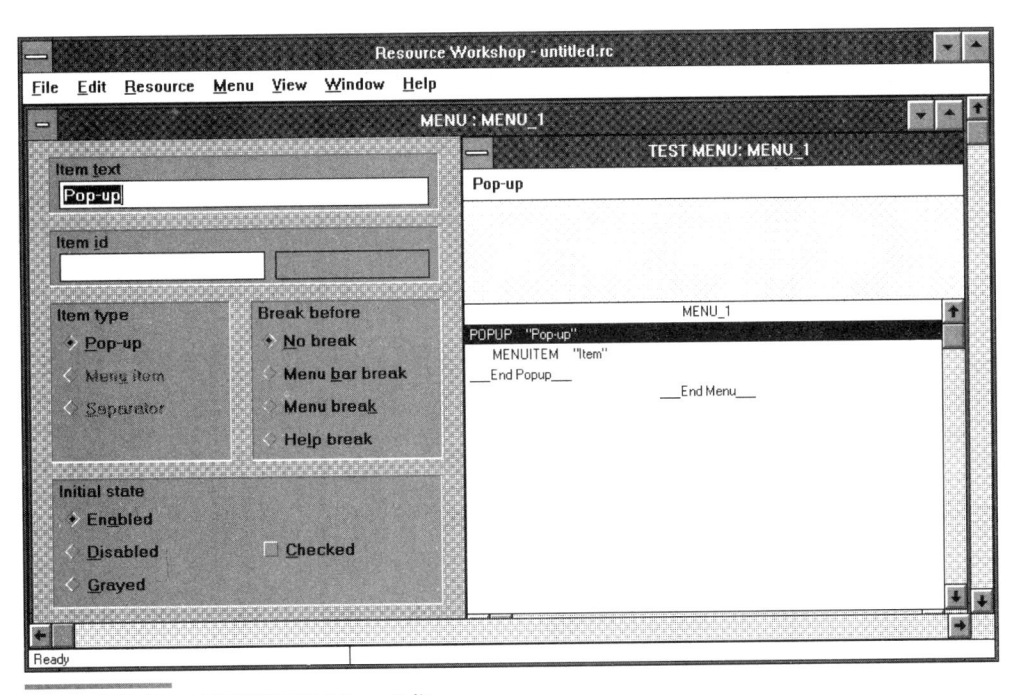

Figure 9-7 The WORKSHOP Menu Editor

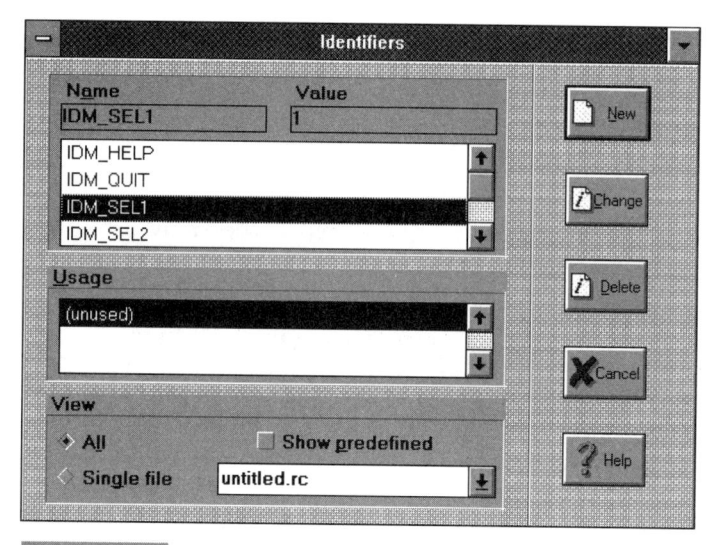

Figure 9-8 The Identifiers Dialog Box

log box to be displayed, as shown in Figure 9-8. You can add and subtract ID values from this dialog box. Select the "OK" button to continue creating the menu.

6. Select the "Item text" edit control at the upper left of the menu editor, and change the text string from the default "Popup" to the string "&First Popup." The ampersand (&) will cause the letter following it (F) to be underlined in the finished menu, and it will make (Alt)-(F) a menu selection shortcut for this item. Press the (Enter) key to cause the change to take effect. Note that the string "First Popup" is reflected in both the example menu and in the menu outline.

7. In the menu outline (lower right window), select the line MENUITEM "Item" with the mouse. The line will be highlighted in reverse video. Back on the left side of the menu editor, change the text to "Selection &1" and the ID value to IDM_SEL1. Press (Enter) to see the changes take place.

8. Select the WORKSHOP menu item "Menu/New separator" to add a separator line to the menu definition. The menu outline should appear as shown in Figure 9-9 at this point.

9. Select the editor menu item "Menu/New Item" to add another menu item below the separator. Edit this item to reflect the string "Selection &2" with the ID value IDM_SEL2. Click the "Checked" button at the lower left part of the editor window in the section labeled "Initial state." This will give the menu item the CHECKED status.

10. Add another menu item "Selection &3" with the ID value IDM_SEL3. Select the "Checked" and "Grayed" options for this item.

11. Select the "__End Popup__" item in the menu outline. This positions the highlighted item so that the "Quit" and "Help" menu items can be added outside of the popup menu definition.

12. Select the editor menu item "Menu/New Item" again, and add a menu item "&Quit" with the ID value IDM_QUIT.

13. Complete the menu by adding the menu item "&Help" with the ID value IDM_HELP. The finished demonstration menu and menu outline should appear as shown in Figure 9-10. If there are differences, you can edit menu items by simply selecting one in the outline, and then changing the values.

14. Select the "File/Save file as..." menu item. Select the file type "RC resource script," select the correct subdirectory, and save the file as TEST.RC. You can also save the menu definition in compiled form (ready to link to your program) by selecting the file type "RES resource object," and saving the file as TEST.RES.

Figure 9-9 Menu Outline after Adding a Separator

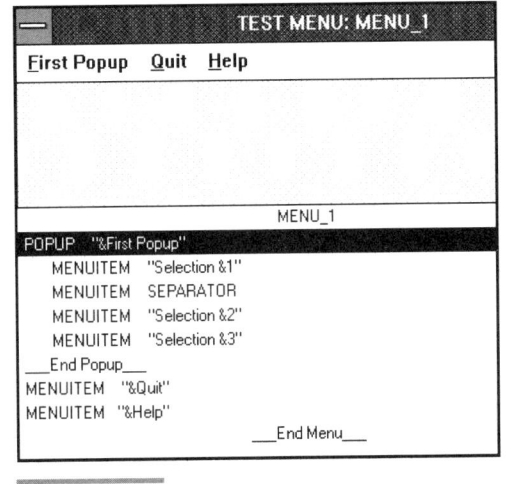

Figure 9-10 The Completed Menu

WORKSHOP will create a resource script file as shown in Listing 9-4. The structure of the menu is identical to what you would create by editing the resource script file yourself. WORKSHOP automatically adds the header file include statement to the top of the resource script file. The only editing you might want to do is to add a comment to the top of the TEST.RC file, giving the name of the file.

Listing 9-4 TEST.RC Created by WORKSHOP

```
#include "test.h"

ExampleMenu MENU
BEGIN
   POPUP "&First Popup"
   BEGIN
      MENUITEM "Selection &1", IDM_SEL1
      MENUITEM SEPARATOR
      MENUITEM "Selection &2", IDM_SEL2, CHECKED
      MENUITEM "Selection &3", IDM_SEL3, GRAYED, CHECKED
   END

   MENUITEM "&Quit", IDM_QUIT
   MENUITEM "&HELP", IDM_HELP
END
```

WORKSHOP will compile the menu directly to the .RES format if you select this file type from the "File/Save as..." menu selection. The .RES file is ready to be included in your application.

An Example with a Complex Menu

The first example program in this chapter is called MENU1, and it demonstrates a number of the menu features. Figure 9-11 shows MENU1 in action, with one of the menu items being selected. MENU1 has two levels of popup menus. The first level of popup menu contains four items, Selection 1 through 3 and the title of the second-level popup. The second-level popup is interesting in that its two items are arranged horizontally. MENU1 also demonstrates a checked and a grayed menu item.

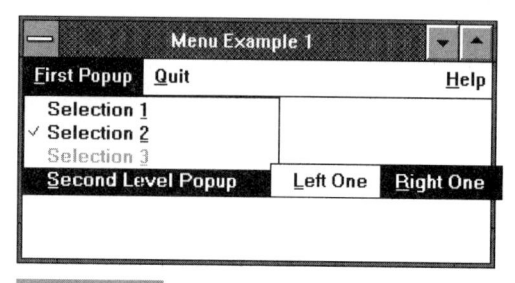

Figure 9-11 The MENU1 Program

The MENU1 menu is defined in the program's resource script file, as shown in Listing 9-5. The menu is named "BigMenu," and it uses most of the possible menu features that can be defined in a resource script file. "Selection 2" is set to CHECKED, and "Selection 3" is set to GRAYED. The GRAYED status means that "Selection 3" will not be active (cannot be selected) when the menu first appears. The status of that item will be changed as the program runs, as we will see in a moment.

Listing 9-5 MENU1.RC Resource Script File

```
/* menu1.rc resource file */

#include    "menu1.h"

MyIcon    ICON    menu1.ico

BigMenu  MENU
BEGIN
    POPUP "&First Popup"
    BEGIN
      MENUITEM "Selection &1",     IDM_SEL1
      MENUITEM "Selection &2",     IDM_SEL2, CHECKED
      MENUITEM "Selection &3",     IDM_SEL3, GRAYED
      POPUP "&Second level popup"
      BEGIN
         MENUITEM "&Left One",     IDM_LEFT
         MENUITEM "&Right One",    IDM_RIGHT, MENUBARBREAK
      END
    END
    MENUITEM "&Quit",              IDM_QUIT
    MENUITEM "\a&Help",            IDM_HELP
END
```

296 *Windows Programming Primer Plus*

The secret to the second-level popup menu appearing in the horizontal format is the MENUBARBREAK statement. This key word instructs the resource compiler to put a vertical line in front of the item and to split the menu at that point. If the menu is horizontal (the main menu bar), the menu is split into two lines. If the menu is vertical (any popup menu), the menu is split into two side-by-side halves at that point. The last menu item in Listing 9-5 is the "Help" selection. Help items are often placed at the far right side of the menu (see Figure 9-11). This is accomplished by putting the special code "\a" in the help item's text string ("a" for align).

MENU1 defines the menu item ID numbers in a header file, MENU1.H, which is shown in Listing 9-6. Note again that the title strings for popup menus do not have ID numbers. Only MENUITEMs have ID numbers and result in WM_COMMAND messages being sent to the program.

Listing 9-6 MENU1.H Header File

```
/* menu1.h  header file */

#define IDM_SEL1    1
#define IDM_SEL2    2
#define IDM_SEL3    3
#define IDM_LEFT    4
#define IDM_RIGHT   5
#define IDM_QUIT    6
#define IDM_HELP   10

long FAR PASCAL WndProc (HWND, WORD, WORD, LONG) ;
```

Listing 9-7 shows the MENU1.C program. This program was designed to exercise the menu items, changing one item from checked to unchecked and allowing another to be alternately grayed and activated. All of this logic is done in the WndProc() function's processing of WM_COMMAND messages generated by the menu items being selected. Note in the WinMain() function that the program's menu name "BigMenu" is specified for the main window class and, therefore, becomes the main program window's menu.

Listing 9-7 MENU1.C

```
/* menu1.c   Windows program with a complex menu */

#include <windows.h>
#include "menu1.h"

int PASCAL WinMain (HANDLE hInstance, HANDLE hPrevInstance, LPSTR lpszCmdLine,
   int nCmdShow)
{
    HWND       hWnd ;      /* the window's "handle" */
    MSG        msg ;       /* a message structure */
    WNDCLASS   wndclass ;  /* window class structure */
```

```c
    if (!hPrevInstance)
    {
        wndclass.style         = CS_HREDRAW | CS_VREDRAW ;
        wndclass.lpfnWndProc   = WndProc ;
        wndclass.cbClsExtra    = 0 ;
        wndclass.cbWndExtra    = 0 ;
        wndclass.hInstance     = hInstance ;
        wndclass.hIcon         = LoadIcon (hInstance, "MyIcon") ;
        wndclass.hCursor       = LoadCursor (NULL, IDC_ARROW) ;
        wndclass.hbrBackground = GetStockObject (WHITE_BRUSH) ;
        wndclass.lpszMenuName  = "BigMenu" ;
        wndclass.lpszClassName = "MyClass" ;
                    /* register the window class */
        if (!RegisterClass (&wndclass))
            return 0 ;
    }

    hWnd = CreateWindow ("MyClass", "Menu Example 1", WS_OVERLAPPEDWINDOW,
        CW_USEDEFAULT, CW_USEDEFAULT, CW_USEDEFAULT, CW_USEDEFAULT,
        NULL, NULL, hInstance, NULL) ;
    ShowWindow (hWnd, nCmdShow) ;      /* display the window */

    while (GetMessage (&msg, NULL, NULL, NULL))   /* message loop */
    {
        TranslateMessage (&msg) ;      /* translate keyboard messages */
        DispatchMessage (&msg) ;       /* send message to WndProc() */
    }
    return (msg.wParam) ;
}

long FAR PASCAL WndProc (HWND hWnd, WORD wMessage, WORD wParam, LONG lParam)
{
    static BOOL  bCheckOnOff = TRUE ;
    HMENU        hMenu ;

    switch (wMessage)      /* process windows messages */
    {
        case WM_COMMAND:
          switch (wParam)
          {
                case IDM_SEL1:                  /* menu items */
                    MessageBox (hWnd, "Selection 1 enables Selection 3",
                        "Surprise!", MB_OK) ;
                    hMenu = GetMenu (hWnd) ;    /* get menu handle */
                    EnableMenuItem (hMenu, IDM_SEL3,
                        MF_BYCOMMAND | MF_ENABLED ) ;
                    break ;
                case IDM_SEL2:                  /* this one can be checked */
                    bCheckOnOff = (bCheckOnOff ? FALSE : TRUE) ;
                    hMenu = GetMenu (hWnd) ;    /* get menu handle */
                    if (bCheckOnOff)
                        CheckMenuItem (hMenu, IDM_SEL2,
                            MF_BYCOMMAND | MF_CHECKED) ;
                    else
                        CheckMenuItem (hMenu, IDM_SEL2,
                            MF_BYCOMMAND | MF_UNCHECKED) ;
                    break ;
                case IDM_SEL3:                  /* initially grayed */
                    MessageBox (hWnd, "Selection 3 now enabled.", "", MB_OK) ;
```

```
            break ;
        case IDM_RIGHT:
            MessageBox (hWnd, "Right side disables Selection 3.",
                "Surprise!", MB_OK) ;
            hMenu = GetMenu (hWnd) ;   /* get menu handle */
            EnableMenuItem (hMenu, IDM_SEL3,
                MF_BYCOMMAND | MF_GRAYED ) ;
            break ;
        case IDM_LEFT:
            MessageBox (hWnd, "Left side just beeps.", "", MB_OK) ;
            MessageBeep (0) ;
            break ;
        case IDM_HELP:
            MessageBox (hWnd, "Try selecting any menu item.",
                "Not much help", MB_OK) ;
            break ;
        case IDM_QUIT:                  /* Quit menu item */
            DestroyWindow (hWnd) ;      /* destroy window, */
            break ;                     /* terminating application */
        default:                        /* otherwise, let Windows process it */
            return (DefWindowProc (hWnd, wMessage, wParam, lParam)) ;
        }
        break ;
    case WM_DESTROY:                    /* stop application */
        PostQuitMessage (0) ;
        break ;
    default:        /* default windows message processing */
        return (DefWindowProc (hWnd, wMessage, wParam, lParam)) ;
    }
    return (0L) ;
}
```

Menu Functions

Let's go through each of the MENU1.C menu item's actions, as defined in the WndProc() function's processing of WM_COMMAND messages. The "Selection 1" menu item has the ID number IDM_SEL1 and, therefore, generates WM_COMMAND messages with *wParam* set to IDM_SEL1. When this message is received, the WndProc() function executes the following code:

```
        case IDM_SEL1:                  /* menu items */
            MessageBox (hWnd, "Selection 1 enables Selection 3",
                "Surprise!", MB_OK) ;
            hMenu = GetMenu (hWnd) ;   /* get menu handle */
            EnableMenuItem (hMenu, IDM_SEL3,
                MF_BYCOMMAND | MF_ENABLED ) ;
            break ;
```

The MessageBox() function just puts a message on the screen, so that the user knows what action will take place. Next, the handle of the menu, *hMenu*, is obtained using the GetMenu() function. GetMenu() obtains the handle of the menu attached to a window. The menu's definition is in memory somewhere, and can be moved by Windows because the FIXED memory option was not specified. The menu handle allows us to work with the menu definition, without worrying about where Windows physically places the menu data in memory.

Given the menu's handle, the EnableMenuItem() function can be called to enable or disable the menu item. EnableMenuItem() must be told which of the menu items to enable or disable. There are two ways to specify the menu item, by menu item ID number or by the position of the menu item in the menu. WINDOWS.H has two binary flags defined to specify the selection option, MF_BYCOMMAND and MF_BYPOSITION. The following two EnableMenuItem() function calls are equivalent:

```
EnableMenuItem (hMenu, IDM_SEL3, MF_BYCOMMAND | MF_ENABLED) ;
EnableMenuItem (hMenu, 2, MF_BYPOSITION | MF_ENABLED) ;
```

The menu item position is relative to the top-most, left-most item, which has position number zero. It is more difficult to keep track of the position of a menu item than the ID number, so the MF_BYPOSITION option is almost never used. The MF_BYCOMMAND option is used in all of the examples in this book.

Having specified the menu item, you must also tell EnableMenuItem() whether to make the menu item enabled, disabled, or grayed. These possibilities are specified with three additional binary flag values defined in WINDOWS.H, MF_ENABLED, MF_DISABLED, and MF_GRAYED. You will probably never use MF_DISABLED, as this disables the menu item without graying the menu item's text string. MF_GRAYED both disables and grays the menu item, and is a better choice. MF_ENABLED both enables and removes graying from a menu item.

The second menu item in the popup has the ID value IDM_SEL2. This item is defined as CHECKED in the MENU1.RC file. The program logic in MENU1.C switches the check mark on and off each time the menu IDM_SEL2 item is selected. MENU1.C uses a static BOOL variable *bCheckOnOff* to keep track of whether the IDM_SEL2 item is checked or unchecked. The logic for switching the item between checked and unchecked is shown below. The C language inline conditional statement (? :) is used to flip the *bXCheckOnOff* value between the TRUE and FALSE value each time the IDM_SEL2 item is selected. This type of logic is commonly referred to as a "toggle," an analogy to common electrical toggle switches.

```
        case IDM_SEL2:             /* this one can be checked */
            bCheckOnOff = (bCheckOnOff ? FALSE : TRUE) ;
            hMenu = GetMenu (hWnd) ; /* get menu handle */
            if (bCheckOnOff)
                CheckMenuItem (hMenu, IDM_SEL2,
                    MF_BYCOMMAND | MF_CHECKED) ;
            else
                CheckMenuItem (hMenu, IDM_SEL2,
                    MF_BYCOMMAND | MF_UNCHECKED) ;
            break ;
```

The CheckMenuItem() function switches menu items between the checked and unchecked states. Like EnableMenuItem(), CheckMenuItem() must be passed a handle to the menu, obtained with the GetMenu() function. CheckMenuItem() can reference a specific item, either by position in the menu (MF_BYPOSITION flag) or by ID number (MF_BYCOMMAND). The MF_BYCOMMAND is almost always used. The other two binary flags that CheckMenuItem() understands are MF_CHECKED and MF_UNCHECKED. You will always combine either MF_BYPOSITION or MF_BYCOMMAND with one of the MF_CHECKED or MF_UNCHECKED flags when calling CheckMenuItem().

Other Files for MENU1

To complete the MENU1 example, you will also need to create the MENU1.DEF module definition file, a project file, and a program icon. These are shown in Listings 9-8 to 9-10 and Figure 9-12 respectively.

Figure 9-12
MENU1.ICO
Icon Image

Listing 9-8 MENU1.DEF Module Definition File

```
NAME         menu1
DESCRIPTION  'Demo complex menu'
EXETYPE      WINDOWS
STUB         'WINSTUB.EXE'
CODE         PRELOAD MOVEABLE DISCARDABLE
DATA         PRELOAD MOVEABLE MULTIPLE
HEAPSIZE     1024
STACKSIZE    5120
EXPORTS      WndProc
```

Listing 9-9 Turbo C++ Project File for MENU1

```
menu1.c
menu1.def
menu1.res
```

Listing 9-10 MENU1

```
menu1.c
menu1.def
menu1.rc
```

Determining Menu Item Status

Normally, your program logic will control the menu item status as checked or grayed, and you can track the status of any item using static variables (such as *bCheckOnOff* in MENU1.C). However, Windows provides an alternative. You can determine the status of a menu item as the program runs using the GetMenuState() function. GetMenuState() returns a WORD value which encodes the status of a menu item as a combination of MF_CHECKED, MF_DISABLED, MF_ENABLED, MF_GRAYED, or MF_UNCHECKED. Here is a typical program fragment which determines if the menu item IDM_MENUID is currently checked:

Chapter 9 • Menus 301

```
HMENU hMenu ;
WORD wStatus ;

hMenu = GetMenu (hWnd) ;
wStatus = GetMenuState (hMenu, IDM_MENUID, MF_BYCOMMAND) ;
if (wStatus & MF_CHECKED)
   /* item is checked */
else
   /* item is not checked */
```
[Other program lines]

You can also determine the character string of a menu item at runtime using the GetMenuString() function. This is useful in cases where the program allows the user to add new menu items, such as user-defined macros. Here is a simple example using GetMenuString(), which copies the menu item IDM_MENUID's string into the character buffer *cBuf[]*:

```
HMENU hMenu ;
char  cBuf [128] ;

hMenu = GetMenu (hWnd) ;
GetMenuString (hMenu, IDM_MENUID, cBuf, 128, MF_BYPOSITION) ;
```
[Other program lines]

Creating a Menu as the Program Operates

Most programs have a fixed menu structure defined in the resource script file, and use that menu as long as the program is operating. There are two situations where you will want to create and destroy menus and/or menu items as the program operates:

1. If certain operations are not always possible, and you want to delete the menu items when the action is not possible, rather than just graying the item.

2. If you want to use a bitmap graphical image in place of text for one or more popup menu items. This is particularly useful for tool selections, such as picking a brush image for painting. Graphical menu items cannot be defined in the resource script file, but can be created as the program runs.

Windows provides several functions that allow you to create and destroy menu items, which are summarized in Table 9-2.

CreateMenu()	Creates a new menu, ready to add items.
CreatePopupMenu()	Creates a new popup menu, ready to add items.
SetMenu()	Attaches a menu to a window. This is frequently used with LoadMenu() to switch between two or more menus used by the program.
AppendMenu()	Adds a new menu item or popup to the end of a menu.
InsertMenu()	Inserts a new menu item or popup into a menu or popup menu.

DeleteMenu()	Removes a menu item from a menu or popup menu.
DestroyMenu()	Deletes an entire menu, removing it from memory. This is only necessary if the menu has been loaded, but is not attached to a window. Menus attached to windows are removed automatically from memory when the window is destroyed.
DrawMenuBar()	Draws the menu bar (the main menu line, right below the window's caption), making any recent changes visible.
LoadMenu()	Loads a menu from the program's resource data, ready to be attached to a window with SetMenu(). You can define more than one menu in the resource data, and switch between menus as the program operates. LoadMenu() will load only one copy of each menu into memory, no matter how often the function is called.

Table 9-2 Menu Creation Functions

The basic sequence of creating a new menu is:

1. Use CreateMenu() to create a new, empty menu with which to start. CreateMenu() returns a handle to the new menu in memory.
2. Use AppendMenu() and/or InsertMenu() to add menu items as needed.
3. Use SetMenu() to attach the menu to a window, so that it can be used.

If the main menu contains popup menus, the popups are created separately, and then attached to the menu as follows:

1. Use CreatePopupMenu() to create a new, empty popup menu. CreatePopupMenu() returns a handle to the popup menu in memory.
2. Use AppendMenu() and/or InsertMenu() to add menu items to the popup as needed.
3. Use AppendMenu() and/or InsertMenu() to add the finished popup menu to the main menu.

If the menu, including all popups, is attached to the window when the window is destroyed, the menu will automatically be removed from memory. If the menu is not attached to a window, it must be explicitly destroyed using the DestroyMenu() function. Otherwise, the menu data will remain in memory for the duration of the Windows session.

You can also insert and delete menu items as the program operates, using the InsertMenu() and DeleteMenu() functions. This is frequently simpler than creating an entire menu from scratch every time a change to the menu is needed, and more flexible than defining multiple menus in the program's resource script file and switching between them with LoadMenu() and SetMenu().

As mentioned previously, menus can be created at runtime in order to include graphics images as menu items. The steps needed to create a menu including bitmap images are:

1. Create the image as a bitmap using either the Microsoft Image Editor or the Borland Resource Workshop. Both tools allow you to "paint" bitmaps, just like creating icon images and cursor shapes. The difference is that bitmaps are stored with the ".BMP" file extension. A 32 by 32 pixel 16-color bitmap is a standard size and color resolution, while 64 by 64 pixel bitmaps provide a larger image.
2. Include the bitmaps in the program's resource data. We will see an example of this in the next program, MENU2.
3. Load the bitmap data into memory while the program is running. The LoadBitmap() function does this and returns a handle to the bitmap in memory.
4. Use AppendMenu() and/or InsertMenu() to add the bitmap to the menu as a menu item.
5. When the program is about to terminate, or has no further use for the bitmap, use DeleteObject() to remove the bitmap data from memory.

The next example program, MENU2, will illustrate these menu operations by creating two graphic menu items, and by allowing a whole section of the menu to be deleted and restored as the program operates.

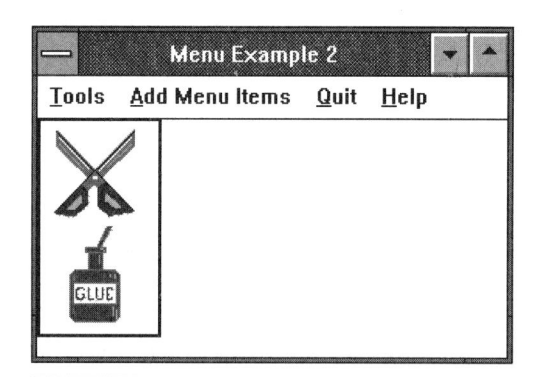

Figure 9-13 The MENU2 Program's Graphic Popup Menu

The MENU2 Program

The MENU2 program does not have a menu defined in its resource script file. Instead, the program's main menu is created as the program starts operation when the WndProc() function receives a WM_CREATE message. Figure 9-13 shows the MENU2 program in operation, with its initial popup menu item displayed. The popup menu item consists of two bitmap images. Bitmap files are created with an editor, such as the Microsoft Image Editor, or the Borland Resource Workshop. The bitmap images are then included in the program's resource data. Listing 9-11 shows the MENU2.RC resource script file, which includes an icon file, two bitmaps, and two cursor files, all created with the same editor, but saved as separate files. Selecting either of the bitmap menu items in MENU2 causes the cursor shape to change. The cursor files are needed for the cursor shapes, as Bitmaps have a different file format and cannot be used as cursors. We will explore more complex operations with bitmaps in Chapter 16, *Bitmaps*, but for now simply creating the bitmap pictures and adding them to the resource script file will allow us to use them in creating a menu.

Listing 9-11 MENU2.RC Resource Script File

```
/* menu2.rc resource file */

#include "menu2.h"

MyIcon      ICON    menu2.ico       /* program icon file */

CutBmp      BITMAP  scissor.bmp     /* bitmap files */
PasteBmp    BITMAP  glue.bmp

CutCur      CURSOR  scissor.cur     /* cursor files */
GlueCur     CURSOR  glue.cur
```

Creating a Menu Containing Bitmaps

Before looking at the entire MENU2.C program, let's examine the portion that creates the menu structure that is visible in Figure 9-13. Listing 9-12 shows the creation of the menu as the MENU2.C program processes the WM_CREATE message. First, the main menu and popup menu are created using the CreateMenu() and CreatePopupMenu() functions respectively. Both of these functions return a handle to the memory area where the menu data will be stored. Next the two bitmaps are loaded into memory from the resource data using the LoadBitmap() function. Again, handles to the bitmaps are returned by the LoadBitmap() function. The bitmaps are appended to the popup menu using the AppendMenu() function. The AppendMenu() function uses the MF_BITMAP flag to signify bitmap menu items, assigns them the menu item ID numbers IDM_CUT and IDM_PASTE, and passes handle to the bitmap data as the last parameter. The handle to the bitmap data is cast to a LPSTR to avoid a compiler warning message, as normally the last parameter in AppendMenu() is a pointer to a character string. Finally, the popup menu is appended to the main menu with another call to AppendMenu(), using the MF_POPUP flag. When appending a popup menu, the third parameter in AppendMenu() is the handle to the popup menu, and the fourth parameter is the character string title for the popup.

Listing 9-12 Creating the MENU2 Program Menu

```
HBITMAP     hCut, hPaste ;
HMENU       hMenu, hSubmenu ;
HANDLE      hInstance ;

switch (wMessage)       /* process windows messages */
{
    case WM_CREATE:     /* program starting - create menu from scratch */
            /* create a main menu and a popup menu - initially empty */
        hMenu = CreateMenu () ;
        hSubmenu = CreatePopupMenu () ;
            /* get bitmap handles from resource data */
        hInstance = GetWindowWord (hWnd, GWW_HINSTANCE) ;
        hCut = LoadBitmap (hInstance, "CutBmp") ;
```

```
            hPaste = LoadBitmap (hInstance, "PasteBmp") ;
                /* add to bitmap items to the popup menu */
            AppendMenu (hSubmenu, MF_BITMAP, IDM_CUT,
               (LPSTR)(LONG) hCut) ;
            AppendMenu (hSubmenu, MF_BITMAP, IDM_PASTE,
               (LPSTR)(LONG) hPaste) ;
                /* create the first entry on the main menu, attach popup */
            AppendMenu (hMenu, MF_POPUP, hSubmenu, "&Tools") ;
                /* add other text items to main menu */
            AppendMenu (hMenu, MF_STRING, IDM_ADD, "&Add Menu Items") ;
            AppendMenu (hMenu, MF_STRING, IDM_QUIT, "&Quit") ;
            AppendMenu (hMenu, MF_STRING, IDM_HELP, "&Help") ;
                /* attach menu to window */
            SetMenu (hWnd, hMenu) ;
            break;
```
[Other program lines]

The remainder of the code in Listing 9-12 adds three more menu items to the main menu, and then attaches the entire menu structure to the program's window using SetMenu(). Without the SetMenu() call, the menu structure would be defined in memory, but would not be related in any way to the program's window. In fact, the menu definition would continue to exist in memory after the program terminated, or until the DestroyMenu() function was used to remove it.

As you can see from this example, creating a menu as the program operates is more work than just defining it as part of the resource script file. Use the resource script file, unless you are using graphics in the menu. You can also use a combination of resource data and menu commands, by defining all of the text menu items in the resource script file, and then only appending the graphics elements of the menu as the program starts operating.

Other MENU2 Files

Listing 9-13 shows the complete MENU2.C program. There are a few other points worth noting, besides the creation of the graphics menu items. In the WinMain() function, the window's class definition has NULL for the class menu. This is inevitable, because there is no menu defined in the resource script file. Unless the SetMenu() function is called, the MENU2.C program will appear without a menu bar, because no menu exists for this window class. Another point of interest is in the processing of the WM_COMMAND message. The IDM_ADD menu item causes a whole new popup menu to be added to the main menu. This is created just like we created the initial program menu, using AppendMenu() commands to add each menu item. Note that the DrawMenuBar() function is called after the popup is added to redraw the menu bar with the new entry. Otherwise, the menu bar will not change until Windows updates the nonclient area of the window.

After the user has selected the IDM_ADD menu item one time, that menu item is grayed, deactivating the menu item. This makes it impossible to add the popup menu more than once. The variable *bAddedItem* keeps track of whether the popup menu has been added. The added popup is deleted when the IDM_REMOVE menu item is activated. The DeleteMenu() function removes the popup menu. Again, DrawMenuBar()

must be called after the menu bar is restructured so that the changes are visible. MENU2.C processes the WM_COMMAND messages from the two graphics menu items, and uses them to change the cursor shape. The current cursor shape is stored in the static variable *nCursor*, which is examined when processing the WM_SETCURSOR message, to change the cursor shape. This portion of the program follows the examples in Chapter 6, *Taming the Mouse*.

Listing 9-13 MENU2.C

```
/* menu2.c   graphics menu items, and changing the menu structure */

#include <windows.h>
#include "menu2.h"

int PASCAL WinMain (HANDLE hInstance, HANDLE hPrevInstance, LPSTR lpszCmdLine,
    int nCmdShow)
{
    HWND        hWnd ;          /* the window's "handle" */
    MSG         msg ;           /* a message structure */
    WNDCLASS    wndclass ;      /* window class structure */

    if (!hPrevInstance)
    {
        wndclass.style         = CS_HREDRAW | CS_VREDRAW ;
        wndclass.lpfnWndProc   = WndProc ;
        wndclass.cbClsExtra    = 0 ;
        wndclass.cbWndExtra    = 0 ;
        wndclass.hInstance     = hInstance ;
        wndclass.hIcon         = LoadIcon (hInstance, "MyIcon") ;
        wndclass.hCursor       = LoadCursor (NULL, IDC_ARROW) ;
        wndclass.hbrBackground = GetStockObject (WHITE_BRUSH) ;
        wndclass.lpszMenuName  = NULL ;    /* no class menu */
        wndclass.lpszClassName = "MyClass" ;
                /* register the window class */
        if (!RegisterClass (&wndclass))
            return 0 ;
    }

    hWnd = CreateWindow ("MyClass", "Menu Example 2", WS_OVERLAPPEDWINDOW,
        CW_USEDEFAULT, CW_USEDEFAULT, CW_USEDEFAULT, CW_USEDEFAULT,
        NULL, NULL, hInstance, NULL) ;
    ShowWindow (hWnd, nCmdShow) ;   /* display the window */

    while (GetMessage (&msg, NULL, NULL, NULL))   /* message loop */
    {
      TranslateMessage (&msg) ;  /* translate keyboard messages */
      DispatchMessage (&msg) ;   /* send message to WndProc() */
    }
    return (msg.wParam) ;
}

long FAR PASCAL WndProc (HWND hWnd, WORD wMessage, WORD wParam, LONG lParam)
{
    HBITMAP     hCut, hPaste ;
    HMENU       hMenu, hSubmenu ;
```

```c
        HANDLE          hInstance ;
        HCURSOR         hCursor ;
        static BOOL     bAddedItems = FALSE, bSelTwoOn = FALSE ;
        static int      nCursor = ARROWCURSOR ;

        switch (wMessage)       /* process windows messages */
        {
            case WM_CREATE:     /* program starting - create menu from scratch */
                /* create a main menu and a popup menu - initially empty */
                hMenu = CreateMenu () ;
                hSubmenu = CreatePopupMenu () ;
                    /* get bitmap handles from resource data */
                hInstance = GetWindowWord (hWnd, GWW_HINSTANCE) ;
                hCut = LoadBitmap (hInstance, "CutBmp") ;
                hPaste = LoadBitmap (hInstance, "PasteBmp") ;
                    /* add to bitmap items to the popup menu */
                AppendMenu (hSubmenu, MF_BITMAP, IDM_CUT, (LPSTR)(LONG) hCut) ;
                AppendMenu (hSubmenu, MF_BITMAP, IDM_PASTE,
                    (LPSTR)(LONG) hPaste) ;
                    /* create the first entry on the main menu, attach popup */
                AppendMenu (hMenu, MF_POPUP, hSubmenu, "&Tools") ;
                    /* add other text items to main menu */
                AppendMenu (hMenu, MF_STRING, IDM_ADD, "&Add Menu Items") ;
                AppendMenu (hMenu, MF_STRING, IDM_QUIT, "&Quit") ;
                AppendMenu (hMenu, MF_STRING, IDM_HELP, "&Help") ;
                    /* attach menu to window */
                SetMenu (hWnd, hMenu) ;
                break;
            case WM_COMMAND:
                switch (wParam)
                {
                    case IDM_ADD:           /* add new text items to menu as popup */
                        if (!bAddedItems)
                        {
                        hMenu = GetMenu (hWnd) ;    /* get menu handle */
                            /* create new popup menu */
                        hSubmenu = CreatePopupMenu () ;
                            /* insert popup into in front of IDM_ADD */
                        InsertMenu (hMenu, IDM_ADD, MF_BYCOMMAND | MF_POPUP,
                            hSubmenu, "Added &Popup Menu") ;
                            /* now put in two text menu items under popup */
                        AppendMenu (hSubmenu, MF_STRING | MF_CHECKED,
                            IDM_SEL1, "New Selection &1, toggles next item") ;
                        AppendMenu (hSubmenu, MF_STRING | MF_GRAYED,
                            IDM_SEL2, "New Selection &2, beeps if active") ;
                        bSelTwoOn = FALSE ;     /* keep track if on or off */
                        AppendMenu (hSubmenu, MF_STRING, IDM_REMOVE,
                            "&Delete this entire popup menu.") ;
                            /* gray the "Add" menu item, as can't add twice */
                        EnableMenuItem (hMenu, IDM_ADD,
                            MF_BYCOMMAND | MF_GRAYED) ;
                        bAddedItems = TRUE ;
                        DrawMenuBar (hWnd) ;    /* redraw menu bar */
                        }
                        break ;
                    case IDM_REMOVE:        /* menu item that removes a popup menu */
                        hMenu = GetMenu (hWnd) ;    /* get menu handle */
                        if (bAddedItems)            /* if the popup exists */
                        {                           /* delete entire popup */
```

```
                DeleteMenu (hMenu, 1, MF_BYPOSITION) ;
                    /* activate the "Add" menu item, can add again */
                EnableMenuItem (hMenu, IDM_ADD,
                    MF_BYCOMMAND | MF_ENABLED) ;
                DrawMenuBar (hWnd) ;     /* redraw menu bar */
                    bAddedItems = FALSE ;
                }
                break ;
            case IDM_SEL1:              /* ID of first added menu item */
                    /* toggle item SEL2 on/off */
                bSelTwoOn = (bSelTwoOn ? FALSE : TRUE) ;
                hMenu = GetMenu (hWnd) ;   /* get menu handle */
                if (bSelTwoOn)          /* ungray sel 2, uncheck sel 1 */
                {
                    EnableMenuItem (hMenu, IDM_SEL2,
                        MF_BYCOMMAND | MF_ENABLED) ;
                    CheckMenuItem (hMenu, IDM_SEL1,
                        MF_BYCOMMAND | MF_UNCHECKED) ;
                }
                else                    /* gray sel 2, check sel 1 */
                {
                    EnableMenuItem (hMenu, IDM_SEL2,
                        MF_BYCOMMAND | MF_GRAYED) ;
                    CheckMenuItem (hMenu, IDM_SEL1,
                        MF_BYCOMMAND | MF_CHECKED) ;
                }
                break ;
            case IDM_SEL2:              /* ID of second added menu item */
                MessageBeep (0) ;       /* just beep to prove it's active */
                break ;
            case IDM_CUT:               /* ID of scissors bitmap menu item */
                nCursor = CUTCURSOR ;
                break ;
            case IDM_PASTE:
                nCursor = GLUECURSOR ;
                break ;
            case IDM_HELP:
                MessageBox (hWnd, "Try selecting any menu item.",
                    "Not much help", MB_OK) ;
                break ;
            case IDM_QUIT:              /* Quit menu item */
                DestroyWindow (hWnd) ;  /* destroy window, */
                break ;                 /* terminating application */
            default:                    /* otherwise, let Windows process it */
                return (DefWindowProc (hWnd, wMessage, wParam, lParam)) ;
        }
        break ;
    case WM_SETCURSOR:                  /* time to change cursor shape */
        hInstance = GetWindowWord (hWnd, GWW_HINSTANCE) ;
        switch (nCursor)
        {
            case ARROWCURSOR:
                hCursor = LoadCursor (NULL, IDC_ARROW) ;
                break ;
            case CUTCURSOR:
                hCursor = LoadCursor (hInstance, "CutCur") ;
                break ;
            case GLUECURSOR:
                hCursor = LoadCursor (hInstance, "GlueCur") ;
```

```
                break ;
            }
            SetCursor (hCursor) ;
            break ;
        case WM_DESTROY:                    /* stop application */
            DeleteObject (hPaste) ;         /* remove bitmap data from memory */
            DeleteObject (hCut) ;
            PostQuitMessage (0) ;
            break ;
        default:                            /* default windows message processing */
            return (DefWindowProc (hWnd, wMessage, wParam, lParam)) ;
    }
    return (0L) ;
}
```

MENU2 requires the usual header file, module definition file, and project file. These files are shown in Listings 9-14 to 9-17. The icon, cursor, and bitmap files used in MENU2.RC are also shown in Figure 9-14.

a) MENU2.ICO
Icon Image

b) GLUE.CUR
Cursor Image

c) SCISSOR.CUR
Cursor Image

d) GLUE.BMP
Bitmap Image

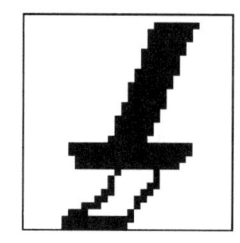

e) SCISSOR.BMP
Bitmap Image

Figure 9-14 MENU2 Icon, Cursor, and Bitmap Images

Listing 9-14 MENU2.H Header File

```
/* menu2.h header file */

#define IDM_CUT    1    /* menu item ID numbers */
#define IDM_PASTE  2
#define IDM_ADD    3
#define IDM_SEL1   4
#define IDM_SEL2   5
```

```
#define IDM_QUIT    6
#define IDM_TOOLS   7
#define IDM_REMOVE  8
#define IDM_ARROW   9
#define IDM_HELP    10

#define ARROWCURSOR 1     /* keep track of cursor shape */
#define GLUECURSOR  2
#define CUTCURSOR   3

long FAR PASCAL WndProc (HWND, WORD, WORD, LONG) ;
```

Listing 9-15 MENU2.DEF Module Definition File

```
NAME         menu2
DESCRIPTION  'Menu example 2'
EXETYPE      WINDOWS
STUB         'WINSTUB.EXE'
CODE         PRELOAD MOVEABLE DISCARDABLE
DATA         PRELOAD MOVEABLE MULTIPLE
HEAPSIZE     1024
STACKSIZE    5120
EXPORTS      WndProc
```

Listing 9-16 Turbo C++ Project File for MENU2

```
menu2.c
menu2.def
menu2.res
```

Listing 9-17 QuickC Project File for MENU2

```
menu2.c
menu2.def
menu2.rc
```

The System Menu

The system menu is an important built-in feature of Windows. Main program windows have a system menu box at their upper left corner. Clicking this box once displays the system menu, or you can use the Alt-Spacebar key combination to activate the system menu for the window which has the input focus. Figure 9-15a shows the system menu for the Notepad application. Notepad uses the default system menu, which is used by most applications. The primary purpose of the system menu is to provide a keyboard alternative for actions like moving the window or minimizing the program to an icon.

The system menu is also displayed if the program is minimized to an icon and the icon is clicked once with the mouse. This is shown in Figure 9-15b, again for the

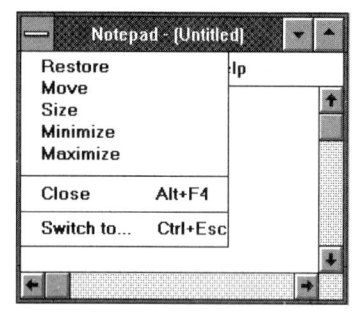

a) Displayed While Program Is Active

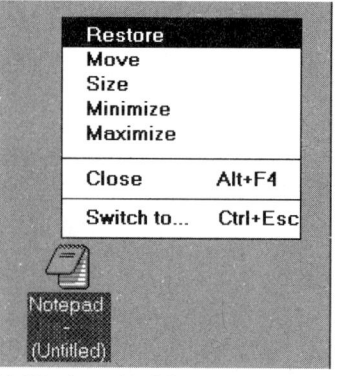

b) Displayed While Program Is Minimized ⇓ System Menu Box

Figure 9-15 The Notepad Application's System Menu

Notepad application. This brings up a reason that you might want to use the system menu. If the program is never allowed to be any bigger than an icon, the system menu is the only menu that will ever be visible. Adding to and modifying the system menu are ideal ways to add functionality to a miniature program.

System menus are attached to the program window by including the WS_SYSMENU window style when calling CreateWindow(). WS_SYSMENU is part of the WS_OVERLAPPEDWINDOW style used to create most main program windows, so the system menu will be added to your program's main window if you use the WS_OVERLAPPEDWINDOW style. You can explicitly add the WS_SYSMENU style to child and popup windows.

The key to working with the system menu is the GetSystemMenu() function. GetSystemMenu() returns the menu handle of a window's system menu. You can then operate on the system menu, as you would any other menu, adding items with AppendMenu(), graying them with EnableMenuItem(), etc. If you want to modify the default system menu items, you will need to know their menu item ID values. These values are defined in WINDOWS.H and summarized in Table 9-3.

ID VALUE	DISPLAYED IN SYSTEM MENU AS
SC_CLOSE	Close
SC_MAXIMIZE (or SC_ZOOM)	Maximize
SC_MINIMIZE (or SC_ICON)	Minimize
SC_MOVE	Move
SC_RESTORE	Restore
SC_SIZE	Size
SC_TASKLIST	Switch To...

Table 9-3 System Menu Item ID Values

When the user selects an item in the system menu, Windows sends WM_SYS-COMMAND messages, not WM_COMMAND messages (which are sent for program menu items). Just like WM_COMMAND messages, WM_SYSCOMMAND messages have the system menu item ID number (Table 9-3) as the *wParam* parameter passed with the message.

Something important to remember when processing WM_SYSCOMMAND messages is that the WM_SYSCOMMAND messages *must* be sent on to the DefWindowProc() function if they are not handled by the program's own logic. Otherwise, the default logic for sizing and moving the program's window will be disrupted.

An Example That Changes the System Menu

The last example in this chapter is named SYSMENU. This program is a bit of fun, as it creates an icon-sized space ship that appears to "fly" around on the screen. When the space ship hits the edge of the screen, it changes course and keeps going. The space ship icon goes over inactive windows and under active ones as it travels around the screen area. The program's image never gets bigger than an icon, and it can only be controlled via the program's system menu. Figure 9-16 shows what the SYSMENU icon looks like on the screen with the program's system menu displayed. Note that several of the default system menu entries ("Restore," "Size," and "Maximize") have been removed, and two new entries ("Start" and "Stop") have been added at the bottom. If the "Start" menu item is selected, the icon begins moving, while "Stop" stops the movement.

SYSMENU employs a couple of tricks to keep the program window from being enlarged from the icon size. The "Restore," "Size," and "Maximize" system menu items are deleted to prevent the user from trying to resize the program window. In addition, if the WM_SIZE message is received, meaning that the program window has been resized (perhaps by the user

Figure 9-16 The SYSMENU Program with Its System Menu Displayed

double clicking the icon), the ShowWindow() function is executed to reduce the window back to an icon. This is a brute force way to keep a program iconized, but it works. You can also process the WM_QUERY OPEN message to stop an iconic window from being enlarged.

Setting A Timer

The movement of the program icon on the screen is done with the MoveWindow() function, which was introduced in Chapter 8, *Child and Popup Windows*. In order to make the SYSMENU icon move at a steady rate, the program must call MoveWindow() at a fixed time interval. This is done by using Window's timer functions, SetTimer() and KillTimer(). SetTimer() allows up to 16 timers to be set at one time. The limit of 16 applies to the sum of all the timers set by every application running on the system, not just to one program. Once a program calls SetTimer(), the program begins receiving WM_TIMER messages at a fixed time interval.

To start a timer that will send the program WM_TIMER messages once per second, use the following code:

```
static int nTimer ;

nTimer = SetTimer (hWnd, 1, 1000, NULL) ;    /* timer 1, 1000 milliseconds */
if (nTimer == 0)      /* == 0 if can't start timer */
   MessageBox (hWnd, "No timers left.", "Message", MB_OK) ;
```

SetTimer() takes four parameters. The first is the window handle of the window that will receive the WM_TIMER messages. The second parameter is the timer's ID number. This value will end up as the *wParam* parameter passed to the program with each WM_TIMER message. The ID value allows you to set more than one timer in an application, perhaps for separate activities that take place on different times. You can distinguish which timer caused the WM_TIMER message by checking the *wParam* value. The third parameter is the number of milliseconds Windows should wait between WM_TIMER messages. A value of 1000 is a one second time interval. The fourth parameter for the SetTimer() function is usually set to NULL. (You can put the procedure-instance address of a separate function that will receive the WM_TIMER messages as the fourth parameter of SetTimer(). We will not use that technique in this book.)

SetTimer() will return zero if all 16 timers have been used. This is a distinct possibility, so be sure to check whether the timer was set, and alert the user if the system has used all 16 timers. Normally, the user will be able to close at least one application, such as a clock, and then have access to another timer.

When the timer is no longer needed, remove it from memory with the KillTimer() function. This must be done explicitly, as terminating the program will not automatically remove the timer. KillTimer() requires the window handle and the timer number as parameters. Here is a typical function call:

```
if (nTimer)    /* if the timer is active */
{
   KillTimer (hWnd, 1) ;  /* kill timer 1 */
   nTimer = 0 ;
}
```

Timers have all sorts of uses. You will probably find that you use timers more often in Windows than in DOS programming because they are a convenient way to make sure some activity happens, without having a program take over the system. The maximum accuracy for a timer is about 1/18 of a second. Timer accuracy down to 1 millisecond is possible using the Multimedia extensions to Windows, but this requires special attention so as not to bog down the system with the overhead of processing the timer calls. Windows will not put more than one WM_TIMER message in a program's message queue, so there is no danger of having WM_TIMER messages "pile up" waiting to be processed. Nevertheless, it is always better to use a long time interval if possible, to minimize the effect of the timer on the overall performance of the system.

SYSMENU Program Files

Listing 9-18 shows the SYSMENU.C program. As only the program's icon will be visible, the main program window class can be pretty simple, with no cursor, background brush, or class menu defined. We *will* use the system menu, which is created automatically by Windows when the CreateWindow() function is called. Note that the ShowWindow() call in the WinMain() function of SYSMENU.C uses the SW_SHOWMINIMIZED flag, starting the program in its minimized form. This is different from most programs, which pass the *nCmdShow* parameter to WinMain() to ShowWindow(). Again, SYSMENU is designed to always appear minimized, so we do not want ShowWindow() to get any instructions to the contrary from Windows.

The modifications to the SYSMENU.C program's system menu are done while processing the WM_CREATE message as the program first starts running. AppendMenu() is used to add a separator bar and the "Stop" and "Start" menu items to the bottom of the system menu. DeleteMenu() is then called to remove the standard "Maximize," "Restore," and "Size" menu items. The dimensions of the screen and an icon are also determined using GetSystemMetrics(), as this information will be needed to move the icon.

WM_SYSCOMMAND messages are processed in the WndProc() function to detect when the user selects either the "Start" or "Stop" menu items that were added to the system menu. "Start" sets timer number one going, with an interval of 100 milliseconds (1/10 of a second) between WM_TIMER messages. "Stop" simply stops the timer by calling the KillTimer() function. KillTimer() is also called when processing WM_DESTROY messages, to make sure that the timer is not left "On" when the program terminates. Note that WM_SYSCOMMAND messages that do not correspond to the "Start" and "Stop" menu items are sent to the DefWindowProc() function for processing. This is important, as otherwise all of the built-in actions for moving and terminating an application will not work.

The movement of the icon on the screen occurs when the WM_TIMER messages are processed by the WndProc() function. The MoveWindow() function moves the icon. The direction of movement is reversed if the icon reaches an edge of the screen. This movement logic is identical to the bouncing ball example in Chapter 4, *Text and Graphics Output*, except that the entire screen serves as the boundaries for the icon's movement, instead of the client area of a window.

A couple of other messages are processed in the SYSMENU.C WndProc() function. WM_MOVE messages are used to determine the position of the icon on the screen. This is needed when the program first starts, to find out where the program's icon is positioned by Windows, and if the user moves the icon using the mouse. WM_SIZE messages are processed to stop the program from being resized. Each time a WM_SIZE message is received, the ShowWindow() function is used to minimize the program back to an icon. This makes it impossible for the program window to become any larger than an icon.

Listing 9-18 SYSMENU.C

```c
/* sysmenu.c    flies an icon around the screen - modifies the system menu */

#include <windows.h>
#include "sysmenu.h"

int PASCAL WinMain (HANDLE hInstance, HANDLE hPrevInstance, LPSTR lpszCmdLine,
   int nCmdShow)
{
   HWND       hWnd ;         /* the window's "handle" */
   MSG        msg ;          /* a message structure */
   WNDCLASS   wndclass ;     /* window class structure */

   if (!hPrevInstance)
   {
      wndclass.style         = CS_HREDRAW | CS_VREDRAW ;
      wndclass.lpfnWndProc   = WndProc ;
      wndclass.cbClsExtra    = 0 ;
      wndclass.cbWndExtra    = 0 ;
      wndclass.hInstance     = hInstance ;
      wndclass.hIcon         = LoadIcon (hInstance, "MyIcon") ;
      wndclass.hCursor       = NULL ;    /* no class cursor */
      wndclass.hbrBackground = NULL ;    /* never paint background */
      wndclass.lpszMenuName  = NULL ;    /* no menu */
      wndclass.lpszClassName = "MyClass" ;
                    /* register the window class */
      if (!RegisterClass (&wndclass))
          return 0 ;
   }

   hWnd = CreateWindow ("MyClass", "SysMenu", WS_OVERLAPPEDWINDOW,
      0, 0, 1, 1, NULL, NULL, hInstance, NULL) ;
   ShowWindow (hWnd, SW_SHOWMINIMIZED) ;   /* display minimized */

   while (GetMessage (&msg, NULL, NULL, NULL))   /* message loop */
   {
      TranslateMessage (&msg) ;      /* translate keyboard messages */
      DispatchMessage (&msg) ;       /* send message to WndProc() */
   }
   return (msg.wParam) ;
}

long FAR PASCAL WndProc (HWND hWnd, WORD wMessage, WORD wParam, LONG lParam)
{
   HMENU            hSysMenu ;
   static int       nTimer = 0, nXpos, nYpos, nXvel = 1, nYvel = 1,
                    nScreenX, nScreenY, nIconX, nIconY ;
   POINT            *pMinMaxInfo ;

   switch (wMessage)       /* process windows messages */
   {
      case WM_CREATE:
         hSysMenu = GetSystemMenu (hWnd, NULL) ; /* get system menu handle */
            /* add new start and stop menu items to system menu */
         AppendMenu (hSysMenu, MF_SEPARATOR, 0, NULL) ;
         AppendMenu (hSysMenu, MF_STRING, IDM_STOP, "Sto&p") ;
```

316 Windows Programming Primer Plus®

```c
            AppendMenu (hSysMenu, MF_STRING, IDM_START, "Sta&rt") ;
               /* remove system menu items cause size change */
            DeleteMenu (hSysMenu, SC_MAXIMIZE, MF_BYCOMMAND) ;
            DeleteMenu (hSysMenu, SC_RESTORE, MF_BYCOMMAND) ;
            DeleteMenu (hSysMenu, SC_SIZE, MF_BYCOMMAND) ;
               /* save the screen and icon dimensions */
            nScreenX = GetSystemMetrics (SM_CXSCREEN) ;
            nScreenY = GetSystemMetrics (SM_CYSCREEN) ;
            nIconX = GetSystemMetrics (SM_CXICON) ;
            nIconY = GetSystemMetrics (SM_CYICON) ;
            break ;
     case WM_SYSCOMMAND:              /* system menu items */
         switch (wParam)
         {
            case IDM_START:           /* start timer, so WM_TIMER msgs start */
               if (nTimer == 0)       /* only start one timer */
               {
               nTimer = SetTimer (hWnd, 1, 100, NULL) ;
               if (nTimer == 0)       /* == 0 if can't start timer */
                   MessageBox (hWnd, "No timers left.", "Message", MB_OK) ;
               }
               return (0) ;
            case IDM_STOP: /* stop timer, so WM_TIMER msgs stop */
               if (nTimer)
               {
               KillTimer (hWnd, 1) ;
               nTimer = 0 ;
               }
               return (0) ;
            default:                  /* pass other system commands to: */
               return (DefWindowProc (hWnd, wMessage, wParam, lParam)) ;
         }
     case WM_MOVE:          /* get position of window - needed at startup */
         nXpos = LOWORD (lParam) ;
         nYpos = HIWORD (lParam) ;
         break ;
     case WM_SIZE:                    /* don't let size get bigger than icon */
         ShowWindow (hWnd, SW_SHOWMINIMIZED) ;
         break ;
     case WM_TIMER:                   /* got a timer message, move the icon */
         nXpos += nXvel ;
         nYpos += nYvel ;
         if (nXpos <= 0 || nXpos >= nScreenX - nIconX)
             nXvel *= -1 ;            /* reverse direction if at a side */
         if (nYpos <= 0 || nYpos >= nScreenY - nIconY)
             nYvel *= -1 ;            /* reverse direction if at top/bottom */
         MoveWindow (hWnd, nXpos, nYpos, 1, 1, TRUE) ;
         break ;
     case WM_DESTROY:                 /* stop application */
         if (nTimer)
            KillTimer (hWnd, 1) ;
         PostQuitMessage (0) ;
         break ;
     default:                         /* default windows message processing */
         return (DefWindowProc (hWnd, wMessage, wParam, lParam)) ;
   }
   return (0L) ;
}
```

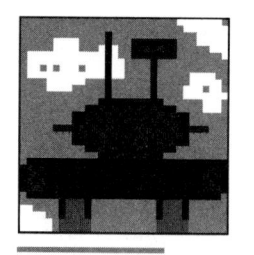

Figure 9-17 The SYSMENU.ICO Icon Image

The remaining files for the SYSMENU program are pretty simple. There are only two menu item ID numbers, used for the two added items in the system menu. If you look in WINDOWS.H, you will find that the ID numbers for the default system menu items are above 0xF000 hexadecimal, so normal numbering of menu items between 0 and 100 will not overlap the default system menu item ID values.

Listings 9-19 to 9-25 show the support files for SYSMENU. The program's icon is shown in Figure 9-17.

Listing 9-19 SYSMENU.H Header File

```
/* sysmenu.h header file */

#define IDM_STOP    1
#define IDM_START   2

long FAR PASCAL WndProc (HWND, WORD, WORD, LONG) ;
```

Because SYSMENU does not have a menu, the only resource data included is the icon's image.

Listing 9-20 SYSMENU.RC Resource Script File

```
/* sysmenu.rc resource file */

MyIcon     ICON    sysmenu.ico    /* program icon file */
```

Listing 9-21 SYSMENU.DEF Module Definition File

```
NAME            sysmenu
DESCRIPTION     'system menu demo'
EXETYPE         WINDOWS
STUB            'WINSTUB.EXE'
CODE            PRELOAD MOVEABLE DISCARDABLE
DATA            PRELOAD MOVEABLE MULTIPLE
HEAPSIZE        1024
STACKSIZE       5120
EXPORTS         WndProc
```

Listing 9-22 Turbo C++ Project File for SYSMENU

```
sysmenu.c
sysmenu.def
sysmenu.res
```

Listing 9-23 QuickC Project File for SYSMENU

sysmenu.c
sysmenu.def
sysmenu.rc

Summary

Menus are normally defined in the program's resource script file. By default, menu data is loaded into memory when needed (LOADONCALL) and moved and discarded from memory if Windows needs to make room for other programs or data (MOVEABLE, DISCARDABLE). You can override these default memory options, but there is seldom any reason to do so.

The two basic building blocks of menus are menu items and popup menus. Menu items are the only objects that can be selected and that generate WM_COMMAND messages. Popup menus are used to create "drop-down" menus, containing additional menu items. You can create popups within popups in popups, down to eight levels, but this tends to be confusing for the user. Normally, only one level of popup menus is used.

Individual menu items can be either enabled (can be selected), checked or unchecked, grayed or disabled. Graying is used to stop a menu item from being active when a menu operation is not possible or appropriate. The EnableMenuItem() function allows menu items to be switched between enabled, grayed, and disabled as the program runs. CheckMenuItem() allows the program to change a menu item from checked to unchecked.

Menus can also be created and destroyed as the program operates. The CreateMenu() and CreatePopupMenu() functions create empty main and popup menus respectively. New menu items can be appended to the end of the menu or inserted, using AppendMenu() and InsertMenu(). Menus are attached to a window with the SetMenu() function. When a menu is attached to a window, the menu data will be removed from memory when the program terminates. Otherwise, the DestroyMenu() function must be used to remove a menu from memory once it has been loaded or created. One of the advantages of adding menu items while the program operates is that bitmap images can be used as menu items in place of text strings.

Main program windows, child windows, and popup window, can also have a system menu. The system menu is activated by clicking the system menu box at the topleft corner of the window's caption area, or by selecting a program icon with a single mouse click, or by using the (Alt)-(Spacebar) key combination. A handle to the system menu can be obtained using GetSystemMenu(). The normal menu functions (EnableMenuItem(), DeleteMenu(), and AppendMenu()) can then be used to modify the program's system menu.

Windows provides a handy feature to allow a program to set timers. Up to 16 timers can be active on the system at one time. Timers result in WM_TIMER messages being sent to the program at fixed intervals. The SetTimer() function starts a timer, and KillTimer() removes the timer.

QUESTIONS

1. The default load option for a menu defined in a program's resource script file is _____. The default memory options are _____ and _____.
2. The only two types of statements that can be placed between the BEGIN and END statements for a menu in a resource script file are _____ and _____.
3. The CHECKED and DISABLED menu item options cannot be used together because CHECKED items are always ENABLED. (True/False)
4. To insert a line between two items in a popup menu, use a MENUITEM _____ menu item.
5. To break a popup menu horizontally, use the a) MENUBARBREAK; b) MENUBREAK; c) a and b; d) neither.
6. The _____ function obtains a handle to a window's main menu. The _____ function obtains a handle to a window's system menu.
7. Main menus generate _____ messages when a menu item is selected. System menus generate _____ messages. Both messages encode the menu item ID number as the _____ parameter.
8. Timers are created with the _____ function, and destroyed with the _____ function. When a timer is operating, it generates _____ messages.
9. Only one timer can be started in a program at any one time. (True/False)
10. If changes are made to a main program menu as the program is running, the _____ function must be called to make the changes visible.
11. The _____ function deletes a menu item. The _____ function removes the entire menu from memory.
12. WM_SYSCOMMAND messages must be passed on to the _____ function to avoid disabling many default program actions.

EXERCISES

1. Modify the MENU2 program so that there is a third menu item in the popup containing the two bitmaps. The new menu item should have the ID value IDM_ARROW and should contain the text "Default Arrow." Selecting this menu item should cause the cursor to switch back to the normal arrow shape.
2. Modify the MENU2 program again to make the new, third menu item a bitmap image of the default arrow shape.

ANSWERS TO QUESTIONS

1. LOADONCALL, MOVEABLE, DISCARDABLE.
2. MENUITEM, POPUP.
3. False. Checked items are not always enabled. It is up the the program logic to determine the implications of checking a menu item.
4. SEPARATOR.
5. C.
6. GetMenu(), GetSystemMenu().
7. WM_COMMAND, WM_SYSCOMMAND, *wParam*.
8. SetTimer(), KillTimer(), WM_TIMER.
9. False. You can have up to 16 timers in use at one time. However, there is a limit of 16 timers maximimum between all running applications on the system.
10. DrawMenuBar().
11. DeleteMenu(), DestroyMenu().
12. DefWindowProc().

SOLUTIONS TO EXERCISES

1. The MENU2 program already has the IDM_ARROW ID value defined in the header file, and it already has the code to switch the cursor to the default arrow shape if the static integer *nCursor* is set equal to ARROWCURSOR. All that is needed is to add the new menu item and process WM_COMMAND messages when the new item is selected. Add the third menu item to the popup menu using the AppendMenu() function:

```
AppendMenu (hSubmenu, MF_BITMAP, IDM_CUT, (LPSTR)(LONG) hCut) ;
AppendMenu (hSubmenu, MF_BITMAP, IDM_PASTE, (LPSTR)(LONG) hPaste) ;
AppendMenu (hSubmenu, MF_STRING, IDM_ARROW, "Default &Arrow") ;
/* new line */
   /* create the first entry on the main menu, attach popup */
AppendMenu (hMenu, MF_POPUP, hSubmenu, "&Tools") ;
```
[Other program lines]

Insert a new case in the processing of the WM_COMMAND message as follows:

```
case IDM_CUT:            /* ID of scissors bitmap menu item */
    nCursor = CUTCURSOR ;
    break ;
case IDM_PASTE:
    nCursor = GLUECURSOR ;
    break ;
case IDM_ARROW:          /* added menu item */
    nCursor = ARROWCURSOR ;
    break ;
```
[Other program lines]

SOLUTIONS TO EXERCISES (cont'd)

The complete solution is under the file name C9EXER1 on the optional source code disks.

2. First, you will need to create a bitmap image of an arrow. Use either the Microsoft Image Editor, or the Borland Resource Workshop, to create a file ARROW.BMP. A 64 by 64 pixel 16-color bitmap will match the other two items. Add this file to the data in the program's resource file as follows:

```
/* c09exer2.rc  resource file */

#include "c09exer2.h"

MyIcon        ICON    c09exer2.ico   /* program icon file */

CutBmp        BITMAP  scissor.bmp    /* bitmap files */
PasteBmp      BITMAP  glue.bmp
ArrowBmp      BITMAP  arrow.bmp      /* new bitmap file */

CutCur        CURSOR  scissor.cur    /* cursor files */
GlueCur       CURSOR  glue.cur
```

Finally, the AppendMenu() function call must be modified to add a bitmap in place of a character string. The new code is:

```
AppendMenu (hSubmenu, MF_BITMAP, IDM_CUT, (LPSTR)(LONG) hCut) ;
AppendMenu (hSubmenu, MF_BITMAP, IDM_PASTE,
    (LPSTR)(LONG) hPaste) ;
AppendMenu (hSubmenu, MF_BITMAP, IDM_ARROW,  /* add new bitmap item */
    (LPSTR)(LONG) hArrow) ;
     /* create the first entry on the main menu, attach popup */
AppendMenu (hMenu, MF_POPUP, hSubmenu, "&Tools") ;
```
[Other program lines]

The complete solution is under the file name C9EXER2 on the optional source code disks.

CHAPTER 10

Dialog Boxes

In Chapter 8, *Child and Popup Windows*, we created a program with a popup window. Popup windows are most commonly used to prompt the user for specific information. For example, popup windows can allow the user to select a file and subdirectory, can prompt for input of a string at the start of a search operation, and can be used to configure a program using groups of selection buttons. In these cases, the popup window can be constructed entirely of child window controls, such as list boxes, buttons, and edit controls.

Adding popup windows to an application is such a common task that Windows provides the programmer with a shortcut called a "dialog box." Dialog boxes can be designed using a dialog box editor. The editor is a Windows program that allows you to quickly position child window controls on the dialog box screen and save the final positions as a dialog box template. The resource compiler reads these template files and creates a dialog box definition that is added to the finished program as resource data. Using a dialog box editor is much faster than designing a popup window by hand.

Windows does not automate the process of running the dialog box after it is created. You still need to write a message processing function for each dialog box. In this chapter, we will explore designing and creating several types of dialog boxes, with their associated message processing logic. The advantages of the newer dialog box functions, introduced with Windows 3.0, will be demonstrated with examples using both "old style" and "new style" functions.

Concepts Covered

Using the Dialog Box Editor
Dialog Base Units
Procedure-Instance Address
Dialog Box Function
Avoiding Global Variables
Modal Dialog Boxes
System Modal Dialog Boxes
Modeless Dialog Boxes

Keywords Covered

FARPROC
DIALOG
DS_SYSMODAL
WS_DLGFRAME

Functions Covered

DialogBox()
EndDialog()
MakeProcInstance()
FreeProcInstance()
SendDlgItemMessage()
DialogBoxParam()
CreateDialog()
CreateDialogParam()
IsDialogMessage()

Messages Covered

WM_INITDIALOG

What Is a Dialog Box?

Dialog boxes are nothing more than popup windows. Any time you need a small window to appear for user information or input, you can use a popup window (as we demonstrated in Chapter 8, *Child and Popup Windows*) or you can use a dialog box. The advantage to using a dialog box is that the dialog box can be constructed quickly using a dialog box editor program. Both Microsoft QuickC and Microsoft C++ have the Dialog Box Editor application for this purpose. Borland C++ and Turbo C++ have the Resource Workshop (WORKSHOP), which includes a dialog box editor with a number of advanced features. The only restriction when using a dialog box editor is that the dialog box must be constructed entirely of child window controls. There is no facility for painting designs on the dialog box window using the editors, although painting can be done by including WM_PAINT message processing logic in the dialog box function. Normally, dialog boxes are constructed entirely with child window controls, such as buttons, list boxes, static text, and icons.

Creating and using a dialog box in a Windows program requires several steps. Here is an outline of the most common case:

1. Design the dialog box using the dialog box editor. The dialog box definition is written to a file, usually named with the extension .DLG. (With the Borland WORKSHOP you can take a shortcut by saving all of the program's resources in a single .RC or .RES file, skipping the .DLG file. To maintain consistency with the Microsoft tools, the examples in this chapter use WORKSHOP to create a separate .DLG file.)

2. Each of the child window controls within the dialog box is given an ID number. These ID numbers are given names in a header file, to make them easier to remember. The header file can be maintained within the dialog box editor.

3. Each dialog box requires a message processing function to be added to the program. These functions are similar to the child window message processing functions we saw in the last chapter, but there are a few differences. These differences will be explained in a moment.

4. The dialog box message processing function must be listed in the EXPORTS section of the program's module definition file (.DEF file).

5. The program activates the dialog box by calling the DialogBox() function, passing the dialog box name and dialog box function address as parameters.

6. The dialog box stays on the screen until the EndDialog() function is called from within the dialog box function. This closes the dialog box and returns control to the window that called the DialogBox() function.

Dialog boxes started with the DialogBox() function take control from the parent window. When the dialog box is visible, you can switch to another program, but not back to the parent window. The dialog box message processing function gets all of the Windows messages while the dialog box is visible. When you kill the dialog box window, usually by clicking a button on the dialog box, the dialog box goes away and control returns to the parent window. Internally, the dialog box message processing function executes the EndDialog() function to kill the dialog box window and return control to the parent window.

How Dialog Boxes Work

When you design a dialog box with a dialog box editor, the final design is saved as a text file, usually with the extension ".DLG." This is called a "dialog box template." The template file consists of a series of command lines that define the dialog box window and each of its controls. Listing 10-1 shows an example. Normally, you will not need to examine these template files directly, as the dialog box editor applications take care of these chores. However, templates are fairly simple to read once you get used to the for-

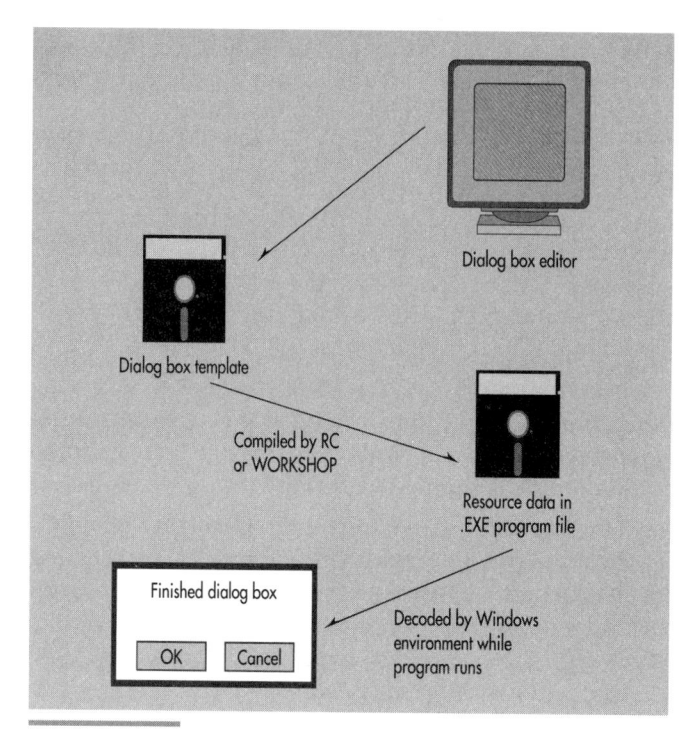

Figure 10-1 Creation of a Dialog Box

mat. The template in Listing 10-1 defines a dialog box named "FIRSTDIALOG." The dialog box will be located at position 11,19 on its parent's client area, and will be 173 units wide by 56 units high. The dialog box will have a WS_DLGFRAME frame (thick blue line) and will be a popup window. Inside the dialog box will be four controls: a DEFPUSHBUTTON labeled "OK" (default push button that gets activated if the user presses the (Enter) key), a regular button labeled "Not OK," a static icon named "dialg1," and a static text control containing the string "Simple Dialog Box."

Listing 10-1 DIALG1.DLG Dialog Box Template File

```
FIRSTDIALOG DIALOG LOADONCALL MOVEABLE DISCARDABLE 11, 19, 173, 56
STYLE WS_DLGFRAME | WS_POPUP
BEGIN
    CONTROL "OK", DLI_OK, "button",
      BS_DEFPUSHBUTTON | WS_TABSTOP | WS_CHILD, 72, 36, 38, 14
    CONTROL "Not Ok", DLI_NOTOK, "button",
      BS_PUSHBUTTON | WS_TABSTOP | WS_CHILD, 124, 36, 39, 14
    CONTROL "dialg1", DLI_ICON, "static",
      SS_ICON | WS_CHILD, 11, 19, 16, 16
    CONTROL "Simple Dialog Box", -1, "static",
      SS_CENTER | WS_CHILD, 50, 10, 74, 10
END
```

This dialog box definition will be used in the DIALG1 example program. You can see what this dialog box looks like when created by peeking ahead to Figure 10-2.

Dialog Base Units

One of the peculiarities of dialog box templates is the system of units used to size the dialog box and all of the child window controls. Dialog box templates use "dialog base units." Vertical sizes are measured in eighths of the height of a character. Horizontal heights are measured in fourths of the width of a character. Using the character size makes the dialog box automatically proportion itself when displayed on monitors with different resolutions. A side effect is that you can change the size of the entire dialog box and every control by just changing the font being used. The dialog box editor will allow you to change the font, although normally the default system font is fine.

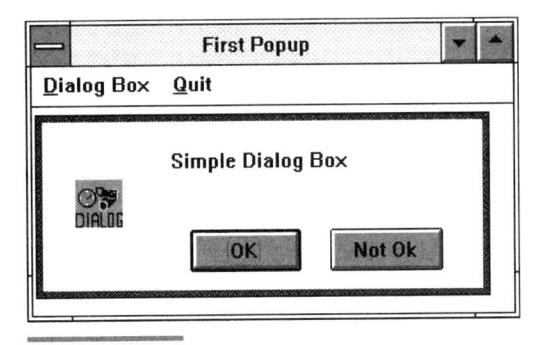

Figure 10-2 The DIALG1 Program's Dialog Box

Compiling a Dialog Box

To make the dialog box template usable by Windows, it must be compiled using the resource compiler (WORKSHOP with the Borland tools, RC.EXE or RCW.EXE with the Microsoft tools). The compiled dialog box definition data becomes part of the program's resource data, and is added to the finished program (.EXE file). When the program needs to display the dialog box, the dialog box data is loaded into memory. Windows decodes the resource data and creates the dialog box and all of the child window controls from the information in the resource data. Figure 10-1 shows the chain of events leading to the appearance of a dialog box on the screen.

This probably sounds like a roundabout way to create a popup window. The advantage to the programmer is that the dialog box editor makes the design of a dialog box very simple. Also, the dialog box definition is added to the program's resource data, and by default, only gets brought into memory if the dialog box needs to be displayed. This makes dialog boxes memory efficient. If you need to have the dialog box pre-loaded into memory, you can override the default behavior by changing settings within the dialog box editor. The default settings are used in 99% of all dialog boxes, and are only loaded into memory when needed.

Designing a Dialog Box

To see how all of this works, let's create a simple program with one dialog box. Figure 10-2 shows the DIALG1 program in action, with its dialog box visible. The dialog box becomes visible when the user clicks the "Dialog Box" menu item. The dialog box appears above the parent window's client area and consists of four window controls. The dialog box uses a static text control for the string "Simple Dialog Box," a static icon control to display the program's icon on the left side, and two push button controls with the captions "OK" and "Not OK." The "OK" button causes the dialog box to vanish. The "Not OK" button causes the computer's speaker to beep.

Note that the static icon in the dialog box is not directly related to the program icons that appear when an application is minimized. The static icon is just added to the dialog box to provide some visual interest. The dialog box cannot be minimized and will never display this icon except when the entire dialog box is visible. Static icons are just a handy way to add small bitmap images to dialog boxes.

Dialog boxes are defined by a text file, called a "dialog box template," which becomes part of the program's resource script (.RC) file. The common naming conventions are to use the ".RC" suffix for complete resource script files, and the ".DLG" suffix if the file only defines a dialog box template. The exact steps you take to design the dialog box for the DIALG1 program will depend on which dialog box editor you are using. The following two sections give you a step-by-step guide for the Microsoft editor and the Resource Workshop that comes with the Turbo C++ and Borland C++ compilers.

Using the Microsoft Dialog Editor

This section is specific to the Microsoft tools, so skip ahead to the section titled *Using the Borland Resource Workshop Dialog Editor* if you will be using the Borland tools.

The Microsoft Dialog Box Editor (DBE) is a self-contained application that automates designing dialog boxes. The DBE includes a tool menu attached to a small popup window that makes it easy to select different types of controls as you are editing. The DBE also has the ability to store the finished dialog box definition as an already compiled .RES file. We will not take advantage of this option in this book, as there is no good way to show the dialog box definition in print without looking at the script form (.RC or .DLG file format).

It is easier to use the DBE if you prepare a small header file before starting the DBE session. The header file defines the ID numbers for the controls in the dialog box. You can edit the header file from within the DBE to create or change ID numbers as needed. This same header file can be included in your C program, so that the C compiler gets the same definitions for all of the dialog box ID numbers. For the DIALG1 program, create a header file named DIALG1D.H, as shown in Listing 10-2.

Listing 10-2 DIALG1D.H Header File for Dialog Box Control ID Numbers

```
#define DLI_OK     100
#define DLI_NOTOK  101
#define DLI_ICON   102
```

When your first start the DBE, you will be presented with a blank work area, containing the tool menu. Select the "File/New" menu item to create an empty dialog box as a starting point. To let the DBE know about the header file, select the "File/Set Include" menu item and load the DIALG1D.H file. You will see the header file name at the top of the DBE screen. You are now ready to create a dialog box, using the graphical tools.

The DBE default style for the dialog box frame has a caption bar and a system menu button. The dialog box will be shown on the emtpy "target" dialog box in the DBE edit area. Before controls are added, the dialog box style needs to be changed to match our needs. The combination of caption bar and system menu button is a good style for many dialog boxes, but not for our DIALG1 example. DIALG1 needs a simple dialog box frame without a caption bar or system menu. Double click the target dialog box to cause the DBE to display the options for a dialog box. The DBE will display the "Dialog Styles" box, as shown in Figure 10-3. Turn off the "Caption" and "System Menu" styles, and select the "Dialog" frame style. Click the "OK" button to save the style information and return to the DBE main window. Note that the position of the target dialog box in the editor screen will determine where the dialog box shows up when it appears "above" the parent window's client area when the dialog box is displayed. You can move the target dialog box by dragging it with the mouse.

Figure 10-3 Specifying the Dialog Box Style Using the 3.1 DBE

One of the automatic features of the DBE is the generation of ID numbers for objects like controls and the target dialog box. This is not always helpful. The target dialog box will be automatically assigned the ID number of 100. Every control added will receive a default ID number one greater than the last (100, 101, 102...). Because we have already loaded the header file, the target dialog box ID number gets translated

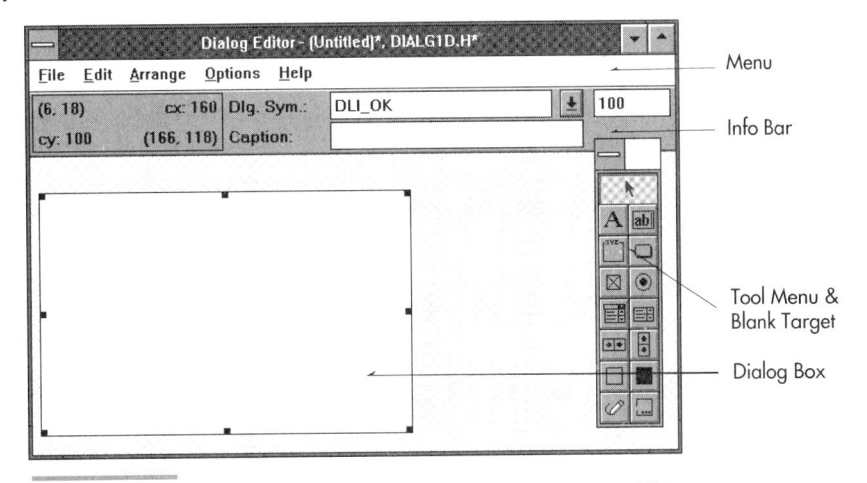

Figure 10-4 The 3.1 DBE Showing an Initial Assignment of ID 100 to the Target Dialog Box

Chapter 10 • Dialog Boxes

into the DLI_OK, which we set equal to 100 in DIALG1D.H. This incorrect ID number assignment shows up in the upper right portion of Figure 10-4, just below the menu. The easiest way to get around this type of problem is to invent a new ID number, and assign it to the target dialog box. Unfortunately, this makes the ID *number* the name of the dialog box, not the character string name. Unless you want your dialog box to have a name like "100," the Dialog Symbol needs to be changed to a character string that does *not* have a numeric definition in the header file.

To name the dialog box "FIRSTDIALOG," the "Dlg. Sym." (dialog symbol) item in the extended menu area must be changed to "FIRSTDIALOG," and the number to the right of it erased. The white rectangles to the right of "Dlg. Sym." in the info bar are actually edit controls, so you can select them with the mouse, and edit their contents. The info bar should be as shown in Figure 10-5 when you correctly specify the dialog box name as "FIRSTDIALOG."

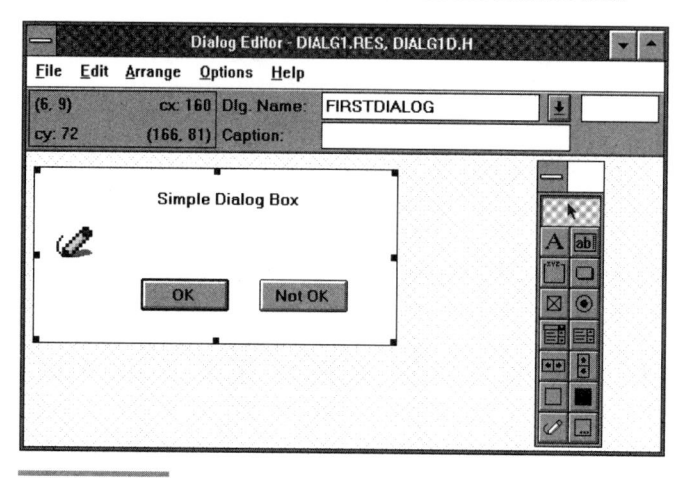

Figure 10-5 The DBE Screen with the FIRSTDIALOG Dialog Box Defined

Now you can go ahead and add all of the controls to the dialog box. Select the button from the tool menu, and place it in the lower center of the dialog box. The button does not appear until you click the left mouse button. If you double click the new button control, the "Push Button Styles" dialog box will appear. Selecting the "Default" push button style gives the button a highlighted border. Select the "OK" button to go back to the main DBE window. The button's text and ID numbers are specified in the gray info bar area, below the editor's menu. Change the first button's ID number DLI_OK with a text field of "OK." The second button is added the same way and assigned an ID number of DLI_NOTOK, with a text field of "Not OK." Only one button can have the "Default" push button style, as the default button is usually the one that is activated when the user presses the return key, and it would not be logical for two buttons to be activated if the user pressed (Enter).

The icon tool looks like a small pencil at the bottom left of the tool menu. To continue with our example, you should place an icon on the left side of the target dialog box. When you select an icon, the upper menu area of the DBE changes wording, reflecting that an icon is currently selected. In the gray info bar area, you will want to make the "Symbol" field equal to DLI_ICON and the "Icon Name" equal to DIALG1, the name of the icon in the program's resource script file. Finally, add a static text field containing the text "Simple Dialog Box" to the top center of the target dialog box. You can select the "(Unused)" symbol name for the static text field, as this ID value is not important. "Unused" gets translated to an ID value of -1. With all of the controls in place, your DBE screen will look approximately like Figure 10-5.

When you have added all of the controls, you can save the dialog box definition and any changes to the header file. Select the "File/Save As" menu item. Two dialog boxes will appear in sequence, the first one captioned "Save Include File." Clicking the "OK" button will save any changes to DIALG1D.H. The second dialog box will then appear, captioned "Save Resource File," and allow you to save the dialog box definition in either compiled (.RES) form or as a dialog box definition. Change the file name to "DIALG1.RES." The DBE will save the dialog box data as both the compiled DIALG1.RES and the resource script format DIALG1.DLG automatically. Listing 10-3 shows the output of the DBE for the example dialog box.

Listing 10-3 DIALG1.DLG Dialog Box Definition File

```
DLGINCLUDE RCDATA DISCARDABLE
BEGIN
    "DIALG1D.H\0"
END

FIRSTDIALOG DIALOG 6, 9, 160, 72
STYLE WS_POPUP | WS_VISIBLE | WS_DLGFRAME
FONT 8, "Helv"
BEGIN
    DEFPUSHBUTTON    "OK", DLI_OK, 46, 46, 40, 14
    PUSHBUTTON       "Not OK", DLI_NOTOK, 100, 46, 40, 14
    ICON             "DIALG1", DLI_ICON, 8, 21, 16, 16
    LTEXT            "Simple Dialog Box", -1, 53, 7, 78, 15
END
```

The top four lines add the dialog box header file name to the program's resource data. This wastes a little space, but it allows the DBE to find the header file from the compiled version of the dialog box definition by reading the header file name out of the resource data. We will examine other uses for including raw data in a program's resources in the next chapter. For now, you can ignore these lines in the .DLG file. The DBE also defaults to adding a FONT statement to the dialog box definition, selecting an eight point Helvetica font. Because dialog base units are fractions of the font size, selecting a small font, such as Helvetica 8, reduces the size of the dialog box on the screen. Helvetica 8 is used by all of the Microsoft applications supplied with Windows.

Using the Borland Resource Workshop Dialog Editor

This section is specific to the Borland Resource Workshop, so skip ahead to the section titled *Using the Dialog Box* if you are not using the Borland tools.

The Resource Workshop (WORKSHOP) coordinates all of the activities involving a program's resources, including dialog boxes, icons, cursors, and bitmaps. WORKSHOP assumes that you will want to put all of the resource data into a single resource file.

This assumption works well for everything except menu item and dialog box control ID numbers. The ID numbers are needed in both the resource file and in the C program, so that the C program can reference individual controls. It is best to put the ID numbers for all of the controls in a separate header file. The header file can then be included in both the resource file and in the C program. Before starting the WORKSHOP, create a header file like DIALG1D.H which is shown in Listing 10-4. You can edit this file from within the WORKSHOP, but you cannot create a header file from scratch from within WORKSHOP (at least not with the WORKSHOP release version 1.01).

Listing 10-4 DIALG1D.H Header File for Dialog Box Control ID Numbers

```
#define DLI_OK     100
#define DLI_NOTOK  101
#define DLI_ICON   102
```

When you first start WORKSHOP, you will have a blank work area with no editing features visible. Each type of resource (dialog boxes, icons, menus, etc.) has a separate editor that can be accessed from the WORKSHOP work area window. To start the dialog editor, select the "File/New Project" menu item. A dialog box giving you a choice of file types will appear. Select the ".RC" file type and click the "OK" button. At this point, a child window will appear on the right of the WORKSHOP with the title "untitled.rc." This child window will keep track of each object that you add to the resource file. To change the name of the resource file and specify the working directory to use, select the "File/Save project" menu item, and save the file as DIALG1.RC in your working directory.

To make the WORKSHOP aware of the DIALG1D.H header file, select the "File\Add to project" menu item. The "Add file to project" dialog box will appear. Select the file type "H c header," and the file name DIALG2D.H. If you do not see the DIALG2D.H header file, you will need to change the working directory by going back to the "File/Save project" menu item, saving the project file as DIALG1.RC, and then going back to the "Add file to project" menu item to include the header file. You can add and remove items from the header file from within the WORKSHOP by using the "Resource/Identifiers" menu item. This will produce the "Identifiers" dialog box, as shown in Figure 10-6. Make sure that the head file ID definitions (DLI_ICON, etc.) are visible in the "Identifiers" dialog box before proceeding.

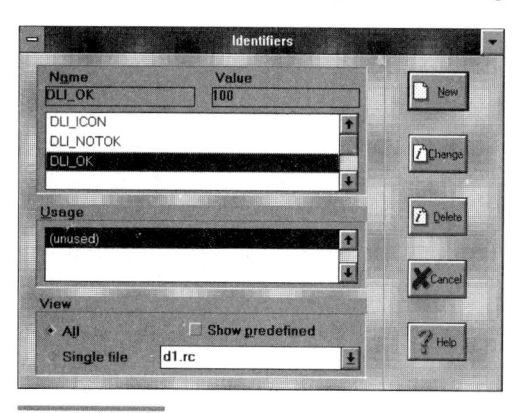

Figure 10-6 Editing the DIALG1D.H Header File Inside WORKSHOP

To start the WORKSHOP dialog box editor, select the "Resource/New" menu item. The "New Resource" dialog box will appear, providing a choice of resource types. Select "Dialog Box," and then the "OK" button. The dialog box editor will then appear inside of the WORKSHOP window, complete with several tool bar popup menus as shown in Figure 10-7. Initially, an empty dialog box (the "target" dialog box) with a caption bar and system menu button is

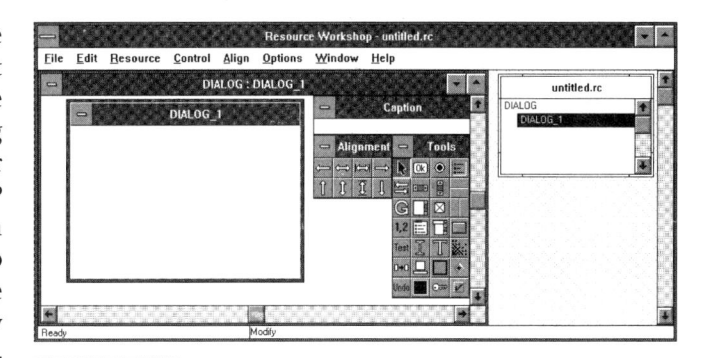

Figure 10-7 The Borland WORKSHOP Dialog Editor

displayed in the edit area. The combination of caption bar and system menu button is a good style for many dialog boxes, but not for our simple DIALG1 example. DIALG1 needs a simple border without a caption bar or system menu.

To set the properties of the dialog box frame, double click the top caption bar of the target dialog box. The "Window Style" dialog box will appear. From this dialog box, you can click the "Dialog frame" item to remove the caption, click the "System Menu" item to remove the system menu, and make sure the only selections from the other available options are "Popup" "and "Modal frame." You can go ahead and delete the caption string because it will not be used. These changes will specify a dialog box without a caption or system menu, but with a thick blue frame. This is the standard style for an "About Box," or a simple dialog box that the user will have no reason to move on the screen. Retaining the dialog box style with a caption bar and system menu button is more appropriate for larger dialog boxes, where the user may want to reposition the dialog box using the caption bar.

Now we are ready to add the controls to the dialog box window. To get started, try adding the title string as a static text control. You can do this either by selecting the "Control/Static Text" menu item, or by selecting the tool button labeled "T" from the tools menu. The cursor shape will change to a cross. (If you can't select the "T" button, go up to the WORKSHOP main menu and select the "Resource/Edit" menu item to get back into the edit mode.) Click the left mouse button to position the upper left corner of the title string, and then drag the lower right corner of the rectangle to position the lower right corner. Initially, the text string will appear outlined, containing the string "Text." Double click the text, and a dialog box will appear similar to Figure 10-8. Change the text string to "Simple Dialog Box," and leave the ID number set to -1. Static text controls cannot be selected when the dialog box is running and do not generate WM_COMMAND messages. The ID value is, therefore, never used, so -1 can be used to signify that no ID value is assigned. Click the "OK" button when you are done editing the static text control.

Next, you can add an icon control to the left side of the dialog box. Select the "Control\Icon" menu item, or the icon tool button (it looks like two white rectangles), and use the mouse to position the icon on the left side of the dialog box window area. Double click the icon outline to make the "Static Style" dialog box appear again (Figure 10-8). Set

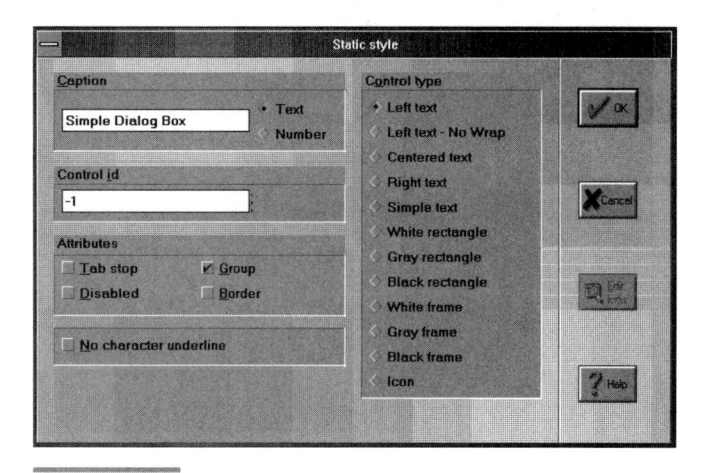

Figure 10-8 Changing a Static Text Control's String and ID Number

the caption string to "DIALG1" and the Item ID value to DLI_ICON. You can get away without an ID number for icons (set it to -1) if you like, as icons are static items and cannot be selected. The DIALG1 example follows the convention of giving icons an ID value, which is sometimes handy if you want to change the icon image as the program runs. Click the OK button to go back to the main edit window.

To add the push buttons to the bottom of the target dialog box, select the "Control\Button" menu item, or the button tool labeled "OK," to create a push button control. Position this control with the mouse in the lower half of the center of the dialog box window. Double click the control to make the "Button style" dialog box appear, change the text string to "OK," and the item ID value to DLI_OK. Also select the "Default push button" style option for this button, which gives the button a dark border. Add a second, regular push button on the lower right side of the dialog box window and change its text string to "Not OK" and its ID value to DLI_NOTOK.

So far, the target dialog box has used the default name of "DIALOG_1." To name the dialog box, select the "Resource/Rename" menu item and change the dialog box name to "FIRSTDIALOG." You will be prompted to see if you want to create a new identifier "FIRSTDIALOG." Select the "No" button, as we do not want "FIRSTDIALOG" to become an ID value. FIRSTDIALOG should be the name of our dialog box. To save the dialog box definition, select the "File\Save file as" menu item. You will have a choice of saving the file as a .RC resource script file or as a .DLG dialog box definition file. For our purposes, save the file as DIALG1.DLG in the same directory with your header file.

If you look at the dialog box definition file you just created, it will be approximately as shown in Listing 10-5. The exact numbers for sizing and positioning each control will be slightly different, depending on where you placed each control.

Listing 10-5 DIALG1.DLG Dialog Box Definition File Created by the WRT

```
FIRSTDIALOG DIALOG 10, 8, 150, 72
CAPTION "FIRSTDIALOG"
STYLE DS_MODALFRAME | WS_POPUP | WS_DLGFRAME
```

```
BEGIN
    LTEXT "Simple Dialog Box", -1, 37, 6, 66, 10, WS_CHILD | WS_VISIBLE | WS_GROUP
    ICON "DIALG1", DLI_ICON, 7, 25, 16, 16, WS_CHILD | WS_VISIBLE
    DEFPUSHBUTTON "OK", DLI_OK, 49, 55, 35, 14, WS_CHILD | WS_VISIBLE | WS_TABSTOP
    PUSHBUTTON "Not OK", DLI_NOTOK, 101, 55, 32, 14, WS_CHILD | WS_VISIBLE |
WS_TABSTOP
END
```

The Resource Workshop dialog box editor is so powerful that you will probably never need to modify the dialog box definition (like Listing 10-5) directly. You can let the WORKSHOP go ahead and compile all of the resources into a finished .RES file, ready to be added to the Windows program.

Using the Dialog Box

All we have done so far is to create the dialog box template. We still need to write the message processing logic for the dialog box, and add it to our program. We also need to make sure that the dialog box template is compiled by the resource compiler, and added to the finished program. Let's start with the header files. We created a separate header file with the ID numbers for the dialog box controls using the dialog box editor. Listing 10-6 shows this header file.

Listing 10-6 DIALG1D.H Header file for Dialog Box ID Numbers

```
#define DLI_ICON    102
#define DLI_NOTOK   101
#define DLI_OK      100
```

It is easier to work with the dialog box ID numbers from within the dialog box editor if the dialog box IDs are maintained in a separate header file, like DIALG1D.H. This still leaves the normal header file for the program. A handy trick here (which was also used in Chapter 9, *Menus*) is to include the dialog box ID header file in the header file that you make for the C program. Listing 10-7 shows the main DIALG1.H header file. Any time the DIALG1.H header file is included in another program, the DIALG1D.H header file (Listing 10-4) will also be included. This is simpler than always needing to include both the DIALG1.H and DIALG1D.H header files.

Listing 10-7 DIALG1.H Header file

```
/* dialg1.h header file */

#include "dialg1d.h"        /* add the dialog box ID values */
                            /* by including this file */
#define IDM_DIALOG  1       /* main menu ID values */
#define IDM_QUIT    10

                            /* function declarations */
long FAR PASCAL WndProc (HWND, WORD, WORD, LONG) ;
BOOL FAR PASCAL DialogProc (HWND, WORD, WORD, LONG) ;
```

Note that the DialogProc() dialog box message processing function is declared in the header file. Dialog box functions have the same parameters as window procedures, but dialog box functions return a BOOL value instead of a LONG value.

The dialog box definition created with the dialog box editor must be added to the program's resources. Listing 10-8 shows a simple way to do this. The dialog box template file DIALG1.DLG is added using the include directive. Note that the header file is included before the dialog box template, as the resource compiler needs the ID values from the DIALG1D.H header file to make sense out of the dialog box template.

Listing 10-8 DIALG1.RC Resource Script File

```
/* dialg1.rc resource file */

#include "windows.h"
#include "dialg1.h"          /* dialg1.h includes dialg1d.h */
#include "dialg1.dlg"        /* dialog box definition */

dialg1     ICON    dialg1.ico

MyMenu    MENU
BEGIN
    MENUITEM "&Dialog Box",  IDM_DIALOG
    MENUITEM "&Quit",        IDM_QUIT
END
```

DIALG1.C

The DIALG1.C program file is shown in Listing 10-9. The WinMain() function is pretty standard. Unlike the examples in Chapter 8, *Child and Popup Windows*, no extra window classes are defined, as this is not necessary when using dialog boxes. In the DIALG1.C program, the dialog box is shown when the user selects a menu item with the ID value IDM_DIALOG. The DialogBox() function displays the dialog box and switches the message processing to the dialog box function while the dialog box is visible.

The DialogBox() function requires four parameters. The first parameter is the program's instance handle, which is used by Windows to find the dialog box resource data. The second parameter is the name of the dialog box definition in the resource data. We called this dialog box "FIRSTDIALOG" when it was defined using the dialog box editor, so this is the dialog box name. Next is the parent window's handle, *hWnd*. Finally, there is the address of the dialog box function that will process messages for the dialog box control.

```
        FARPROC    lpfnDlgProc ;    /* far pointer to a function */

        lpfnDlgProc = MakeProcInstance (DialogProc, hInstance) ;
        DialogBox (hInstance, "FIRSTDIALOG", hWnd, lpfnDlgProc) ;
        FreeProcInstance (lpfnDlgProc) ;
```

When passing a function's address in Windows, you cannot just pass the current memory address as you would in a DOS program. This is because the Windows environment can move the program's code in memory while the program is running to make room for other programs and data. Windows allows you to establish a logical address called a "procedure-instance address" to make it simple to call a dialog box function, regardless of where the function is physically located in memory. Internally, Windows maintains data tables to track where the function is actually located in memory. Instead of passing a physical memory address of the dialog box function, we can use the MakeProcInstance() function to obtain the procedure-instance address of the function. The internal data table that Windows maintains for each procedure-instance address takes a bit of memory, so the FreeProcInstance() function is called when the address is no longer needed to free the memory used by Windows to track a procedure-instance address.

The result of calling the DialogBox() function is that the dialog box definition is extracted from the program's resources, interpreted by Windows, and displayed on the screen. While the dialog box is visible, all messages for the program pass to the dialog box function, which is known to Windows because we passed the function's procedure-instance address to DialogBox(). When the dialog box vanishes, control passes back to the main program window's WndProc() function. The next instruction executed when the dialog box is gone is the FreeProcInstance() function, which frees the small amount of memory associated with creating a procedure-instance address for the dialog box function.

Listing 10-9 DIALG1.C

```
/* dialg1.c   Creating a simple dialog box */

#include <windows.h>
#include "dialg1.h"

int PASCAL WinMain (HANDLE hInstance, HANDLE hPrevInstance, LPSTR lpszCmdLine,
   int nCmdShow)
{
   HWND        hWnd ;               /* the window's "handle" */
   MSG         msg ;                /* a message structure */
   WNDCLASS    wndclass ;           /* window class structure */

   if (!hPrevInstance)
   {                                /* define the parent window class */
     wndclass.style         = CS_HREDRAW | CS_VREDRAW ;
     wndclass.lpfnWndProc   = WndProc ;
     wndclass.cbClsExtra    = 0 ;
     wndclass.cbWndExtra    = 0 ;
     wndclass.hInstance     = hInstance ;
     wndclass.hIcon         = LoadIcon (hInstance, "dialg1") ;
     wndclass.hCursor       = LoadCursor (NULL, IDC_ARROW) ;
     wndclass.hbrBackground = GetStockObject (WHITE_BRUSH) ;
     wndclass.lpszMenuName  = "MyMenu" ;
     wndclass.lpszClassName = "MyClass" ;
              /* register the parent window class */
     if (!RegisterClass (&wndclass))
         return (0) ;
```

```
    }
    hWnd = CreateWindow ("MyClass","Dialog Box Example 1", WS_OVERLAPPEDWINDOW,
        CW_USEDEFAULT, CW_USEDEFAULT, CW_USEDEFAULT, CW_USEDEFAULT,
        NULL, NULL, hInstance, NULL) ;
    ShowWindow (hWnd, nCmdShow) ;        /* display the window */

    while (GetMessage (&msg, NULL, NULL, NULL))   /* message loop */
    {
        TranslateMessage (&msg) ;        /* translate keyboard messages */
        DispatchMessage (&msg) ;         /* send message to WndProc() */
    }
    return (msg.wParam) ;
}

long FAR PASCAL WndProc (HWND hWnd, WORD wMessage, WORD wParam, LONG lParam)
{
    FARPROC     lpfnDlgProc ;            /* far pointer to a function */
    HANDLE      hInstance ;

    switch (wMessage)                    /* process windows messages */
    {
        case WM_COMMAND:                 /* menu items */
            switch (wParam)
            {
                case IDM_DIALOG:         /* run the dialog box procedure */
                    hInstance = GetWindowWord (hWnd, GWW_HINSTANCE) ;
                    lpfnDlgProc = MakeProcInstance (DialogProc, hInstance) ;
                    DialogBox (hInstance, "FIRSTDIALOG", hWnd, lpfnDlgProc) ;
                    FreeProcInstance (lpfnDlgProc) ;
                    break ;
                case IDM_QUIT:
                    DestroyWindow (hWnd) ;   /* destroy window, */
                    break ;                  /* terminating application */
            }
            break ;
        case WM_DESTROY:                 /* stop application */
            PostQuitMessage (0) ;
            break ;
        default:                         /* default windows message processing */
            return DefWindowProc (hWnd, wMessage, wParam, lParam) ;
    }
    return (0L) ;
}

/* Dialog box message processing function. */

BOOL FAR PASCAL DialogProc (HWND hDlg, WORD wMessage, WORD wParam, LONG lParam)
{
    switch (wMessage)                        /* process messages */
    {
        case WM_INITDIALOG:
            return (TRUE) ;
        case WM_COMMAND:    /* controls in dialog box activated */
            switch (wParam)
            {
                case DLI_OK:                 /* OK button */
                    EndDialog (hDlg, 0) ;    /* exit the dialog box */
                    return (TRUE) ;
                case DLI_NOTOK:              /* Not OK button */
```

```
                    MessageBeep (0) ;        /* just beep */
                    return (TRUE) ;
                }
            break ;
        }
    return (FALSE) ;    /* return FALSE to signify message not processed */
}
```

The Dialog Box Function

The dialog box function for DIALG1.C is called DialgProc() and is shown at the end of Listing 10-9. Dialog box functions are similar to WndProc() message processing functions for child and parent windows. There are a few differences:

1. Dialog box functions are of the type BOOL FAR PASCAL, not the LONG FAR PASCAL function type used for window functions. This means that the dialog box function will return either TRUE (nonzero) or FALSE (zero). The TRUE or FALSE value will be returned each time a message is sent to the dialog box function. With one exception, the dialog box function should return TRUE if the message was processed, and FALSE if the message was not processed by the dialog box function. The exception is the WM_INITDIALOG message. In processing this message, always return TRUE. WM_INITDIALOG is similar to WM_CREATE for windows and child windows. This message is processed before the dialog box is made visible, and it is an ideal place to do initialization routines, such as filling list box controls.

2. Dialog box functions do not pass messages to DefWindowProc() if the message is not processed within the dialog box function. Simply returning FALSE alerts Windows that the message was not processed. The default message processing happens automatically.

3. Instead of calling DestroyWindow() to terminate a dialog box, use EndDialog(). This destroys the dialog box and returns control to the window function that called DialogBox(). EndDialog() takes two parameters, the dialog box window handle (*hDlg*) and an integer. The integer value ends up being returned by the DialogBox() function when the dialog is done. This is a way to return a value to the calling program, based on the user's actions when the dialog box was visible. We will take advantage of this feature in our next example.

Other than these exceptions, you can do almost anything in a dialog box function that might otherwise be done in a child window. The window handle passed to the dialog box function (*hDlg* in Listing 10-9's DialogProc() function) is the window handle to the dialog box window. You can use this handle just like any other window handle, to obtain a device context, to paint on the dialog box client area, or to create another dialog box from within the dialog box function. Dialog boxes get WM_COMMAND messages when child window controls are activated, or when menu items in the dialog box window are selected. Menus on dialog boxes are unusual, but certainly possible.

In the DialogProc() function in Listing 10-9, the WM_INITDIALOG message is processed to return TRUE, but no actions occur. The two button controls generate

Figure 10-9
DIALG1.ICO
Icon Image

WM_COMMAND messages. The "OK" button results in the dialog box being terminated by calling EndDialog(). The "Not OK" button results in a beep on the computer's speaker. The dialog box message processing function is called from within the Windows environment when you call DialogBox(). The dialog box function must be listed in the EXPORTS section of the program's module definition file. Listings 10-10 to 10-12 show the DIALG1.DEF file and project files respectively. The program's icon is shown in Figure 10-9.

Listing 10-10 DIALG1.DEF Module definition file

```
NAME         dialg1
EXETYPE      WINDOWS
STUB         'WINSTUB.EXE'
CODE         PRELOAD MOVEABLE
DATA         PRELOAD MOVEABLE MULTIPLE
HEAPSIZE     1024
STACKSIZE    5120
EXPORTS      WndProc
             DialogProc
```

Listing 10-11 Turbo C++ Project File for DIALG1

```
dialg1.c
dialg1.def
dialg1.res
```

Listing 10-12 QuickC Project File for DIALG1

```
dialg1.c
dialg1.def
dialg1.rc
```

The first time you use a dialog box function, it seems like an incredible amount of work. After you have done a few of them, the steps become almost automatic. The dialog box editor comes in handy when you need to update a dialog box you worked on months ago, and you no longer remember the ID numbers for the controls. The dialog box function in DIALG1.C (DialogProc()) is an ideal starting point for any dialog box. Copy this function to your next project as a starting point, and then modify it to fit the controls you add. Our next example will do this, adding radio buttons and a check box to the dialog box template.

Exchanging Data with a Dialog Box — Global Variable Method

The dialog box in DIALG1.C did not do anything besides appear and beep the computer's speaker. Most dialog boxes are designed to get information from the user. This means that the dialog box function will need to exchange information with the WndProc() function of the program. The simplest way to exchange data between functions is to use C language global variables. Global variables are defined outside of any function, and they are available to all functions at any time. This allows the dialog box function to change the values, and it also allows the WndProc() function to read the current settings.

The next example, DIALG2.C, is designed to illustrate using global variables with a dialog box function. Figure 10-10 shows the program running with the dialog box visible. This dialog box has a caption bar with a system menu button on the upper left corner. The caption bar allows the dialog box to be moved on the screen. This is a handy feature if the user may need to see what is under the dialog box to fill in the dialog box data. The dialog box allows the user to make two choices. The first is a selection between one of two radio button controls labeled "Choice 1" and "Choice 2." The two radio buttons are surrounded in a group box control to indicate that the radio buttons are related. Group boxes are rectangular outlines, with a

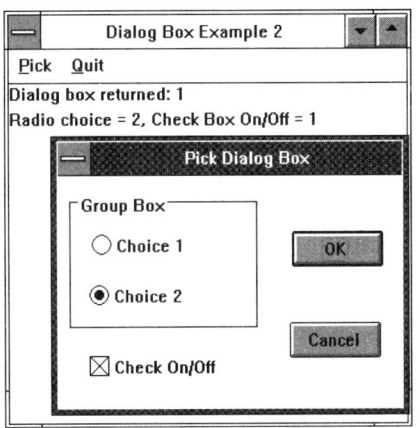

Figure 10-10 The DIALG2 Program's Dialog Box

title at the top left corner. The radio buttons within the group box are set up so that if one is selected, the other radio button is automatically de-selected.

Below the group box is a check box control. Check boxes typically are used for options that are either on or off, although a three-state check box (on, off, grayed) is possible. In this case, the check box has the text string "Check On/Off." The dialog box also has two button controls, "OK" and "Cancel." The DIALG2 program's main window (see Figure 10-10) displays the most recent selections from the radio buttons, check box, and "OK" and "Cancel" buttons in the window's client area. The program's WndProc() function must be able to determine which selections were made in the dialog box to update the window's client area. We will examine the program logic to do this in a moment.

Creating the DIALG2 Dialog Box

The first step in creating the DIALG2 program is to design the dialog box. This time, the step-by-step instructions for operating the dialog box editor will not be given. However, here is an outline of the steps you should take to create the dialog box template:

1. Create a header file defining the ID numbers for the dialog box controls in advance. The header file for DIALG2 is called DIALG2D.H and is shown in Listing 10-13.

Listing 10-13 DIALG2D.H Header File

```
#define DLI_CHECKBOX      104
#define DLI_RADIO2        103
#define DLI_RADIO1        102
#define DLI_PICKCANCEL    101
#define DLI_PICKOK        100
```

2. Use your dialog box editor to define a dialog box named PICKDIALOG with the appearance shown in Figure 10-10. You will need to specify the "Caption" and "System Menu" styles for the dialog box window. The group box control can have an ID value of -1, as this control is never selected. The other controls should use the ID values defined in the DIALG2D.H header file. The output of the dialog box editor should be similar to the DIALG2.DLG Listing 10-14. The exact dimensions and placement of each control are not critical, so the numbers at the end of each definition line in DIALG2.DLG for your version will be slightly different. Note that the format of the dialog box definition file is slightly different for the Microsoft and Borland dialog box editors, although both compile to create the same dialog box.

Listing 10-14 DIALG2.DLG Dialog Box Definition File

```
#include "dialg2d.h"

PICKDIALOG DIALOG 18, 18, 142, 92
CAPTION "Pick Dialog Box"
STYLE DS_MODALFRAME | WS_POPUP | WS_CAPTION | WS_SYSMENU
BEGIN
    DEFPUSHBUTTON "OK", DLI_PICKOK, 96, 22, 38, 14, WS_CHILD | WS_VISIBLE |
        WS_TABSTOP
    PUSHBUTTON "Cancel", DLI_PICKCANCEL, 95, 58, 38, 14, WS_CHILD | WS_VISIBLE |
        WS_TABSTOP
    RADIOBUTTON "Choice 1", DLI_RADIO1, 14, 21, 54, 12, WS_CHILD | WS_VISIBLE |
        WS_TABSTOP
    RADIOBUTTON "Choice 2", DLI_RADIO2, 13, 41, 61, 12, WS_CHILD | WS_VISIBLE |
        WS_TABSTOP
    CHECKBOX "Check On/Off", DLI_CHECKBOX, 13, 69, 68, 12, WS_CHILD | WS_VISIBLE |
        WS_TABSTOP
    CONTROL "Group Box", -1, "button", BS_GROUPBOX | WS_CHILD | WS_VISIBLE,
        5, 6, 77, 54
END
```

Creating the DIALG2.C Program

The DIALG2.C program is similar to the DIALG1.C program. The primary changes are to the dialog box function that handles the selection of the radio buttons and check box controls. Listing 10-15 shows the complete DIALG2.C program, with changes from DIALG1.C highlighted. One significant change is the addition of two global variables to track the current selections in the dialog box. The *nRadioChoice* and *nCheckOnOff* variables are defined outside of any function and are, therefore, global variables. Global variables are stored in the program's local heap, just like static variables. The difference is that global variables can be referenced from within any function, while static variables are defined inside a function and are only available to that function. Both global and static variables are "nonvolatile," meaning that their values will not be invalidated when a function returns. This is in contrast to automatic variables, which use the stack for temporary storage, but become invalid as soon as the function returns. In Windows, global and static variables remain valid as the program (and data) is moved in memory.

```
int    nRadioChoice = 0;      /* global variables */
int    nCheckOnOff = 0;
```

Because *nRadioChoice* and *nCheckOnOff* are global variables, their values can be changed within the dialog box function and accessed within the WndProc() function. In DIALG2.C, the WndProc() function displays the current status of the global variables when processing WM_PAINT messages. In addition, the WM_PAINT logic shows the current status of the static variable *nRetVal*. This value is updated when the dialog box is finished.

Within the WndProc() function, you will find the lines:

```
hInstance = GetWindowWord (hWnd, GWW_HINSTANCE) ;
lpfnDlgProc = MakeProcInstance (PickDialogProc, hInstance) ;
nRetVal = DialogBox (hInstance, "PICKDIALOG", hWnd,
    lpfnDlgProc ) ;
FreeProcInstance (lpfnDlgProc) ;
```

Note that the DialogBox() function returns a value that is stored in *nRetVal*. If the user selects the "OK" button in the dialog box, the DialogBox() function returns one. If the user selects the "Cancel" button, the DialogBox() function returns zero. This is another way for data to be exchanged between a dialog box function and WndProc(). The logic that returns this value in the dialog box function [PickDialogProc()] is discussed below.

Listing 10-15 DIALG2.C Program File

```
/* dialg2.c   using global variables to exchange data with a dialog box */

#include <windows.h>
#include "dialg2.h"      /* includes dialg2d.h automatically */

int PASCAL WinMain (HANDLE hInstance, HANDLE hPrevInstance, LPSTR lpszCmdLine,
    int nCmdShow)
{
```

```
    HWND        hWnd ;              /* the window's "handle" */
    MSG         msg ;               /* a message structure */
    WNDCLASS    wndclass ;          /* window class structure */

    if (!hPrevInstance)
    {                               /* define the parent window class */
        wndclass.style          = CS_HREDRAW | CS_VREDRAW ;
        wndclass.lpfnWndProc    = WndProc ;
        wndclass.cbClsExtra     = 0 ;
        wndclass.cbWndExtra     = 0 ;
        wndclass.hInstance      = hInstance ;
        wndclass.hIcon          = LoadIcon (hInstance, "MyIcon") ;
        wndclass.hCursor        = LoadCursor (NULL, IDC_ARROW) ;
        wndclass.hbrBackground  = GetStockObject (WHITE_BRUSH) ;
        wndclass.lpszMenuName   = "MyMenu" ;
        wndclass.lpszClassName  = "MyClass" ;
                /* register the parent window class */
        if (!RegisterClass (&wndclass))
            return (0) ;
    }
    hWnd = CreateWindow ("MyClass", "Dialog Box Example 2",
        WS_OVERLAPPEDWINDOW, CW_USEDEFAULT, CW_USEDEFAULT, CW_USEDEFAULT,
        CW_USEDEFAULT, NULL, NULL, hInstance, NULL) ;
    ShowWindow (hWnd, nCmdShow) ;   /* display the window */

    while (GetMessage (&msg, NULL, NULL, NULL))    /* message loop */
    {
        TranslateMessage (&msg) ;       /* translate keyboard messages */
        DispatchMessage (&msg) ;        /* send message to WndProc() */
    }
    return (msg.wParam) ;
}

int     nRadioChoice = 0;           /* global variables */
int     nCheckOnOff = 0;

long FAR PASCAL WndProc (HWND hWnd, WORD wMessage, WORD wParam, LONG lParam)
{
    FARPROC         lpfnDlgProc ;   /* far pointer to a function */
    HANDLE          hInstance ;
    static int      nRetVal = 0 ;
    PAINTSTRUCT     ps ;
    char            cBuf [128] ;

    switch (wMessage)               /* process windows messages */
    {
        case WM_COMMAND:            /* menu items */
            switch (wParam)
            {
                case IDM_PICK:      /* run the choice dialog procedure */
                    hInstance = GetWindowWord (hWnd, GWW_HINSTANCE) ;
                    lpfnDlgProc = MakeProcInstance (PickDialogProc, hInstance) ;
                    nRetVal = DialogBox (hInstance, "PICKDIALOG", hWnd,
                        lpfnDlgProc ) ;
                    FreeProcInstance (lpfnDlgProc) ;
                    InvalidateRect (hWnd, NULL, TRUE) ;  /* force WM_PAINT */
                    break ;
                case IDM_QUIT:
```

```c
                        DestroyWindow (hWnd) ;      /* destroy window, */
                        break ;                     /* terminating application */
                }
                break ;
        case WM_PAINT:
                BeginPaint (hWnd, &ps) ;
                TextOut (ps.hdc, 0, 0, cBuf, wsprintf (cBuf,
                    |Dialog box returned: "d", nRetVal)) ;
                TextOut (ps.hdc, 0, 20, cBuf, wsprintf (cBuf,
                    |Radio choice = %d, Check Box On/Off = "d",
                    nRadioChoice + 1, nCheckOnOff)) ;
                EndPaint (hWnd, &ps) ;
                break ;
        case WM_DESTROY:                            /* stop application */
                PostQuitMessage (0) ;
                break ;
        default:            /* default windows message processing */
            return DefWindowProc (hWnd, wMessage, wParam, lParam) ;
    }
    return (0L) ;
}

BOOL FAR PASCAL PickDialogProc (HWND hDlg, WORD wMessage, WORD wParam, LONG lParam)
{
    switch (wMessage)                   /* process messages */
    {
      case WM_INITDIALOG:
            SetRadioButtons (hDlg, nRadioChoice) ;
            SendDlgItemMessage (hDlg, DLI_CHECKBOX, BM_SETCHECK, nCheckOnOff, 0L) ;
            return (TRUE) ;
      case WM_COMMAND:                  /* controls in dialog box activated */
            switch (wParam)
            {
                case DLI_PICKOK:            /* OK button */
                    EndDialog (hDlg, TRUE) ;   /* exit the dialog box */
                    return (TRUE) ;            /* returning TRUE */
                case DLI_PICKCANCEL:        /* Cancel button */
                    EndDialog (hDlg, FALSE) ; /* exit the dialog box */
                    return (TRUE) ;            /* returning FALSE */
                case DLI_RADIO1:            /* top radio button */
                    nRadioChoice = 0 ;
                    SetRadioButtons (hDlg, nRadioChoice) ;
                    return (TRUE) ;
                case DLI_RADIO2:            /* bottom radio button */
                    nRadioChoice = 1 ;
                    SetRadioButtons (hDlg, nRadioChoice) ;
                    return (TRUE) ;
                case DLI_CHECKBOX:          /* checkbox toggle on/off */
                    nCheckOnOff = (nCheckOnOff ? 0 : 1) ;   /* opposite */
                    SendDlgItemMessage (hDlg, DLI_CHECKBOX, BM_SETCHECK,
                        nCheckOnOff, 0L) ;
                    return (TRUE) ;
            }
            break ;
    }
    return (FALSE) ;    /* return FALSE to signify message not processed */
}
```

```
void SetRadioButtons (HWND hDlg, int nButtonOn)
{
   if (nButtonOn == 1)    /* if bottom one is on, then top one is off */
   {
      SendDlgItemMessage (hDlg, DLI_RADIO1, BM_SETCHECK, 0, 0L) ;
      SendDlgItemMessage (hDlg, DLI_RADIO2, BM_SETCHECK, 1, 0L) ;
   }
   else                   /* if top one is on, then bottom one is off */
   {
      SendDlgItemMessage (hDlg, DLI_RADIO1, BM_SETCHECK, 1, 0L) ;
      SendDlgItemMessage (hDlg, DLI_RADIO2, BM_SETCHECK, 0, 0L) ;
   }
}
```

Working with Controls in a Dialog Box Function

The PickDialogProc() function in DIALG2.C (Listing 10-15) handles the message processing logic for the program's dialog box. The dialog box contains two radio buttons and a check box that must be manipulated. These buttons are child window controls, and they are handled by sending messages to the controls just as we did in Chapter 5, *Window Controls*. The problem is that the SendMessage() function needs the control's window handle to send a message. We do not know the window handles for the controls in a dialog box, as the controls are created automatically by Windows, based on the definition of the dialog box in the program's resource data.

Windows provides two solutions to this problem. A roundabout way to send a message to a control in a dialog box is to first get the window handle of the control using the GetDlgItem() function, and then send a message using SendMessage(). For example, to turn the check mark on for the DLI_CHECKBOX control in a dialog box by sending a BM_SETCHECK message would require the following lines:

```
HWND    hControl ;

hControl = GetDlgItem (hDlg, DLI_CHECKBOX) ;
SendMessage (hControl, BM_SETCHECK, 1, 0L) ;
```

Sending a message to a control in a dialog box is such a common task that Windows provides a shortcut method. The SendDlgItemMessage() function uses the dialog box control's ID number to figure out the control's window handle, and then sends the message. The equivalent function call using SendDlgItemMessage() to turn on the check mark for the DLI_CHECKBOX control is:

```
SendDlgItemMessage (hDlg, DLI_CHECKBOX, BM_SETCHECK, 1, 0L) ;
```

This is done when the dialog box is first created and the WM_INITDIALOG message is processed. In the PickDialogProc() function, the status of the check box is determined by using the global variable *nCheckOnOff*.

```
SendDlgItemMessage (hDlg, DLI_CHECKBOX, BM_SETCHECK, nCheckOnOff, 0L) ;
```

This function call is used twice in PickDialogProc() to update the check box control. When the user selects the check box control, Windows sends a WM_COMMAND message to the dialog box function with the *wParam* value set equal to the control's ID number. This is the same ID number we specified in the dialog box definition, DLI_CHECKBOX for the check box control. Receiving this WM_COMMAND message activates the toggle. The check box control gets updated by sending it a BM_SETCHECK message.

The currently selected radio button is stored in the global variable *nRadioChoice*. This value is changed when the user selects a radio button control, which generates a WM_COMMAND message with the control's ID value as the *wParam* parameter. Radio buttons are always used to show a series of mutually exclusive choices. The exclusivity does not happen automatically. You must send each of the radio buttons in group messages in order to set or de-select a check mark. To avoid duplicate code, the DIALG2.C program puts the logic for setting the two radio buttons in a separate function called SetRadioButtons(). SendDlgItemMessage() is again used to send the BM_SETCHECK messages.

Other Files for the DIALG2 Program

The complete DIALG2 program requires the usual collection of support files. Listing 10-16 shows the main header file, DIALG2.H. Note that this header file includes the DIALG2D.H file containing the dialog box control ID numbers. Also note that both the dialog box function PickDialogProc() and the SetRadioButtons() function have function prototypes.

Listing 10-16 DIALG2.H Header File

```
/* dialg2.h header file */

#include "dialg2d.h"          /* add the dialog box ID values */
                              /* by including this file */
#define IDM_PICK    1         /* menu item ID numbers */
#define IDM_QUIT   10
                              /* function declarations */
long FAR PASCAL WndProc (HWND, WORD, WORD, LONG) ;
BOOL FAR PASCAL PickDialogProc (HWND, WORD, WORD, LONG) ;
void SetRadioButtons (HWND hDlg, int nButtonOn) ;
```

The dialog box function name must be listed in the EXPORTS section of the program's module definition file (Listing 10-17), as this function is called by Windows from outside of the program. The SetRadioButtons() function is not listed in the EXPORTS section, as this function is only called from within the DIALG2.C program.

Listing 10-17 DIALG2.DEF Module Definition File

```
NAME        dialg2
EXETYPE     WINDOWS
```

```
STUB            'WINSTUB.EXE'
CODE            PRELOAD MOVEABLE
DATA            PRELOAD MOVEABLE MULTIPLE
HEAPSIZE        1024
STACKSIZE       5120
EXPORTS         WndProc
                PickDialogProc
```

The dialog box definition is included in the program's resource script file, DIALG2.RC, which is shown in Listing 10-18. Note how both the program's header file DIALG2.H and the dialog box ID number header file DIALG2D.H are included in the resource script file. Listings 10-19 and 10-20 show the project files. The program's icon is shown in Figure 10-11.

Listing 10-18 DIALG2.RC Resource Script File

```
/* dialg2.rc */

#include <windows.h>
#include "dialg2.h"       /* menu item ID's */
#include "dialg2d.h"      /* dlg item ID's */
#include "dialg2.dlg"     /* dialog box template */

MyIcon ICON dialg2.ico    /* program icon file */

MyMenu MENU               /* menu definition */
BEGIN
    MENUITEM "&Pick", IDM_PICK
    MENUITEM "&Quit", IDM_QUIT
END
```

Figure 10-11
DIALG2.ICO
Icon Image

Listing 10-19 Turbo C++ Project File for DIALG2

```
dialg2.c
dialg2.def
dialg2.res
```

Listing 10-20 QuickC Project File for DIALG2

```
dialg2.c
dialg2.def
dialg2.rc
```

Problems with Using Global Variables

The DIALG2 program succeeds in exchanging data between the dialog box and the main program window. However, using global variables to do the data exchange is not a good practice. Global variables are acceptable in small programs, written by a single person, when none of the program code is expected to be used in another project. If you start working with more than one programmer, or want to write reusable code, global variables are a major headache. Some of the problems that occur with global variables are:

1. Imagine that the same dialog box, which changes global variables, is used in several parts of the program. Each part of the program is being written by a different person. One person can write code that changes the global variables, without informing the other person of the changes. This will invalidate the assumptions other programmers make about the status of the global variables, with potentially disastrous results.

2. If you want to reuse the dialog box that uses global variables in another program, that program will have to use the same names for the global variables. These names may conflict with other variable names already in use in the project.

3. As the program becomes larger, the list of global variables increases. This makes the program very difficult to document, as global variables defined in one file, may be used in a series of other files.

Problems like these have lead to the development of better computer languages, such as the evolution of C into C++. These "object oriented" languages provide ways to "hide" global variables so that they can be used effectively without compromising the performance or clarity of the program code. This book does not take advantage of the C++ extensions (no matter how tempting it may be to the author), but it is possible to achieve similar results by using more advanced C programming methods. The next example program, DIALG3, shows a more advanced way to exchange data with a dialog box function, avoiding the use of global variables.

Exchanging Data with a Dialog Box — Pointer Method

Prior to Windows 3.0, global variables were the only method of exchanging data with a dialog box. Windows 3.0 and 3.1 include new dialog box calling functions that allow exchange of data without using global variables. The most common of these is the DialogBoxParam() function. DialogBoxParam() is used identically to the DialogBox() function, except that it is called with one additional parameter, a DWORD value named *dwInitParam*. Listing 10-21 shows the function declaration for DialogBoxParam(). The *dwInitParam* parameter can be used to pass any information to the dialog box function that will fit within the size of a DWORD (four bytes). Normally, the DWORD value is used to pass a pointer to data that the dialog box can use. The *dwInitParam* value is passed to the dialog box function as the *lParam* parameter when the dialog box function receives the WM_INITDIALOG message.

Listing 10-21 DialogBoxParam() Function Declaration

```
int FAR PASCAL DialogBoxParam(HANDLE hInstance, LPSTR lpszTemplateName, HWND hWndParent,
FARPROC lpfnDlgProc, DWORD dwInitParam);
```

To understand how DialogBoxParam() is used, consider a dialog box like the one shown in Figure 10-12. The dialog box consists of a list box and two button controls. This is a general purpose dialog box that might be used in a number of programs. The key to making it useful in the future is not to "hard code" the list items into the dialog box definition. Ideally, we would like to send the list box a list of items to display, and then find out which one the user selected when the "OK" button is selected.

To make the list dialog box as reusable as possible, the code will be defined in a separate C program, with its own header file and dialog box definition file. The header file, LISTDLG.H, is shown in Listing 10-22. The header file defines the ID numbers for the dialog box controls, and has the function prototype for the dialog box function ListDialogProc(). More important is the definition of a new data type, using the C language typedef statement. The CHARARRAY data type consists of three integers, and a far pointer to a character string. This data type is designed to allow any program to pass an array of character strings to the dialog box function for the list box. The dialog box can then display the list, and allow the user to make a selection. This is done in the DIALG3.C example program, which we will get to in a moment.

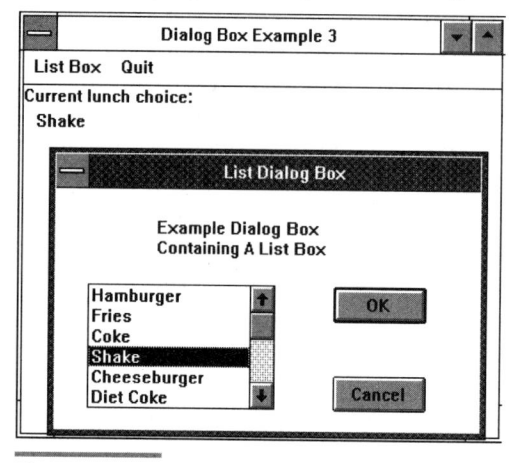

Figure 10-12 The DIALG3 Program

Listing 10-22 LISTDLG.H Header File

```
/* listdlg.h header file for list dialog box */

#define DLI_LISTBOX      2000
#define DLI_LISTOK       2001
#define DLI_LISTCANCEL   2002

typedef struct tagCharArray   /* define a structure to hold a character */
{                             /* array */
    int   nCharWidth ;        /* chars in each array element */
    int   nItemCount ;        /* number of items */
    int   nSelection ;        /* current selection number */
    char FAR *cBuf ;          /* place holder for character array */
} CHARARRAY ;

BOOL FAR PASCAL ListDialogProc (HWND, WORD, WORD, LONG) ;
```

To take advantage of this new data type, we will call the DialogBoxParam() function, passing a pointer to the CHARARRY data as the *dwInitParam* parameter. A typical code fragment that calls the dialog box function is shown in Listing 10-23. Declaring the variable *caMenu* to be a "static CHARARRAY" causes the compiler to set aside room for one CHARARRAY structure in the local heap. The CHARARRAY structure is just three integers and a far pointer and does not contain the actual character data. The character strings that will make up the list box contents are stored in a static array named *cMenuNames*. This character data is also placed in the local heap by the compiler.

Figure 10-13 shows the relationship of the CHARARRAY structure and the character string data in the local heap. Before a pointer to the CHARARRAY structure is passed to the DialogBoxParam() data structure, each element of the structure is initialized (see Listing 10-23). The *cBuf* member of the CHARARRAY structure is set equal to the address of the character strings. The result is that a pointer to the *caMenu* CHARARRAY data structure provides access to both the integer elements, as well as access to the array of character strings. This is ideal for passing information to the DialogBoxParam() function, as one pointer provides access to all of the data.

Listing 10-23 Passing the CHARARRAY Data to the Dialog Box Function

```
FARPROC          lpfnDlgProc ;         /* far pointer to a function */
HANDLE           hInstance ;
static    CHARARRAY caMenu ;           /* defined in listdlg.h */
static    char FAR  cMenuNames [3][10] = {"First", "Second", "Third"} ;

                                       /* initialize CHARARRAY elements */
     caMenu.nCharWidth = 10 ;          /* width of each char string */
     caMenu.nItemCount = 3 ;           /* number of char strings */
     caMenu.nSelection = 0 ;           /* the currently selected item */
/* have the cBuf member of the structure point to the string array */
     caMenu.cBuf = (char FAR *) cMenuNames ;
                                       /* now run the dialog box */
     hInstance = GetWindowWord (hWnd, GWW_HINSTANCE) ;
     lpfnDlgProc = MakeProcInstance (ListDialogProc, hInstance) ;
                              /* run dlg box, passing pointer to caMenu */
     DialogBoxParam (hInstance, "LISTDIALOG", hWnd, lpfnDlgProc,
          (DWORD) (LPSTR) &caMenu ) ;  /* pass pointer to CHARARRAY data */
     FreeProcInstance (lpfnDlgProc) ;
```

The dialog box procedure for the list box is defined in the LISTDLG.C file (Listing 10-24). This is a separate C program that we will include in the program compilation when we need the ListDialgProc() dialog box function to run the list dialog box. Because this dialog procedure is called by DialogBoxParam() instead of DialogBox(), the DWORD value passed as the last parameter in the DialogBoxParam() function call ends up as the *lParam* value when the dialog box function receives the WM_INITDIALOG message. In the ListDialogProc() function, *lParam* is decoded as a pointer to a CHARARRAY data structure. The CHARARRAY elements provide the number of character items (*nItemCount*), the width of each character string (*nCharWidth*), and a pointer to the character string data. This allows the ListDialogProc() function to extract all of the strings and add them to the list box using the LB_ADDSTRING message.

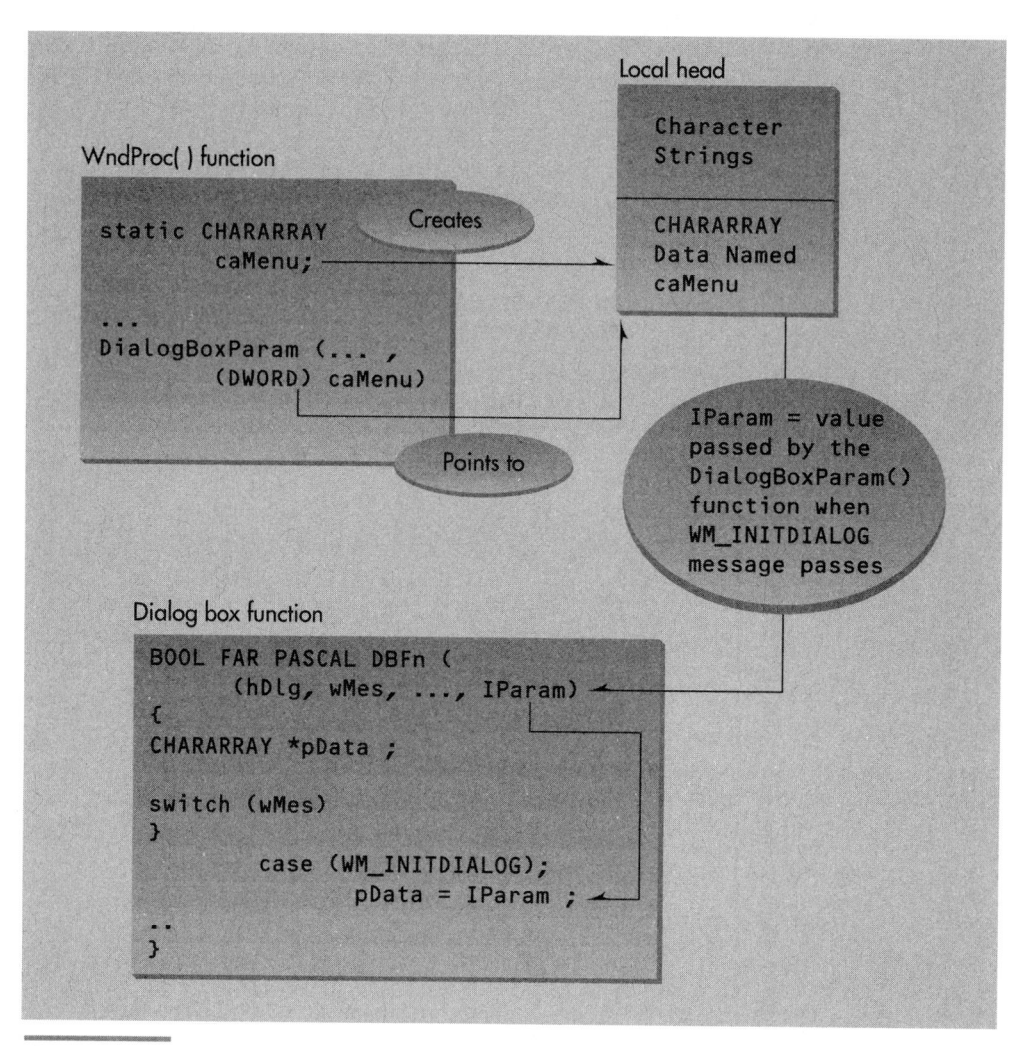

Figure 10-13 How DialogBoxParam() Receives a Pointer to Data

Local head
Character Strings
CHARARRAY Data Named caMenu

WndProc( ) function
```
static CHARARRAY
       caMenu;
...
DialogBoxParam (... ,
       (DWORD) caMenu)
```
Creates →
Points to →

lParam = value passed by the DialogBoxParam() function when WM_INITDIALOG message passes

Dialog box function
```
BOOL FAR PASCAL DBFn (
       (hDlg, wMes, ..., lParam)
{
CHARARRAY *pData ;

switch (wMes)
}
       case (WM_INITDIALOG);
              pData = lParam ;
..
}
```

Listing 10-24 LISTDLG.C

```
/* listdlg.c  dialog box function for list box */
/* always include listdlg.h if using this file */
/* also export the function ListDialogProc() */

#include <windows.h>
#include "listdlg.h"

BOOL FAR PASCAL ListDialogProc (HWND hDlg, WORD wMessage, WORD wParam, LONG lParam)
{
```

```
    static CHARARRAY far *pcaListArray ;    /* defined in listdlg.h */
    int                  i ;
    LPSTR                lpszItem ;

    switch (wMessage)       /* process messages */
    {
       case WM_INITDIALOG:
           pcaListArray = (CHARARRAY far *) lParam ;
           lpszItem = pcaListArray->cBuf ;
           for (i = 0 ; i < pcaListArray->nItemCount ; i++) /* add strings */
           {                                                /* to dialog box */
              SendDlgItemMessage (hDlg, DLI_LISTBOX, LB_ADDSTRING, 0,
                  (DWORD) lpszItem) ;
              lpszItem += pcaListArray->nCharWidth ;     /* advance to next item */
           }
           return (TRUE) ;
       case WM_COMMAND:     /* controls in dialog box activated */
           switch (wParam)
           {
              case DLI_LISTOK:                            /* OK button */
                  EndDialog (hDlg, TRUE) ;                /* exit the dialog box */
                  return (TRUE) ;
              case DLI_LISTCANCEL:                        /* Cancel button */
                  EndDialog (hDlg, FALSE) ;
                  return (TRUE) ;
              case DLI_LISTBOX:                           /* list box activity */
                  if (HIWORD (lParam) == LBN_SELCHANGE) /* selection made */
                  {
                       i = (int) SendDlgItemMessage (hDlg, DLI_LISTBOX,
                          LB_GETCURSEL, 0, 0L) ;
                       pcaListArray->nSelection = i ;
                  }
                   return (TRUE) ;
           }
           break ;
    }
    return (FALSE) ;   /* return FALSE to signify message not processed */
}
```

When the user selects an item in the dialog box, Windows sends a WM_COMMAND message to the ListDilogProc() function, with the high-order word of *lParam* set equal to LBN_SELCHANGE. If this is unfamiliar, look at the list box example in Chapter 5, *Window Controls*. The ListDialogProc() function writes the current selection back into the CHARARRAY data structure, as the *nSelection* member. The function calling the dialog box will be able to access this item to find out which of the strings was selected.

Note that by writing to the data structure, global variables were completely avoided. Several different parts of the program could use the list dialog box procedure, each passing a pointer to a different CHARARRAY data structure. There would never be a chance of one portion of the program interfering with another portion's data.

One last way that the ListDialogProc() function communicates with the function that called the DialogBoxParam() function is by returning a value. If the user selects the "OK" button, the EndDialog() function returns TRUE. If the user selects the "Cancel" button, EndDialog() returns FALSE. This returned value could be used to undo any recent selections, if the "Cancel" button was selected.

The dialog box must also be defined as a dialog box template. The LISTDLG.DLG template shown in Listing 10-25 was created using a dialog box editor. The dialog box name is "ListDialog." The WS_CAPTION and WS_SYSMENU styles were used so that the list box could be moved on the screen. Note that the LISTDLG.H header file (Listing 10-22) is included for the control ID number definitions.

Listing 10-25 LISTDLG.DLG Dialog Box Template File

```
/* listdlg.dlg  dialog box definition for listdlg.c */

#include "listdlg.h"

ListDialog DIALOG 9, 21, 174, 95
CAPTION "List Dialog Box"
STYLE DS_MODALFRAME | WS_POPUP | WS_CAPTION | WS_SYSMENU
BEGIN
    CONTROL "", DLI_LISTBOX, "LISTBOX", LBS_NOTIFY | LBS_HASSTRINGS | WS_CHILD |
WS_VISIBLE | WS_BORDER | WS_VSCROLL, 14, 38, 76, 53
    DEFPUSHBUTTON "OK", DLI_LISTOK, 114, 38, 38, 14, WS_CHILD | WS_VISIBLE |
WS_TABSTOP
    PUSHBUTTON "Cancel", DLI_LISTCANCEL, 114, 73, 38, 14, WS_CHILD | WS_VISIBLE |
WS_TABSTOP
    CONTROL "Example Dialog Box Containing A List Box", -1, "STATIC", SS_LEFT |
WS_CHILD | WS_VISIBLE, 41, 11, 78, 20
END
```

Listing 10-26 shows the complete DIALG3.C program that calls the "ListDialog" dialog box. Note that the LISTDLG.H header file is included to provide the definition of the CHARARRAY data type. A longer list of character strings, corresponding to a junk-food menu, are used in this example. The current selection is also displayed in the parent window's client area when processing WM_PAINT messages.

Listing 10-26 DIALG3.C Program Using the LISTDLG Dialog Box

```
/* dialg3.c   Using DialogBoxParam() */

#include <windows.h>
#include "dialg3.h"      /* program's header file */
#include "listdlg.h"     /* header file for listdlg.c */

int PASCAL WinMain (HANDLE hInstance, HANDLE hPrevInstance, LPSTR lpszCmdLine,
    int nCmdShow)
{
    HWND       hWnd ;        /* the window's "handle" */
    MSG        msg ;         /* a message structure */
    WNDCLASS   wndclass ;    /* window class structure */

    if (!hPrevInstance)
    {                        /* define the parent window class */
        wndclass.style        = CS_HREDRAW | CS_VREDRAW ;
        wndclass.lpfnWndProc  = WndProc ;
```

```
        wndclass.cbClsExtra     = 0 ;
        wndclass.cbWndExtra     = 0 ;
        wndclass.hInstance      = hInstance ;
        wndclass.hIcon          = LoadIcon (hInstance, "MyIcon") ;
        wndclass.hCursor        = LoadCursor (NULL, IDC_ARROW) ;
        wndclass.hbrBackground  = GetStockObject (WHITE_BRUSH) ;
        wndclass.lpszMenuName   = "MyMenu" ;
        wndclass.lpszClassName  = "MyClass" ;
                   /* register the parent window class */
        if (!RegisterClass (&wndclass))
            return (0) ;
    }
    hWnd = CreateWindow ("MyClass","Dialog Box Example 3",
        WS_OVERLAPPEDWINDOW, CW_USEDEFAULT, CW_USEDEFAULT, CW_USEDEFAULT,
        CW_USEDEFAULT, NULL, NULL, hInstance, NULL) ;
    ShowWindow (hWnd, nCmdShow) ;    /* display the window */

    while (GetMessage (&msg, NULL, NULL, NULL))   /* message loop */
    {
        TranslateMessage (&msg) ;       /* translate keyboard messages */
        DispatchMessage (&msg) ;        /* send message to WndProc() */
    }
    return (msg.wParam) ;
}

long FAR PASCAL WndProc (HWND hWnd, WORD wMessage, WORD wParam, LONG lParam)
{
    FARPROC             lpfnDlgProc ;/* far pointer to a function */
    HANDLE              hInstance ;
    static  CHARARRAY   caMenu ;     /* defined in listdlg.h */
    static  char FAR    cMenuNames [NUMMENU][ARRAYWIDE] =
                        {"Hamburger", "Fries", "Coke", "Shake",
                         "Cheeseburger", "Diet Coke", "Onion rings"} ;
    PAINTSTRUCT         ps ;

    switch (wMessage)                /* process windows messages */
    {
        case WM_CREATE:              /* program just starting, initialize data */
            caMenu.nCharWidth = ARRAYWIDE ;
            caMenu.nItemCount = NUMMENU ;
            caMenu.nSelection = -1 ;
            caMenu.cBuf = (char FAR *) cMenuNames ;
            break ;
        case WM_COMMAND:             /* menu items */
            switch (wParam)
            {
                case IDM_LIST:       /* run the list box dialog procedure */

                    hInstance = GetWindowWord (hWnd, GWW_HINSTANCE) ;
                    lpfnDlgProc = MakeProcInstance (ListDialogProc, hInstance) ;
                           /* run dlg box, passing pointer to caMenu */
                    DialogBoxParam (hInstance, "LISTDIALOG", hWnd,
                        lpfnDlgProc, (DWORD) (LPSTR) &caMenu ) ;
                    FreeProcInstance (lpfnDlgProc) ;
                    InvalidateRect (hWnd, NULL, TRUE) ; /* force WM_PAINT */
                    break ;
                case IDM_QUIT:
                    DestroyWindow (hWnd) ;   /* destroy window, */
```

Chapter 10 • Dialog Boxes   355

```
                    break ;                 /* terminating application */
                }
                break ;
        case WM_PAINT:
                BeginPaint (hWnd, &ps) ;
                TextOut (ps.hdc, 0, 0, "Current lunch choice:", 21) ;
                if (caMenu.nSelection == -1)
                    TextOut (ps.hdc, 10, 20, "Have not chosen yet.", 20) ;
                else
                    TextOut (ps.hdc, 10, 20, cMenuNames [caMenu.nSelection],
                        lstrlen (cMenuNames [caMenu.nSelection])) ;
                EndPaint (hWnd, &ps) ;
                break ;
        case WM_DESTROY:                    /* stop application */
                PostQuitMessage (0) ;
                break ;
        default:                            /* default windows message processing */
                return DefWindowProc (hWnd, wMessage, wParam, lParam) ;
    }
    return (0L) ;
}
```

As usual, the menu item ID numbers and the function declaration for the WndProc() function are stored in a header file. DIALG3.H (Listing 10-27) also contains the definition of the NUMMENU and ARRAYWIDE constants that are used in DIALG3.C to size the CHARARRAY data. Listings 10-28 to 10-30 show the other support files for DIALG3. The program's icon is shown in Figure 10-14.

Figure 10-14
DIALG3.ICO
Icon Image

Listing 10-27 DIALG3.H Header File

```
/* dialg3.h header file */

#define IDM_LIST    1    /* menu item ID numbers */
#define IDM_QUIT    10

#define NUMMENU     7    /* number of items that will show in list box */
#define ARRAYWIDE   15   /* width of items that will be added to list box */

    /* function declarations */
long FAR PASCAL WndProc (HWND, WORD, WORD, LONG) ;
```

Listing 10-28 DIALG3.RC Resource Script File

```
/* dialg3.rc */

#include <windows.h>
#include "diag3.h"
#include "listdlg.dlg"
```

```
MyIcon ICON dialg3.ico

MyMenu MENU
BEGIN
    MENUITEM "List Box",        IDM_LIST
    MENUITEM "Wuite",           IDM_LIST
```

Listing 10-29 Turbo C++ Project File for DIALG3

```
dialg3.c
dialg3.def
listdlg.c
dialg3.res
```

Listing 10-30 QuickC Project File for DIALG3

```
dialg3.c
dialg3.def
listdlg.c
dialg3.rc
```

The DIALG3.C and LISTDLG.C example programs provide an outline of how dialog box functions can be designed to exchange data with the main program, while avoiding the use of global variables. The LISTDLG.C program is a reasonable first effort at producing a program module that could be used in many applications. To make the dialog box more general, it would be nice to also pass character strings for the dialog box caption and static text fields, which would be changed to reflect the specific list being displayed.

Modal, Modeless, and System Modal Dialog Boxes

The dialog boxes created in the previous three examples are technically known as "modal" dialog boxes. A modal dialog box takes control from the application while it is visible. The user can switch to other running applications, but cannot switch to another window in the same application that created the dialog box. Modal dialog boxes are ideal for prompting the user to make a selection, or enter a small amount of data, before returning the rest of the program.

In a few rare cases, you will want to prohibit the user from switching to another program or program window. "System modal" dialog boxes take over the entire Windows environment and will not allow any other application to receive messages or gain the input focus until the system modal dialog box disappears. System modal dialog boxes should only be used for serious error messages, as taking over the system violates the basic principle that Windows programs should cooperate and allow other applications to run.

You can create a system modal dialog box by selecting the "System Modal" style for the dialog box window when you are using the dialog box editor. Both the Microsoft and Borland dialog box editors have this selection in their editor's "dialog style" or "window style" dialog boxes respectively. Selecting "system modal" results in the DS_SYSMODAL style being added to the dialog box template, as shown in Listing 10-31. When Windows creates the dialog box, this style information is recognized by Windows, and only the system modal dialog box receives messages while it is visible.

Listing 10-31 A System Modal Dialog Box Template

```
SYSMODALEXAMPLE DIALOG 6, 18, 160, 100
STYLE DS_SYSMODAL | DS_MODALFRAME | WS_POPUP | WS_VISIBLE
FONT 8, "Helv"
BEGIN
     /* control's defined here */
END
```

The other extremes in dialog boxes are "modeless" dialog boxes. They are basically popup windows that remain on the screen for extended periods of time. Modeless dialog boxes allow the user to switch to other applications, and to other windows in the application that created the dialog box. Modeless dialog boxes are frequently used for small "tool" windows, which can be moved on the screen. Modeless dialog boxes are defined in the dialog box template exactly the same as regular modal dialog boxes — there is not a special style that defines a modeless dialog box. Instead, you use a different function to make the dialog box visible on the screen. In place of DialogBox(), use CreateDialog(); and in place of DialogBoxParam(), use CreateDialogParam() when making a modeless dialog box visible. The CreateDialog() functions alert Windows that the dialog box is going to be around for an indefinite period of time, and that other windows can gain the input focus while the modeless dialog box is visible.

Modeless dialog boxes are not as independent as real popup windows, like the popup window we created in Chapter 8, *Child and Popup Windows*. Messages for modeless dialog boxes are sent to the parent window, not directly to the dialog box message processing function. You will need to modify the program's message loop to divert messages to the dialog box function if the message is intended for the dialog box. The specialized IsDialogMessage() function is provided to do this diversion. A typical message loop for a program that uses a modeless dialog box is shown in Listing 10-32. A message received by GetMessage() is sent directly to the dialog box function by IsDialogMessage() if the dialog box window exits and IsDialogMessage() returns TRUE. Otherwise, the message is not for the dialog box, and the normal TranslateMessage() and DispatchMessage() functions process the message and send it on to the program's WndProc() function.

Listing 10-32 Message Loop for a Program Using a Modeless Dialog Box

```
HWND    hModeless = NULL ;      /* modeless dialog window handle */

while (GetMessage (&msg, NULL, NULL, NULL))   /* message loop */
{
    if (hModeless == NULL ||            /* check if msg->modeless dlg */
      !IsDialogMessage (hModeless, &msg))
    {                                   /* if not, send to WndProc() */
        TranslateMessage (&msg) ;       /* translate keyboard messages */
        DispatchMessage (&msg) ;        /* send message to WndProc() */
    }
}
return (msg.wParam) ;
```

One last difference between modeless and modal dialog boxes concerns the way they are eliminated. In modal and system modal dialog boxes, the EndDialog() function is used to remove the dialog box and return control back to the program window that created the dialog box. Modeless dialog boxes do not retain control all of the time, so EndDialog() will not work properly. Instead, simply use the DestroyWindow() function to remove the modeless dialog box, just as you would for a popup or child window.

If the modeless dialog box includes a system menu button (modeless dialog boxes should), the user can select the close menu option by clicking the system button. This sends a WM_CLOSE message to the dialog box function, but no default actions occur. To make the modeless dialog box vanish when the user selects WM_CLOSE from the system menu, use the WM_CLOSE message in the dialog box function to initiate calling DestroyWindow(). A typical code fragment accomplishing this is as follows:

```
case WM_CLOSE:                  /* close selected from system menu */
    DestroyWindow (hDlg) ;      /* destroy the dialog box */
    return (TRUE) ;
```

It is up to you to decide between a popup window or modeless dialog box, as both accomplish the same thing. Generally, modeless dialog boxes are easier to use if the dialog box is created entirely from child window controls that the dialog box editor can manipulate. Popup windows are better if you will be painting or otherwise modifying the client area of the popup window.

Creating a Modeless Dialog Box

The last example in this chapter creates a modeless dialog box which displays three cursor shapes. The user can select a cursor shape from this list, which results in the new cursor being used within the program's window. Figure 10-15 shows the MDIALG program in action, with the modeless dialog box overlapping the program's main window. The modeless dialog box acts like a popup window. It can be moved on the screen, it always appears to be "above" the parent's main program window, but it can be covered up

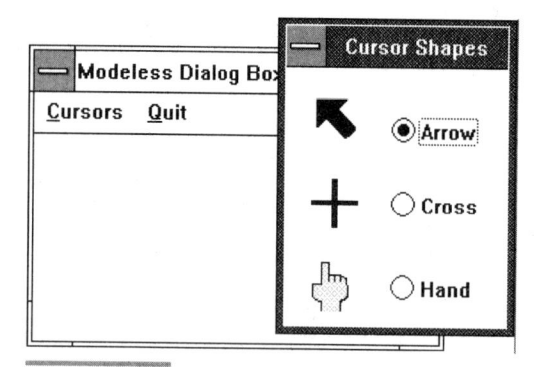

Figure 10-15 The MDIALG Program

by other program's windows. The modeless dialog box disappears when its parent window is minimized, and reappears when the parent is restored.

Defining the Modeless Dialog Box

Before you can create the modeless dialog box template, you will need to create three icon images that will be used to show graphical images of the cursor shapes within the dialog box. Use the Microsoft Image Editor or the Borland Resource Workshop icon editor to create the icons. The example icons provided with the source code disks use the default 32 by 32 pixel, 16-color format, and are shown in Figure 10-16. Note that although we are displaying pictures of cursors, you cannot use a "cursor" as a static image in a dialog box. Icons are used to display the cursor images. The arrow and cross cursors are stock cursors, always available within Windows. The hand cursor image must be created twice, once as an icon file and once as a cursor file, with both files added to the program's resources. Review Chapter 6, *Taming the Mouse*, if you are not familiar with defining a new cursor shape. The hand cursor should look like the hand icon in Figure 10-16c.

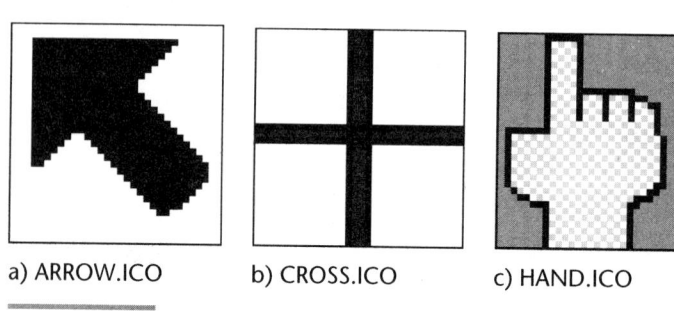

a) ARROW.ICO   b) CROSS.ICO   c) HAND.ICO

Figure 10-16 Icon Images for MDIALG

The ID numbers for the dialog box controls are stored in a separate file, MDIALGD.H, shown in Listing 10-33. It is easier to use the dialog box editors if the header file is created in advance.

Listing 10-33 MDIALGD.H Header File

```
#define DLI_ARROW    100
#define DLI_HAND     101
#define DLI_CROSS    102
#define HANDICON     103
#define CROSSICON    104
#define ARROWICON    105
```

The modeless dialog box is defined using the dialog box editor. Listing 10-34 shows the MDIALG.DLG dialog template. There will be a couple of other lines at the top of the file if you use the Microsoft dialog box editor, as that application saves the dialog box template file name with the resource data. The MDIALG.DLG dialog box definition is identical to what the definition would be if a normal modal dialog box were being defined. No special style values are added for a modeless dialog box. The dialog box definition includes six controls: the three icons, and three radio buttons. The dialog box window itself has both a caption and system menu box included. They are important for modeless dialog boxes, as the user will need to move the dialog box on the screen.

Listing 10-34 MDIALG.DLG Dialog Template File

```
DLGINCLUDE RCDATA DISCARDABLE  /* this section is only created by the Microsoft */
BEGIN                          /* dialog box editor */
    "MDIALGD.DLG\0"
END

MODELESS DIALOG 6, 18, 75, 84
STYLE DS_MODALFRAME | WS_POPUP | WS_VISIBLE | WS_CAPTION | WS_SYSMENU
CAPTION "Cursor Shapes"
FONT 10, "System"
BEGIN
    ICON        "ArrowIcon", -1, 9, 9, 16, 16
    ICON        "CrossIcon", -1, 9, 36, 16, 16
    ICON        "HandIcon", -1, 9, 63, 16, 16
    CONTROL     "Arrow", DLI_ARROW, "Button", BS_AUTORADIOBUTTON, 36, 15,
                39, 10
    CONTROL     "Cross", DLI_CROSS, "Button", BS_AUTORADIOBUTTON, 36, 39,
                39, 10
    CONTROL     "Hand", DLI_HAND, "Button", BS_AUTORADIOBUTTON, 36, 66,
                39, 10
END
```

The dialog box template is included in the program's resource script file, along with the header files, icon, and cursor data. Listing 10-35 shows the MDIALG.RC file, including the definition of the program's menu.

Listing 10-35 MDIALG.RC Resource Script File

```
/* mdialg.rc */

#include <windows.h>
#include "mdialg.h"
#include "mdialgd.h"
#include "mdialg.dlg"

ProgIcon     ICON     mdialg.ico        /* the program's icon */
ArrowIcon    ICON     arrow.ico         /* icons for the dialog box */
CrossIcon    ICON     cross.ico
HandIcon     ICON     hand.ico
HandCursor   CURSOR   hand.cur          /* the hand cursor shape */
```

```
MainMenu MENU
BEGIN
    POPUP    "&Cursors"
    BEGIN
      MENUITEM "&Create Modeless Dlg Box",   IDM_CREATE
      MENUITEM "&Destroy Modeless Dlg Box",  IDM_DESTROY
    END
    MENUITEM "&Quit",        IDM_QUIT
END
```

Calling the Modeless Dialog Box

Listing 10-36 shows the MDIALG.C program, including both the WndProc() function and the dialog box function named DialogProc(). A global variable *_hModeless* is defined at the top of MDIALG.C listing to hold the window handle of the modeless dialog box. Global variables are difficult to avoid when using modeless dialog boxes because the dialog box window handle is needed within the WinMain() function to process messages, and needed within the WndProc() function to allow the creation and destruction of the dialog box window. MDIALG.C uses the convention of preceding the global variable name with an underscore character. This makes it obvious that the variable is global in scope anywhere in the listing.

The message loop in the WinMain() function has been modified to include the IsDialogMessage() function. Without this function, the dialog box message processing function would not receive messages. The dialog box is not created until the user selects the menu item with the ID value IDM_CREATE. The CreateDialogParam() function creates the modeless dialog box and returns a handle to the dialog box window, which is stored in the *_hModeless* global variable. The CreateDialogParam() function allows a DWORD value to be passed to the dialog box function. In this case, the value is just the address (a pointer) of the *nCursorSel* static variable that keeps track of what type of cursor is selected. The DWORD value ends up being the *lParam* parameter passed to the dialog box function when the function receives the WM_INITDIALOG message. This is just like the DialogBoxParam() function we used in DIALG3.C, except that DialogBoxParam() creates a modal dialog box and CreateDialogParam() creates a modeless dialog box.

To make the cursor change shape, the WndProc() function also processes WM_SETCURSOR messages. Different cursor shapes are loaded, depending on the value in the *nCursorSel* static variable. This gives you a clue as to how the dialog box will be able to change the cursor shape for the main program window. The dialog box function receives a pointer to the *nCursorSel* variable when the WM_INITDIALOG message is received. The dialog box can change the value of *nCursorSel*, based on which cursor the user selects in the dialog box. The dialog box function saves the selection in the *nCursorSel* address, which immediately changes the cursor shape the next time the WM_SETCURSOR message is processed by the WndProc() function. The same effect could have been achieved by making *nCursorSel* a global variable, but the pointer method is cleaner.

Listing 10-36 MDIALG.C

```c
/* mdialg.c   Creating a modeless dialog box */

#include <windows.h>
#include "mdialg.h"

HWND        hModeless = NULL ;      /* global variable - modeless dialog window */

int PASCAL WinMain (HANDLE hInstance, HANDLE hPrevInstance, LPSTR lpszCmdLine,
   int nCmdShow)
{
    HWND        hWnd ;              /* the window's "handle" */
    MSG         msg ;               /* a message structure */
    WNDCLASS    wndclass ;          /* window class structure */

    if (!hPrevInstance)
    {                               /* define the parent window class */
        wndclass.style          = CS_HREDRAW | CS_VREDRAW ;
        wndclass.lpfnWndProc    = WndProc ;
        wndclass.cbClsExtra     = 0 ;
        wndclass.cbWndExtra     = 0 ;
        wndclass.hInstance      = hInstance ;
        wndclass.hIcon          = LoadIcon (hInstance, "ProgIcon") ;
        wndclass.hCursor        = LoadCursor (NULL, IDC_ARROW) ;
        wndclass.hbrBackground  = GetStockObject (WHITE_BRUSH) ;
        wndclass.lpszMenuName   = "MainMenu" ;
        wndclass.lpszClassName  = "MyClass" ;
                /* register the parent window class */
        if (!RegisterClass (&wndclass))
            return (0) ;
    }
    hWnd = CreateWindow ("MyClass","Modeless Dialog Box Example",
        WS_OVERLAPPEDWINDOW, CW_USEDEFAULT, CW_USEDEFAULT, CW_USEDEFAULT,
        CW_USEDEFAULT, NULL, NULL, hInstance, NULL) ;
    ShowWindow (hWnd, nCmdShow) ;       /* display the window */

    while (GetMessage (&msg, NULL, NULL, NULL))   /* modified message loop */
    {
        if (_hModeless == NULL ||       /* check if msg->modeless dlg */
           !IsDialogMessage (_hModeless, &msg))
        {                               /* if not, send to WndProc() */
            TranslateMessage (&msg) ;   /* translate keyboard messages */
            DispatchMessage (&msg) ;    /* send message to WndProc() */
        }
    }
    return (msg.wParam) ;
}

long FAR PASCAL WndProc (HWND hWnd, WORD wMessage, WORD wParam, LONG lParam)
{
    static  FARPROC     lpfnDlgProc = NULL ;    /* far pointer to a function */
    HANDLE              hInstance ;
    static  int         nCursorSel = 0 ;        /* holds current cursor selection */
```

Chapter 10 • Dialog Boxes **363**

```c
    switch (wMessage)                  /* process windows messages */
    {
      case WM_COMMAND:                 /* menu items */
          switch (wParam)
          {
              case IDM_CREATE:         /* create the modeless dialog box */
                  if (!_hModeless)
                  {
                      hInstance = GetWindowWord (hWnd, GWW_HINSTANCE) ;
                      lpfnDlgProc = MakeProcInstance (DialogProc, hInstance) ;
                      hModeless = CreateDialogParam (hInstance, "MODELESS",
                        hWnd, lpfnDlgProc, (DWORD) (LPVOID) &nCursorSel) ;
                  }
                  break ;
              case IDM_DESTROY:        /* remove the modeless dialog box */
                  if (_hModeless)
                  {
                      DestroyWindow (_hModeless) ;         /* remove dlg box */
                      hModeless = NULL ;
                      FreeProcInstance (lpfnDlgProc) ;     /* free dlg box function */
                                                           /* procedure instance */
                      lpfnDlgProc = NULL ;
                  }
                  break ;
              case IDM_QUIT:
                  DestroyWindow (hWnd) ;    /* destroy window, */
                  break ;                   /* terminating application */
          }
          break ;
      case WM_SETCURSOR:               /* change cursor shape */
          switch (nCursorSel)
          {
              case 0:                  /* arrow cursor */
                  SetCursor (LoadCursor (NULL, IDC_ARROW)) ;
                  break ;
              case 1:                  /* cross cursor */
                  SetCursor (LoadCursor (NULL, IDC_CROSS)) ;
                  break ;
              case 2:
                  SetCursor (LoadCursor (
                    GetWindowWord (hWnd, GWW_HINSTANCE),
                    "HandCursor")) ;
                  break ;
          }
          break ;
      case WM_DESTROY:                 /* stop application */
          if (lpfnDlgProc)
              FreeProcInstance (lpfnDlgProc) ;/* free dlg box function */
                                              /* procedure instance */
          PostQuitMessage (0) ;
          break ;
      default:                         /* default windows message processing */
          return DefWindowProc (hWnd, wMessage, wParam, lParam) ;
    }
    return (0L) ;
}

/* Dialog box (message processing) function. */
```

```
BOOL FAR PASCAL DialogProc (HWND hDlg, WORD wMessage, WORD wParam, LONG lParam)
{
    static int  *nCursorSel ;

    switch (wMessage)           /* process messages */
    {
       case WM_INITDIALOG:      /* get pointer to int holding cursor selection val */
            nCursorSel = (int *) lParam ;
            SetCursorButton (hDlg, *nCursorSel) ;
            return (TRUE) ;
       case WM_COMMAND:    /* controls in dialog box activated */
            switch (wParam)
            {
                case DLI_ARROW:
                     *nCursorSel = 0 ;
                     SetCursorButton (hDlg, *nCursorSel) ;
                     break ;
                case DLI_CROSS:
                     *nCursorSel = 1 ;
                     SetCursorButton (hDlg, *nCursorSel) ;
                     break ;
                case DLI_HAND:
                     *nCursorSel = 2 ;
                     SetCursorButton (hDlg, *nCursorSel) ;
                     break ;
            }
            return (TRUE) ;
       case WM_MOUSEMOVE:        /* change cursor shape */
          switch (*nCursorSel)
          {
                case 0:          /* arrow cursor */
                     SetCursor (LoadCursor (NULL, IDC_ARROW)) ;
                     break ;
                case 1:          /* cross cursor */
                     SetCursor (LoadCursor (NULL, IDC_CROSS)) ;
                     break ;
                case 2:
                     SetCursor (LoadCursor (
                          GetWindowWord (GetParent (hDlg), GWW_HINSTANCE),
                          "HandCursor")) ;
                     break ;
          }
            return (FALSE) ;          /* let other mouse activities go on */
       case WM_CLOSE:                 /* close selected from system menu */
            DestroyWindow (hDlg) ;    /* destroy the dialog box */
            hModeless = NULL ;        /* stops message loop from sending */
            return (TRUE) ;           /* messages to dialog box function */
    }
    return (FALSE) ;   /* return FALSE to signify message not processed */
}

/* SetCursorButton() checks the correct button in the dialog box */

void SetCursorButton (HWND hDlg, int nSelection)
{
    switch (nSelection)
    {
       case 0:                              /* arrow cursor */
```

```
                SendDlgItemMessage (hDlg, DLI_ARROW, BM_SETCHECK, 1, 0L) ;
                SendDlgItemMessage (hDlg, DLI_CROSS, BM_SETCHECK, 0, 0L) ;
                SendDlgItemMessage (hDlg, DLI_HAND, BM_SETCHECK, 0, 0L) ;
                return ;
        case 1:     /* cross cursor */
                SendDlgItemMessage (hDlg, DLI_ARROW, BM_SETCHECK, 0, 0L) ;
                SendDlgItemMessage (hDlg, DLI_CROSS, BM_SETCHECK, 1, 0L) ;
                SendDlgItemMessage (hDlg, DLI_HAND, BM_SETCHECK, 0, 0L) ;
                return ;
        case 2:
                SendDlgItemMessage (hDlg, DLI_ARROW, BM_SETCHECK, 0, 0L) ;
                SendDlgItemMessage (hDlg, DLI_CROSS, BM_SETCHECK, 0, 0L) ;
                SendDlgItemMessage (hDlg, DLI_HAND, BM_SETCHECK, 1, 0L) ;
                return ;
        }
}
```

The message processing function for the modeless dialog box, DialogProc(), is shown near the end of Listing 10-36. The WM_INITDIALOG message is processed to obtain the address of the *nCursorSel* variable. When the user selects one of the radio button choices, Windows sends a WM_COMMAND message to DialogProc(). The selection is saved as *nCursorSel* and the radio buttons are updated. The checking of the correct radio button in the modeless dialog box is handled by the SetCursorButton() function at the bottom of Listing 10-36. The radio buttons are checked or unchecked by sending the BM_SETCHECK message using the SendDlgItemMessage() function.

One inconsistency in the program is that the dialog box changes the cursor shape used by the program's main window, but does not automatically change the cursor shape used within the dialog box itself. MDIALG.C partially overcomes this by having the dialog box function process WM_MOUSEMOVE messages, changing the cursor shape each time the mouse is moved. You cannot use the WM_SETCURSOR message within a dialog box function, as the built-in logic in Windows for dialog boxes keeps changing the cursor back to the arrow shape. Processing WM_MOUSEMOVE messages forces the cursor shape back to the shape we would like to show each time the mouse is moved, but the cursor shows a slight flicker. The cursor changes back to an arrow shape anytime it is over one of the radio button controls. That is because the radio buttons are small child windows, not part of the dialog box window. (To fully change the cursor shape in all of the dialog box window requires modifying the behavior of standard windows controls via an advanced technique called "window subclassing." See the SetWindowLong() function description in Chapter 3 of *The Waite Group's Windows API Bible* if you need to use this technique.)

The usual header, program icon, module definition, and project files are required to complete MDIALG, and are shown in Listings 10-37 to 10-40. They are pretty standard, as all of the program code is in one C program, MDIALG.C. Figure 10-17 shows the program's icon.

Figure 10-17
MDIALG.ICO
Icon Image

Listing 10-37 MDIALG.H Header File

```
/* mdialg.h header file */

#include "mdialgd.h"            /* add the dialog box ID values */
                                /* by including this file */
#define IDM_CREATE  1           /* main menu ID values */
#define IDM_DESTROY 2
#define IDM_QUIT    10
                                /* function declarations */
long FAR PASCAL WndProc (HWND, WORD, WORD, LONG) ;
BOOL FAR PASCAL DialogProc (HWND, WORD, WORD, LONG) ;
void SetCursorButton (HWND hDlg, int nSelection) ;
```

Listing 10-38 MDIALG.DEF Module Definition File

```
NAME        mdialg
EXETYPE     WINDOWS
STUB        'WINSTUB.EXE'
CODE        PRELOAD MOVEABLE
DATA        PRELOAD MOVEABLE MULTIPLE
HEAPSIZE    1024
STACKSIZE   5120
EXPORTS     WndProc
            DialogProc
```

Listing 10-39 Turbo C++ Project File for MDIALG

```
mdialg.c
mdialg.def
mdialg.res
```

Listing 10-40 QuickC Project File for MDIALG

```
mdialg.c
mdialg.def
mdialg.rc
```

Summary

Dialog boxes are defined in a dialog box template file, usually saved with the file extension ".DLG." These files are created using a dialog box editor, which speeds the process of creating and positioning child window controls. The dialog box template data is compiled by the resource compiler, and added to the finished Windows program as resource data. Windows creates the dialog box from the resource data and displays it on the screen. Although the dialog box editor automates the process of designing the dialog box, the message processing logic for each dialog box must be written by the programmer. The message processing function for a dialog box is usually called the "dialog box function."

Dialog boxes are invoked using the DialogBox() function. The procedure-instance address of the dialog box function must be passed to the Dialog Box() function so that Windows knows where to send message data when the dialog box is on the screen. Procedure-instance addresses are used rather than absolute addresses in memory, as Windows keeps the procedure-instance address valid where the code is moved in memory. The MakeProcInstance() function creates a procedure-instance address that can be passed to DialogBox(), and FreeProcInstance() frees the procedure-instance data from memory.

The DialogBox() function has the disadvantage of not allowing data to be passed between the function (usually WndProc()) that calls DialogBox() and the dialog box function. The DialogBoxParam() function improves on DialogBox() by allowing a single DWORD value to be passed to the dialog box function when the WM_INITDIALOG message is received. This DWORD value is normally used to pass a pointer to a data structure that the dialog box can use for reading and writing data.

There are actually three kinds of dialog boxes. The normal type of dialog box created with DialogBox() or DialogBoxParam() is called a "modal" dialog box. The user cannot switch the input focus to any other portion of the program while a modal dialog box is visible, although another program can be selected. If the DS_SYSMODAL style is added to the dialog box definition, the dialog box becomes "system modal." System modal dialog boxes take over the entire system and do not allow any other window or application to receive messages or gain the input focus. System modal dialog boxes should only be used for critical error messages.

The third type of dialog box is the "modeless" dialog box. Modeless dialog boxes are similar to popup windows, in that they remain on the screen for extended periods of time, and can gain and lose the input focus based on the user's actions. Modeless dialog boxes are frequently used to display small tool bars and other utility windows. Modeless dialog boxes are created by using the CreateDialog() and CreateDialogParam() functions in place of DailogBox() and DialogBoxParam(), respectively. To use a modeless dialog box, the main program's message loop must be modified to include the IsDialogMessage() function to route messages meant for the dialog box function to the dialog box message processing function.

QUESTIONS

1. To allow a dialog box to be moved on the screen, include a _____ in the dialog box style.
2. Only modeless dialog boxes can be moved on the screen. (True/False).
3. The dialog box function must: a) Be declared BOOL FAR PASCAL; b) Have a function prototype listed in a header file or the top of the C program listing; c) Be included in the EXPORTS section of the program's module definition file; d) All of the above.
4. The dialog box template is converted into instructions Windows can read by the _____ _____.
5. When a child window control in a dialog box is activated, Windows sends a _____ message to the dialog box function. The ID value for the child window is passed as the _____ parameter with the message.
6. If the DialogBoxParam() or CreateDialogParam() functions are used to create a dialog box, a DWORD value can be passed to the dialog box function. This DWORD value becomes the _____ parameter when the dialog box function receives the _____ message.
7. The _____ function is used to create a _____ _____ address of the dialog box function that can be passed to the DialogBox() function so that Windows can send messages directly to the dialog box function.
8. The _____ function sends messages to the dialog box function for a modeless dialog box.
9. The _____ function is used to free the memory required to store a procedure-instance address when it is no longer needed.
10. Modal and system modal dialog boxes are destroyed by calling the _____ function from within the dialog box function. Modeless dialog boxes are destroyed by calling the _____ function.

EXERCISES

1. Modify the DIALG1.C example so that the dialog box paints a light gray rectangle from location 10,20 to 60,30 in the dialog box window. Although this could be done using a static control, do this example by processing WM_PAINT messages received by the dialog box function. Is the rectangle output using dialog base units or client coordinates?
2. Improve the DIALG3 example by:
    a. Making the caption of the dialog box a parameter that can be specified before the dialog box is displayed. Make the title "Select some junk food."
    b. Start the dialog box with the current selection highlighted. (Hint: The LB_SETCURSEL message sets the current selection in a list box control to the item specified by the wParam parameter sent with the message. 0 for the first item, 1 for the second, etc.).

ANSWERS TO QUESTIONS

1. caption or WS_CAPTION.
2. False. All types of dialog boxes can be moved if they are created with a caption bar.
3. D.
4. Resource compiler or Resource Workshop.
5. WM_COMMAND, *wParam*.
6. *lParam*, WM_INITDIALOG.
7. MakeProcInstance(), procedure-instance.
8. IsDialogMessage().
9. FreeProcInstance().
10. EndDialog(), DestroyWindow().

SOLUTIONS TO EXERCISES

1. The only change necessary is to add the WM_PAINT logic to the dialog box function. Listing 10-41 shows the complete DialogProc() function. The complete solution is included under the file name C10EXER1 on the source code disks. The resulting dialog box appears, as shown in Figure 10-18. The rectangle is output using normal client coordinates (pixels from the upper left corner). Dialog box units are used only by the dialog box editor and in the dialog box template. Once the dialog box window is created, it is a window like any other window.

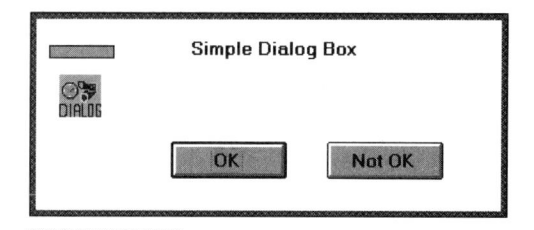

Figure 10-18 Solution to Exercise 10-1

Listing 10-41 Modified Dialog Box Function

```
BOOL FAR PASCAL DialogProc (HWND hDlg, WORD wMessage, WORD wParam, LONG lParam)
{
   PAINTSTRUCT     ps ;

   switch (wMessage)     /* process messages */
   {
       case WM_INITDIALOG:
         return (TRUE) ;
       case WM_PAINT:    /* added WM_PAINT logic */
```

Windows Programming Primer Plus®

SOLUTIONS TO EXERCISES (cont'd)

```
            BeginPaint (hDlg, &ps) ;
            SelectObject (ps.hdc, GetStockObject (LTGRAY_BRUSH)) ;
            Rectangle (ps.hdc, 10, 20, 60, 30) ;
            EndPaint (hDlg, &ps) ;
            return (TRUE) ;
         case WM_COMMAND:     /* controls in dialog box activated */
            switch (wParam)
            {
                case DLI_OK:                /* OK button */
                    EndDialog (hDlg, 0) ;   /* exit the dialog box */
                    return (TRUE) ;
                case DLI_NOTOK:             /* Not OK button */
                    MessageBeep (0);        /* just beep */
                    return (TRUE) ;
            }
            break ;
    }
    return (FALSE) ;   /* return FALSE to signify message not processed */
}
```

2. Passing a title string to the dialog box function requires that the data structure used to pass the data be modified to add one additional parameter, a pointer to the character string containing the title. The necessary changes to LISTDLG.H are shown in Listing 10-42. The complete solution to this exercise are under the names C10exer2 and LISTDLG2 on the source code disks.

Listing 10-42 Changes to LISTDLG.H

```
/* listdlg2.h  header file for list dialog box */

#define             DLI_LISTBOX    2000
#define             DLI_LISTOK     2001
#define             DLI_LISTCANCEL 2002

typedef struct tagCharArray   /* define a structure to hold a character */
{                             /* array */
    int     nCharWidth ;      /* chars in each array element */
    int     nItemCount ;      /* number of items */
    int     nSelection ;      /* current selection number */
    char FAR *cBuf ;          /* pointer to list box character array */
    char FAR *cCaption ;      /* pointer to dialog box caption */
} CHARARRAY ;

BOOL FAR PASCAL ListDialogProc (HWND, WORD, WORD, LONG) ;
```

The LISTDLG.C program must also be changed to take advantage of this new parameter, and to send the LB_SETCURSEL message when the dialog box is first started, highlighting the current selection. Listing 10-43 shows the top portion of LISTDLG.C, with the changes highlighted. The remainder of LISTDLG.C is not affected.

SOLUTIONS TO EXERCISES (cont'd)

Listing 10-43 Changes to LISTDLG.C

```
BOOL FAR PASCAL ListDialogProc (HWND hDlg, WORD wMessage, WORD wParam, LONG
lParam)
{
   static CHARARRAY far   *pcaListArray ;   /* defined in listdlg.h */
   int                    i ;
   LPSTR                  lpszItem ;

   switch (wMessage)   /* process messages */
   {
      case WM_INITDIALOG:
           pcaListArray = (CHARARRAY far *) lParam ;
           lpszItem = pcaListArray->cBuf ;
           for (i = 0 ; i < pcaListArray->nItemCount ; i++) /* add strings */
           {                          /* to dialog box */
              SendDlgItemMessage (hDlg, DLI_LISTBOX, LB_ADDSTRING, 0,
                                  (DWORD) lpszItem) ;
              lpszItem += pcaListArray->nCharWidth ;  /* advance to next item */
           }
           SetWindowText (hDlg, pcaListArray->cCaption) ; /* change dlg caption */
           SendDlgItemMessage (hDlg, DLI_LISTBOX, LB_SETCURSEL,
              pcaListArray->nSelection, 0L) ;                 /* select current item */
           return (TRUE) ;
```
[Other program lines]

Finally, the DIALG3.C program must be changed to specify the new caption string as part of the CHARARRAY data passed to the dialog box. Listing 10-44 shows the top portion of the WndProc() function of DIALG3, with the caption string added. Figure 10-19 shows the result of the changes on the dialog box. With these changes, the LISTDLG dialog box is not specific to any program, and could be useful in other programming projects.

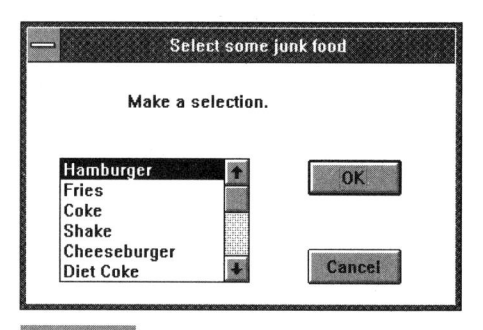

Figure 10-19 The Modified Dialog Box in Action

SOLUTIONS TO EXERCISES (cont'd)

Listing 10-44 Changes to the WndProc() Function of DIALG3.C

```
long FAR PASCAL WndProc (HWND hWnd, WORD wMessage, WORD wParam, LONG lParam)
{
    FARPROC          lpfnDlgProc ;         /* far pointer to a function */
    HANDLE           hInstance ;
    static  CHARARRAY caMenu ;             /* defined in listdlg.h */
    static  char     cMenuNames [NUMMENU][ARRAYWIDE] =
                     {"Hamburger", "Fries", "Coke", "Shake",
                      "Cheeseburger", "Diet Coke", "Onion rings"} ;
    static  char     cCaption [] = {"Select some junk food"} ;
    PAINTSTRUCT      ps ;

    switch (wMessage)              /* process windows messages */
    {
        case WM_CREATE:            /* program just starting, initialize data */
            caMenu.nCharWidth = ARRAYWIDE ;
            caMenu.nItemCount = NUMMENU ;
            caMenu.nSelection = 0 ; /* start with the first item selected */
                                    /* specify the dialog box caption string */
            caMenu.cCaption = (char FAR *) cCaption ;
            caMenu.cBuf = (char FAR *) cMenuNames ;
            break ;
```
[Other program lines]

CHAPTER 11

Other Resources

This is the last of the chapters on resources. So far the focus has been on the most common types of resources: menus, dialog boxes, icons, and bitmaps. These common resource types are usually created interactively, using the editing tools provided by Borland, Microsoft, and other companies. Resource files can contain more than these predefined types of resources. Essentially any type of static data (data that does not change as the program runs) can be stored as part of the program's resources. There are several advantages to storing static data in resources, compared with storing the data as part of the program's code. Resource data makes full use of Windows' memory optimization functions and can be loaded and unloaded from memory as needed to make room for other objects. Resources are also convenient for the programmer because they group all of the static data in a single location, which makes updating the program more straightforward. You can even have different versions of the resource data for different languages (French, Spanish, etc.) without changing the C language portion of the program.

This chapter's examples will cover several types of resource data, including grouping all of the program's text in a string table, adding a raw text file to the resource script file, and storing numeric data as resources. The last subject will introduce managing objects in memory. This chapter will limit the discussion to managing resource data, which leads into the broader discussion in the next chapter of allocating and manipulating memory blocks for all types of data.

Concepts Covered

String Tables
Conditional Compilation
User-Defined Resources

Resources in Separate Files
"Back-words" Storage Format of Numbers in Memory

Keywords Covered

STRINGTABLE
RCDATA
#ifdef

#else
#endif

Functions Covered

DrawText()
SetRect()
LoadString()
FindResource()

LoadResource()
LockResource()
GlobalUnlock()

String Tables

Up to this point, the example programs have put character strings directly into the C program source code with statements like:

```
static char  szMessage [] = "This string will become static data." ;
```

The C language "static" key word is included just for clarity here, as the character string will become static data without explicitly declaring *szMessage[]* as a static variable. In a Windows program, static variables are stored in the program's local heap. (Refer back to Chapter 1, *How Windows Works*, if you need to review the way Windows uses the local heap.) Windows keeps the local heap in memory as long as the program is running, so this character string will use up memory space whether or not it is about to be displayed. Programs with extensive text and other static data hog a lot of memory if all of the data is stored as static variables.

Another problem with putting character strings in the C program source code is that they are difficult to maintain. Imagine that your company decides to market the program in France and Canada and, therefore, wants all of the text that the user will see translated into French. The text strings will be scattered throughout the program, intermixed with program comments that you probably do not want translated. Worse, if you have the static text strings translated, you will end up with a different C program for English than for French. Every time you want to make a change in the program, you need to make the change in two different files, and compile twice. Wait until the boss asks for a German version....

Defining String Tables

Fortunately, Windows includes an easy to use method of storing text strings with the resource data, separate from the program's code. String tables are just what they sound like, a table or list of strings. The syntax for defining a string table in the resource script file is as follows:

```
STRINGTABLE [load option] [memory option]
BEGIN
    idNumber, "Text string 1 here"
    idNumber, "Text string 2 here"
    ...
END
```

There can be only one string table in a resource script file, so it is not given a title other than the "STRINGTABLE" key word. As with all resources, the string table can use either PRELOAD or LOADONCALL as the load options, and can use MOVEABLE, DISCARDABLE, or FIXED as memory options. The defaults are LOADONCALL, MOVEABLE, and DISCARDABLE, which are almost always what you will want with a string table, so you can just leave the load and memory options blank. Each line between the BEGIN and END statements defines a string. The string's ID number is defined first, followed by a comma, and the text string in double quotes.

Conditional Compilation of Resources

Although you can compile only one string table in a program's resources, you can include more than one string table definition in the program's resource script statement by taking advantage of *conditional compilation.* This is done using the resource compiler key words #ifdef, #else, and #endif. The idea is that if a constant is defined, one portion of the resource script file is compiled. If the constant is not defined, the alternative portion of the file is compiled. This is ideal for cases where you want to have more than one language in the same resource script file for menus, string tables, dialog boxes, and so on.

Listing 11-1 shows a short resource file including a string table, with three character strings defined. In this case, there are two alternative string tables, one for a French version of the program and a second for an English version. Remember that the resource compiler can only compile one string table in a resource script file. Only one of these two string tables will be used, as they are surrounded in the #ifdef, #else, and #endif conditional statements. With the second line defining the constant FRENCH, the French language portion of the resource script file is compiled. If the constant FRENCH is not defined, the lower (English) string table will be added to the program's resources.

Listing 11-1 Example String Tables

```
/* example.rc  resource script file using string tables and two languages */

#define  FRENCH       /* define the constant FRENCH */
#include "example.h"  /* include the header file */

#ifdef FRENCH         /* compile this section if FRENCH is defined */

STRINGTABLE
BEGIN
    S_HELP ,            "Utiliser F1 pour l'assistance."
    S_PROGRAMCAPTION,   "Programme Fou"
    S_SERIOUSTEXT,      "Trouvais une problème sérieux - Progamme s'arrête"
END

#else                 /* otherwise compile this section */

STRINGTABLE
BEGIN
    S_HELP ,            "Hit the F1 key for help"
    S_PROGRAMCAPTION,   "Silly Program"
    S_SERIOUSTEXT,      "Encountered a serious error - program to terminate."
END

#endif
```

Note in Listing 11-1 that the same ID numbers are used for both the English and French versions, so no change to the program's code will be needed, regardless of which language is being used. The ID numbers are defined in the program's header file, as shown in Listing 11-2.

Listing 11-2 Header File Containing String Table ID Numbers

```
/* example.h  header file */

#define S_HELP            1
#define S_PROGRAMCAPTION  2
#define S_SERIOUSTEXT     3
```

You can also use conditional compilation in C programs for similar purposes. A common use is to surround debugging portions of the program with #ifdef DEBUG and #endif statements. Unless the constant DEBUG is defined, the debug code is left out of the program.

Using the String Data

Within the body of the program, you will use the LoadString() function to load a string table into memory. The program's instance handle is passed to LoadString() so that Windows knows where to find the string table data, the ID number of the string, a pointer to a character buffer to hold the string, and the maximum length of the string to copy to buffer (so as not to write past the end of the buffer). The string is then loaded from the program's resource data and copied into the buffer. Listing 11-3 shows a typical program excerpt, loading the string with the ID value S_SERIOUSTEXT.

Listing 11-3 Displaying a String from a String Table

```
HANDLE     hInstance ;
char       cBuf [128] ;     /* automatic variable, stored on program's stack */
int        nTextLong ;

hInstance = GetWindowWord (hWnd, GWW_HINSTANCE) ;
nTextLong = LoadString (hInstance, S_SERIOUSTEXT, cBuf, sizeof (cBuf)) ;
TextOut (hDC, 0, 0, cBuf, nTextLong) ;
```
[Other program lines]

LoadString() returns the number of characters loaded. This number will be equal to or less than the size of the buffer passed to LoadString() as the fourth parameter. Note in Listing 11-3 that the C language sizeof() function is used to pass the length of the *cBuf[]* buffer to LoadString(). If the string in the string table is longer than *cBuf[]*, it is simply truncated to fit.

Note that the string is copied to an automatic variable *cBuf[]*, which is stored on the program's stack. Automatic variables are ideal for temporarily storing strings, as the stack gets reused (deleting the string) as soon as execution passes to another function in the program. Loading all of strings from the string table into a group of static text buffers would be a complete waste, as the data would still end up occupying space in the local heap.

A String Table Example

The first example program in this chapter is called STRTAB, short for string table. STRTAB demonstrates using string tables for three purposes: setting the program's title, displaying text in the program's client area, and specifying text for a message box. Figure 11-1 shows STRTAB in action, with the message box and client area strings visible.

All of the text visible in Figure 11-1, including the menu and the program's caption, is defined in the STRTAB.RC resource script file, shown in Listing 11-4. The first string in the string table demonstrates how to embed unprintable characters into the string in a string table. The resource compiler recognizes three digits preceded by a "\" character as an octal constant. Unlike hexadecimal numbers (0x4A26), octal constants can be embedded in a string and are interpreted as a number by the resource compiler, rather than as just character data. Octal numbers use base eight and were once commonly used by computer programmers, but no longer much in use. The only three characters you are likely to need are

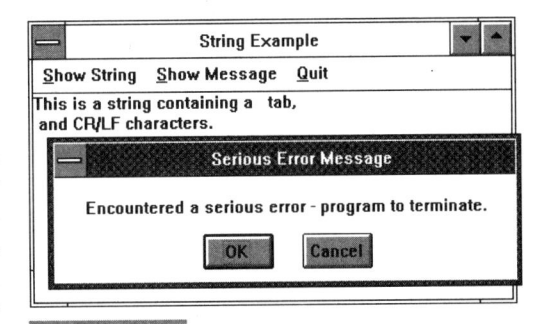

Figure 11-1 The STRTAB Program

the tab character (\011 octal) and the carriage return, line feed combination to start a new line (\012\015 octal). You can see the effect of these unprintable characters on the text in the main Windows' client area in Figure 11-1.

Listing 11-4 STRTAB.RC Resource Script File

```
/* strtab.rc resource file */

#include "strtab.h"

MyIcon      ICON    strtab.ico

MyMenu      MENU
BEGIN
    MENUITEM "&Show String",    IDM_MES1
    MENUITEM "&Show Message",   IDM_MES2
    MENUITEM "&Quit",           IDM_QUIT
END

STRINGTABLE
BEGIN
    S_GENERAL, "This is a string containing a \011tab,\012\015 and CR/LF characters."
    S_SERIOUSTITLE, "Serious Error Message"
    S_SERIOUSTEXT, "Encountered a serious error - program to terminate."
    S_PROGRAMCAPTION, "String Example"
END
```

STRTAB also needs a header file to define the menu item and string table ID numbers. Listing 11-5 shows the STRTAB.H file. The header file also includes the function declarations, including the declaration of the StringTableMessage() function, which is defined in the STRTAB.C program.

Listing 11-5 STRTAB.H Header File

```
/* strtab.h header file */

#define IDM_QUIT            1   /* menu item id number */
#define IDM_MES1            2
#define IDM_MES2            3

#define S_GENERAL           1   /* string table ID numbers */
#define S_SERIOUSTITLE      2
#define S_SERIOUSTEXT       3
#define S_PROGRAMCAPTION    4

long FAR PASCAL WndProc (HWND, WORD, WORD, LONG) ;
int StringTableMessage (HWND hWnd, int nTitleString, int nTextString) ;
```

The STRTAB.C Program

Listing 11-6 shows STRTAB.C, with the program lines specific to string tables highlighted. The string S_PROGRAMCAPTION is loaded in WinMain() to pass the program title to the CreateWindow() function.

The S_GENERAL string, containing the embedded tab and CR/LF characters, is output when the user selects the IDM_MES1 menu item. The normal TextOut() function will not expand tabs or show multiple lines, so it is not used here. The TabbedTextOut() function will expand tabs, but is also restricted to one line of output. To show the complete S_GENERAL text string, a more sophisticated text output function is used: DrawText(). DrawText() outputs text within the bounds of a rectangle, expands tabs, starts new lines after CR/LF pairs, and will add extra CR/LF pairs as needed to fit the text into a rectangle.

To keep the example simple, the bounding rectangle for the DrawText() function is set using the SetRect() function. SetRect() allows you to set all four values of a RECT data structure in one function call. In case you have forgotten about the RECT data structure (it was introduced in Chapter 4, *Text and Graphics Functions*), it is defined in WINDOWS.H as follows:

```
typedef struct tagRECT
  {
    int    left;
    int    top;
    int    right;
    int    bottom;
  } RECT;
#endif

typedef RECT          *PRECT;
typedef RECT NEAR     *NPRECT;
typedef RECT FAR      *LPRECT;
```

The RECT data structure defines a rectangle in terms of its upper left and lower right corners. You can skip the SetRect() function, and enter the values for each of the elements of a RECT structure individually. The two examples in Table 11-1 are equivalent, although SetRect() saves some wear and tear on the keyboard when you type in a program.

SETTING EACH MEMBER	USING THE SETRECT() FUNCTION
RECT rRectangle ; rRectangle.left = 10 ; rRectangle.right = 20 ; rRectangle.right = 30 ; rRectangle.bottom = 40 ;	RECT rRectangle ; SetRect (&rRectangle, 10, 20, 30, 40) ;

Table 11-1 Setting the Values for a RECT Data Structure

When the user selects the menu item with the IDM_MES2 ID value, STRTAB executes the StringTableMessage() function, defined at the bottom of the listing. StringTableMessage() is a handy function that displays a message box with a caption and text string defined by two string table ID values. The message box also displays an "OK" and "Cancel" button. After the user selects one of the two buttons, StringTableMessage() will return an integer, with a value being equal to either IDOK or IDCANCEL. IDOK and

IDCANCEL are defined in WINDOWS.H as predefined values that the MessageBox() function can return. You will find StringTableMessage() useful in any application that uses string tables.

Listing 11-6 STRTAB.C

```c
/* strtab.c   using a string table */

#include <windows.h>
#include "strtab.h"

int PASCAL WinMain (HANDLE hInstance, HANDLE hPrevInstance, LPSTR lpszCmdLine,
    int nCmdShow)
{
    HWND       hWnd ;           /* the Windows' "handle" */
    MSG        msg ;            /* a message structure */
    WNDCLASS   wndclass ;       /* window class structure */
    char       cBuf [128] ;     /* to hold text string */

    if (!hPrevInstance)
    {
        wndclass.style         = CS_HREDRAW | CS_VREDRAW ;
        wndclass.lpfnWndProc   = WndProc ;
        wndclass.cbClsExtra    = 0 ;
        wndclass.cbWndExtra    = 0 ;
        wndclass.hInstance     = hInstance ;
        wndclass.hIcon         = LoadIcon (hInstance, "MyIcon") ;
        wndclass.hCursor       = LoadCursor (NULL, IDC_ARROW) ;
        wndclass.hbrBackground = GetStockObject (WHITE_BRUSH) ;
        wndclass.lpszMenuName  = "MyMenu" ;
        wndclass.lpszClassName = "MyClass" ;
                    /* register the window class */
        if (!RegisterClass (&wndclass))
            return 0 ;
    }
        /* load program caption from string table */
    LoadString (hInstance, S_PROGRAMCAPTION, cBuf, sizeof (cBuf)) ;

    hWnd = CreateWindow ("MyClass", cBuf, WS_OVERLAPPEDWINDOW,
        CW_USEDEFAULT, CW_USEDEFAULT, CW_USEDEFAULT, CW_USEDEFAULT,
        NULL, NULL, hInstance, NULL) ;
    ShowWindow (hWnd, nCmdShow) ;      /* display the window */

    while (GetMessage (&msg, NULL, NULL, NULL))   /* message loop */
    {
        TranslateMessage (&msg) ;      /* translate keyboard messages */
        DispatchMessage (&msg) ;       /* send message to WndProc() */
    }
    return (msg.wParam) ;
}

long FAR PASCAL WndProc (HWND hWnd, WORD wMessage, WORD wParam, LONG lParam)
{
    HANDLE   hInstance ;
    char     cBuf [128] ;
```

```
    HDC     hDC ;
    RECT    rDrawRectangle ;

    switch (wMessage)           /* process windows messages */
    {
      case WM_COMMAND:
          switch (wParam)
          {
            case IDM_MES1:   /* demo tabbed string to client area */
                SetRect (&rDrawRectangle, 0, 0, 400, 100) ;
                hDC = GetDC (hWnd) ;
                hInstance = GetWindowWord (hWnd, GWW_HINSTANCE) ;
                LoadString (hInstance, S_GENERAL, cBuf, sizeof (cBuf)) ;
                DrawText (hDC, cBuf, lstrlen (cBuf), &rDrawRectangle,
                    DT_EXPANDTABS) ;
                ReleaseDC (hWnd, hDC) ;
                break ;
            case IDM_MES2:          /* demo using a string table in msg box */
                StringTableMessage (hWnd, S_SERIOUSTITLE, S_SERIOUSTEXT) ;
                break ;
            case IDM_QUIT:          /* Quit menu item */
                DestroyWindow (hWnd) ;   /* destroy window, */
                break ;                  /* terminating application */
            default:                     /* otherwise, let Windows process it */
                return (DefWindowProc (hWnd, wMessage, wParam, lParam)) ;
          }
          break ;
      case WM_DESTROY:              /* stop application */
          PostQuitMessage (0) ;
          break ;
      default:                       /* default windows message processing */
          return (DefWindowProc (hWnd, wMessage, wParam, lParam)) ;
    }
    return (0L) ;
}

/* put a message box on screen, using title and text from string table */

int StringTableMessage (HWND hWnd, int nTitleString, int nTextString)
{
    HANDLE  hInstance ;
    char    cTitle [128], cText [128] ;

    hInstance = GetWindowWord (hWnd, GWW_HINSTANCE) ;
    LoadString (hInstance, nTitleString, cTitle, sizeof (cTitle)) ;
    LoadString (hInstance, nTextString, cText, sizeof (cText)) ;
    return (MessageBox (hWnd, cText, cTitle, MB_OKCANCEL)) ;
}
```

STRTAB requires the usual module definition file, project file, and program icon to be complete. These are shown in Listing 11-7 to 11-9 and Figure 11-2 respectively.

Listing 11-7 STRTAB.DEF Module Definition File

```
NAME            strtab
DESCRIPTION     'String table example'
```

```
EXETYPE       WINDOWS
STUB          'WINSTUB.EXE'
CODE          PRELOAD MOVEABLE
DATA          PRELOAD MOVEABLE MULTIPLE
HEAPSIZE      1024
STACKSIZE     5120
EXPORTS       WndProc
```

Listing 11-8 Turbo C++ Project File for STRTAB

```
strtab.c
strtab.def
strtab.res
```

Figure 11-2
STRTAB.ICO
Icon Image

Listing 11-9 QuickC Project File for STRTAB

```
strtab.c
strtab.def
strtab.rc
```

User-Defined Resources

String tables are ideal for single line text entries, but they run out of steam when you need to include a larger block of text. Windows does not include any other predefined way to store blocks of text, but does allow you to define your own resource types. The next example does this, creating the new resource type called "TEXT."

As an example, imagine that you need to display one or more paragraphs of text in a part of a program, perhaps as instructions for the user. There are several ways to go about doing this. One is to add the block of data right into the program's code as static text. The introduction to string tables earlier in this chapter explained why this approach is not such a good idea. You could also keep the text in a separate file, and read the file from disk when it is needed. This method gets messy if you have a lot of little files that need to be available for your program to work, and it complicates program maintenance and installation.

An almost ideal solution is to add the text data to the program's resources. This makes the text part of the program, so the end user does not end up with a lot of little files on his or her hard disk. Resources can be set to be LOADONCALL and MOVEABLE plus DISCARDABLE (the default values), so they do not have the memory consumption problems of static text strings.

Resource Data in a Separate File

The next example program, named RESOR1, includes a block of text that is added to the program as resource data. During program development, the text is stored in a separate file, although it is added to the finished program during the compilation phase. The initial TESTTEXT.TXT file (shown in Listing 11-10) is a standard ANSI text file, which can be created with the Notepad application. The only thing special about the file is that the end of the file is marked with a tilde (~) character. The tilde will be used by the RESOR1 program to locate the end of the text data when it is loaded into memory.

Listing 11-10 TESTTEXT.TXT Text File

```
This is a bunch of text created with the notepad
application. Each line ends in a CR/LF pair.
This data is arbitrary, but allows the program
RESOR1 to demonstrate loading special resource
data that is not of a predefined resource type.
The end of the file is marked with a tilde.~
```

The text data can be easily added to a program's resource file. Listing 11-11 shows the RESOR1.RC resource script file. The TESTTEXT.TXT file is assigned the resource type "TEXT," and given the resource name "paragraph." "TEXT" is not a standard resource type like MENU, ICON, or STRINGTABLE, so RESOR1.RC invents this new resource type by simply using it as shown in Listing 11-11. The effect is that the text file is inserted into the program's resource data, assigned the name "paragraph," and assigned the resource type "TEXT." We use the "paragraph" and "TEXT" words defined in the resource script file to find and load this special data into memory when the RESOR1 program needs it.

Listing 11-11 RESOR1.RC Resource Script File

```
/* resor1.rc resource file */

#include "resor1.h"

MyIcon      ICON      resor1.ico       /* standard resource type ICON */
paragraph   TEXT      testtext.txt     /* custom resource type TEXT */

MyMenu      MENU
BEGIN
    MENUITEM "&Quit",      IDM_QUIT
END

STRINGTABLE
BEGIN
    S_PROGRAMCAPTION, "Custom Resource Example"
END
```

The rest of the RESOR1.RC program is pretty standard, with a simple menu and string table defined, along with the program's icon. You may notice the parallel between the inclusion of the icon data and the text data. ICON happens to be a predefined key word that the resource compiler recognizes, but the effect is the same. The data from the icon file RESOR1.ICO is added to the program's resources, and assigned the name "MyIcon" and the resource type "ICON." The only difference is that Windows does not have a special loading function like LoadIcon() for the text data, because TEXT is not a standard resource type. The TEXT data will need to be loaded into memory using lower level functions.

Locating and Loading a Custom Resource

To use the text data in the program, we need three general purpose functions for dealing with resources: FindResource(), LoadResource(), and LockResource(). These functions take the place of the specialized resource functions LoadAccelerators(), LoadBitmap(), LoadCursor(), LoadIcon(), LoadMenu(), and LoadString() which work for the predefined resource types, but which will not handle user-defined resources, such as the TEXT resource type created in RESOR1.RC.

The basic sequence to load a user-defined resource into memory is:

1. Use the FindResource() function to locate the specific resource in the program's resource data. FindResource() returns a handle to the relative location of the resource in the resource data. This is not a handle to the resource in memory.
2. Use LoadResource() to load the resource data into memory. LoadResource() returns a handle to the data in memory.
3. Use LockResource() to lock the data in memory before it is accessed. Otherwise, the resource data could be moved by Windows. LockResource() returns a pointer to the data in memory.
4. Use UnlockResource() to free the resource data as soon as possible, so that it does not inhibit Windows' memory optimization.

If you want to deliberately purge a resource from memory, use the FreeResource() function. Windows automatically frees all resource data associated with a program instance when the program terminates, so you do not have to call FreeResource(). By default, resources are both moveable and discardable and do not get in the way of Windows' memory optimization efforts, except for the brief period of time from when you call LockResource() to access the data until you call UnlockResource() to make the data moveable (and discardable) again. You will want LockResource() and UnlockResource() to be as close together in your program's code as possible to minimize the amount of time that the resource is fixed in memory.

Listing 11-12 shows a typical program fragment which accesses a custom resource of the type "TEXT" named "paragraph," and outputs the first 25 characters to the device context.

Listing 11-12 Loading and Accessing the "TEXT" Custom Resource "OneLine"

```
HANDLE   hInstance, hResTemp, hResourceData ;
LPSTR    lpResData ;              /* a pointer to data in memory */
HDC      hDC ;                    /* divide context handle for TextOut() */

hDC = GetDC (hWnd) ;
hInstance = GetWindowWord (hWnd, GWW_HINSTANCE) ;

hResTemp = FindResource (hInstance, "paragraph", "TEXT") ;
hTextResource = LoadResource (hInstance, hResTemp) ;
if (hTextResource)      /* if found resource data */
{
                /* lock resource in memory */
```

```
    lpResData = LockResource (hTextResource);
    /* lpResData now points to locked data in memory */

    TextOut (hDC, 0, 0, lpResData, 25);
                /* unlock resource in memory */
    GlobalUnlock (hTextResource);
                /* explicit purge from memory */
    FreeResource (hTextResource);
}
```
[Other program lines]

For clarity, Listing 11-12 shows the FindResource() function returning the *hResTemp* handle to the resource data, and the handle is then passed on to LoadResource() to load the data into memory. The *hResTemp* variable does not accomplish anything, so most programmers use a shorthand notation, combining the FindResource() and LoadResource() function calls into one program phrase:

```
hTextResource = LoadResource (hInstance,
    FindResource (hInstance, "OneLine", "TEXT"));
```

One basic rule that must be obeyed is that resource data, even resource data locked in memory, is read-only. You cannot modify resource data. If you want to do anything other than read the data, copy the resource data into a local memory buffer, and then make the changes.

The RESOR1 Program

The RESOR1.C program (Listing 11-13) puts the techniques discussed in the previous section to work to load the paragraph of TEXT data defined in the RESOR1.RC resource script file, and displays the text on the screen. The result is shown in Figure 11-3, which shows the RESOR1 program in action, correctly displaying the text data.

One complication when loading user-defined resource data is that there is no predefined way for Windows to find the end of the data. Windows includes a SizeofResource() function, but this function returns the minimum size the resource will occupy in memory, not the actual size of the resource data. Windows deals with user-defined resources in blocks of memory sized at multiples of 512 bytes, so the text resource will occupy 512 bytes in memory, even though there are less than 512 characters in the file. SizeofResource() will return 512, not the length of the text.

To get around this problem, the end of the text data is marked with an unusual character, in this case a tilde (~). Any character not used in the body of the text would do. RESOR1 then reads through the resource data until it finds the tilde, to find the length of the text string. This can be done only after the resource data has been loaded and locked in memory with LockResource().

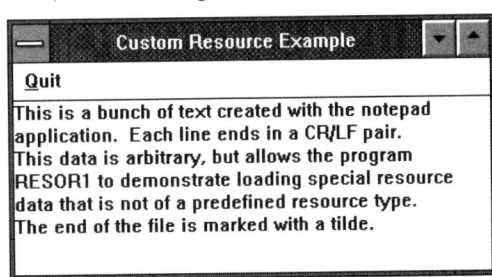

Figure 11-3 The RESOR1 Program

The pointer to the locked resource data and the length of the string are passed to the DrawText() function to actually display the text data.

Note in the RESOR1.C program that the resource data is not copied to a local character buffer before determining the location of the tilde character, or before sending the data to the DrawText() function to display it. Locating the tilde and using DrawText() are both read-only activities that do not attempt to modify the resource data in memory. As long as you do not attempt to write to the resource data, you can treat a locked resource like any other memory address, just as if the text were stored as static data. Just remember not to attempt to change any of the resource data, and don't forget to unlock the data as soon as you have finished reading it.

Listing 11-13 RESOR1.C

```
/* resor1.c   Loading a custom resource */

#include <windows.h>
#include "resor1.h"

int PASCAL WinMain (HANDLE hInstance, HANDLE hPrevInstance, LPSTR lpszCmdLine,
    int nCmdShow)
{
    HWND        hWnd ;              /* the Windows' "handle" */
    MSG         msg ;               /* a message structure */
    WNDCLASS    wndclass ;          /* window class structure */
    char        cBuf [128] ;        /* to hold text string */

    if (!hPrevInstance)
    {
        wndclass.style          = CS_HREDRAW | CS_VREDRAW ;
        wndclass.lpfnWndProc    = WndProc ;
        wndclass.cbClsExtra     = 0 ;
        wndclass.cbWndExtra     = 0 ;
        wndclass.hInstance      = hInstance ;
        wndclass.hIcon          = LoadIcon (hInstance, "MyIcon") ;
        wndclass.hCursor        = LoadCursor (NULL, IDC_ARROW) ;
        wndclass.hbrBackground  = GetStockObject (WHITE_BRUSH) ;
        wndclass.lpszMenuName   = "MyMenu" ;
        wndclass.lpszClassName  = "MyClass" ;
                /* register the window class */
        if (!RegisterClass (&wndclass))
            return 0 ;
    }
        /* load program caption from string table */
    LoadString (hInstance, S_PROGRAMCAPTION, cBuf, sizeof (cBuf)) ;

    hWnd = CreateWindow ("MyClass", cBuf, WS_OVERLAPPEDWINDOW,
        CW_USEDEFAULT, CW_USEDEFAULT, CW_USEDEFAULT, CW_USEDEFAULT,
        NULL, NULL, hInstance, NULL) ;
    ShowWindow (hWnd, nCmdShow) ;    /* display the window */

    while (GetMessage (&msg, NULL, NULL, NULL))   /* message loop */
    {
        TranslateMessage (&msg) ;    /* translate keyboard messages */
```

```
            DispatchMessage (&msg) ;        /* send message to WndProc() */
    }
    return (msg.wParam) ;
}

long FAR PASCAL WndProc (HWND hWnd, WORD wMessage, WORD wParam, LONG lParam)
{
    PAINTSTRUCT      ps ;
    HANDLE           hTextResource, hInstance ;
    int              nTextLong ;
    LPSTR            lpResData, lpStr ;
    static RECT      rClient ;

    switch (wMessage)      /* process windows messages */
    {
        case WM_SIZE :     /* save client area size as RECT */
            SetRect (&rClient, 0, 0, LOWORD (lParam), HIWORD (lParam)) ;
            break ;
        case WM_PAINT:
            hInstance = GetWindowWord (hWnd, GWW_HINSTANCE) ;
            hTextResource = LoadResource (hInstance,
                FindResource (hInstance, "paragraph","TEXT")) ;
            if (hTextResource)              /* if found resource data */
                                            /* determine length */
            {                               /* lock resource in memory */
                lpResData = LockResource (hTextResource) ;
                nTextLong = 0 ;
                lpStr = lpResData ;
                while (*lpStr++ != _~ )     /* count chars to tilde */
                    nTextLong++ ;
                BeginPaint (hWnd, &ps) ;    /* output text */
                DrawText (ps.hdc, lpResData, nTextLong, &rClient,
                    DT_EXPANDTABS | DT_WORDBREAK) ;
                EndPaint (hWnd, &ps) ;
                                            /* unlock resource in memory */
                GlobalUnlock (hTextResource) ;
            }
            break ;
        case WM_COMMAND:
            switch (wParam)
            {
                case IDM_QUIT:              /* Quit menu item */
                    DestroyWindow (hWnd) ;  /* destroy window, */
                    break ;                 /* terminating application */
            }
            break ;
        case WM_DESTROY:                    /* stop application */
            PostQuitMessage (0) ;
            break ;
        default:           /* default windows message processing */
            return (DefWindowProc (hWnd, wMessage, wParam, lParam)) ;
    }
    return (0L) ;
}
```

You may have noticed that RESOR1.C does not include a call to FreeResource(). Instead the program takes advantage of Windows automatically removing all of the resources associated with the RESOR1 program when the program terminates.

Chapter 11 • *Other Resources*   389

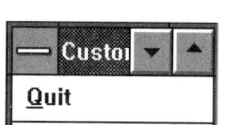

Exercising DrawText()

One extra bit of logic thrown into the RESOR1.C program is used to size the rectangle the text must fit into based on the size of the Windows' client area. WM_SIZE messages are processed, and the client area width and height are extracted from the low-order and high-order WORDS of the *lParam* value passed with WM_SIZE. The client area size is stored in the RECT data structure *rClient*, ready to be passed to the DrawText function. If the client area is larger than the one that the block of text occupies, DrawText() respects the CR/LF hard carriage return characters in the resource data and breaks each line at those positions. However, if the client area is narrower than the text lines, DrawText() inserts additional CR/LF pairs to make the text fit the space available. Figure 11-4 shows an example, with the RESOR1 window sized with a narrow width. You can use the power of the DrawText() function to format long character strings that do not have embedded CR/LF pairs.

Figure 11-4 The RESOR1 Program with a Narrow Client Area

Figure 11-5 RESOR1.ICO Icon Image

Other Program Files for RESOR1

Listings 11-14 to 11-17 show the support files for RESOR1. The program's icon is shown in Figure 11-5.

Listing 11-14 RESOR1.H Header File

```
/* resor1.h header file */

#define IDM_QUIT              1       /* menu item id number */
#define S_PROGRAMCAPTION      2       /* string table id value */

long FAR PASCAL WndProc (HWND, WORD, WORD, LONG) ;
```

Listing 11-15 RESOR1.DEF Module Definition File

```
NAME            resor1
DESCRIPTION     'User-defined resource example'
EXETYPE         WINDOWS
STUB            'WINSTUB.EXE'
CODE            PRELOAD MOVEABLE DISCARDABLE
DATA            PRELOAD MOVEABLE MULTIPLE
HEAPSIZE        1024
STACKSIZE       5120
EXPORTS         WndProc
```

Listing 11-16 Turbo C++ Project File for RESOR1

```
resor1.c
resor1.def
resor1.res
```

Listing 11-17 QuickC Project File for RESOR1

```
resor1.c
resor1.def
resor1.rc
```

The RCDATA Statement

The RESOR1 program demonstrated how to include user-defined resources that are located in separate files in the program's resource data. This is frequently the most convenient way to add text and tables of numbers to a program's resources, but there is a drawback. Because the user-defined data (the paragraph of text) is kept in a separate file, the programmer will need to keep track of this file during future program updates. If there are many such files included in the program's resources, updates can be complicated, because each of the files must be updated separately. Putting resource data in separate files is not a problem to the end user of the program, as the data is ultimately included in the program's resources, and becomes part of the finished program's .EXE file.

Windows provides the alternative method of including user-defined data directly in the resource script file. The RCDATA statement can be used in the program's resource script file to include any collection of numeric and/or character data desired. The complete syntax of the RCDATA statement is as follows:

```
ResName RCDATA [load option] [memory option]
BEGIN
    /* the data goes here */
END
```

As always, you can specify a load option of either PRELOAD or LOADONCALL, and a memory option of FIXED, MOVEABLE, or MOVEABLE and DISCARDABLE. The defaults are LOADONCALL, MOVEABLE, and DISCARDABLE. The actual data between the BEGIN and END statements is limited to integers and characters, which are the only two types of entries the resource compiler understands. You cannot put floating point (decimal) numbers directly in the resource data because any digits after the decimal will be ignored. Each entry in the resource data is separated from the previous one with a comma. Character strings are surrounded in double quotes. Integers can be shown in decimal notation (1234), hexadecimal (0x24b7), and octal preceded by a "\" character (\015).

Our next example program uses the RCDATA statement to include three integer values and a character string as a single block of resource data. Listing 11-18 shows the RCDATA.RC resource script file, which includes the RCDATA statement at the end of the listing. In this case, the resource data is given the name "Arbitrary," and specifically assigned the memory options PRELOAD and MOVEABLE. Because the DISCARDABLE memory option was not selected, the "Arbitrary" data will be moveable in memory, but will not be discarded if Windows runs short on memory space. The selection of PRELOAD and MOVEABLE in RCDATA.RC is purely for demonstration purposes. Normally, you will use the default LOADONCALL, MOVEABLE, and DISCARDABLE options.

Listing 11-18 RCDATA.RC Resource Script File

```
/* rcdata.rc  resource file */

#include "rcdata.h"

MyIcon     ICON    rcdata.ico

MyMenu     MENU
BEGIN
    MENUITEM "&Show Data",      IDM_SHOW
    MENUITEM "&Quit",           IDM_QUIT
END

STRINGTABLE
BEGIN
    S_PROGRAMCAPTION, "RCDATA Example"
    S_DATAHEADING, "Here is the RCDATA in hexadecimal and ANSI:"
END

Arbitrary RCDATA PRELOAD MOVEABLE
BEGIN
    5, 11056, 0x2d,              /* three integers */
    "A String\0"                 /* null terminated string */
END
```

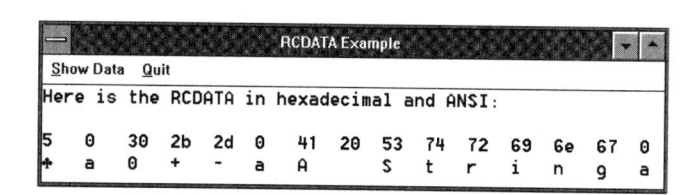

Figure 11-6 The RCDATA Program

Figure 11-6 shows the RCDATA program in operation, after the user has selected the "Show Data" menu item. The upper line of data shows every byte from the resource in hexadecimal notation. The lower line shows each byte interpreted as a character. Neither representation is appropriate for all of the data, as the data consists of both numbers and characters. One thing you may notice in looking at the hexadecimal representation of the numbers is that they are stored in reverse order. The least significant byte (word) is stored before the most significant byte. This "back-words" storage format for integer data in resources matches the way that integers are stored in memory for computers with the 80x86 CPU chips that Windows runs on. The resource data can, therefore, be used without changing the order of the bytes.

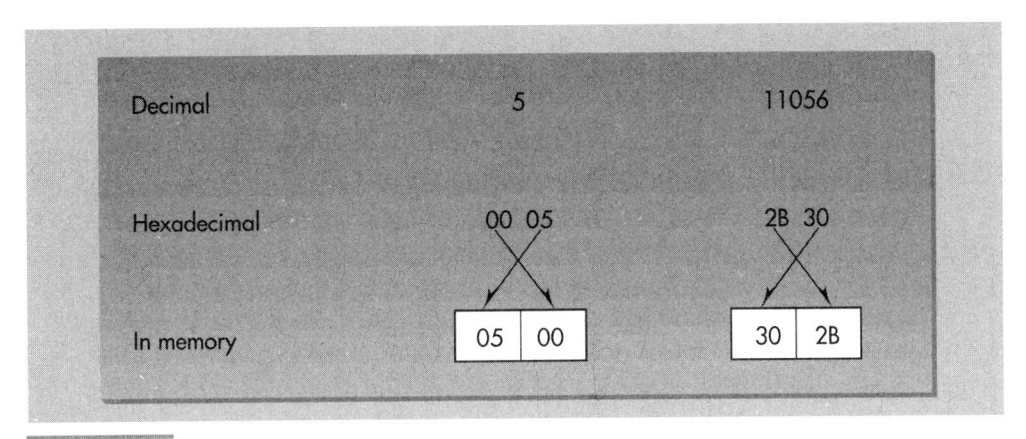

Decimal	5	11056
Hexadecimal	00 05	2B 30
In memory	05 00	30 2B

Figure 11-7 How Integers are Stored in Memory and in Resource Data

Figure 11-7 shows the "back-words" storage format breakdown for the first two integers stored in the resource data, 5 and 11056 decimal. You can match the "in memory" representation with the output of the RCDATA program in Figure 11-7. The first six characters shown below the hexadecimal numbers in Figure 11-7 are the characters that happen to be defined for these byte values in the ANSI_FIXED_FONT character set used in the example. They are only meaningful for the character data "A String" defined at the end of the resource data.

The key thing to realize from the RCDATA example is that the resource data ends up as a block of bytes. There is no internal structure to the data, other than the order which you specify in the RCDATA statement in the program's resource script file. The program must interpret each byte of data as either character or numeric data when the resource data is read into memory.

The RCDATA Example Program

Continuing with the example, Listing 11-19 shows the RCDATA.C program. RCDATA.C is similar to the last example RESOR1.C. The main difference is that the output data is only displayed when the user selects the "Show Data" menu item with RCDATA, while RESOR1 processed WM_PAINT messages to keep the client area painted with the resource text data. The loading of the resource data is almost identical for data stored in the resource script file using the RCDATA statement, as compared with loading a user-defined resource stored in a separate file. The sequence of function calls to load the RCDATA is as follows:

1. FindResource() is used to locate the data in the program's resources. WINDOWS.H defines the special flag RT_RCDATA which is used as the last parameter when calling FindResource() to locate data stored as RCDATA in the program's resource script file.
2. LoadResource() is used to load the resource data into memory.
3. LockResource() is used to fix the resource data in memory, and returns a pointer (the address) of the data in memory.

4. The data is read, but cannot be written to.
5. GlobalUnlock() is used to allow Windows to move the resource data in memory, and discard the data if the resource is discardable.
6. FreeResource() can be used to explicitly remove the resource data from memory. Otherwise, the data will be removed from memory when the program terminates.

RCDATA.C in Listing 11-19 follows this pattern exactly, although the FreeResource() function is not used to explicitly remove the resource data from memory. The TextOut() function is used to display each byte of data in the resource data, using the wsprintf() function to format the data first as hexadecimal digits, and second as text characters.

Listing 11-19 RCDATA.C

```
/* rcdata.c   loading a custom resource */

#include <windows.h>
#include "rcdata.h"

int PASCAL WinMain (HANDLE hInstance, HANDLE hPrevInstance, LPSTR lpszCmdLine,
    int nCmdShow)
{
    HWND       hWnd ;            /* the Windows' "handle" */
    MSG        msg ;             /* a message structure */
    WNDCLASS   wndclass ;        /* window class structure */
    char       cBuf [128] ;      /* to hold text string */

    if (!hPrevInstance)
    {
        wndclass.style         = CS_HREDRAW | CS_VREDRAW ;
        wndclass.lpfnWndProc   = WndProc ;
        wndclass.cbClsExtra    = 0 ;
        wndclass.cbWndExtra    = 0 ;
        wndclass.hInstance     = hInstance ;
        wndclass.hIcon         = LoadIcon (hInstance, "MyIcon") ;
        wndclass.hCursor       = LoadCursor (NULL, IDC_ARROW) ;
        wndclass.hbrBackground = GetStockObject (WHITE_BRUSH) ;
        wndclass.lpszMenuName  = "MyMenu" ;
        wndclass.lpszClassName = "MyClass" ;
                /* register the window class */
        if (!RegisterClass (&wndclass))
          return 0 ;
    }
    /* load program caption from string table */
    LoadString (hInstance, S_PROGRAMCAPTION, cBuf, sizeof (cBuf)) ;

    hWnd = CreateWindow ("MyClass", cBuf, WS_OVERLAPPEDWINDOW,
        CW_USEDEFAULT, CW_USEDEFAULT, CW_USEDEFAULT, CW_USEDEFAULT,
        NULL, NULL, hInstance, NULL) ;
    ShowWindow (hWnd, nCmdShow) ;       /* display the window */
```

```c
    while (GetMessage (&msg, NULL, NULL, NULL))   /* message loop */
    {
        TranslateMessage (&msg) ;       /* translate keyboard messages */
        DispatchMessage (&msg) ;        /* send message to WndProc() */
    }
    return (msg.wParam) ;
}

long FAR PASCAL WndProc (HWND hWnd, WORD wMessage, WORD wParam, LONG lParam)
{
    HANDLE      hInstance, hData ;
    char        cBuf [128] ;
    HDC         hDC ;
    int         i, nCharX, nCharY ;
    LPSTR       lpData ;
    TEXTMETRIC  tm ;

    switch (wMessage)           /* process windows messages */
    {
        case WM_COMMAND:
            switch (wParam)     /* menu selections */
            {
                case IDM_SHOW:          /* show RCDATA in client area */
                    hDC = GetDC (hWnd) ;
                                /* select a fixed pitch font for spacing */
                    SelectObject (hDC, GetStockObject (OEM_FIXED_FONT)) ;
                                /* get character font sizes */
                    GetTextMetrics (hDC, &tm) ;
                    nCharX = tm.tmAveCharWidth * 4 ; /* horz spacing */
                    nCharY = tm.tmHeight + tm.tmExternalLeading ;
                                /* get instance handle for program */
                    hInstance = GetWindowWord (hWnd, GWW_HINSTANCE) ;
                                /* show heading from string table */
                    LoadString (hInstance, S_DATAHEADING, cBuf,
                            sizeof (cBuf)) ;
                    TextOut (hDC, 0, 0, cBuf, lstrlen (cBuf)) ;
                                /* show data in hexadecimal and ANSI */
                    hData = LoadResource (hInstance,
                            FindResource (hInstance, "Arbitrary", RT_RCDATA)) ;
                    if (hData)      /* if found resource data */
                    {               /* lock resource data in memory */
                        lpData = LockResource (hData) ;
                                /* display as both hex and char */
                        for (i = 0 ; i < 15 ; i++)
                        {           /* first output each byte as hexadecimal */
                            TextOut (hDC, i * nCharX, 2 * nCharY, cBuf,
                                wsprintf (cBuf, "%x", *lpData)) ;
                                /* then output as a character */
                            TextOut (hDC, i * nCharX, 3 * nCharY, cBuf,
                                wsprintf (cBuf, "%c", *lpData++)) ;
                        }
                        GlobalUnlock (hData) ; /* unlock data */
                    }
                    ReleaseDC (hWnd, hDC) ;
                    break ;
                case IDM_QUIT:          /* Quit menu item */
                    DestroyWindow (hWnd) ; /* destroy window, */
```

Chapter 11 • Other Resources

```
                    break ;            /* terminating application */
                default:               /* otherwise, let Windows process it */
                    return (DefWindowProc (hWnd, wMessage, wParam, lParam)) ;
            }
            break ;
        case WM_DESTROY:               /* stop application */
            PostQuitMessage (0) ;
            break ;
        default:                       /* default windows message processing */
            return (DefWindowProc (hWnd, wMessage, wParam, lParam)) ;
    }
    return (0L) ;
}
```

Listings 11-20 to 11-23 show the support files for RCDATA. The program's icon is shown in Figure 11-8.

Listing 11-20 RCDATA.H Header File

```
/* rcdata.h header file */

#define IDM_QUIT          1         /* menu item ID number */
#define IDM_SHOW          2

#define S_PROGRAMCAPTION  1         /* string table ID numbers */
#define S_DATAHEADING     2

long FAR PASCAL WndProc (HWND, WORD, WORD, LONG) ;
```

Figure 11-8
RCDATA.ICO
Icon Image

Listing 11-21 RCDATA.DEF Module Definition File

```
NAME            rcdata
DESCRIPTION     'RCDATA example'
EXETYPE         WINDOWS
STUB            'WINSTUB.EXE'
CODE            PRELOAD MOVEABLE DISCARDABLE
DATA            PRELOAD MOVEABLE MULTIPLE
HEAPSIZE        1024
STACKSIZE       5120
EXPORTS         WndProc
```

Listing 11-22 Turbo C++ Project File for RCDATA

```
rcdata.c
rcdata.def
rcdata.res
```

Listing 11-23 QuickC Project File for RCDATA

```
rcdata.c
rcdata.def
rcdata.rc
```

Summary

The Windows design encourages programmers to separate the program's code and static data. Resource data is used to store static data for Windows programs, in place of static data defined in the body of the C program. Using resources improves Windows' ability to optimize memory, and also makes the program easier to maintain. Essentially any type of data can be stored as resources, including the predefined resource types, such as menus, icons, accelerators, bitmaps, cursors, and string tables, as well as data in any arbitrary format using either the RCDATA statement, or by using a special user-defined resource type created by the program.

The resource compiler converts the raw .RC resource script file into the .RES format and attaches the .RES data to the program. The resource compiler has the ability to conditionally compile only portions of a resource script file by using the #ifdef, #else, and #endif conditional statements within the body of the resource script file.

String tables provide a convenient way to put all of the character strings used by a program into the resource script file. Larger blocks of data can be included in the resource data either by writing the data using an RCDATA block, or by including a separate file in the resource data as a user-defined data type. User-defined resources and RCDATA must be loaded using the FindResource(), LoadResource(), LockResource() function sequence because specialized functions, such as LoadIcon() and LoadMenu(), only exist for the predefined resource types.

By default, resource data is stored as moveable and discardable blocks of data in memory, and is only loaded into memory when needed. These default memory options should be used whenever possible to make the best use of available memory while the program is running. User-defined and RCDATA resource data must be locked in memory before it is read, and then immediately unlocked. Resource data can be read from memory after it is locked, but the locked memory block cannot be written to. The GlobalUnlock() function is used to unlock resource data in memory, so that Windows can move and possibly discard the data after it has been used. FreeResource() is used to explicitly remove a resource from memory, although Windows will do this automatically when the program terminates.

QUESTIONS

1. Static variables, such as static text, are stored in the program's: a) stack; b) local heap ; c) resources ; d) none of the above.
2. The default load and memory options for resources are: a) LOADONCALL; b) MOVEABLE; c) DISCARDABLE; d) all of the above.
3. You must load a string from a string table into a local memory buffer using LoadString() before modifying the string data. (True/False)
4. The following line in a program's resource script file:

    SomeData   NUMB   datatab.txt

    would load the data file _____ as a user-defined resource of type _____ .
5. The handle returned by the FindResource() function is passed to LoadResource() to load the resource data into memory. (True/False)
6. There is no reason to lock discardable resource data in memory before reading the data. (True/False)
7. The RCDATA statement in a resource script file allows you to put user-defined data in the block between the BEGIN and END statements following RCDATA. This data can consist of a) integers; b) character strings; c) floating-point numbers; d) a and b; e) a,b, and c).

EXERCISES

1. Change the resource data in the RESOR1 example program so that rather than being loaded from a separate text file, the resource data is included in the program's .RC file as RCDATA.
2. Add the integers 45, 33, 88, 982, and -12 to a program's RCDATA resources. Read the data into an array of integers, and then display each of the integer values in the program's client area. You can modify the RCDATA program for this example.

ANSWERS TO QUESTIONS

1. b.
2. d.
3. True.
4. DATATAB.TXT, NUMB.
5. True.
6. False. The block must be locked.
7. d. Floating point numbers are not correctly parsed by the resource compiler.

SOLUTIONS TO EXERCISES

1. The program's resource script file will need to be modified as shown in Listing 11-24. Each line of text must be surrounded in quotes, and the terminating CR/LF pairs added with octal constants to produce the same stored data as the separate text file.

Listing 11-24 Resource Script File for Exercise 1

```
/* c11exer1.rc  resource file */

#include "c11exer1.h"

MyIcon     ICON    c11exer1.ico              /* standard resource type ICON */

paragraph  RCDATA                            /* put paragraph in as RCDATA */
BEGIN
    "This is a bunch of text created with the notepad\012\015"
    "application. Each line ends in a CR/LF pair.\012\015"
    "This data is arbitrary, but allows the program\012\015"
    "RESOR1 to demonstrate loading special resource\012\015"
    "data that is not of a predefined resource type.\012\015"
    "The end of the file is marked with a tilde.~"
END

MyMenu     MENU
BEGIN
   MENUITEM "&Quit",      IDM_QUIT
END

STRINGTABLE
BEGIN
   S_PROGRAMCAPTION, "Custom Resource Example"
END
```

The only other change is to modify the FindResource() function call so that data of type RCDATA is being located, not a user-defined resource type.

```
hTextResource = LoadResource (hInstance,
FindResource (hInstance, "paragraph", RT_RCDATA)) ;
```

Otherwise, the C program is not changed. The complete solution is stored on the source code disks as C11EXER1.

2. The five integer values can be defined in the program's resource script file as follows:

```
Arbitrary RCDATA
BEGIN
   45, 33, 88, 982, -12
END
```

Chapter 11 • Other Sources   399

SOLUTIONS TO EXERCISES (cont'd)

Listing 11-25 shows the top portion of the modified RCDATA.C program's WndProc() function, which copies the resource data into the array *nArray[]*, and then displays the integers using the TextOut() and wsprintf() functions.

Listing 11-25 WndProc() Function for Exercise 2

```
long FAR PASCAL WndProc (HWND hWnd, WORD wMessage, WORD wParam, LONG lParam)
{
   HANDLE      hInstance, hData ;
   char        cBuf [128] ;
   HDC         hDC ;
   int         i, nArray [5] ;
   int FAR     *lpIntData ;

   switch (wMessage)                   /* process windows messages */
   {
      case WM_COMMAND:
         switch (wParam)               /* menu selections */
         {
            case IDM_SHOW:             /* show c11exer2 in client area */
               hDC = GetDC (hWnd) ;
               hInstance = GetWindowWord (hWnd, GWW_HINSTANCE) ;
               hData = LoadResource (hInstance,
                   FindResource (hInstance, "Arbitrary", RT_RCDATA)) ;
               if (hData)              /* if found resource data */
               {                       /* lock resource data in memory */
                  lpIntData = (int FAR *) LockResource (hData) ;
                  /* load resource data into array */
                  for (i = 0 ; i < 5 ; i++)
                     nArray [i] = *lpIntData++ ;
                  GlobalUnlock (hData) ; /* unlock data */
                  TextOut (hDC, 0, 0, cBuf, wsprintf (cBuf,
                     "The resource data read was %d %d %d %d %d",
                     nArray [0], nArray [1], nArray [2], nArray [3],
                     nArray [4])) ;

               else
                  TextOut (hDC, 0, 0,
                     "Could not find resource data.", 29) ;
               }
               ReleaseDC (hWnd, hDC) ;
               break ;
```
[Other program lines]

The key change is to make the pointer to the locked resource data in memory a pointer to an integer rather than a pointer to a character. *lpIntData* is declared "int FAR *," which matches the format of the five integers in memory. The complete solution is under the file name C11EXER2 on the source code disks.

CHAPTER 12

Managing Memory

Programs perform work by manipulating data in memory, so managing the computer's memory is fundamental to writing efficient programs. Windows provides the programmer with advanced memory management functions, which manage both memory local to the program and global memory blocks. Although the graphical and windowing functions are more visible to the user, it is the memory management functions that give Windows the ability to efficiently run multiple programs.

Windows allows three basic types of memory blocks to be created: fixed, moveable, and discardable. Moveable and discardable blocks are preferable because they allow Windows to optimize memory use. Fixed memory blocks are like putting posts in the middle of a slalom course—they get in the way of Windows' memory optimization efforts, but do have their uses. This chapter will explain how all three types of memory are created and used. The last two examples in this chapter will create several memory blocks with different attributes and show their locations in memory before and after Windows attempts to make room for a large object.

Because Windows moves objects in memory, the memory management functions under Windows are a bit more complex to use than those of a DOS program, in which memory blocks remain fixed in one location. The Windows approach to memory management revolves around the use of handles to memory blocks, rather than the absolute addresses in memory. This chapter will give you a number of examples using handles and the related functions that provide direct access to the full power of Windows' memory management capabilities.

Concepts Covered

Local and Global Memory
Locking Memory Blocks
Lock Count
Using Discardable Memory
Using Memory Handles

Fixed Memory Blocks
Passing Handles to Other Functions
Changing the Size of a Memory Block
System Resources

Keywords Covered

LMEM_MOVEABLE
LMEM_DISCARDABLE
LMEM_FIXED
GMEM_MOVEABLE
GMEM_DISCARDABLE

GMEM_FIXED
LHND
LPTR
GHND
GPTR

Functions Covered

LocalAlloc()
LocalReAlloc()
LocalFree()
LocalLock()
LocalUnlock()
LocalCompact()
LocalFlags()

GlobalAlloc()
GlobalReAlloc()
GlobalFree()
GlobalLock()
GlobalUnlock()
GlobalCompact()
GlobalFlags()

Local Versus Global Memory

Under Windows, programs can allocate blocks of memory for their own use in two locations, the program's own local heap and the global memory area. The local heap is a portion of the program's private data segment, an area in memory limited to a maximum of 64K that the program uses for its stack, static data, and local heap. The global

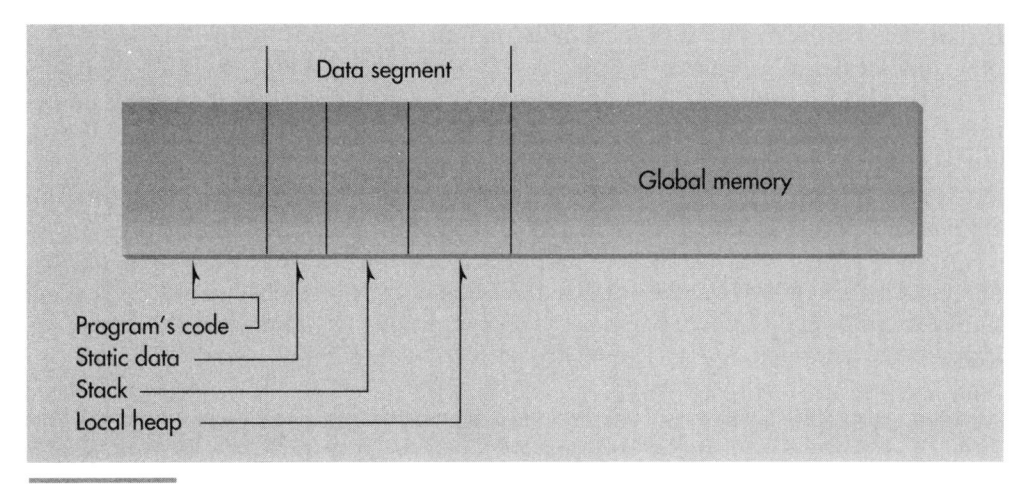

Figure 12-1 Memory Available to a Windows Program

heap is all of the free memory in the system, outside of any program's code or local data segment. Figure 12-1 shows a simplified diagram of what memory looks like to a single running program, ignoring other programs and parts of the Windows system that may be occupying other areas of memory.

All of the data on the stack (automatic variables), static data, and data in the local heap, resides within a single segment. If you remember the discussion on segments and offsets from Chapter 2, *Setting Up Your System*, you will recall that data in a single segment requires only the offset to specify an address. Using the C compiler conventions, addresses in the program's local data segment are "near" addresses and use near pointers. Addresses in the global memory area will have different segments and offsets and must, therefore, use the full segment/offset address. These are "far" addresses, requiring far pointers to memory. The advantage of using the local data segment is that access to a memory location is faster, as only the offset must be specified. The advantage of the global memory area

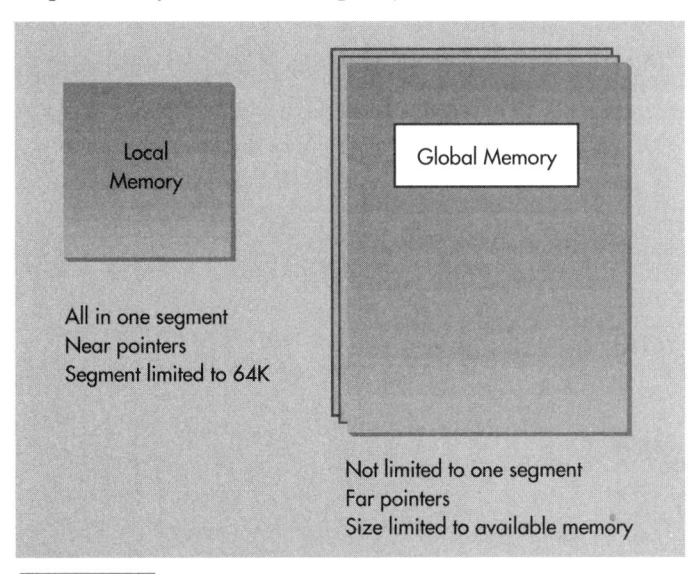

Figure 12-2 Local Versus Global Memory

Chapter 12 • Managing Memory **403**

is that it is limited only by the available memory space, not by the 64K limit to a program's local data segment.

In general, you will use the local data segment for small chunks of memory, something like a scratch pad or sticky note. Access is fast, but the amount of room is limited. The global memory area is for big objects and objects that will stay in memory for a while. Global memory blocks are like a full notebook for your program to write on. Figure 12-2 summarizes the differences.

In this chapter, local memory functions will be explored thoroughly before global memory allocations are covered. The functions that operate on global memory blocks are similar to the ones for local memory, so the programming techniques used to create, enlarge, and destroy memory blocks apply to both types of memory.

Windows Pointer Conventions

Windows programmers use a couple of handy shortcuts when defining variables that are pointers to memory locations. The normal C language declaration for a pointer to a character string is:

```
char * pCharString ;      /* declaring a near pointer to a character string */
```

If the program is compiled with the small memory model, this is a "near" pointer, meaning that only the offset value is saved, not the segment. Near pointers are used with memory blocks in a single data segment, such as a memory block allocated in the local heap. You can be more explicit in the declaration and use the "near" compiler key word to show that it is a near pointer ("near" is the default case, so most programmers leave out the "near" key word when declaring near pointers).

```
char near * pCharString ; /* same effect, but uses explicit "near" declaration */
```

Pointers to characters are so common that WINDOWS.H includes a shorthand notation for this variable type. If you look in WINDOWS.H near the beginning of the file, you will see the definitions:

```
typedef unsigned char    BYTE;
typedef unsigned int     WORD;
typedef unsigned long    DWORD;
typedef char near        *PSTR;
typedef char near        *NPSTR;
typedef char far         *LPSTR;
typedef BYTE near        *PBYTE;
typedef BYTE far         *LPBYTE;
typedef int near         *PINT;
typedef int far          *LPINT;
typedef WORD near        *PWORD;
typedef WORD far         *LPWORD;
typedef long near        *PLONG;
typedef long far         *LPLONG;
typedef DWORD near       *PDWORD;
typedef DWORD far        *LPDWORD;
typedef void far         *LPVOID;
```

> **Windows Pointer Conventions (cont'd)**
>
> With WINDOWS.H included in your C program file, you can use these handy definitions to shorten variable declarations. For example, a near pointer to a character can be declared:
>
> PSTR pChar ;
>
> The PSTR declaration takes care of the "char near" and the "*" all in one short word. Similarly, if you are working with global memory blocks, you will need to declare far pointers to memory. The following two declarations are equivalent:
>
> ```
> LPSTR     lpChar ;      /* normal Windows convention */
> char far  *lpChar ;     /* spelled out version - does the same thing */
> ```
>
> Almost all Windows programmers take advantage of the definitions in the WINDOWS.H file to make their declarations short and clear.

Local Memory Blocks

Because Windows frequently moves things around in memory, the address of an object is only meaningful while the object is locked in place. This leaves the problem of how to keep track of a memory block as it moves around in memory. Windows solves this problem by using handles to identify each memory block, regardless of where the block is located in memory. The handle of a memory block remains the same, even though the physical location (address) of the block may change many times. If you have been programming under MS-DOS or a similar operating system, you will need to get used to using the handle of a memory block to track it, rather than a physical address.

Let's imagine that you need to store the character string "ABCDEFG" at some point in a program. This is a small piece of data, so a local memory block is ideal. The LocalAlloc() function is used to request a memory block in the program's local data segment, and the function returns the handle of the memory block. LocalAlloc() allows you to specify whether you want the memory block to be fixed in memory, moveable in memory (the normal case), or moveable and discardable, meaning the Windows can purge the data from memory if Windows needs more room. These options are specified with LocalAlloc() flags like LMEM_MOVEABLE and LMEM_ZEROINIT, which are defined in WINDOWS.H and summarized in Table 12-1. Here is an example, allocating a little block of 10 bytes, specifying that the block will be moveable in memory, and initially filled with null bytes (zeros).

```
static HANDLE hMem ;   /* handle of memory block as a static variable */

hMem = LocalAlloc (LMEM_MOVEABLE | LMEM_ZEROINIT, 10) ;
if (hMem == NULL)
   MessageBox (hWnd, "No more room in the local heap!", "Warning", MB_OK) ;
```

LocalAlloc() will return zero (NULL) if it could not allocate the memory block, meaning that there is no more room in the program's data segment. This is certainly possible, as the combination of the program's stack, static data, and any allocated local memory blocks must fit within the 64K limit of a single segment, so be sure to check that a valid handle (any value not equal to zero) was returned before attempting to use the block.

VALUE	MEANING
LMEM_DISCARDABLE	Allocates memory that can be discarded if Windows needs to make room. Used only with LMEM_MOVEABLE.
LMEM_FIXED	Allocates fixed memory. Do not use this unless necessary. Fixed memory limits Windows' ability to optimize memory use.
LMEM_MOVEABLE	Allocates moveable memory.
LMEM_NOCOMPACT	Allocates memory in the local heap that is not compacted or discarded to make room for the new memory block.
LMEM_NODISCARD	Allocates memory in the local heap that is not discarded to make room for the new memory block.
LMEM_ZEROINIT	Initializes the new allocated memory block contents to zero.

Table 12-1 LocalAlloc() Flags

Note that the handle returned by LocalAlloc() is stored in a static variable. The handle will be used to reference this block later in the program when we need to access the memory space. In order to read or write data in the block, the block must be fixed in memory. Otherwise, the block might be moved during a reading or writing operation, causing the program to attempt to read or write on an old memory location that no longer belongs to the program. Windows will detect this and terminate the offending program to protect any other programs from being written over. (This is what is happening when you see a message box on the screen describing an "Application Error," and the program or all of Windows terminates.) To avoid this problem, the block is locked with LocalLock(), accessed, and then unlocked (allowed to move) using LocalUnlock(). Here is an example:

```
PSTR  pStr ;                /* a near pointer to a character string */

pStr = LocalLock (hMem) ;   /* lock the block in memory */
lstrcpy (pStr, "ABCDEFG") ; /* copy the character string to the block in memory */
LocalUnlock (hMem) ;        /* allow the block to be moveable again */
```

The lstrcpy() Windows function copies the character string "ABCDEFG" into the memory location of the block. During the brief period when the block is locked, it is a fixed memory location and can be accessed using normal C language pointer operations and functions like lstrcpy(). The block is then unlocked, allowing Windows to move it if necessary. As soon as LocalUnlock() is called, the value of the pointer *pStr* becomes unreliable, as Windows may move the block to a new location. If Windows moves the memory block, the data in the block will be copied to the new location. This means that the string "ABCDEFG" will continue to be in the memory block, regardless of where the block is located. Later, the program might need to output the string to a device context. To read the data, the block must again be locked.

```
PSTR  pStr ;              /* a near pointer to a character string */

pStr = LocalLock (hMem) ; /* lock the block in memory */
TextOut (hDC, 0, 0, pStr, lstrlen (pStr)) ;
LocalUnlock (hMem) ;      /* allow the block to be moveable again */
```

When the program no longer needs the memory block, it can be freed from the system. The LocalFree() function releases the memory block, so that Windows can use the space for other local storage needs.

```
LocalFree(hMem) ;         /* free the block.  hMem now has no meaning */
```

The Lock Count

If more than one part of a program accesses the same memory block, it is likely that LocalLock() will be called several times in sequence, without a call to LocalUnlock(). This is not a problem, as Windows keeps track of each call to LocalLock() as the block's "lock count." Every time LocalLock() is called, the lock count is increased by one. Every time LocalUnlock() is called, the lock count is reduced by one. When the lock count is zero, the block is unlocked. As long as every call to LocalLock() has a matching call to LocalUnlock() following it, Windows will keep the block locked until the "last" LocalUnlock() function is called.

Passing Handles to Functions

Handles can be passed as parameters to functions. For example, you might want to create a function to output a character string stored in a local memory block. A simple function named OutLocalText() is shown below. OutLocalText() will output a string stored in a memory block whose handle is *hMem* at the location *X,Y* on the device context.

```
void OutLocalText (HWND hWnd, int X, int Y, HANDLE hMem)
{
    HDC   hDC ;
    PSTR  pStr ;

    pStr = LocalLock (hMem) ;
    hDC = GetDC (hWnd) ;
    TextOut (hDC, X, Y, pStr, lstrlen (pStr)) ;
    ReleaseDC (hWnd, hDC) ;
    LocalUnlock (hMem) ;
}
```

The program wanting to call the OutLocalText() function would need to allocate the memory block, put the character data in it, and then call OutLocalText(). Here is a simple example.

```
static   HANDLE hMem ;
PSTR     pStr ;
```

```
hMem = LocalAlloc (LMEM_MOVEABLE, 64) ;
if (hMem == NULL)
        /* output a warning message */
else
{
    pStr = LocalLock (hMem) ;
    lstrcpy (pStr, "Text to output") ;
    LocalUnlock (hMem) ;
    OutLocalText (hWnd, 10, 15, hMem) ;
    LocalFree (hMem) ;
}
```

This example is a bit oversimplified, because the string "Text to output" would be stored in the program's local heap as static data. There is no pressing reason to allocate a memory block to store it twice, unless the OutLocalText() function was so convenient that it justified these extra steps. Normally, memory blocks are allocated for data that the program does not know in advance, such as input from the user.

Storing Other Types of Data

The examples so far have stored character data, but any type of data can be put in a memory block. For example, to store the integers from 1 to 25 in a local memory block, use code similar to that shown below. The C language sizeof() function comes in handy when calculating the amount of space to set aside.

```
static   HANDLE  hMem ;
int      *pInt ;

hMem = LocalAlloc (LMEM_MOVEABLE, 25 * sizeof (int)) ;
if (hMem == NULL)
        /* output an error message */
else
{
    pInt = LocalLock (hMem) ;
    for (i = 1 ; i <= 25 ; i++)
        *pInt++ = i ;   /* copy integers 1 to 25 to memory block */
    LocalUnlock (hMem) ;
}
```

This example again demonstrates that during the brief period when the memory block is locked, the block can be dealt with like any other address, using pointer operations as shown here, or functions which access a memory location such as lstrcpy() in the string examples.

Using Fixed Memory Blocks

Although you will normally avoid fixed memory blocks, there are situations where they can be used without having a negative impact on Windows' memory performance. Basically, fixed memory blocks are suitable for occasions when you only need a memory block for a very short period of time, and then immediately free the space. The advantage of a fixed block is that you save the time of locking and unlocking the block before and after use. Fixed blocks are always locked and, therefore, always at the same address. Fixed blocks are also used in applications where the program must access a block extremely rapidly, such as in processing a signal from data acquisition equipment. Using a fixed block avoids the time delay in locking and unlocking a memory block, but at the cost of reduced efficiency in Windows' use of memory.

One of the interesting side effects of using a fixed local memory block is that the block's handle value equals the address of the block. This allows you to skip calling LocalLock() to just get the address of a fixed memory block, as you can use the value returned by LocalAlloc() as an address. The following example shows how a fixed block can be used for a "quicky" way to store the 26 letters of the alphabet, output them, and then immediately free the block.

```
HDC   hDC ;
PSTR  pStr1, pStr2 ;
int   i ;

pStr1 = (PSTR) LocalAlloc (LMEM_FIXED | LMEM_ZEROINIT, 27) ;
pStr2 = pStr1 ;

for (i = 0 ; i < 26 ; i++)
  *pStr2++ = 'A' + i ;
hDC = GetDC (hWnd) ;
TextOut (hDC, 0, 0, pStr1, lstrlen (pStr1)) ;
ReleaseDC (hWnd, hDC) ;
LocalFree ((HANDLE) pStr1) ;
```

Note that the handle value returned by LocalAlloc() is cast to a PSTR to use it as a pointer, and then cast back to a HANDLE to call LocalFree(). The pointer *pStr1* will remain valid until the block is freed with LocalFree(). If the block were to be used for a longer period of time, *pStr1* would be saved as a static variable and used to access the block elsewhere in the program. There is no reason to call LocalLock() to access a locked memory block — it is already locked!

Another trick here is to use the LMEM_ZEROINIT flag, which fills the block with null characters, saving you the trouble of filling in the terminal null for a character string. The combination of LMEM_FIXED and LMEM_ZEROINIT is so common, that WINDOWS.H has a shortcut definition LPTR for "local pointer." This allows you to shorten the call to LocalAlloc() shown above down to just:

```
pStr1 = (PSTR) LocalAlloc (LPTR, 27) ; /* a locked, zero-initialized block */
```

There are four of these memory combinations defined in WINDOWS.H. The definitions cover the most common cases of moveable and fixed blocks in local and global memory, all initialized to zero.

```
#define LHND       (LMEM_MOVEABLE | LMEM_ZEROINIT)
#define LPTR       (LMEM_FIXED | LMEM_ZEROINIT)
#define GHND       (GMEM_MOVEABLE | GMEM_ZEROINIT)
#define GPTR       (GMEM_FIXED | GMEM_ZEROINIT)
```

An Example Allocating Local Memory

The first full example in this chapter is the MEM1 program. Figure 12-3 shows MEM1 in action, displaying the lowercase alphabet. Selecting the "Change" menu item causes MEM1 to display the uppercase alphabet. The 26 letters of the alphabet are stored in a local memory block. Initially, the memory block contains the lowercase letters, but they are written over with the uppercase letters when the "Change" menu item is selected. This demonstrates allocating a memory block, and both reading and writing data as the program operates.

Listing 12-1 shows the MEM1.C program. The WinMain() function is taken directly from the examples in Chapter 11, *Other Resources*, and obtains the main program window's caption from a string table resource. The new material is all in the WndProc() function. The memory block that will contain the alphabet is allocated when the program first starts and processes the WM_CREATE message. After the block is allocated, it is locked in memory with LocalLock(), and the lowercase alphabet characters are copied into the block. LocalUnlock() is then called to unlock the memory block, and the block is left unlocked in memory as the program operates.

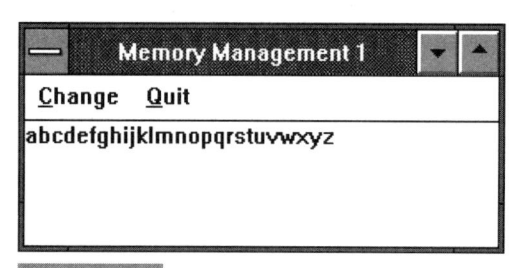

Figure 12-3 The MEM1 Program

When the user selects the "Change" menu item, the memory block is again locked, and the uppercase letters are copied into the same space, overwriting the previous lowercase letters. One other point in the program that must lock and unlock the memory block is the logic for displaying the 26 letters on the parent window's client area. This is done while processing WM_PAINT messages. The TextOut() function needs a pointer to a string, which is the address of the memory block after it is locked in memory. As usual, the block is immediately unlocked after the TextOut() function has finished with the data.

The memory block continues to exist as long as the program is running. The block is removed from memory before the program terminates by calling LocalFree() when the program processes the WM_DESTROY message. This is a convenient point to do any clean-up activities, such as deleting memory blocks.

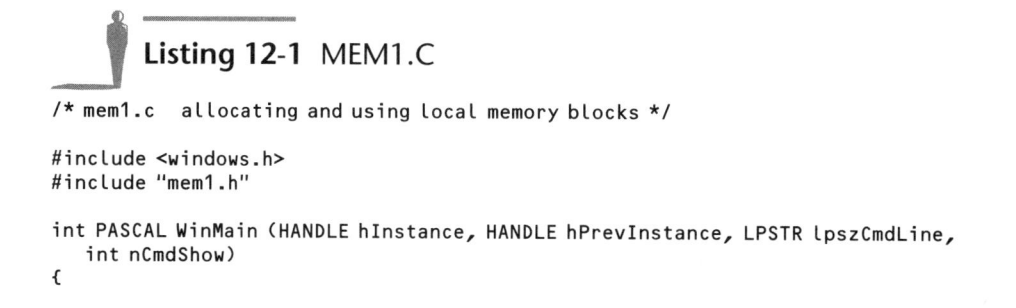

Listing 12-1 MEM1.C

```
/* mem1.c   allocating and using local memory blocks */

#include <windows.h>
#include "mem1.h"

int PASCAL WinMain (HANDLE hInstance, HANDLE hPrevInstance, LPSTR lpszCmdLine,
    int nCmdShow)
{
```

```
    HWND       hWnd ;       /* the window's "handle" */
    MSG        msg ;        /* a message structure */
    WNDCLASS   wndclass ;   /* window class structure */
    char       cBuf [128] ; /* character buffer */

    if (!hPrevInstance)
    {
       wndclass.style         = CS_HREDRAW | CS_VREDRAW ;
       wndclass.lpfnWndProc   = WndProc ;
       wndclass.cbClsExtra    = 0 ;
       wndclass.cbWndExtra    = 0 ;
       wndclass.hInstance     = hInstance ;
       wndclass.hIcon         = LoadIcon (hInstance, "MyIcon") ;
       wndclass.hCursor       = LoadCursor (NULL, IDC_ARROW) ;
       wndclass.hbrBackground = GetStockObject (WHITE_BRUSH) ;
       wndclass.lpszMenuName  = "MyMenu" ;
       wndclass.lpszClassName = "MyClass" ;
                  /* register the window class */
       if (!RegisterClass (&wndclass))
            return 0 ;
    }
    LoadString (hInstance, S_PROGRAMCAPTION, cBuf, sizeof (cBuf)) ;

    hWnd = CreateWindow ("MyClass", cBuf, WS_OVERLAPPEDWINDOW,
       CW_USEDEFAULT, CW_USEDEFAULT, CW_USEDEFAULT, CW_USEDEFAULT,
       NULL, NULL, hInstance, NULL) ;
    ShowWindow (hWnd, nCmdShow) ;     /* display the window */

    while (GetMessage (&msg, NULL, NULL, NULL))   /* message loop */
    {
       TranslateMessage (&msg) ;     /* translate keyboard messages */
       DispatchMessage (&msg) ;      /* send message to WndProc() */
    }
    return (msg.wParam) ;
}

long FAR PASCAL WndProc (HWND hWnd, WORD wMessage, WORD wParam, LONG lParam)
{
    static  HANDLE hMem ;
    PSTR           pStr ;
    int            i ;
    PAINTSTRUCT    ps ;

    switch (wMessage)              /* process windows messages */
    {
       case WM_CREATE:    /* program just starting, allocate local block */
            hMem = LocalAlloc (LMEM_MOVEABLE, 27) ;    /* allocate block */
            pStr = LocalLock (hMem) ;
            for (i = 0 ; i < 26 ; i++)   /* put lowercase letters in block */
                *pStr++ = (char)(_a + i) ;
            *pStr = 0 ;              /* end string with null character */
            LocalUnlock (hMem) ;
            break ;
       case WM_COMMAND:
            switch (wParam)                           /* menu items */
            {
               case IDM_CHANGE:                       /* "Change" menu item */
                    pStr = LocalLock (hMem) ;         /* lock block */
```

```
                for (i = 0 ; i < 26 ; i++)
                    *pStr++ = (char)(_A + i) ;         /* now uppercase */
                *pStr = 0 ;                            /* null terminate */
                LocalUnlock (hMem) ;                   /* unlock block */
                InvalidateRect (hWnd, NULL, TRUE) ;    /* force WM_PAINT */
                break ;
            case IDM_QUIT:                             /* "Quit" menu item */
                DestroyWindow (hWnd) ;                 /* destroy window, */
                break ;     /* terminating application */
            default:        /* otherwise, let Windows process it */
                return (DefWindowProc (hWnd, wMessage, wParam, lParam)) ;
            }
            break ;
        case WM_PAINT:
            BeginPaint (hWnd, &ps) ;
            pStr = LocalLock (hMem) ;                  /* lock block */
            TextOut (ps.hdc, 0, 0, pStr, lstrlen (pStr)) ;
            LocalUnlock (hMem) ;                       /* unlock block */
            EndPaint (hWnd, &ps) ;
            break ;
        case WM_DESTROY:                               /* stop application */
            LocalFree (hMem) ;                         /* get rid of block */
            PostQuitMessage (0) ;
            break ;
        default:        /* default windows message processing */
            return (DefWindowProc (hWnd, wMessage, wParam, lParam)) ;
    }
    return (0L) ;
}
```

The rest of the files needed to create the MEM1 program are shown in Listings 12-2 to 12-6. The program's icon is shown in Figure 12-4.

Listing 12-2 MEM1.H Header File

```
/* mem1.h header file */

#define   IDM_CHANGE         1     /* menu item ID numbers */
#define   IDM_QUIT           2

#define   S_PROGRAMCAPTION   1     /* string table ID numbers */

long FAR PASCAL WndProc (HWND, WORD, WORD, LONG) ;
```

Figure 12-4
MEM1.ICO
Icon Image

Listing 12-3 MEM1.RC Resource Script File

```
/* mem1.rc resource file */

#include "mem1.h"

MyIcon      ICON    mem1.ico
```

412 Windows Programming Primer Plus®

```
MyMenu      MENU
BEGIN
    MENUITEM "&Change",      IDM_CHANGE
    MENUITEM "&Quit",        IDM_QUIT
END

STRINGTABLE
BEGIN
    S_PROGRAMCAPTION   "Memory Management 1"
END
```

Listing 12-4 MEM1.DEF Module Definition File

```
NAME            mem1
DESCRIPTION     'memory use example 1'
EXETYPE         WINDOWS
STUB            'WINSTUB.EXE'
CODE            PRELOAD MOVEABLE DISCARDABLE
DATA            PRELOAD MOVEABLE MULTIPLE
HEAPSIZE        1024
STACKSIZE       5120
EXPORTS         WndProc
```

Listing 12-5 Turbo C++ Project File for MEM1

```
mem1.c
mem1.def
mem1.res
```

Listing 12-6 QuickC Project File for MEM1

```
mem1.c
mem1.def
mem1.res
```

Changing the Size of a Memory Block

In many cases, you will need to change the size of a memory block after it has been created. For example, a memory block containing the text for a word processor will need to be increased in size as more text is entered. Windows makes this easy to do, by providing the LocalReAlloc() function. LocalReAlloc() can either increase or decrease the size of a memory block, after the block has been created with the LocalAlloc() function. If the block is increased in size, the data in the "old" part of the block is not changed. If the block is decreased in size, the data in the end of the block is lost as the block is reduced in size. Figure 12-5 shows the effects of increasing and decreasing the size of a small memory block containing the letters of the alphabet.

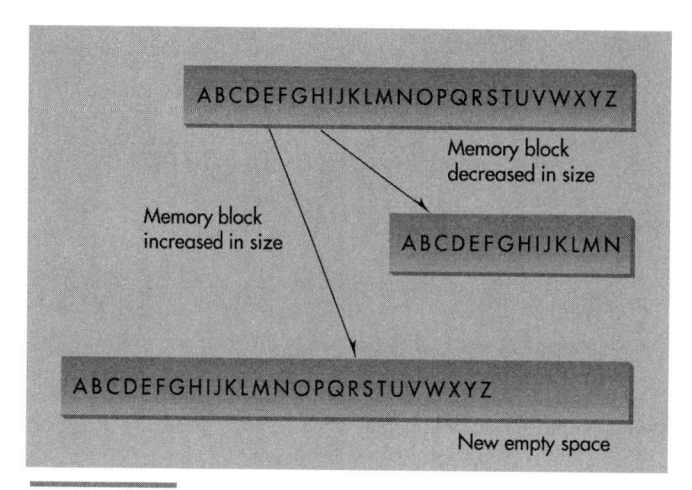

Figure 12-5 LocalReAlloc() Effects

A typical code sequence that creates a memory block and later increases it in size is shown below. In this case, the memory block is initially allocated with a size of 512 bytes, but later reallocated to 1,024 bytes.

```
static HANDLE hMem ;

hMem = LocalAlloc (LMEM_MOVEABLE, 512) ;
```
[Other program lines]
```
hMem = LocalReAlloc (hMem, 1024, LMEM_MOVEABLE) ;
```

Both LocalAlloc() and LocalReAlloc() can be used to allocate a memory block with a size of zero bytes. This sounds silly at first, as obviously the block cannot be used to store any data. However, the handle to the block remains a valid handle even when the block has a size of zero. The usual reason for allocating zero length memory buffers is that it is convenient to allocate the blocks before their size is known. The blocks can be allocated with an initial size of zero, and then reallocated as needed when data becomes available. The next example uses this approach to store a data block which is gradually enlarged.

An Example Using LocalReAlloc()

The next example, MEM2, demonstrates using LocalReAlloc() to both enlarge and shrink a memory block. The memory block is used to hold a character string, containing the digit characters. Initially, the memory block is allocated with zero bytes. Each time the user clicks the "Add" menu item, the memory block is enlarged by ten bytes, and the added space is filled with digit characters using each digit character in sequence. Figure 12-6 shows the MEM2 program after the user has selected the "Add" menu item three times. Selecting the "Delete" menu item reallocates the memory block back to zero bytes, eliminating all of the added digits.

Listing 12-7 shows the MEM2.C program. The zero-length buffer is initially allocated when the WM_CREATE message is processed. The LocalReAlloc() function is called every time the "Add" menu item is selected to add ten more bytes to the memory block. One extra byte is always included to make room for the terminating null character. The added buffer length is filled with digit characters after being locked. The portion of the code that moves to the start of the new portion of the memory block is worth reviewing, and is shown here:

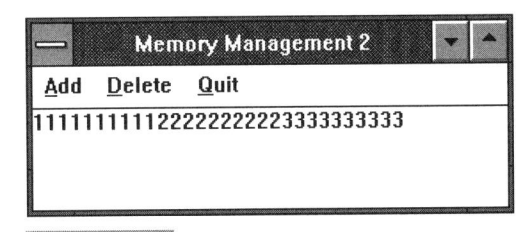

Figure 12-6 MEM2 Program After Selecting "Add" Three Times

```
pStr = LocalLock (hMem) ;       /* lock block */
    /* pStr points to start of block, now move to start */
pStr += nBlockSize - 10 ;       /* of new portion added on */
for (i = 0 ; i < 10 ; i++)
    *pStr++ = '0' + nBlockSize/10 ; /* fill with text */
*pStr = 0 ;                     /* null terminate */
LocalUnlock (hMem) ;            /* unlock block */
```

LocalLock() returns the address (a pointer) to the start of the memory block. The static variable *nBlockSize* keeps track of the length of the block, so the address of the end of the block is *pStr + nBlockSize*, and the address of the start of the new portion of the block is *pStr + nBlockSize* - 10. This type of simple address arithmetic works because the block is locked, and because each character occupies exactly one byte.

When the user selects the "Delete" menu item, LocalReAlloc() is called again to set the block size back to zero bytes. The "Add" and "Delete" menu items can be selected as often as desired, so long as "Add" is not selected so many times that it fills up the local heap. The block is not deleted from memory with the LocalFree() function until the WM_DESTROY message is processed.

Listing 12-7 MEM2.C

```
/* mem2.c   reallocating memory blocks */

#include <windows.h>
#include "mem2.h"

int PASCAL WinMain (HANDLE hInstance, HANDLE hPrevInstance, LPSTR lpszCmdLine,
   int nCmdShow)
{
    HWND       hWnd ;        /* the window's "handle" */
    MSG        msg ;         /* a message structure */
    WNDCLASS   wndclass ;    /* window class structure */
    char       cBuf [128] ;  /* character buffer */

    if (!hPrevInstance)
    {
```

```
        wndclass.style          = CS_HREDRAW | CS_VREDRAW ;
        wndclass.lpfnWndProc    = WndProc ;
        wndclass.cbClsExtra     = 0 ;
        wndclass.cbWndExtra     = 0 ;
        wndclass.hInstance      = hInstance ;
        wndclass.hIcon          = LoadIcon (hInstance, "MyIcon") ;
        wndclass.hCursor        = LoadCursor (NULL, IDC_ARROW) ;
        wndclass.hbrBackground  = GetStockObject (WHITE_BRUSH) ;
        wndclass.lpszMenuName   = "MyMenu" ;
        wndclass.lpszClassName  = "MyClass" ;
                /* register the window class */
        if (!RegisterClass (&wndclass))
           return 0 ;
    }
    LoadString (hInstance, S_PROGRAMCAPTION, cBuf, sizeof (cBuf)) ;

    hWnd = CreateWindow ("MyClass", cBuf, WS_OVERLAPPEDWINDOW,
        CW_USEDEFAULT, CW_USEDEFAULT, CW_USEDEFAULT, CW_USEDEFAULT,
        NULL, NULL, hInstance, NULL) ;
    ShowWindow (hWnd, nCmdShow) ;   /* display the window */

    while (GetMessage (&msg, NULL, NULL, NULL))   /* message loop */
    {
       TranslateMessage (&msg) ;        /* translate keyboard messages */
       DispatchMessage (&msg) ;         /* send message to WndProc() */
    }
    return (msg.wParam) ;
}

long FAR PASCAL WndProc (HWND hWnd, WORD wMessage, WORD wParam, LONG lParam)
{
    static  HANDLE  hMem ;
    PSTR            pStr ;
    int             i ;
    static int      nBlockSize ;
    PAINTSTRUCT     ps ;

    switch (wMessage)       /* process windows messages */
    {
       case WM_CREATE:      /* program just starting, allocate local block */
            hMem = LocalAlloc (LMEM_MOVEABLE, 0) ;  /* initially 0 bytes */
            nBlockSize = 0 ;
            break ;
       case WM_COMMAND:
            switch (wParam)                         /* menu items */
            {
               case IDM_ADD:                        /* "Add" menu item */
                    nBlockSize += 10 ;              /* set new size of mem block */
                    /* allocate one additional byte for terminal null char */
                    hMem = LocalReAlloc (hMem, nBlockSize + 1, LMEM_MOVEABLE) ;
                    if (hMem == NULL)
                        MessageBox (hWnd, "Ran out of local memory",
                                "Message", MB_OK) ;
                    else
                    {
                        pStr = LocalLock (hMem) ;           /* lock block */
                        /* pStr points to start of block, now move to start */
```

```
                    pStr += nBlockSize - 10 ;          /* of new portion */
                    for (i = 0 ; i < 10 ; i++)         /* fill w. text */
                        *pStr++ = (char)(_0 + nBlockSize/10) ;
                    *pStr = 0 ;                        /* null terminate */
                    LocalUnlock (hMem) ;               /* unlock block */
                    InvalidateRect (hWnd, NULL, TRUE) ; /* force WM_PAINT */
                }
                break ;
            case IDM_DELETE:                  /* resize mem block to zero */
                nBlockSize = 0 ;
                LocalReAlloc (hMem, 0, LMEM_MOVEABLE) ;
                InvalidateRect (hWnd, NULL, TRUE) ;    /* force WM_PAINT */
                break ;
            case IDM_QUIT:                             /* "Quit" menu item */
                DestroyWindow (hWnd) ;                 /* destroy window, */
                                          /* terminating application */
                break ;
            default:                      /* otherwise, let Windows process it */
                return (DefWindowProc (hWnd, wMessage, wParam, lParam)) ;
            }
            break ;
        case WM_PAINT:     /* output the entire string in mem block */
            BeginPaint (hWnd, &ps) ;
            if (nBlockSize > 0)
            {
                pStr = LocalLock (hMem) ;              /* lock block */
                TextOut (ps.hdc, 0, 0, pStr, lstrlen (pStr)) ;
                LocalUnlock (hMem) ;                   /* unlock block */
            }
            EndPaint (hWnd, &ps) ;
            break ;
        case WM_DESTROY:                               /* stop application */
            LocalFree (hMem) ;                         /* get rid of block */
            PostQuitMessage (0) ;
            break ;
        default:                       /* default windows message processing */
            return (DefWindowProc (hWnd, wMessage, wParam, lParam)) ;
    }
    return (0L) ;
}
```

Listings 12-8 to 12-12 show the support files for MEN2. The program's icon is shown in Figure 12-7.

Listing 12-8 MEM2.H Header File

```
/* mem2.h  header file */

#define IDM_ADD             1      /* menu item ID numbers */
#define IDM_DELETE          2
#define IDM_QUIT            3

#define S_PROGRAMCAPTION    1      /* string table ID numbers */

long FAR PASCAL WndProc (HWND, WORD, WORD, LONG) ;
```

Figure 12-7
MEM2.ICO
Icon Image

Listing 12-9 MEM2.RC Resource Script File

```
/* mem2.rc resource file */

#include "mem2.h"

MyIcon      ICON    mem2.ico

MyMenu      MENU
BEGIN
    MENUITEM "&Add",        IDM_ADD
    MENUITEM "&Delete",     IDM_DELETE
    MENUITEM "&Quit",       IDM_QUIT
END

STRINGTABLE
BEGIN
    S_PROGRAMCAPTION    "Memory Management 2"
END
```

Listing 12-10 MEM2.DEF Module Definition File

```
NAME            mem2
DESCRIPTION     'memory use example 2'
EXETYPE         WINDOWS
STUB            'WINSTUB.EXE'
CODE            PRELOAD MOVEABLE DISCARDABLE
DATA            PRELOAD MOVEABLE MULTIPLE
HEAPSIZE        1024
STACKSIZE       5120
EXPORTS         WndProc
```

Listing 12-11 Turbo C++ Project File for MEM2

```
mem2.c
mem2.def
mem2.res
```

Listing 12-12 QuickC Project File for MEM2

```
mem2.c
mem2.def
mem2.rc
```

Discardable Memory Blocks

Discardable blocks are the least memory consuming of all of the memory options. If Windows needs to find room for another program or data, it follows the following procedure:

1. Windows scans the available memory and looks for a block of sufficient size. If Windows finds one, this space is allocated and no other blocks are moved or discarded.
2. If a block of sufficient size is not available, Windows attempts to make room by relocating moveable code and data to make room. If a big enough space can be created by moving objects, no discardable data is removed.
3. If there still is not enough room in memory, Windows makes room by discarding discardable objects. The most recently accessed objects are the last to be discarded.
4. If there is still not enough room in memory after discarding every discardable block, LocalAlloc() will return zero, indicating that there is not enough room to allocate the requested size block. Most programs display a message box at this point, telling the user that the system is out of memory and that other applications should be terminated before trying again.

When a data block is discarded, the data is no longer available in memory, but the handle to the data block remains valid. The handle points to a data block containing zero bytes. LocalReAlloc() can be used to restore the block back to its former size when it is again needed.

Discardable blocks are best suited to data that can either be loaded again from disk if needed, or that can be recreated in memory on demand. Resources are almost always discardable, as the data is always defined in the program's disk file. Discardable blocks are also useful for temporary files and for saving portions of large databases in memory, where the database can be large enough to exceed available memory requirements.

Using Discardable Blocks

Discardable blocks are always moveable, so the LocalAlloc() function call to create a discardable block combines the LMEM_MOVEABLE and LMEM_DISCARDABLE flags. To allocate a block of 100 bytes and copy some characters to the beginning of the block, use the following code:

```
static    HANDLE  hMem ;
PSTR              pStr ;

hMem = LocalAlloc (LMEM_MOVEABLE | LMEM_DISCARDABLE, 100) ;
if (hMem)
{
    pStr = LocalLock (hMem) ;
    lstrcpy (pStr, "abcdefg") ;
    LocalUnlock (hMem) ;
}
```

When you need to access a discardable data block, it is important to make sure that the data is still there, and has not been discarded. The LocalFlags() function does this, returning a WORD value that contains both the lock count for the block in the low-order byte, and the LMEM_DISCARDED and/or LMEM_DISCARDABLE flags as the high-order byte. Be sure to check that the data has not been discarded before attempting to read from a discardable block, as shown in this typical code fragment:

```
char    cBuf [128] ;    /* automatic character buffer (uses stack) */
PSTR    pStr ;

if (LMEM_DISCARDED & LocalFlags (hMem))     /* has block been discarded? */
{                                           /* if so, reallocate block */
    hMem = LocalReAlloc (hMem, 100, LMEM_MOVEABLE | LMEM_DISCARDABLE)
    /* reload or recreate the data */
}
else                                        /* if block was not discarded */
{                                           /* can read data from block */
    pStr = LocalLock (hMem) ;
    lstrcpy (cBuf, pStr) ;
    LocalUnlock (hMem) ;
}
```

When LocalUnlock() is called for a discardable block, the block is made both moveable and discardable again. When the program is done with the discardable block, use LocalFree() to permanently remove it from memory. LocalFree() makes the handle to the block invalid, so the block cannot be restored with LocalReAlloc(). If another discardable block is needed, it must be created from scratch with LocalAlloc(). You can also deliberately discard a discardable block without invalidating the block's handle by calling the LocalDiscard() function. Normally, you will let Windows decide when memory is full, and not bother with LocalDiscard().

An Example Using Discardable Blocks

The next example is designed to illustrate both discardable and moveable memory blocks in more detail. The MEM3 program allocates four blocks of 512 bytes in the local heap and displays the handles, addresses, and discardable status for each block in the window's client area. Figure 12-8 shows the MEM3 program right after it was started. Note that blocks 0 and 2 are discardable, while blocks 1 and 3 are only moveable. Block 0 is allocated first, and ends up at the highest address in memory, with each successive block added below it in the local heap.

The handles and addresses output by the MEM3 program are in decimal, not hexadecimal. If you do a little arithmetic on the address values, you will note that the blocks are actually 520 bytes apart (9458 - 8938 = 520), not the exact 512 bytes requested for each block. The extra eight bytes is taken up by a small header that Windows uses to keep track of the size and status of each local memory block. This is all internal to Windows, and does not affect our considering each block to contain 512 bytes of usable storage. As usual, Windows is doing a number of "low-level" tasks automatically, leaving the programmer to concentrate on the more important issues.

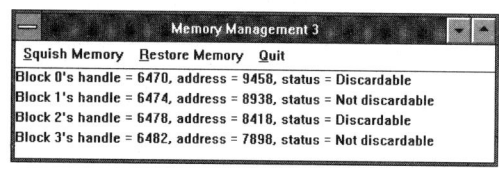

Figure 12-8 The MEM3 Program Immediately After Startup

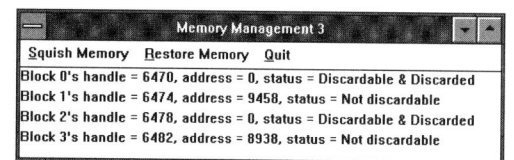

Figure 12-9 The MEM3 Program After "Squish Memory" was Selected

If the user selects the "Squish Memory" menu item, MEM3 compacts the local heap by calling the LocalCompact() function. LocalCompact() discards all discardable blocks, and moves all moveable blocks to the high end of the local heap. This makes the maximum amount of room available in the local heap for allocating a new memory block, but discards every discardable block in the process. Figure 12-9 shows the MEM3 program after the "Squish Memory" menu item was selected. Blocks 0 and 2 are discarded, which results in their address being zero (NULL), but their handles remain unchanged. Note that blocks 1 and 3 have been moved, and their addresses now correspond to the previous locations of blocks 0 and 1 in memory. Windows has moved these two moveable (but not discardable) blocks to the high end of the local heap.

Figure 12-10 The MEM3 Program After "Restore Memory" Was Selected

The "Restore Memory" menu item in MEM3 reallocates the two discardable blocks, restoring them to their 512 byte size. Figure 12-10 shows the MEM3 program after "Restore Memory" was selected. The discardable blocks end up with new addresses, located below (lower address values) the moveable, but not discardable, blocks in memory.

Figure 12-11 shows a diagram of what Windows did with each of the memory blocks allocated by MEM3 during each activity. Initially, the blocks are located in consecutive addresses at the top of the local heap. When the LocalCompact() function is used to com-

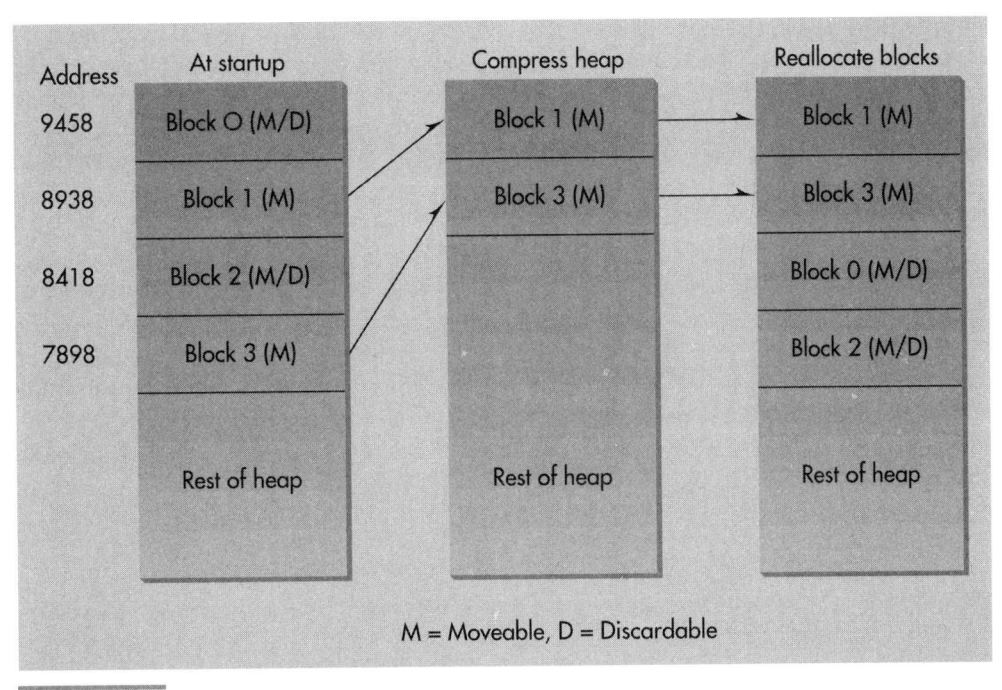

Figure 12-11 Local Heap Organization of MEM3

Chapter 12 • Managing Memory   421

press the heap, blocks 0 and 2 are discarded, and blocks 1 and 3 moved to the top end of the heap. This makes the maximum amount of room available in the remainder of the local heap. When the two discardable blocks are restored using the LocalReAlloc() function, they are positioned at the highest free locations in the local heap. Note that there is no reason for Windows to move blocks 1 and 3 when the discardable blocks are restored.

Throughout all of these memory movements, the handles of the memory blocks remained the same. Even the discardable memory blocks, which were purged from memory, and then recreated at new locations, retained valid memory handles. As a programmer, you will normally not be concerned with the physical address of a memory block. Keeping track of the memory handle is enough to assure access to the block regardless of where it is located.

The MEM3 Program

Listing 12-13 shows the MEM3.C program. Most of this example is similar to MEM1.C and MEM2.C, but there are a few new items worth noting. To keep the example as short as possible, the memory blocks are created, but no data is copied to the blocks. MEM3.C uses the LocalCompact() function to compact the local heap, resulting in both discardable memory blocks being discarded. This requires two calls to LocalCompact(), as shown here:

```
wFree = LocalCompact (0) ;          /* find amount of free mem */
LocalCompact (wFree + 500) ;        /* force compact */
InvalidateRect (hWnd, NULL, TRUE) ; /* force WM_PAINT */
```

LocalCompact() is first called with an argument of zero, which results in a returned value of the amount of free memory that could be made available after compacting. LocalCompact() is then called a second time, requesting more than the available memory room. This forces Windows to compact the memory block, discarding any discardable data in the local heap. InvalidateRect() is called to force a WM_PAINT message to be sent to MEM3, as all of the logic for showing the handles and address values is in the WM_PAINT logic of MEM3.C.

When the user selects the "Restore Memory" menu item, MEM3.C checks the two discardable memory blocks to see if they have been discarded using the LocalFlags() function.

```
if (LocalFlags (hMem [0]) | LMEM_DISCARDED)
{
  LocalReAlloc (hMem [0], 512,
      LMEM_MOVEABLE | LMEM_DISCARDABLE) ;
}
if (LocalFlags (hMem [2]) | LMEM_DISCARDED)
{
  LocalReAlloc (hMem [2], 512,
      LMEM_MOVEABLE | LMEM_DISCARDABLE) ;
}
```

The LocalFlags() function is also used in the WM_PAINT logic to determine the status of each of the memory blocks as either discarded, discardable but not discarded, or moveable. The only way to determine the address of a memory block is to lock it, so the WM_PAINT logic also calls LocalLock() for each block to determine its address, outputs the address data using TextOut(), and then calls LocalUnlock() to unlock the data block. This is done for all four blocks. Locking and unlocking each memory block does not cause Windows to move the blocks, so there is no reason to lock all four blocks at once before displaying their addresses.

```
case WM_PAINT:
    BeginPaint (hWnd, &ps) ;
    for (i = 0 ; i < 4 ; i++)
    {
       wStatus = LocalFlags (hMem [i]) ;     /* find block's status */
       if (!(wStatus & (LMEM_DISCARDED | LMEM_DISCARDABLE)))
           lstrcpy (cStatus, "Not discardable") ;
       else
       {
           lstrcpy (cStatus, "") ;           /* start with empty string */
           if (wStatus & LMEM_DISCARDABLE)
              lstrcat (cStatus, "Discardable ") ;
           if (wStatus & LMEM_DISCARDED)
              lstrcat (cStatus, "& Discarded") ;
       }
       pStr = LocalLock (hMem [i]) ;         /* lock block */
       TextOut (ps.hdc, 0, 20 * i, cBuf, wsprintf (cBuf,
           "Block %d's handle = %d, address = %u, status = %s",
           i, hMem [i], pStr, (LPSTR) cStatus)) ;
       LocalUnlock (hMem [i]) ;              /* unlock block */
    }
    EndPaint (hWnd, &ps) ;
    break ;
```

The memory blocks are not removed from memory using LocalFree() until the WM_DESTROY message is processed as the program is terminating.

Listing 12-13 MEM3.C

```
/* mem3.c   experiment with moveable and discardable memory blocks */

#include <windows.h>
#include "mem3.h"

int PASCAL WinMain (HANDLE hInstance, HANDLE hPrevInstance, LPSTR lpszCmdLine,
   int nCmdShow)
{
    HWND       hWnd ;         /* the window's "handle" */
    MSG        msg ;          /* a message structure */
    WNDCLASS   wndclass ;     /* window class structure */
    char       cBuf [128] ;   /* character buffer */

    if (!hPrevInstance)
    {
      wndclass.style          = CS_HREDRAW | CS_VREDRAW ;
      wndclass.lpfnWndProc    = WndProc ;
```

```
        wndclass.cbClsExtra        = 0 ;
        wndclass.cbWndExtra        = 0 ;
        wndclass.hInstance         = hInstance ;
        wndclass.hIcon             = LoadIcon (hInstance, "MyIcon") ;
        wndclass.hCursor           = LoadCursor (NULL, IDC_ARROW) ;
        wndclass.hbrBackground     = GetStockObject (WHITE_BRUSH) ;
        wndclass.lpszMenuName      = "MyMenu" ;
        wndclass.lpszClassName     = "MyClass" ;
                    /* register the window class */
        if (!RegisterClass (&wndclass))
             return 0 ;
    }
    LoadString (hInstance, S_PROGRAMCAPTION, cBuf, sizeof (cBuf)) ;

    hWnd = CreateWindow ("MyClass", cBuf, WS_OVERLAPPEDWINDOW,
        CW_USEDEFAULT, CW_USEDEFAULT, CW_USEDEFAULT, CW_USEDEFAULT,
        NULL, NULL, hInstance, NULL) ;
    ShowWindow (hWnd, nCmdShow) ;    /* display the window */

    while (GetMessage (&msg, NULL, NULL, NULL))   /* message loop */
    {
       TranslateMessage (&msg) ;     /* translate keyboard messages */
       DispatchMessage (&msg) ;      /* send message to WndProc() */
    }
    return (msg.wParam) ;
}


long FAR PASCAL WndProc (HWND hWnd, WORD wMessage, WORD wParam, LONG lParam)
{
    static  HANDLE  hMem [4] ;      /* an array of handles */
    PSTR            pStr ;          /* pointer to near data */
    int             i ;
    PAINTSTRUCT     ps ;
    char            cBuf [128], cStatus [64] ;
    WORD            wStatus, wFree ;

    switch (wMessage)               /* process windows messages */
    {
       case WM_CREATE:              /* program just starting, allocate local blocks */
            hMem [0] = LocalAlloc (LMEM_MOVEABLE | LMEM_DISCARDABLE, 512) ;
            hMem [1] = LocalAlloc (LMEM_MOVEABLE, 512) ;
            hMem [2] = LocalAlloc (LMEM_MOVEABLE | LMEM_DISCARDABLE, 512) ;
            hMem [3] = LocalAlloc (LMEM_MOVEABLE, 512) ;
            break ;
       case WM_COMMAND:
            switch (wParam)         /* menu items */
            {
               case IDM_SQUISH:     /* request more memory than is available */
                    wFree = LocalCompact (0) ;      /* find amount of free mem */
                    LocalCompact (wFree + 500) ;    /* force compact */
                    InvalidateRect (hWnd, NULL, TRUE) ;   /* force WM_PAINT */
                    break ;
               case IDM_RESTORE:    /* restore the two discardable blocks */
                    if (LocalFlags (hMem [0]) | LMEM_DISCARDED)
                    {
                        LocalReAlloc (hMem [0], 512,
                            LMEM_MOVEABLE | LMEM_DISCARDABLE) ;
                    }
```

```
            if (LocalFlags (hMem [2]) | LMEM_DISCARDED)
            {
                LocalReAlloc (hMem [2], 512,
                    LMEM_MOVEABLE | LMEM_DISCARDABLE) ;
            }
            InvalidateRect (hWnd, NULL, TRUE) ;    /* force WM_PAINT */
            break ;
        case IDM_QUIT:                      /* "Quit" menu item */
            DestroyWindow (hWnd) ;          /* destroy window, */
            break ;                         /* terminating application */
        default:                  /* otherwise, let Windows process it */
            return (DefWindowProc (hWnd, wMessage, wParam, lParam)) ;
        }
        break ;
    case WM_PAINT:
        BeginPaint (hWnd, &ps) ;
        for (i = 0 ; i < 4 ; i++)
        {
            wStatus = LocalFlags (hMem [i]) ;  /* find block s status */
            if (!(wStatus & (LMEM_DISCARDED | LMEM_DISCARDABLE)))
                lstrcpy (cStatus, "Not discardable") ;
            else
            {
                lstrcpy (cStatus, "") ;         /* start with empty string */
                if (wStatus & LMEM_DISCARDABLE)
                    lstrcat (cStatus, |Discardable |) ;
                if (wStatus & LMEM_DISCARDED)
                    lstrcat (cStatus, "& Discarded") ;
            }
            pStr = LocalLock (hMem [i]) ;         /* lock block */
            TextOut (ps.hdc, 0, 20 * i, cBuf, wsprintf (cBuf,
               "Block %d's handle = %d, address = %u, status = %s",
               i, hMem [i], pStr, (LPSTR) cStatus)) ;
            LocalUnlock (hMem [i]) ;              /* unlock block */
        }
        EndPaint (hWnd, &ps) ;
        break ;
    case WM_DESTROY:                              /* stop application */
        for (i = 0 ; i < 4 ; i++)
            LocalFree (hMem [i]) ;                /* get rid of block */
        PostQuitMessage (0) ;
        break ;
    default:                 /* default windows message processing */
        return (DefWindowProc (hWnd, wMessage, wParam, lParam)) ;
    }
    return (0L) ;
}
```

An important detail in creating the MEM3 program is to provide enough room in the local heap for the four memory blocks. This is done in the program's module definition file, MEM3.DEF, shown in Listing 12-14. The HEAPSIZE statement sets the size of the local heap when the program starts. MEM3.DEF uses a HEAPSIZE of 4,096 bytes, which is more than enough for the four blocks of 512 bytes. Failing to set the heap large enough will cause the discardable memory blocks to be discarded to make room for the moveable blocks as the moveable blocks are allocated. If the discardable memory blocks are allocated after the moveable blocks, Windows will enlarge the local heap to make room. If the discardable memory blocks are allocated first, they will be discarded as the other blocks are allocated, because Windows will attempt to keep the heap size down to the size specified in the module definition file. One of the exercises at the end of this chapter experiments with this effect by changing the HEAPSIZE value.

Listing 12-14 MEM3.DEF Module Definition File

```
NAME            mem3
DESCRIPTION     'memory use example 3'
EXETYPE         WINDOWS
STUB            'WINSTUB.EXE'
CODE            PRELOAD MOVEABLE DISCARDABLE
DATA            PRELOAD MOVEABLE MULTIPLE
HEAPSIZE        4096
STACKSIZE       5120
EXPORTS         WndProc
```

Figure 12-12
MEM3.ICO
Icon Image

The remaining files needed to create MEM3 are shown in Listings 12-15 to 12-18. There are no new concepts lurking in these files. Figure 12-12 shows the program's icon.

Listing 12-15 MEM3.H Header File

```
/* mem3.h header file */

#define IDM_SQUISH        1          /* menu item ID numbers */
#define IDM_RESTORE       2
#define IDM_QUIT         10

#define S_PROGRAMCAPTION  1          /* string table ID numbers */

long FAR PASCAL WndProc (HWND, WORD, WORD, LONG) ;
```

Listing 12-16 MEM3.RC Resource Script File

```
 /* mem3.rc resource file */

#include "mem3.h"

MyIcon    ICON    mem3.ico

MyMenu    MENU
BEGIN
    MENUITEM "&Squish Memory",     IDM_SQUISH
    MENUITEM "&Restore Memory",    IDM_RESTORE
    MENUITEM "&Quit",              IDM_QUIT
END
```

```
STRINGTABLE
BEGIN
   S_PROGRAMCAPTION   "Memory Management 3"
END
```

Listing 12-17 Turbo C++ Project File for MEM3

```
mem3.c
mem3.def
mem3.res
```

Listing 12-18 QuickC Project File for MEM3

```
mem3.c
mem3.def
mem3.rc
```

Global Memory Allocation

So far we have been looking only at allocation of memory blocks in the local heap. It may be a pleasant surprise to find out that allocating blocks in the global memory area is done in exactly the same way. Windows has a parallel set of functions for global memory allocation, which have the function names changed from "Local" to "Global." Table 12-2 summarizes the key memory allocation functions.

LOCAL HEAP FUNCTION	GLOBAL HEAP FUNCTION	PURPOSE
LocalAlloc()	GlobalAlloc()	Allocate a memory block.
LocalLock()	GlobalLock()	Lock a memory block, return its address.
LocalUnlock()	GlobalUnlock()	Unlock a memory block.
LocalFree()	GlobalFree()	Free a memory block, return space to system.
LocalFlags()	GlobalFlags()	Determine if a block is discardable, or already discarded.
LocalReAlloc()	GlobalReAlloc()	Change the size of a memory block.
LocalDiscard()	GlobalDiscard()	Discard a discardable memory block.
LocalCompact()	GlobalCompact()	Determine the amount of memory space available, optionally moving and discarding memory blocks to make room.

Table 12-2 Memory Allocation Functions

A couple of the global memory functions should look a bit familiar, as the GlobalUnlock() and GlobalFree() functions were used in Chapter 11, *Other Resources*, to unlock and free resource data. Resource data is stored in the global memory area, and resources have similar functions for loading and locking memory blocks, such as LoadResource() and LockResource(), which are used for custom resource data.

The main difference you will need to remember is that global memory blocks are not all in the same data segment and, therefore, must use far pointers to memory. A typical program excerpt that allocates 64 bytes of global memory, and copies character data to it, is shown here.

```
static HANDLE   hgMem ;
LPSTR           lpStr ;

hgMem = GlobalAlloc (GMEM_MOVEABLE, 64) ;
if (hgMem)
{
    lpStr = GlobalLock (hgMem) ;
    lstrcpy (lpStr, "Some data here.") ;
    GlobalUnlock (hgMem) ;
}
```

Global memory blocks are tracked by using handles, just like local memory blocks. There is no obvious difference between a handle for a local block and a handle for a global one, so it is a good idea to use a variable name for a global handle that contains a "g" or some other marker that makes it obvious what type of object the handle refers to. Also note that the pointer to the character data is a far pointer (LPSTR == "char far *" in WINDOWS.H), as the GlobalLock() function returns a pointer to far memory. One final difference between local and global memory allocation is that the GlobalAlloc() function's memory flags start with "GMEM" instead of the "LMEM" flags used by LocalAlloc(). Table 12-3 summarizes the most common global memory flags.

FLAG	MEANING
GMEM_DISCARDABLE	Allocates memory that can be discarded if Windows needs to make room. Used only with GMEM_MOVEABLE.
GMEM_FIXED	Allocates fixed memory. Do not use this unless absolutely necessary. Fixed memory limits Windows' ability to optimize memory use.
GMEM_MOVEABLE	Allocates moveable memory.
GMEM_NOCOMPACT	Allocates memory in the global heap that is not compacted or discarded to make room for the new memory block.
GMEM_NODISCARD	Allocates memory in the global heap that is not discarded to make room for the new memory block.
GMEM_ZEROINIT	Initializes the new allocated memory block contents to zero.

Table 12-3 Global Memory Flags

When the program needs to access the data in the memory block, the block is locked with GlobalLock(), which returns the address of the locked data. Here is an example:

```
LPSTR     lpStr ;           /* a far pointer to character data */
char      cBuf [64] ;       /* the buffer (on the stack) that will receive the data */

lpStr = GlobalLock (hgMem) ;    /* lock/determine the address of the block */
lstrcpy (cBuf, lpStr) ;         /* copy its contents to cBuf[] */
GlobalUnlock (hgMem) ;          /* unlock block */
```

You can change the size of a global memory block, using the GlobalReAlloc() function, as the program operates. For example, to increase the size of the global block to 128 bytes, you would use the following code:

```
GlobalReAlloc (hgMem, 128, GMEM_MOVEABLE) ;
```

Increasing the size of a global memory block does not affect the data already stored in the block. Decreasing the size of the block causes any data in the end of the block to be lost, but does not affect the data in the portion of the block that remains after resizing. When the memory block is no longer needed, GlobalFree() is used to remove it from memory, freeing Windows to use the block for other purposes. The handle becomes invalid after GlobalFree() is called.

```
GlobalFree (hMem) ;
```

Global memory blocks can also be allocated with the GMEM_DISCARDABLE flag set, which allows Windows to discard the block if it cannot make enough room in the global memory area for a new program or data by simply moving global objects. This option is demonstrated in the next program example.

An Example Allocating Global Memory Blocks

The last example program in this chapter is called GMEM1, and it demonstrates a number of global memory options. GMEM1 is identical to the previous example program (MEM3) except that GMEM1 uses global memory blocks exclusively. This provides an interesting contrast between the address values used for local and global memory. Figure 12-13 shows the GMEM1 program in action, having allocated four global memory blocks, each 1,024 bytes long. The first thing you may notice is the size of the address values. Far address values are shown here in decimal notation (not hexadecimal). Note also that the address values for blocks 1 and 3 which are moveable, but not discardable, are located at lower address value than the two discardable blocks. Windows puts the discardable blocks in the high end of memory, where they can be discarded with a minimum impact on the rest of the memory objects. We will look at a diagram of this in a moment.

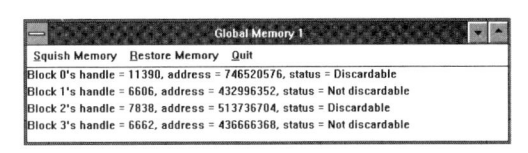

Figure 12-13 The GMEM1 Program at Startup

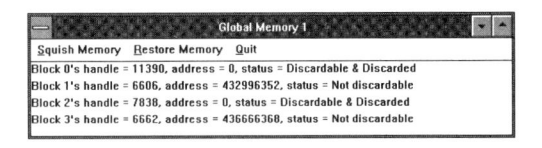

Figure 12-14 The GMEM1 Program After Selecting "Squish Memory"

Chapter 12 • Managing Memory

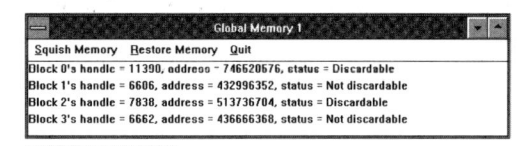

Figure 12-15 The GMEM1 Program After Selecting "Restore Memory"

If the user selects the "Squish Memory" menu item, GMEM1 uses the GlobalCompact() function to compact the global heap. This takes a second or more, depending on the amount of memory in the system and the speed of the computer. Figure 12-14 shows the result, with blocks 0 and 2 discarded, while blocks 1 and 3 remain down in the lower portion of the global heap (lower address values). Note again that the handles of the discardable memory blocks remain valid, even though any data in the blocks has been discarded.

Selecting the "Restore Memory" menu item causes the two discarded memory blocks to be restored, using the GlobalReAlloc() function to pump blocks 0 and 2 back up to 1,024 bytes of room. Figure 12-15 shows the result. Windows takes a shortcut and reallocates the 1,024 bytes for blocks 0 and 2 back at their old memory locations. These happen to be free in the example, as compressing the global heap moved other objects lower in memory, leaving the old positions of blocks 0 and 2 still available in memory. If another program, or more data, were loaded into memory before the "Restore Memory" menu item was selected, Windows would have needed to find a new address for one or both of the reallocated blocks.

Figure 12-16 shows a rough impression of what is happening to the global heap as GMEM1 compresses the global memory space, and then recreates the two discardable memory blocks. Compressing the global heap results in all discardable objects being discarded, which will include all of the menus, icons, and other resources that programs have loaded, in addition to the two discardable blocks that GMEM1 allocates. Compressing the global heap makes a maximum amount of continuous space available to load a big object into memory. When the two discardable blocks are reallocated, they are simply put back at their old locations in memory. Windows can move them later if needed to make a large space available, or it can discard them if moving objects does not free up enough space. Other programs will reload their menus, icons, etc. when these resources are needed.

The GMEM1 Program

Listing 12-19 shows the GMEM1.C program. This should look pretty familiar, as it is directly copied from the MEM3.C program file, changing all of the "Local..." functions to "Global..." ones. A couple of other changes are also necessary. The pointer to the memory address in the global heap (*lpStr*) must be a far pointer (LPSTR). GlobalCompact () returns a DWORD value instead of the WORD that LocalAlloc() returns, so the DWORD variable *dwFree* is used to store the amount of free memory available. Finally, the memory flags for GlobalAlloc() and GlobalReAlloc() start with "GMEM" instead of "LMEM" for the local heap allocation functions.

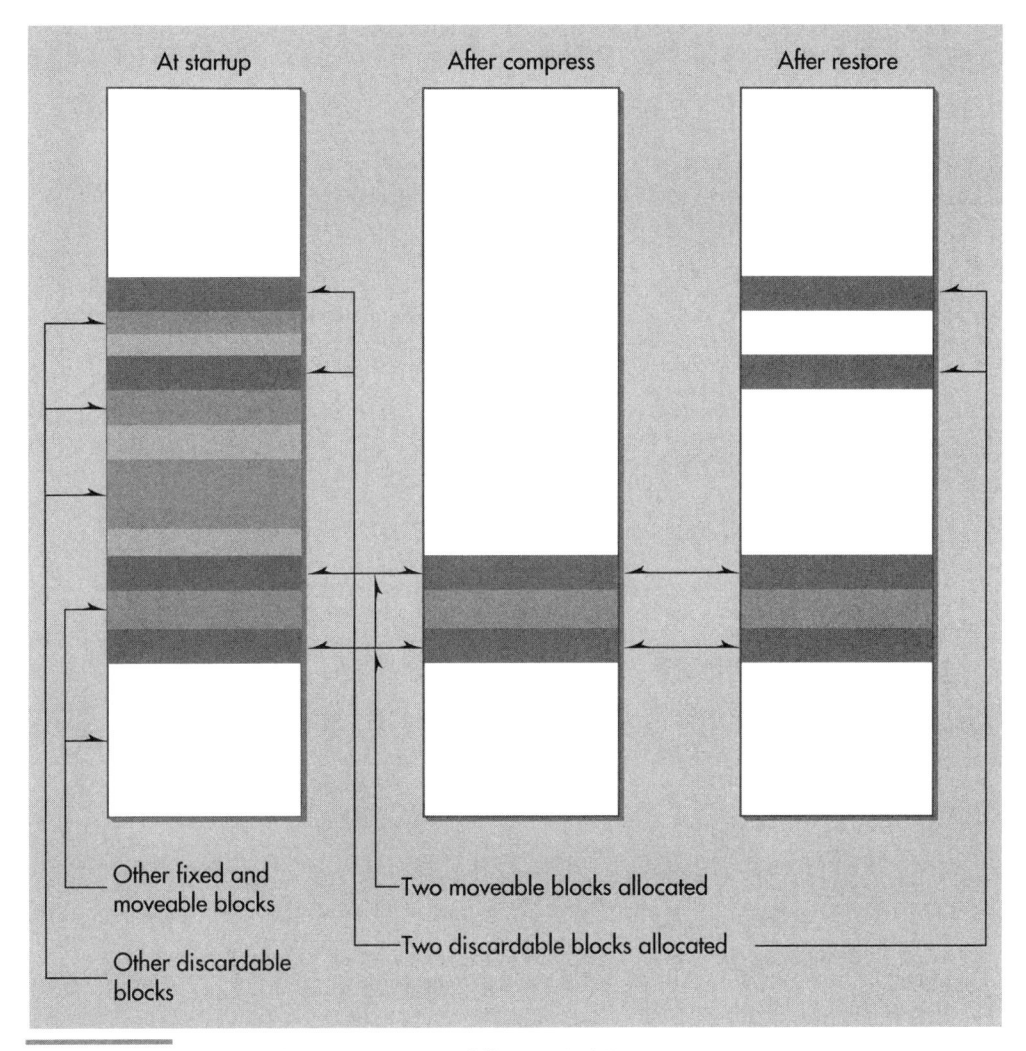

Figure 12-16 The Global Memory Heap While GMEM1 Runs

Listing 12-19 GMEM1.C

```
/* gmem1.c   experiment with global memory blocks */

#include <windows.h>
#include "gmem1.h"

int PASCAL WinMain (HANDLE hInstance, HANDLE hPrevInstance, LPSTR lpszCmdLine,
    int nCmdShow)
{
```

Chapter 12 • Managing Memory

```
    HWND       hWnd ;          /* the window's "handle" */
    MSG        msg ;           /* a message structure */
    WNDCLASS   wndclass ;      /* window class structure */
    char       cBuf [128] ;    /* character buffer */

    if (!hPrevInstance)
    {
        wndclass.style          = CS_HREDRAW | CS_VREDRAW ;
        wndclass.lpfnWndProc    = WndProc ;
        wndclass.cbClsExtra     = 0 ;
        wndclass.cbWndExtra     = 0 ;
        wndclass.hInstance      = hInstance ;
        wndclass.hIcon          = LoadIcon (hInstance, "MyIcon") ;
        wndclass.hCursor        = LoadCursor (NULL, IDC_ARROW) ;
        wndclass.hbrBackground  = GetStockObject (WHITE_BRUSH) ;
        wndclass.lpszMenuName   = "MyMenu" ;
        wndclass.lpszClassName  = "MyClass" ;
                    /* register the window class */
        if (!RegisterClass (&wndclass))
             return 0 ;
    }
    LoadString (hInstance, S_PROGRAMCAPTION, cBuf, sizeof (cBuf)) ;

    hWnd = CreateWindow ("MyClass", cBuf, WS_OVERLAPPEDWINDOW,
        CW_USEDEFAULT, CW_USEDEFAULT, CW_USEDEFAULT, CW_USEDEFAULT,
        NULL, NULL, hInstance, NULL) ;
    ShowWindow (hWnd, nCmdShow) ;    /* display the window */

    while (GetMessage (&msg, NULL, NULL, NULL))    /* message loop */
    {
        TranslateMessage (&msg) ;    /* translate keyboard messages */
        DispatchMessage (&msg) ;     /* send message to WndProc() */
    }
    return (msg.wParam) ;
}

long FAR PASCAL WndProc (HWND hWnd, WORD wMessage, WORD wParam, LONG lParam)
{
    static  HANDLE  hgMem [4] ;     /* an array of handles */
    LPSTR           lpStr ;         /* far pointer to data */
    int             i ;
    DWORD           dwFree ;
    PAINTSTRUCT     ps ;
    char            cBuf [128], cStatus [64] ;
    WORD            wStatus ;

    switch (wMessage)               /* process windows messages */
    {
        case WM_CREATE:             /* program just starting, allocate global blocks */
            hgMem [0] = GlobalAlloc (GMEM_MOVEABLE | GMEM_DISCARDABLE, 1024) ;
            hgMem [1] = GlobalAlloc (GMEM_MOVEABLE, 1024) ;
            hgMem [2] = GlobalAlloc (GMEM_MOVEABLE | GMEM_DISCARDABLE, 1024) ;
            hgMem [3] = GlobalAlloc (GMEM_MOVEABLE, 1024) ;
            break ;
        case WM_COMMAND:
            switch (wParam)         /* menu items */
            {
```

```c
            case IDM_SQUISH:        /* request more memory than is available */
                dwFree = GlobalCompact (0) ;    /* find amount of free mem */
                GlobalCompact (dwFree + 1) ;                /* force compact */
                InvalidateRect (hWnd, NULL, TRUE) ;   /* force WM_PAINT */
                break ;
            case IDM_RESTORE:   /* restore the two discardable blocks */
                if (GlobalFlags (hgMem [0]) | GMEM_DISCARDED)
                {
                    GlobalReAlloc (hgMem [0], 1024,
                        GMEM_MOVEABLE | GMEM_DISCARDABLE) ;
                }
                if (GlobalFlags (hgMem [2]) | GMEM_DISCARDED)
                {
                    GlobalReAlloc (hgMem [2], 1024,
                        GMEM_MOVEABLE | GMEM_DISCARDABLE) ;
                }
                InvalidateRect (hWnd, NULL, TRUE) ; /* force WM_PAINT */
                break ;
            case IDM_QUIT:                  /* "Quit" menu item */
                DestroyWindow (hWnd) ;      /* destroy window, */
                break ;                     /* terminating application */
            default:            /* otherwise, let Windows process it */
                return (DefWindowProc (hWnd, wMessage, wParam, lParam)) ;
        }
        break ;
    case WM_PAINT:
        BeginPaint (hWnd, &ps) ;
        for (i = 0 ; i < 4 ; i++)
        {           /* create string containing block s status */
            wStatus = GlobalFlags (hgMem [i]) ;  /* find block s status */
            if (!(wStatus & (GMEM_DISCARDED | GMEM_DISCARDABLE)))
                lstrcpy (cStatus, "Not discardable") ;
            else
            {
                lstrcpy (cStatus, "") ;         /* start with empty string */
                if (wStatus & GMEM_DISCARDABLE)
                    lstrcat (cStatus, |Discardable |) ;
                if (wStatus & GMEM_DISCARDED)
                    lstrcat (cStatus, "& Discarded") ;
            }
            lpStr = GlobalLock (hgMem [i]) ;   /* lock block */
            TextOut (ps.hdc, 0, 20 * i, cBuf, wsprintf (cBuf,
                "Block %d" s handle = %d, address = %lu, status = %s",
                i, hgMem [i], lpStr, (LPSTR) cStatus)) ;
            GlobalUnlock (hgMem [i]) ;         /* unlock block */
        }
        EndPaint (hWnd, &ps) ;
        break ;
    case WM_DESTROY:                            /* stop application */
        for (i = 0 ; i < 4 ; i++)
            GlobalFree (hgMem [i]) ;            /* get rid of block */
        PostQuitMessage (0) ;
        break ;
    default:        /* default windows message processing */
        return (DefWindowProc (hWnd, wMessage, wParam, lParam)) ;
    }
    return (0L) ;
}
```

Listings 12-20 to 12-24 show the support files for GMEM1. Figure 12-17 shows the program's icon.

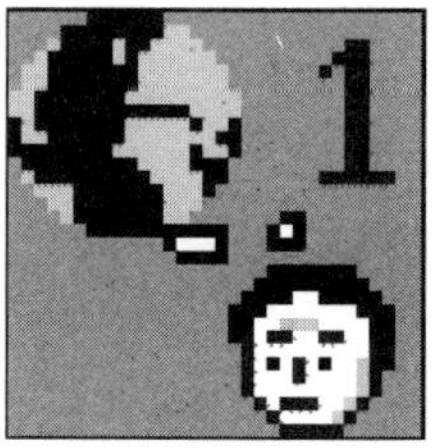

Listing 12-20 GMEM1.H Header File

```
/* gmem1.h header file */

#define IDM_SQUISH          1       /* menu item ID numbers */
#define IDM_RESTORE         2
#define IDM_QUIT           10

#define S_PROGRAMCAPTION    1       /* string table ID numbers */

long FAR PASCAL WndProc (HWND, WORD, WORD, LONG) ;
```

Figure 12-17
GMEM1.ICO
Icon Image

Listing 12-21 GMEM1.RC Resource Script File

```
/* gmem1.rc resource file */

#include "gmem1.h"

MyIcon      ICON    gmem1.ico

MyMenu      MENU
BEGIN
    MENUITEM "&Squish Memory",      IDM_SQUISH
    MENUITEM "&Restore Memory",     IDM_RESTORE
    MENUITEM "&Quit",               IDM_QUIT
END

STRINGTABLE
BEGIN
    S_PROGRAMCAPTION    "Global Memory 1"
END
```

Listing 12-22 GMEM1.DEF Module Definition File

```
NAME            gmem1
DESCRIPTION     'global memory example'
EXETYPE         WINDOWS
STUB            'WINSTUB.EXE'
CODE            PRELOAD MOVEABLE DISCARDABLE
DATA            PRELOAD MOVEABLE MULTIPLE
HEAPSIZE        1024
STACKSIZE       5120
EXPORTS         WndProc
```

Windows Programming Primer Plus®

Listing 12-23 Turbo C++ Project File for GMEM1

```
gmem1.c
gmem1.def
gmem1.res
```

Listing 12-24 QuickC Project File for GMEM1

```
gmem1.c
gmem1.def
gmem1.rc
```

What Windows Is Actually Doing with Memory

This chapter has focused on the mechanics of creating and using memory blocks in the local and global heaps. The techniques discussed are all that you will need for the vast majority of Windows applications. However, there are a few situations that you might run into that require a deeper understanding of what Windows is really doing when you allocate and lock memory blocks. As a primer, this book cannot cover every possibility you may encounter, but at least you will be aware of situations that require a bit more work.

When you call the LocalLock() or GlobalLock() functions, the value returned is an address. You have probably assumed that the returned value is the actual numeric location of a place in memory. Back in the Windows 2.0 days (and with the Windows 3.0 "real mode"), the returned address *was* the actual location of the block of data in memory. With Windows 3.0 and 3.1, things are not so simple. Windows now uses what is called "protected mode" memory addressing, so that Windows programs can access the entire computer's memory, not just the 640K of memory that Windows 2.0 used. When running on a 80386 computer or better, Windows can now run in "Enhanced" mode, meaning that free disk space can be used as "virtual memory," allowing Windows programs to behave as if there is much more memory than is actually installed in the system.

Deep down inside Windows, there is a lot of logic that handles all the complexity of virtual memory and protected mode addressing. As a Windows programmer, you get all of that sophistication without doing any extra work. We can treat the address value returned by LocalLock() and GlobalLock() just as if it were a "real" address in memory. The fact that Windows is doing all sorts of things to figure out if the block is physically located in memory, or has been temporarily stored on the computer's hard disk, is transparent to the programmer.

The only time you will need to be aware of the low-level realities of Window's memory management operations is when you need to directly access the computer's hardware, or when you need to have a Windows program respond to a non-Windows application, such as a device driver for a hardware data acquisition package. In these rare cases, you cannot make the assumption that an address returned by GlobalLock() is the "real" address in memory. You must work with the physical address locations that the hardware works with.

The designers of Windows deliberately did not put access functions for "real" address locations into the standard Windows Software Development Kit (SDK). The low-level functions needed for this type of project are separately documented by Microsoft in the *Windows Device Drivers Development Kit* (DDDK). If you get involved in a hardware intensive Windows project, be sure to get a copy of the DDDK. *Windows API Primer*, and most other books on Windows, do not cover these advanced subjects.

System Memory and System Resources

While on the subject of the inner workings of Windows, you may be curious about a couple of numbers that show up in the Windows Program Manager "About box." Figure 12-18 shows a typical group of settings in the about box, in this case for a beta-test version of Windows 3.1. The figure shows that over 39 megabytes of memory are available. The system running Windows at this time had 16 megabytes of RAM memory, not the 39 megabytes of memory indicated in the about box. The memory value shown in the about box includes disk space that Windows can take advantage of as virtual memory. The "Memory" value represents the amount of room available to store memory objects, including disk space that Windows will automatically use if it is in 386 enhanced mode. 80286 computers do not use virtual memory management under Windows, and will only show the true amount of RAM memory available.

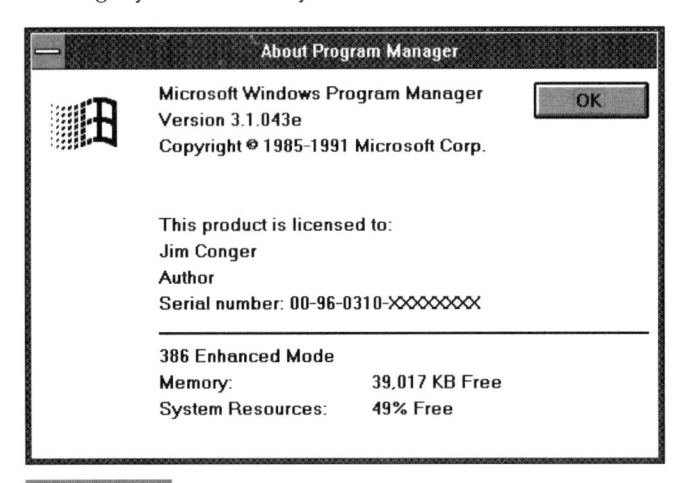

Figure 12-18 The Windows 3.1 Program Manager "About Box"

The other interesting entry is the "System Resources" percent free. This is the amount of room left in the local memory heaps of two parts of Windows, the USER and GDI portions. USER and GDI are just Windows programs (actually dynamic link libraries) that contain many of the functions we have been using, such as CreateSolidBrush() and Rectangle(). When you create a brush, the data for the brush is stored in the local heap of the GDI module. Similarly, menus, window classes, and many other basic pieces of data that Windows needs are stored in the local heap of the USER module. If you create too many pens, brushes, window classes, etc., you can use up the local memory space of the USER and GDI modules of Windows. After all, like all other Windows programs, USER and GDI are each limited to 64K for their respective local heaps.

The point of this discussion is that Windows does not have unlimited room to store vast numbers of objects. Most Windows applications only create a few objects, and delete them as soon as possible. Check the system resources entry before and after your program is run, and make sure that it is not using up big chunks of these limited areas. A classic error is to create more than one menu, but then forget that only the menus attached to a window are deleted when the window is destroyed. The extra menus will remain stored in the USER module's heap, taking up space until the Windows session is ended. Similar problems occur if you forget to destroy pens and brushes. Errors like this are easy to spot, as the system resources value will not return to its previous value when the program is terminated.

Summary

Windows allows you to allocate blocks of memory for the program to use in both the local data segment and in the global heap. In either case, the blocks can be specified as fixed in memory, moveable, or both moveable and discardable. Fixed blocks are generally avoided, as they reduce Windows' ability to optimize memory use. Normally, programs use a combination of moveable and discardable memory blocks.

Because Windows can move objects in memory, the address of the block may change. Windows programs keep track of memory blocks using the block's handle, not the address. When the program needs to read or write to the block, the block is first fixed in memory with either LocalLock() or GlobalLock() and then accessed. The locking functions return the current address of the memory block, so that normal memory operations can be performed. Once the data has been used, the block is unlocked using LocalUnlock() or GlobalUnlock(), and again freed to move in memory. When the block is no longer needed, it can be freed with LocalFree() or GlobalFree().

The size of a block can be changed as the program runs using LocalReAlloc() or GlobalReAlloc(). If the block is enlarged, the existing data in the block is not affected by reallocating additional room. Of course, shrinking the block truncates any data in the far end of the block as it is reduced in size. Discardable blocks must be reallocated if Windows has discarded the data. The handle to a discardable block remains valid even if the data has been discarded. Use LocalFlags() or GlobalFlags() to determine if a discardable block still contains data, or if it has been discarded.

Local memory blocks are all within one data segment and use near pointers for addresses. Global memory blocks are outside of the program's data segment and must use far pointers. The WINDOWS.H file provides handy abbreviations for common pointers, such as PSTR for a near pointer to a character string and LPSTR for a far pointer to a character string.

QUESTIONS

1. If a program has a 5K stack and no static data, what is the largest memory block that can be allocated in the program's local data segment? a) 5K; b) 16K; c) 64K; d) about 59K.

2. Write the full declaration for the following data types defined in WINDOWS.H.
   BYTE = _____, PSTR = _____, PBYTE = _____,
   LPINT = _____.

3. Call the _____ function to determine the address of a moveable memory block in the local heap.

4. Handles cannot be passed to other functions because the data may move in memory. (True/False).

5. Because memory is allocated in units of bytes, only byte-sized data, such as characters, can be stored in allocated memory. (True/False).

6. The handle returned by LocalAlloc() is equal to the allocated block's address if a fixed memory block is allocated (True/False).

7. Use the _____ function to determine if a discardable global memory block has been discarded.

8. Use the _____ function to change the size of a global memory block that has already been allocated.

9. Successively allocated memory blocks will always start out next to each other in memory (True/False).

10. Near pointers can be used for addresses of small global memory blocks, as long as the blocks fit into one segment (less than 64K).

EXERCISES

1. Modify the MEM3 program so that the program starts with a heap size of 1,024 bytes. Are all four of the memory blocks still allocated when the program starts? Can you still restore and discard the two discardable blocks using the menu commands?

2. Modify the MEM1 program so that the program stores 50 integers in a local memory block. Initially, set the integers to be the sequence from 0 to 49. When the "Change" menu item is selected, change the values to range from 100 to 149. Modify the WM_PAINT message processing logic to display the integers in the window's client area.

ANSWERS TO QUESTIONS

1. D.
2. BYTE = unsigned char; PSTR = char near *; PBYTE = unsigned char near *; LPINT = int far *.
3. LocalLock().
4. False. The handle remains valid regardless of where Windows locates the block in memory, so handles can be passed as valid parameters to functions.
5. False. Memory blocks are allocated in units of bytes, but any type of data can be stored in the memory block after the block is allocated.
6. True.
7. GlobalFlags().
8. GlobalReAlloc().
9. False. Windows may place successively allocated blocks next to each other, or separated if there is not enough continuous room in memory for the next block.
10. False. Near pointers can be used if the address is within the program's local heap (local memory). A small block allocated outside of the program's heap would require a far pointer.

SOLUTIONS TO EXERCISES

1. The only change needed to MEM3 is to edit the program's module definition file, and change the HEAPSIZE statement to show 1,024 bytes. Listing 12-25 shows the modified file, listed under the file name C12EXER1.DEF on the source code disks.

Listing 12-25 C12EXER1.DEF

```
NAME            c12exer1
DESCRIPTION     'exercise 1 chapter 12'
EXETYPE         WINDOWS
STUB            'WINSTUB.EXE'
CODE            PRELOAD MOVEABLE DISCARDABLE
DATA            PRELOAD MOVEABLE MULTIPLE
HEAPSIZE        1024
STACKSIZE       5120
EXPORTS         WndProc
```

The result of changing the heapsize is that Windows discards the two discardable blocks on startup in an effort to fit the two moveable, but not discardable, blocks into the limited heap space. Selecting the "Restore Memory" menu item forces Windows to reallocate the two moveable blocks. Windows ex-

SOLUTIONS TO EXERCISES (cont'd)

pands the heap to over 4K at this point, making room for all four blocks in memory. Figure 12-19 shows the C12EXER1 program on startup, which you can compare to Figure 12-8 for the MEM3 program which starts with a larger heap size defined in the program's .DEF file.

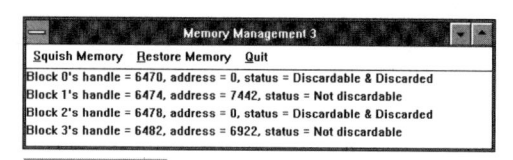

Figure 12-19 The C12EXER1 Program on Startup

Note that during startup, when the blocks are first allocated, each of the discardable blocks is allocated before a moveable block is allocated. The discardable blocks are briefly allocated in memory, but then immediately discarded as Windows attempts to allocate another block in the small local heap, and finds a discardable block that can be discarded to make room.

2. The main change is to allocate room for 50 integers, and then fill the memory block with integer data. Listing 12-26 shows the modifications to the WndProc() function of the MEM1.C file. No changes to the other program files are needed. The full solution is under the file name C12EXER2 on the source code disks. Note that the pointer to the memory block returned by LocalLock() is cast to a PINT (near pointer to an integer).

Listing 12-26 Solution to Exercise 2

```
long FAR PASCAL WndProc (HWND hWnd, WORD wMessage, WORD wParam, LONG lParam)
{
    static  HANDLE      hMem ;
    PINT                pInt ;              /* pointer to a near integer */
    int                 i, nRow, nCol ;
    PAINTSTRUCT         ps ;
    char                cBuf [128] ;

    switch (wMessage)                       /* process windows messages */
    {
        case WM_CREATE:         /* program just starting, allocate local block */
            hMem = LocalAlloc (LMEM_MOVEABLE, 50 * sizeof (int)) ;
            pInt = (PINT) LocalLock (hMem) ;   /* lock the block in mem */
            for (i = 0 ; i < 50 ; i++)
                *pInt++ = i ;       /* put integers in block */
            LocalUnlock (hMem) ;    /* unlock the block */
            break ;
        case WM_COMMAND:
            switch (wParam)                 /* menu items */
            {
                case IDM_CHANGE:    /* "Change" menu item */
                    pInt = (PINT) LocalLock (hMem) ;    /* lock block */
```

Windows Programming Primer Plus®

SOLUTIONS TO EXERCISES (cont'd)

```
                    for (i = 0 ; i < 50 ; i++)
                        *pInt++ = 100 + i ;    /* now numbers from 100 to 150 */
                    LocalUnlock (hMem) ;       /* unlock block */
                    InvalidateRect (hWnd, NULL, TRUE) ; /* force WM_PAINT */
                    break ;
                case IDM_QUIT:                 /* "Quit" menu item */
                    DestroyWindow (hWnd) ;     /* destroy window, */
                    break ;       /* terminating application */
                default:            /* otherwise, let Windows process it */
                    return (DefWindowProc (hWnd, wMessage, wParam, lParam)) ;
            }
            break ;
        case WM_PAINT:
            BeginPaint (hWnd, &ps) ;
            pInt = (PINT) LocalLock (hMem) ;   /* lock block */
            nRow = nCol = 0 ;
            for (i = 0 ; i < 50 ; i++)
            {
                TextOut (ps.hdc, nCol, nRow, cBuf, wsprintf (cBuf,
                    " %d", *pInt++)) ;
                nCol += 40 ;
                if (nCol > 400)
                {
                    nCol = 0 ;
                    nRow += 20 ;
                }
            }
            LocalUnlock (hMem) ;               /* unlock block */
            EndPaint (hWnd, &ps) ;
            break ;
        case WM_DESTROY:                       /* stop application */
            LocalFree (hMem) ;                 /* get rid of block */
            PostQuitMessage (0) ;
            break ;
        default:    /* default windows message processing */
            return (DefWindowProc (hWnd, wMessage, wParam, lParam)) ;
    }
    return (0L) ;
}
```

When started, the solution to Exercise 2 appears as shown in Figure 12-20. The solution shown takes the shortcut of using fixed character spacing for the numbers. A more complete solution would use GetTextMetrics() to determine the size of the characters before doing any output.

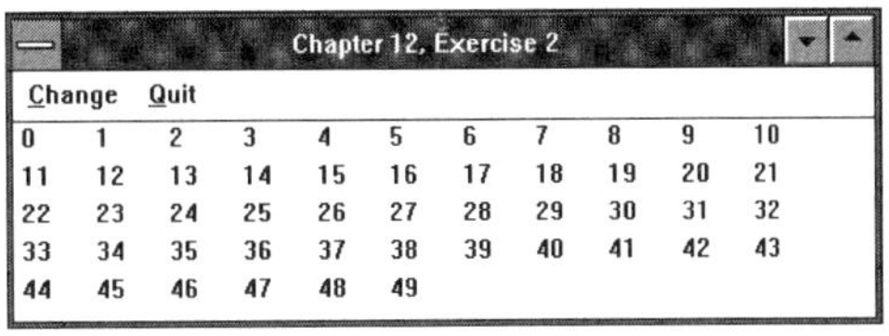

Figure 12-20 C12EXER2 Program on Startup

CHAPTER 13

The Device Context

The use of device contexts was introduced in Chapter 4, *Text and Graphics Output*, to demonstrate text and graphics output to the screen. Screen output is the most common use of device contexts, but not the only one. Windows programs are expected to output text and graphics to a wide range of printers, plotters, and video equipment.

The concept of a device context is used to provide the connection between Windows' graphics functions and the "real world" of computer hardware. Windows programs can use the same graphical functions, such as TextOut() and Rectangle(), to output to any device context. Windows handles the chore of translating the function calls into commands that a printer, plotter, or video board will understand. A handy feature of Windows' device context logic is the ability to describe the output surface (screen, printer page, etc.) with different sets of units. You can specify a location using inches, millimeters, printer's units (twips), or pixels (dots). You can even create your own arbitrary system of units. Windows also allows the origin of the device context to be relocated, which is a simple way to move an image without changing the graphics function calls.

One other subject discussed in this chapter is the technique of saving device context settings with a window's private data. This technique allows you to save the current set of pens, brushes, and units with the window's data, rather than having to recreate the settings each time a painting operation is done. Saving the device context data uses memory, but speeds up the program's graphics output.

Concepts Covered

A Window's Private Device Context
Device Units
Logical Units
Mapping Modes
Moving the Origin
Text Alignment
Scalable Mapping Modes

Keywords Covered

CS_OWNDC
CS_CLASSDC
CS_PARENTDC
MM_ANISOTROPIC
MM_HIENGLISH
MM_HIMETRIC
MM_ISOTROPIC
MM_LOENGLISH
MM_LOMETRIC
MM_TEXT
MM_TWIPS

Functions Covered

SetMapMode()
SetWindowOrg()
SetViewportOrg()
SetWindowExt()
SetViewportExt()
GetWindowExt()

Private Device Contexts

In all of the examples so far in this book, we have created a device context each time the program needed to output to its window's client area. The BeginPaint() function is used when processing WM_PAINT messages, and the GetDC() function is used everywhere else in the program to retrieve a handle to the window's device context. Here is a typical example of a sequence of function calls used to output an ellipse to the window's client area:

```
HDC     hDC ;
HPEN    hPen, hOldPen ;

hDC = GetDC (hWnd) ;     /* create a device context for Window's client area */
hPen = CreatePen (PS_SOLID, 3, RGB (255, 0, 0)) ; /* create a red pen 3 dots wide */
hOldPen = SelectObject (hDC, hPen) ;            /* select pen into dc */
```

```
Ellipse (hDC, 10, 10, 100, 80) ;           /* draw ellipse */
SelectObject (hDC, hOldPen) ;              /* displace new pen from dc */
DeleteObject (hPen) ;                      /* delete new pen */
ReleaseDC (hWnd, hDC) ;                    /* free the device context */
```

When the GetDC() function is called, Windows sets aside a memory area for the device context data and initializes it with the default settings for the video equipment in use. The call to CreatePen() sets aside another memory area to store the data for the pen. Selecting the pen into the device context modifies the data in the device context memory block, providing the device context with a pointer to the pen data in memory. The data is put to use when the Ellipse() function is called, and then purged from memory by calling DeleteObject() and ReleaseDC().

This type of logic is fine for simple graphical output, but becomes cumbersome if you are changing many device context settings. It is also slow, because Windows must set up the device context each time graphics output is needed. To speed things up, you can create a private device context for the window, which will store all device context settings while the window exists. This also means that you can save a set of pens, brushes, fonts, etc. with the device context, rather than having to recreate them each time they are needed.

The trade-off in using a private device context is an increase in memory use. Saving a device context requires about 800 bytes of memory, plus the memory consumed by the pens, brushes, and other objects. This memory room comes out of the local data heap maintained by the KERNEL and USER portions of Windows, and shows up as a reduction in the amount of free "system resources" when you check the "About" box on the Windows Program Manager. The Windows environment can definitely run out of system resource space, so use private device contexts with discretion.

You will probably find that a private device context is most appropriate when the application requires that many changes be made to the default settings of the device context before it is used. Private device contexts are also convenient if your application uses a number of child windows created from the same window class. Each child window ends up with the same background brush, pen, font, system of units, and so on, which gives every child window created from the window class a consistent appearance.

Creating a Private Device Context

To create a window with its own private device context, add the CS_OWNDC window class style when registering the window's class in the WinMain() function. Here is an example:

```
if (!hPrevInstance)
{
    wndclass.style          = CS_HREDRAW | CS_VREDRAW | CS_OWNDC ;
    wndclass.lpfnWndProc    = WndProc ;
    wndclass.cbClsExtra     = 0 ;
    wndclass.cbWndExtra     = 0 ;
    wndclass.hInstance      = hInstance ;
    wndclass.hIcon          = LoadIcon (hInstance, "MyIcon") ;
    wndclass.hCursor        = LoadCursor (NULL, IDC_ARROW) ;
    wndclass.hbrBackground  = GetStockObject (WHITE_BRUSH) ; ;
```

```
        wndclass.lpszMenuName    = "MyMenu" ;
        wndclass.lpszClassName   = "MyClass" ;
                    /* register the window class */
        if (!RegisterClass (&wndclass))
            return 0 ;
}
```

The CS_OWNDC style instructs Windows to set aside a memory area large enough to hold the device context settings for each window created from this class. If you will be creating a number of similar windows that can share the same device context, use the CS_CLASSDC style in place of CS_OWNDC. CS_CLASSDC tells Windows to reserve only one memory area for a device context, and let every window from the class share that group of device context settings. One last option is CS_PARENTDC, which can be used for child windows. Child windows created from a class using the CS_PARENTDC style use their parent's device context. This presumes the parent was created with either the CS_OWNDC or CS_CLASSDC style, so that the child has data to read.

Using a Private Device Context

With a private device context created, the program can save all sorts of settings into the device context, and then use the modified device context as desired. The device context data will continue to exist in memory until the window is destroyed. For example, the device context for the parent window can be initialized when the program first starts as follows:

```
static HPEN     hPen ;
static HBRUSH   hBrush ;

case WM_CREATE:                             /* program starting - set dc settings */
    hDC = GetDC (hWnd) ;                    /* get dc handle */
    SetTextColor (hDC, RGB (0, 0, 255)) ;   /* set text color to blue */
                                            /* select objects into dc */
    hPen = CreatePen (PS_SOLID, 3, RGB (255, 0, 0)) ;
    SelectObject (hDC, hPen) ;
    hBrush = CreateSolidBrush (RGB (255, 200, 0)) ;
    SelectObject (hDC, hBrush) ;
    break ;                                 /* note no ReleaseDC() call */
```

The GetDC() function simply returns a handle to the device context data in memory. GetDC() does not need to create a new device context because the function checks that the *hWnd* window was created with the CS_OWNDC style and, therefore, already has a device context set aside. The device context is modified by changing the color of any text displayed using the SetTextColor() function, and by selecting a new pen and brush into the device context. Note that the pen and brush handles are saved as static variables. These handles will be needed when the program terminates to delete these objects so that they do not continue to occupy space in memory. Also note that the ReleaseDC() function is not called after the changes to the private device context. ReleaseDC() will not do anything if the device context is owned by a window.

At some other point in the program's operation, the device context can be used to output text and graphics. If output is done in the course of processing a WM_PAINT message, BeginPaint() is used to retrieve a handle to the device context. In any other part of the program, GetDC() is used, as shown here:

```
hDC = GetDC (hWnd) ;                /* get a handle to the dc data for the window */
TextOut (hDC, 0, 0, "Some text.", 10) ;
Rectangle (hDC, 20, 0, 100, 200) ;
break ;                             /* no call to ReleaseDC() */
```

The text and rectangle will be output based on the device context settings in memory. Because the previous code changed the text color and selected a new pen and brush, the result will be blue text and a rectangle painted with a red outline and a magenta center. The same effect could be obtained when processing a WM_PAINT message. In this case, both the BeginPaint() and EndPaint() functions are required. EndPaint() stops the painting process, but does not free the device context if the DC is owned by the window.

```
case WM_PAINT:
    BeginPaint (hWnd, &ps) ;
    TextOut (hDC, 0, 0, "Some text.", 10) ;
    Rectangle (hDC, 20, 0, 100, 200) ;
    EndPaint (hWnd, &ps) ;
    break ;
```

The private device context will be destroyed automatically when the window that owns it is destroyed. You can use the DeleteDC() function to explicitly delete a device context, but normally you will want the DC to exist as long as the window is active, so DeleteDC() is seldom used. Don't forget to use DeleteObject() to delete any pens, brushes, or fonts before the program terminates. Otherwise, these objects will stay in memory after the program is gone, taking up valuable system memory space.

An Example with a Private Device Context

The first example program in this chapter, OWNDC, demonstrates a program window with its own private device context. Figure 13-1 shows OWNDC in operation. Initially,

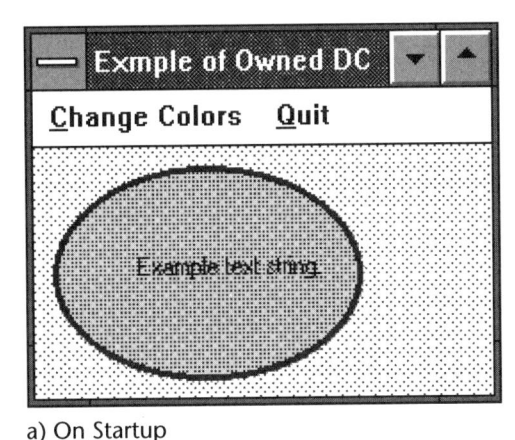

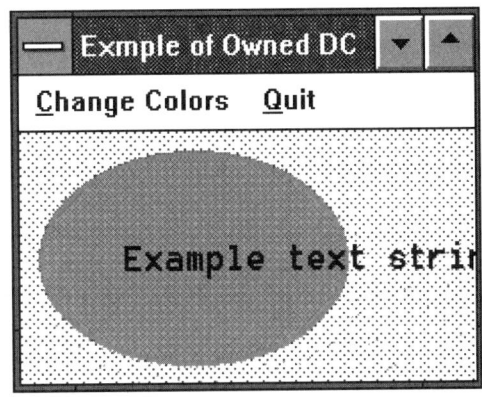

a) On Startup

b) After Selecting "Change Colors"

Figure 13-1 The OWNDC Program

the program window displays an ellipse filled with a yellow brush, outlined with a red pen, and containing small blue text characters. Selecting the "Change Colors" menu item causes the ellipse to be filled with a turquoise brush, surrounded by a green pen, and changes the text font. The color changes are not obvious in Figure 13-1, but the change to the text font shows up clearly.

The interesting thing about the graphics in Figure 13-1 is that both images are drawn with exactly the same WM_PAINT logic. The changes to the colors and fonts are made by changing the settings in the program window's private device context. That device context's settings are used to paint the window's client area, so any change to the DC shows up when graphics functions are used.

OWNDC.C

Listing 13-1 shows the complete OWNDC.C program, which demonstrates several new techniques. One change is that the main program window uses a custom brush for the background color. The brush is created with CreateSolidBrush() at the top of the WinMain() function, and deleted when the program terminates at the end of WinMain(). The custom brush results in the window's client area being painted a light magenta color.

Another change is that OWNDC uses the CS_OWNDC class style when registering the parent window's class. This creates a private device context for any window created from this class. The device context is initialized when the program starts (when the WM_CREATE message is processed) by calling SetBkMode() to make the text background transparent, using SetTextColor() to set the text color to blue, and by selecting a red pen and yellow brush. All of these changes are saved in the private device context.

```
case WM_CREATE:             /* program starting - set dc settings */
    hDC = GetDC (hWnd) ;                /* get dc handle */
    SetBkMode (hDC, TRANSPARENT) ;      /* set painting mode */
    SetTextColor (hDC, RGB (0, 0, 255)) ;   /* set text color to blue */
                                        /* select objects into dc */
    SelectObject (hDC, GetStockObject (ANSI_VAR_FONT)) ;
    hPen = CreatePen (PS_SOLID, 3, RGB (255, 0, 0)) ;
    SelectObject (hDC, hPen) ;
    hBrush = CreateSolidBrush (RGB (255, 200, 0)) ;
    SelectObject (hDC, hBrush) ;
    break ;                             /* note no ReleaseDC() call */
```

The WM_PAINT logic ends up being fairly simple, as the device context is already set with the correct pens, brushes, and so on. All the program needs to do when a WM_PAINT message is received is to call Ellipse() to paint the ellipse, and call TextOut() to output the text string. In this case, the text string is stored in the program's resource data as a string table entry, so LoadString() is also used to fetch the character string.

```
case WM_PAINT:
    BeginPaint (hWnd, &ps) ;
    Ellipse (ps.hdc, 10, 10, 160, 110) ;
    hInstance = GetWindowWord (hWnd, GWW_HINSTANCE) ;
    LoadString (hInstance, S_CENTERTEXT, cBuf, sizeof (cBuf)) ;
```

```
        TextOut (ps.hdc, 50, 50, cBuf, lstrlen (cBuf)) ;
        EndPaint (hWnd, &ps) ;
        break ;
```

When the user selects the "Change Color" menu item, the device context settings are altered. The previously created pen and brush are displaced out of the device context by selecting stock objects, and then deleted. A new pen and brush are then created and selected into the DC. Also, the stock OEM_FIXED_FONT is selected into the DC to change the text font used. All of these changes are stored in the Window's private DC, and take effect in any subsequent painting operations.

```
    case IDM_CHANGE:                    /* change device context settings */
        hDC = GetDC (hWnd) ;            /* get dc handle */
                                        /* displace pen and brush out of the dc */
        SelectObject (hDC, GetStockObject (BLACK_PEN)) ;
        SelectObject (hDC, GetStockObject (BLACK_BRUSH)) ;
        DeleteObject (hPen) ;           /* get rid of old pen */
        DeleteObject (hBrush) ;         /* and brush */
                                        /* create new pen and brush */
        hPen = CreatePen (PS_SOLID, 3, RGB (0, 255, 0)) ;
        SelectObject (hDC, hPen) ;      /* select into dc */
        hBrush = CreateSolidBrush (RGB (0, 200, 200)) ;
        SelectObject (hDC, hBrush) ;
                                        /* and select new font */
        SelectObject (hDC, GetStockObject (OEM_FIXED_FONT)) ;
                                        /* force WM_PAINT */
        InvalidateRect (hWnd, NULL, TRUE) ;
        break ;                         /* note no ReleaseDC() call */
```

Because the pen and brush are used by the Window's private device context, they must be saved until the program terminates. DeleteObject() is used in processing the WM_DESTROY message to delete the pen and brush from memory just before the OWNDC program exits. If a new font is created and used by a private device context, it will also need to be deleted with DeleteObject() to avoid tying up memory.

Listing 13-1 OWNDC.C

```
/* owndc.c   example with window owning a device context */

#include <windows.h>
#include "owndc.h"

int PASCAL WinMain (HANDLE hInstance, HANDLE hPrevInstance, LPSTR lpszCmdLine,
    int nCmdShow)
{
    HWND        hWnd ;          /* the Window's "handle" */
    MSG         msg ;           /* a message structure */
    WNDCLASS    wndclass ;      /* window class structure */
    char        cBuf [128] ;    /* character buffer */
    HBRUSH      hBrush ;
                                /* create a magenta brush for background */
    hBrush = CreateSolidBrush (RGB (255, 230, 255)) ;
```

```c
        if (!hPrevInstance)
        {
            wndclass.style          = CS_HREDRAW | CS_VREDRAW | CS_OWNDC ;
            wndclass.lpfnWndProc    = WndProc ;
            wndclass.cbClsExtra     = 0 ;
            wndclass.cbWndExtra     = 0 ;
            wndclass.hInstance      = hInstance ;
            wndclass.hIcon          = LoadIcon (hInstance, "MyIcon") ;
            wndclass.hCursor        = LoadCursor (NULL, IDC_ARROW) ;
            wndclass.hbrBackground  = hBrush ;
            wndclass.lpszMenuName   = "MyMenu" ;
            wndclass.lpszClassName  = "MyClass" ;
                    /* register the window class */
            if (!RegisterClass (&wndclass))
                return 0 ;
        }
        LoadString (hInstance, S_PROGRAMCAPTION, cBuf, sizeof (cBuf)) ;

        hWnd = CreateWindow ("MyClass", cBuf, WS_OVERLAPPEDWINDOW,
            CW_USEDEFAULT, CW_USEDEFAULT, CW_USEDEFAULT, CW_USEDEFAULT,
            NULL, NULL, hInstance, NULL) ;
        ShowWindow (hWnd, nCmdShow) ; /* display the window */

        while (GetMessage (&msg, NULL, NULL, NULL))   /* message loop */
        {
            TranslateMessage (&msg) ;  /* translate keyboard messages */
            DispatchMessage (&msg) ;   /* send message to WndProc() */
        }
        DeleteObject (hBrush) ;        /* delete the background brush */
        return (msg.wParam) ;
}

long FAR PASCAL WndProc (HWND hWnd, WORD wMessage, WORD wParam, LONG lParam)
{
        PAINTSTRUCT     ps ;
        char            cBuf [128] ;
        HANDLE          hInstance ;
        HDC             hDC ;
        static  HPEN    hPen ;
        static  HBRUSH  hBrush ;

        switch (wMessage)              /* process windows messages */
        {
            case WM_CREATE:            /* program starting - set dc settings */
                hDC = GetDC (hWnd) ;               /* get dc handle */
                SetBkMode (hDC, TRANSPARENT) ;     /* set painting mode */
                SetTextColor (hDC, RGB (0, 0, 255)) ;  /* set text color to blue */
                                                   /* select objects into dc */
                SelectObject (hDC, GetStockObject (ANSI_VAR_FONT)) ;
                hPen = CreatePen (PS_SOLID, 3, RGB (255, 0, 0)) ;
                SelectObject (hDC, hPen) ;
                hBrush = CreateSolidBrush (RGB (255, 200, 0)) ;
                SelectObject (hDC, hBrush) ;
                break ;                /* note no ReleaseDC() call */
            case WM_COMMAND:
                switch (wParam)                    /* menu items */
                {
```

```
            case IDM_CHANGE:              /* change device context settings */
                hDC = GetDC (hWnd) ;      /* get dc handle */
                /* displace pen and brush out of the dc */
                SelectObject (hDC, GetStockObject (BLACK_PEN)) ;
                SelectObject (hDC, GetStockObject (BLACK_BRUSH)) ;
                DeleteObject (hPen) ;     /* get rid of old pen */
                DeleteObject (hBrush) ;   /* and brush */
                                          /* create new pen and brush */
                hPen = CreatePen (PS_SOLID, 3, RGB (0, 255, 0)) ;
                SelectObject (hDC, hPen) ; /* select into dc */
                hBrush = CreateSolidBrush (RGB (0, 200, 200)) ;
                SelectObject (hDC, hBrush) ;
                                          /* and select new font */
                SelectObject (hDC, GetStockObject (OEM_FIXED_FONT)) ;
                                          /* force WM_PAINT */
                InvalidateRect (hWnd, NULL, TRUE) ;
                break ;                   /* note no ReleaseDC() call */
            case IDM_QUIT:
                DestroyWindow (hWnd) ;
                break ;
        }
        break ;
    case WM_PAINT:
        BeginPaint (hWnd, &ps) ;
        Ellipse (ps.hdc, 10, 10, 160, 110) ;
        hInstance = GetWindowWord (hWnd, GWW_HINSTANCE) ;
        LoadString (hInstance, S_CENTERTEXT, cBuf, sizeof (cBuf)) ;
        TextOut (ps.hdc, 50, 50, cBuf, lstrlen (cBuf)) ;
        EndPaint (hWnd, &ps) ;
        break ;
    case WM_DESTROY:                      /* stop application */
        DeleteObject (hPen) ;             /* delete pen and brush */
        DeleteObject (hBrush) ;
        PostQuitMessage (0) ;
        break ;
    default:    /* default windows message processing */
        return (DefWindowProc (hWnd, wMessage, wParam, lParam)) ;
    }
    return (0L) ;
}
```

Listings 13-2 to 13-6 show the support files for OWNDC.H. Figure 13-2 shows the program's icon.

Listing 13-2 OWNDC.H Header File

```
/* owndc.h header file */

#define    IDM_CHANGE         1    /* menu item ID numbers */
#define    IDM_QUIT          10

#define    S_CENTERTEXT       1    /* string table ID numbers */
#define    S_PROGRAMCAPTION   2

long FAR PASCAL WndProc (HWND, WORD, WORD, LONG) ;
```

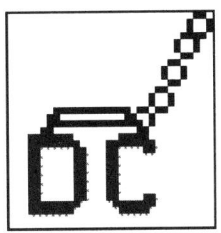

Figure 13-2
OWNDC.ICO
Icon Image

Listing 13-3 OWNDC.RC Resource Script File

```
/* owndc.rc  resource file */

#include "owndc.h"

MyIcon      ICON    owndc.ico

MyMenu      MENU
BEGIN
   MENUITEM "&Change Colors",   IDM_CHANGE
   MENUITEM "&Quit",            IDM_QUIT
END

STRINGTABLE
BEGIN
   S_PROGRAMCAPTION, "Example of Owned DC "
   S_CENTERTEXT, "Example text string."
END
```

Listing 13-4 OWNDC.DEF Module Definition File

```
NAME            owndc
DESCRIPTION     'owndc program'
EXETYPE         WINDOWS
STUB            'WINSTUB.EXE'
CODE            PRELOAD MOVEABLE DISCARDABLE
DATA            PRELOAD MOVEABLE MULTIPLE
HEAPSIZE        1024
STACKSIZE       5120
EXPORTS         WndProc
```

Listing 13-5 Turbo C++ Project File for OWNDC

```
owndc.c
owndc.def
owndc.res
```

Listing 13-6 QuickC Project File for OWNDC

```
owndc.c
owndc.def
owndc.rc
```

Mapping Modes

Graphics and text output functions, such as Rectangle() and TextOut(), must be passed coordinates in the device context to specify where the object should be painted. So far, we have used the default system of units called "device units." Using a video screen as an example, device units are the number of pixels measured from the upper left corner of a window area to a point on the screen. Positive values for X are to the right, and positive values for Y are downward. For a printer, device units are the number of printer dots measured from the upper left corner of a printed page.

The problem with device units is that not all pixels and dots are the same size. If you create a nice looking picture on the screen and then try to output the same picture to a high-resolution laser printer, the whole picture will end up about the size of a postage stamp. That is because the printer's dots are a lot closer together than a video screen's pixels. You could go to all sorts of trouble to figure out how much bigger to draw every object on the printer, but fortunately Windows provides a more elegant solution — mapping modes.

Mapping modes allow you to create a logical system of units for use in text and graphics functions, and then let Windows figure out how to "map" the output to any real device. When you use a mapping mode, function calls, such as Rectangle() and TextOut(), will be in "logical units." "Logical units" is a fancy way to say that Windows does not know exactly how big your video screen is. If you specify a logical location 100 millimeters to the left, Windows will make an intelligent guess as to how big a logical millimeter is on an average screen, and plot the point there. This will not be exactly 100 millimeters to the left on your screen, but it will be close. For printers, the location will be very close to 100 millimeters, as Windows can determine the spacing of the printer's dots by requesting information from the printer driver (printer drivers are explained in the next chapter).

Table 13-1 summarizes the most common mapping modes available in Windows. The default mapping mode is called MM_TEXT. The MM_TEXT mode is the only mode that moves locations downward as the Y values increase. That is because text lines are typically numbered from top to bottom. All of the other modes move the location upward as the Y values increase, which is typical of mathematical coordinate systems. The MM_LOMETRIC and MM_LOENGLISH modes are the most commonly used. The "LO" prefix stands for "low resolution," while "HI" stands for "high resolution." MM_TWIPS uses printers units, and is the most appropriate if you are working with primarily text.

MM_HIENGLISH	Each logical unit is 0.001 inch. X increases to the right. Y increases upward.
MM_HIMETRIC	Each logical unit is 0.01 millimeter. X increases to the right. Y increases upward.
MM_LOENGLISH	Each logical unit is 0.01 inch. X increases to the right. Y increases upward.
MM_LOMETRIC	Each logical unit is 0.1 millimeter. X increases to the right. Y increases upward.
MM_TEXT	This is the default mapping mode. Each unit equals one pixel. X increases to the right. Y increases downward.

continued

Table 13-1 (cont'd)

MM_TWIPS	Each logical unit is 1/20 point, or 1/1440 of an inch. X increases to the right. Y increases upward. This is typically used with text fonts.

Table 13-1 Fixed Size Mapping Modes

Figure 13-3 shows how logical units are interpreted for several mapping modes. Any graphics or text output function that specifies a location will interpret the location using the current mapping mode for the device context. For example, in Figure 13-3 the MoveTo(hDC, 50, 90) function call is interpreted as a location in pixels in the MM_TEXT mapping mode, a location in tenths of a millimeter in the MM_LOMETRIC mapping mode, and a location in hundredths of an inch in the MM_LOENGLISH mapping mode. Note that only the MM_TEXT mapping mode has Y values increasing downward.

The SetMapMode() function changes the mapping mode of a device context. A typical sequence of function calls to set the MM_LOMETRIC mapping mode is as follows:

```
HDC     hDC ;

hDC = GetDC (hWnd) ;
SetMapMode (hDC, MM_LOMETRIC) ;
Rectangle (hDC, 100, -100, 300, -50) ;
ReleaseDC (hWnd, hDC) ;
```

In this case, the mapping mode is changed before the Rectangle() function is called, so the parameters passed to the Rectangle() function will be interpreted as sizing the rectangle in tenths of a millimeter, not in pixels. If the window has its own private device context, the mapping mode is saved along with all of the other data stored with the DC, and the ReleaseDC() function call is not required.

Text and Mapping Modes

One thing to be aware of in setting mapping modes is that text is handled slightly differently than graphical objects. If you change the mapping mode, the location where

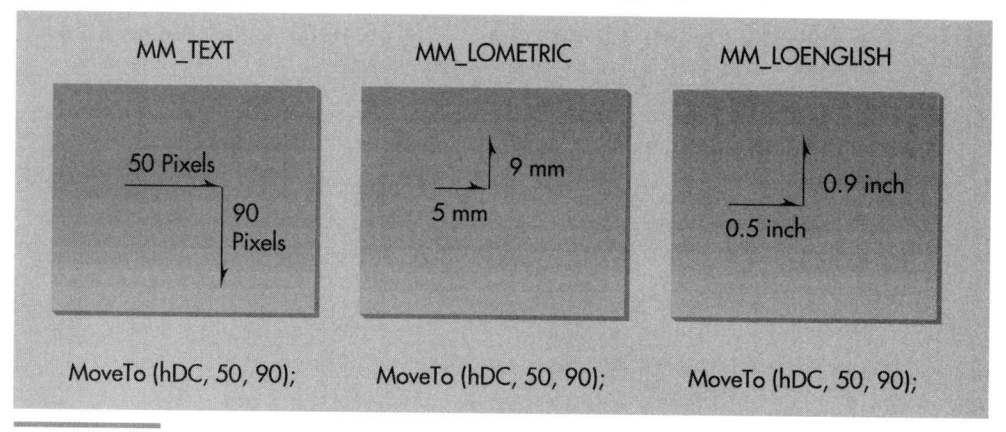

Figure 13-3 Three Mapping Modes

the text will be placed will be interpreted using the logical coordinate system. For example, if you set the MM_LOMETRIC mapping mode and then call TextOut(hDC, 10, 20,...), the position that the text string will start on will be interpreted as $X = 1$ mm and $Y = 2$ mm. However, the size of the text will be determined by the font in use. Changing the mapping mode changes the location of the text, but not its size. Create and select a different font if you want to change the size of the characters.

Moving the Origin

A default value for a device context that can lead to a lot of confusion is the location of the origin for the mapping modes. All of the modes start with the origin (0,0 point) at the upper left corner of the screen, or the upper left corner of the page for a printer or plotter. This works fine for the default MM_TEXT mapping mode, but means that positive X,Y locations for the other mapping modes are not visible, as they appear above the top of the screen or page. You can spend hours trying to figure out what happened to your output if you forget this simple fact. Figure 13-4 illustrates the result of attempting to draw a rectangle at location 100, 100 using the different mapping modes. Only the MM_TEXT mapping mode will produce a visible result.

The most obvious way to get around the problem of the location of the origin for the mapping modes, such as MM_LOMETRIC, is to use negative Y values. Painting the rectangle starting at location 100, -100 would make the rectangle appear in the client area. A more elegant solution is to just move the origin of the logical coordinate sys-

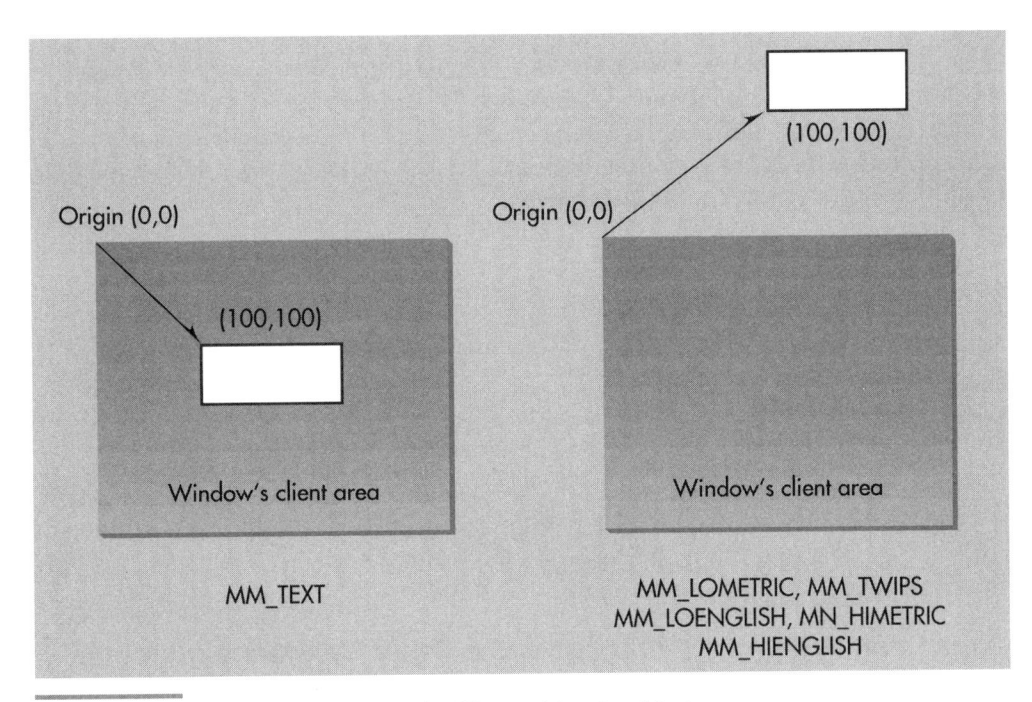

Figure 13-4 Drawing a Rectangle with Different Mapping Modes

tem. Windows provides two functions for doing this, SetWindowOrg() and SetViewportOrg(). The reason for having two functions to do the same task is that SetViewportOrg() moves the origin using device units (pixels), while SetWindowOrg() uses whatever logical units are currently selected into the device context. The window origin is an offset from the viewport origin, as shown in Figure 13-5. "Viewport" is just a made-up word that describes the logical coordinate system of a device context.

It is common to use SetWindowOrg() to move the logical origin on the screen to the bottom left corner of the window's client area, and then use SetViewportOrg() to move the origin using the logical units. The GetWindowExt() function is used to determine the height of a window's client area, prior to moving the origin. GetWindowExt() returns a DWORD value, with the high-order word containing the height of the client area in logical units, and the low-order word containing the width. If GetWindowExt() is called before the mapping mode is changed, the default MM_TEXT mapping mode will be in place, and logical units will be equal to pixels. Here is a typical sequence of function calls, setting the mapping mode to MM_LOENGLISH and moving the origin to the bottom left corner of the client area.

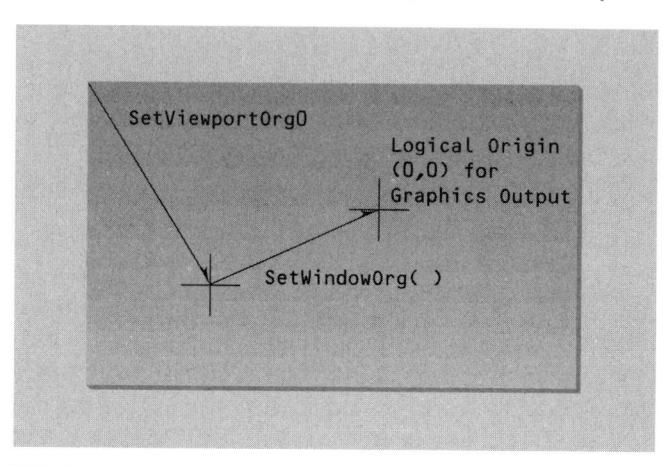

Figure 13-5 The Window and Viewport Origins

```
HDC     hDC ;
DWORD   dwWindowExtent ;

hDC = GetDC (hWnd) ;
dwWindowExtent = GetWindowExt (hDC) ;   /* get X and Y size of Window's client area */
SetViewportOrg (hDC, 0, HIWORD (dwWindowExtent)) ; /* move origin to bottom left */
SetMapMode (hDC, MM_LOENGLISH) ;        /* switch to Loenglish mapping mode */
TextOut (hDC, 100, 100, "Text string.", 12) ;
ReleaseDC (hWnd, hDC) ;
```

After the origin is moved, all painting operations are relative to the new origin. You can move an image on the screen by simply moving the origin and repainting. A common application of moving the origin is as a simple way to implement scrolling the client area.

An Example Program That Changes the Origin and Mapping Mode

The next example program, MAPMODE, demonstrates three of the mapping modes and moving the origin. Figure 13-6 shows MAPMODE displaying a rectangle and a line of text, each drawn at the same logical coordinates, but using three different mapping modes. The logical origin is also drawn with a cross in each mapping mode.

One difference between the three examples shown in Figure 13-6 is that in the text mapping mode, the text and rectangle end up below the origin, while in the MM_LOMETRIC and MM_LOENGLISH mapping modes, the text and rectangle end up above the origin. The reason for this difference is that the MM_TEXT mapping mode is the only case where *Y* values increase downward. In the other mapping modes, *Y* values increase upward. The text and rectangle both start at logical location 50,50, which will be below the origin in the MM_TEXT mapping mode, but above the origin in the other modes.

a) MM_TEXT Mapping Mode

b) MM_LOMETRIC Mapping Mode

c) MM_LOENGLISH Mapping Mode

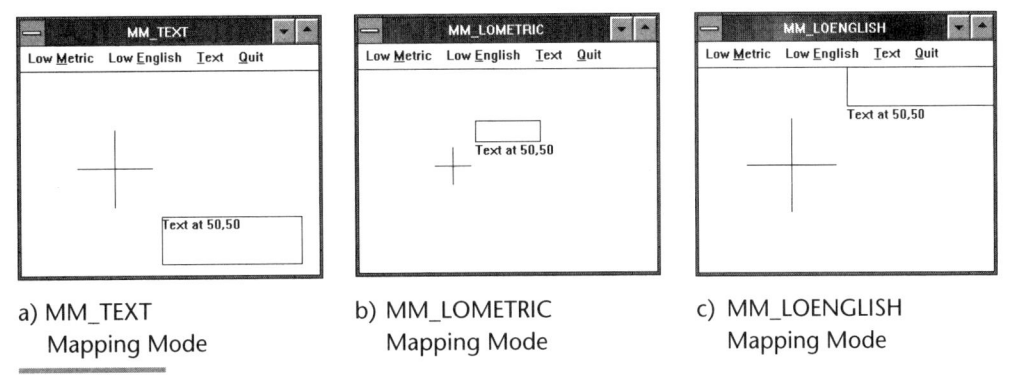

Figure 13-6 The MAPMODE Program

The physical size of the rectangle and its location are also different in the three mapping modes. In each case, the rectangle is created with the function call:

```
Rectangle (ps.hdc, 50, 50, 200, 100);
```

In the MM_TEXT mapping mode, this results in a rectangle that is 150 pixels wide (200 - 50) by 50 pixels tall (100 - 50). In the MM_LOMETRIC mapping mode, the rectangle is 150 * 0.1 = 15 logical millimeters wide by 50 * 0.1 = 5 logical millimeters tall (approximate sizes—remember that Windows does not know the exact size of your video screen). In the MM_LOENGLISH mapping mode, the rectangle is 1.5 logical inches wide by 0.5 logical inches tall.

Another difference between the examples in Figure 13-6 is that the text falls inside the rectangle in the MM_TEXT mapping mode, but below the rectangle in the MM_LOMETRIC and MM_LOENGLISH modes. This is because the default basis for text alignment for a device context is the upper left corner of the first letter in a string. Figure 13-7 shows how the text and rectangle are positioned in two of the mapping modes. In both cases, the text extends downward from the logical location 50,50 on the device context. In the MM_TEXT mapping mode, the rectangle also extends downward, as *Y* values increase downward. In the other mapping modes, the rectangle extends upward, so the text ends up below the rectangle.

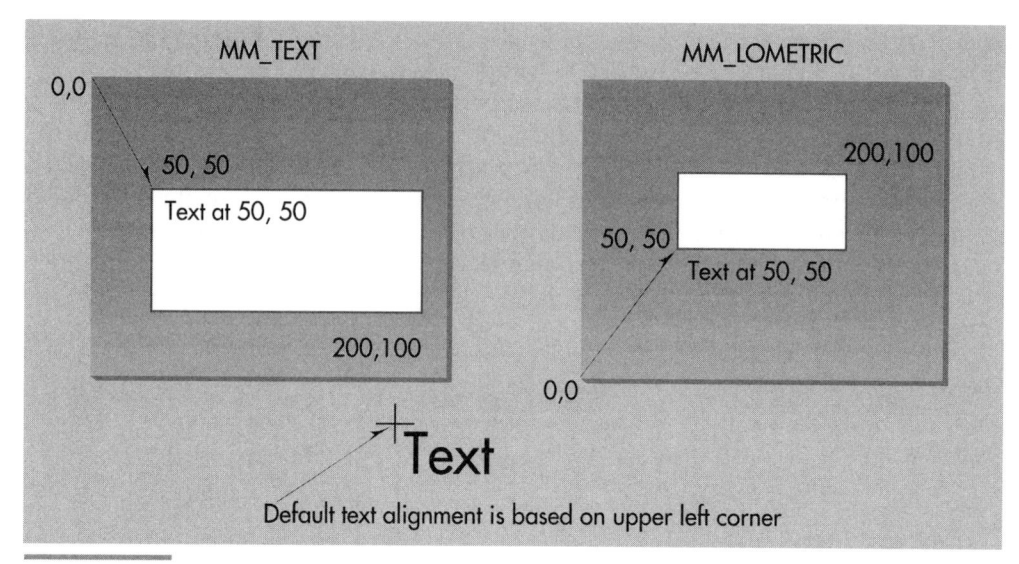

Figure 13-7 Text Alignment

By the way, Windows will allow you to change the text alignment for the device context. The SetTextAlign() function will change the basis for the vertical alignment of the first character to the top, middle, or bottom, and the horizontal alignment to left, center, or right. Usually, the default alignment at the upper left corner works fine, but you need to remember this position if you are combining text and graphics. The text alignment is yet another device context setting that can be saved if a window has its own private device context.

MAPMODE Program Listings

Listing 13-7 shows the MAPMODE.C program. MAPMODE does not use a private device context for the main program window, so the device context must be initialized every time output is performed. All of the output logic is done in processing WM_PAINT messages. Besides setting the mapping mode with SetMapMode(), the WM_PAINT logic moves the origin using SetViewportOrg(). The new origin is located at 100, 100 relative to the top left corner of the client area. The origin is marked with a cross, formed by two lines drawn with the MoveTo() and LineTo() functions. Finally, the rectangle and text are output, starting at location 50,50 with the new mapping mode and origin.

Listing 13-7 MAPMODE.C

```
/* mapmode.c    example changing mapping mode of a device context */

#include <windows.h>
#include "mapmode.h"
```

458   Windows Programming Primer Plus®

```c
int PASCAL WinMain (HANDLE hInstance, HANDLE hPrevInstance, LPSTR lpszCmdLine,
   int nCmdShow)
{
    HWND       hWnd ;           /* the window's "handle" */
    MSG        msg ;            /* a message structure */
    WNDCLASS   wndclass ;       /* window class structure */
    char       cBuf [128] ;     /* character buffer */

    if (!hPrevInstance)
    {
        wndclass.style         = CS_HREDRAW | CS_VREDRAW ;
        wndclass.lpfnWndProc   = WndProc ;
        wndclass.cbClsExtra    = 0 ;
        wndclass.cbWndExtra    = 0 ;
        wndclass.hInstance     = hInstance ;
        wndclass.hIcon         = LoadIcon (hInstance, "MyIcon") ;
        wndclass.hCursor       = LoadCursor (NULL, IDC_ARROW) ;
        wndclass.hbrBackground = GetStockObject (WHITE_BRUSH) ;
        wndclass.lpszMenuName  = "MyMenu" ;
        wndclass.lpszClassName = "MyClass" ;
                   /* register the window class */
        if (!RegisterClass (&wndclass))
            return 0 ;
    }
    LoadString (hInstance, S_PROGRAMCAPTION, cBuf, sizeof (cBuf)) ;

    hWnd = CreateWindow ("MyClass", cBuf, WS_OVERLAPPEDWINDOW,
        CW_USEDEFAULT, CW_USEDEFAULT, CW_USEDEFAULT, CW_USEDEFAULT,
        NULL, NULL, hInstance, NULL) ;
    ShowWindow (hWnd, nCmdShow) ; /* display the window */

    while (GetMessage (&msg, NULL, NULL, NULL)) /* message loop */
    {
        TranslateMessage (&msg) ; /* translate keyboard messages */
        DispatchMessage (&msg) ;  /* send message to WndProc() */
    }
    return (msg.wParam) ;
}

long FAR PASCAL WndProc (HWND hWnd, WORD wMessage, WORD wParam, LONG lParam)
{
    PAINTSTRUCT   ps ;
    char          cBuf [128] ;
    static int    nMapMode = IDM_TEXT ;
    HANDLE        hInstance ;
    int           i ;

    switch (wMessage)              /* process windows messages */
    {
        case WM_COMMAND:
            switch (wParam)                   /* menu items */
            {
                case IDM_LOMETRIC:
                    hInstance = GetWindowWord (hWnd, GWW_HINSTANCE) ;
                    LoadString (hInstance, S_LOMETRIC, cBuf,
                                sizeof (cBuf)) ;
                    SetWindowText (hWnd, cBuf) ;
                    nMapMode = IDM_LOMETRIC ;
```

```
            InvalidateRect (hWnd, NULL, TRUE) ;   /* force WM_PAINT */
            break ;
        case IDM_LOENGLISH:
            hInstance = GetWindowWord (hWnd, GWW_HINSTANCE) ;
            LoadString (hInstance, S_LOENGLISH, cBuf,
                        sizeof (cBuf)) ;
            SetWindowText (hWnd, cBuf) ;
            nMapMode = IDM_LOENGLISH ;
            InvalidateRect (hWnd, NULL, TRUE) ;   /* force WM_PAINT */
            break ;
        case IDM_TEXT:
            hInstance = GetWindowWord (hWnd, GWW_HINSTANCE) ;
            LoadString (hInstance, S_TEXT, cBuf, sizeof (cBuf)) ;
            SetWindowText (hWnd, cBuf) ;
            nMapMode = IDM_TEXT ;
            InvalidateRect (hWnd, NULL, TRUE) ;   /* force WM_PAINT */
            break ;
        case IDM_QUIT:                    /* "Quit" menu item */
            DestroyWindow (hWnd) ;        /* destroy window, */
            break ;                       /* terminating application */
    }
    break ;
case WM_PAINT:
    BeginPaint (hWnd, &ps) ;
    switch (nMapMode)       /* set mapping mode of dc */
    {
        case IDM_TEXT:
            SetMapMode (ps.hdc, MM_TEXT) ;
            break ;
        case IDM_LOMETRIC:
            SetMapMode (ps.hdc, MM_LOMETRIC) ;
            break ;
        case IDM_LOENGLISH:
            SetMapMode (ps.hdc, MM_LOENGLISH) ;
            break ;
    }
        /* set background painting mode to transparent */
    SetBkMode (ps.hdc, TRANSPARENT) ;
        /* change the viewport origin to 100, 100 */
    SetViewportOrg (ps.hdc, 100, 100) ;
        /* paint X,Y origin cross */
    MoveTo (ps.hdc, 0, -40) ;
    LineTo (ps.hdc, 0, 40) ;
    MoveTo (ps.hdc, -40, 0) ;
    LineTo (ps.hdc, 40, 0) ;
        /* output text and rectangle at same location, but */
        /* mapping mode will be different */
    Rectangle (ps.hdc, 50, 50, 200, 100) ;
        /* load text string from resource data */
    hInstance = GetWindowWord (hWnd, GWW_HINSTANCE) ;
    LoadString (hInstance, S_OUTTEXT, cBuf, sizeof (cBuf)) ;
    TextOut (ps.hdc, 50, 50, cBuf, lstrlen (cBuf)) ;
    EndPaint (hWnd, &ps) ;
    break ;
case WM_DESTROY:                          /* stop application */
    PostQuitMessage (0) ;
    break ;
default:                   /* default windows message processing */
```

```
               return (DefWindowProc (hWnd, wMessage, wParam, lParam)) ;
     }
     return (0L) ;
}
```

One nice touch in MAPMODE.C is that the program's caption is changed to reflect the current mapping mode. The SetWindowText() function changes the Window's caption. Each of the caption strings is stored in the program's resource script file in the string table. The ID values for the string table items and menu items are all defined in the program's header file, MAPMODE.H.

Listings 13-8 to 13-12 show the support files for MAPMODE. The program's icon is shown in Figure 13-8.

Listing 13-8 MAPMODE.H Header File

```
/* mapmode.h  header file */

#define IDM_LOMETRIC       1       /* menu item ID numbers */
#define IDM_LOENGLISH      2
#define IDM_TEXT           3
#define IDM_QUIT          10

#define S_PROGRAMCAPTION   1       /* string table ID numbers */
#define S_OUTTEXT          2
#define S_TEXT             3
#define S_LOMETRIC         4
#define S_LOENGLISH        5

long FAR PASCAL WndProc (HWND, WORD, WORD, LONG) ;
```

Figure 13-8
MAPMODE.ICO
Icon Image

Listing 13-9 MAPMODE.RC Resource Script File

```
/* mapmode.rc  resource file */

#include "mapmode.h"

MyIcon     ICON    mapmode.ico

MyMenu     MENU
BEGIN
    MENUITEM "Low &Metric",      IDM_LOMETRIC
    MENUITEM "Low &English",     IDM_LOENGLISH
    MENUITEM "&Text",            IDM_TEXT
    MENUITEM "&Quit",            IDM_QUIT
END

STRINGTABLE
BEGIN
    S_PROGRAMCAPTION         "Mapping Mode Example"
    S_TEXT                   "MM_TEXT"
    S_LOMETRIC               "MM_LOMETRIC"
```

```
    S_LOENGLISH             "MM_LOENGLISH"
    S_OUTTEXT               "Text at 50,50"
END
```

Listing 13-10 MAPMODE.DEF Module Definition File

```
NAME            mapmode
DESCRIPTION     'mapmode program'
EXETYPE         WINDOWS
STUB            'WINSTUB.EXE'
CODE            PRELOAD MOVEABLE DISCARDABLE
DATA            PRELOAD MOVEABLE MULTIPLE
HEAPSIZE        1024
STACKSIZE       5120
EXPORTS         WndProc
```

Listing 13-11 Turbo C++ Project File for MAPMODE

```
mapmode.c
mapmode.def
mapmode.res
```

Listing 13-12 QuickC Project File for MAPMODE

```
mapmode.c
mapmode.def
mapmode.rc
```

Scalable Mapping Modes

There are two additional mapping modes that you may find useful. The MM_ISOTROPIC and MM_ANISOTROPIC mapping modes allow the axes to have any desired scaling or orientation. They are summarized in Table 13-2. Think of these to modes as ways to stretch or compress the coordinate system. The basic difference is that the MM_ISOTROPIC mapping mode maintains the same proportion for both the vertical and horizontal directions. MM_ANISOTROPIC allows either axis to be set with any arbitrary scaling.

MM_ISOTROPIC	Arbitrary scaling of the axes, but the *X* and *Y* scaling must be the same.
MM_ANISOTROPIC	This is the most flexible system of units. Either axis can have any scaling factor.

Table 13-2 Mapping Modes That Can Be Scaled

Windows uses the SetWindowExt() and SetViewportExt() functions together to set the scaling of the device context coordinate system when either the MM_ISOTROPIC or MM_ANISOTROPIC mapping mode is in effect. For example, to create a coordinate system where each logical unit is two pixels (twice the default device unit coordinates), use the following code:

```
HDC     hDC ;

hDC = GetDC (hWnd) ;
SetMapMode (hDC, MM_ISOTROPIC) ;        /* same in both directions */
SetWindowExt (hDC, 1, 1) ;
SetViewportExt (hDC, 2, 2) ;
```

The reason for using two sets of *X,Y* values to set the scaling of the device context is that the ratio of the integer values passed for SetWindowExt() and SetViewportExt() is used to set the scaling factors. This could have been done using single floating-point values rather than integers. Windows does not use floating-point values for any function's parameters, but uses the ratios of the integers to pass the scaling factors.

You can reverse the orientation of the axes in the MM_ANISOTROPIC and MM_ISOTROPIC mapping modes by changing the sign of one of the scaling integers. For example, to create a coordinate system where one logical unit is one fourth of a pixel, and *Y* values increase upward, use the following code:

```
HDC     hDC ;

hDC = GetDC (hWnd) ;
SetMapMode (hDC, MM_ISOTROPIC) ;        /* same in both directions */
SetWindowExt (hDC, 4, -4) ;             /* reverse Y orientation, Y increases up */
SetViewportExt (hDC, 1, 1) ;
```

With the MM_ANISOTROPIC mapping mode, you can have different scalings for the horizontal and vertical axes. The most common use of this mode is to create a coordinate system where the window's client area always has the same logical height and width. For example, to create a coordinate system where the client area is always 1,000 logical units high and wide, and where *Y* values increase upward:

```
HDC     hDC ;
DWORD   dwClientExt ;

hDC = GetDC (hWnd) ;
dwClientExt = GetWindowExt (hDC) ;      /* get client area size */
SetMapMode (hDC, MM_ANISOTROPIC) ;      /* allow X,Y axes to have different scalings */
SetWindowExt (hDC, 1000, -1000) ;       /* 1000 logical units wide and tall, Y reversed */
SetViewportExt (hDC, LOWORD (dwClientExt), HIWORD (dwClientExt)) ;
```

Note that GetWindowExt() always returns the client area size in device units, so it is not affected by the current mapping mode. The DWORD value returned by GetWindowExt() contains the width of the client area as the low-order word, and the height of the client area as the high-order word, which is ideal for passing these values on to SetViewportExt(). Having the client area always scaled to be 1,000 by 1,000 logical units is convenient for complex graphics operations, as the graphics functions can all be "hard coded" to fit a 1,000 by 1,000 space. The image is then scaled to the actual client area size by Windows' mapping logic.

You can also move the origin using SetWindowOrg() and SetViewportOrg() with the MM_ISOTROPIC and MM_ANISOTROPIC mapping modes. Just remember that SetViewportOrg() uses device units regardless of the mapping mode, while SetWindowOrg() uses logical units, which will change depending on the mapping mode in effect.

Text and Scalable Mapping Modes

As with the fixed-size mapping modes, text character sizing is not scaled as you change the device context mapping mode with the MM_ANISOTROPIC and MM_ISOTROPIC modes. The location where the text string starts *will* use the logical coordinate system, but the sizing of the text characters is determined by the font selected into the device context, not the scaling of the mapping mode. This is normally just what you will want, but it can cause problems if you expect an image consisting of both text and graphics to be smoothly scaled as the mapping mode is changed. You can come close by creating different font sizes with CreateFont() as needed to scale the text. Review Chapter 7, *Character Sets, Fonts, and the Keyboard*, if you have forgotten how to use the CreateFont() function.

An MM_ANISOTROPIC Example

The last example program in this chapter is called ANISO. Figure 13-9 shows the ANISO program in operation, with two different sizings of the main program window. The rectangle and the ellipse are always sized to fit the client area. The interesting thing about ANISO is that the Ellipse() and Rectangle() function calls that draw these figures are always drawn with the same dimensions specified:

```
Ellipse (ps.hdc, 0, 0, 100, 100) ;
Rectangle (ps.hdc, 20, 20, 80, 80) ;
```

The ellipse is always drawn from logical location 0,0 to 100,100, and the rectangle from location 20,20 to 80,80. The reason that the ellipse and rectangle continue to exactly fit the window's client area exactly is that the logical coordinate system for the

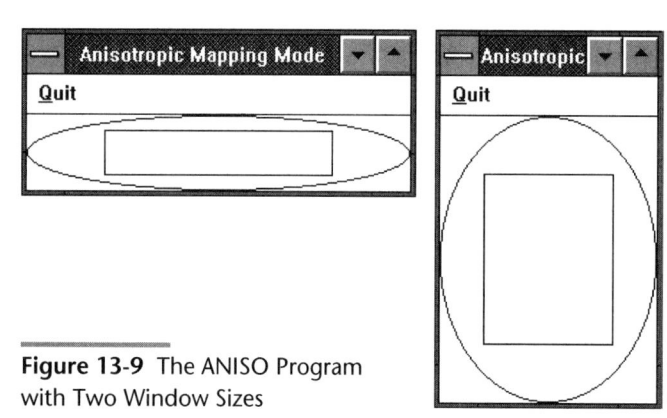

Figure 13-9 The ANISO Program with Two Window Sizes

client area is always scaled to be a 100 by 100 logical units square. Any output to this device context uses the logical units in place and, therefore, is deformed to fit.

The actual code to accomplish the scaling is remarkably short. The size of the window's client area is saved in two static variables *nX* and *nY* when processing the WM_SIZE message. WM_SIZE message is sent any time the window's size is changed, including when the program's window is first created. The WM_PAINT logic sets the mapping mode as MM_ANISOTROPIC, and then scales the viewport extent to map 100 by 100 logical units. This requires a call to both SetViewportExt() and SetWindowExt(). The Ellipse() and Rectangle() function calls occur after the device context mapping mode and scaling have been set and, therefore, use the new logical coordinate system.

```
case WM_SIZE:         /* save client area size */
    nX = LOWORD (lParam) ;
    nY = HIWORD (lParam) ;
    break ;
case WM_PAINT:
    BeginPaint (hWnd, &ps) ;
    SetMapMode (ps.hdc, MM_ANISOTROPIC) ;
    SetViewportExt (ps.hdc, nX, nY) ;      /* scale coordinates so */
    SetWindowExt (ps.hdc, 100, 100) ;      /* client area is 100x100 */
    Ellipse (ps.hdc, 0, 0, 100, 100) ;
    Rectangle (ps.hdc, 20, 20, 80, 80) ;
    EndPaint (hWnd, &ps) ;
    break ;
```

Note in this example that the sign of the *Y* axis was not reversed, so the logical coordinate system continues to have *Y* values increase downward. Listing 13-13 shows the complete ANISO.C program.

Listing 13-13 ANISO.C

```
/* aniso.c   example using anisotropic mapping mode */

#include <windows.h>
#include "aniso.h"

int PASCAL WinMain (HANDLE hInstance, HANDLE hPrevInstance, LPSTR lpszCmdLine,
    int nCmdShow)
{
    HWND        hWnd ;              /* the window's "handle" */
    MSG         msg ;               /* a message structure */
    WNDCLASS    wndclass ;          /* window class structure */
    char        cBuf [128] ;        /* character buffer */

    if (!hPrevInstance)
    {
        wndclass.style          = CS_HREDRAW | CS_VREDRAW ;
        wndclass.lpfnWndProc    = WndProc ;
        wndclass.cbClsExtra     = 0 ;
        wndclass.cbWndExtra     = 0 ;
        wndclass.hInstance      = hInstance ;
        wndclass.hIcon          = LoadIcon (hInstance, "MyIcon") ;
        wndclass.hCursor        = LoadCursor (NULL, IDC_ARROW) ;
```

```c
        wndclass.hbrBackground = GetStockObject (WHITE_BRUSH) ;
        wndclass.lpszMenuName  = "MyMenu" ;
        wndclass.lpszClassName = "MyClass" ;
                /* register the window class */
        if (!RegisterClass (&wndclass))
            return 0 ;
    }
    LoadString (hInstance, S_PROGRAMCAPTION, cBuf, sizeof (cBuf)) ;

    hWnd = CreateWindow ("MyClass", cBuf, WS_OVERLAPPEDWINDOW,
        CW_USEDEFAULT, CW_USEDEFAULT, CW_USEDEFAULT, CW_USEDEFAULT,
        NULL, NULL, hInstance, NULL) ;
    ShowWindow (hWnd, nCmdShow) ;      /* display the window */

    while (GetMessage (&msg, NULL, NULL, NULL))   /* message loop */
    {
        TranslateMessage (&msg) ;      /* translate keyboard messages */
        DispatchMessage (&msg) ;       /* send message to WndProc() */
    }
    return (msg.wParam) ;
}

long FAR PASCAL WndProc (HWND hWnd, WORD wMessage, WORD wParam, LONG lParam)
{
    PAINTSTRUCT   ps ;
    char          cBuf [128] ;
    static  int   nX, nY ;

    switch (wMessage)                  /* process windows messages */
    {
        case WM_COMMAND:
            switch (wParam)            /* menu items */
            {
                case IDM_QUIT:                /* "Quit" menu item */
                    DestroyWindow (hWnd) ;    /* destroy window, */
                    break ;                   /* terminating application */
            }
            break ;
        case WM_SIZE:                         /* save client area size */
            nX = LOWORD (lParam) ;
            nY = HIWORD (lParam) ;
            break ;
        case WM_PAINT:
            BeginPaint (hWnd, &ps) ;
            SetMapMode (ps.hdc, MM_ANISOTROPIC) ;
            SetViewportExt (ps.hdc, nX, nY) ;       /* scale coordinates so */
            SetWindowExt (ps.hdc, 100, 100) ;       /* client area is 100x100 */
            Ellipse (ps.hdc, 0, 0, 100, 100) ;
            Rectangle (ps.hdc, 20, 20, 80, 80) ;
            EndPaint (hWnd, &ps) ;
            break ;
        case WM_DESTROY:                      /* stop application */
            PostQuitMessage (0) ;
            break ;
        default:              /* default windows message processing */
            return (DefWindowProc (hWnd, wMessage, wParam, lParam)) ;
    }
    return (0L) ;
}
```

Listings 13-14 to 13-18 show the support files for ANISO. The program's icon is shown in Figure 13-10.

Listing 13-14 ANISO.H Header File

```
/* aniso.h  header file */

#define IDM_QUIT         10       /* menu item id numbers */

#define S_PROGRAMCAPTION 1

long FAR PASCAL WndProc (HWND, WORD, WORD, LONG) ;
```

Figure 13-10
ANISO.ICO
Icon Image

Listing 13-15 ANISO.RC Resource Script File

```
/* aniso.rc  resource file */

#include "aniso.h"

MyIcon      ICON    aniso.ico

MyMenu      MENU
BEGIN
    MENUITEM "&Quit",          IDM_QUIT
END

STRINGTABLE
BEGIN
    S_PROGRAMCAPTION    "Anisotropic Mapping Mode"
END
```

Listing 13-16 ANISO.DEF Module Definition File

```
NAME            aniso
DESCRIPTION     'aniso program'
EXETYPE         WINDOWS
STUB            'WINSTUB.EXE'
CODE            PRELOAD MOVEABLE DISCARDABLE
DATA            PRELOAD MOVEABLE MULTIPLE
HEAPSIZE        1024
STACKSIZE       5120
EXPORTS         WndProc
```

Listing 13-17 Turbo C++ Project File for ANISO

```
aniso.c
aniso.def
aniso.res
```

Chapter 13 • The Device Context

Listing 13-18 QuickC Project File for ANISO

```
aniso.c
aniso.def
aniso.rc
```

Summary

Windows uses the data in a device context to translate calls to functions, such as TextOut() and Rectangle(), into commands that an output device, such as a video board or a printer, will understand. Device contexts can be scaled to use different systems of coordinates by changing the mapping mode in effect. The MM_TEXT mapping mode is the default mode for a device context, but it has the disadvantage of displaying different sized images depending on the resolution of the output device (how big the pixels are on the output surface). MM_TEXT is also unusual in that *Y* values increase downward. The fixed-scaling mapping modes, such as MM_LOMETRIC and MM_LOENGLISH, are very useful, as they will produce images which are almost exactly the same size on any output device. All of the mapping modes except MM_TEXT use increasing values for *Y* to reference locations higher on the output surface, the normal convention for measurement in mathematics.

The MM_ANISOTROPIC and MM_ISOTROPIC mapping modes are interesting in that you can create your own system of units with any arbitrary scaling. This is a convenient way to stretch or expand graphics images. MM_ISOTROPIC always keeps the *X* and *Y* axes in proportion, while MM_ANISOTROPIC allows arbitrary scaling of both axes. The SetWindowExt() and SetViewportExt() functions are used with these two mapping modes to scale the device context.

Besides changing the scaling of the device context, you can also move the origin. SetWindowOrg() and SetViewportOrg() are used for this purpose. SetViewportOrg() uses device units (pixels), and SetWindowOrg() uses the logical coordinate system based on the current mapping mode. Moving the origin causes any subsequent graphics output to be based on the new location of the origin.

If a number of changes are made to a device context, it is desirable to save the settings so that they do not need to be recreated each time output occurs. You can create a private device context for a window or class of windows by changing the class definition for the window, and adding the CS_CLASSDC, CS_OWNDC or CS_PARENTDC class styles to the *style* member of the WNDCLASS structure before calling RegisterClass(). Private device contexts take up about 800 bytes of memory, but save time during graphics output. Private device contexts are usually used in programs that make many changes to the device context settings.

QUESTIONS

1. Every window created from a window class using the CS_OWNDC class style will have the same shared device context. (True/False)
2. If you are processing WM_PAINT messages for a window with its own private device context, you must use the BeginPaint() but not the EndPaint() function. (True/False)
3. If you are outputting text outside of the WM_PAINT logic for a window with its own private device context, you will use the GetDC() function, but can skip the ReleaseDC() function, as the device context will continue to be stored in memory. (True/False)
4. If you want to save a new pen with the device context data for a window with a private device context, you will need to: a) Create the pen with CreatePen(); b) Select it into the device context with SelectObject(); c) Not destroy the pen until the window is destroyed; d) a, b, and c.
5. Objects should be displaced out of the device context by selecting another object of the same type before the object is deleted. (True/False)
6. The default mapping mode for a device context is _____ .
7. Text character sizes change when you change the mapping mode of a device context. (True/False)
8. If the mapping mode is changed, locations on the device context are measured in _____ units. They are only the same as _____ units in the MM_TEXT mapping mode.
9. If you move the origin of the device context for a window's client area, but do not re-draw the image, the image will not move on the screen. (True/False)
10. In the MM_LOMETRIC mapping mode, a location $X = 100$, $Y = 300$ will be _____ mm to the right and _____ mm above the logical origin of the device context.
11. With the MM_ANISOTROPIC and MM_ISOTROPIC mapping modes, you use both the _____ and _____ functions to set the scaling of the device context.
12. Only the _____ mapping mode allows both the horizontal and vertical axes to be scaled independently.

EXERCISES

1. Change the mapping mode in the ANISO.C program to the MM_ISOTROPIC mapping mode. What happens to the image as the window's sizing is changed?
2. Change the MAPMODE program to use the CS_CLASSDC style, for a private device context. Change the program logic in the WndProc() function to take advantage of the private device context.

ANSWERS TO QUESTIONS

1. False. (The CS_CLASSDC class style value allows all the windows created from a single window class to share the same device context data. CS_OWNDC provides each window with its own device context.)
2. False. EndPaint() is required. Outside of the WM_PAINT logic, you can use GetDC() and not call ReleaseDC(), if the program is using a private device context.
3. True.
4. D.
5. True.
6. MM_TEXT.
7. False. Select a different font size to change the text character size.
8. logical, device.
9. True.
10. 10, 30.
11. SetWindowExt(), SetViewportExt().
12. MM_ANISOTROPIC.

SOLUTIONS TO EXERCISES

1. The only change in the program's code is to change the mapping mode specified in the SetMapMode() function call as follows:

   `SetMapMode (ps.hdc, MM_ISOTROPIC) ;`

   The result of this change is that the image will always be displayed in proportion, regardless of the relative sizing of the window's horizontal and vertical extents. Figure 13-11 shows the program with the MM_ISOTROPIC mapping mode in effect. The complete solution is given under the C13EXER1 file name on the source code disks.

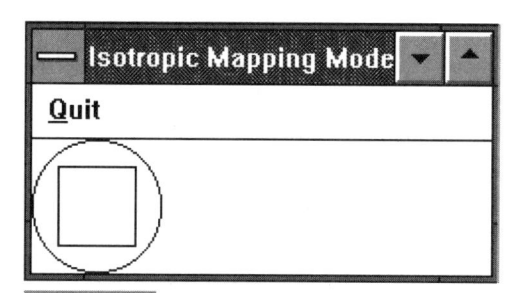

   Figure 13-11 Solution to Exercise 1, Chapter 13

2. Listing 13-19 shows the modified MAPMODE program, with the changes highlighted. Because the device context is saved, the device context can be altered outside of the WM_PAINT logic. The initialization of the device context is done in processing the WM_CREATE message. The mapping mode is changed directly by calling SetMapMode() when the menu items are selected. The complete solution is under the file name C13EXER2 on the optional source code disks.

SOLUTIONS TO EXERCISES (cont'd)

Listing 13-19 Solution to Exercise 2

```
/* c13exer2.c   solution to exercise 2, chapter 13 */

#include <windows.h>
#include "c13exer2.h"

int PASCAL WinMain (HANDLE hInstance, HANDLE hPrevInstance, LPSTR lpszCmdLine,
   int nCmdShow)
{
    HWND       hWnd ;          /* the window's "handle" */
    MSG        msg ;           /* a message structure */
    WNDCLASS   wndclass ;      /* window class structure */
    char       cBuf [128] ;    /* character buffer */

    if (!hPrevInstance)
    {
       wndclass.style          = CS_HREDRAW | CS_VREDRAW | CS_CLASSDC ;
       wndclass.lpfnWndProc    = WndProc ;
       wndclass.cbClsExtra     = 0 ;
       wndclass.cbWndExtra     = 0 ;
       wndclass.hInstance      = hInstance ;
       wndclass.hIcon          = LoadIcon (hInstance, "MyIcon") ;
       wndclass.hCursor        = LoadCursor (NULL, IDC_ARROW) ;
       wndclass.hbrBackground  = GetStockObject (WHITE_BRUSH) ;
       wndclass.lpszMenuName   = "MyMenu" ;
       wndclass.lpszClassName  = "MyClass" ;
                       /* register the window class */
       if (!RegisterClass (&wndclass))
            return 0 ;
    }
    LoadString (hInstance, S_PROGRAMCAPTION, cBuf, sizeof (cBuf)) ;

    hWnd = CreateWindow ("MyClass", cBuf, WS_OVERLAPPEDWINDOW,
        CW_USEDEFAULT, CW_USEDEFAULT, CW_USEDEFAULT, CW_USEDEFAULT,
        NULL, NULL, hInstance, NULL) ;
    ShowWindow (hWnd, nCmdShow) ;     /* display the window */

    while (GetMessage (&msg, NULL, NULL, NULL))   /* message loop */
    {
       TranslateMessage (&msg) ;      /* translate keyboard messages */
       DispatchMessage (&msg) ;       /* send message to WndProc() */
    }
    return (msg.wParam) ;
}
long FAR PASCAL WndProc (HWND hWnd, WORD wMessage, WORD wParam, LONG lParam)
{
    PAINTSTRUCT   ps ;
    char          cBuf [128] ;
    HANDLE        hInstance ;
    HDC           hDC ;
    int           i ;

    switch (wMessage)              /* process windows messages */
    {
        case WM_CREATE:            /* initialize device context settings */
             hDC = GetDC (hWnd) ;
             SetBkMode (hDC, TRANSPARENT) ;
                     /* change the viewport origin to 100, 100 */
             SetViewportOrg (hDC, 100, 100) ;
```

SOLUTIONS TO EXERCISES (cont'd)

```
              break ;
        case WM_COMMAND:
              switch (wParam)                          /* menu items */
              {
        case IDM_LOMETRIC:
              hInstance = GetWindowWord (hWnd, GWW_HINSTANCE) ;
              LoadString (hInstance, S_LOMETRIC, cBuf,
                  sizeof (cBuf)) ;
              SetWindowText (hWnd, cBuf) ;
              hDC = GetDC (hWnd) ;
              SetMapMode (hDC, MM_LOMETRIC) ;
              InvalidateRect (hWnd, NULL, TRUE) ;      /* force WM_PAINT */
              break ;
        case IDM_LOENGLISH:
              hInstance = GetWindowWord (hWnd, GWW_HINSTANCE) ;
              LoadString (hInstance, S_LOENGLISH, cBuf,
                  sizeof (cBuf)) ;
              SetWindowText (hWnd, cBuf) ;
              hDC = GetDC (hWnd) ;
              SetMapMode (hDC, MM_LOENGLISH) ;
              InvalidateRect (hWnd, NULL, TRUE) ;      /* force WM_PAINT */
              break ;
        case IDM_TEXT:
              hInstance = GetWindowWord (hWnd, GWW_HINSTANCE) ;
              LoadString (hInstance, S_TEXT, cBuf, sizeof (cBuf)) ;
              SetWindowText (hWnd, cBuf) ;
              hDC = GetDC (hWnd) ;
              SetMapMode (hDC, MM_TEXT) ;
              InvalidateRect (hWnd, NULL, TRUE) ;      /* force WM_PAINT */
              break ;
        case IDM_QUIT:                   /* "Quit" menu item */
              DestroyWindow (hWnd) ;     /* destroy window, */
              break ;                    /* terminating application */
        default:                         /* otherwise, let Windows process it */
              return (DefWindowProc (hWnd, wMessage, wParam, lParam)) ;
        }
              break ;
        case WM_PAINT:          /* paint using current DC settings */
              BeginPaint (hWnd, &ps) ;
              MoveTo (ps.hdc, 0, -40) ;
              LineTo (ps.hdc, 0, 40) ;
              MoveTo (ps.hdc, -40, 0) ;
              LineTo (ps.hdc, 40, 0) ;
                  /* output text and rectangle at same location, but */
                  /* mapping mode will be different */
              Rectangle (ps.hdc, 50, 50, 200, 100) ;
                  /* load text string from resource data */
              hInstance = GetWindowWord (hWnd, GWW_HINSTANCE) ;
                LoadString (hInstance, S_OUTTEXT, cBuf, sizeof (cBuf)) ;
                TextOut (ps.hdc, 50, 50, cBuf, lstrlen (cBuf)) ;
                EndPaint (hWnd, &ps) ;
                break ;
        case WM_DESTROY:                 /* stop application */
                PostQuitMessage (0) ;
                break ;
        default:                         /* default windows message processing */
                return (DefWindowProc (hWnd, wMessage, wParam, lParam)) ;
    }
    return (0L) ;
}
```

CHAPTER 14

Printing

Under MS-DOS, programs interact with the printer by sending commands directly to the printer hardware. Every type of printer has its own set of commands for setting tab stops, drawing graphic symbols, ejecting a page, and so on. DOS programs need to have all of these commands "hard wired" into the program logic, or in separate printer driver files which are copied to your hard disk when you install the program. Each DOS program has its own set of printer drivers to support every type of printer.

The situation is different under Windows. It is the Windows environment that supports the printer, not Windows application programs. The user chooses one or more printers when Windows is first installed, or when the user selects a new printer using the Windows Control Panel application. From that point on, the installation of a printer applies to all of the Windows applications on the system, not to just one program. This frees you (the programmer) to concentrate on what the output should look like, not the specifics of a printer's commands. When you want the program you are writing to output text or graphics to a printer, your program obtains a device context handle for the printer, and then uses standard output functions, such as TextOut() and Rectangle(), to output to the device.

Even though Windows takes care of all of the printer logic for you, there are differences between sending output to a printer or plotter and sending output to the screen. You may need to find out the paper sizes that the printer supports, and if it supports color output. You will probably also want to allow the user to quit in the middle of a printing job if the paper jams, or some other problem occurs. These operations are all possible under Windows, without ever needing to know the specifics of a printer's internal commands.

Concepts Covered

Printer Drivers

WIN.INI File

Printer Device Context

Abort Procedures

Accessing Data Stored in the Device Context

Determining Output Device Physical Characteristics

Calling Functions in the Printer Device Driver

Keywords Covered

STARTDOC

NEWFRAME

ENDDOC

ABORTDOC

SETABORTPROC

DC_DRIVER

DC_PAPERS

DC_PAPERSIZE

DM_PROMPT

Functions Covered

CreateDC()

DeleteDC()

GetProfileString()

Strtok()

EnableWindow()

GetDeviceCaps()

ExtDeviceMode()

DeviceCapabilities()

GetWindowsDirectory()

GetSystemDirectory()

How Windows Supports Printers

Windows supports printers and other output devices by using special Windows programs called "drivers." These programs (which are actually dynamic link library files) are stored in the Windows system directory, which by default will have the directory name "C:\WINDOWS\SYSTEM." In this directory, you will find a number of files with the extension ".DRV." If you install a printer, a new .DRV file will be copied to the system directory, such as PSCRIPT.DRV for a PostScript printer. The driver file contains all of the program logic that converts from the Windows graphics commands to the specific printer instructions that a printer understands. If you have more than one type of printer installed on your system, there will be more than one driver file. Figure 14-1 shows how the driver file is used in the Windows environment.

If you look in your Windows system directory, you will notice a number of other driver files such as MOUSE.DRV for the mouse driver, and VGA.DRV if you have a normal 16-color VGA display. Driver files are a general approach that Windows uses for supporting hardware. When new hardware comes along, only a driver file needs to be written, without any modification to the core logic of Windows. Microsoft Corp. encourages hardware manufacturers to write Windows drivers by supplying the documentation for writing device drivers (called the "Device Driver Development Kit") at a reasonable cost.

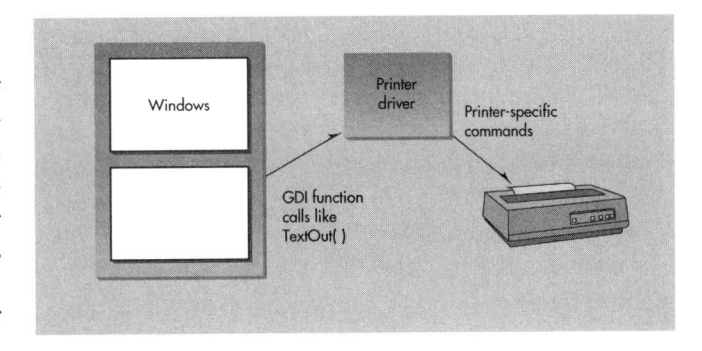

Figure 14-1 Windows Printer Drivers

The other impact of installing a printer is that the WIN.INI file is modified. WIN.INI is a special file that Windows reads when it first starts to find out what type of equipment is installed, and to find startup values for various programs. The key line that determines what type of printer is installed is in a section labeled "[windows]," which is usually at the top of WIN.INI. The key lines for a printer look something like:

```
[windows]
...           ; any number of other lines here
device=HP LaserJet IIP PostScript,pscript,LPT1:
```

This line informs Windows on startup that a device with the name "HP LaserJet IIP PostScript" is installed, which uses the driver file PSCRIPT.DRV and outputs to the serial port LPT1. This is how Windows will know which driver file to run when printer output is requested. You may also find some other information relating to the printer later in the WIN.INI file. For example, the following lines are in the author's WIN.INI file:

```
[HP LaserJet IIP,LPT1]
Memory=2243
Number of Cartridges=0
```

This type of data is written into WIN.INI when you access the printer setup options from within the Windows Control Panel application. When you set up the printer, the choices you make are written into WIN.INI so that they will be "remembered" in subsequent Windows sessions.

Printer Device Contents

So far, all of the example programs in this book have output to the program window's device context. The device context handle for a window is obtained with either GetDC() or BeginPaint(). To output to a printer, you will need to obtain the device context handle for a printer's device context. The CreateDC() function creates a device context for a printer (or plotter) and returns the device context handle. The syntax of the CreateDC() function is as follows.

HDC **CreateDC** (LPSTR *lpDriverName*, LPSTR *lpDeviceName*, LPSTR *lpOutput*, LPDEVMODE *lpInitData*);

lpDriverName	A pointer to a character string containing the printer driver name, such as "PSCRIPT."
lpDeviceName	A pointer to a character string containing the device name, such as "HP LaserJet IIP PostScript."
lpOutput	A pointer to a character string containing the output device name, such as "LPT1."
lpInitData	A pointer to printer initialization data. This is seldom used. Normally, this parameter is just set to NULL.

As you may have noticed from the descriptions of the parameters for the CreateDC() function, all of the character strings needed to call CreateDC() are available from the "device=" line of the WIN.INI file. Windows provides the convenient function GetProfileString() to read lines from WIN.INI. To use GetProfileString(), you specify the heading string (the string that appears in square brackets in WIN.INI such as "windows") and the key word that starts the line (such as "device"). Here is a typical call to GetProfileString(), obtaining the string following "device" in the "[windows]" section of WIN.INI:

```
char    szPrinter [64]

GetProfileString ("windows", "device", "", szPrinter, 64) ;
```

The result is that up to 64 characters of the string following the characters "device=" are copied to the character buffer *szPrinter[]*. The third parameter in GetProfileString() allows you to specify a default string, if no matching value is found in the WIN.INI file. This is just set to the null string ("") in the example.

Reading WIN.INI was easy, but there remains the problem of breaking up the string into the specific device name, driver name, and output device name strings needed by CreateDC(). Fortunately, each element of the "device=" line in WIN.INI is separated from the previous element by a comma.

```
device=HP LaserJet IIP PostScript,pscript,LPT1:
```

You can either write your own string parsing function, or take advantage of the C library function strtok(). The strtok() function parses a string, advancing until it finds a specific character, such as a comma, and returns a pointer to that position in the string.

strtok() is not part of Windows, so you will need to include the compiler library STRING.H if you use this function. Here is the complete sequence of function calls that creates a printer device context based on the device data in WIN.INI:

```
HDC     hDC ;
char    szPrinter [64], *szDriver, *szDevice, *szOutput ;

    /* parse win.ini line to get printer info */
GetProfileString ("windows", "device", "", szPrinter, 64) ;
szDevice = strtok (szPrinter, ",") ;
szDriver = strtok (NULL, ",") ;
szOutput = strtok (NULL, ",") ;
    /* create a device context for the printer */
hDC = CreateDC (szDriver, szDevice, szOutput, NULL) ;
```

Note that the string is not copied into separate smaller strings for the driver name, device name, and so on. The pointers to each portion of the string (*szDriver, szDevice,* and *szOutput*) all point to locations in the *szPrinter[]* character buffer. These three pointers are then passed to CreateDC() to create the printer device context and return its handle. CreateDC() will return NULL (zero) if the printer device context could not be created.

When the printer's device context is created, you can output to the printer using standard functions, such as TextOut() and Rectangle(). This will be demonstrated in a moment in the first example program. When the output is completed, the device context can be purged from memory by calling the DeleteDC() function:

```
DeleteDC (hDC) ;
```

DeleteDC() frees all of the memory associated with the device context. If you fail to call DeleteDC(), the device context data will remain in memory, taking up space. Printer device contexts are not attached to a window, so Windows has no way of knowing when to delete a printer device context automatically. Be sure every call to CreateDC() has a matching call to DeleteDC() when you are creating a program.

Sending Special Commands to a Printer

Although the normal Windows output functions like TextOut() and Rectangle() work fine for any device context, there are a few commands that you will need to send to a printer that do not have an equivalent on a video device. For example, printers need to eject pages when a page break is reached.

Windows provides the Escape() function to send special commands to a printer. Escape() gets its name from the fact that many printers use a series of command bytes starting with the ESC character to initiate actions like setting tabs and ejecting a page. As a Windows programmer, you will not need to be concerned with the specific commands for a printer, as the device driver will take care of those low-level details. You can use the Escape() function to send generic commands to the device driver, and let the driver translate the commands into the specific sequence of bytes the printer will understand.

Table 14-1 summarizes the most common Escape() commands. Under Windows 2.0 and 3.0, there were reasons to use many other Escape() commands, but they have been superseded by more advanced techniques under Windows 3.1. We will examine these advanced techniques at the end of the chapter. The Escape() commands in Table 14-1 are the only ones you are likely to use, unless you are in the business of writing printer drivers. The command names, such as STARTDOC and NEWFRAME, are defined in the WINDOWS.H header file.

Escape (hDC, **STARTDOC**, 4, "Test", NULL) ;

    Starts a printing job. The name of the job is "Test," which is four characters long.

Escape (hDC, **NEWFRAME**, NULL, NULL, NULL) ;

    Ejects a page.

Escape (hDC, **ENDDOC**, NULL, NULL, NULL) ;

    Ends a printing job.

Escape (hDC, **ABORTDOC**, NULL, NULL, NULL) ;

    Stops a printing job, and erases all pending data from memory.

Escape (hDC, **SETABORTPROC**, NULL, lpAbortFunc, NULL) ;

    Sets a procedure that will receive messages during a printing job, so that printing can be stopped in the middle of a print job. This Escape() function call will be demonstrated later in the chapter.

Table 14-1 Common Escape() Function Calls

A Simple Printing Example

The first example program in this chapter is called PRINT1. PRINT1 demonstrates the minimum support that is necessary to output a line of text and a rectangle to the printer. When operating, PRINT1 appears as shown in Figure 14-2, displaying the output text and rectangle in the window's client area. When the "Print" menu item is selected, the same text string and rectangle are output to the printer.

Listing 14-1 shows the full PRINT1.C program. PRINT1.C closely follows the previous discussion of parsing the WIN.INI file to obtain the device names, creating the printer device context, and using the Escape() command. The critical portions are shown here:

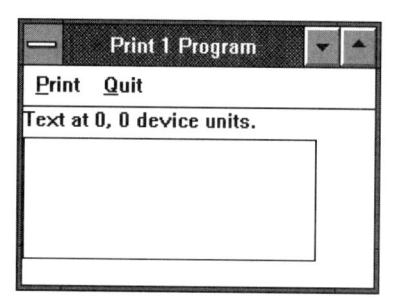

Figure 14-2 The PRINT1 Program

```
   GetProfileString ("windows", "device", "",
      szPrinter, 64) ;
   szDevice = strtok (szPrinter, ",") ;
   szDriver = strtok (NULL, ",") ;
   szOutput = strtok (NULL, ",") ;
      /* create a device context for the printer */
   hDC = CreateDC (szDriver, szDevice, szOutput, NULL) ;
   if (Escape (hDC, STARTDOC, 4, "Test", NULL) > 0)
   {                       /* output to printer */
      OutputStuff (hDC, hInstance) ;
      Escape (hDC, NEWFRAME, NULL, NULL, NULL) ;
      Escape (hDC, ENDDOC, NULL, NULL, NULL) ;
   }
   else
      MessageBox (hWnd, "Could not create printer dc.",
         "Warning", MB_OK) ;
   DeleteDC (hDC) ;
```

Assuming that the printer device context is created (*hDC* is not zero), the output is started using the STARTDOC escape. The output of the text line and rectangle are handled by a small function at the end of PRINT1.C, called OutputStuff(). The output functions are put in the OutputStuff() function, as the same calls to TextOut() and Rectangle() are made to paint the window's client area and to output to the printer. After the output is completed, a page is ejected from the printer with the NEWFRAME escape, and the print job stopped with the ENDDOC escape. Finally, the printer's device context is purged from memory with a call to the DeleteDC() function.

Although this does not look too complex, there are a number of automatic features being accessed as PRINT1 processes its print job. If the "Use Print Manager" option was selected in the Windows Control Panel application (this is the default), the Print Manager application will be loaded automatically when PRINT1 starts output to the printer. The Print Manager application will handle the printing job, along with any other printing jobs that are already in progress. If the Print Manager is not selected, the printer commands will be sent directly to the printer via the printer driver.

If the printer is off line or busy when the PRINT1 program first attempts to print, a warning message box will appear after about 30 seconds. This warning message is generated automatically by the printer driver, without any intervention by the PRINT1 program. Not bad for so simple a program!

Listing 14-1 PRINT1.C

```
/* print1.c   example with simple output to printer */

#include <windows.h>
#include <string.h>     /* needed for strtok() function */
#include "print1.h"

int PASCAL WinMain (HANDLE hInstance, HANDLE hPrevInstance, LPSTR lpszCmdLine,
   int nCmdShow)
{
```

```
    HWND        hWnd ;          /* the window's "handle" */
    MSG         msg ;           /* a message structure */
    WNDCLASS    wndclass ;      /* window class structure */
    char        cBuf [128] ;    /* character buffer */

    if (!hPrevInstance)
    {
        wndclass.style          = CS_HREDRAW | CS_VREDRAW ;
        wndclass.lpfnWndProc    = WndProc ;
        wndclass.cbClsExtra     = 0 ;
        wndclass.cbWndExtra     = 0 ;
        wndclass.hInstance      = hInstance ;
        wndclass.hIcon          = LoadIcon (hInstance, "MyIcon") ;
        wndclass.hCursor        = LoadCursor (NULL, IDC_ARROW) ;
        wndclass.hbrBackground  = GetStockObject (WHITE_BRUSH) ;
        wndclass.lpszMenuName   = "MyMenu" ;
        wndclass.lpszClassName  = "MyClass" ;
                        /* register the window class */
        if (!RegisterClass (&wndclass))
            return 0 ;
    }
    LoadString (hInstance, S_PROGRAMCAPTION, cBuf, sizeof (cBuf)) ;

    hWnd = CreateWindow ("MyClass", cBuf, WS_OVERLAPPEDWINDOW,
        CW_USEDEFAULT, CW_USEDEFAULT, CW_USEDEFAULT, CW_USEDEFAULT,
        NULL, NULL, hInstance, NULL) ;
    ShowWindow (hWnd, nCmdShow) ;       /* display the window */

    while (GetMessage (&msg, NULL, NULL, NULL))     /* message loop */
    {
        TranslateMessage (&msg) ;       /* translate keyboard messages */
        DispatchMessage (&msg) ;        /* send message to WndProc() */
    }
    return (msg.wParam) ;
}

long FAR PASCAL WndProc (HWND hWnd, WORD wMessage, WORD wParam, LONG lParam)
{
    PAINTSTRUCT ps ;
    HDC         hDC ;
    HANDLE      hInstance ;
    char        szPrinter [64], *szDriver, *szDevice, *szOutput ;

    switch (wMessage)       /* process windows messages */
    {
      case WM_COMMAND:
        switch (wParam)                     /* menu items */
        {
            case IDM_PRINT:                 /* output to printer */
                hInstance = GetWindowWord (hWnd, GWW_HINSTANCE) ;
                    /* parse win.ini line to get printer info */
                GetProfileString ("windows", "device", "",
                    szPrinter, 64) ;
                szDevice = strtok (szPrinter, ",") ;
                szDriver = strtok (NULL, ",") ;
                szOutput = strtok (NULL, ",") ;
                    /* create a device context for the printer */
```

```
                    hDC = CreateDC (szDriver, szDevice, szOutput, NULL) ;
                    if (Escape (hDC, STARTDOC, 4, "Test", NULL) > 0)
                        {                       /* output to printer */
                        OutputStuff (hDC, hInstance) ;
                        Escape (hDC, NEWFRAME, NULL, NULL, NULL) ;
                        Escape (hDC, ENDDOC, NULL, NULL, NULL) ;
                        }
                    DeleteDC (hDC) ;
                    break ;
                case IDM_QUIT:                  /* "Quit" menu item */
                    DestroyWindow (hWnd) ;      /* destroy window, */
                    break ;                     /* terminating application */
                }
            break ;
        case WM_PAINT:
            BeginPaint (hWnd, &ps) ;
            hInstance = GetWindowWord (hWnd, GWW_HINSTANCE) ;
            OutputStuff (ps.hdc, hInstance) ; /* do output to screen */
            EndPaint (hWnd, &ps) ;
            break ;
        case WM_DESTROY:                        /* stop application */
            PostQuitMessage (0) ;
            break ;
        default:                /* default windows message processing */
            return (DefWindowProc (hWnd, wMessage, wParam, lParam)) ;
        }
    return (0L) ;
}

                        /* output text and rectangle to dc */
void OutputStuff (HDC hDC, HANDLE hInstance)
{
    char cBuf [128] ;

    Rectangle (hDC, 0, 20, 200, 100) ;
    LoadString (hInstance, S_OUTTEXT, cBuf, sizeof (cBuf)) ;
    TextOut (hDC, 0, 0, cBuf, lstrlen (cBuf)) ;
}
```

Listings 14-2 to 14-6 show the support files for PRINT1. The program's icon is shown in Figure 14-3.

Listing 14-2 PRINT1.H Header File

```
/* print1.h  header file */

#define IDM_PRINT           1       /* menu item ID numbers */
#define IDM_QUIT            10

#define S_OUTTEXT           1       /* string table ID numbers */
#define S_PROGRAMCAPTION    2

long FAR PASCAL WndProc (HWND, WORD, WORD, LONG) ;
void OutputStuff (HDC hDC, HANDLE hInstance) ;
```

Figure 14-3
PRINT1.ICO
Icon Image

Listing 14-3 PRINT1.RC Resource Script File

```
/* print1.rc  resource file */

#include "print1.h"

MyIcon      ICON      print1.ico

MyMenu      MENU
BEGIN
    MENUITEM "&Print",       IDM_PRINT
    MENUITEM "&Quit",        IDM_QUIT
END

STRINGTABLE
BEGIN
    S_PROGRAMCAPTION     "Print 1 Program"
    S_OUTTEXT            "Text at 0, 0 device units."
END
```

Listing 14-4 PRINT1.DEF Module Definition File

```
NAME            print1
DESCRIPTION     'print1 program'
EXETYPE         WINDOWS
STUB            'WINSTUB.EXE'
CODE            PRELOAD MOVEABLE DISCARDABLE
DATA            PRELOAD MOVEABLE MULTIPLE
HEAPSIZE        1024
STACKSIZE       5120
EXPORTS         WndProc
```

Listing 14-5 Turbo C++ Project File for PRINT1

```
print1.c
print1.def
print1.res
```

Listing 14-6 QuickC Project File for PRINT1

```
print1.c
print1.def
print1.rc
```

Problems with PRINT1

If you go ahead and print using the PRINT1 program, the output will appear roughly as shown in Figure 14-4. Although both the text and the rectangle are displayed, their relative size and location do not look like the display on PRINT1 window's client area. This seems odd because the same calls to the Rectangle() and TextOut() functions are made to draw on the client area and printer device contexts. What happened?

The reason the output looks different on the screen and printed page has to do with the interpretation of the default device context units. Remember from the last chapter that when a device context is first created, the default MM_TEXT mapping mode is used. With the MM_TEXT mapping mode, distances are measured in units of pixels. A pixel on a laser printer is a lot smaller than a pixel on a video screen, so the rectangle ends up smaller, and moved closer to the default origin at the upper left corner of the paper.

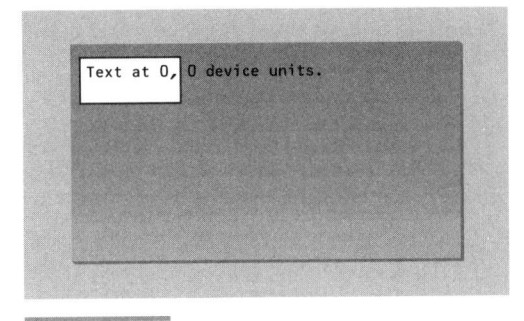

Figure 14-4 Printed Output from PRINT1

Another reason for the change in appearance is that text output is not scaled by the mapping mode in place. Instead, text characters are scaled based on the text font selected into the device context. Windows is smart enough to keep the default system font about the same point size on both the screen and the printer. This means that the text does not end up reduced in size due to the smaller pixel size on the printer.

The solution to these problems is to change the mapping mode of the device contexts for both the printer and video to a mode that uses physical units like inches or millimeters. The text size must also be treated as a variable, determined using the GetTextExtent() function, based on the device context in use. These techniques are demonstrated in the next example program, PRINT2.

Scaling the Printer Output

The key to getting reasonably sized output on a printer is to select one of the five mapping modes that have fixed sizing. They are the MM_LOMETRIC, MM_LOENGLISH, MM_HIMETRIC, MM_HIENGLISH, and MM_TWIPS mapping modes that were discussed in the last chapter. The next example program, PRINT2, modifies the previous example by specifying the MM_LOMETRIC mapping mode. Figure 14-5 shows PRINT2 in action, displaying a text string, a rectangle that exactly surrounds the text string, and a blue circle. In this case, the printed output will be very close to the image in Figure 14-5. There may be a difference in the relative length of the text string, as this is based on the font size, not a physical distance. However, the rectangle will exactly fit the size of the string, and the

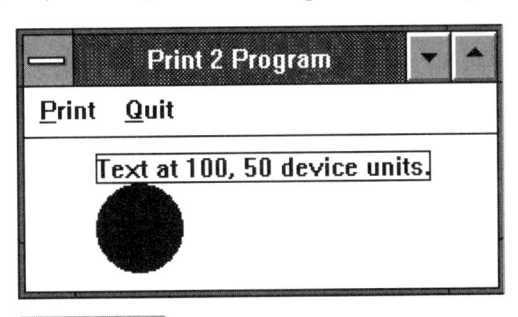

Figure 14-5 The PRINT2 Program

Chapter 14 • Printing   483

text, rectangle, and circle will be properly positioned. Figure 14-6 shows a typical printed output.

Listing 14-7 shows the PRINT2.C program. PRINT2.C is very close to PRINT1.C, except for changing the mapping mode and the different graphics and text string output. Because both the printer device context and window client area device context use the same settings, the mapping mode is set in a separate function called SetDC() at the end of PRINT2.C, and shown here:

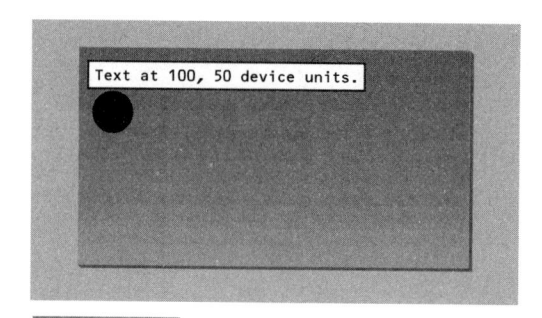

Figure 14-6 PRINT2 Printed Output

```
void SetDC (HDC hDC)    /* change the DC settings (printer and video) */
{
    SetMapMode (hDC, MM_LOMETRIC) ;    /* change map mode */
    SetWindowOrg (hDC, 20, 100) ;      /* move origin down and right */
    /* use null brush so center of rectangle is transparent */
    SelectObject (hDC, GetStockObject (NULL_BRUSH)) ;
    /* align characters based on bottom left */
    SetTextAlign (hDC, TA_LEFT | TA_BOTTOM) ;
}
```

The SetDC() function changes the mapping mode of a device context to MM_LOMETRIC, moves the origin to 20,100, selects the stock NULL_BRUSH for the rectangle, and sets the text alignment to be based on the bottom left corner of the first letter in a string. SetDC() is passed the device context as a parameter, so the function can be used to modify the device context for either a printer or a window's client area DC.

The actual output of the text and graphics is also done in a separate function, OutputStuff(). The function is used for output to both the printer and the client area DC. One of the tricks used in OutputStuff() is to use the GetTextExtent() function to determine the size of the text string on the current device context. This allows the OutputStuff() function to size the rectangle to exactly surround the text string. GetTextExtent() returns the size of the text string using logical units, which is exactly what is needed to call the Rectangle() function. OutputStuff() also temporarily creates a blue brush to paint the circle (using the Ellipse() function), but then restores the old brush and deletes the new brush. This leaves the default NULL_BRUSH installed in the device context when OutputStuff() returns.

```
void OutputStuff (HDC hDC, HANDLE hInstance)
{
    char    cBuf [128] ;
    DWORD   dwTextExtent ;
    HBRUSH  hOldBrush, hNewBrush ;

    LoadString (hInstance, S_OUTTEXT, cBuf, sizeof (cBuf)) ;
    TextOut (hDC, 100, 50, cBuf, lstrlen (cBuf)) ;
    dwTextExtent = GetTextExtent (hDC, cBuf, lstrlen (cBuf)) ;
    Rectangle (hDC, 100, 50, LOWORD (dwTextExtent) + 100,
```

```
            HIWORD (dwTextExtent) + 50) ;
    hNewBrush = CreateSolidBrush (RGB (0, 0, 255)) ;   /* blue */
    hOldBrush = SelectObject (hDC, hNewBrush) ;
    Ellipse (hDC, 100, 50, 200, -50) ;
    SelectObject (hDC, hOldBrush) ;
    DeleteObject (hNewBrush) ;
}
```

The remainder of the PRINT2.C program should look familiar. The same WIN.INI file is used again to get the names of the printer device, etc. for calling CreateDC(). The Escape() function is again used to send the STARTDOC, NEWFRAME, and ENDDOC escapes to the printer.

Listing 14-7 PRINT2.C

```
/* print2.c   output to printer with Iometric mapping mode */

#include <windows.h>
#include <string.h>     /* needed for strtok() function */
#include "print2.h"

int PASCAL WinMain (HANDLE hInstance, HANDLE hPrevInstance, LPSTR lpszCmdLine,
    int nCmdShow)
{
    HWND       hWnd ;          /* the window's "handle" */
    MSG        msg ;           /* a message structure */
    WNDCLASS   wndclass ;      /* window class structure */
    char       cBuf [128] ;    /* character buffer */

    if (!hPrevInstance)
    {
       wndclass.style         = CS_HREDRAW | CS_VREDRAW ;
       wndclass.lpfnWndProc   = WndProc ;
       wndclass.cbClsExtra    = 0 ;
       wndclass.cbWndExtra    = 0 ;
       wndclass.hInstance     = hInstance ;
       wndclass.hIcon         = LoadIcon (hInstance, "MyIcon") ;
       wndclass.hCursor       = LoadCursor (NULL, IDC_ARROW) ;
       wndclass.hbrBackground = GetStockObject (WHITE_BRUSH) ;
       wndclass.lpszMenuName  = "MyMenu" ;
       wndclass.lpszClassName = "MyClass" ;
                 /* register the window class */
       if (!RegisterClass (&wndclass))
          return 0 ;
    }
    LoadString (hInstance, S_PROGRAMCAPTION, cBuf, sizeof (cBuf)) ;

    hWnd = CreateWindow ("MyClass", cBuf, WS_OVERLAPPEDWINDOW,
       CW_USEDEFAULT, CW_USEDEFAULT, CW_USEDEFAULT, CW_USEDEFAULT,
       NULL, NULL, hInstance, NULL) ;
    ShowWindow (hWnd, nCmdShow) ;   /* display the window */

    while (GetMessage (&msg, NULL, NULL, NULL))   /* message loop */
    {
```

```
            TranslateMessage (&msg) ;         /* translate keyboard messages */
            DispatchMessage (&msg) ;          /* send message to WndProc() */
        }
        return (msg.wParam) ;
}


long FAR PASCAL WndProc (HWND hWnd, WORD wMessage, WORD wParam, LONG lParam)
{
        PAINTSTRUCT     ps ;
        HDC             hDC ;
        HANDLE          hInstance ;
        char            szPrinter [64], *szDriver, *szDevice, *szOutput ;

        switch (wMessage)                     /* process windows messages */
        {
          case WM_COMMAND:
                switch (wParam)               /* menu items */
                {
                   case IDM_PRINT:            /* output to printer */
                        hInstance = GetWindowWord (hWnd, GWW_HINSTANCE) ;
                            /* parse win.ini line to get printer info */
                        GetProfileString ("windows", "device", "",
                                szPrinter, 64) ;
                        szDevice = strtok (szPrinter, ",") ;
                        szDriver = strtok (NULL, ",") ;
                        szOutput = strtok (NULL, ",") ;
                            /* create a device context for the printer */
                        hDC = CreateDC (szDriver, szDevice, szOutput, NULL) ;

                        SetDC (hDC) ;         /* change DC settings */
                        if (Escape (hDC, STARTDOC, 4, "Test", NULL) > 0)
                        {                     /* output to printer */
                            OutputStuff (hDC, hInstance) ;
                            Escape (hDC, NEWFRAME, NULL, NULL, NULL) ;
                            Escape (hDC, ENDDOC, NULL, NULL, NULL) ;
                        }
                        else
                        {
                            Escape (hDC, ENDDOC, NULL, NULL, NULL) ;
                            MessageBox (hWnd, "Could not create printer dc.",
                                "Warning", MB_OK) ;
                        }
                        DeleteDC (hDC) ;      /* free printer dc */
                        break ;
                   case IDM_QUIT:             /* "Quit" menu item */
                        DestroyWindow (hWnd) ;  /* destroy window, */
                        break ;               /* terminating application */
                }
                break ;
          case WM_PAINT:
                BeginPaint (hWnd, &ps) ;
                SetDC (ps.hdc) ;              /* change DC settings */
                hInstance = GetWindowWord (hWnd, GWW_HINSTANCE) ;
                OutputStuff (ps.hdc, hInstance) ; /* do output to screen */
                EndPaint (hWnd, &ps) ;
                break ;
```

```c
        case WM_DESTROY:             /* stop application */
            PostQuitMessage (0) ;
            break ;
        default:                 /* default windows message processing */
            return (DefWindowProc (hWnd, wMessage, wParam, lParam)) ;
    }
    return (0L) ;
}

void SetDC (HDC hDC)    /* change the DC settings (printer and video) */
{
    SetMapMode (hDC, MM_LOMETRIC) ;   /* change map mode */
    SetWindowOrg (hDC, 20, 100) ;     /* move origin down and right */
       /* use null brush so center of rectangle is transparent */
    SelectObject (hDC, GetStockObject (NULL_BRUSH)) ;
       /* align characters based on bottom left */
    SetTextAlign (hDC, TA_LEFT | TA_BOTTOM) ;
}

                                /* output text and rectangle to dc */
void OutputStuff (HDC hDC, HANDLE hInstance)
{
    char    cBuf [128] ;
    DWORD   dwTextExtent ;
    HBRUSH  hOldBrush, hNewBrush ;

    LoadString (hInstance, S_OUTTEXT, cBuf, sizeof (cBuf)) ;
    TextOut (hDC, 100, 50, cBuf, lstrlen (cBuf)) ;
    dwTextExtent = GetTextExtent (hDC, cBuf, lstrlen (cBuf)) ;
    Rectangle (hDC, 100, 50, LOWORD (dwTextExtent) + 100,
        HIWORD (dwTextExtent) + 50) ;
    hNewBrush = CreateSolidBrush (RGB (0, 0, 255)) ;   /* blue */
    hOldBrush = SelectObject (hDC, hNewBrush) ;
    Ellipse (hDC, 100, 50, 200, -50) ;
    SelectObject (hDC, hOldBrush) ;
    DeleteObject (hNewBrush) ;
}
```

Listings 14-8 to 14-12 show the support files for PRINT2. The program's icon is shown in Figure 14-7.

Listing 14-8 PRINT2.H Header File

```c
/* print2.h  header file */

#define IDM_PRINT         1     /* menu item ID numbers */
#define IDM_QUIT         10

#define S_OUTTEXT         1     /* string table ID numbers */
#define S_PROGRAMCAPTION  2

long FAR PASCAL WndProc (HWND, WORD, WORD, LONG) ;
void SetDC (HDC hDC) ;
void OutputStuff (HDC hDC, HANDLE hInstance) ;
```

Figure 14-7
PRINT2.ICO
Icon Image

Chapter 14 • Printing   487

Listing 14-9 PRINT2.RC Resource Script File

```
/* print2.rc  resource file */

#include "print2.h"

MyIcon      ICON    print2.ico

MyMenu      MENU
BEGIN
    MENUITEM "&Print",      IDM_PRINT
    MENUITEM "&Quit",       IDM_QUIT
END

STRINGTABLE
BEGIN
    S_PROGRAMCAPTION        "Print 2 Program"
    S_OUTTEXT               "Text at 100, 50 device units."
END
```

Listing 14-10 PRINT2.DEF Module Definition File

```
NAME            print2
DESCRIPTION     'print2 program'
EXETYPE         WINDOWS
STUB            'WINSTUB.EXE'
CODE            PRELOAD MOVEABLE DISCARDABLE
DATA            PRELOAD MOVEABLE MULTIPLE
HEAPSIZE        1024
STACKSIZE       5120
EXPORTS         WndProc
```

Listing 14-11 Turbo C++ Project File for PRINT2

```
print2.c
print2.def
print2.res
```

Listing 14-12 QuickC Project File for PRINT2

```
print2.c
print2.def
print2.rc
```

Allowing Interruption of a Print Job

The PRINT2 program is a good template for a program that has a small amount of printing to do. For larger amounts of printing, it is a good idea to allow the user to cancel the print job while the program is printing. Writing a program which allows a print job to be interrupted requires some fairly sophisticated Windows programming. This section goes through the steps and logic involved, and then demonstrates the techniques with another example program.

The starting point for allowing a printing job to be interrupted is the SETABORTPROC escape command, which is sent by the Escape() function to the printer driver. The SETABORTPROC escape passes the address of an "abort" function to the printer driver. The printer driver then periodically allows messages to be sent to this abort function, instead of the program's normal message loop. The abort function is designed so that it can stop the printing process if necessary.

A typical sequence of commands to alert the printer driver about the abort function is shown below. The SETABORTPROC escape is sent to the printer driver after the printer device context has been created, but before printing is started. A procedure-instance address for the abort function must be created with MakeProcInstance() before the SETABORTPROC escape is called. The abort function's name must also be listed in the EXPORTS section of the program's module definition file, as it will be called from outside of the program.

```
FARPROC lpfnAbortPrint ;

lpfnAbortPrint = MakeProcInstance (PrintAbort, hInstance) ;
Escape (hDC, SETABORTPROC, 0, (LPSTR) lpfnAbortPrint, NULL) ;
```

This form of the Escape() function will compile without a message under Turbo C++, but will result in the warning "cast of a function pointer to a data pointer" under QuickC. Casting the pointer to the function to the LPSTR data type expected by the Escape() function is exactly what we are trying to do, so this warning message is of no consequence.

The abort function will have the form shown below. The function is interesting, as it contains a PeekMessage() loop, similar to the message loop we used in the animated bouncing ball example back in Chapter 4, *Text and Graphics Output*.

```
BOOL FAR PASCAL PrintAbort (HDC hdcPrinter, int nCode)
{
    MSG msg ;

    while (!_bPrintAbort && PeekMessage (&msg, NULL, 0, 0, PM_REMOVE))
    {
      if (!IsDialogMessage (_hDlgPrintAbort, &msg))
      {
          TranslateMessage (&msg) ;
          DispatchMessage (&msg) ;
      }
    }
    return (!_bPrintAbort) ;
}
```

Another key to the printer abort function is that it checks a global variable, *_bPrintAbort*, each time the message loop is accessed. If *_bPrintAbort* is FALSE, PeekMessage() is called, and any pending messages are passed on via the normal TranslateMessage() and DispatchMessage() functions. However, if *_bPrintAbort* is

TRUE, the abort function returns. This is how the printer driver knows that the print job should be terminated.

That leaves us with just one more challenge — how to allow the user to change the value of the global variable *bPrintAbort* while the printing job is in progress. This is typically done by putting a small dialog box on the screen while the printer job is active. The dialog box contains a "Cancel" button. Selecting the "Cancel" button causes the *bPrintAbort* global variable to be changed from FALSE

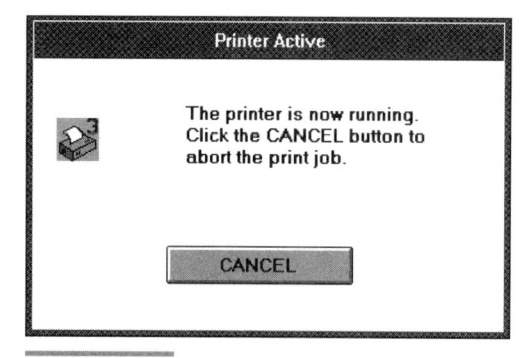

Figure 14-8 The Print Abort Dialog Box from PRINT3

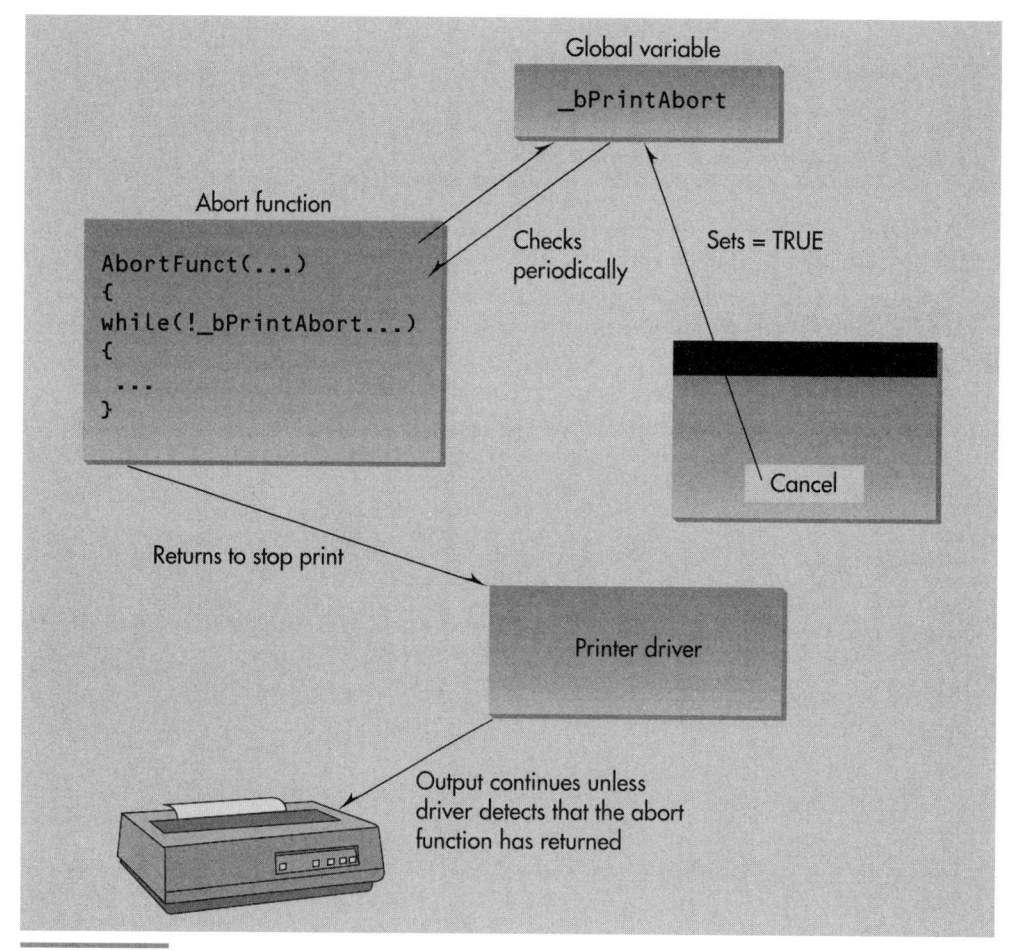

Figure 14-9 Printer Abort Logic Elements

to TRUE, which means that the abort function will return the next time it processes a message. Figure 14-8 shows a typical printer abort dialog box, in this case for the next example program PRINT3.

Figure 14-9 shows the relationship between the different elements involved while a printer session is in progress for a program that has an abort procedure. During printing, the program's normal message loop is shut down by using the EnableWindow() function to disable the main program window. Disabled windows do not receive messages, so only the abort procedure actively processes messages while the printing process is active. Disabling the main program window does not stop the program from running, and the program can continue to send output to the printer. Disabled windows just do not receive messages to their message loops.

Disabling the main program window poses a small problem for the abort dialog box. Common modal dialog boxes (created with the DialogBox() function) take control from the parent window while the dialog box is visible, and they depend on the parent window's message loop to send the dialog box messages. To get around these problems, the printer abort dialog box must be a modeless dialog box, created with the CreateDialog() family of functions. Also, the printer abort procedure (containing the PeekMessage() loop) must include the IsDialogMessage() function to properly process messages for the abort dialog box.

As you can see, setting up a program to allow a print job to be interrupted is not trivial. The reason for the complexity is that the program is basically doing two things at the same time. The printer driver is processing output from the main part of the program, while the abort procedure periodically checks whether the user has selected the cancel button on the abort dialog box.

The PRINT3 Program

Listing 14-13 shows the PRINT3.C program, which includes all of the printer abort logic discussed in the previous section. When running, PRINT3 appears as shown in Figure 14-10, and displays two lines of text in the client area. These two lines are also output on the printer if the "Print" menu item is selected. Both the client area device context and the printer device context are set to the MM_LOMETRIC mapping mode prior to any output, so the output is aligned properly on both devices.

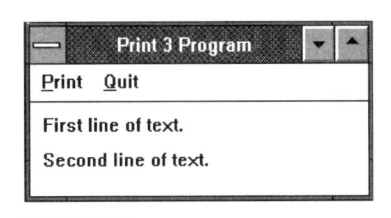

Figure 14-10 The PRINT3 Program

During the printing process, the abort dialog box (see Figure 14-8) is visible above the PRINT3 program window, and the main program window cannot be selected. Disabling the main program window is accomplished by calling the EnableWindow() function as follows:

```
EnableWindow (hWnd, FALSE) ;
```

EnableWindow() takes two parameters. The first is the handle of the window to enable or disable. The second is a BOOL value, TRUE to enable the window and FALSE to disable it. The main program window is enabled after the printing process is completed with a second call to EnableWindow(). During the period when the main program window is disabled, the program's abort dialog box is displayed. The "PrintStop" dialog box is created and displayed with the following function calls:

```
lpfnPrintDlg = MakeProcInstance (PrintStopDlg, hInstance) ;
_hDlgPrintAbort = CreateDialog (hInstance, "PrintStop", hWnd, lpfnPrintDlg) ;
_bPrintAbort = FALSE ;
```

MakeProcInstance() is called to create a procedure-instance address for the dialog box function PrintStopDlg(). CreateDialog() then makes the dialog box visible. Note that the global variable _bPrintAbort is set to FALSE at the time the dialog box is made visible. This is the variable that will be set to TRUE if the user clicks the "Cancel" button on the dialog box, ending the printing process. The abort procedure is established using the SETABORTPROC escape, again passing the procedure-instance address of the abort procedure (the function that will process messages while the printing process is underway).

```
lpfnAbortPrint = MakeProcInstance (PrintAbort, hInstance) ;
Escape (hDC, SETABORTPROC, 0, (LPSTR) lpfnAbortPrint, NULL) ;
```

Output to the printer is then done, starting with the STARTDOC printer escape. When the printing is completed (or terminated), a number of cleanup functions are needed to restore the original environment. DestroyWindow() is used to destroy the modeless dialog box, and EnableWindow() is called to again enable the main program window. SetFocus() is also called to make sure that the main program window has the input focus when the print job is done, in case the user selected some other object on the screen during printing. Finally, FreeProcInstance() is called for both the dialog box procedure and the abort procedure to remove the procedure instances from memory.

```
DestroyWindow (_hDlgPrintAbort) ;      /* kill dlg box */
EnableWindow (hWnd, TRUE) ;            /* enable main window */
SetFocus (hWnd) ;                      /* main window focus */
FreeProcInstance (lpfnPrintDlg) ;      /* free proc. inst's */
FreeProcInstance (lpfnAbortPrint) ;
```

Listing 14-13   PRINT3.C

```
/* print3.c   output to printer an abort dialog box */

#include <windows.h>
#include <string.h>          /* needed for strtok() function */
#include "print3.h"

int PASCAL WinMain (HANDLE hInstance, HANDLE hPrevInstance, LPSTR lpszCmdLine,
    int nCmdShow)
{
    HWND       hWnd ;           /* the window's "handle" */
    MSG        msg ;            /* a message structure */
    WNDCLASS   wndclass ;       /* window class structure */
    char       cBuf [128] ;     /* character buffer */

    if (!hPrevInstance)
    {
```

```
        wndclass.style          = CS_HREDRAW | CS_VREDRAW ;
        wndclass.lpfnWndProc    = WndProc ;
        wndclass.cbClsExtra     = 0 ;
        wndclass.cbWndExtra     = 0 ;
        wndclass.hInstance      = hInstance ;
        wndclass.hIcon          = LoadIcon (hInstance, "MyIcon") ;
        wndclass.hCursor        = LoadCursor (NULL, IDC_ARROW) ;
        wndclass.hbrBackground  = GetStockObject (WHITE_BRUSH) ;
        wndclass.lpszMenuName   = "MyMenu" ;
        wndclass.lpszClassName  = "MyClass" ;
                /* register the window class */
        if (!RegisterClass (&wndclass))
            return 0 ;
    }
    LoadString (hInstance, S_PROGRAMCAPTION, cBuf, sizeof (cBuf)) ;

    hWnd = CreateWindow ("MyClass", cBuf, WS_OVERLAPPEDWINDOW,
        CW_USEDEFAULT, CW_USEDEFAULT, CW_USEDEFAULT, CW_USEDEFAULT,
        NULL, NULL, hInstance, NULL) ;
    ShowWindow (hWnd, nCmdShow) ;       /* display the window */

    while (GetMessage (&msg, NULL, NULL, NULL))  /* message loop */
    {
        TranslateMessage (&msg) ;       /* translate keyboard messages */
        DispatchMessage (&msg) ;        /* send message to WndProc() */
    }
    return (msg.wParam) ;
}
                                        /* global variables */
HWND    hDlgPrintAbort = NULL ;         /* handle of print abort dlg box */
BOOL    bPrintAbort ;                   /* bool is TRUE to abort printing */

long FAR PASCAL WndProc (HWND hWnd, WORD wMessage, WORD wParam, LONG lParam)
{
    PAINTSTRUCT ps ;
    HDC         hDC ;
    HANDLE      hInstance ;
    char        szPrinter [64], *szDriver, *szDevice, *szOutput ;
    FARPROC     lpfnPrintDlg, lpfnAbortPrint ;

    switch (wMessage)                   /* process windows messages */
    {
        case WM_COMMAND:
            switch (wParam)             /* menu items */
            {
                case IDM_PRINT:                 /* output to printer */
                    hInstance = GetWindowWord (hWnd, GWW_HINSTANCE) ;
                        /* parse win.ini line to get printer info */
                    GetProfileString ("windows", "device", "",
                        szPrinter, 64) ;
                    szDevice = strtok (szPrinter, ",") ;
                    szDriver = strtok (NULL, ",") ;
                    szOutput = strtok (NULL, ",") ;
                        /* create a device context for the printer */
                    hDC = CreateDC (szDriver, szDevice, szOutput, NULL) ;
                    SetDC (hDC) ;       /*
    /* set up abort procedure section */
                        /* disable the main window, only dlg box active */
                    EnableWindow (hWnd, FALSE) ;
```

Chapter 14 • Printing

```
                        /* make a procedure instance address for dlg proc. */
                    lpfnPrintDlg = MakeProcInstance (PrintStopDlg,
                            hInstance) ;
                        /* put the modeless dialog box on the screen */
                    hDlgPrintAbort = CreateDialog (hInstance, "PrintStop",
                            hWnd, lpfnPrintDlg) ;
                        /* set the global bool variable FALSE to start */
                    bPrintAbort = FALSE ;
                        /* make procedure instance address for abort proc. */
                    lpfnAbortPrint = MakeProcInstance (PrintAbort,
                            hInstance) ;
                        /* tell Windows to send messages to the */
                        /* PrintAbort() function s message loop */
                    Escape (hDC, SETABORTPROC, 0,
                            (LPSTR) lpfnAbortPrint, NULL) ;
    /* printing starts here */
                    if (Escape (hDC, STARTDOC, 4, "Test", NULL) > 0)
                    {                       /* output to printer */
                        OutputStuff (hDC, hInstance) ;
                        Escape (hDC, NEWFRAME, NULL, NULL, NULL) ;
                        Escape (hDC, ENDDOC, NULL, NULL, NULL) ;
                    }
                    else
                    {
                        Escape (hDC, ENDDOC, NULL, NULL, NULL) ;
                        MessageBox (hWnd, "Could not create printer dc.",
                                "Warning", MB_OK) ;
                    }
                    DestroyWindow (_hDlgPrintAbort) ; /* kill dlg box */
                    EnableWindow (hWnd, TRUE) ;      /* enable main window */
                    SetFocus (hWnd) ;                /* main window focus */
                    FreeProcInstance (lpfnPrintDlg) ; /* free proc. inst s */
                    FreeProcInstance (lpfnAbortPrint) ;
                    DeleteDC (hDC) ;                 /* free printer dc */
                    break ;
                case IDM_QUIT:                       /* "Quit" menu item */
                    DestroyWindow (hWnd) ;           /* destroy window, */
                    break ;                          /* terminating application */
            }
            break ;
        case WM_PAINT:
            BeginPaint (hWnd, &ps) ;
            SetDC (ps.hdc) ;
            hInstance = GetWindowWord (hWnd, GWW_HINSTANCE) ;
            OutputStuff (ps.hdc, hInstance) ;   /* do output to screen */
            EndPaint (hWnd, &ps) ;
            break ;
        case WM_DESTROY:                             /* stop application */
            PostQuitMessage (0) ;
            break ;
        default:             /* default windows message processing */
            return (DefWindowProc (hWnd, wMessage, wParam, lParam)) ;
    }
    return (0L) ;
}

void SetDC (HDC hDC)      /* change the DC settings */
{
```

```
    SetMapMode (hDC, MM_LOMETRIC) ;      /* change map mode */
    SetWindowOrg (hDC, -20, 50) ;        /* move origin down and right */
        /* align characters based on bottom left */
    SetTextAlign (hDC, TA_LEFT | TA_BOTTOM) ;
}

                            /* output two lines of text */
void OutputStuff (HDC hDC, HANDLE hInstance)
{
    char    cBuf [128] ;
    DWORD   dwTextExtent ;

    LoadString (hInstance, S_OUTTEXT1, cBuf, sizeof (cBuf)) ;
        /* output first line of text at 0,0 */
    TextOut (hDC, 0, 0, cBuf, lstrlen (cBuf)) ;
    dwTextExtent = GetTextExtent (hDC, cBuf, lstrlen (cBuf)) ;
    LoadString (hInstance, S_OUTTEXT2, cBuf, sizeof (cBuf)) ;
        /* output second line of text 2 mm below first */
    TextOut (hDC, 0, -1 * HIWORD (dwTextExtent) - 20,
       cBuf, lstrlen (cBuf)) ;
}

    /* this is the dialog box function for the dialog box that is */
    /* shown on the screen while the program is printing */
BOOL FAR PASCAL PrintStopDlg (HWND hDlg, WORD wMessage, WORD wParam,
    LONG lParam)
{
    if (wMessage == WM_COMMAND)     /* there is only one button, so */
    {                               /* any WM_COMMAND comes from it */
        bPrintAbort = TRUE ;        /* changes the global variable */
        return (TRUE) ;             /* _bPrintAbort to TRUE */
    }
    else
        return (FALSE) ;
}

    /* this is the message processing function that gets messages */
    /* while the printer abort dialog box is on the screen */
BOOL FAR PASCAL PrintAbort (HDC hdcPrinter, int nCode)
{
    MSG msg ;
            /* the global variable _bPrintAbort is set to TRUE */
            /* if the user clicks the button on the abort dialog */
            /* box. This exits this message loop, returning */
            /* control back to the program's message loop */
    while (!_bPrintAbort && PeekMessage (&msg, NULL, 0, 0, PM_REMOVE))
    {
        if (!IsDialogMessage (_hDlgPrintAbort, &msg))
        {
            TranslateMessage (&msg) ;
            DispatchMessage (&msg) ;
        }
    }
    return (!_bPrintAbort) ;
}
```

Listings 14-14 to 14-19 show the support files for PRINT3. The program's icon is shown in Figure 14-11.

Listing 14-14 PRINT3.H Header File

```
/* print3.h header file */

#define IDM_PRINT           1       /* menu item ID numbers */
#define IDM_QUIT            10

#define S_OUTTEXT1          1       /* string table ID numbers */
#define S_OUTTEXT2          2
#define S_PROGRAMCAPTION    3

long FAR PASCAL WndProc (HWND, WORD, WORD, LONG) ;
void SetDC (HDC hDC) ;
void OutputStuff (HDC hDC, HANDLE hInstance) ;
BOOL FAR PASCAL PrintStopDlg (HWND hDlg, WORD wMessage, WORD wParam,
    LONG lParam) ;
BOOL FAR PASCAL PrintAbort (HDC hdcPrinter, int nCode) ;
```

Figure 14-11
PRINT3.ICO
Icon Image

Listing 14-15 PRINT3.RC Resource Script File

```
/* print3.rc resource file */

#include "windows.h"
#include "print3.h"
#include "print3d.h"
#include "print3.dlg"

MyIcon      ICON    print3.ico

MyMenu      MENU
BEGIN
    MENUITEM "&Print",      IDM_PRINT
    MENUITEM "&Quit",       IDM_QUIT
END

STRINGTABLE
BEGIN
    S_PROGRAMCAPTION    "Print 3 Program"
    S_OUTTEXT1          "First line of text."
    S_OUTTEXT2          "Second line of text."
END
```

Listing 14-16 PRINT3.DLG Dialog Box Definition

```
DLGINCLUDE RCDATA DISCARDABLE       /* this section is only created using */
BEGIN                               /* the Microsoft SDK dialog box editor */
    "PRINT3D.H\0"
END

PrintStop DIALOG 6, 18, 160, 100
STYLE DS_MODALFRAME | WS_POPUP | WS_VISIBLE | WS_CAPTION
CAPTION "Printer Active"
FONT 8, "Helv"
```

```
    BEGIN
        PUSHBUTTON      "CANCEL", DLI_CANCELBUTTON, 45, 69, 64, 14
        LTEXT           "The printer is now running.  Click the CANCEL button to abort the
print job.",
                        -1, 51, 16, 91, 33
        ICON            "MyIcon", -1, 8, 22, 16, 16
    END
```

Listing 14-17 PRINT3.DEF Module Definition File

```
NAME            print3
DESCRIPTION     'print3 program'
EXETYPE         WINDOWS
STUB            'WINSTUB.EXE'
CODE            PRELOAD MOVEABLE DISCARDABLE
DATA            PRELOAD MOVEABLE MULTIPLE
HEAPSIZE        1024
STACKSIZE       5120
EXPORTS         WndProc
                PrintStopDlg
                PrintAbort
```

Listing 14-18 Turbo C++ Project File for PRINT3

```
print3.c
print3.def
print3.res
```

Listing 14-19 QuickC Project File for PRINT3

```
print3.c
print3.def
print3.rc
```

Getting Information About a Device

Although the device context insulates Windows programs from the low-level details of particular output devices, there are situations where you will want to find out some of the physical details of the printer or video equipment in use. For example, you may want to modify the colors a program uses depending on the number of colors the video board is capable of displaying. It is also valuable to be able to determine the size and resolution of the screen or output surface before deciding how big to make detailed pictures.

There are two basic ways to find out details about a physical output device. One is to create a device context for the device, and then read the values stored by Windows for the device. The GetDeviceCaps() function ("get device capabilities") accesses the device context data, returning any single value requested. The second way to access a device is to call functions in the device driver. For example, Microsoft specifies in its documentation on creating device drivers that the driver must contain the DeviceCapabilities() and ExtDeviceMode() functions which can be called from within a Windows program. We will explore accessing functions in a device driver in the next section, but for now the focus will be on using GetDeviceCaps().

Using GetDeviceCaps()

GetDeviceCaps() is very simple to use. The only requirement is that you must create the device context for the device before running GetDeviceCaps(), as the function reads data stored in the device context block of memory. A typical use of the function is shown here, determining the number of vertical pixels for the video display.

```
HDC    hDC ;
int    nVertPixels ;

hDC = GetDC (hWnd) ;    /* obtain handle to window's device context */
nVertPixels = GetDeviceCaps (hDC, VERTRES) ;
```

Note that although the device context handle was obtained for a window's client area, the device data applies to the entire screen (entire device), not just the portion of the screen occupied by the window. GetDeviceCaps() uses a series of index values, such as VERTRES, to specify the data element requested. These index values are defined in WINDOWS.H, and most are only useful if you are writing a device driver. For example, GetDeviceCaps() will determine if the device has hardware logic for drawing curves or filling areas. The index values that you are most likely to find useful in creating Windows programs are summarized in Table 14-2.

VALUE	MEANING
TECHNOLOGY	Determines the type of device. For common devices, the returned value will be equal to DT_PLOTTER, DT_RASDISPLAY (raster display), or DT_RASPRINTER (raster printer).
HORZSIZE	The approximate width of the physical display in millimeters.
VERTSIZE	The approximate height of the physical display in millimeters.
HORZRES	The number of horizontal pixels.
VERTRES	The number of vertical pixels.
LOGPIXELSX	The number of pixels per logical inch horizontally.
LOGPIXELSY	The number of pixels per logical inch vertically.
BITSPIXEL	The number of adjacent color bits per pixel.
PLANES	The number of color planes.

Table 14-2 Common GetDeviceCaps() Index Values

Two of the GetDeviceCaps() index values are used to determine the number of colors a device, such as a video display, can show simultaneously. Some video displays, such as 16-color VGA boards, store color data for each primary color in separate blocks of memory called "color planes." The other data format stores all of the bits needed to specify a color in adjacent locations in memory. This is typical for higher resolution systems. Any given display will use only one of these two storage techniques, so either the value returned by GetDeviceCaps() of BITSPIXEL will be one, or the value returned for PLANES will be one. The value not equal to one will be the number of bits used per pixel to store colors. You can determine the number of simultaneous colors with this formula:

$$2^{(BITSPIXEL + PLANES - 1)} = \text{Simultaneous Colors}$$

For example, a Super VGA board will typically return eight for BITSPIXEL, and one for PLANES, so the number of simultaneous colors is:

$$2^{(8 + 1 - 1)} = 2^8 = 256 \text{ Simultaneous Colors}$$

An Example Using GetDeviceCaps()

The next example program, called DEVCAP, demonstrates using GetDeviceCaps() for determining physical information about both the video display and the currently selected printer. Figure 14-12 shows DEVCAP in action, displaying information about a system with a Super VGA video board and a HP IIP printer. The horizontal and vertical sizes in millimeters for the video system are just Windows' best estimate for the 1,024 by 768 video resolution. The printer horizontal and vertical sizes are more accurate and refer to the printable region on a page. Note that in Figure 14-12 the video board is a 256 color system (2^8), and the printer is a monochrome (black and white) device.

Listing 14-20 shows the DEVCAP.C program. DEVCAP uses string table entries for all of the text strings that show up in the DEVCAP window's client area. To simplify displaying the string table entries at different locations, DEVCAP defines the OutStringTable() function at the end of the listing that displays a given string at an *X,Y* location on the screen.

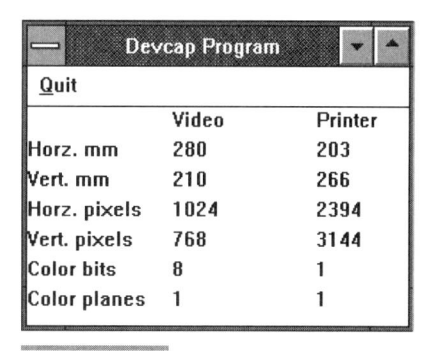

	Video	Printer
Horz. mm	280	203
Vert. mm	210	266
Horz. pixels	1024	2394
Vert. pixels	768	3144
Color bits	8	1
Color planes	1	1

Figure 14-12 The DEVCAP Program

```
void OutStringTable (HDC hDC, HANDLE hInstance, int nString,
    int nX, int nY)
{
    char cBuf [128] ;

    LoadString (hInstance, nString, cBuf, sizeof (cBuf)) ;
    TextOut (hDC, nX, nY, cBuf, lstrlen (cBuf)) ;
}
```

A similar utility function called OutDevCapValue() is defined to output the numeric value for an entry that the GetDeviceCaps() function obtains from a device context at a given *X,Y* location. The OutDevCapValue() is then called a number of times in the WndProc() function of DEVCAP.C to display each of the device capabilities requested at a different location in the window's client area.

Chapter 14 • Printing   499

```
void OutDevCapValue (HDC hDCout, HDC hDCdata, int nIndex,
    int nX, int nY)
{
    char    cBuf [16] ;
    int     nValue ;

    nValue = GetDeviceCaps (hDCdata, nIndex) ;
    TextOut (hDCout, nX, nY, cBuf, wsprintf (cBuf, "%d", nValue)) ;
}
```

DEVCAP.C contains the standard logic for obtaining the installed printer's description from the WIN.INI file. This is done each time a WM_PAINT message is received to create the device context for the printer. The BeginPaint() function obtains the device context for the video system, and these two device contexts are used to obtain device capabilities values for the printer and video system respectively.

Listing 14-20 DEVCAP.C

```
/* devcap.c    demonstrate GetDeviceCaps() function */

#include <windows.h>
#include <string.h>          /* needed for strtok() function */
#include "devcap.h"

int PASCAL WinMain (HANDLE hInstance, HANDLE hPrevInstance, LPSTR lpszCmdLine,
    int nCmdShow)
{
    HWND        hWnd ;          /* the window's "handle" */
    MSG         msg ;           /* a message structure */
    WNDCLASS    wndclass ;      /* window class structure */
    char        cBuf [128] ;    /* character buffer */

    if (!hPrevInstance)
    {
        wndclass.style          = CS_HREDRAW | CS_VREDRAW ;
        wndclass.lpfnWndProc    = WndProc ;
        wndclass.cbClsExtra     = 0 ;
        wndclass.cbWndExtra     = 0 ;
        wndclass.hInstance      = hInstance ;
        wndclass.hIcon          = LoadIcon (hInstance, "MyIcon") ;
        wndclass.hCursor        = LoadCursor (NULL, IDC_ARROW) ;
        wndclass.hbrBackground  = GetStockObject (WHITE_BRUSH) ;
        wndclass.lpszMenuName   = "MyMenu" ;
        wndclass.lpszClassName  = "MyClass" ;
                    /* register the window class */
        if (!RegisterClass (&wndclass))
            return 0 ;
    }
    LoadString (hInstance, S_PROGRAMCAPTION, cBuf, sizeof (cBuf)) ;

    hWnd = CreateWindow ("MyClass", cBuf, WS_OVERLAPPEDWINDOW,
        CW_USEDEFAULT, CW_USEDEFAULT, CW_USEDEFAULT, CW_USEDEFAULT,
        NULL, NULL, hInstance, NULL) ;
    ShowWindow (hWnd, nCmdShow) ;       /* display the window */
```

```c
        while (GetMessage (&msg, NULL, NULL, NULL))     /* message loop */
        {
            TranslateMessage (&msg) ;         /* translate keyboard messages */
            DispatchMessage (&msg) ;          /* send message to WndProc() */
        }
        return (msg.wParam) ;
}

long FAR PASCAL WndProc (HWND hWnd, WORD wMessage, WORD wParam, LONG lParam)
{
    PAINTSTRUCT    ps ;
    HANDLE         hInstance ;
    HDC            hDCprint ;
    char           szPrinter [64], *szDriver, *szDevice, *szOutput,
                   cBuf [128] ;

    switch (wMessage)              /* process windows messages */
    {
        case WM_COMMAND:
            switch (wParam)                    /* menu items */
            {
                case IDM_QUIT:                 /* "Quit" menu item */
                    DestroyWindow (hWnd) ;     /* destroy window, */
                    break ;                    /* terminating application */
            }
            break ;
        case WM_PAINT:
            BeginPaint (hWnd, &ps) ;
            hInstance = GetWindowWord (hWnd, GWW_HINSTANCE) ;
                    /* parse win.ini line to get printer info */
            GetProfileString ("windows", "device", "", szPrinter, 64) ;
            szDevice = strtok (szPrinter, ",") ;
            szDriver = strtok (NULL, ",") ;
            szOutput = strtok (NULL, ",") ;
                    /* create a device context for the printer */
            hDCprint = CreateDC (szDriver, szDevice, szOutput, NULL) ;
                    /* put headings on screen */
            OutStringTable (ps.hdc, hInstance, S_VIDEOTITLE, 100, 0) ;
            OutStringTable (ps.hdc, hInstance, S_PRINTERTITLE, 200, 0) ;
            OutStringTable (ps.hdc, hInstance, S_HORZSIZE, 0, 20 ) ;
            OutStringTable (ps.hdc, hInstance, S_VERTSIZE, 0, 40 ) ;
            OutStringTable (ps.hdc, hInstance, S_HORZRES, 0, 60 ) ;
            OutStringTable (ps.hdc, hInstance, S_VERTRES, 0, 80 ) ;
            OutStringTable (ps.hdc, hInstance, S_BITSPIXEL, 0, 100 ) ;
            OutStringTable (ps.hdc, hInstance, S_PLANES, 0, 120 ) ;
                    /* put values on screen */
            OutDevCapValue (ps.hdc, ps.hdc, HORZSIZE, 100, 20) ;
            OutDevCapValue (ps.hdc, hDCprint, HORZSIZE, 200, 20) ;
            OutDevCapValue (ps.hdc, ps.hdc, VERTSIZE, 100, 40) ;
            OutDevCapValue (ps.hdc, hDCprint, VERTSIZE, 200, 40) ;
            OutDevCapValue (ps.hdc, ps.hdc, HORZRES, 100, 60) ;
            OutDevCapValue (ps.hdc, hDCprint, HORZRES, 200, 60) ;
            OutDevCapValue (ps.hdc, ps.hdc, VERTRES, 100, 80) ;
            OutDevCapValue (ps.hdc, hDCprint, VERTRES, 200, 80) ;
            OutDevCapValue (ps.hdc, ps.hdc, BITSPIXEL, 100, 100) ;
            OutDevCapValue (ps.hdc, hDCprint, BITSPIXEL, 200, 100) ;
            OutDevCapValue (ps.hdc, ps.hdc, PLANES, 100, 120) ;
            OutDevCapValue (ps.hdc, hDCprint, PLANES, 200, 120) ;
```

```
            DeleteDC (hDCprint) ;
            EndPaint (hWnd, &ps) ;
            break ;
        case WM_DESTROY:                /* stop application */
            PostQuitMessage (0) ;
            break ;
        default:       /* default windows message processing */
            return (DefWindowProc (hWnd, wMessage, wParam, lParam)) ;
    }
    return (0L) ;
}

    /* utility function to output a string table entry on DC */
void OutStringTable (HDC hDC, HANDLE hInstance, int nString,
    int nX, int nY)
{
    char cBuf [128] ;

    LoadString (hInstance, nString, cBuf, sizeof (cBuf)) ;
    TextOut (hDC, nX, nY, cBuf, lstrlen (cBuf)) ;
}

    /* utility to display a device caps value on output DC */
    /* hDCout is DC for output, hDCdata is DC source for data */
void OutDevCapValue (HDC hDCout, HDC hDCdata, int nIndex,
    int nX, int nY)
{
    char    cBuf [16] ;
    int     nValue ;

    nValue = GetDeviceCaps (hDCdata, nIndex) ;
    TextOut (hDCout, nX, nY, cBuf, wsprintf (cBuf, "%d", nValue)) ;
}
```

One shortcut taken for clarity in DEVCAP.C is that the physical locations of all of the strings and numeric entries are at fixed X,Y locations on the screen. A more complete program would use the GetTextMetrics() function to determine the character font height and width, and then calculate the text locations accordingly. This would assure that the output was properly spaced on the window's client area, regardless of the video resolution of the system.

Figure 14-13
DEVCAP.ICO
Icon Image

Listings 14-21 to 14-25 show the support files for DEVCAP. The program's icon is shown in Figure 14-13.

Listing 14-21 DEVCAP.H Header File

```
/* devcap.h header file */

#define IDM_QUIT              1        /* menu item ID numbers */

#define S_PROGRAMCAPTION      1        /* string table ID numbers */
```

```
#define S_PRINTERTITLE      2
#define S_VIDEOTITLE        3
#define S_HORZSIZE          4
#define S_VERTSIZE          5
#define S_HORZRES           6
#define S_VERTRES           7
#define S_BITSPIXEL         8
#define S_PLANES            9

long FAR PASCAL WndProc (HWND, WORD, WORD, LONG) ;
void OutStringTable (HDC hDC, HANDLE hInstance, int nString,
   int nX, int nY) ;
void OutDevCapValue (HDC hDCout, HDC hDCdata, int nIndex,
   int nX, int nY) ;
```

Listing 14-22 DEVCAP.RC Resource Script File

```
/* devcap.rc  resource file */

#include "devcap.h"

MyIcon      ICON    devcap.ico

MyMenu      MENU
BEGIN
    MENUITEM "&Quit",       IDM_QUIT
END


STRINGTABLE
BEGIN
    S_PROGRAMCAPTION        "Devcap Program"
    S_PRINTERTITLE          "Printer"
    S_VIDEOTITLE            "Video"
    S_HORZSIZE              "Horz. mm"
    S_VERTSIZE              "Vert. mm"
    S_HORZRES               "Horz. pixels"
    S_VERTRES               "Vert. pixels"
    S_BITSPIXEL             "Color bits"
    S_PLANES                "Color planes"
END
```

Listing 14-23 DEVCAP.DEF Module Definition File

```
NAME            devcap
DESCRIPTION     'devcap program'
EXETYPE         WINDOWS
STUB            'WINSTUB.EXE'
CODE            PRELOAD MOVEABLE DISCARDABLE
DATA            PRELOAD MOVEABLE MULTIPLE
HEAPSIZE        1024
STACKSIZE       5120
EXPORTS         WndProc
```

Listing 14-24 Turbo C++ Project File for DEVCAP

```
devcap.c
devcap.def
devcap.res
```

Listing 14-25 QuickC Project File for DEVCAP

```
devcap.c
devcap.def
devcap.rc
```

Calling Functions in the Printer Driver

The last subject covered in this chapter involves accessing functions that reside in the printer driver file from within another Windows program. This is done to obtain more data about the installed printer and to display the printer setup dialog box. Besides being a practical example that you will probably find useful in many programs, displaying a printer setup dialog box introduces the concept of dynamic link libraries (DLLs) and the open-ended nature of the Windows environment. We will return to this subject in Chapter 18, *Dynamic Link Libraries*, to discuss DLLs in more detail.

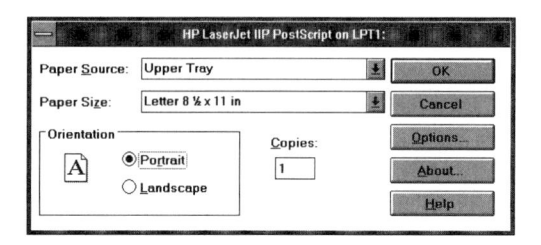

Figure 14-14 A Printer Setup Dialog Box

Back in the Windows 2.0 days, most programs required that the Windows Control Panel be used to change printer settings, such as selecting a different paper size. Most Windows 3.x programs provide the handy shortcut of a "Printer Setup" menu item, so that you can change printer settings quickly from within the program. Figure 14-14 shows a typical printer setup dialog box. The interesting thing about this dialog box is that it is not defined as part of the Windows application program and is not part of Windows. The dialog box definition resides in the printer driver file. The Windows program calls a function in the driver file to display this dialog box. This allows a Windows program to always display the correct dialog box for the current printer driver, without any advance knowledge as to what type of printer the user has selected.

If you think about the concept of calling a function in a printer driver, you may wonder how this is possible. The printer driver is a separate program, and one for which we do not have a source code listing. Under DOS it would be nearly impossible to call a function in another program. There are two secrets to our ability to call a function in the printer driver under Windows. The first is that Microsoft specifies the names of several functions that all printer drivers should support. This is part of the documentation Microsoft provides with the *Windows Device Driver Development Kit*

(DDDK). The specific function that is called to display the printer setup dialog box is always called ExtDeviceMode(). The other key to being able to call the ExtDeviceMode() function is that the printer device driver file is a special type of Windows program, called a Dynamic Link Library, or "DLL" for short. DLLs are collections of functions that can be called by other Windows programs to perform tasks.

Although this is the first time we will explicitly call a function a DLL, all of the programs in this book call functions in DLLs. Every time you use a Windows function such as TextOut() or GetDC(), you are calling a function in a dynamic link library. The common Windows functions reside in DLLs named KERNEL, USER, and GDI. You can find these files in the Windows system directory. Dynamic link libraries are the basic stuff out of which Windows is made. Windows can be added to by simply adding more functions in dynamic link libraries. Printer drivers are a typical example of adding special features to Windows via a DLL. Let's explore how the functions in a printer driver are accessed from within another Windows program.

Accessing the Printer Driver's Functions

Driver files are not part of the main portion of Windows and, therefore, do not use the WINDOWS.H file for constants and function declarations. Instead, the Microsoft and Borland development tools provide a separate header file called DRIVINIT.H. This file contains all of constants, structure definitions, and function declarations needed to work with driver files from an outside program. For example, there is a *typedef* statement for the ExtDeviceMode() function in DRIVINIT.H.

```
typedef WORD FAR PASCAL FNDEVMODE(HWND, HANDLE, LPDEVMODE, LPSTR, LPSTR,
    LPDEVMODE, LPSTR, WORD);

typedef FNDEVMODE FAR * LPFNDEVMODE;  /* typedef for pointer to this function */
```

The function type for ExtDeviceMode() was given the name FNDEVMODE. These declared types are handy when declaring pointers to functions, as you will see in a moment. If you are working with a device driver's functions, be sure to include the DRIVINIT.H file in your Windows' program.

The first step in accessing a function in the printer driver is to load the driver into memory. The LoadLibrary() function does this, and returns a handle to the file in memory. If the printer driver is already loaded, LoadLibrary() just returns a handle to the driver in memory, without loading another copy. As an example, to load the HPPLC.DRV driver file, you would use the following code. (This LoadLibrary() function call is a bit oversimplified. You would seldom know in advance that the user will be using the HPPLC.DRV driver. The complete example program PRTDRIV.C demonstrates a more general technique for calling the LoadLibrary() function, using the currently installed printer driver.)

```
HANDLE   hDriver ;
hDriver = LoadLibrary ("c:\windows\system\hpplc.drv") ;
```

If the value returned by LoadLibrary() is greater than 31, the library was successfully loaded. A returned value less than or equal to 31 means that the library was not loaded, probably because the library path/file name was incorrect. Assuming the library was loaded properly, the next step is to obtain the address of a function in the library so that the function can be called. GetProcAddress() returns the address of a function in a DLL, or returns NULL if the function was not found. This is similar to using the MakeProcInstance() function to obtain a function's address in a Windows program, except GetProcAddress() is used with functions in DLLs.

```
LPFNDEVMODE    lpfnDeviceMode ;
lpfnDeviceMode = (LPFNDEVMODE) GetProcAddress (hDriver, "ExtDeviceMode") ;
```

Note that the *lpfnDeviceMode* value returned from GetProcAddress() is cast to the type LPFNDEVMODE, defined in the DRIVINIT.H header file. This is important, as the next step is to call the function pointed to by the *lpfnDeviceMode* address. The C compiler will do its normal type checking when this function is called, so correctly casting the pointer to the function keeps the compiler satisfied that there has not been an error in the parameter list passed to the function. Here is an example function call to the ExtDeviceMode() function in the HPPLC.DRV printer driver, using the address of the function just obtained with GetProcAddress():

```
DEVMODE DevMode ;    /* calling ExtDeviceMode() using a pointer */

(* lpfnDeviceMode) (hWnd, hDriver, &DevMode, "HP LaserJet IIP", "lpt1",
    NULL, NULL, DM_PROMPT) ;
```

Don't feel bad if this syntax looks a bit odd. You can program in C for years without running into a need to call a function using a pointer to the function. However, this is valid C language (or C++) syntax, and it is equivalent to calling the ExtDeviceMode() function in the printer driver directly:

```
DEVMODE DevMode ;    /* an equivalent ExtDeviceMode() function call */

ExtDeviceMode (hWnd, hDriver, &DevMode, "HP LaserJet IIP", "lpt1",
    NULL, NULL, DM_PROMPT) ;
```

This direct call to the ExtDeviceMode() function would work if you were creating the printer driver, but it is not possible from within another Windows program. The C compiler has no way of knowing the address of the ExtDeviceMode() function in advance and, therefore, could not compile this function call. The address of the function in the driver must be obtained when the program is running (after the driver is loaded into memory so that the address is known) and a pointer is then used to call the ExtDeviceMode() function.

When you are done using the printer driver, you can tell Windows to free the driver from memory with the FreeLibrary() function. The library will only end up physically removed from memory if no other program is currently using the driver.

```
FreeLibrary (hDriver) ;
```

You may have noticed that the call to the ExtDeviceMode() structure passed a pointer to a variable of the type DEVMODE, and also used the constant DM_PROMPT.

Both of these are defined in the DRIVINIT.H header file. DM_PROMPT instructs the driver to display the printer setup dialog box. The DEVMODE data structure is where the printer driver writes information about the printer, so that the program calling the function can determine the printer's characteristics. Listing 14-26 shows the definition of the DEVMODE data structure, taken directly from DRIVINIT.H.

Listing 14-26 The DEVMODE Data Structure

```
/* size of a device name string */
#define CCHDEVICENAME 32

typedef struct _devicemode {
    char    dmDeviceName[CCHDEVICENAME];   /* device name string */
    WORD    dmSpecVersion;      /* driver specification ver. eg. 0x30A = Win 3.1 */
    WORD    dmDriverVersion;    /* OEM driver version number */
    WORD    dmSize;             /* size of the DEVMODE structure */
    WORD    dmDriverExtra;      /* number of bytes following DEVMODE structure */
    DWORD   dmFields;           /* bit filed for which of the following dm */
                                /* values are supported. Bit 0 is one if */
                                /* dmOrientation is supported, etc. */
    short   dmOrientation;      /* DMORIENT_PORTRAIT or DMORIENT_LANDSCAPE */
    short   dmPaperSize;        /* DM_PAPER_LETER, DM_PAPER_LEGAL, DM_PAPER_A4 */
            /* DMPAPER_CSCHEET, DMPAPER_DSCHEET, DMPAPER_ESHEET, DMPAPER_ENV_9 */
            /* DMPAPER_ENV_10, DMPAPER_ENV_11, DMpAPER_ENV_12, etc... */
    short dmPaperLength;        /* overrides dmPaperSize, in mm/10 */
    short dmPaperWidth;         /* overrides dmPaperSize, in mm/10 */
    short dmScale;              /* page is scaled by dmScale/100 */
    short dmCopies;             /* number of copies supported */
    short dmDefaultSource;      /* default paper bin */
    short dmPrintQuality;       /* DMRES_HIGH, DMRES_MEDIUM, DMRES_LOW, */
                                /* or DMRES_DRAFT */
    short dmColor;              /* DMCOLOR_COLOR, or DMCOLOR_MONOCHROME */
    short dmDuplex;             /* DMDUP_SIMPLEX, DMDUP_HORIZONTAL, or */
                                /* DMDUP_VERTICAL */
    short dmYResolution;        /* vertical resolution */
    short dmTTOption;           /* true type option = DMTT_BITMAP, */
                                /* DMTT_DOWNLOAD, DMTT_SUBDEV */
} DEVMODE;
```

As you can see, a wealth of data is available about the specific printer via the DEVMODE structure. You can instruct the ExtDeviceMode() function in the driver to fill in the DEVMODE data instead of displaying the printer setup dialog box by substituting DM_COPY for DM_PROMPT when you call the function:

```
DEVMODE DevMode ;   /* copy printer data in to DevMode */

(* lpfnDeviceMode) (hWnd, hDriver, &DevMode, "HP LaserJet IIP", "lpt1",
    NULL, NULL, DM_COPY) ;
```

ExtDeviceMode() also has the ability to modify the printer's settings, and to permanently record the changes in the WIN.INI file. This book will not explore these options, but they are documented in the *Waite Group's Windows API Bible*, and in the Microsoft Windows SDK documentation.

The DeviceCapabilities() Function

A second function that printer drivers are expected to support is DeviceCapabilities(). This function is also called indirectly by obtaining the function's address in the driver file, and then using a pointer to the address to call the function. The function is declared in the DRIVINIT.H file, with the following statements.

```
typedef DWORD FAR PASCAL FNDEVCAPS(LPSTR, LPSTR, WORD, LPSTR, LPDEVMODE);

typedef FNDEVCAPS FAR * LPFNDEVCAPS;  /* typedef for pointer to this function */
```

The process of calling DeviceCapabilities() is identical to the ExtDeviceMode() function we just examined. Here is a typical example, which determines the number of paper bins the printer supports.

```
HANDLE       hDriver ;
LPFNDEVCAPS  lpfnDeviceCaps ;
DWORD        dwNumBins ;

hDriver = LoadLibrary ("c:\windows\system\hpplc.drv") ;
lpfnDeviceCaps = (LPFNDEVCAPS) GetProcAddress (hDriver, "DeviceCapabilities") ;
dwNumBins = (* lpfnDeviceCaps) ("HP LaserJet IIP", "lpt1", DC_BINS, NULL, NULL) ;
FreeLibrary (hDriver) ;
```

DeviceCapabilities() is an elaborate function, which can return many different pieces of information about an output device. DeviceCapabilities() takes the place of a number of Escape() function calls that were used to determine printer characteristics with Windows versions before Windows 3.0. The full syntax for DeviceCapabilities() is shown below, including a table of all of the index values defined in the DRIVINT.H header file that are used to specify which data value should be returned.

DWORD **DeviceCapabilities** (LPSTR *lpDeviceName*, LPSTR *lpPort*, WORD *nIndex*, LPSTR *lpOutput*, LPDEVMODE *lpDevMode*);

lpDeviceName LPSTR

A pointer to a null-terminated character string containing the printer device name as "PCL/HP LaserJet."

lpPort LPSTR

A pointer to a null-terminated character string containing the name of the port to which the device is connected, such as "LPT1:."

nIndex WORD

Specifies which value to obtain from the device. It can be any of the indices in Table 14-3, all of which are defined in DRIVINIT.H.

lpOutput LPSTR

A pointer to a memory buffer. The data received in the buffer will depend on the *nIndex* value, as described in Table 14-3.

lpDevMode   LPDEVMODE
Normally set to NULL. In this case, DeviceCapabilities() returns the current initialization values for the specified driver. If *lpDevMode* is not NULL, it should contain a pointer to a DEVMODE data structure containing the values to be read by DeviceCapabilities(). DEVMODE is defined in DRIVINIT.H and shown in the previous section.

VALUE	MEANING
DC_BINNAMES	If the printer driver does not support multiple bins, DeviceCapabilities() returns 0. If multiple bins are supported, DeviceCapabilities() returns the number of bins. *lpOutput* should then point to a memory buffer to hold data on the bins. The data consists of an array of integers, each containing the bin ID number (one for each bin). This is followed by the bin names, each 24 characters long. Set *lpOutput* to NULL to simply return the number of bins supported. This is usually done to determine the number of bytes to allocate for the bin numbers and names (26 bytes per bin).
DC_BINS	If *lpOutput* is set to NULL, DeviceCapabilities() returns the number of paper bins that the printer supports. If *lpOuput* is not NULL, it should contain a pointer to a memory buffer. The buffer will receive an array of WORD values, each containing a bin number.
DC_COPIES*	DeviceCapabilities() returns the maximum number of copies that the printer can produce..
DC_DRIVER	DeviceCapabilities() returns the printer driver version number.
DC_DUPLEX	Returns 1 if the printer supports duplex printing, 0 if not.
DC_ENUMRESOLUTIONS*	If *lpOutput* is set to NULL, DeviceCapabilities() returns the number of output resolutions the printer supports. If *lpOuput* is not NULL, it should contain a pointer to a memory buffer. The buffer will receive an array of groups of two LONG integers values, each containing the horizontal and vertical resolution supported.
DC_EXTRA	Returns the number of bytes of device specific data at the end of the DEVMODE structure for the printer driver.
DC_FIELDS	Returns the bit-field value that specifies which features are supported by the printer driver. This is the same as the *dmFields* element of the DEVMODE structure.
DC_FILEDEPENDENCIES*	If *lpOutput* is set to NULL, DeviceCapabilities() returns the number of files which need to be loaded to make the printer work. If *lpOuput* is not NULL, it should contain a pointer to a memory buffer. The buffer will receive an array of 64-character long file names, each containing the file name of a file that must be loaded to support the printer.

continued

Table 14-3 (cont'd)

DC_MAXEXTENT	Returns a POINT structure containing the maximum paper size that the printer can support. These values are the largest that can be placed in the *dmPaperLength* and *dmPaperWidth* elements of the DEVMODE structure.
DC_MINEXTENT	Returns a POINT structure containing the minimum paper size that the printer can support. These values are the smallest that can be placed in the *dmPaperLength* and *dmPaperWidth* elements of the DEVMODE structure.
DC_PAPERS	If *lpOutput* is set to NULL, DeviceCapabilities() returns the number of supported paper sizes. This is the normal use of this flag. If *lpOuput* is not NULL, it should contain a pointer to a memory buffer. The buffer will receive an array of WORD values, each containing a supported paper size.
DC_PAPERSIZE	*lpOutput* should contain a pointer to a memory buffer. The buffer will receive an array of POINT values, each containing the horizontal and vertical size in 1/10 mm for supported paper sizes. Use DC_PAPERS first to determine the size of the data buffer needed to contain the POINT data.
DC_SIZE	DeviceCapabilities() returns the size of the DEVMODE data structure, not including any driver-specific data following the structure. This is the same as the *dmSize* element of the DEVMODE data structure.
DC_VERSION	DeviceCapabilities() returns the Microsoft driver specification number to which the driver conforms.

*Windows 3.1

Table 14-3 DeviceCapabilities() *nIndex* Values

A Printer Driver Access Example

The last example program in this chapter is called PRTDRIV.C. This example demonstrates using both the ExtDeviceMode() and DeviceCapabilities() functions in whatever printer driver is currently installed on your system. Figure 14-15 shows a typical example of PRTDRIV running, with an HP IIP printer installed. If the "Printer Setup" menu item is selected, the printer setup dialog box defined in the printer driver is displayed, as shown in Figure 14-16. The exact dialog box displayed will depend on the printer driver, so expect yours to be somewhat different unless you have an HP IIP printer installed.

Listing 14-27 shows the PRTDRIV.C program. When the WM_CREATE message is processed, PRTDRIV creates a character string consisting of the full path name and file name of the currently installed printer driver. This requires several steps. First, the printer driver and output device name are extracted from the WIN.INI file, using the same techniques used in the previous examples:

```
GetProfileString ("windows", "device", "", szPrinter, 64) ;
szDevice = strtok (szPrinter, ",") ;
szDriver = strtok (NULL, ",") ;
szOutput = strtok (NULL, ",") ;
```

Next, the system directory path name is determined using the handy GetSystemDirectory() function. The system directory is where all of the driver files are stored for use by Windows. Normally, the system directory has the path name "C:\WINDOWS\SYSTEM," but you cannot safely assume this. The user may be using another drive letter, or may have renamed the system directory when he or she installed Windows. GetSystemDirctory() copies the current directory name into a character string, correctly including the current drive letter and directory names. There is also a GetWindowsDirectory() function, if you ever need to know the Windows directory ("C:\WINDOWS" by default).

Figure 14-15 The PRTDRIV Program

```
static char    szSysDir [128]
GetSystemDirectory (szSysDir, 128) ;
```

The last step is to add the driver name to the end of the system directory name to create the full file name for the printer driver. One trick in creating the file name is that a backslash character (\) must be appended to the end of the system directory name before adding the driver name. The backslash has special meanings in C language strings, so two backslash characters are needed to add one "real" backslash to the string. Driver files have the extension ".DRV," so this is also tacked on to the end of the string.

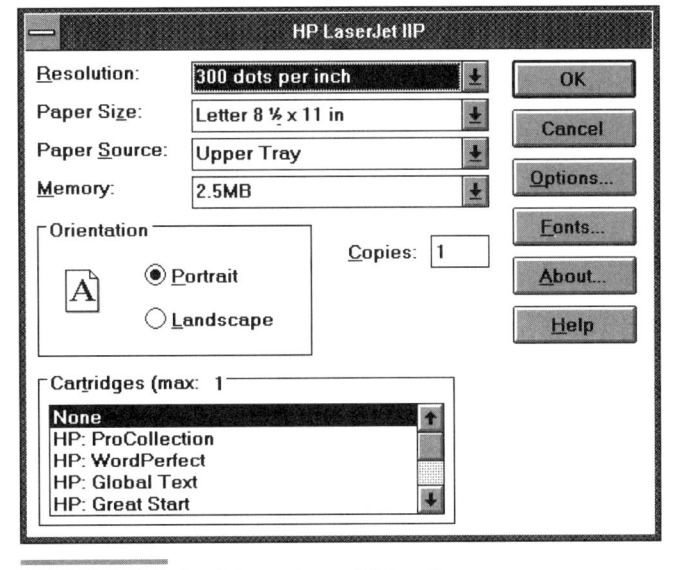

Figure 14-16 The Printer Setup Dialog Box

```
GetSystemDirectory
(szSysDir, 128) ;
lstrcpy (szFullDriver, szSysDir) ;
```

```
lstrcat (szFullDriver, "\\") ;
lstrcat (szFullDriver, szDriver) ;
lstrcat (szFullDriver, ".DRV") ;
    /* load driver and save its handle */
hDriver = LoadLibrary (szFullDriver) ;
```

The result of all of this effort constructs a printer driver file name such as "C:\WINDOWS\SYSTEM\HPPLC.DRV" and uses the full name to load the driver into memory using LoadLibrary(). If everything went well, LoadLibrary() will return a handle to the library in memory, with a handle value greater than 31. If the returned value is less than or equal to 31, some error occurred, and the library cannot be assumed to be loaded into memory.

Displaying the printer setup dialog box is simply a matter of calling the ExtDeviceMode() function in the driver. This must be done indirectly, by first obtaining the function's address in the driver with GetProcAddress(), and then calling the function using the function's address (a pointer).

```
lpfnDeviceMode = (LPFNDEVMODE) GetProcAddress (hDriver, "ExtDeviceMode") ;
if (lpfnDeviceMode)        /* call the function */
    (* lpfnDeviceMode) (hWnd, hDriver, &DevMode, szDevice, szOutput, NULL, NULL,
                   DM_PROMPT) ;
```

The DeviceCapabilities() function is called twice while processing WM_PAINT messages to retrieve the printer driver number, and to fill an array of POINT values with the available paper sizes. Again, the DeviceCapabilities function must be called indirectly, using a pointer to the function obtained with GetProcAddress().

```
            lpfnDeviceCaps = (LPFNDEVCAPS) GetProcAddress (hDriver,
                "DeviceCapabilities") ;
            if (lpfnDeviceCaps)        /* if found the DeviceCapibilites() */
            {                          /* call the function to get driver # */
                dwVersion = (* lpfnDeviceCaps) (szPrinter,
                    szOutput, DC_DRIVER, NULL, NULL) ;
                dwNumPaperSize = (* lpfnDeviceCaps) (szPrinter,
                    szOutput, DC_PAPERSIZE, (LPSTR) PointArray, NULL) ;
```
[Other program lines]

When the program is about to terminate, the printer driver is freed from memory by calling the FreeLibrary() function.

Listing 14-27 PRTDRIV.C

```
/* prtdriv.c   example demonstrating printer setup */

#include <windows.h>
#include <drivinit.h>   /* separate header for driver functions */
#include <string.h>     /* needed for strtok() function */
#include "prtdriv.h"

int PASCAL WinMain (HANDLE hInstance, HANDLE hPrevInstance, LPSTR lpszCmdLine,
    int nCmdShow)
{
```

```c
    HWND        hWnd ;          /* the window's "handle" */
    MSG         msg ;           /* a message structure */
    WNDCLASS    wndclass ;      /* window class structure */
    char        cBuf [128] ;    /* character buffer */

    if (!hPrevInstance)
    {
       wndclass.style         = CS_HREDRAW | CS_VREDRAW ;
       wndclass.lpfnWndProc   = WndProc ;
       wndclass.cbClsExtra    = 0 ;
       wndclass.cbWndExtra    = 0 ;
       wndclass.hInstance     = hInstance ;
       wndclass.hIcon         = LoadIcon (hInstance, "MyIcon") ;
       wndclass.hCursor       = LoadCursor (NULL, IDC_ARROW) ;
       wndclass.hbrBackground = GetStockObject (WHITE_BRUSH) ;
       wndclass.lpszMenuName  = "MyMenu" ;
       wndclass.lpszClassName = "MyClass" ;
                   /* register the window class */
       if (!RegisterClass (&wndclass))
             return 0 ;
    }
    LoadString (hInstance, S_PROGRAMCAPTION, cBuf, sizeof (cBuf)) ;

    hWnd = CreateWindow ("MyClass", cBuf, WS_OVERLAPPEDWINDOW,
        CW_USEDEFAULT, CW_USEDEFAULT, CW_USEDEFAULT, CW_USEDEFAULT,
        NULL, NULL, hInstance, NULL) ;
    ShowWindow (hWnd, nCmdShow) ;   /* display the window */

    while (GetMessage (&msg, NULL, NULL, NULL))   /* message loop */
    {
       TranslateMessage (&msg) ;   /* translate keyboard messages */
       DispatchMessage (&msg) ;    /* send message to WndProc() */
    }
    return (msg.wParam) ;
}
long FAR PASCAL WndProc (HWND hWnd, WORD wMessage, WORD wParam, LONG lParam)
{
    static HANDLE   hDriver ;
    DEVMODE         DevMode ;
    LPFNDEVMODE     lpfnDeviceMode ;    /* data types defined in DRIVINT.H */
    LPFNDEVCAPS     lpfnDeviceCaps ;
    DWORD           dwVersion, dwNumPaperSize ;
    POINT           PointArray [50] ;
    PAINTSTRUCT     ps ;
    int             i ;
    static char     szPrinter [64], szSysDir [128], szFullDriver [256],
    *szDriver,      *szDevice, *szOutput ;
    char            cBuf [128], cBuf2 [128] ;
    static HANDLE   hInstance ;

    switch (wMessage)      /* process windows messages */
    {
       case WM_CREATE:
            hInstance = GetWindowWord (hWnd, GWW_HINSTANCE) ;
                    /* get printer driver info from WIN.INI file */
            GetProfileString ("windows", "device", "", szPrinter, 64) ;
            szDevice = strtok (szPrinter, ",") ;
            szDriver = strtok (NULL, ",") ;
            szOutput = strtok (NULL, ",") ;
```

```
                /* build full driver path/file name */
    GetSystemDirectory (szSysDir, 128) ;
    lstrcpy (szFullDriver, szSysDir) ;
    lstrcat (szFullDriver, "\\") ;
    lstrcat (szFullDriver, szDriver) ;
    lstrcat (szFullDriver, ".DRV") ;
                /* load driver and save its handle */
    hDriver = LoadLibrary (szFullDriver) ;
    if (hDriver < 32)        /* driver not loaded */
    {
        LoadString (hInstance, S_PRINTDRIVERPROBLEM, cBuf,
            sizeof (cBuf)) ;
        MessageBox (hWnd, "cBuf", "", MB_OK) ;
        DestroyWindow (hWnd) ; /* terminate program */
    }
    break ;
case WM_COMMAND:
    switch (wParam)          /* menu items */
    {
        case IDM_SETUP:      /* show setup printer dialog box */
            lpfnDeviceMode = (LPFNDEVMODE)
                GetProcAddress (hDriver, "ExtDeviceMode") ;
            if (lpfnDeviceMode)    /* call the function */
                (* lpfnDeviceMode) (hWnd, hDriver, &DevMode,
                szDevice, szOutput, NULL, NULL, DM_PROMPT) ;
            break ;
        case IDM_QUIT:                /* "Quit" menu item */
            DestroyWindow (hWnd) ;    /* destroy window, */
            break ;                   /* terminating application */
    }
    break ;
case WM_PAINT:                /* show printer info in client area */
    BeginPaint (hWnd, &ps) ;
    TextOut (ps.hdc, 0, 0, szDevice, lstrlen (szDevice)) ;
    lpfnDeviceCaps = (LPFNDEVCAPS) GetProcAddress (hDriver,
        "DeviceCapabilities") ;
    if (lpfnDeviceCaps)       /* if found the DeviceCapibilites() */
    {                         /* call the function to get driver # */
        dwVersion = (* lpfnDeviceCaps) (szPrinter,
            szOutput, DC_DRIVER, NULL, NULL) ;
        dwNumPaperSize = (* lpfnDeviceCaps) (szPrinter,
            szOutput, DC_PAPERSIZE, (LPSTR) PointArray, NULL) ;
        LoadString (hInstance, S_PRINTERHEADING, cBuf2,
            sizeof (cBuf2)) ;
        TextOut (ps.hdc, 0, 20, cBuf, wsprintf (cBuf,
            cBuf2, dwVersion)) ;
        for (i = 0 ; i < (int) dwNumPaperSize ; i++)
            TextOut (ps.hdc, 0, 40 + (i * 20), cBuf,
                wsprintf (cBuf, "%d:  %dmm X %dmm",
                i + 1, PointArray [i].x / 10,
                PointArray [i].y / 10)) ;
    }
    EndPaint (hWnd, &ps) ;
    break ;
case WM_DESTROY:              /* stop application */
    FreeLibrary (hDriver) ;
    PostQuitMessage (0) ;
    break ;
default:            /* default windows message processing */
```

```
          return (DefWindowProc (hWnd, wMessage, wParam, lParam)) ;
     }
     return (0L) ;
}
```

One shortcut taken in the PRTDRIV.C program is that the paper sizes are copied to an array of POINT structures called *PointArray[]*. This is not an ideal practice because no matter how big you make the array, there is always the chance that someone will build a printer with even more paper sizes supported. The preferred practice is to allocate a memory block big enough to hold all of the paper sizes after the number of paper sizes has been determined. This technique is demonstrated in one of the exercises at the end of this chapter. Listing 14-28 shows the PRTDRIV.H header file.

Listing 14-28 PRTDRIV.H Header File

```
/* prtdriv.h header file */

#define IDM_SETUP              1       /* menu item ID numbers */
#define IDM_QUIT              10

#define S_PROGRAMCAPTION       1       /* string table ID numbers */
#define S_PRINTDRIVERPROBLEM   2
#define S_PRINTERHEADING       3

long FAR PASCAL WndProc (HWND, WORD, WORD, LONG) ;
```

Note in the PRTDRIV.RC resource file (Listing 14-29) that S_PRINTERHEADING is a string that is passed to the wsprintf() function as a formatting string. The "%d" characters encode the wsprintf() place holder for a decimal number. String tables can be used to pass formatting strings to wsprintf(), maintaining all of the text in the resource script file.

The remaining support files for PRTDRIV are shown in Listings 14-29 to 14-32. Figure 14-17 shows the program's icon.

Figure 14-17
PRTDRIV.ICO
Icon Image

Listing 14-29 PRTDRIV.RC Resource Script File

```
/* prtdriv.rc resource file */

#include "prtdriv.h"

MyIcon      ICON     prtdriv.ico

MyMenu      MENU
BEGIN
    MENUITEM "&Printer Setup",  IDM_SETUP
    MENUITEM "&Quit",           IDM_QUIT
END

STRINGTABLE
```

```
BEGIN
    S_PROGRAMCAPTION           "Printer Setup Example"
    S_PRINTDRIVERPROBLEM       "Could not load Printer Driver, terminating."
    S_PRINTERHEADING           "Driver No. %d, Paper sizes:"
END
```

Listing 14-30 PRTDRIV.DEF Module Definition File

```
NAME            prtdriv
DESCRIPTION     'prtdriv program'
EXETYPE         WINDOWS
STUB            'WINSTUB.EXE'
CODE            PRELOAD MOVEABLE DISCARDABLE
DATA            PRELOAD MOVEABLE MULTIPLE
HEAPSIZE        1024
STACKSIZE       5120
EXPORTS         WndProc
```

Listing 14-31 Turbo C++ Project File for PRTDRIV

```
prtdriv.c
prtdriv.def
prtdriv.res
```

Listing 14-32 QuickC Project File for PRTDRIV

```
prtdriv.c
prtdriv.def
prtdriv.rc
```

Summary

Windows supports printers and plotters by using specialized support files called printer drivers. When a printer is installed, the printer driver is added to the Windows system directory, and the driver name added to the WIN.INI file. When a program outputs text or graphics to the printer, the driver converts the GDI function calls into instructions that the printer understands. During output of text and graphics, the driver is not directly accessed. Simply obtaining a device context handle to the printer with the CreateDC() function allows all of the text and graphics commands to be sent to the printer instead of the screen. Normally, you will want to use a device context mapping mode with fixed scaling, such as MM_LOMETRIC, when working with a printer to avoid having the proportions of the output change depending on the resolution of the printer.

Printers require special commands which have no equivalent when output is sent to the screen, such as when ejecting a page. Windows provides the Escape() function to send these commands, as well as to notify the printer driver that a print job is starting or stopping. The Escape() function also can be used to notify the printer driver of a function that should process messages while the print job is in progress. This function, called an "abort" function, allows a Windows program to interrupt the print job while it is in progress.

It is sometimes necessary to obtain information about a printer or plotter to determine if it supports color output, what paper sizes are available, and so on. There are two general approaches to obtaining this type of data. The GetDeviceCaps() function allows a program to determine limited information about the printer or plotter, based on the values stored in the device context data. For more complete information and to allow the user to access the printer setup dialog box, it is necessary to call functions in the printer's device driver. This is done indirectly by first loading the printer driver into memory with LoadLibrary(), obtaining the address of a function in the driver with GetProcAddress(), and then calling the function. The two functions in the driver file that you are most likely to use are ExtDeviceMode() and DeviceCapabilities(). The DRIVINIT.H header file is provided with both the Borland and Microsoft programming tools to simplify working with device driver functions.

QUESTIONS

1. The driver file for a printer is stored in the _____ directory. The WIN.INI file is stored in the _____ directory.
2. The line in the WIN.INI file that contains the name of the printer, the printer driver name, and the output device name, starts with the word _____ followed by an equal sign. This will be in the section of WIN.INI which is named _____, surrounded in square brackets.
3. Use the _____ function to create a device context for a printer.
4. The easy way to read a line from the WIN.INI file is to call the _____ function.
5. When printing is complete, use the a) DeleteDC(), b) ReleaseDC(), c) EndPaint(), d) a or b, function to remove the printer device context from memory.
6. Use the a) STARTDOC, b) NEWFRAME, c) SETABORTPROC, d) ENDDOC printer escape to begin a printing job.
7. Which mapping mode would be the best choice for printing an image which is also displayed in the program's main window client area? a) MM_ISOTROPIC; b) MM_ANISOTROPIC; c) MM_HIMETRIC; d) a or b.
8. The dialog box that displays the print job "Cancel" button must be created with which of the following functions? a) DialogBox(); b) CreateDialog(); c) CreateWindow(); d) b or c.
9. The abort procedure is basically a a) GetMessage() loop; b) PeekMessage() loop; c) a dialog box procedure; d) a built-in Windows function.
10. The GetDeviceCaps() function retrieves information about a printer or other output device from: a) the printer driver; b) the WIN.INI file; c) the device context data; d) the Windows environment.
11. Function prototypes and constant definitions used with printer drivers are declared in the _____ file.
12. The _____ function loads the printer driver into memory. _____ removes it from memory.
13. The _____ function returns the address of a function in a driver or dynamic link library loaded into memory.

EXERCISES

1. The PRTDRIV.C program takes a shortcut by using an array of POINT structures to store the paper sizes obtained from the DeviceCapabilities() function in the printer driver. This is not an ideal solution, as it is always possible that there will be more paper sizes supported than the number of POINT structures in the array, which will cause the program to terminate when Windows detects an attempt to write past the end of the array. Improve PRTDRIV.C so that the array of POINT

EXERCISES (cont'd)

data returned by DeviceCapabilities() is stored in a local memory block, allocated with LocalAlloc(). (Hint: You will need to call DeviceCapabilities() twice, once to obtain the number of paper sizes and a second time to fill the paper size data into the allocated memory block.)

2. Modify the PRINT3.C program so that the caption of the printer abort dialog box flashes between the normal caption string and "Got Message!" every time a message is processed while the dialog box is visible. When are messages received during printing?

ANSWERS TO QUESTIONS

1. system, windows.
2. device=, [windows].
3. CreateDC().
4. GetProfileString().
5. a.
6. a.
7. c.
8. b.
9. b.
10. c.
11. DRIVINIT.H
12. LoadLibrary(), FreeLibrary().
13. GetProcAddress().

SOLUTIONS TO EXERCISES

1. The complete solution is given under the name C14EXER1 on the source code disks. The changes are summarized in the modified WM_PAINT logic shown in Listing 14-33. The key to using an allocated memory block to store the paper size data is that you must determine the number of paper sizes before the block is allocated, so that you know how much space to reserve. This is done by first calling the DeviceCapabilities() function in the printer driver with the DC_PAPERS flag. The returned value is the number of paper sizes supported. A fixed, local memory block of that size is then allocated with LocalAlloc(). The example uses the shortcut of a fixed memory block, which means that the value of the handle returned by LocalAlloc() is equal to the address of the memory block in the local heap. The second call to the DeviceCapabilities() function uses the DC_PAPERS flag, and copies the paper sizes into the memory block.

SOLUTIONS TO EXERCISES (cont'd)

Listing 14-33 Modifications to PRTDRIV.C

```
POINT            *pPointArray ;
[Other program lines]
    case WM_PAINT:                      /* show printer info in client area */
        BeginPaint (hWnd, &ps) ;
        TextOut (ps.hdc, 0, 0, szDevice, lstrlen (szDevice)) ;
        lpfnDeviceCaps = (LPFNDEVCAPS) GetProcAddress (hDriver,
            "DeviceCapabilities") ;
        if (lpfnDeviceCaps)    /* if found the DeviceCapabilites() */
        {                      /* call the function to get driver # */
            dwVersion = (* lpfnDeviceCaps) (szPrinter,
                szOutput, DC_DRIVER, NULL, NULL) ;
                               /* first find number of paper sizes */
            dwNumPaperSize = (* lpfnDeviceCaps) (szPrinter,
                szOutput, DC_PAPERS, NULL, NULL) ;
                               /* allocate local memory block */
            pPointArray = (POINT *) LocalAlloc (LPTR,
                dwNumPaperSize * sizeof (POINT)) ;
            if (pPointArray)
            {                  /* copy paper sizes into mem. block */
                (* lpfnDeviceCaps) (szPrinter, szOutput, DC_PAPERSIZE,
                    (LPSTR) pPointArray, NULL) ;
                LoadString (hInstance, S_PRINTERHEADING, cBuf2,
                    sizeof (cBuf2)) ;
                TextOut (ps.hdc, 0, 20, cBuf, wsprintf (cBuf,
                    cBuf2, dwVersion)) ;
                for (i = 0 ; i < (int) dwNumPaperSize ; i++)
                    TextOut (ps.hdc, 0, 40 + (i * 20), cBuf,
                        wsprintf (cBuf, "%d:  %dmm X %dmm",
                        i + 1, pPointArray [i].x / 10,
                        pPointArray [i].y / 10)) ;
                               /* free the memory block */
                LocalFree ((HANDLE) pPointArray) ;
            }
        }
        EndPaint (hWnd, &ps) ;
        break ;
```

Note the interesting shortcut in the TextOut() function at the bottom of the WM_PAINT logic in Listing 14-33. Array notation is used to reference the specific POINT value in the *pPointArray* memory block, even though *pPointArray* was only declared as a pointer to POINT data (POINT *pPointArray), not as an array of POINT data (POINT pPointArray[]). The C compiler will allow you to use array notation based on a pointer to a block of data, as long as the data type for the pointer and array notation is the same. Array notation makes it easier to access specific elements of an array, rather than always using and incrementing pointers.

SOLUTIONS TO EXERCISES (cont'd)

2. The only changes needed to have the caption of the dialog box change when messages are received are to the printer abort procedure. Listing 14-34 shows the modified printer abort procedure, which changes the dialog box caption briefly to "Got Message!" and then back, each time a message is processed by the PeekMessage() loop. The printer abort function will process all the messages for the program while the printer abort dialog box is visible. Changing the dialog box title is relatively easy in this example, as the handle to the dialog box window is stored in a global variable, _hDlgPrintAbort, ready to be used by the GetWindowText() and SetWindowText() functions which retrieve and set the window caption.

Listing 14-34 Modified Printer Abort Procedure

```
BOOL FAR PASCAL PrintAbort (HDC hdcPrinter, int nCode)
{
   MSG    msg ;
   char   cBuf [128] ;
          /* the global variable _bPrintAbort is set to TRUE */
          /* if the user clicks the button on the abort dialog */
          /* box. This exits this message loop, returning */
          /* control back to the program's message loop */
   while (!_bPrintAbort && PeekMessage (&msg, NULL, 0, 0, PM_REMOVE))
   {
      GetWindowText (_hDlgPrintAbort, cBuf, 128) ;
      SetWindowText (_hDlgPrintAbort, "Got Message!") ;
      SetWindowText (_hDlgPrintAbort, cBuf) ;
      if (!IsDialogMessage (_hDlgPrintAbort, &msg))
      {
         TranslateMessage (&msg) ;
         DispatchMessage (&msg) ;
      }
   }
   return (!_bPrintAbort) ;
}
```

If you turn your printer off and then run the modified PRINT3 program, you will have enough time to experiment with the program while the print abort dialog box is visible (after about 30 seconds the printer driver will quit trying to print, and it will display a message box). While the printer abort dialog box is visible you may note that no messages are processed unless some action is taken (such as moving the mouse, or using the keyboard.) These actions generate messages, which are then processed by the PrintAbort() function. The messages interrupt any processing being done by the printer driver, and they provide an opportunity to cancel the printer job by selecting the "Cancel" button in the dialog box.

The complete solution is given under the file name C14EXER2 on the source code disks.

CHAPTER 15

Disk File Access

Reading and writing data to and from disk files in a Windows program is done by accessing file functions in MS-DOS. DOS is always loaded into memory when Windows is operating, so the DOS file functions are always available. The advantage of using the DOS file system is that files created by Windows programs use the same disk format that DOS programs use, so data can easily be exchanged between DOS programs and Windows applications. The disadvantage of using DOS file support is that disk file names are restricted to eight letters, plus an optional three character extension (like "FILENAME.TXT").

In this chapter, we will examine both the low-level details of reading and writing data from a disk file, and the higher level functions for providing the user with easy-to-use methods of locating and selecting a file. File selection under Windows involves setting up a dialog box, which has list boxes for selecting subdirectories and specific files. Because accessing a disk file is such a common requirement, the dialog box functions will be stored in a separate C program, so that the same functions can be easily added to your future Windows projects. The dialog box function will be tested by creating a simple text editor, which will allow reading, modifying, and storing of text data in disk files.

You will notice that starting with this chapter, the example programs are somewhat longer than those in the previous chapters. The longer examples will provide more complete programs that you will be able to apply to your own projects. The last example program in this chapter is a functioning text editor, although it lacks locate, cut, and paste operations. They will be added in Chapter 17, *The Clipboard*.

Concepts Covered

DOS Disk Access
Opening a File
Reading File Data
Writing to a File
Moving to a Different Location
 in the File

Closing a File
Creating a File Selection Dialog Box
DOS File Attributes
The Current Working Directory
Attaching a Memory Block to
 an Edit Control

Keywords Covered

OFSTRUCT
OF_CREATE
OF_READ

OF_WRITE
File Pointer
File Handle

Functions Covered

OpenFile()
_lclose()
_llseek()
_lopen()
_lread()

_lwrite()
_lcreat()
DlgDirList()
DlgDirSelect()

Messages Covered

EM_SETHANDLE

EM_GETHANDLE

How Windows Programs Access Disk Files

For most operations, Windows contains its own programming logic for accessing the computer's hardware. For example, all of the graphics output in the Windows GDI bypasses DOS, and directly accesses the computer's video hardware. However, Windows uses DOS to access disk files. DOS is always loaded in memory when Windows is running, so taking advantage of DOS saves memory space by not duplicating these functions. Using DOS functions also allows Windows to maintain 100% file compatibility with DOS programs, which is a key selling point for the Windows environment. Figure 15-1 shows a comparison between the program logic for graphics output under Windows and that for disk file access.

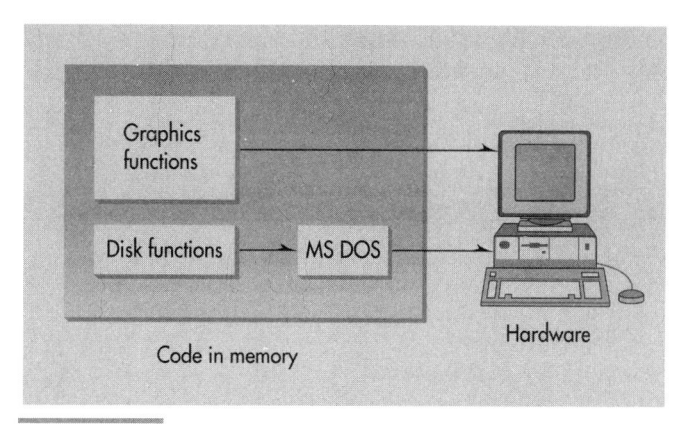

Figure 15-1 Windows Use of DOS File Functions

The History of Windows File Function Name

One thing you may find puzzling as you start looking at the file access functions is that most of the file function names start with an underscore character, like "_lread()." Back in the early days of Windows programming, the DOS file functions were accessed using C compiler library functions. Windows 2.0 included file access functions, but the functions were not officially documented. Reflecting their "unofficial" status, the file functions all had function names starting with an underscore character. So many people began using these functions that Microsoft made them official with the 3.0 release of Windows, but left the underscore characters in front of the function names to be consistent with earlier programming practices.

Opening a Disk File

Before you can take any action on a file, you must alert DOS that the file will be accessed. This is called "opening" a file. DOS returns an integer value, called the "file handle" after a file is opened. This handle is then used in all subsequent file operations to reference the file. You can open several files at the same time, and use the file handles to keep track of which file you want to access at any particular time. By default, an application can have a maximum of 20 files open at one time, although you can increase this to a maximum of 255 using the SetHandleCount() function in Windows.

The simplest way to open a file is with the _lopen() function. A typical call to _lopen() is as follows:

```
int hFileHandle ;

hFileHandle = _lopen ("testfile.txt", OF_READ) ;
```

This opens the file TESTFILE.TXT for reading data, and returns the file handle as an integer. If the file could not be opened, the file handle will be equal to -1. The OF_READ value is defined in WINDOWS.H, and instructs the _lopen() function to open the file for reading data from the file. You would use the OF_WRITE flag to open the file for writing.

Chapter 15 • Disk File Access   525

If the file you want to write to does not already exist, you will need to create a new one. The _lcreat() function does this, with a syntax similar to the _lopen() function.

```
int hFileHandle ;

hFileHandle = _lcreat ("testfile.txt", 0) ;
```

The _lopen() and _lcreat() functions are fairly primitive, and they are seldom used by Windows programmers. A more useful function is OpenFile(), which can open an existing file, delete a file, or create a new one. A typical call to OpenFile(), opening an existing file for both reading and writing, would be as follows:

```
int         hFileHandle ;
OFSTRUCT    of ;

hFileHandle = OpenFile ("testfile.txt", &of, OF_READWRITE) ;
```

Like _lopen() and _lcreat(), OpenFile() will return -1 if the file could not be accessed. Otherwise, OpenFile() returns the file handle for the opened file. OpenFile() uses the OFSTRUCT data structure, which is defined in WINDOWS.H and shown in Listing 15-1. The member of the structure that you are most likely to use is the *szPathName* character array. When OpenFile() returns, this array will contain the path and file name for the opened file.

Listing 15-1 The OFSTRUCT Structure

```
/* OpenFile() Structure */
typedef struct tagOFSTRUCT
{
    BYTE    cBytes;             /* size of OFSTRUCT structure */
    BYTE    fFixedDisk;         /* zero if removable, 1 if fixed disk */
    WORD    nErrCode;           /* the DOS error code */
    BYTE    reserved[4];
    BYTE    szPathName[128];    /* the full path name where the file was found */
} OFSTRUCT;
typedef OFSTRUCT        *POFSTRUCT;
typedef OFSTRUCT NEAR   *NPOFSTRUCT;
typedef OFSTRUCT FAR    *LPOFSTRUCT;
```

The third value passed to the OpenFile() function specifies what action the function is to take. The options that apply to a single-user system (not including local area network file options) are shown in Table 15-1. The OpenFile() options are actually binary flags, and can be combined. For example, to open a file for reading and writing data, with the option of displaying a dialog box saying "File not found. Insert a new disk in A:," with both "OK" and "Cancel" buttons, use the following code:

```
int         hFileHandle ;
OFSTRUCT    of ;

hFileHandle = OpenFile ("testfile.txt", &of, OF_READWRITE | OF_PROMPT | OF_CANCEL) ;
```

VALUE	MEANING
OF_CANCEL	Only used with the OF_PROMPT style. Adds a Cancel button to the file not-found dialog box.
OF_CREATE	Creates a new file. If the file already exists, the file is opened and truncated to zero bytes.
OF_DELETE	Deletes a file.
OF_EXIST	Checks if the file exists. The file is opened, and then immediately closed.
OF_PARSE	Fills in the OFSTRUCT data structure, but does not open or close the file. Useful for determining the full path name.
OF_PROMPT	Displays a dialog box if the requested file does not exist. The dialog box requests the user to put a disk in drive A and retry. This is seldom a reasonable action.
OF_READ	The file is opened for reading only.
OF_READWRITE	The file is opened for reading and writing.
OF_REOPEN	Opens the file specified in the *szPathName* field of the OFSTRUCT. This assures that the same file is opened that was originally open when OpenFile() was first called. Otherwise, changing the default subdirectory could result in changing which of several files with the same name, but residing in different subdirectories, is opened.
OF_VERIFY	Verifies that the date and time of the file on the disk are the same as the data in the OFSTRUCT data structure. This assumes that OpenFile() has already been called at least once to fill in the data.
OF_WRITE	Opens the file for writing data only.

Table 15-1 OpenFile Flag Values

Reading and Writing Data

When you have the file open and have a valid file handle, you can read and write data to the disk file. There are three functions that you will use to do these operations: _lread() to read data from the file, _lwrite() to write data to the file, and _llseek() to move to a new location in the file. Figure 15-2 shows the relationship between these functions. _llseek() is used to go to a specific location in the file prior to reading or writing data.

For example, to create a new file EXAMPLE.TXT and copy a character string to the file, you would use the following code:

```
int        hFileHandle ;
OFSTRUCT   of ;
char       szData [] = "This is text to be copied to the file."

hFileHandle = OpenFile ("example.txt", &of, OF_CREATE) ;
```

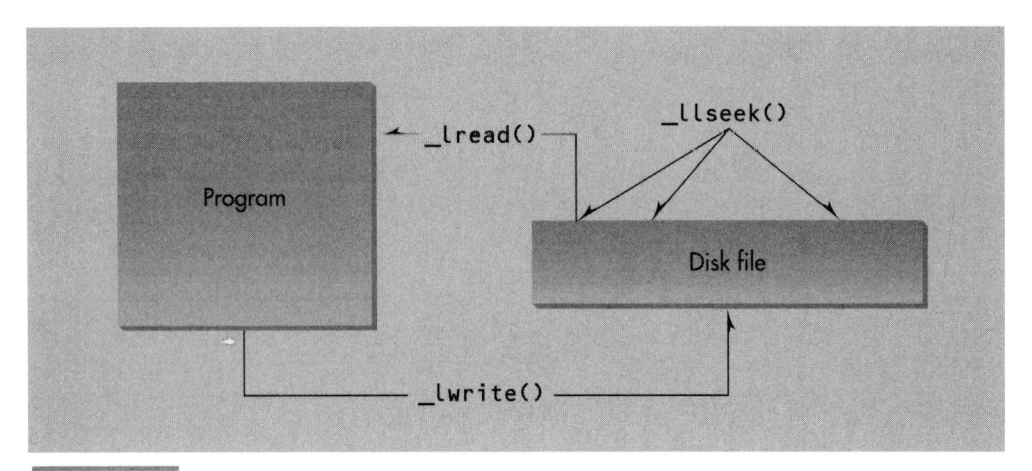

Figure 15-2 Reading and Writing Data

```
if (hFileHandle != -1)
{
   _lwrite (hFileHandle, szData, sizeof (szData)) ;
   _lclose (hFileHandle) ;
}
```

The first parameter passed to _lwrite() is the file's handle. Parameter two is a pointer to the data, and parameter three gives the number of bytes to write to the file. The _lclose() function closes the file after access is complete. When the file is closed, the handle to the file is no longer valid, and the file must be reopened again before another file operation can take place. For example, to copy the first ten characters from the EXAMPLE.TXT file to a character buffer:

```
int        hFileHandle ;
OFSTRUCT   of ;
char       cBuf [128] ;

hFileHandle = OpenFile ("example.txt", &of, OF_CREATE) ;
if (hFileHandle != -1)
{
   _lread (hFileHandle, cBuf, 10) ;
   _lclose (hFileHandle) ;
}
```

The DOS file system keeps track of where a program is "pointing" in a disk file, maintaining a file "location pointer." The next read or write operation will start at this location. When a file is first opened, the file pointer will point to the beginning of the file. Any call made to _lread() or _lwrite() will start on the first byte, and move forward in the file as bytes are read or written. Often, you will want to move to a specific location in the file prior to reading or writing data. This is done with the _llseek() function, which moves the file pointer forward or backwards in the file. Here is an example, which moves to byte number 10 in the file, and then reads the next five bytes:

```
int          hFileHandle ;
OFSTRUCT     of ;
char         cBuf [128] ;

hFileHandle = OpenFile ("example.txt", &of, OF_CREATE) ;
if (hFileHandle != -1)
{
   _llseek (hFileHandle, 10, 0) ;
   _lread (hFileHandle, cBuf, 5) ;
   _lclose (hFileHandle) ;
}
```

The _llseek() function has the following syntax:

LONG **_llseek** (int *hFile*, long *lOffset*, int *nOrigin*) ;

hFile   The file handle.

lOffset   The number of bytes to move. Positive values move forward in the file, negative values move backwards (towards the start of the file).

nOrigin   The starting position to move the pointer. 0 for the start of the file, 1 for the current location, and 2 for the end of the file.

The returned value from the _llseek() function is the current position in the file, relative to the start of the file. _llseek() can be used in a number of ways. A common use is to determine the length of a file by moving to the end of the file. This is frequently done to determine how large a memory buffer to allocate to hold the file's contents. For a small file that will fit in a local memory buffer, use code similar to the following to allocate a memory block to hold a disk file's contents:

```
int nFileLong ;

              /* find out file length */
nFileLong = (int) _llseek (nFileHandle, 0L, 2) ;
              /* go back to beginning of file */
_llseek (nFileHandle, 0L, 0) ;
              /* allocate memory block */
pStr = (PSTR) LocalAlloc (LPTR, nFileLong) ;
```

You can move backwards and forwards in a file using _llseek(). Here are a few examples:

```
           /* go to end of file */
_llseek (nFileHandle, 0L, 2) ;
           /* move 20 backward from the end of the file */
_llseek (nFileHandle, -20L, 2) ;
           /* move 5 forward from the current location */
_llseek (nFileHandle, 5L, 1) ;
           /* move to 25 after the beginning of the file */
_llseek (nFileHandle, 25L, 0) ;
```

When using these functions, keep in mind that disk files do not have any intrinsic organization, and should be considered as just a series of byte values. It is up to your program to define the organization of the data in a disk file, and consistently use the same structure for both reading and writing data. In some cases, such as text documents, the organization is simple: every byte is a character in the document. In other cases, such as databases and spreadsheets, the meaning of each byte will depend on its location in the file.

Closing a File

It is easy to forget to close a disk file after it has been opened or created. Until a file is closed, the data is not fully registered on the disk drive. If you forget to close a file, other disk operations may write over some or all of the disk file. You may also run out of DOS file handles if the program continues to open, but not close, files.

Closing a file is simple — just call the _lclose() function. Once the file is closed, the file handle is no longer valid. If you want to do another operation on the file, you must open it again to obtain the new file handle.

```
_lclose (hFileHandle) ;
```

The SMARTDRV.SYS Program

When you install Windows, the installation program will add a line to the CONFIG.SYS file on your root directory (C:\ directory) that will cause the SMARTDRV.SYS program to be loaded into memory. SMARTDRV is a disk caching program. What this means is that SMARTDRV can speed up disk operations by saving recently loaded portions of disk files in memory, rather than always reading and writing from the disk surface. The memory allocated to saving disk file contents is called a "cache." A typical call to load SMARTDRV.SYS is as follows:

```
DEVICE=C:\DOS\smartdrv.sys 2048 512
```

This line in CONFIG.SYS will run the SMARTDRV.SYS program, with a maximum cache size of 2 megabytes and a minimum cache size of 512K bytes. The physical size limits of the cache that are optimum for your system will depend on how much memory you have installed.

SMARTDRV has no way of knowing in advance which files you will be using, and it is only effective once a file has been opened. When a disk file is opened, its contents are copied into the SMARTDRV cache. For small files, the entire file will be copied into the cache. For larger files, the portions of the file that are accessed, and which will fit within the limits of the cache size, will be copied into the cache. Subsequent disk reading operations that access the portions of the file in the cache will read only the memory contents, and will not physically read from the disk file. You can verify this by noting that the disk drive light does not flash during these file operations.

The result of disk caching is that repeated access to the same files or file portions is very fast. This is a big advantage for Windows applications, which typically store a variety of items as resource data (menus, string tables, etc.) and which may have a number of different elements of the program loaded and unloaded from the disk as the program operates.

A File Access Example

The first example program in this chapter, imaginatively named FILE1, demonstrates several file operations. Figure 15-3 shows the FILE1 program in operation. When the "Write File" menu item is selected, FILE1 writes the capital letters A-Z to a file named TESTFILE.TXT in the same drive/directory that the FILE1 program resides. Selecting the "Read File" option opens the TEST-FILE.TXT file, reads its contents, and displays the contents in the FILE1 window's client area. This is the status shown in Figure 15-3.

Figure 15-3 The FILE1 Program After "Write File" and "Read File" Menu Items Were Selected

The "Append File" menu item also opens the TESTFILE.TXT file, this time to add the digits 0-9 to the end of the file. If the "Read File" menu item is selected after "Append File" is selected once, FILE1 will appear as shown in Figure 15-4. Each time "Append File" is selected, another set of 0-9 digits is appended to the file, lengthening the file and the resultant string displayed when "Read File" is selected.

Figure 15-4 The FILE1 Program After "Append File" and "Read File" Menu Items Were Selected

How FILE1 Works

FILE1 puts the OpenFile(), _lwrite(), _lclose(), _lread(), and _llseek() functions all to work. The only shortcut taken in FILE1 is that the file name for all input and output is fixed as TESTFILE.TXT, and the disk subdirectory is always the same as the FILE1.EXE subdirectory. (The next example program will demonstrate how to have the user select a file name and subdirectory.) Listing 15-2 shows the complete FILE1.C program. One function you will see at a number of locations in FILE1.C is StringTableMessageBox(). This is a custom function defined at the end of FILE1.C that displays a message box, with both the message box caption and central text defined in the program's string table. The definition of StringTableMessageBox() is as follows:

```
int StringTableMessageBox (HWND hWnd, int nString, int nCaption, WORD
    wFlags)
{
    char    cBuf1 [128], cBuf2 [128] ;
    HANDLE  hInstance ;

    hInstance = GetWindowWord (hWnd, GWW_HINSTANCE) ;
    LoadString (hInstance, nString, cBuf1, sizeof (cBuf1)) ;
    LoadString (hInstance, nCaption, cBuf2, sizeof (cBuf2)) ;
    return (MessageBox (hWnd, cBuf1, cBuf2, wFlags)) ;
}
```

StringTableMessageBox() is convenient if you want to display message boxes, but want to keep all of the program's text defined in the resource script file. StringTableMessageBox() is used to display an error message if the TESTFILE.TXT file cannot be opened or created. Here is an example, accessed when the user selects the "Write File" menu item:

```
nFileHandle = OpenFile ("testfile.txt", &of, OF_CREATE) ;
if (nFileHandle == -1)
    StringTableMessageBox (hWnd, S_NOCREATE, S_FILEERROR, MB_OK | MB_ICONHAND) ;
```

You are not likely to see this particular error message because OpenFile() will create a new TESTFILE.TXT file if it does not already exist, or it will open the file and truncate it to zero bytes if it does already exist. Assuming that the file was created or opened without error, FILE1 copies the uppercase alphabet to the file. This is done by first allocating a local memory buffer, copying the alphabet to the buffer, and then writing the entire buffer to the disk file.

```
pStr2 = pStr = (PSTR) LocalAlloc (LPTR, 27) ; /* allocate string buffers */
for (i = 0 ; i < 26 ; i++)
    *pStr2++ = 'A' + i ;        /* copy letters to block */
*pStr2 = 0 ;                    /* null terminate string */
                                /* write data to file */
_lwrite (nFileHandle, pStr, lstrlen (pStr) + 1) ;
_lclose (nFileHandle) ;         /* close file */
LocalFree ((HANDLE) pStr) ;     /* free memory block */
```

The memory space is allocated in the local memory heap as a fixed block (LPTR is defined equal to LMEM_FIXED | LMEM_ZEROINIT in WINDOWS.H). There is no penalty for using a fixed memory block in this case, as the block only exists for the short period of time when the file is being created and then is immediately freed. Note that a terminating null character is added to the end of the data copied to the file. This will be handy when the file data is read and displayed using TextOut().

Reading the disk file uses similar logic. The data in the file is copied to a fixed local memory buffer prior to being displayed. The _llseek() function is used to find out how big the disk file is by simply locating the end of the file. _llseek() returns the byte number of the current position in the file, so the number of the last byte in the file is equal to the file length. The file length is then used to specify how big a memory buffer to allocate, prior to reading the data.

```
nFileHandle = OpenFile ("testfile.txt", &of, OF_READ) ;
if (nFileHandle == -1)
    StringTableMessageBox (hWnd, S_NOREAD,
        S_FILEERROR, MB_OK | MB_ICONHAND) ;
else
{                               /* find out file length */
    nFileLong = (int) _llseek (nFileHandle, 0L, 2) ;
                                /* go back to front of file */
    _llseek (nFileHandle, 0L, 0) ;
                                /* allocate memory block */
    pStr = (PSTR) LocalAlloc (LPTR, nFileLong) ;
                                /* copy file data to block */
```

```
    _lread (nFileHandle, pStr, nFileLong) ;
    _lclose (nFileHandle) ;
    hDC = GetDC (hWnd) ;    /* display the file content */
    TextOut (hDC, 0, 0, pStr, lstrlen (pStr)) ;
    ReleaseDC (hWnd, hDC) ;
    LocalFree ((HANDLE) pStr) ; /* free mem. block */
}
```

The last file operation done by FILE1 is to append the digits 0-9 to the end of the TESTFILE.TXT file. This provides a simple demonstration of writing to a file starting at a location other than the first byte. To append the digits, the terminal null character in the existing file data must be written over. Otherwise, the string will have a null character in the center, and functions like lstrlen() will only detect the portion of the string up to the null. The _llseek() function is used to move to a location one byte before the end of the file by using an offset of -1 and a file location basis of 2 for the end of the file.

```
_llseek (nFileHandle, -1L, 2) ;      /* move to one byte before the end of file */
```

Note that the offset of -1 is specified as a LONG value, as _llseek() expects a long integer as the second parameter. The remaining logic for copying the digits to the end of the file is similar to creating the file from scratch. The digits are copied to a fixed local memory buffer prior to being copied to the disk file.

```
    /* allocate a memory block */
pStr2 = pStr = (PSTR) LocalAlloc (LPTR, 11) ;
for (i = 0 ; i < 10 ; i++)
    *pStr2++ = '0' + i ; /* copy digits to block */
*pStr2 = 0 ;              /* null terminate string */
                          /* open file */
nFileHandle = OpenFile ("testfile.txt", &of, OF_READWRITE) ;
if (nFileHandle == -1)
    StringTableMessageBox (hWnd, S_NOOPEN,
        S_FILEERROR, MB_OK | MB_ICONHAND) ;
else
{   /* move to one before end of file (all but end null) */
    _llseek (nFileHandle, -1L, 2) ;
                        /* write data at file end */
    _lwrite (nFileHandle, pStr, lstrlen (pStr) + 1) ;
    _lclose (nFileHandle) ; /* close file */
}
LocalFree ((HANDLE) pStr) ; /* free memory block */
```

One shortcut taken in all of these examples is that the local memory buffer is assumed to be allocated without error. This is fine in a short example like FILE1.C, where the amount of data allocated is much smaller than the available room in the local heap. In a larger program with many portions allocating memory blocks, you would want to verify that the value returned by LocalAlloc() is not equal to null before attempting to write data to the block.

FILE1 Program Listings

The complete listing for the FILE1.C program is shown in Listing 15-2, followed by the support files. Notice the similarity in the program logic for each of the sections containing file operations (each of the menu selections.) Each section starts with a call to OpenFile() and ends with a call to _lclose(). Data is always exchanged between the file and a memory buffer. The only differences are the location chosen to start disk operations (either at the start of the file, or at another location specified with the _llseek() function), and whether data is written to the file with _lwrite() or read from the file with _lread().

Listing 15-2 FILE1.C

```c
/* file1.c    file access example */

#include <windows.h>
#include "file1.h"

int PASCAL WinMain (HANDLE hInstance, HANDLE hPrevInstance, LPSTR lpszCmdLine,
    int nCmdShow)
{
    HWND        hWnd ;          /* the window's "handle" */
    MSG         msg ;           /* a message structure */
    WNDCLASS    wndclass ;      /* window class structure */
    char        cBuf [128] ;    /* character buffer */

    if (!hPrevInstance)
    {
        wndclass.style          = CS_HREDRAW | CS_VREDRAW ;
        wndclass.lpfnWndProc    = WndProc ;
        wndclass.cbClsExtra     = 0 ;
        wndclass.cbWndExtra     = 0 ;
        wndclass.hInstance      = hInstance ;
        wndclass.hIcon          = LoadIcon (hInstance, "MyIcon") ;
        wndclass.hCursor        = LoadCursor (NULL, IDC_ARROW) ;
        wndclass.hbrBackground  = GetStockObject (WHITE_BRUSH) ;
        wndclass.lpszMenuName   = "MyMenu" ;
        wndclass.lpszClassName  = "MyClass" ;
                        /* register the window class */
        if (!RegisterClass (&wndclass))
            return 0 ;
    }
    LoadString (hInstance, S_PROGRAMCAPTION, cBuf, sizeof (cBuf)) ;

    hWnd = CreateWindow ("MyClass", cBuf, WS_OVERLAPPEDWINDOW,
        CW_USEDEFAULT, CW_USEDEFAULT, CW_USEDEFAULT, CW_USEDEFAULT,
        NULL, NULL, hInstance, NULL) ;
    ShowWindow (hWnd, nCmdShow) ;       /* display the window */

    while (GetMessage (&msg, NULL, NULL, NULL))  /* message loop */
    {
       TranslateMessage (&msg) ;        /* translate keyboard messages */
       DispatchMessage (&msg) ;         /* send message to WndProc() */
    }
    return (msg.wParam) ;
}

long FAR PASCAL WndProc (HWND hWnd, WORD wMessage, WORD wParam, LONG lParam)
{
```

```c
        int             i ;
        OFSTRUCT        of ;
        int             nFileHandle, nFileLong ;
        PSTR            pStr, pStr2 ;
        HDC             hDC ;

    switch (wMessage)       /* process windows messages */
    {
        case WM_COMMAND:
            switch (wParam)                 /* menu items */
            {
                case IDM_WRITE:             /* write to the file */
                    nFileHandle = OpenFile ("testfile.txt", &of, OF_CREATE) ;
                    if (nFileHandle == -1)
                        StringTableMessageBox (hWnd, S_NOCREATE,
                            S_FILEERROR, MB_OK | MB_ICONHAND) ;
                    else
                    {                       /* allocate memory block */
                        pStr2 = pStr = (PSTR) LocalAlloc (LPTR, 27) ;
                        for (i = 0 ; i < 26 ; i++)/* copy letters to block */
                            *pStr2++ = (char)(_A + i) ;
                        *pStr2 = 0 ;        /* null terminate string */
                                            /* write data to file */
                        _lwrite (nFileHandle, pStr, lstrlen (pStr) + 1) ;
                        _lclose (nFileHandle) ;     /* close file */
                        LocalFree ((HANDLE) pStr) ; /* free memory block */
                        StringTableMessageBox (hWnd, S_CREATED,
                            S_MESSAGE, MB_OK | MB_ICONINFORMATION) ;
                    }
                    break ;
                case IDM_READ:
                    nFileHandle = OpenFile ("testfile.txt", &of, OF_READ) ;
                    if (nFileHandle == -1)
                            StringTableMessageBox (hWnd, S_NOREAD,
                                S_FILEERROR, MB_OK | MB_ICONHAND) ;
                    else
                    {                       /* find out file length */
                        nFileLong = (int) _llseek (nFileHandle, 0L, 2) ;
                                            /* go back to front of file */
                        _llseek (nFileHandle, 0L, 0) ;
                                            /* allocate memory block */
                        pStr = (PSTR) LocalAlloc (LPTR, nFileLong) ;
                                            /* copy file data to block */
                        _lread (nFileHandle, pStr, nFileLong) ;
                        _lclose (nFileHandle) ;
                        hDC = GetDC (hWnd) ; /* display the file content */
                        TextOut (hDC, 0, 0, pStr, lstrlen (pStr)) ;
                        ReleaseDC (hWnd, hDC) ;
                        LocalFree ((HANDLE) pStr) ;    /* free mem. block */
                    }
                    break ;
                case IDM_ADD:               /* append data to file end */
                                            /* allocate a memory block */
                    pStr2 = pStr = (PSTR) LocalAlloc (LPTR, 11) ;
                    for (i = 0 ; i < 10 ; i++)/* copy digits to block */
                        *pStr2++ = (char)(_0 + i) ;
                    *pStr2 = 0 ;            /* null terminate string */
                                            /* open file */
```

```
                    nFileHandle = OpenFile ("testfile.txt", &of, OF_READWRITE) ;
                    if (nFileHandle == -1)
                        StringTableMessageBox (hWnd, S_NOOPEN,
                            S_FILEERROR, MB_OK | MB_ICONHAND) ;
                    else
                    {   /* move to one before end of file (all but end null) */
                        lseek (nFileHandle, -1L, 2) ;
                                        /* write data at file end */
                        lwrite (nFileHandle, pStr, lstrlen (pStr) + 1) ;
                        lclose (nFileHandle) ; /* close file */
                    }
                    LocalFree ((HANDLE) pStr) ; /* free memory block */
                    StringTableMessageBox (hWnd, S_NOWTRY,
                        S_MESSAGE, MB_OK | MB_ICONINFORMATION) ;
                    break ;
                      case IDM_QUIT:              /* "Quit" menu item */
                    DestroyWindow (hWnd) ;  /* destroy window, */
                    break ;                 /* terminating application */
            }
            break ;
        case WM_DESTROY:                    /* stop application */
            PostQuitMessage (0) ;
            break ;
        default:        /* default windows message processing */
            return (DefWindowProc (hWnd, wMessage, wParam, lParam)) ;
    }
    return (0L) ;
}

/* display a message box based on two string table entries */

int StringTableMessageBox (HWND hWnd, int nString, int nCaption, WORD
    wFlags)
{
    char    cBuf1 [128], cBuf2 [128] ;
    HANDLE  hInstance ;

    hInstance = GetWindowWord (hWnd, GWW_HINSTANCE) ;
    LoadString (hInstance, nString, cBuf1, sizeof (cBuf1)) ;
    LoadString (hInstance, nCaption, cBuf2, sizeof (cBuf2)) ;
    return (MessageBox (hWnd, cBuf1, cBuf2, wFlags)) ;
}
```

Listings 15-3 to 15-7 show the support files for FILE1. The program's icon is shown in Figure 15-5.

Figure 15-5
FILE1.ICO
Icon Image

Listing 15-3 FILE1.H Header File

```
/* file1.h header file */

#define IDM_WRITE       1       /* menu item ID numbers */
#define IDM_READ        2
#define IDM_ADD         3
#define IDM_QUIT        10
```

536 Windows PROGRAMMING Primer Plus®

```
#define S_PROGRAMCAPTION  1       /* string table ID numbers */
#define S_NOCREATE        2
#define S_FILEERROR       3
#define S_CREATED         4
#define S_MESSAGE         5
#define S_NOREAD          6
#define S_NOOPEN          7
#define S_NOWTRY          8

long FAR PASCAL WndProc (HWND, WORD, WORD, LONG) ;
int StringTableMessageBox (HWND hWnd, int nString, int nCaption, WORD
    wFlags) ;
```

Listing 15-4 FILE1.RC Resource Script File

```
/* file1.rc resource file */

#include "file1.h"

MyIcon      ICON    file1.ico

MyMenu      MENU
BEGIN
    MENUITEM "&Write File",     IDM_WRITE
    MENUITEM "&Read File",      IDM_READ
    MENUITEM "&Append File",    IDM_ADD
    MENUITEM "&Quit",           IDM_QUIT
END

STRINGTABLE
BEGIN
    S_PROGRAMCAPTION    "File 1 Program"
    S_NOCREATE          "Could not create file TESTFILE.TXT"
    S_FILEERROR         "File Error"
    S_CREATED           "Created file TESTFILE.TXT"
    S_MESSAGE           "Message"
    S_NOREAD            "Could not read file TESTFILE.TXT"
    S_NOOPEN            "Could not open file TESTFILE.TXT"
    S_NOWTRY            "Now try reading file"
END
```

Listing 15-5 FILE1.DEF Module Definition File

```
NAME            file1
DESCRIPTION     'file1 program'
EXETYPE         WINDOWS
STUB            'WINSTUB.EXE'
CODE            PRELOAD MOVEABLE DISCARDABLE
DATA            PRELOAD MOVEABLE MULTIPLE
HEAPSIZE        1024
STACKSIZE       5120
EXPORTS         WndProc
```

Listing 15-6 Turbo C++ Project File for FILE1

file1.c
file1.def
file1.res

Listing 15-7 QuickC Project File for FILE1

file1.c
file1.def
file1.rc

Creating a File Selection Dialog Box

One of the hallmarks of a good Windows application is the relative ease in selecting a file and in changing disk subdirectories. Gone are the days of early DOS programs that required you to remember subdirectory and file names. Most Windows programs allow file and subdirectory selection with a simple dialog box, such as the one shown in Figure 15-6. Drive letters and subdirectories are selected with the right list box, and files with the left one. File names can also be entered by typing in the edit control at the upper left corner. Note that a static text field in the upper right corner of the dialog box shows the currently selected subdirectory. This static text control is updated as new disks, subdirectories, and files are selected.

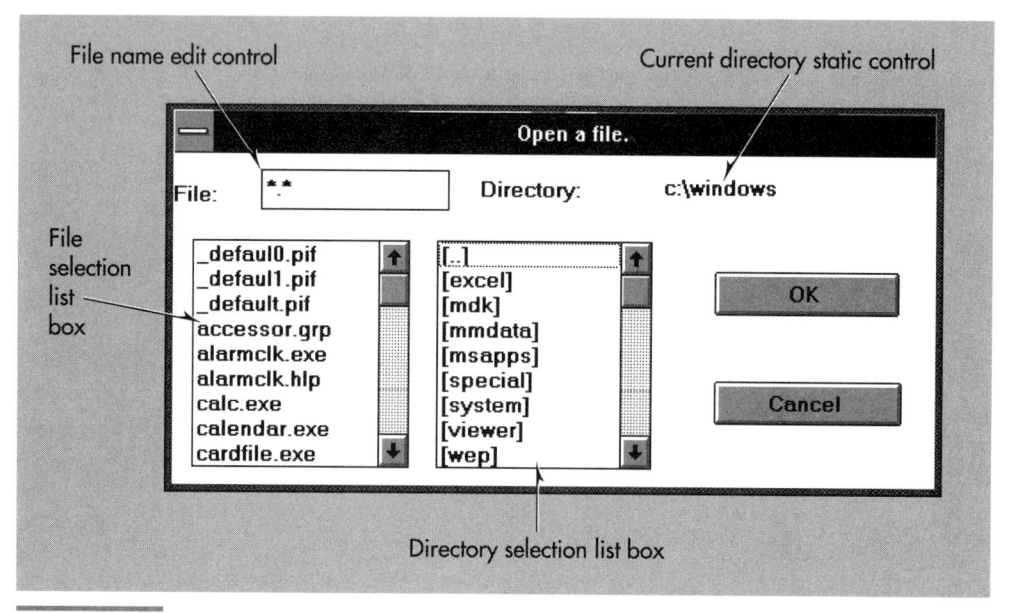

Figure 15-6 A File Selection Dialog Box

538 Windows Programming Primer Plus®

The DlgDirList() Function

There are two functions that make creating a file selection dialog box like the one shown in Figure 15-6 relatively simple. The DlgDirList() function fills a dialog box with a list of files and/or disk and subdirectory names. DlgDirSelect() works with DlgDirList() and copies a selected file or subdirectory name into a memory buffer. For the two functions to work properly, they must share a common character buffer that will hold the currently selected subdirectory name. The syntax for the DlgDirList() function is shown below:

int **DlgDirList**(HWND *hDlg*, LPSTR *lpPathSpec*, int *nIDListBox*, int *nIDStaticPath*,
       WORD *wFileType*);

hDlg HWND
The dialog box handle.

lpPathSpec LPSTR
A pointer to a character string containing the path/file search specification. For example, "C:\WINDOWS*.TXT" locates all files with the .TXT extension in the Windows subdirectory. The character buffer holding this string should also be used by the DlgDirSelect() function as the *lpString* parameter, so that DlgDirSelect() can update the entry based on the user's selections.

nIDListBox int
The dialog box ID value for the list box control. Normally, the list box will have the LBS_SORT style, so that the files are listed in ASCII sort order.

nIDStaticPath int
The dialog box ID value for a static text control that will be updated with the current path name. The updating is automatic. This is how the drive/directory/file name shown at the upper right corner of the dialog box in Figure 15-6 is updated.

wFileType WORD
The DOS file attribute value. Only files with the selected attributes will be displayed. The DOS file attributes are summarized in Table 15-2 and can be combined using the C language binary OR operator (|). For example, to show only drive and subdirectory names, combine the exclusive flag with the drive and subdirectory flags: 0x8000 | 0x4000 | 0x0010 = 0xC010.

VALUE	MEANING
0x0000	Read/write data files with no other attributes set (normal files.)
0x0001	Read only files.
0x0002	Hidden files.
0x0004	System files.
0x0010	Subdirectories.
0x0020	Archived files.

continued

Table 15-2 (cont'd)

0x2000	LB_DIR flag. This places messages associated with filling the list box on the application's message queue, rather than sending them directly.
0x4000	Drives (A, B, C, ...).
0x8000	Exclusive bit. If this is set, only the specified file attribute type is recovered. If not set, normal files are displayed in addition to the types listed.

Table 15-2 DOS File Attributes

The DlgDirSelect() Function

The DlgDirSelect() function takes the most recently selected entry in a list box that was filled by DlgDirList() and copies the selection into the character buffer pointed to by *lpString*. DlgDirSelect() does some cleaning up of the selections in the list box before copying the selection. For example, drive names will show up in the list box surrounded by square brackets, like "[C:]." The square brackets are stripped away by DlgDirSelect() before the string is copied. The resultant string will always be a valid DOS search string, ready to be passed back to DlgDirList() to update the list box with the newly selected drive/directory/file selections. The full syntax of the DlgDirSelect() function is shown below:

BOOL **DlgDirSelect**(HWND *hDlg*, LPSTR *lpString*, int *nIDListBox*);

hDlg   HWND
                The dialog box handle.

lpString   LPSTR
                A pointer to a memory buffer that will hold the name of file or subdirectory selected. Subdirectories will be displayed with square brackets surrounding the subdirectory name. The brackets are not copied to the memory buffer.

nIDListBox   int
                The ID value for the list box control in the dialog box.

Creating a File Selection Dialog Box

File selection is such a common activity that you can expect to need a similar dialog box in many application programs. The ideal approach here is to write the dialog box procedure in a general way, so that the code can be used without modification in any future project. This section will show how to create the FILEDLG program, which will contain the dialog box definition and dialog box function for a file selection dialog box. The next section will put those functions to work by creating a simple text editor, which will read and write text files from the disk.

Writing a file selection dialog box function that can be applied to many projects requires a little foresight. Different programs start with different default subdirectories, and they do different things with the file once it is selected. To make the FILEDLG functions as general as possible, the following design criteria will be applied:

1. File selection will occur in the dialog box function, but the file will not be opened. The dialog box function will return the selected drive/directory/file name, but will

leave any operations on the selected file to the calling program (the "calling program" is the program using the file selection dialog box).
2. The calling program will specify the starting subdirectory and the starting file search string (like "*.EXE"). This will allow the calling program to specify a default subdirectory, or save previously selected subdirectory names for the next file operation.
3. The calling program will also specify the title of the dialog box, so that the same dialog box can be used for different operations, such as "Select a file to open," "Select a file to delete," etc.
4. The dialog box will have "OK" and "Cancel" buttons. The dialog box function will return FALSE if the user selected "Cancel," and "TRUE" if the user selected "OK."
5. Double clicking a file name in the file list box will be equivalent to selecting a file (single mouse click) and then selecting the "OK" button.

If you remember the discussion in Chapter 10, *Dialog Boxes*, you will recall that there are two general methods used to exchange data between a dialog box and the calling program. One method is to use global variables and the simple DialogBox() function. This is not the preferred method, as global variables are difficult to track in large programming projects with multiple source files. The second method is to pass information to the dialog box using the DialogBoxParam() function, by passing a pointer to a data structure containing data that the dialog box function will use. This is the preferred technique.

The FILEDLG program uses the DialogBoxParam() function to pass the starting path name, file name, and dialog box caption to the dialog box function. This requires that a specialized structure be defined to hold these character strings. The FILEOPENDATA structure is defined in the FILEDLG.H header file, shown in Listing 15-8. The calling program (the program that uses the FILEDLG dialog box) fills in the character data in the FILEOPENDATA structure, and then calls the file selection dialog box. When the user selects a file, the dialog box function returns, after copying the selected file and drive/directory name into the FILEOPENDATA structure. This is how the calling program will determine the names of the file and drive/directory that the user selected when the dialog box was displayed.

Listing 15-8 FILEDLG.H

```
/* filedlg.h header file for filedlg.c */

#define DLI_EDIT          101     /* dialog box ID numbers */
#define DLI_DIRECT        102
#define DLI_OK            103
#define DLI_CANCEL        104
#define DLI_DIRLIST       105
#define DLI_FILELIST      106

#define FILENAMELONG       13     /* constants for string lengths */
#define PATHNAMELONG      128
#define FILEOPENCAPTIONLONG 32

typedef struct tagFILEOPENDATA    /* structure use to pass data */
{                                 /* to/from dialog box proc. */
```

```
    char    szPath [PATHNAMELONG] ;
    char    szFile [FILENAMELONG] ;
    char    szCaption [FILEOPENCAPTIONLONG] ;
} FILEOPENDATA ;

BOOL FAR PASCAL FileOpenProc (HWND hDlg, WORD wMessage, WORD wParam, LONG lParam) ;
void CombinePathFile (LPSTR szFileName, LPSTR szDir, LPSTR szFile) ;
void SplitPathFile (LPSTR lpSource, LPSTR lpPath, LPSTR lpFile) ;
```

A dialog box definition is also required to create the file selection dialog box. Listing 15-9 shows the dialog box definition for FILEDLG.RC. Note that both of the list boxes in the dialog box definition use the LBS_SORT style, so that all entries are sorted in alphabetical order. The DlgDirList() function surrounds drive letters in square brackets, so they end up at the end of the list. The dialog box image is shown in Figure 15-7, inside the Microsoft Dialog Box Editor.

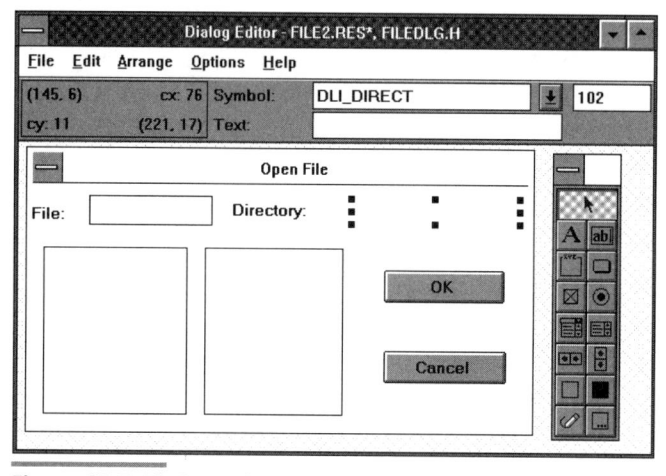

Figure 15-7 FileOpenDlg() Image in Microsoft Dialog Box Editor

Listing 15-9 FILEDLG.RC Resource Script File

```
/* filedlg.rc */

#include <windows.h>
#include "filedlg.h"

FileOpenDlg DIALOG 6, 18, 225, 106
STYLE DS_MODALFRAME | WS_POPUP | WS_VISIBLE | WS_CAPTION | WS_SYSMENU
CAPTION "Open File"
FONT 8, "Helv"
BEGIN
    EDITTEXT        DLI_EDIT, 26, 5, 56, 13, ES_AUTOHSCROLL
    LISTBOX         DLI_FILELIST, 6, 28, 64, 74, LBS_SORT | WS_VSCROLL |
                    WS_TABSTOP
    PUSHBUTTON      "OK", DLI_OK, 160, 37, 54, 14
    PUSHBUTTON      "Cancel", DLI_CANCEL, 160, 72, 55, 14
    LTEXT           "File:", -1, 0, 9, 20, 12
    LTEXT           "Directory:", -1, 91, 7, 38, 11
    LTEXT           "", DLI_DIRECT, 145, 6, 76, 11
    LISTBOX         DLI_DIRLIST, 79, 28, 62, 74, LBS_SORT | WS_VSCROLL |
                    WS_TABSTOP
END
```

542 Windows Programming Primer Plus®

The File Selection Dialog Box Function

Before looking at the FILEDLG.C program containing the dialog box function, let's look at how the dialog box will be used. The calling program will pass the starting subdirectory, file search string, and dialog box window title to the dialog box function by copying the data into the FILEOPENDATA structure. A simple example of this is shown here:

```
static FILEOPENDATA  FOD ;         /* must be static */
HANDLE               hInstance ;
FARPROC              lpfnDlgProc ;

hInstance = GetWindowWord (hWnd, GWW_HINSTANCE) ;
lpfnDlgProc = MakeProcInstance (FileOpenProc, hInstance) ;
lstrcpy (FOD.szPath, "c:\\windows") ;    /* start in the c:\windows subdirectory */
lstrcpy (FOD.szFile, "*.*") ;            /* select all files */
lstrcpy (FOD.szCaption, "Open any file you like!") ;
bFileStatus = DialogBoxParam (hInstance, "FileOpenDlg",
    hWnd, lpfnDlgProc, (DWORD)(LPSTR) &FOD) ;   /* pass the FOD data to dlg box */
FreeProcInstance (lpfnDlgProc) ;
```

The subdirectory name, file search string ("*.*") and window caption are copied to the appropriate member elements of the FILEOPENDATA structure. The address of the FILEOPENDATA structure is then passed as a DWORD value when DialogBoxParam() is called. When the dialog box function starts and the WM_INITDIALOG message is processed by the dialog box function, the address of the FILEOPENDATA will be passed as the *lParam* value sent with the message. Review Chapter 10, *Dialog Boxes*, if this is not familiar.

The full FILEDLG.C program is shown in Listing 15-10. The dialog box function is named FileOpenProc(). The first thing FileOpenProc() must do is to read the data from the FILEOPENDATA structure when processing the WM_INITDIALOG message. The two list boxes are filled with file and drive/directory names at this point by calling the DlgDirList() function for each list box.

```
        static FILEOPENDATA * pFOD ;
        static char           szPathFile [PATHNAMELONG] ; /* working buffer */

    case WM_INITDIALOG:
        pFOD = (FILEOPENDATA *) lParam ;   /* get the pointer to data */
        SetWindowText (hDlg, pFOD->szCaption) ;
                                           /* initialize working buffer */
        CombinePathFile (szPathFile, pFOD->szPath, pFOD->szFile) ;
                                           /* fill both list boxes */
        DlgDirList (hDlg, szPathFile, DLI_FILELIST, DLI_EDIT, 0) ;
        DlgDirList (hDlg, szPathFile, DLI_DIRLIST, DLI_DIRECT, 0xC010) ;
        SetDlgItemText (hDlg, DLI_EDIT, pFOD->szFile) ;
        bMadeSel = FALSE ; /* keep track of if file was selected */
        return (FALSE) ;
```

One little complication the FileOpenProc() function must deal with is that the FILEOPENDATA structure contains the file name and drive/directory name as separate character strings. The DlgDirList() function expects a single complete path/file name, such as "C:\WINDOWS*.*," so the file and drive/directory names must be combined. A helper function called CombinePathFile(), which is defined at the end of the FILEDLG.C listing, combines the two strings to make a single file search string. The same search string is passed to the DlgDirList() function to fill each of the list boxes. The only differences are that the left list box is filled with a file attribute value of zero (last parameter passed to DlgDirList()), selecting all normal files, while the right list box uses a file attribute value of 0x0C10, selecting exclusively subdirectories and drive letters.

Note that the file search string is stored in a static buffer *szPathFile[]*. This is important for the functioning of the DlgDirSelect() function. When the user selects an item from one of the dialog boxes, DlgDirSelect() is used to copy the current selection into the *szPathFile[]* buffer, ready for the next call to DlgDirList(). For example, when the user selects an item from the left file name list box, the following code is executed:

```
      case DLI_FILELIST:             /* the file list box */
          switch (HIWORD (lParam))
          {
              case LBN_SELCHANGE:    /* picked a file name */
                                     /* get user's selection */
                  DlgDirSelect (hDlg, szPathFile, DLI_FILELIST) ;
                  SplitPathFile (szPathFile, szPathName,
                       szFileName) ;    /* display selected file */
                  SetDlgItemText (hDlg, DLI_EDIT, szFileName) ;
                  bMadeSel = TRUE ;
                  break ;
```

This all works fine, except for a little detail. The file name copied into the *szPathFile[]* buffer will be the full path/file name like "C:\WINDOWS\MYTEXT.DOC." To show only the file name in the edit control at the top left of the dialog box, the file name must be separated from the complete path/file name. This is done with the second helper function, SplitPathFile(), which splits a complete path/file name into two separate strings. Only the file name is copied into the edit buffer.

While the dialog box function is active, a static variable *bMadeSel* keeps track of whether the user has selected or typed in a file name. *bMadeSel* is TRUE if a file has been selected or typed, or FALSE if a selection has not been made. When the user selects the "OK" button or double clicks a file name, the dialog box ends by calling EndDialog(). Before stopping, the dialog box function copies the current file and subdirectory names back into the FILEOPENDATA structure. That structure resides back in the calling program's local heap (it was declared as a static variable in the calling program's code), so the calling program will be able to read the data after the dialog box disappears.

```
      case DLI_OK:                   /* OK button */
          GetDlgItemText (hDlg, DLI_EDIT, pFOD->szFile,
              FILENAMELONG) ;
          getcwd (pFOD->szPath, PATHNAMELONG) ;
          EndDialog (hDlg, bMadeSel) ;
```

Note that the C compiler library function getcwd() (get current working subdirectory) is used to determine the subdirectory name, and copy it to the FILEOPENDATA structure. You will need to include the DIRECT.H header file to use this library function. If the user selects a subdirectory name in the right side list box, the DOS working subdirectory for the drive will change. DOS keeps track of the working directory name for each disk drive on the system. The getcwd() function is just a handy way to retrieve the current working directory name.

EndDialog() passes the *bMadeSel* value as its second parameter. This ends up being the value returned by the DialogBoxParam() function when the dialog box disappears. The calling program can check the returned value to determine if a file was selected. If so, the file name and subdirectory name are stored in the FILEOPENDATA data structure, ready to be used.

The remainder of the FileOpenProc() function in Listing 15-10 follows the basic pattern outlined above. You will probably find the SplitPathFile() and CombinePathFile() functions at the bottom of the listing handy in many programs that work with file names.

Listing 15-10 FILEDLG.C

```c
/* filedlg.c   example with simple output to printer */

#include <windows.h>
#include <string.h>      /* needed for strtok() function */
#include <direct.h>      /* needed for getcwd() function */
#include "filedlg.h"

/* FileOpenProc() function runs the FileDlg dialog box, defined in filedlg.rc */
/* FileOpenProc() should be called using the DialogBoxParam() function, */
/* passing a pointer to a FILEOPENDATA structure containing the starting */
/* caption, path name and file search strings (like "c:\\", and  "*.*"). */
/* The returned value is TRUE if a file was selected, FALSE if not */
/* No attempt is made to open the file within this procedure. */
/* Don't forget to show FileOpenProc in the EXPORTS section of the calling */
/* program's .DEF file, and to include filedlg.h as a header file. */

BOOL FAR PASCAL FileOpenProc (HWND hDlg, WORD wMessage, WORD wParam, LONG lParam)
{
    static FILEOPENDATA * pFOD ;
    char           szPathName [PATHNAMELONG],   szFileName [FILENAMELONG] ;
    static char    szPathFile [PATHNAMELONG] ;  /* working buffer */
    static BOOL    bMadeSel ;

    switch (wMessage)
    {
      case WM_INITDIALOG:
          pFOD = (FILEOPENDATA *) lParam ;       /* get the pointer to data */
          SetWindowText (hDlg, pFOD->szCaption) ;
                                                 /* initialize working buffer */
          CombinePathFile (szPathFile, pFOD->szPath, pFOD->szFile) ;
                                                 /* fill both list boxes */
          DlgDirList (hDlg, szPathFile, DLI_FILELIST, DLI_EDIT, 0) ;
          DlgDirList (hDlg, szPathFile, DLI_DIRLIST, DLI_DIRECT, 0xC010) ;
          SetDlgItemText (hDlg, DLI_EDIT, pFOD->szFile) ;
          bMadeSel = FALSE ;   /* keep track of if file was selected */
          return (FALSE) ;
      case WM_COMMAND:
          switch (wParam)
          {
            case DLI_OK:                         /* OK button */
                GetDlgItemText (hDlg, DLI_EDIT, pFOD->szFile,
                  FILENAMELONG) ;
```

```c
                    getcwd (pFOD->szPath, PATHNAMELONG) ;
                    EndDialog (hDlg, bMadeSel) ;
                    break ;
                case DLI_CANCEL:                    /* cancel button */
                    EndDialog (hDlg, FALSE) ;
                    break ;
                case DLI_EDIT:                      /* the edit control */
                    if (HIWORD (lParam) == EN_CHANGE)
                        bMadeSel = TRUE ;           /* user entered file */
                    break ;
                case DLI_FILELIST:                  /* the file list box */
                    switch (HIWORD (lParam))
                    {
                        case LBN_SELCHANGE:         /* picked a file name */
                                                    /* get user's selection */
                            DlgDirSelect (hDlg, szPathFile, DLI_FILELIST) ;
                            SplitPathFile (szPathFile, szPathName,
                                szFileName) ;       /* display selected file */
                            SetDlgItemText (hDlg, DLI_EDIT, szFileName) ;
                            bMadeSel = TRUE ;
                            break ;
                        case LBN_DBLCLK:            /* double clicked file */
                            GetDlgItemText (hDlg, DLI_EDIT, pFOD->szFile,
                                FILENAMELONG) ;
                            getcwd (pFOD->szPath, PATHNAMELONG) ;
                            EndDialog (hDlg, bMadeSel) ;
                            break ;
                    }
                    break ;
                case DLI_DIRLIST:                   /* subdirectory list box */
                    switch (HIWORD (lParam))
                    {
                        case LBN_SELCHANGE:         /* picked a dir name */
                                                    /* get user's selection */
                            DlgDirSelect (hDlg, szPathFile, DLI_DIRLIST) ;
                                                    /* refresh dir list */
                            DlgDirList (hDlg, szPathFile, DLI_DIRLIST,
                                DLI_DIRECT, 0xC010) ;
                            /* if subdirectory name is just \.. */
                            if (strstr (szPathFile, "..") ||
                                lstrlen (szPathFile) == 0)
                                lstrcpy (szPathFile, "*.*") ;
                                                    /* refresh file list */
                            DlgDirList (hDlg, szPathFile, DLI_FILELIST,
                                DLI_EDIT, 0) ;
                            SplitPathFile (szPathFile, szPathName,
                                szFileName) ;
                                                    /* show new file spec */
                            SetDlgItemText (hDlg, DLI_EDIT, szFileName) ;
                            bMadeSel = FALSE ; /* reset file selection */
                            break ;
                    }
                    break ;
            }
            return (TRUE) ;
    }
    return (FALSE) ;
}
```

```c
void SplitPathFile (LPSTR lpSource, LPSTR lpPath, LPSTR lpFile)
{
    LPSTR    lpChar ;

    lpChar = lpSource + (long) lstrlen (lpSource) ; /* point to end */
        /* move backwards through string looking for : or \ chars */
    while (*lpChar != ':' && *lpChar != '\\' && lpChar > lpSource)
        lpChar-- ;
    if (*lpChar != ':' && *lpChar != '\\') /* none found ? */
    {
       lstrcpy (lpFile, lpChar) ;       /* copy file name from end */
       *lpPath = 0 ;                    /* did not find subdirectory */
       return ;
    }
    else    /* found : or \, so can copy file and path names */
    {
       lstrcpy (lpFile, lpChar + 1) ;   /* copy file name from end */
       *(lpChar + 1) = 0 ;              /* end path before file starts */
       lstrcpy (lpPath, lpSource) ;
    }
}
void CombinePathFile (LPSTR szFileName, LPSTR szDir, LPSTR szFile)
{
    lstrcpy (szFileName, szDir) ;
    if (szFileName [lstrlen (szFileName) - 1] != '\\')
       lstrcat (szFileName, "\\") ;
    lstrcat (szFileName, szFile) ;
}
```

The FILEDLG.C program does not do anything on its own. To use the file selection dialog box, you will need to create a program that calls the dialog box to select a file. The next example program demonstrates this by creating a simple text editor.

Creating a Text Editor

The last example program in this chapter is called FILE2. FILE2 is a simple text editor, which puts the FILEDLG functions to use for the "Open File" and "Save File" dialog boxes. Figure 15-8 shows the FILE2 program at work, editing the CONFIG.SYS file. Structurally, FILE2 contains a big edit control that occupies the entire client area. The edit control displays any text file that is loaded into memory and allows the text to be edited. From a programming point of view, essentially all of the FILE2.C program will consist of the logic to read and write disk file data. The built-in logic of the edit control will handle just about everything else.

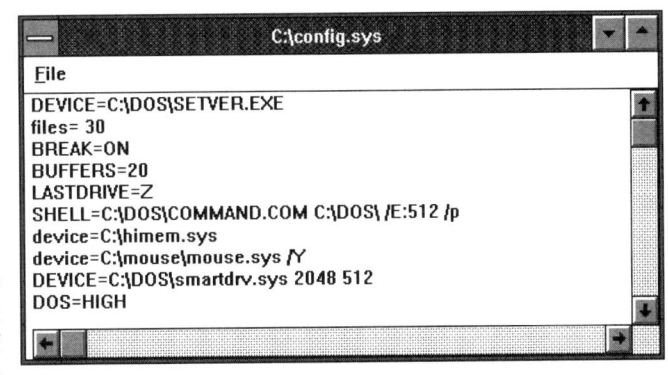

Figure 15-8 The FILE2 Program

Creating the Edit Control

The complete FILE2.C program is shown in Listing 15-12. The edit control is created when FILE2 first starts running and the WM_CREATE message is processed. The CreateWindow() function call takes nine window flag values to fully specify a multiline edit control with both vertical and horizontal scroll bars. When the edit control is first created, it is not sized to fit the window's client area. The edit control is sized when processing WM_SIZE messages, which is discussed below.

Listing 15-11 WM-CREATE TITLE

```
case WM_CREATE:     /* create edit window, and link mem buffer */
    hInstance = GetWindowWord (hWnd, GWW_HINSTANCE) ;
    hEditWindow = CreateWindow ("EDIT", "",
        WS_CHILD | WS_VISIBLE | ES_AUTOVSCROLL | ES_MULTILINE |
        ES_LEFT | ES_NOHIDESEL | WS_VSCROLL| ES_AUTOHSCROLL |
        WS_HSCROLL, 0, 0, 1, 1, hWnd, NULL, hInstance, NULL) ;
                /* get rid of default edit buffer */
    hEditBuf = (HANDLE) SendMessage (hEditWindow,
        EM_GETHANDLE, 0, 0L) ;
    if (hEditBuf)
        LocalFree (hEditBuf) ;
                /* allocate a new edit buffer */
    hEditBuf = LocalAlloc (LMEM_MOVEABLE | LMEM_ZEROINIT, 100) ;
    PostMessage (hEditWindow, EM_SETHANDLE, hEditBuf, 0L) ;
    break ;
```

A key activity in the creation of the edit control is to associate a local memory handle with the control. This is done by sending the EM_SETHANDLE message to the edit control window. Initially, the memory block for FILE2's edit control is arbitrarily sized at 100 bytes, although Windows will automatically increase the size of the memory block if the user types in more than 100 characters.

Prior to associating a new memory block with the edit control, FILE2 retrieves the handle to the default memory buffer created by Windows by sending the EM_GETHANDLE message to the edit control, and then it frees the default memory buffer from memory. Previous examples using edit controls did not associate a memory block with the edit control. They used the default memory block created by Windows for each edit control. The reason FILE2 allocates its own memory block for the edit control is to ensure that the memory block has the correct attributes (moveable and initialized to all zeros). Knowing the handle of the edit control's memory block makes it easy to copy the entire memory block to a disk file if the user decides to save the edit control's contents.

FILE2 processes WM_SIZE messages to keep the edit control sized to fit inside the parent window's client area. Actually, the edit control starts five pixels from the left side of the parent window's border. This five pixel space keeps text in the edit control from being right next to the border, which would be difficult to read.

```
case WM_SIZE:       /* keep edit control filling client area */
    MoveWindow (hEditWindow, 5, 0, LOWORD (lParam) - 5,
        HIWORD (lParam), TRUE) ;
    break ;
```

Using the File Selection Dialog Box

The most interesting parts of the FILE2.C program deal with reading and writing disk files. Both the "Open File" and "Save File" menu items use the file selection dialog box described in the last section. The dialog box function is passed the current working subdirectory (obtained with the getcwd() C compiler library function) and the file search specification "*.*," as elements of the FILEOPENDATA structure passed to the dialog box function when DialogBoxParam() is called. The caption for the dialog box is also copied to the FILEOPENDATA structure, after loading the text from the program's resource string table. If the user selects a file, the dialog box function returns the selected file name as the *szFile* member of the FILEOPENDATA structure when the dialog box function returns.

```
case IDM_OPEN:
    hInstance = GetWindowWord (hWnd, GWW_HINSTANCE) ;
    lpfnDlgProc = MakeProcInstance (FileOpenProc,
            hInstance) ;
    getcwd (cBuf, PATHNAMELONG) ;
    lstrcpy (FOD.szPath, cBuf) ;
    lstrcpy (FOD.szFile, "*.*") ;
    LoadString (hInstance, S_FILEOPEN, cBuf,
            sizeof (cBuf)) ;
    lstrcpy (FOD.szCaption, cBuf) ;
    bFileStatus = DialogBoxParam (hInstance, "FileOpenDlg",
            hWnd, lpfnDlgProc, (DWORD)(LPSTR) &FOD) ;
    FreeProcInstance (lpfnDlgProc) ;
```

As you may recall from the discussion of the file FILEDLG.C program, if a file is typed in or selected, DialogBoxParam() returns TRUE. Selecting the "Cancel" button or not selecting a file results in a returned value of FALSE. A returned value of TRUE does not guarantee that a valid file was selected. There is always the possibility that the user typed in a file name that does not exist, or which is not in the current subdirectory. OpenFile() is called to open the file for reading, as well as to verify that the file exists. If OpenFile() returns -1, the file could not be opened and an error message is displayed.

```
    if (bFileStatus)            /* if a file was selected */
    {
        CombinePathFile (cBuf, FOD.szPath, FOD.szFile) ;
        nFileHandle = OpenFile (cBuf, &of, OF_READ) ;
        if (nFileHandle == -1)   /* file could not be opened */
        {
            LoadString (hInstance, S_FILENOTOPEN, cBuf2,
                sizeof (cBuf2)) ;
            MessageBox (hWnd, cBuf, cBuf2,
                MB_OK | MB_ICONHAND) ;
        }
```

If OpenFile() did not return -1, the file was opened and can be read. Before any data is read from the file, the file length is determined with a call to _llseek(). Also the old memory buffer attached to the edit control is freed, in effect deleting any data that was being edited.

One of the little tricks in working with edit controls is that the edit control looks for two adjacent null characters to mark the end of the text string displayed in the buffer. To leave room for these terminating null bytes, a local memory buffer two bytes larger than the length of the file is allocated. The file is then read into this buffer using _lread(), and then the last two bytes are set equal to zero (null). Finally, the EM_SETHANDLE message is sent to the edit control, attaching the buffer containing the file data to the control. This makes the text data in the memory buffer visible inside the edit control.

```
        else
        {                               /* determine the file length */
            nFileLong = (int) _llseek (nFileHandle, 0L, 2) ;
                                        /* go back to front of file */
            _llseek (nFileHandle, 0L, 0) ;
                                        /* delete old edit buffer */
            LocalFree (hEditBuf) ;
                                        /* allocate new block */
            hEditBuf = LocalAlloc (LMEM_MOVEABLE,
                    nFileLong + 2) ;
            if (hEditBuf)
            {
                pStr = LocalLock (hEditBuf) ;
                                        /* copy file data to block */
                _lread (nFileHandle, pStr, nFileLong) ;
                _lclose (nFileHandle) ;
                pStr2 = pStr + nFileLong ;
                *pStr2++ = 0 ;
                *pStr2 = 0 ;            /* append two nulls at end */
                LocalUnlock ((HANDLE) pStr) ;
                PostMessage (hEditWindow, EM_SETHANDLE,
                    hEditBuf, 0L) ;
            }
            else
                StringTableMessageBox (hWnd, S_NOTALLOC,
                    S_MEMERROR, MB_OK | MB_ICONHAND) ;
        }
    }
    break ;
```

Writing the data in the edit control's memory buffer requires a similar series of steps. Again the file selection dialog box is used to allow the user to type or select a file name for saving the edit control's data. The entire contents of the edit control's memory buffer (up to the first null character) is copied to the opened file using the _lwrite() function. The logic is so similar to the previous discussion of opening a file, that it will not be repeated here. You can examine the coding in Listing 15-12 under the IDM_SAVE menu item ID number for specific details.

Listing 15-12 FILE2.C

```
/* file2.c   Example using filedlg dialog box procedure */

#include <windows.h>
#include <string.h>       /* needed for strtok() function */
#include <direct.h>       /* needed for getcwd() function */
#include "file2.h"
#include "filedlg.h"      /* needed for structure definition and funct prototype */

int PASCAL WinMain (HANDLE hInstance, HANDLE hPrevInstance, LPSTR lpszCmdLine,
    int nCmdShow)
{
```

```
    HWND        hWnd ;                  /* the window's "handle" */
    MSG         msg ;                   /* a message structure */
    WNDCLASS    wndclass ;              /* window class structure */
    char        cBuf [128] ;/* character buffer */

    if (!hPrevInstance)
    {
        wndclass.style          = CS_HREDRAW | CS_VREDRAW ;
        wndclass.lpfnWndProc    = WndProc ;
        wndclass.cbClsExtra     = 0 ;
        wndclass.cbWndExtra     = 0 ;
        wndclass.hInstance      = hInstance ;
        wndclass.hIcon          = LoadIcon (hInstance, "MyIcon") ;
        wndclass.hCursor        = LoadCursor (NULL, IDC_ARROW) ;
        wndclass.hbrBackground  = GetStockObject (WHITE_BRUSH) ;
        wndclass.lpszMenuName   = "MyMenu" ;
        wndclass.lpszClassName  = "MyClass" ;
                        /* register the window class */
        if (!RegisterClass (&wndclass))
            return 0 ;
    }
    LoadString (hInstance, S_PROGRAMCAPTION, cBuf, sizeof (cBuf)) ;

    hWnd = CreateWindow ("MyClass", cBuf, WS_OVERLAPPEDWINDOW,
        CW_USEDEFAULT, CW_USEDEFAULT, CW_USEDEFAULT, CW_USEDEFAULT,
        NULL, NULL, hInstance, NULL) ;
    ShowWindow (hWnd, nCmdShow) ;           /* display the window */

    while (GetMessage (&msg, NULL, NULL, NULL))  /* message loop */
    {
        TranslateMessage (&msg) ;           /* translate keyboard messages */
        DispatchMessage (&msg) ;            /* send message to WndProc() */
    }
    return (msg.wParam) ;
}

long FAR PASCAL WndProc (HWND hWnd, WORD wMessage, WORD wParam, LONG lParam)
{
    static FILEOPENDATA FOD ;               /* defined in filedlg.h */
    HANDLE              hInstance ;
    static  HANDLE      hEditBuf ;
    FARPROC             lpfnDlgProc ;
    static HWND         hEditWindow ;
    BOOL                bFileStatus ;
    int                 nFileHandle, nFileLong ;
    OFSTRUCT            of ;
    char                cBuf [PATHNAMELONG], cBuf2 [128] ;
    PSTR                pStr, pStr2 ;

    switch (wMessage)       /* process windows messages */
    {
        case WM_CREATE:     /* create edit window, and link mem buffer */
            hInstance = GetWindowWord (hWnd, GWW_HINSTANCE) ;
            hEditWindow = CreateWindow ("EDIT", "",
                WS_CHILD | WS_VISIBLE | ES_AUTOVSCROLL | ES_MULTILINE |
                ES_LEFT | ES_NOHIDESEL | WS_VSCROLL| ES_AUTOHSCROLL |
                WS_HSCROLL, 0, 0, 1, 1, hWnd, NULL, hInstance, NULL) ;
                        /* get rid of default edit buffer */
            hEditBuf = (HANDLE) SendMessage (hEditWindow,
```

```
                    EM_GETHANDLE, 0, 0L) ;
            if (hEditBuf)
                LocalFree (hEditBuf) ;
                            /* allocate a new edit buffer */
            hEditBuf = LocalAlloc (LMEM_MOVEABLE | LMEM_ZEROINIT, 100) ;
            PostMessage (hEditWindow, EM_SETHANDLE, hEditBuf, 0L) ;
            break ;
        case WM_SIZE:       /* keep edit control filling client area */
            MoveWindow (hEditWindow, 5, 0, LOWORD (lParam) - 5,
                HIWORD (lParam), TRUE) ;
            break ;
        case WM_COMMAND:
            switch (wParam)                         /* menu items */
            {
                case IDM_OPEN:
                    hInstance = GetWindowWord (hWnd, GWW_HINSTANCE) ;
                    lpfnDlgProc = MakeProcInstance (FileOpenProc,
                            hInstance) ;
                    getcwd (cBuf, PATHNAMELONG) ;
                    lstrcpy (FOD.szPath, cBuf) ;
                    lstrcpy (FOD.szFile, "*.*") ;
                    LoadString (hInstance, S_FILEOPEN, cBuf,
                            sizeof (cBuf)) ;
                    lstrcpy (FOD.szCaption, cBuf) ;
                    bFileStatus = DialogBoxParam (hInstance, "FileOpenDlg",
                            hWnd, lpfnDlgProc, (DWORD)(LPSTR) &FOD) ;
                    FreeProcInstance (lpfnDlgProc) ;
                    if (bFileStatus)                /* if a file was opened */
                    {
                        CombinePathFile (cBuf, FOD.szPath, FOD.szFile) ;
                        nFileHandle = OpenFile (cBuf, &of, OF_READ) ;
                        if (nFileHandle == -1)
                        {
                            LoadString (hInstance, S_FILENOTOPEN, cBuf2,
                                    sizeof (cBuf2)) ;
                            MessageBox (hWnd, cBuf, cBuf2,
                                    MB_OK | MB_ICONHAND) ;
                        }
                        else            /* file is open, so read it */
                        {               /* file name = window title */
                            SetWindowText (hWnd, cBuf) ;
                                        /* find the length of file */
                            nFileLong = (int) _llseek (nFileHandle, 0L, 2) ;
                                        /* go back to front of file */
                            _llseek (nFileHandle, 0L, 0) ;
                                        /* delete old edit buffer */
                            LocalFree (hEditBuf) ;
                                        /* allocate new block */
                            hEditBuf = LocalAlloc (LMEM_MOVEABLE,
                                    nFileLong + 2) ;
                            if (hEditBuf)
                            {
                                pStr = LocalLock (hEditBuf) ;
                                            /* copy file data to block */
                                _lread (nFileHandle, pStr, nFileLong) ;
                                _lclose (nFileHandle) ;
                                pStr2 = pStr + nFileLong ;
                                *pStr2++ = 0 ;
```

```
                        *pStr2 = 0 ;    /* append two nulls at end */
                        LocalUnlock ((HANDLE) pStr) ;
                        PostMessage (hEditWindow, EM_SETHANDLE,
                                hEditBuf, 0L) ;
                    }
                    else
                        StringTableMessageBox (hWnd, S_NOTALLOC,
                                S_MEMERROR, MB_OK | MB_ICONHAND) ;
                }
            }
            break ;
        case IDM_SAVE:
            hInstance = GetWindowWord (hWnd, GWW_HINSTANCE) ;
            lpfnDlgProc = MakeProcInstance (FileOpenProc,
                hInstance) ;
            getcwd (cBuf, PATHNAMELONG) ;
            lstrcpy (FOD.szPath, cBuf) ;
            lstrcpy (FOD.szFile, "*.*") ;
            LoadString (hInstance, S_FILEWRITE, cBuf,
                sizeof (cBuf)) ;
            lstrcpy (FOD.szCaption, cBuf) ;
            bFileStatus = DialogBoxParam (hInstance, "FileOpenDlg",
                hWnd, lpfnDlgProc, (DWORD)(LPSTR) &FOD) ;
            FreeProcInstance (lpfnDlgProc) ;
            if (bFileStatus)                /* if a file was opened */
            {
                CombinePathFile (cBuf, FOD.szPath, FOD.szFile) ;
                nFileHandle = OpenFile (cBuf, &of, OF_CREATE) ;
                if (nFileHandle == -1)
                {
                    LoadString (hInstance, S_FILENOTCREATE, cBuf2,
                        sizeof (cBuf2)) ;
                    MessageBox (hWnd, cBuf, cBuf2,
                        MB_OK | MB_ICONHAND) ;
                }
                else
                {                       /* file name = window title */
                    SetWindowText (hWnd, cBuf) ;
                                        /* copy whole edit buffer to file */
                    nFileLong = FindEditSize (hEditBuf) ;
                    pStr = LocalLock (hEditBuf) ;
                    _lwrite (nFileHandle, pStr, nFileLong) ;
                    _lclose (nFileHandle) ;
                    LocalUnlock (hEditBuf) ;
                }
            }
            break ;
        case IDM_ABOUT:
            StringTableMessageBox (hWnd, S_ABOUTTEXT, S_ABOUTCAPTION,
                MB_OK | MB_ICONINFORMATION) ;
            break ;
        case IDM_QUIT:                  /* "Quit" menu item */
            DestroyWindow (hWnd) ;      /* destroy window, */
            break ;                     /* terminating application */
        }
        break ;
    case WM_DESTROY:                    /* stop application */
        LocalFree (hEditBuf) ;
```

```
                PostQuitMessage (0) ;
                break ;
        default:                            /* default windows message processing */
                return (DefWindowProc (hWnd, wMessage, wParam, lParam)) ;
    }
    return (0L) ;
}

/* display a message box based on two string table entries */

int StringTableMessageBox (HWND hWnd, int nString, int nCaption, WORD
    wFlags)
{
    char    cBuf1 [128], cBuf2 [128] ;
    HANDLE  hInstance ;

    hInstance = GetWindowWord (hWnd, GWW_HINSTANCE) ;
    LoadString (hInstance, nString, cBuf1, sizeof (cBuf1)) ;
    LoadString (hInstance, nCaption, cBuf2, sizeof (cBuf2)) ;
    return (MessageBox (hWnd, cBuf1, cBuf2, wFlags)) ;
}

/* find the end of the edit buffer text by locating null byte */

WORD FindEditSize (HANDLE hEditBuf)
{
    int     i ;
    PSTR    pStr ;

    i = 0 ;
    pStr = LocalLock (hEditBuf) ;
    while (*pStr++ != 0)
        i++ ;

    LocalUnlock (hEditBuf) ;
    return (i) ;
}
```

Listing 15-13 shows the FILE2.H header file.

Listing 15-13 FILE2.H Header File

```
/* file2.h */

#define IDM_OPEN            1       /* menu item ID numbers */
#define IDM_SAVE            2
#define IDM_ABOUT           3
#define IDM_QUIT            10

#define S_PROGRAMCAPTION    1       /* string table ID numbers */
#define S_FILENOTOPEN       2
#define S_NOTALLOC          3
#define S_MEMERROR          4
#define S_ABOUTTEXT         5
```

```
#define S_ABOUTCAPTION    6
#define S_FILENOTCREATE   7
#define S_FILEOPEN        8
#define S_FILEWRITE       9

long FAR PASCAL WndProc (HWND, WORD, WORD, LONG) ;
int StringTableMessageBox (HWND hWnd, int nString, int nCaption, WORD
   wFlags) ;
WORD FindEditSize (HANDLE hEditBuf) ;
```

Note in Listing 15-14 that the FILE2.RC file includes the FILEDLG.RC resource script file. This compiles the resource data from FILEDLG.RC along with the FILE2 program's own resources, adding the file selection dialog box to the finished program.

Listing 15-14 FILE2.RC Resource Script File

```
/* file2.rc  resource file */

#include <windows.h>
#include "file2.h"
#include "filedlg.h"
#include "filedlg.rc"       /* add the filedlg resources */

MyIcon      ICON    file2.ico

MyMenu      MENU
BEGIN
    POPUP   "&File"
    BEGIN
        MENUITEM "&Open File",   IDM_OPEN
        MENUITEM "&Save File",   IDM_SAVE
        MENUITEM SEPARATOR
        MENUITEM "&About",       IDM_ABOUT
        MENUITEM "&Quit",        IDM_QUIT
    END
END

STRINGTABLE
BEGIN
    S_PROGRAMCAPTION    "File 2 - Simple Editor"
    S_FILENOTOPEN       "Could Not Open File"
    S_NOTALLOC          "Could not allocate memory."
    S_MEMERROR          "Memory Error"
    S_ABOUTTEXT         "Simple Editor Application"
    S_ABOUTCAPTION      "File 2 Program"
    S_FILENOTCREATE     "Could not open or create file."
    S_FILEOPEN          "Open a file."
    S_FILEWRITE         "Write data to a file."
END
```

The FileOpenProc() function name must be included in the calling program's module definition file (Listing 15-15), so that this function name can be passed to the DialogBoxParam() function.

Listing 15-15 FILE2.DEF Module Definition File

```
NAME            file2
DESCRIPTION     'file2 program'
EXETYPE         WINDOWS
STUB            'WINSTUB.EXE'
CODE            PRELOAD MOVEABLE DISCARDABLE
DATA            PRELOAD MOVEABLE MULTIPLE
HEAPSIZE        1024
STACKSIZE       5120
EXPORTS         WndProc
                FileOpenProc
```

Note that both the FILE2.C and FILEDLG.C programs are compiled, and added to the final program in the linking step, as part of the logic in the project files (Listings 15-16 and 15-17). The program's icon is shown in Figure 15-9

Listing 15-16 Turbo C++ Project File for FILE2

```
file2.c
filedlg.c
file2.def
file2.res
```

Figure 15-9
FILE2.ICO
Icon Image

Listing 15-17 QuickC Project File for FILE2

```
file2.c
filedlg.c
file2.def
file2.rc
```

A Bug

There is an odd bug in the edit control logic under Windows 3.0 and 3.1. For some reason, the fourth character in the edit control will be reduced by one when a memory block is passed to the control using the EM_SETHANDLE message. This is easy to get around, and the "fix" will be presented in Chapter 17, *The Clipboard*, when the simple editor application reaches its last stage of completion. For now, realize that FILE2 needs a bit of work to be a finished editor.

Summary

Windows programs use DOS for disk file operations. This reduces the amount of memory consumed by Windows, as DOS is always loaded before Windows is started. Using DOS file operations also ensures that files created with Windows applications are compatible at the operating system level with files created with DOS programs. The actual organization of the data within the file may be different between DOS and Windows programs, just as different DOS programs have different structures within their file data.

Accessing a disk file is fairly straightforward. The OpenFile() function is used to open an existing file, or to create a new one. OpenFile() returns an integer value, which is called the "file handle," or -1 if the file could not be opened. The file handle is used in all subsequent disk operations. The _llseek() function allows you to move to different locations in the file. The _lread() function reads data from the file, and _lwrite() writes data to the file. When file operations are complete, the _lclose() function must be used to close the file, ensuring that the data is properly recorded on the disk. The file handle no longer refers to the file after a file is closed. If you need to do additional reading and/or writing to the file, the file must be again opened with OpenFile(), and the new file handle used for disk operations. If more than one file is opened at one time, each file will have a different handle value returned by OpenFile().

Windows programs generally make it easy for the user to select a file and/or file subdirectory using a file selection dialog box. Windows provides the DlgDirList() function to fill a list box in a dialog box with a set of file names, and the DlgDirSelect() function to update a character string with the currently selected file name. These two functions are always used together, and must share the same character buffer holding the current drive/path/file selection string (like "C:\WINDOWS*.*"). The FILEDLG program example in this chapter is generalized enough that you should be able to use it in other programs without modification. (Users of Microsoft C++ 7.0 will find a similar function as part of the common dialog tools—a rather nice file selection dialog box, including bitmap images of file folders in the list boxes).

QUESTIONS

1. Windows provides two functions that can be used to open an existing file, _____ and _____ .
2. Windows also provides two functions that can be used to create a new file, _____ and _____ .
3. When file operations are complete, the _____ function must be called to ensure that the file is closed, and that all data is physically recorded on the disk media.
4. To move to a location in an open file 25 bytes before the end of the file, use the following call to the _llseek() function: a) _llseek(hFile, 25, 0) ; b) _llseek (hFile, -25, 0) ; c) _llseek (hFile, -25, 2) ; d) none of the above.
5. To link a local memory buffer containing text to an edit control, send the following message to the edit control window: a) EM_SETHANDLE; b) EM_GETHANDLE; c) EM_SETSEL ; d) WM_COPY.
6. OpenFile() will return a value of _____ if the file could not be opened.
7. To add new data to the end of an existing file, the entire contents of the file must be created in a memory block, and then copied to the disk file. (True/False).
8. To fill a list box in a dialog box with only the names of valid drive letters, you would use the following call to DlgDirList():

    a) DlgDirList (hDlg, "C:*.*", DLI_LIST, DLI_STATIC, 0xC000) ;
    b) DlgDirList (hDlg, "", DLI_LIST, DLI_STATIC, 0xC000) ;
    c) DlgDirList (hDlg, "", DLI_LIST, DLI_STATIC, 0x4000) ;
    d) a or b.

9. Selecting a new drive or subdirectory from a dialog box filled with DlgDirList(), and updated with DlgDirSelect(), will result in the current working subdirectory for the drive. This may impact the subdirectory that other Windows programs first display in their file selection dialog boxes. (True/False).
10. To determine the current working drive/directory, use the _____ function, which is a C compiler library function, not a part of Windows.

EXERCISES

1. Modify the FILE1.C program so that the initial character string copied to the TESTFILE.TXT file is a string table entry in the program's resource script file, rather than the alphabet.
2. Modify the FILE1.C program so that the "Append File" menu item causes every other character to be changed to lowercase in the disk file, as shown in Figure 15-10. Make the changes to the disk file without reading the file into memory. In other words, write the new lowercase characters to the disk file individually.

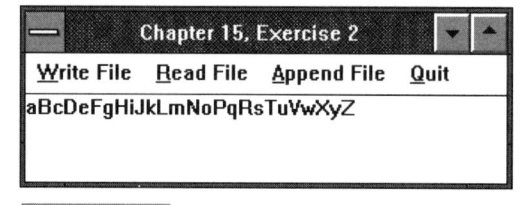

Figure 15-10 The C15EXER2 Program

ANSWERS TO QUESTIONS

1. OpenFile(), _lopen().
2. OpenFile(), _lcreat().
3. _lclose().
4. c.
5. a.
6. -1.
7. False. You can append data to an existing file without changing the current file contents.
8. d.
9. True.
10. getcwd().

SOLUTIONS TO EXERCISES

1. First, add a new entry in the program's header file for the ID number of the new string table entry:

   ```
   #define S_FILETEXT       9
   ```

   Second, add the new string table entry to the program's resource script file:

   ```
   S_FILETEXT      "This is a stringtable text entry."
   ```

   Finally, modify the program so that the string table entry is copied to a buffer, and the buffer is then copied to the disk file. You can either allocate a local memory buffer, or just use a character array, as shown in this program excerpt:

   ```
   char        cBuf [128] ;
   HANDLE      hInstance ;

   switch (wMessage)                    /* process windows messages */
   {
      case WM_COMMAND:
          switch (wParam)       /* menu items */
          {
              case IDM_WRITE: /* write to the file */
                nFileHandle = OpenFile ("testfile.txt", &of,
                OF_CREATE) ;
                if (nFileHandle == -1)
                StringTableMessageBox (hWnd, S_NOCREATE,
                S_FILEERROR, MB_OK | MB_ICONHAND) ;
              else
              {
                hInstance = GetWindowWord (hWnd, GWW_HINSTANCE) ;
                LoadString (hInstance, S_FILETEXT, cBuf,
                sizeof (cBuf)) ;
                          /* write data to file */
   ```

Chapter 15 • Disk File Access

SOLUTIONS TO EXERCISES (cont'd)

```
            _lwrite (nFileHandle, cBuf, lstrlen (cBuf)) ;
            _lclose (nFileHandle) ;    /* close file */
            StringTableMessageBox (hWnd, S_CREATED,
                S_MESSAGE, MB_OK | MB_ICONINFORMATION) ;
        }
        break ;
```
[Other program lines]

The complete solution is given under the file name C15EXER1 on the source code disks.

2. The key to changing every other character in the disk file is to repeatedly call the _llseek() function to move forward in the file. Listing 15-18 shows the modifications to the FILE1.C program, for the portion that handles the selection of the "Append File" menu item. _lwrite() is called to write only one character at a time. Writing a character advances the file position pointer one byte in the file. To write on every second location, _llseek() is then called to advance one more byte.

Listing 15-18 Solution to Chapter 15, Exercise 2

```
case IDM_ADD:
    nFileHandle = OpenFile ("testfile.txt", &of, OF_READWRITE) ;
    if (nFileHandle == -1)
        StringTableMessageBox (hWnd, S_NOOPEN,
            S_FILEERROR, MB_OK | MB_ICONHAND) ;
    else
    {       /* write lower case letter at alternate locations */
        for (i = 0 ; i < 26 ; i += 2)
        {           /* write 1 char, then move forward */
            cBuf [0] = 'a' + i ;
            _lwrite (nFileHandle, cBuf, 1) ;
            _llseek (nFileHandle, 1L, 1) ;
        }
        _lclose (nFileHandle) ; /* close file */
    }
```
[Other program lines]

The complete solution is given under the file name C15EXER2 on the source code disks.

CHAPTER 16

Bitmaps

So far the example programs using graphics in this book have called GDI functions, such as Ellipse() and Rectangle(), to do the drawing. GDI functions are ideal for geometric shapes, but are not convenient for a realistic image like a person's face. More realistic images can be created with painting programs, like the Windows Paint application, that allow the color of each pixel to be edited. These images are known as bitmaps, as each color "bit" of the picture is stored individually. We have been using a limited form of bitmap for the program icon images that were created with the Borland Resource Workshop or Microsoft Image Editor. Icons are small bitmaps, but limited to certain sizes that Windows can conveniently display when an application is minimized. The image editors will also allow you to create and save images of any size using the Windows bitmap format, limited only by the resolution of your system's video equipment.

Bitmaps are records of each pixel's color in a picture drawn on a computer's screen. Bitmaps have the advantage of being able to save any picture, no matter how complex. The disadvantage of bitmaps is that they take up a lot of space, as every pixel's color must be recorded individually.

Windows provides a number of useful functions for manipulating bitmap images. You can use a bitmap as a brush pattern, stretch and compress bitmap images, and paste them on the screen with different effects depending on the screen image "under" the bitmap.

Bitmaps also find their way into animated graphics. Windows allows you to "draw" on a memory bitmap. Memory bitmaps imitate the screen's organization for saving each pixel's color. When all of the drawing is completed, the memory bitmap can be "pasted" onto the screen, making the complete image visible at once. This has the advantage that the drawing operations take place in the background, so the user sees the complete new image appear in one quick action.

Concepts Covered

Loading a Bitmap Resource
Creating a Memory
   Device Context
Displaying a Bitmap

Stretching or Shrinking a Bitmap
Raster Operation Codes
Filling an Area with a Bitmap Brush
Device Dependent vs. Device Independent
   Bitmaps

Keywords Covered

BLACKNESS
DSTINVERT
MERGECOPY
MERGEPAINT
NOTSRCCOPY
NOTSRCERASE
PATCOPY
PATINVERT
PATPAINT

SRCAND
SRCCOPY
SRCERASE
SRCINVERT
SRCPAINT
WHITENESS
BITMAP
DIB

Functions Covered

LoadBitmap()
CreateCompatibleDC()
BitBlt()

StretchBlt()
CreatePatternBrush()
PatBlt()

How Bitmaps Store Images

Imagine that you have been using the Windows Paintbrush application to draw a picture. Although Paintbrush allows you to draw rectangles, lines, and other objects, the actual data for the picture is recorded one pixel at a time. Each pixel can have a different color, so if you save the color of each pixel, you have captured the entire image. This is exactly what Paintbrush does, when it saves a picture as a bitmap file. Figure 16-1 illustrates the relationship between a picture and the bitmap data that stores the image.

The amount of data that it takes to store a bitmap depends on the size of the picture, and on the number of colors the bitmap uses. For black and white systems, only one bit is needed for each pixel. The bit can be set to one for white, and to zero for black. For color images, more bits are required. A 16-color VGA display requires four bits per pixel, while a "true color" display will need three bytes (24 bits) per pixel to specify each color.

Bitmaps are not efficient ways to store large images. For example, saving a VGA screen requires 640 X 480 X 4 = 806,400 bits, or about 100K bytes of storage. Normally, you will use bitmaps for smaller images, particularly images that are difficult to recreate using GDI functions, such as Rectangle() and Ellipse(). Bitmaps are easy to create. You can use the Windows Paintbrush application, or the graphic editor that comes with your Windows development tools. Microsoft calls its editor the "Image Editor," and the Borland editor is part of the Resource Workshop. These are the same tools we used to create custom cursors and icons in previous chapters. All of these applications save the images you create as bitmap files, with the extension ".BMP."

Loading a Bitmap File

The most common use of bitmaps is to display small images as part of a program's operations. Bitmaps normally do not change as the program operates (bitmaps are static data), so the ideal place to store bitmap information is with the program's resource data. First, create the bitmap image using your favorite editor, and save it in the

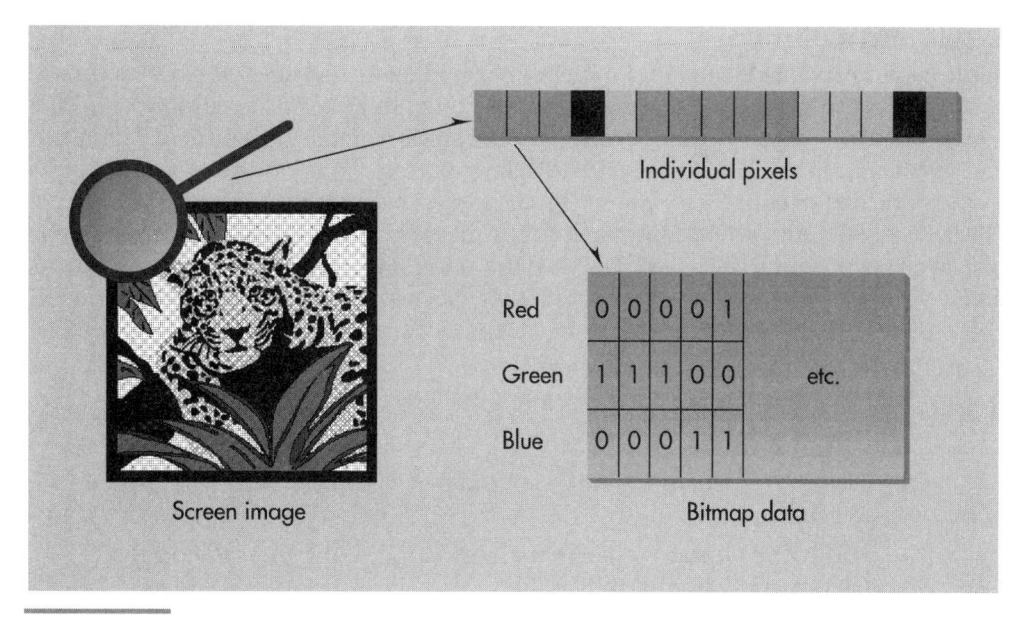

Figure 16-1 How a Bitmap Stores Image Data

same subdirectory that you will use for your program files. Second, add a BITMAP line to your program's resource script file, as follows:

```
ImageBmp    BITMAP    image.bmp
```

This adds the data in the IMAGE.BMP bitmap file to the program's resources and gives the bitmap data the name "ImageBmp." The format of this line in the resource script statement should look familiar; it is identical to the way in which cursor images and icons are added to a program's resources. Cursor images and icons are actually just specialized forms of bitmaps, which must use certain sizes and limited colors. Bitmap data is the most flexible, as the bitmap can have any size and can take advantage of high resolution color equipment.

```
ImageBmp    BITMAP    image.bmp    /* loading a bitmap file into the resource data */
HandCurs    CURSOR    hand.cur     /* loading a cursor file into the resource data */
ProgIcon    ICON      test.ico     /* loading an icon file into the resource data */
```

When you want to display a bitmap, the bitmap data must be read from the program's resource data and loaded into memory. The LoadBitmap() function does this, and it returns a handle to the bitmap data in memory.

```
HBITMAP     hBitmap ;
HANDLE      hInstance ;

hInstance = GetWindowWord (hWnd, GWW_HINSTANCE) ;
hBitmap = LoadBitmap (hInstance, "HouseBmp") ;
```

Displaying a Bitmap

With the bitmap data loaded into memory, you are ready to display the bitmap image on the screen. This is a little more involved than you might expect. Windows uses the concept of a *memory device context* to convert from the format of the bitmap data file to the physical format used by the screen display or printer. A memory device context is just like the device context for the screen or printer, except that it is not tied to a specific device. You must select a bitmap into the memory device context, before it can be displayed on a physical device. Selecting the bitmap into a memory device context gives Windows a chance to figure out whether the color data needs to be organized in color planes (like a VGA card uses) or needs to use adjacent color bits.

The steps needed to display a bitmap are:

1. Load the bitmap data into memory with LoadBitmap().
2. Create a memory device context with CreateCompatibleDC().
3. Select the bitmap into the memory device context with SelectObject().
4. Copy the bitmap from the memory device context to the output device context with BitBlt().

Figure 16-2 shows a graphical image of how these functions interact to produce the final bitmap image. The CreateCompatibleDC() function creates a memory device con-

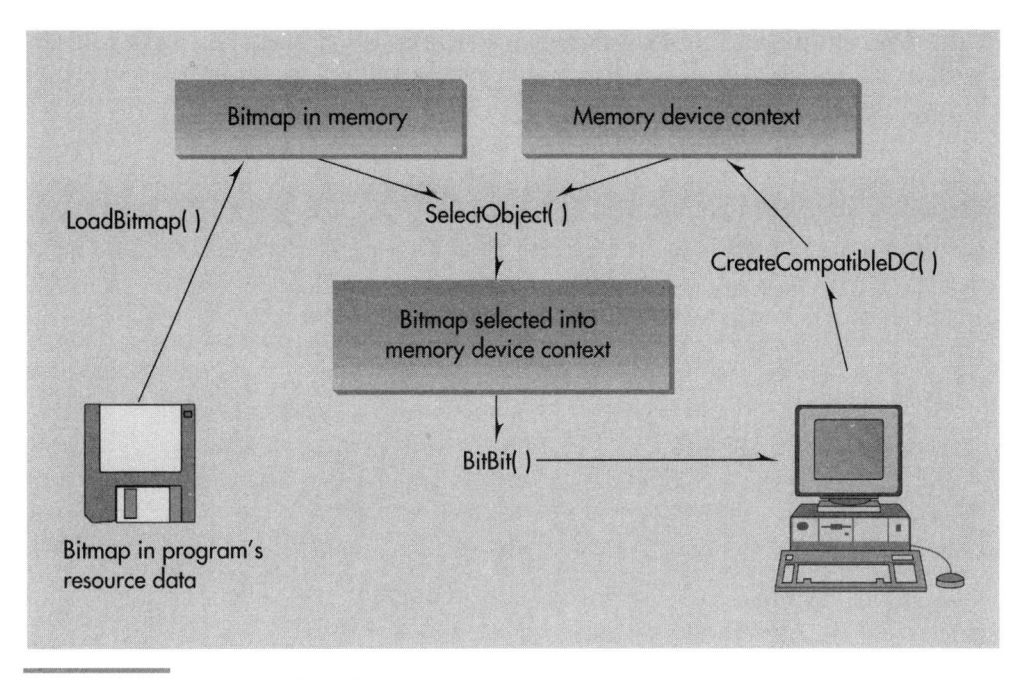

Figure 16-2 Steps to Display a Bitmap Image

text with the same physical attributes as the device context of your video system or printer. When you call SelectObject() and select the bitmap into the memory device context, Windows sets up the bitmap data with the exact sequence of data needed to display the data on the physical device. This makes the last step, calling BitBlt(), very fast. BitBlt() stuffs the bitmap bits from the memory device context right into the output device. Here is a typical sequence of function calls to display a bitmap.

```
HDC        hDC, hMemDC ;
HBITMAP    hBitmap ;
HANDLE     hInstance ;

hInstance = GetWindowWord (hWnd, GWW_HINSTANCE) ;    /* get the instance handle */
hBitmap = LoadBitmap (hInstance, "Bitmap32by32") ;   /* load the bitmap resource */

hDC = GetDC (hWnd) ;                                 /* get DC for client area */
hMemDC = CreateCompatibleDC (hDC) ;                  /* create memory DC */
SelectObject (hMemDC, hBitmap) ;                     /* select bitmap into mem DC */
BitBlt (hDC, 10, 20, 32, 32, hMemDC, 0, 0, SRCCOPY) ; /* paint bitmap onto screen */
DeleteDC (hMemDC) ;                                  /* clean up */
ReleaseDC (hWnd, hDC) ;
DeleteObject (hBitmap) ;
```

BitBlt() takes a number of parameters, which can be understood by looking at this example. The bitmap was created as a 32 by 32 pixel image and stored as resource data. BitBlt() is called to display the image at location 10,20 on the window's client area, with an output height and width of 32 pixels each. The bitmap data is obtained from the hMemDC memory device context, starting with the upper left corner of the bitmap (0,0) point). The flag "SRCCOPY" tells BitBlt() to copy the bitmap to the output device context, covering up any pixels under the bitmap's 32 by 32 square. Here is the full syntax of the BitBlt() function:

BOOL **BitBlt**(HDC *hDC*, int *X*, int *Y*, int *nWidth*, int *nHeight*, HDC *hSrcDC*,
 int *XSrc*, int *YSrc*, DWORD *dwRop*);

hDC   HDC

The device context handle to receive the bitmap.

X   int

The logical X coordinate of the upper left corner of the destination rectangle.

Y   int

The logical Y coordinate of the upper left corner of the destination rectangle.

nWidth   int

The width in logical units of the destination rectangle.

nHeight   int

The height in logical units of the destination rectangle.

hSrcDC   HDC

The device context from which the bitmap will be copied. This is normally a memory device context created with CreateCompatibleDC(). A bitmap is loaded into the memory device context using SelectObject().

XSrc   int

The logical X coordinate of the upper left corner in the source bitmap. Normally 0, for the whole bitmap.

YSrc   int

The logical Y coordinate of the upper right corner in the source bitmap. Normally 0, for the whole bitmap.

dwRop   DWORD

One of the raster operation codes. Fifteen of the 256 possibilities have names defined in WINDOWS.H. You will most often use the SRCCOPY code for this parameter. The remainder are explained later in this chapter under the heading *Raster Operation Codes*.

An Example Program Using BitBlt()

The BITMAP1 program demonstrates loading a bitmap from a program's resource data and displaying the bitmap using a memory device context and BitBlt(). Figure 16-3 shows the BITMAP1 program in action, after the "Show" menu item has been selected.

The bitmap is a 64 by 64 pixel, 16-color bitmap created with the Microsoft Image Editor or Borland Resource Workshop. The center image in Figure 16-3 is the complete bitmap. The left and right images demonstrate the BitBlt() function's ability to display portions of a bitmap image. The left image is the upper left quarter of the bitmap, while the right image shows the lower right quarter.

Figure 16-3 The BITMAP1 Program

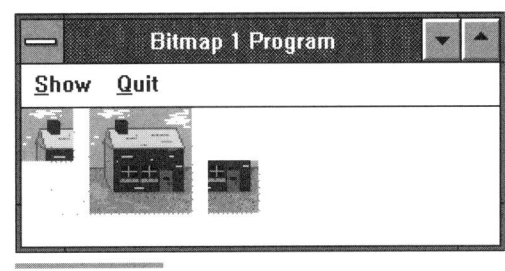

The first step in creating the BITMAP1 program is to create a 64 by 64 pixel bitmap to display. The source code disks include a bitmap named HOUSE.BMP. Figure 16-4 shows a blowup of the HOUSE bitmap in the work area of the Microsoft Image Editor application. The Borland editor in the Resource Workshop is almost identical.

With the bitmap saved as the HOUSE.BMP file, you are ready to add the bitmap data to the program's resources. Listing 16-1 shows the BITMAP1.RC file, which includes both the program's icon file and the HOUSE.BMP file as resource data, along with a simple menu definition and a short string table.

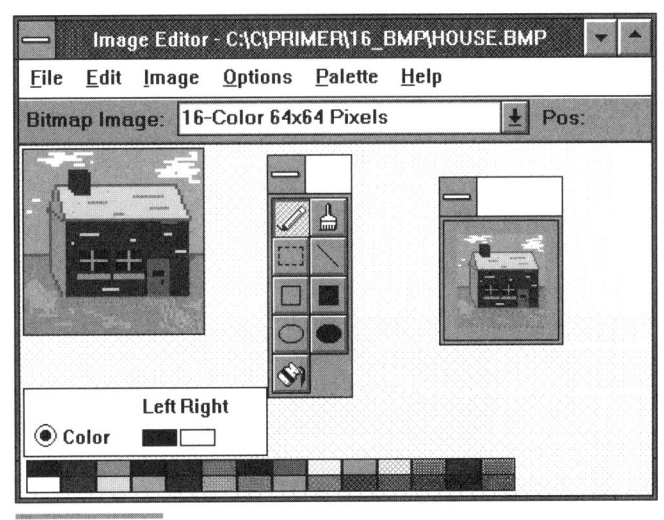

Figure 16-4 Creating the HOUSE Bitmap

Listing 16-1 BITMAP1.RC Resource Script File

```
/* bitmap1.rc resource file */

#include "bitmap1.h"

MyIcon      ICON     bitmap1.ico
HouseBmp    BITMAP   house.bmp

MyMenu      MENU
BEGIN
    MENUITEM "&Show",       IDM_SHOW
    MENUITEM "&Quit",       IDM_QUIT
END
```

```
STRINGTABLE
BEGIN
    S_PROGRAMCAPTION   "Bitmap 1 Program"
END
```

The BITMAP1.C program (Listing 16-2) follows the previous discussion of loading and displaying bitmaps closely. The only change is that three calls to the BitBlt() function are made to display different portions of the HOUSE bitmap.

Listing 16-2 BITMAP1.C

```
/* bitmap1.c   BitBlt() example */

#include <windows.h>
#include "bitmap1.h"

int PASCAL WinMain (HANDLE hInstance, HANDLE hPrevInstance, LPSTR lpszCmdLine,
    int nCmdShow)
{
    HWND        hWnd ;              /* the window's "handle" */
    MSG         msg ;               /* a message structure */
    WNDCLASS    wndclass ;          /* window class structure */
    char        cBuf [128] ;

    if (!hPrevInstance)
    {
      wndclass.style         = CS_HREDRAW | CS_VREDRAW ;
      wndclass.lpfnWndProc   = WndProc ;
      wndclass.cbClsExtra    = 0 ;
      wndclass.cbWndExtra    = 0 ;
      wndclass.hInstance     = hInstance ;
      wndclass.hIcon         = LoadIcon (hInstance, "MyIcon") ;
      wndclass.hCursor       = LoadCursor (NULL, IDC_ARROW) ;
      wndclass.hbrBackground = GetStockObject (WHITE_BRUSH) ;
      wndclass.lpszMenuName  = "MyMenu" ;
      wndclass.lpszClassName = "MyClass" ;
                       /* register the window class */
      if (!RegisterClass (&wndclass))
          return 0 ;
    }
    LoadString (hInstance, S_PROGRAMCAPTION, cBuf, sizeof (cBuf)) ;

    hWnd = CreateWindow ("MyClass", cBuf, WS_OVERLAPPEDWINDOW,
        CW_USEDEFAULT, CW_USEDEFAULT, CW_USEDEFAULT, CW_USEDEFAULT,
        NULL, NULL, hInstance, NULL) ;
    ShowWindow (hWnd, nCmdShow) ;     /* display the window */

    while (GetMessage (&msg, NULL, NULL, NULL))   /* message loop */
    {
       TranslateMessage (&msg) ;     /* translate keyboard messages */
       DispatchMessage (&msg) ;      /* send message to WndProc() */
    }
    return (msg.wParam) ;
}
```

```
long FAR PASCAL WndProc (HWND hWnd, WORD wMessage, WORD wParam, LONG lParam)
{
    HDC             hDC, hMemDC ;
    HBITMAP         hBitmap ;
    HANDLE          hInstance ;

    switch (wMessage)       /* process windows messages */
    {
        case WM_COMMAND:
            switch (wParam)
            {
                case IDM_SHOW:
                    hInstance = GetWindowWord (hWnd, GWW_HINSTANCE) ;
                    hBitmap = LoadBitmap (hInstance, "HouseBmp") ;
                    hDC = GetDC (hWnd) ;
                    hMemDC = CreateCompatibleDC (hDC) ;
                    SelectObject (hMemDC, hBitmap) ;
                            /* show top left corner at 0,0 */
                    BitBlt (hDC, 0, 0, 32, 32, hMemDC, 0, 0, SRCCOPY) ;
                            /* show entire 64x64 bitmap at 42,0 */
                    BitBlt (hDC, 42, 0, 64, 64, hMemDC, 0, 0, SRCCOPY) ;
                            /* show bottom right corner at 116,32 */
                    BitBlt (hDC, 116, 32, 32, 32, hMemDC, 32, 32, SRCCOPY) ;
                    DeleteDC (hMemDC) ;
                    ReleaseDC (hWnd, hDC) ;
                    DeleteObject (hBitmap) ;
                    break ;
                case IDM_QUIT:                  /* Quit menu item */
                    DestroyWindow (hWnd) ;      /* destroy window, */
                    break ;         /* terminating application */
            }
            break ;
        case WM_DESTROY:    /* stop application */
            PostQuitMessage (0) ;
            break ;
        default:                /* default windows message processing */
            return (DefWindowProc (hWnd, wMessage, wParam, lParam)) ;
    }
    return (0L) ;
}
```

Listings 16-3 to 16-6 show the remaining support files for BITMAP1. The program's icon is shown in Figure 16-5.

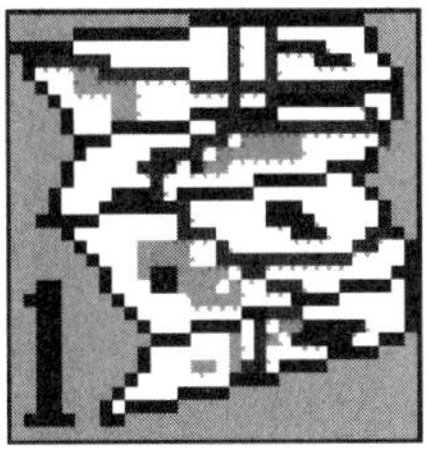

Listing 16-3 BITMAP1.H Header File

```
/* bitmap1.h header file */

#define IDM_SHOW            1       /* menu item ID numbers */
#define IDM_QUIT            10

#define S_PROGRAMCAPTION    1       /* string table ID numbers */

long FAR PASCAL WndProc (HWND, WORD, WORD, LONG) ;
```

Figure 16-5
BITMAP1.ICO
Icon Image

Listing 16-4 BITMAP1.DEF Module Definition File

```
NAME            bitmap1
DESCRIPTION     'bitmap1 application'
EXETYPE         WINDOWS
STUB            'WINSTUB.EXE'
CODE            PRELOAD MOVEABLE DISCARDABLE
DATA            PRELOAD MOVEABLE MULTIPLE
HEAPSIZE        1024
STACKSIZE       5120
EXPORTS         WndProc
```

Listing 16-5 Turbo C++ Project File for BITMAP1

```
bitmap1.c
bitmap1.def
bitmap1.res
```

Listing 16-6 QuickC Project File for BITMAP1

```
bitmap1.c
bitmap1.def
bitmap1.rc
```

Stretching and Compressing a Bitmap

The BitBlt() function is delightfully fast, once the bitmap data has been selected into a memory device context. You can happily "blit" the same image all over the output device context. Although BitBlt() can output pieces of a bitmap, it cannot increase or reduce the size of a bitmap. Windows includes the StretchBlt() function as an alternative to BitBlt() when the bitmap needs to be changed in size. StretchBlt() takes the same parameters as BitBlt(), plus two more. You specify not only the location of the top left corner of the output bitmap, but also its width and length. The source bitmap will be stretched or compressed to fill out the specified size. Here is the syntax of the StretchBlt() function:

BOOL **StretchBlt**(HDC *hDestDC*, int *X*, int *Y*, int *nWidth*, int *nHeight*, HDC *hSrcDC*, int *XSrc*, int *YSrc*, int *nSrcWidth*, int *nSrcHeight*, DWORD *dwRop*);

hDestDC	HDC
	The output device context handle. This is typically the device context for a window's client area, or the printer.
X	int
	The logical *X* coordinate of the upper left corner of the bitmap on the output device context.

Y	int

The logical Y coordinate of the upper left corner of the bitmap on the output.

nWidth	int

The width in logical units of the output bitmap.

nHeight	int

The height in logical units of the output bitmap.

hSrcDC	HDC

The device context from which the bitmap will be copied. This is normally a memory device context created with CreateCompatibleDC(). A bitmap is loaded into the memory device context using SelectObject().

XSrc	int

The logical X coordinate of the upper left corner of the source bitmap. Normally zero.

YSrc	int

The logical Y coordinate of the upper right corner of the source bitmap. Normally zero.

nSrcWidth	int

The width of the source bitmap in logical units. If the default coordinate system is being used for *hSrcDC*, this is the width in pixels.

nSrcHeight	int

The height of the source bitmap in logical units. If the default coordinate system is being used for *hSrcDC*, this is the height in pixels.

dwRop	DWORD

One of the raster operation codes. Fifteen of the 256 possibilities have names defined in WINDOWS.H. You will most often use the code SRCCOPY for this parameter. The remaining codes are explained later in this chapter, under the heading *Raster Operation Codes*.

Using StretchBlt()

The BITMAP2 example program demonstrates the StretchBlt() function, by both shrinking and expanding the HOUSE.BMP bitmap image used in the last example. Figure 16-6 shows the BITMAP2 program in operation. From left to right, the images are: 1) half size; 2) full size; 3) doubled size; and 4) four times original size, but only displaying the upper left corner of the image. All of these images are created with calls to the StretchBlt() function, shrinking and expanding the same bitmap image after it has been selected into a memory device context.

If you examine the diagonal lines in Figure 16-6, you will notice that the lines become increasingly jagged as the image is enlarged. This is inevitable, as the StretchBlt()

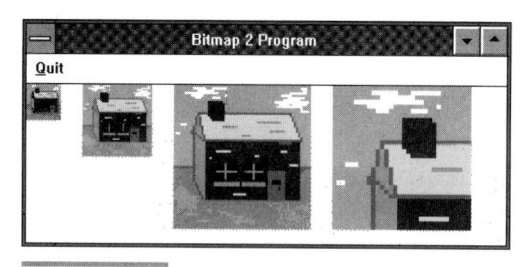

Figure 16-6 The BITMAP2 Program

function simply adds pixels with the same colors as the original pixels, to fill in the image as it is expanded. Although it is not obvious in looking at the smallest image in Figure 16-6, StretchBlt() eliminates pixels when the image is reduced in size. You can change the logic used to eliminate pixels using the SetStretch-BltMode() function, but no matter what you do, pixels must disappear for an image to become smaller. As a general rule, bitmaps become unacceptably altered when they are increased or decreased in size by more than a factor of two. If you need broader scaling than this, consider storing multiple bitmaps of the same image, each with different sizes.

Listing 16-7 shows the BITMAP2.C program. BITMAP2.C is almost identical to the previous BITMAP1.C example, except that the StretchBlt() function has been substituted for the BitBlt() function. StretchBlt() is not as fast as BitBlt(), so you will only want to use StretchBlt() if the bitmap must be changed in scale. The other change to BITMAP2.C is that the painting logic has been placed in the WM_PAINT message processing section, so that the images are repainted automatically.

Listing 16-7 BITMAP2.C

```
/* bitmap2.c   stretching a bitmap example */

#include <windows.h>
#include "bitmap2.h"

int PASCAL WinMain (HANDLE hInstance, HANDLE hPrevInstance, LPSTR lpszCmdLine,
    int nCmdShow)
{
    HWND         hWnd ;             /* the window's "handle" */
    MSG          msg ;              /* a message structure */
    WNDCLASS     wndclass ;         /* window class structure */
    char         cBuf [128] ;

    if (!hPrevInstance)
    {
        wndclass.style          = CS_HREDRAW | CS_VREDRAW ;
        wndclass.lpfnWndProc    = WndProc ;
        wndclass.cbClsExtra     = 0 ;
        wndclass.cbWndExtra     = 0 ;
        wndclass.hInstance      = hInstance ;
        wndclass.hIcon          = LoadIcon (hInstance, "MyIcon") ;
        wndclass.hCursor        = LoadCursor (NULL, IDC_ARROW) ;
        wndclass.hbrBackground  = GetStockObject (WHITE_BRUSH) ;
        wndclass.lpszMenuName   = "MyMenu" ;
        wndclass.lpszClassName  = "MyClass" ;
               /* register the window class */
        if (!RegisterClass (&wndclass))
            return 0 ;
```

```
        }
        LoadString (hInstance, S_PROGRAMCAPTION, cBuf, sizeof (cBuf)) ;

        hWnd = CreateWindow ("MyClass", cBuf, WS_OVERLAPPEDWINDOW,
            CW_USEDEFAULT, CW_USEDEFAULT, CW_USEDEFAULT, CW_USEDEFAULT,
            NULL, NULL, hInstance, NULL) ;
        ShowWindow (hWnd, nCmdShow) ;       /* display the window */

        while (GetMessage (&msg, NULL, NULL, NULL))   /* message loop */
        {
            TranslateMessage (&msg) ;       /* translate keyboard messages */
            DispatchMessage (&msg) ;        /* send message to WndProc() */
        }
        return (msg.wParam) ;
}

long FAR PASCAL WndProc (HWND hWnd, WORD wMessage, WORD wParam, LONG lParam)
{
    HBITMAP         hBitmap ;
    HANDLE          hInstance ;
    PAINTSTRUCT     ps ;
    HDC             hMemDC ;

    switch (wMessage)                       /* process windows messages */
    {
        case WM_COMMAND:
            switch (wParam)
            {
                case IDM_QUIT:              /* Quit menu item */
                    DestroyWindow (hWnd) ;  /* destroy window, */
                    break ;                 /* terminating application */
            }
            break ;
        case WM_PAINT:
            BeginPaint (hWnd, &ps) ;
            hInstance = GetWindowWord (hWnd, GWW_HINSTANCE) ;
            hBitmap = LoadBitmap (hInstance, "HouseBmp") ;
            hMemDC = CreateCompatibleDC (ps.hdc) ;
            SelectObject (hMemDC, hBitmap) ;
            StretchBlt (ps.hdc, 0, 0, 32, 32, hMemDC, 0, 0, 64, 64, SRCCOPY) ;
            StretchBlt (ps.hdc, 52, 0, 64, 64, hMemDC, 0, 0, 64, 64, SRCCOPY) ;
            StretchBlt (ps.hdc, 136, 0, 128, 128, hMemDC, 0, 0, 64, 64, SRCCOPY) ;
            StretchBlt (ps.hdc, 284, 0, 128, 128, hMemDC, 0, 0, 32, 32, SRCCOPY) ;
            EndPaint (hWnd, &ps) ;
            DeleteDC (hMemDC) ;
            DeleteObject (hBitmap) ;
            break ;
        case WM_DESTROY:                    /* stop application */
            PostQuitMessage (0) ;
            break ;
        default:                            /* default windows message processing */
            return (DefWindowProc (hWnd, wMessage, wParam, lParam)) ;
    }
    return (0L) ;
}
```

Listings 16-8 to 16-12 show the support files for BITMAP2. The program's icon is shown in Figure 16-7

Listing 16-8 BITMAP2.H Header File

```
/* bitmap2.h header file */
#define IDM_QUIT       10         /* menu item ID numbers */
#define S_PROGRAMCAPTION  1  /* string table ID numbers */
long FAR PASCAL WndProc (HWND, WORD, WORD, LONG) ;
```

Figure 16-7
BITMAP2.ICO
Icon Image

Listing 16-9 BITMAP2.RC Resource Script File

```
/* bitmap2.rc resource file */
#include "bitmap2.h"

MyIcon        ICON       bitmap2.ico
HouseBmp      BITMAP     house.bmp

MyMenu        MENU
BEGIN
    MENUITEM "&Quit",              IDM_QUIT
END

STRINGTABLE
BEGIN
    S_PROGRAMCAPTION    "Bitmap 2 Program"
END
```

Listing 16-10 BITMAP2.DEF Module Definition File

```
NAME           bitmap2
DESCRIPTION    'bitmap2 application'
EXETYPE        WINDOWS
STUB           'WINSTUB.EXE'
CODE           PRELOAD MOVEABLE DISCARDABLE
DATA           PRELOAD MOVEABLE MULTIPLE
HEAPSIZE       1024
STACKSIZE      5120
EXPORTS        WndProc
```

Listing 16-11 Turbo C++ Project File for BITMAP2

```
bitmap2.c
bitmap2.def
bitmap2.res
```

Listing 16-12 QuickC Project File for BITMAP2

```
bitmap2.c
bitmap2.def
bitmap2.rc
```

Raster Operation Codes

In the examples above, the BitBlt() and StretchBlt() functions were called using the SRCCOPY constant. For example, in the BITMAP2 program, the first picture is drawn with the function call:

StretchBlt (ps.hdc, 0, 0, 32, 32, hMemDC, 0, 0, 64, 64, SRCCOPY) ;

SRCCOPY is a constant defined in WINDOWS.H, which is referred to as a "raster operation code." Raster operations are those that take place on a raster device, which is a device that draws using individual dots. The opposite of a raster device is a vector device, which draws using lines. The most common vector device is a plotter, which moves pens in lines to draw images. Bitmaps are clearly associated with raster devices, as a bitmap is just a method of storing the color of each pixel on the screen.

When using functions like BitBlt() and StretchBlt(), it is possible to do more than just copy the bitmap onto the output device. These functions can look at the pixels currently on the screen, and combine those pixel colors with the bitmap's pixel colors to produce the final image. The screen pixels and the bitmap pixels are combined using binary logic (binary AND, OR, NOT, etc.), sometimes called "raster" logic. Figure 16-8 shows a couple of examples, using a simple monochrome bitmap for both the source bitmap and the destination screen. The same type of logic can be applied to color bitmaps by taking the red, green, and blue elements of each pixel's color individually.

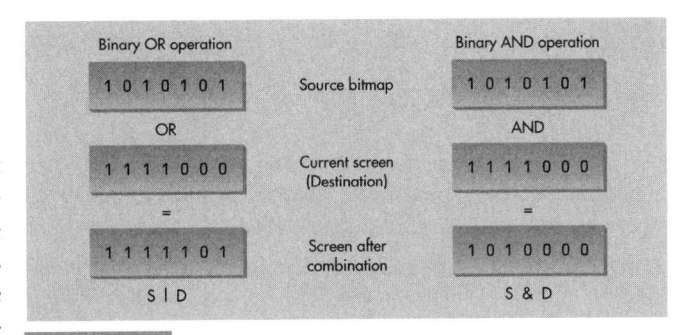

Figure 16-8 Raster Logic for a Monochrome Bitmap

To make life even more interesting, Windows also can include the currently selected brush pattern in the binary logic. With three bitmaps (source bitmap, destination bitmap, and the brush patter), there are a total of 256 possible combinations that can be created. Fortunately, you are unlikely to need more than two or three of these combinations. The WINDOWS.H header file gives names to the fifteen most common raster operations, which are listed in Table 16-1. For the Boolean codes, "S" is the source bitmap, "D" is the destination bitmap (usually the screen), and "P" is the currently selected brush (called a "pattern") of the output device context. The Boolean operators follow the C language conventions: AND = &, NOT = ~, OR = |, and XOR = ^ .

VALUE	MEANING
BLACKNESS	Turns all output black. (0)
DSTINVERT	Inverts the destination bitmap. (~D)

continued

Table 16-1 (cont'd)

MERGECOPY	The source and destination bitmaps are combined with the Boolean AND operator. (D & S)
MERGEPAINT	The inverted source and destination bitmaps are combined with the Boolean OR operator. (~S | D)
NOTSRCCOPY	Inverts the source bitmap, then copies it to the destination. (~S)
NOTSRCERASE	Inverts the result of combining the source and destination bitmaps using the Boolean OR operator. (~(S | D))
PATCOPY	Copies the pattern to the destination. (P)
PATINVERT	Combines the destination bitmap with the pattern using the Boolean OR operator. (P ^ D)
PATPAINT	P | ~(S | D)
SRCAND	Combines the source and destination bitmaps with the Boolean AND operator. (S & D)
SRCCOPY	Copies the source to the destination. (S)
SRCERASE	S & ~ D
SRCINVERT	Combines the source and destination bitmaps using the Boolean XOR operator. (S ^ D)
SRCPAINT	Combines the source and destination bitmaps using the Boolean OR operator. (S | D)
WHITENESS	Turns all output white. This is a quick way to blank a device context. (1)

Table 16-1 Raster Operation Codes for BitBlt() and StretchBlt()

Several of the raster operation codes in Table 16-1 deserve special mention. The SRCCOPY operator just copies the bitmap onto the destination, which is the most common requirement. The BLACKNESS and WHITENESS operators make the bitmap area all black or all white respectively. They have the advantage of being able to set the bitmap handle to NULL, as the bitmap is not used to create the final image. DSTINVERT, PATINVERT, and SCRINVERT all have the interesting property that painting the same bitmap at the same location repeatedly causes the bitmap to disappear and reappear.

An Example Using Raster Operation Codes

The next example program, named BITMAP3, demonstrates all 15 of the raster operation codes listed in Table 16-1. Figure 16-9 shows the BITMAP3 program in operation. The black and white illustration does not do the program justice, so be sure to create and run this example to get the full visual effect. The same bitmap is displayed all 15 times, but it appears differently in each case because a different raster operation code is applied. The unadulterated source bitmap can be seen in the lower left corner, above the SRCCOPY raster operation code. The background is a black and white bitmap pattern with tiles which on the screen appear roughly like bricks. The inverted image above the DSTINVERT raster code shows the brick pattern more clearly because the colors are reversed. The logical pattern (selected brush) is a blue diagonal cross pattern, visible above the PATCOPY raster code.

An interesting experiment you can do with BITMAP2 is to select the "Show" menu item more than once. Figure 16-10 shows the result after a second click. The bitmap images drawn with the DSTINVERT, PATINVERT, and SRCINVERT raster codes all disappear, and several others change colors. The reason for these changes is that in painting the second time, the raster codes that involve comparisons with the screen now have a different starting point. Selecting "Show" a third time restores all of the bitmaps to their previous states.

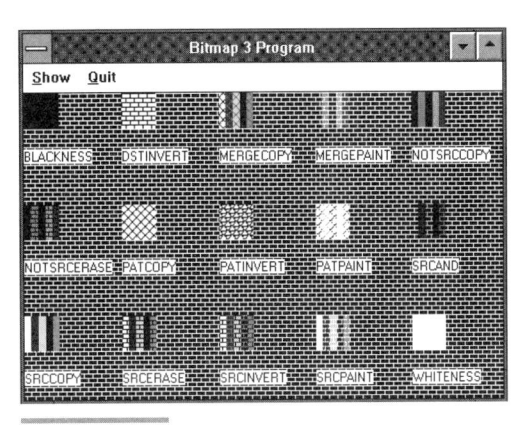

Figure 16-9 The BITMAP3 Program After Selection of the "Show" Menu Item

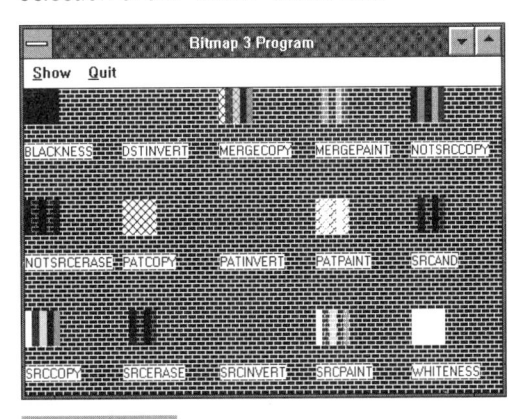

Figure 16-10 The BITMAP3 Program After the "Show" Menu Item Was Selected a Second Time

The BITMAP3 Program

The BITMAP3.C program (Listing 16-13) includes a couple of new programming techniques. One is the use of a small bitmap to paint the client area with a brick pattern. The brick bitmap was created with the image editor and stored as a bitmap file. BITMAP3 includes this bitmap in its resource data. The two keys to painting with a bitmap brush are to use the CreatePatternBrush() function to create a brush from a bitmap, and to use the PatBlt() function to fill an area using the currently selected brush. These operations take place in the WM_PAINT logic portion of BITMAP3.C.

```
case WM_PAINT:
    BeginPaint (hWnd, &ps) ;
    hInstance = GetWindowWord (hWnd, GWW_HINSTANCE) ;
    hBitmap = LoadBitmap (hInstance, "BrickBrush") ;
    hBrush = CreatePatternBrush (hBitmap) ;
    hOldBrush = SelectObject (ps.hdc, hBrush) ;
    PatBlt (ps.hdc, 0, 0, nXclient, nYclient, PATCOPY) ;
    SelectObject (ps.hdc, hOldBrush) ;
    DeleteObject (hBrush) ;
    EndPaint (hWnd, &ps) ;
    DeleteObject (hBitmap) ;
    break ;
```

The PatBlt() function has a limited set of raster operation codes, which are listed in Table 16-2. PatBlt() only works with the destination bitmap and the current brush pattern, and it does not use a second bitmap like BitBlt() and StretchBlt(). PatBlt(), therefore, has fewer possible raster operation codes.

VALUE	MEANING
BLACKNESS	Turns all output black. (0)
DSTINVERT	Inverts the destination bitmap. (~D)
PATCOPY	Copies the pattern to the destination. (P)
PATINVERT	Combines the destination bitmap with the pattern using the Boolean OR operator. (P ^ D)
WHITENESS	Turns all output white. This is a quick way to blank a device context. (1)

Table 16-2 Raster Operation Codes for PatBlt()

The bitmap images are not displayed until the user selects the "Show" menu item. The bitmap is selected into the memory device context, while the crosshatched brush is selected into the output device context, prior to painting the 15 copies of the bitmap image.

```
case IDM_SHOW:
    hInstance = GetWindowWord (hWnd, GWW_HINSTANCE) ;
    hBitmap = LoadBitmap (hInstance, "ColorsBmp") ;
    hDC = GetDC (hWnd) ;
    SelectObject (hDC, GetStockObject (ANSI_VAR_FONT)) ;
    hBrush = CreateHatchBrush (HS_DIAGCROSS, RGB (0, 0, 255)) ;
    hOldBrush = SelectObject (hDC, hBrush) ;
    hMemDC = CreateCompatibleDC (hDC) ;
    SelectObject (hMemDC, hBitmap) ;
```

All 15 of the predefined raster operation codes in WINDOWS.H are loaded into a static DWORD array *dwRasterOp[]*. This makes it easy for BitBlt() to be called 15 times, each time with a different raster operation code. In addition, the name of the raster operation code is displayed under each bitmap. The raster operation code names are defined as consecutive entries in the program's stringtable in the resource script file. The StringAtPoint() function defined at the end of BITMAP3.C writes each string under the bitmap.

```
for (i = 0 ; i < 5 ; i++)         /* count 5 across per row */
{
    for (j = 0 ; j < 3 ; j++)     /* count 3 rows of bitmaps */
    {
        BitBlt (hDC, 90 * i, 100 * j, 32, 32,
            hMemDC, 0, 0, dwRasterOp [i + (5*j)] ) ;
        StringAtPoint (hDC, hInstance, 90 * i,
            50 + (100 * j),
            S_BLACKNESS + i + (5 * j)) ;
    }
}
```

The bitmaps for both the brick brush and the colored square were created using a bitmap editor. Figures 16-11 and 16-12 show the two images. The color bands in the 64 by 64 pixel COLORS.BMP bitmap are (from left to right) white, red, yellow, blue, and green. The BRIKBRSH bitmap is black and white, and only eight by eight pixels in size. If you attempt to use a larger bitmap with the CreatePatternBrush() function, only the upper left eight by eight pixel square will end up in the brush pattern.

Listing 16-13 shows the complete BITMAP-3.C program. The support files are shown in Listings 16-14 to 16-18. The program's icon is shown in Figure 16-13.

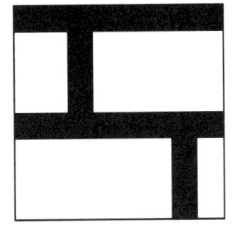

Figure 16-11 BRIKBRSH.BMP

Figure 16-12 COLORS.BMP

Figure 16-13 BITMAP3.ICO Icon Image

Listing 16-13 BITMAP3.C

```
/* bitmap3.c   demonstration of 15 raster operation codes */

#include <windows.h>
#include "bitmap3.h"

int PASCAL WinMain (HANDLE hInstance, HANDLE hPrevInstance, LPSTR lpszCmdLine,
    int nCmdShow)
{
    HWND        hWnd ;          /* the window's "handle" */
    MSG         msg ;           /* a message structure */
    WNDCLASS    wndclass ;      /* window class structure */
    char        cBuf [128] ;

    if (!hPrevInstance)
    {
        wndclass.style          = CS_HREDRAW | CS_VREDRAW ;
        wndclass.lpfnWndProc    = WndProc ;
        wndclass.cbClsExtra     = 0 ;
        wndclass.cbWndExtra     = 0 ;
        wndclass.hInstance      = hInstance ;
        wndclass.hIcon          = LoadIcon (hInstance, "MyIcon") ;
        wndclass.hCursor        = LoadCursor (NULL, IDC_ARROW) ;
        wndclass.hbrBackground  = GetStockObject (WHITE_BRUSH) ;
        wndclass.lpszMenuName   = "MyMenu" ;
        wndclass.lpszClassName  = "MyClass" ;
                /* register the window class */
      if (!RegisterClass (&wndclass))
         return 0 ;
    }
    LoadString (hInstance, S_PROGRAMCAPTION, cBuf, sizeof (cBuf)) ;

    hWnd = CreateWindow ("MyClass", cBuf, WS_OVERLAPPEDWINDOW,
        CW_USEDEFAULT, CW_USEDEFAULT, CW_USEDEFAULT, CW_USEDEFAULT,
        NULL, NULL, hInstance, NULL) ;
    ShowWindow (hWnd, nCmdShow) ;     /* display the window */
```

```
    while (GetMessage (&msg, NULL, NULL, NULL))   /* message loop */
    {
        TranslateMessage (&msg) ;       /* translate keyboard messages */
        DispatchMessage (&msg) ;        /* send message to WndProc() */
    }
    return (msg.wParam) ;
}

long FAR PASCAL WndProc (HWND hWnd, WORD wMessage, WORD wParam, LONG lParam)
{
    HDC             hDC, hMemDC ;
    HBITMAP         hBitmap ;
    HBRUSH          hBrush, hOldBrush ;
    HANDLE          hInstance ;
    PAINTSTRUCT     ps ;
    static int      nXclient, nYclient ;
    static DWORD    dwRasterOp [15] = {BLACKNESS, DSTINVERT, MERGECOPY,
        MERGEPAINT, NOTSRCCOPY, NOTSRCERASE, PATCOPY, PATINVERT, PATPAINT,
        SRCAND, SRCCOPY, SRCERASE, SRCINVERT, SRCPAINT, WHITENESS} ;
    int             i, j ;

    switch (wMessage)        /* process windows messages */
    {
        case WM_COMMAND:
            switch (wParam)
            {
                case IDM_SHOW:
                    hInstance = GetWindowWord (hWnd, GWW_HINSTANCE) ;
                    hBitmap = LoadBitmap (hInstance, "ColorsBmp") ;
                    hDC = GetDC (hWnd) ;
                    SelectObject (hDC, GetStockObject (ANSI_VAR_FONT)) ;
                    hBrush = CreateHatchBrush (HS_DIAGCROSS, RGB (0, 0, 255)) ;
                    hOldBrush = SelectObject (hDC, hBrush) ;
                    hMemDC = CreateCompatibleDC (hDC) ;
                    SelectObject (hMemDC, hBitmap) ;
                    for (i = 0 ; i < 5 ; i++)
                    {
                        for (j = 0 ; j < 3 ; j++)
                        {
                            BitBlt (hDC, 90 * i, 100 * j, 32, 32,
                                hMemDC, 0, 0, dwRasterOp [i + (5*j)] ) ;
                            StringAtPoint (hDC, hInstance, 90 * i,
                                50 + (100 * j),
                                S_BLACKNESS + i + (5 * j)) ;
                        }
                    }
                    SelectObject (hDC, hOldBrush) ;
                    DeleteObject (hBrush) ;
                    DeleteDC (hMemDC) ;
                    ReleaseDC (hWnd, hDC) ;
                    DeleteObject (hBitmap) ;
                    break ;
                case IDM_QUIT:              /* Quit menu item */
                    DestroyWindow (hWnd) ;  /* destroy window, */
                    break ;     /* terminating application */
                default:        /* otherwise, let Windows process it */
                    return (DefWindowProc (hWnd, wMessage, wParam, lParam)) ;
            }
            break ;
```

```c
        case WM_SIZE:
            nXclient = LOWORD (lParam) ;
            nYclient = HIWORD (lParam) ;
            break ;
        case WM_PAINT:
            BeginPaint (hWnd, &ps) ;
            hInstance = GetWindowWord (hWnd, GWW_HINSTANCE) ;
            hBitmap = LoadBitmap (hInstance, "BrickBrush") ;
            hBrush = CreatePatternBrush (hBitmap) ;
            hOldBrush = SelectObject (ps.hdc, hBrush) ;
            PatBlt (ps.hdc, 0, 0, nXclient, nYclient, PATCOPY) ;
            SelectObject (ps.hdc, hOldBrush) ;
            DeleteObject (hBrush) ;
            EndPaint (hWnd, &ps) ;
            DeleteObject (hBitmap) ;
            break ;
        case WM_DESTROY:    /* stop application */
            PostQuitMessage (0) ;
            break ;
        default:            /* default windows message processing */
            return (DefWindowProc (hWnd, wMessage, wParam, lParam)) ;
    }
    return (0L) ;
}
/* display a string table entry at an X,Y location on a DC */

void StringAtPoint (HDC hDC, HANDLE hInstance, int nX, int nY, int nString)
{
    char    cBuf [128] ;

    LoadString (hInstance, nString, cBuf, sizeof (cBuf)) ;
    TextOut (hDC, nX, nY, cBuf, lstrlen (cBuf)) ;
}
```

Listing 16-14 BITMAP3.H Header File

```c
/* bitmap3.h  header file */

#define IDM_SHOW    1              /* menu item ID numbers */
#define IDM_QUIT    10

#define S_PROGRAMCAPTION    1      /* string table ID numbers */
#define S_BLACKNESS         2
#define S_DSTINVERT         3
#define S_MERGECOPY         4
#define S_MERGEPAINT        5
#define S_NOTSRCCOPY        6
#define S_NOTSRCERASE       7
#define S_PATCOPY           8
#define S_PATINVERT         9
#define S_PATPAINT          10
#define S_SRCAND            11
#define S_SRCCOPY           12
#define S_SRCERASE          13
#define S_SRCINVERT         14
#define S_SRCPAINT          15
#define S_WHITENESS         16
```

```
long FAR PASCAL WndProc (HWND, WORD, WORD, LONG) ;
void StringAtPoint (HDC hDC, HANDLE hInstance, int nX, int nY, int nString) ;
```

Listing 16-15 BITMAP3.RC Resource Script File

```
/* bitmap3.rc resource file */

#include "bitmap3.h"

MyIcon       ICON     bitmap3.ico
BrickBrush   BITMAP   brikbrsh.bmp
ColorsBmp    BITMAP   colors.bmp

MyMenu  MENU
BEGIN
    MENUITEM "&Show",       IDM_SHOW
    MENUITEM "&Quit",       IDM_QUIT
END

STRINGTABLE
BEGIN
    S_PROGRAMCAPTION    "Bitmap 3 Program"
    S_BLACKNESS         "BLACKNESS"
    S_DSTINVERT         "DSTINVERT"
    S_MERGECOPY         "MERGECOPY"
    S_MERGEPAINT        "MERGEPAINT"
    S_NOTSRCCOPY        "NOTSRCCOPY"
    S_NOTSRCERASE       "NOTSRCERASE"
    S_PATCOPY           "PATCOPY"
    S_PATINVERT         "PATINVERT"
    S_PATPAINT          "PATPAINT"
    S_SRCAND            "SRCAND"
    S_SRCCOPY           "SRCCOPY"
    S_SRCERASE          "SRCERASE"
    S_SRCINVERT         "SRCINVERT"
    S_SRCPAINT          "SRCPAINT"
    S_WHITENESS         "WHITENESS"
END
```

Listing 16-16 BITMAP3.DEF Module Definition File

```
NAME            bitmap3
DESCRIPTION     'bitmap3 application'
EXETYPE         WINDOWS
STUB            'WINSTUB.EXE'
CODE            PRELOAD MOVEABLE DISCARDABLE
DATA            PRELOAD MOVEABLE MULTIPLE
HEAPSIZE        1024
STACKSIZE       5120
EXPORTS         WndProc
```

Listing 16-17 Turbo C++ Project File for BITMAP3

```
bitmap3.c
bitmap3.def
bitmap3.res
```

Listing 16-18 QuickC Project File for BITMAP3

```
bitmap3.c
bitmap3.def
bitmap3.rc
```

Drawing on a Memory Bitmap

So far in this book we have used the GDI functions like LineTo() and Rectangle() to output GDI commands to "real" devices for the screen and the printer. It turns out that you can also use the GDI functions to "draw" on a memory device context. You can do all sorts of output on the memory device context, and then copy the finished image all at once to a "real" device context using BitBlt(). Although you can use the GDI functions to draw on a bitmap file/resource loaded into memory, normally you will want to create a blank bitmap in memory before using the GDI functions. The CreateCompatibleBitmap() function creates a blank memory bitmap. Here is a typical program fragment, which creates a 200 pixel wide by 100 pixel high memory bitmap, draws a rectangle on the memory bitmap, and then copies it to the screen device context:

```
HDC  hDC, hMemDC ;

hDC = GetDC (hWnd) ;
hMemDC = CreateCompatibleDC (hDC) ;
hBitmap = CreateCompatibleBitmap (hDC, 200, 100) ;
SelectObject (hMemDC, hBitmap) ;
Rectangle (hMemDC, 10, 10, 30, 50) ;
BitBlt (hDC, 0, 0, 200, 100, hMemDC, 0, 0, SRCCOPY) ;
```
[Other program lines]

Drawing on a memory bitmap probably sounds like a roundabout way to produce an image. Normally, it is easier to just draw on the output device context and skip the intermediate steps required to create a memory bitmap. However, there are situations where doing all of the drawing on a memory bitmap and then copying the final picture to the output device with a single call to BitBlt() produces a much better effect. The advantage of drawing to the memory bitmap is that all of the GDI operations are invisible to the user. The drawing is only made visible when the final bitmap is copied to the output device context with BitBlt() or StretchBlt(). BitBlt() is a fast function, much faster than the GDI functions, such as Rectangle() and Ellipse(). By drawing on a memory bitmap, and then "blitting" the finished image to the output device, the image appears in an instant, rather than gradually taking shape as each GDI function does its work.

Memory Bitmaps and Animation

The most common situation that demands the use of memory bitmaps is animation. Even simple animated sequences are jittery if you attempt to move objects by painting and repainting each object using GDI functions directly on the output device. A much better way to animate is to do all of the changes on a memory bitmap, and then "blit" the finished picture onto the screen. This technique can be applied to the entire screen at once, or for individual portions which are changing.

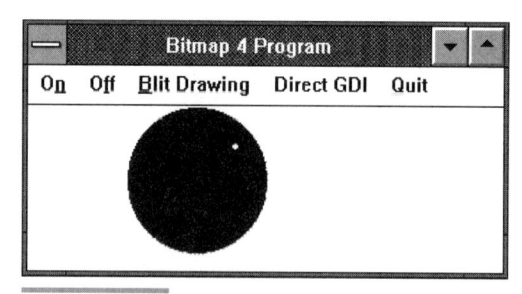

Figure 16-14 The BITMAP4 Program

The last example program in this chapter, BITMAP4, demonstrates the advantages of using memory bitmaps for animation by animating a moving ball image. BITMAP4 uses both direct GDI function calls to the screen and a memory bitmap to paint in the background, so you can compare the two techniques. Figure 16-14 shows the running BITMAP4 program. Selecting the "On" menu item causes a large blue ball to move from the left to the right of an area in the window's client area. If the "Blit Drawing" menu item has been selected (this is the default choice), the ball appears to move steadily. If the "Direct GDI" menu item is selected, the ball moves faster, but the image of the ball becomes fuzzy and is constantly changing.

The reason the "Blit Drawing" option shows a clear image of the ball moving is that all of the drawing operations are done on a memory bitmap. When the image is complete, the finished picture of the ball at a new location is "blit" onto the screen. With the "Direct GDI" option, the ball is drawn on the screen's device context. Each GDI action, erasing the ball at the old location and drawing it again at the new location, is visible to the user, and results in the ball appearing to flicker on the screen as it moves.

Coding the BITMAP4 Program

The complete BITMAP4.C program is shown in Listing 16-19. The animation of the moving ball in the BITMAP4 program requires that a PeekMessage() loop be used in place of the usual GetMessage() loop in the WinMain() function. PeekMessage() was used back in Chapter 4, *Text And Graphics Output*, for another animation example. The difference between PeekMessage() and GetMessage() is that GetMessage() will only be activated if there is a message waiting for the program. If there are no pending messages, GetMessage() returns control to Windows. However, PeekMessage() keeps checking for messages and will continue to be called periodically by the Windows environment even if there are no pending messages for the program. This is ideal for animation, as we can process messages (if any have been sent) and use periods when there are no messages to do the animation of the image.

The structure of the message loop using PeekMessage() is a bit different from a GetMessage() loop, as we want to do something even if there are no waiting messages. The message loop for the BITMAP4.C program is shown below. PeekMessage() returns TRUE if there is a message waiting, and FALSE if not. If there is a message, the message is sent on to the WndProc() function using the usual TranslateMessage(), DispatchMessage() function pair. If there is not a message, the animation functions are called to draw the ball at a new location.

```
while (TRUE)                            /* peek message loop */
{
    if (PeekMessage (&msg, NULL, 0, 0, PM_REMOVE))
    {
        if (msg.message == WM_QUIT)     /* if WM_QUIT, quit! */
            return msg.wParam ;
        else                            /* else, process message */
        {
            TranslateMessage (&msg) ;
            DispatchMessage (&msg) ;
        }
    }   /* no message waiting, so paint the ball if drawing enabled */
    else if (_bDrawOn)
    {
        if (_bBlitOn)
            DrawBallBlt (_hDC, _hMemDC) ;
        else
            DrawBallGDI (_hDC) ;
    }
}
```

Note that when using PeekMessage(), you must explicitly check for the WM_QUIT message to stop the program. GetMessage() has the handy feature of returning FALSE (zero) when the WM_QUIT message is received, but this is not the case for PeekMessage().

BITMAP4.C stores the handles of the window's client area device context, and of a memory device context, in the global variables _hDC and _hMemDC. The device context handles are obtained when the user selects the "On" menu item:

```
case IDM_ON:            /* turn on animation */
    _bDrawOn = TRUE ;
    _hDC = GetDC (hWnd) ;
                        /* create memory DC */
    _hMemDC = CreateCompatibleDC (_hDC) ;
    hBitmap = CreateCompatibleBitmap (_hDC, BITMAPWIDE,
        BITMAPTALL) ;                   /* create mem bitmap */
    SelectObject (_hMemDC, hBitmap) ;
    break ;
```

Note that a memory bitmap is created and selected into the memory device context at this stage. The memory bitmap is created using the CreateCompatibleBitmap() function, and given a size of BITMAPWIDE horizontally and BITMAPTALL vertically. The constants BITMAPWIDE and BITMAPTALL are defined as 200 and 100 respectively in the BITMAP4.H header file.

The ball is actually drawn when the PeekMessage() loop executes, and does not find a waiting message. If the global variable _bBlitOn is TRUE, the drawing is done with the DrawBallBlt() function, which uses the memory device context approach. If _bBlitOn is FALSE, the DrawBallGDI() function is used to draw the ball, which draws directly on the window's client area. DrawBallBlt() and DrawBallGDI() are identical, except that DrawBallBlt() draws on a memory bitmap in a memory device context rather than directly to the screen. Here is the DrawBallBlt() function:

```c
void DrawBallBlt (HDC hDC, HDC hMemDC)
{
    static  int nXpos = 0 ;
    int         nX, nY ;
    HBRUSH      hBrush ;
                                                /* move to left */
    nXpos = (nXpos > BITMAPWIDE ? -1 * BITMAPTALL : nXpos + 2) ;

    SelectObject (hMemDC, GetStockObject (WHITE_BRUSH)) ;
    SelectObject (hMemDC, GetStockObject (WHITE_PEN)) ;
    Rectangle (hMemDC, 0, 0, BITMAPWIDE, BITMAPTALL) ;
    hBrush = CreateSolidBrush (RGB (0, 0, 255)) ;   /* make blue brush */
    SelectObject (hMemDC, hBrush) ;                 /* draw blue ball */
    Ellipse (hMemDC, nXpos, 0, nXpos + BITMAPTALL, BITMAPTALL) ;
    SelectObject (hMemDC, GetStockObject (WHITE_BRUSH)) ;
    DeleteObject (hBrush) ;                         /* delete blue brush */
    SelectObject (hMemDC, GetStockObject (WHITE_PEN)) ;
    nX = nXpos + ((3 * BITMAPTALL) / 4) ;
    nY = BITMAPTALL / 4 ;           /* put small white highlight on ball */
    Ellipse (hMemDC, nX, nY, nX + 4, nY + 4) ;
                                    /* now copy entire mem DC to screen DC */
    BitBlt (hDC, 0, 0, BITMAPWIDE, BITMAPTALL, hMemDC, 0, 0, SRCCOPY) ;
}
```

DrawBallBlt() keeps track of the current location of the ball with a static variable *nXpos*. Prior to drawing the ball, the entire memory bitmap is erased by drawing a white rectangle with a white border on the bitmap. The ball is then drawn using the Ellipse() function. A small white highlight is also added to the ball to improve its appearance. Once the drawing is completed, the BitBlt() function copies the entire memory bitmap to the window's client area.

BITMAP4 Program Listings

The complete listings for the BITMAP4 program are shown below. Note the similarity between the DrawBallGDI() and DrawBallBlt() functions at the end of BITMAP4.C (Listing 16-19). Drawing on a memory bitmap is just like drawing on a "real" device.

Listing 16-19 BITMAP4.C

```c
/* bitmap4.c    drawing on a memory bitmap */

#include <windows.h>
#include "bitmap4.h"

BOOL    _bDrawOn = FALSE ;      /* global variables */
BOOL    _bBlitOn = TRUE ;
HDC     _hDC, _hMemDC ;

int PASCAL WinMain (HANDLE hInstance, HANDLE hPrevInstance, LPSTR lpszCmdLine,
    int nCmdShow)
{
    HWND        hWnd ;          /* the window's "handle" */
    MSG         msg ;           /* a message structure */
    WNDCLASS    wndclass ;      /* window class structure */
    char        cBuf [128] ;
```

```c
    if (!hPrevInstance)
    {
        wndclass.style         = CS_HREDRAW | CS_VREDRAW ;
        wndclass.lpfnWndProc   = WndProc ;
        wndclass.cbClsExtra    = 0 ;
        wndclass.cbWndExtra    = 0 ;
        wndclass.hInstance     = hInstance ;
        wndclass.hIcon         = LoadIcon (hInstance, "MyIcon") ;
        wndclass.hCursor       = LoadCursor (NULL, IDC_ARROW) ;
        wndclass.hbrBackground = GetStockObject (WHITE_BRUSH) ;
        wndclass.lpszMenuName  = "MyMenu" ;
        wndclass.lpszClassName = "MyClass" ;
                    /* register the window class */
        if (!RegisterClass (&wndclass))
            return 0 ;
    }
    LoadString (hInstance, S_PROGRAMCAPTION, cBuf, sizeof (cBuf)) ;

    hWnd = CreateWindow ("MyClass", cBuf, WS_OVERLAPPEDWINDOW,
        CW_USEDEFAULT, CW_USEDEFAULT, CW_USEDEFAULT, CW_USEDEFAULT,
        NULL, NULL, hInstance, NULL) ;
    ShowWindow (hWnd, nCmdShow) ;           /* display the window */

    while (TRUE)                            /* peek message loop */
    {
        if (PeekMessage (&msg, NULL, 0, 0, PM_REMOVE))
        {
            if (msg.message == WM_QUIT)     /* if WM_QUIT, quit! */
                return msg.wParam ;
            else                            /* else, process message */
            {
                TranslateMessage (&msg) ;
                DispatchMessage (&msg) ;
            }
        }   /* no message waiting, so paint the ball if drawing enabled */
        else if (_bDrawOn)
        {
            if (_bBlitOn)
                DrawBallBlt (_hDC, _hMemDC) ;
            else
                DrawBallGDI (_hDC) ;
        }
    }
}

long FAR PASCAL WndProc (HWND hWnd, WORD wMessage, WORD wParam, LONG lParam)
{
    static HBITMAP   hBitmap ;

    switch (wMessage)       /* process windows messages */
    {
        case WM_COMMAND:
            switch (wParam)
            {
                case IDM_ON:    /* turn on animation */
                    bDrawOn = TRUE ;
                    hDC = GetDC (hWnd) ;
                                /* create memory DC */
                    hMemDC = CreateCompatibleDC (_hDC) ;
                    hBitmap = CreateCompatibleBitmap (_hDC, BITMAPWIDE,
```

```
                        BITMAPTALL) ;              /* create mem bitmap */
                    SelectObject (_hMemDC, hBitmap) ;
                    break ;
                case IDM_OFF:     /* turn off animation */
                    _bDrawOn = FALSE ;
                    DeleteDC (_hMemDC) ;
                    DeleteObject (hBitmap) ;
                    ReleaseDC (hWnd, _hDC) ;
                    break ;
                case IDM_BLIT:    /* use Blit drawing */
                    _bBlitOn = TRUE ;
                    InvalidateRect (hWnd, NULL, TRUE) ; /* clear */
                    break ;
                case IDM_GDI:     /* use GDI functions directly */
                    _bBlitOn = FALSE ;
                    InvalidateRect (hWnd, NULL, TRUE) ; /* clear */
                    break ;
                case IDM_QUIT:                    /* Quit menu item */
                    DestroyWindow (hWnd) ;   /* destroy window, */
                    break ;      /* terminating application */
            }
            break ;
        case WM_DESTROY:          /* stop application */
            if (_bDrawOn == TRUE)
            {
                    DeleteDC (_hMemDC) ;
                    DeleteObject (hBitmap) ;
                    ReleaseDC (hWnd, _hDC) ;
            }
            PostQuitMessage (0) ;
            break ;
        default:        /* default windows message processing */
            return (DefWindowProc (hWnd, wMessage, wParam, lParam)) ;
    }
    return (0L) ;
}

        /* draw moving ball on memory bitmap, then blit it to screen DC */
void DrawBallBlt (HDC hDC, HDC hMemDC)
{
    static  int nXpos = 0 ;
    int         nX, nY ;
    HBRUSH      hBrush ;
                                                /* move to left */
    nXpos = (nXpos > BITMAPWIDE ? -1 * BITMAPTALL : nXpos + 2) ;

    SelectObject (hMemDC, GetStockObject (WHITE_BRUSH)) ;
    SelectObject (hMemDC, GetStockObject (WHITE_PEN)) ;
    Rectangle (hMemDC, 0, 0, BITMAPWIDE, BITMAPTALL) ;
    hBrush = CreateSolidBrush (RGB (0, 0, 255)) ;   /* make blue brush */
    SelectObject (hMemDC, hBrush) ;                 /* draw blue ball */
    Ellipse (hMemDC, nXpos, 0, nXpos + BITMAPTALL, BITMAPTALL) ;
    SelectObject (hMemDC, GetStockObject (WHITE_BRUSH)) ;
    DeleteObject (hBrush) ;                      /* delete blue brush */
    SelectObject (hMemDC, GetStockObject (WHITE_PEN)) ;
    nX = nXpos + ((3 * BITMAPTALL) / 4) ;
    nY = BITMAPTALL / 4 ;      /* put small white highlight on ball */
    Ellipse (hMemDC, nX, nY, nX + 4, nY + 4) ;
                            /* now copy entire mem DC to screen DC */
```

```
        BitBlt (hDC, 0, 0, BITMAPWIDE, BITMAPTALL, hMemDC, 0, 0, SRCCOPY) ;
    }

        /* draw moving ball using GDI calls, direct to screen DC */
void DrawBallGDI (HDC hDC)
{
    static  int nXpos = 0 ;
    int         nX, nY ;
    HBRUSH      hBrush ;
                                                /* move to left */
    nXpos = (nXpos > BITMAPWIDE ? -1 * BITMAPTALL : nXpos + 2) ;

    SelectObject (hDC, GetStockObject (WHITE_BRUSH)) ;
    SelectObject (hDC, GetStockObject (WHITE_PEN)) ;
    Rectangle (hDC, 0, 0, BITMAPWIDE + BITMAPTALL, BITMAPTALL) ;
    hBrush = CreateSolidBrush (RGB (0, 0, 255)) ;    /* make blue brush */
    SelectObject (hDC, hBrush) ;                     /* draw blue ball */
    Ellipse (hDC, nXpos, 0, nXpos + BITMAPTALL, BITMAPTALL) ;
    SelectObject (hDC, GetStockObject (WHITE_BRUSH)) ;
    DeleteObject (hBrush) ;                          /* delete blue brush */
    SelectObject (hDC, GetStockObject (WHITE_PEN)) ;
    nX = nXpos + ((3 * BITMAPTALL) / 4) ;
    nY = BITMAPTALL / 4 ;             /* put small white highlight on ball */
    Ellipse (hDC, nX, nY, nX + 4, nY + 4) ;
}
```

The support files for BITMAP4 are shown in Listings 16-20 to 16-24. Figure 16-15 shows the program's icon.

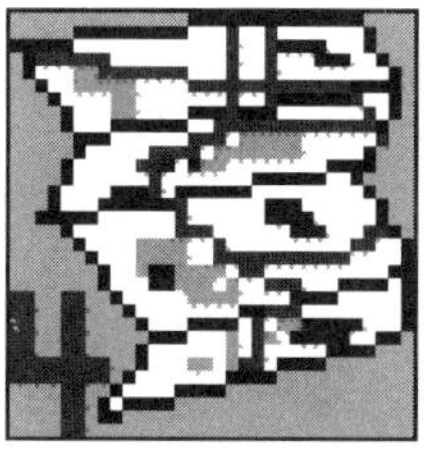

Listing 16-20 BITMAP4.H Header File

```
/* bitmap4.h  header file */

#define BITMAPWIDE      200     /* defines size of memory bitmap */
#define BITMAPTALL      100

#define IDM_ON          1       /* menu item ID numbers */
#define IDM_OFF         2
#define IDM_BLIT        3
#define IDM_GDI         4
#define IDM_QUIT        10

#define S_PROGRAMCAPTION 1      /* string table ID numbers */

long FAR PASCAL WndProc (HWND, WORD, WORD, LONG) ;
void DrawBallBlt (HDC hDC, HDC hMemDC) ;
void DrawBallGDI (HDC hDC) ;
```

Figure 16-15
BITMAP4.ICO
Icon Image

Listing 16-21 BITMAP4.RC Resource Script File

```
/* bitmap4.rc  resource file */

#include "bitmap4.h"

MyIcon      ICON    bitmap4.ico
```

```
MyMenu      MENU
BEGIN
    MENUITEM "O&n",                 IDM_ON
    MENUITEM "O&ff",                IDM_OFF
    MENUITEM "&Blit Drawing",       IDM_BLIT
    MENUITEM "Direct GDI",          IDM_GDI
    MENUITEM "&Quit",               IDM_QUIT
END

STRINGTABLE
BEGIN
    S_PROGRAMCAPTION    "Bitmap 4 Program"
END
```

Listing 16-22 BITMAP4.DEF Module Definition File

```
NAME            bitmap4
DESCRIPTION     'bitmap4 application'
EXETYPE         WINDOWS
STUB            'WINSTUB.EXE'
CODE            PRELOAD MOVEABLE DISCARDABLE
DATA            PRELOAD MOVEABLE MULTIPLE
HEAPSIZE        1024
STACKSIZE       5120
EXPORTS         WndProc
```

Listing 16-23 Turbo C++ Project File for BITMAP4

```
bitmap4.c
bitmap4.def
bitmap4.res
```

Listing 16-24 QuickC Project File for BITMAP4

```
bitmap4.c
bitmap4.def
bitmap4.rc
```

BITMAP Data Format

Up to this point, we have managed to manipulate bitmaps without being concerned with the internal format of the BITMAP data. It turns out that there are two different data formats used by Windows to store bitmap data. For the most part, Windows converts automatically between these two formats, so you will not deal with the data in the bitmap structure directly in most cases. However, you may run into the terminology used to describe the different types of bitmaps, and you may occasionally need to deal with the bitmap data directly.

The simplest type of bitmap is the BITMAP format, which is sometimes called the "device dependent bitmap" (DDB) format. The BITMAP format is device-dependent because the data stored with the bitmap has the numeric values for the color of each pixel, but does not have data to specify the color of each possible pixel color value (how "red" red is, etc.). In other words, the BITMAP format assumes that you will be displaying the bitmap on the same type of display that was used to create the BITMAP. If the bitmap is displayed on another type of display, with a different color resolution, the colors of the bitmap image may end up completely wrong. Because of this problem, the BITMAP format is used primarily for manipulating images in memory, but not for storing bitmap data on disk files. The BITMAP data structure is defined in WINDOWS.H as follows:

```
BITMAP Structure
typedef struct tagBITMAP
  {
    int     bmType;           /* always zero */
    int     bmWidth;          /* width in pixels */
    int     bmHeight;         /* height in pixels */
    int     bmWidthBytes;     /* bytes per line of data */
                              /* must be a multiple of 2 */
    BYTE    bmPlanes;         /* the number of color planes */
    BYTE    bmBitsPixel;      /* the number of bits per pixel */
    LPSTR   bmBits;           /* far pointer to the bitmap data */
  } BITMAP;
typedef BITMAP            *PBITMAP;
typedef BITMAP NEAR       *NPBITMAP;
typedef BITMAP FAR        *LPBITMAP;
```

The BITMAP structure has two different ways to specify the number of color bits used in the pixel data. *bmPlanes* is the number of color planes a device, such as a VGA display, may use. If this value is used, then *bmBitsPixel* will be set to one. *bmBitsPixel* is the number of color bits per pixel for a device that does not use color planes, such as a high-end "true color" display. If this value is used, *bmPlanes* will be set to one. The CreateCompatibleBitmap() function sets these color values to match a physical device, so that you do not have to know in advance how the colors are stored by the video system. The actual pixel data is stored in a memory buffer pointed to by *bmBits*. This buffer is usually right after the header data in memory, as shown in Figure 16-16.

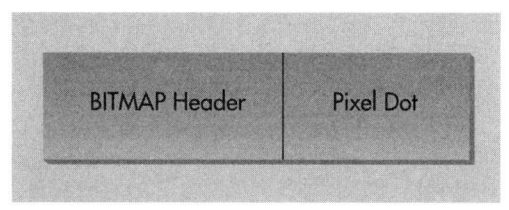

Figure 16-16 The DDB Bitmap Format in Memory

The DIB Format

The device-independent bitmap was introduced with Windows 3.0 as a solution to the shortcomings of the old BITMAP (DDB) format. The difference between DIBs and DDBs is that DIBs include a table of the colors the bitmap will use. This allows a program to read the color data, adjust the color palette being used on the screen, and then display the bitmap image. Adjusting the color palette is an advanced subject, and not covered in this book (see Chapter 12 of *The Waite Group's Windows API Bible* for a discussion of color palette control). However, we used the DIB format indirectly in the examples in this chapter, as Windows uses this format for bitmap disk files. The Paintbrush application and the Microsoft and Borland image editors save their output as DIB data. The DIB bitmap data is automatically converted to the BITMAP (DDB) format when the data is loaded into memory with the LoadBitmap() function.

An important difference between the BITMAP and DIB formats is that only the BITMAP format can be selected into a device context. Think of the DIB format as a disk file format, used to preserve the color information. The BITMAP format is the low-level data about an image, which can be directly "blit" to a location on the screen.

The header format for a DIB is more complex than for the simple BITMAP. The DIB format consists of three sections, shown in Figure 16-17. This is the format if you were to load raw DIB data into memory with LoadResource(), instead of automatically converting the DIB data to BITMAP format using LoadBitmap().

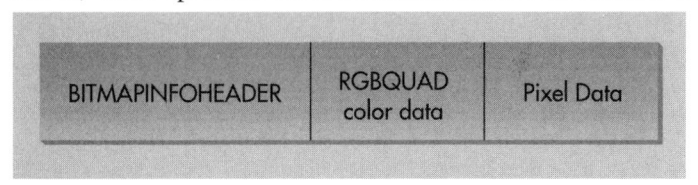

Figure 16-17 Device Independent Bitmap (DIB) Format in Memory

WINDOWS.H has the definitions for both the BITMAPINFOHEADER and RGBQUAD structures.

```
typedef struct tagBITMAPINFOHEADER{
    DWORD   biSize;             /* size of BITMAPINFOHEADER */
    DWORD   biWidth;            /* width in pixels */
    DWORD   biHeight;           /* height in pixels */
    WORD    biPlanes;           /* always 1 */
    WORD    biBitCount;         /* color bits per pixel */
                                /* must be 1, 4, 8 or 24 */
    DWORD   biCompression;      /* BI_RGB, BI_RLE8 */
                                /* or BI_RLE4 */
    DWORD   biSizeImage;        /* total bytes in image */
    DWORD   biXPelsPerMeter;    /* 0, or opt. h res. */
    DWORD   biYPelsPerMeter;    /* 0, or opt. v res. */
    DWORD   biClrUsed;          /* normally 0, can set a */
                                /* lower no. colors than biBitCount */
    DWORD   biClrImportant;     /* normally 0 */
} BITMAPINFOHEADER;

typedef BITMAPINFOHEADER FAR *LPBITMAPINFOHEADER;
typedef BITMAPINFOHEADER *PBITMAPINFOHEADER;
```

Although similar to the BITMAP header structure, BITMAPINFOHEADER contains some added fields. The *biBitCount* element contains the number of color bits per pixel, 1, 4, 8 or 24 bits. Table 16-3 describes the meaning of these values.

COLOR BITS	NUMBER OF COLORS
1	A monochrome bitmap. Each bit in the bitmap data will represent one pixel.

4	A bitmap with 16 colors. Each pixel requires four bits of information in the bitmap data. The four bits represent an index in the color table.
8	A bitmap with 256 colors. Each pixel requires a byte of information in the bitmap data. The byte value represents an index into the color table.
24	A bitmap with 2^{24} colors. Each pixel requires three bytes of information, representing the RGB (Red, Green, Blue) color bytes.

Table 16-3 Color Resolutions

The *biCompression* element contains a value to define how the bitmap data is compressed to save space. If it is set to BI_RGB, no compression is used. BI_RLE4 is a 4 bits-per-pixel run length encoding compression. BI_RLE8 is an 8 bits-per-pixel compression.

biSizeImage is the bitmap size in bytes. Each row of pixels data must terminate on a 32-bit (DWORD) boundary. If a row of pixels, with the specified number of color bits per pixel, does not end at an even 32-bit number, the remainder is padded with zero bits.

The *biXPelsPerMeter* and *biYPelsPerMeter* values can be used to encode the bitmap resolution in pixels per meter, although these values are not required (can be set to zero). *biClrUsed* specifies the number of color values in the color table (described below) that are actually used. It is normally set to zero, meaning that all colors are used. This value must be set to zero if the bitmap is compressed. *biClrImportant* specifies the number of critical colors. It is normally set to zero, meaning that all of the colors are important.

After the BITMAPINFOHEADER structure, a DIB will contain the color table. This is a set of RGBQUAD data structures, holding the RGB color for each of the colors used in the bitmap. There will be as many RGBQUAD entries as there are color choices in the bitmap. For example, if *biBitCount* is four, there will be 16 color possibilities, requiring 16 RGBQUAD elements to define, taking up 16 * 4 = 64 bytes of space. This assumes *biClrUsed* is set to zero. If *biClrUsed* is set to a value above zero, that will be the number of RGBQUAD elements.

```
typedef struct tagRGBQUAD {
    BYTE  rgbBlue;        /* blue intensity, 0 - 255 */
    BYTE  rgbGreen;       /* green intensity, 0 - 255 */
    BYTE  rgbRed;         /* red intensity, 0 - 255 */
    BYTE  rgbReserved;    /* reserved, set to zero */
} RGBQUAD;
```

WINDOWS.H includes two other structure definitions that are useful in manipulating DIBs. The BITMAPINFO structure simply combines the first two parts of a DIB into one structure:

```
typedef struct tagBITMAPINFO {
    BITMAPINFOHEADER  bmiHeader;
    RGBQUAD           bmiColors[1];
} BITMAPINFO;
typedef BITMAPINFO FAR   *LPBITMAPINFO;
typedef BITMAPINFO       *PBITMAPINFO;
```

The last structure is used only when DIBs are stored to disk. The BITMAPFILEHEADER structure is the first part of a bitmap stored as a disk file. This is

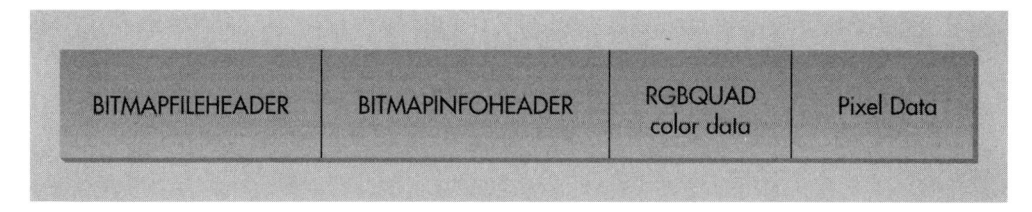

Figure 16-18 Device Independent Bitmap Format as a Disk File

how the Windows PaintBrush and SDKPaint applications store their outputs. Figure 16-18 shows how the DIB data is arranged in a disk file.

```
typedef struct tagBITMAPFILEHEADER {
    WORD    bfType;         /* always equal to 'BM' */
    DWORD   bfSize;         /* size of file in DWORDs */
    WORD    bfReserved1;    /* set to zero */
    WORD    bfReserved2;    /* set to zero */
    DWORD   bfOffBits;      /* byte offset from BITMAPFILEHEADER to */
                            /* bitmap pixel data in the file */
} BITMAPFILEHEADER;
typedef BITMAPFILEHEADER FAR    *LPBITMAPFILEHEADER;
typedef BITMAPFILEHEADER        *PBITMAPFILEHEADER;
```

Summary

Bitmaps record every pixel of an image drawn with a raster device, such as a video screen. Bitmaps have the advantage of being able to store any image, but they take up a lot of space. The amount of memory and/or disk space consumed by a bitmap depends on the size of the image stored, and on the number of colors possible per pixel. Bitmaps are commonly used to store smaller images, but they take too much disk space and memory to store large amounts of graphic data, such as long sequences of complete screen images.

The most common way Windows programs use bitmaps is to include bitmap files in the program's resource data. Bitmaps can be created with the image editors that come with the Windows programming tools, or with the Windows PaintBrush application that is supplied with the Windows. Bitmap files are included in the resource data by using the BITMAP statement. The LoadBitmap() function loads the bitmap into memory from the resource data, and returns a handle to the bitmap data. To display the bitmap, the bitmap must be selected into a memory device context created with CreateCompatibleDC(), and then copied to the device context of the screen or printer using BitBlt() or StretchBlt(). BitBlt() merely copies the bitmap to a device, while StretchBlt() can stretch or compress the image as it is copied.

When a bitmap image is copied to a device context, the bitmap pixels can be altered depending on the colors of the pixels that will be covered up by the bitmap, and by the colors of the brush currently selected into the output device context. The different possible combinations of these three colors are controlled using raster operation codes. The most common raster operation code is SRCCOPY, which simply copies the bitmap to the output device without considering the color of the current pixels on the device, or the current brush. Other raster codes are given names in WINDOWS.H and perform more complex operations when BitBlt() or StretchBlt() is called.

One other use of bitmaps is to allow drawing on a memory bitmap. This is ideal for animation and complex drawing operations. Drawing on a memory bitmap allows all of the drawing to be done in the background, and then the final image to be "blit" to the screen using BitBlt() or StretchBlt(). The CreateCompatibleBitmap() function creates a memory bitmap, which can be selected into a memory device context created with CreateCompatibleDC(). Normal GDI functions like LineTo() and Rectangle() can be used to draw on a bitmap in memory, just like any other device context.

QUESTIONS

1. When a bitmap file is included in a program's resource script file, the bitmap is given a name. This name does not have to be the same as the bitmap file name, and it is used to locate the bitmap data in the finished program's resources. (True/False)

2. The _____ function loads a bitmap into memory and returns a handle to the bitmap's data in memory.

3. Before a bitmap can be displayed, it must be selected into a _____ device context created with the _____ function.

4. The BitBlt() function copies a bitmap from the _____ to a physical output device. a) bitmap in the resource data; b) bitmap in memory; c) bitmap selected into a memory device context; d) bitmap file.

5. The BitBlt() function also has the ability to stretch or compress a bitmap image. (True/False).

6. The raster operation code to copy the source bitmap to the destination device without changing the source bitmap is _____ .

7. Which of the following raster operation codes would make the source bitmap alternately appear and disappear is it was repeatedly "blit" onto the output device context? a) SRCERASE; b) SRCINVERT; c) SRCCOPY; d) SRCAND.

8. The _____ function fills a rectangular area with the currently selected pattern brush.

9. Which function is used to load an 8 by 8 pixel bitmap from resources and convert it into a brush that can be used in GDI painting operations? a) LoadBitmap(); b) CreatePatternBrush(); c) SelectObject(); d) a, b, and c.

10. Like GetMessage(), the PeekMessage() function returns FALSE when the WM_QUIT message is received. (True/False)

11. Use the _____ function to create a blank memory bitmap that can be selected into a memory device context for drawing.

EXERCISES

1. Modify the BITMAP2 program so that the HOUSE.BMP file is displayed only once, but is stretched to fill the client area.

2. Modify the BITMAP4 program so that the DrawBallGDI() function erases the "old" part of the moving ball image by painting a thick white border around the blue circle of the ball. Does this improve the image of the animation? If so, why?

ANSWERS TO QUESTIONS

1. True.
2. LoadBitmap().
3. memory, CreateCompatibleDC().
4. c.
5. False. The StretchBlt() function stretches and compresses bitmap images.
6. SRCCOPY.
7. b.
8. PatBlt().
9. d.
10. False. Only GetMesage() returns FALSE when a WM_QUIT message is processed.
11. CreateCompatibleBitmap().

SOLUTIONS TO EXERCISES

1. The only changes needed are to process WM_SIZE messages to determine the window's client area dimensions, and to use these values when calling StretchBlt(). Save the client area width and height as static variables:

   ```
   static int     nXclient, nYclient ;
   ```

   The StretchBlt() function stretches the 64 by 64 pixel source bitmap to fit between the upper left corner (0,0) and the bottom right corner of the client area:

   ```
   case WM_SIZE:
       nXclient = LOWORD (lParam) ;
       nYclient = HIWORD (lParam) ;
       break ;
   case WM_PAINT:
       BeginPaint (hWnd, &ps) ;
       hInstance = GetWindowWord (hWnd, GWW_HINSTANCE) ;
       hBitmap = LoadBitmap (hInstance, "HouseBmp") ;
       hMemDC = CreateCompatibleDC (ps.hdc) ;
       SelectObject (hMemDC, hBitmap) ;
       StretchBlt (ps.hdc, 0, 0, nXclient, nYclient,
           hMemDC, 0, 0, 64, 64, SRCCOPY) ;
       EndPaint (hWnd, &ps) ;
       DeleteDC (hMemDC) ;
       DeleteObject (hBitmap) ;
       break ;
   ```

   The complete solution is under the file name C16EXER1 on the source code disks.

SOLUTIONS TO EXERCISES (cont'd)

2. A thick white border can be drawn around the blue circle of the moving ball by selecting a thick white pen into the device context before the blue circle is drawn. The thick border paints over the "old" edges of the previous location of the ball. Here is the modified DrawBallGDI() function, using the thick white pen:

```
void DrawBallGDI (HDC hDC)
{
    static   int nXpos = 0 ;
    int      nX, nY ;
    HBRUSH   hBrush ;
    HPEN     hPen ;
                                        /* move to left */
    nXpos = (nXpos > BITMAPWIDE ? -1 * BITMAPTALL : nXpos + 2) ;

    hPen = CreatePen (PS_SOLID, 4, RGB (255, 255, 255)) ;
    SelectObject (hDC, hPen) ;     /* make white pen */
    hBrush = CreateSolidBrush (RGB (0, 0, 255)) ;  /* make blue brush */
    SelectObject (hDC, hBrush) ; /* draw blue ball */
    Ellipse (hDC, nXpos, 0, nXpos + BITMAPTALL, BITMAPTALL) ;
    SelectObject (hDC, GetStockObject (WHITE_BRUSH)) ;
    DeleteObject (hBrush) ;        /* delete blue brush */
    SelectObject (hDC, GetStockObject (WHITE_PEN)) ;
    DeleteObject (hPen) ;          /* delete white pen */
    nX = nXpos + ((3 * BITMAPTALL) / 4) ;
    nY = BITMAPTALL / 4 ;          /* put small white highlight on ball */
    Ellipse (hDC, nX, nY, nX + 4, nY + 4) ;
}
```

Drawing the moving ball this way is an improvement over the BITMAP4.C method, as the entire ball is not erased. This reduces the flicker in the image as it moves. This approach will only work to animate simple images moving over a solid color background. For more complex images and backgrounds, painting the memory device context, and then "blitting" the image to the screen is the only reasonable approach. The complete solution to this exercise is under the name C16EXER2 on the source code disks.

CHAPTER 17

The Clipboard

One of the pleasures of using the Windows environment is being able to cut text and graphics from one application and paste it into another application. This ability is shared by almost all Windows applications, as the Windows environment provides a common mechanism for exchanging data in memory, called the "Clipboard." The Clipboard is just a memory block that Windows maintains. Applications can pass data to the Clipboard, or read the contents of the Clipboard. Because the Clipboard is maintained by the Windows environment, its contents are available to any running application.

The most common types of data exchanged via the Clipboard are text and bitmaps. There are a number of data formats available for clipboard data, and you can invent your own formats for specialized data, such as spreadsheet cells. Although the Clipboard is most often used to exchange data between separate programs, you may find that the Clipboard is convenient within a single program for cut and paste operations.

This chapter will demonstrate several uses of the Clipboard, including copying and retrieving both text and graphics. The simple text editor introduced in Chapter 15, *Disk File Access*, is also improved at the end of the chapter by adding cut, paste, copy, and delete functions that take advantage of the Clipboard. The final result, called SIMPEDIT, is a basic text editor that you can include in other programming projects.

Concepts Covered

Clipboard Viewers
Passing a Memory Block to the Clipboard
Clipboard Formats
Reading Clipboard Data
Delayed Rendering of Clipboard Data
Passing Text from an Edit Control to and from the Clipboard

Keywords Covered

CF_TEXT
CF_BITMAP
CF_OEMTEXT

Functions Covered

OpenClipboard()
CloseClipboard()
EmptyClipboard()
SetClipboardData()
GetClipboardData()
IsClipboardFormatAvailable()
RegisterClipboardFormat()
GetObject()

Messages Covered

WM_COPY
WM_CUT, WM_PASTE
WM_RENDERALLFORMATS
WM_RENDERFORMAT
WM_DESTROYCLIPBOARD

How the Clipboard Works

One thing to clear up right away is that the Windows application called CLIPBRD.EXE that comes with Windows is *not* the Clipboard. CLIPBRD.EXE (shown in Figure 17-1) is a clipboard viewer, not the Clipboard itself. Clipboard viewer applications show you what type of data is currently in the Clipboard. For example, Figure 17-1b shows the clipboard viewer displaying some bitmap data.

When you use the "Copy" or "Cut" menu items in Paintbrush, Notepad, or Windows Write, you are copying data to the Clipboard. If you have the clipboard viewer running, the data will show up in CLIPBRD's client area. If the data selected was text, text will appear in CLIPBRD's client area. If the data selected was a bitmap image, the bitmap will be displayed by CLIPBRD. When you select the "Paste" menu item from these applications, you are copying data from the Clipboard to the application. Windows keeps track of the type of data being stored in the Clipboard as the "clipboard format." Typical formats are named CF_TEXT for text data and CF_BITMAP for bitmaps.

For all types of data, the data being transferred is stored in a global memory block. If the application needs to send some

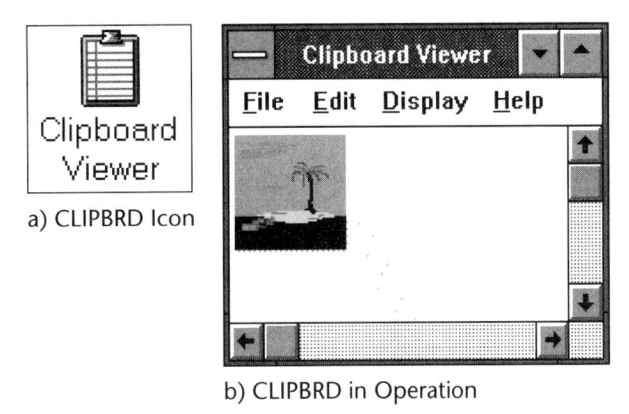

a) CLIPBRD Icon

b) CLIPBRD in Operation

Figure 17-1 The CLIPBRD.EXE Clipboard Viewer

data to the Clipboard, the data is first copied into the global memory block. The data block is then transferred to the Windows Clipboard, which takes ownership of the block. When Windows owns the block, the data in the block is said to be "in the Clipboard." Figure 17-2 illustrates the process of transferring a data block to Windows. Keep in mind that Windows, the application program(s), and the memory block, are all in memory before and after the block is transferred to the Clipboard. It is the ownership of the block that is transferred to Windows.

Once the memory block has been transferred to the Windows Clipboard, it is no longer related to the program that created the block. The Windows environment has complete ownership of the clipboard data. Any application can request access to the data in the Clipboard, although the data can only be read, not modified. The block will continue to be attached to the Windows Clipboard until a program empties the Clipboard, or passes another block with the same type of data to Windows. Windows can only keep

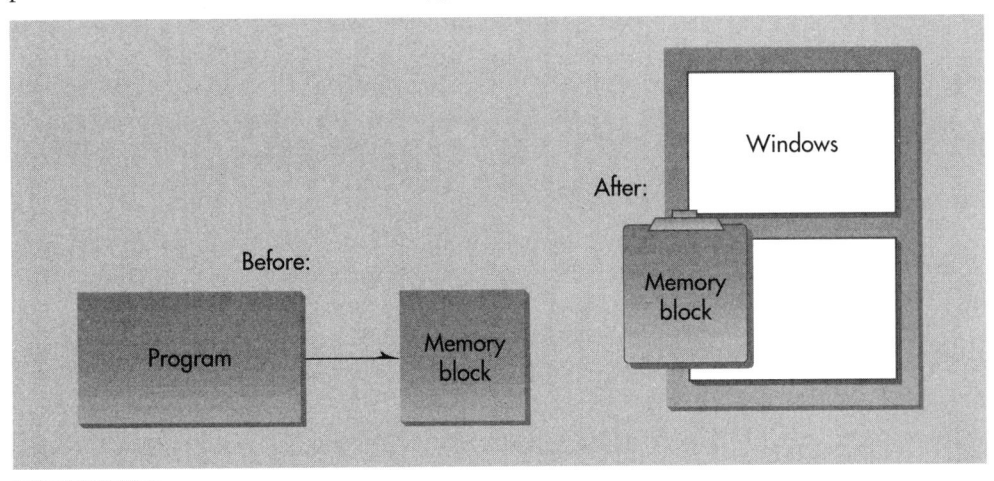

Figure 17-2 Transferring a Memory Block to the Clipboard

one memory block at a time for any given clipboard format, so any new data displaces the old data block. Windows automatically frees the old global memory block when it is displaced from the Clipboard.

Basic Clipboard Functions

From a programming standpoint, the Clipboard is easy to use and boils down to understanding five functions:

OpenClipboard()   -   Opens the Clipboard for access by the program.
EmptyClipboard()   -   Frees all data now in the Clipboard.
GetClipboardData()   -   Retrieves a handle to read-only data in the Clipboard.
SetClipboardData()   -   Passes a memory block to the Clipboard.
CloseClipboard()   -   Closes the Clipboard.

As an example, let's copy some text into the Clipboard. The first step is to allocate a global memory block and copy the text into the block. Once the block is ready, the Clipboard is opened with OpenClipboard(). Only one application can open the Clipboard at any one time, so OpenClipboard() both opens the Clipboard and keeps any other application from accessing the Clipboard. If the Clipboard is available (not currently opened by another application), OpenClipboard() will return TRUE. The Clipboard is emptied of all data with EmptyClipboard(), and then given the new data block with SetClipboardData(). Finally, the Clipboard is closed using CloseClipboard(), so that other programs can again access the clipboard.

```
HANDLE    hGmem ;
LPSTR     lpStr ;

hGmem = GlobalAlloc (GHND, 32) ;           /* allocate a global block 32 bytes long */
lpStr = GlobalLock (hGmem) ;               /* lock the block */
lstrcpy (lpStr, "Some text to copy.") ;    /* copy some text into the block */
GlobalUnlock (hGmem) ;                     /* leave the block unlocked */
if (OpenClipboard (hWnd))                  /* open the clipboard */
{
    EmptyClipboard () ;                    /* remove all formats now in clipboard */
    SetClipboardData (CF_TEXT, hGmem) ;    /* block to clipboard with CF_TEXT format */
    CloseClipboard () ;                    /* close the clipboard */
}
```

The same application will probably need to be able to read the Clipboard data. The only trick to remember is that the data in the Clipboard belongs to Windows, so the block is read-only data once it is in the Clipboard. If you are going to modify the Clipboard data in any way, you will need to copy the Clipboard data to a memory buffer within your program before the data is used. Here is a typical example, which copies the Clipboard text data into the character buffer *cBuf[]*:

```
HANDLE    hClipMem ;
LPSTR     lpClip ;
char      cBuf [128] ;
```

```
if (OpenClipboard (hWnd))
{                      /* get handle to clipboard data */
    hClipMem = GetClipboardData (CF_TEXT) ;
    if (hClipMem)   /* if there is CF_TEXT data */
    {
        lpClip = GlobalLock (hClipMem) ;
        lstrcpy (cBuf, lpClip) ;
        GlobalUnlock (hClipMem) ;
    }
    CloseClipboard () ;
}
```

This is a simplified example. Normally, you could not be certain that the data in the Clipboard would not exceed the *cBuf[]* buffer size. Typically, the program will allocate a new memory block and copy the Clipboard data to that block, after determining the size of the clipboard data with the GlobalSize() function. This way you can make sure that the allocated block is big enough to hold the entire Clipboard contents. This technique is demonstrated in the first example program, which will be described shortly.

Clipboard Formats

You probably noticed in the previous section that the SetClipboardData() and GetClipboardData() functions used the CF_TEXT constant. CF_TEXT is a Clipboard format for simple text data, which is defined in WINDOWS.H. Table 17-1 shows the most common predefined clipboard formats.

VALUE	MEANING
CF_BITMAP	A bitmap handle (HBITMAP).
CF_DIB	A memory block containing a device-independent bitmap (DIB). The block will contain a BITMAPINFO data structure followed by the bitmap bits (see Chapter 16, *Bitmaps*).
CF_DIF	Software Arts' Data Interchange Format.
CF_METAFILEPICT	A metafile picture. See Chapter 23 of *The Waite Group's Windows API Bible* for a description of metafiles.
CF_OEMTEXT	A memory block containing only OEM text characters. Each line is ended with a CR-LF pair. A NULL byte marks the end of the text. This is the format Windows uses to transfer data between non-Windows and Windows applications.
CF_OWNERDISPLAY	The Clipboard owner is responsible for painting the Clipboard.
CF_PALETTE	A handle to a color palette.
CF_TEXT	A memory block containing text characters. Each line is ended with a CR-LF pair. A NULL byte marks the end of the text. This is the standard format for exchanging text between Windows applications.
CF_TIFF	Tag Image File Format.

Table 17-1 Predefined Clipboard Formats

In addition to the predefined clipboard formats, an application can create a special clipboard format. Spreadsheet programs typically create their own clipboard format for cutting and pasting the contents of spreadsheet cells. The RegisterClipboardFormat() function creates a clipboard format, based on a text name string. As soon as the new clipboard format is registered, the returned value from RegisterClipboardFormat() can be used in place of a predefined format such as CF_TEXT when calling SetClipboardData() and GetClipboardData(). (A custom clipboard format will be demonstrated in the second example program in this chapter.)

```
static WORD         wClipFormat ;

wClipFormat = RegisterClipboardFormat ("SpreadCell") ;
if (OpenClipboard (hWnd))
{
     hClipMem = GetClipboardData (wClipFormat) ;
```
[Other program lines]

The most obvious reason for clipboard formats is to make sure that the data in the Clipboard is in the format that the program expects. It would be a disaster for a program to expect to read text data, but have the memory block contain a bitmap. A more subtle reason for using clipboard formats is that a program can save data to the Clipboard in more than one format at the same time. Although the Clipboard can hold only one memory block at a time with the CF_TEXT format, the Clipboard can contain several memory blocks at once, as long as each has a different format. Figure 17-3 shows this situation, with three clipboard memory formats in place at one time.

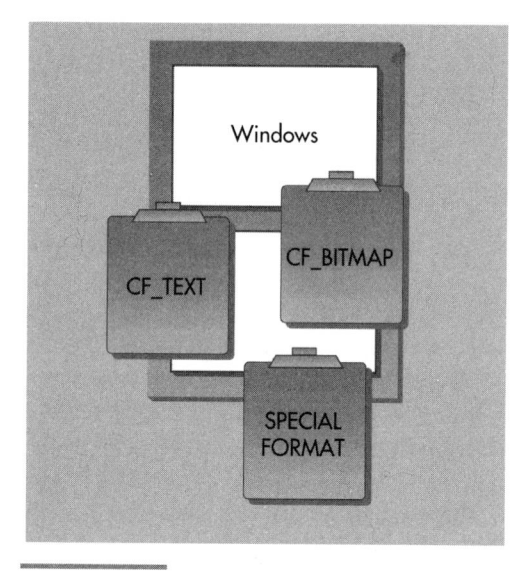

Figure 17-3 Multiple Clipboard Formats

A program that wants to read the clipboard data can look to see which formats are available. The IsClipboardFormatAvailable() function comes in handy to see what data is in the Clipboard to be read. The program can start out with the most desirable format, and load it if it is available. For example, the spreadsheet would read the specialized format for storing a spreadsheet cell in preference to the simple CF_TEXT format, as the CF_TEXT format would just pass the cell's contents, and not any special formatting information. If the most desirable format is not available, the program can use a less sophisticated format.

```
     if (IsClipboardFormatAvailable (CF_TEXT))
          /* read that data */
```

```
else if (IsClipboardFormatAvailable (CF_OEMTEXT))
    /* second choice, read OEM text */
```

Many Windows applications take advantage of multiple clipboard formats. For example, Word for Windows loads five different formats into the Clipboard when a selection of text is copied or cut. The most desirable format is the special "Rich text format" that Word for Windows uses to cut and paste text, including all text formatting information. Word for Windows also copies the selected text in the CF_TEXT and CF_OEMTEXT formats, so that other programs, which do not support the rich text format, can at least copy the text characters from data placed on the Clipboard. Word for Windows will also read and write several forms of graphical data including DDB and DIB bitmaps, allowing the user to paste pictures directly into a document via the Clipboard.

Clipboard Limitations

There is a basic limitation to the Clipboard that you should keep in mind when designing Windows applications. The Clipboard is designed to hold only data from one program at any one time. If the application supports multiple clipboard formats, the contents in each of the formats is expected to reflect the same basic data. For example, if you copy text into the Clipboard using Word for Windows, the same text string will be saved in several clipboard formats. The CF_TEXT format block will contain just the text characters, while special clipboard formats (such as "Rich Text") will contain the text *and* formatting data (font, boldface, underline, etc.).

If you have several applications running at the same time, copying data to the Clipboard from one application will result in any data currently in the Clipboard being lost. This is because applications call EmptyClipboard() before copying their own data to the Clipboard. Every running application can then read the new data from the Clipboard, if the application supports one of the formats in the Clipboard.

A simple way to describe this limitation from the user's point of view is: The Clipboard only holds one object at a time. As a programmer you will realize that the "one object" may be stored using several clipboard formats. There is no reason to burden the user with this knowledge. He or she can happily cut and paste data between applications without any thought of the subtle differences in data formats used by different programs.

A Simple Clipboard Example

The first example program in this chapter is called CLIPBRD1, and it demonstrates the basic clipboard functions. Figure 17-4 shows CLIPBRD1 running, after both the "Copy to Clipboard" and "Get Clipboard Text" menu items were selected. CLIPBRD1 copies the uppercase alphabet to a memory block, and sends the block to the Clipboard, when "Copy to Clipboard" is selected.

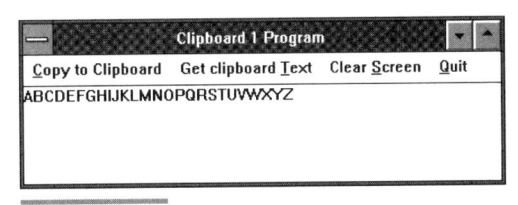

Figure 17-4 The CLIPBRD1 Program

Because CLIPBRD1 uses the Clipboard to copy and retrieve data, the text is available to other applications. Here are some experiments that you can try using CLIPBRD1:

1. After selecting the "Copy to Clipboard" menu item in CLIPBRD1, start the Notepad or Windows Write application, and select "Paste." The uppercase alphabet will be copied from the Clipboard into your document.
2. Start the Windows clipboard viewer application while CLIPBRD1 is running. The contents inside the clipboard viewer will change to the alphabet when "Copy to Clipboard" is selected in CLIPBRD1.
3. Highlight a block of text from within the Notepad application, and then select Notepad's "Copy" menu item. The next time the "Get Clipboard Text" menu item is selected in CLIPBRD1, the text copied in Notepad will be displayed in CLIPBRD1's client area. The text will end up all on one line, as CLIPBRD1 makes no attempt to format text data.

As you can see from these examples, CLIPBRD1 succeeds in exchanging text data with a wide range of other applications. Windows makes it so easy to use the Clipboard that it is almost criminal not to support the Clipboard in a Windows application.

CLIPBRD1 Listings

The complete CLIPBRD1.C program is shown in Listing 17-1. This is about as simple as a program that supports the Clipboard can be, as only the CF_TEXT format is supported. The uppercase alphabet is copied into a global memory block before the Clipboard is opened. The block is then passed to the Clipboard using SetClipboardData() and the CF_TEXT clipboard format.

```
                /* allocate global memory block */
hGmem = GlobalAlloc (GHND, 32) ;
lpStr = GlobalLock (hGmem) ;
                /* copy 26 letters to block */
for (i = 0 ; i < 26 ; i++)
    *lpStr++ = (char)('A' + i) ;
GlobalUnlock (hGmem) ;
if (OpenClipboard (hWnd))
{               /* give clipboard data as CF_TEXT */
    EmptyClipboard () ;
    SetClipboardData (CF_TEXT, hGmem) ;
    CloseClipboard () ;
}
```

When reading the Clipboard contents, CLIPBRD1 follows the typical practice of copying the contents of the Clipboard into a memory block allocated by CLIPBRD1, prior to doing anything with the data. The GlobalSize() function returns the size of the memory block currently in the Clipboard, so that CLIPBRD1 knows how big a block to allocate. As soon as the Clipboard data is copied into the new memory block, CLIPBRD1 displays it as text using the TextOut() function.

```
        hDC = GetDC (hWnd) ;
        if (OpenClipboard (hWnd))
        {                      /* get handle to clipboard data */
            hClipMem = GetClipboardData (CF_TEXT) ;
            if (hClipMem)      /* if there is CF_TEXT data */
            {                  /* create 2nd block, sized for data */
                hGmem = GlobalAlloc (GHND, GlobalSize (hClipMem)) ;
                if (hGmem)
                {              /* copy data from clipboard */
                    lpStr = GlobalLock (hGmem) ;
                    lpClip = GlobalLock (hClipMem) ;
                    lstrcpy (lpStr, lpClip) ;
                    TextOut (hDC, 0, 0, lpStr, lstrlen (lpStr)) ;
                    GlobalUnlock (hGmem) ;
                    GlobalUnlock (hClipMem) ;
                    GlobalFree (hGmem) ;
                }
            }
            CloseClipboard () ;
        }
        ReleaseDC (hWnd, hDC) ;
        break ;
```

Note that when GetClipboardData() is called with the CF_TEXT clipboard style, the returned value will be NULL if data with the CF_TEXT format is not currently selected into the Clipboard. This keeps CLIPBRD1 from attempting to display bitmap, or other nontext data if CF_TEXT data is not available.

Listing 17-1 CLIPBRD1.C

```
/* clipbrd1.c    simple clipboard example */

#include <windows.h>
#include "clipbrd1.h"

int PASCAL WinMain (HANDLE hInstance, HANDLE hPrevInstance, LPSTR lpszCmdLine,
    int nCmdShow)
{
    HWND        hWnd ;          /* the window's "handle" */
    MSG         msg ;           /* a message structure */
    WNDCLASS    wndclass ;      /* window class structure */
    char        cBuf [128] ;

    if (!hPrevInstance)
    {
        wndclass.style           = CS_HREDRAW | CS_VREDRAW ;
        wndclass.lpfnWndProc     = WndProc ;
        wndclass.cbClsExtra      = 0 ;
        wndclass.cbWndExtra      = 0 ;
        wndclass.hInstance       = hInstance ;
        wndclass.hIcon           = LoadIcon (hInstance, "MyIcon") ;
        wndclass.hCursor         = LoadCursor (NULL, IDC_ARROW) ;
        wndclass.hbrBackground   = GetStockObject (WHITE_BRUSH) ;
        wndclass.lpszMenuName    = "MyMenu" ;
```

```
            wndclass.lpszClassName = "MyClass" ;
                        /* register the window class */
            if (!RegisterClass (&wndclass))
                return 0 ;
    }
    LoadString (hInstance, S_PROGRAMCAPTION, cBuf, sizeof (cBuf)) ;

    hWnd = CreateWindow ("MyClass", cBuf, WS_OVERLAPPEDWINDOW,
        CW_USEDEFAULT, CW_USEDEFAULT, CW_USEDEFAULT, CW_USEDEFAULT,
        NULL, NULL, hInstance, NULL) ;
    ShowWindow (hWnd, nCmdShow) ;    /* display the window */

    while (GetMessage (&msg, NULL, NULL, NULL))    /* message loop */
    {
        TranslateMessage (&msg) ;   /* translate keyboard messages */
        DispatchMessage (&msg) ;    /* send message to WndProc() */
    }
    return (msg.wParam) ;
}

long FAR PASCAL WndProc (HWND hWnd, WORD wMessage, WORD wParam, LONG lParam)
{
    HDC         hDC ;
    HANDLE      hGmem, hClipMem ;
    LPSTR       lpStr, lpClip ;
    int         i ;

    switch (wMessage)       /* process windows messages */
    {
        case WM_COMMAND:
            switch (wParam)
            {
                case IDM_SENDCLIP:  /* copy text to the clipboard */
                                    /* allocate global memory block */
                    hGmem = GlobalAlloc (GHND, 32) ;
                    lpStr = GlobalLock (hGmem) ;
                                /* copy 26 letters to block */
                    for (i = 0 ; i < 26 ; i++)
                        *lpStr++ = (char) (_A + i) ;
                    GlobalUnlock (hGmem) ;
                    if (OpenClipboard (hWnd))
                    {           /* give clipboard data as CF_TEXT */
                        EmptyClipboard () ;
                        SetClipboardData (CF_TEXT, hGmem) ;
                        CloseClipboard () ;
                    }
                    break ;
                case IDM_GETCLIP:       /* read the clipboard data */
                    hDC = GetDC (hWnd) ;
                    if (OpenClipboard (hWnd))
                    {           /* get handle to clipboard data */
                        hClipMem = GetClipboardData (CF_TEXT) ;
                        if (hClipMem)   /* if there is CF_TEXT data */
                        {           /* create 2nd block, sized for data */
                            hGmem = GlobalAlloc (GHND, GlobalSize (hClipMem)) ;
                            if (hGmem)
                            {           /* copy data from clipboard */
                                lpStr = GlobalLock (hGmem) ;
                                lpClip = GlobalLock (hClipMem) ;
```

```
                    lstrcpy (lpStr, lpClip) ;
                    TextOut (hDC, 0, 0, lpStr, lstrlen (lpStr)) ;
                    GlobalUnlock (hGmem) ;
                    GlobalUnlock (hClipMem) ;
                    GlobalFree (hGmem) ;
                  }
                }
                CloseClipboard () ;
              }
              ReleaseDC (hWnd, hDC) ;
              break ;
            case IDM_CLEAR:          /* clear the client area */
              InvalidateRect (hWnd, NULL, TRUE) ;
              break ;
            case IDM_QUIT:               /* Quit menu item */
              DestroyWindow (hWnd) ;   /* destroy window, */
              break ;            /* terminating application */
        }
        break ;
    case WM_DESTROY:             /* stop application */
        PostQuitMessage (0) ;
        break ;
    default:        /* default windows message processing */
        return (DefWindowProc (hWnd, wMessage, wParam, lParam)) ;
  }
  return (0L) ;
}
```

The support files for CLIPBRD1 are shown in Listings 17-2 to 17-6. The program's icon is shown in Figure 17-5.

Listing 17-2 CLIPBRD1.H Header File

```
/* clipbrd1.h header file */

#define IDM_SENDCLIP      1      /* menu item ID numbers */
#define IDM_GETCLIP       2
#define IDM_CLEAR         3
#define IDM_QUIT         10

#define S_PROGRAMCAPTION  1      /* string table ID numbers */

long FAR PASCAL WndProc (HWND, WORD, WORD, LONG) ;
```

Figure 17-5
CLIPBRD1.ICO Icon Image

Listing 17-3 CLIPBRD1.RC Resource Script File

```
/* clipbrd1.rc resource file */

#include "clipbrd1.h"

MyIcon    ICON    clipbrd1.ico

MyMenu    MENU
BEGIN
```

```
        MENUITEM "&Copy to Clipboard",      IDM_SENDCLIP
        MENUITEM "Get clipboard &Text",     IDM_GETCLIP
        MENUITEM "Clear &Screen",           IDM_CLEAR
        MENUITEM "&Quit",                   IDM_QUIT
    END


    STRINGTABLE
    BEGIN
        S_PROGRAMCAPTION      "Clipboard 1 Program"
    END
```

Listing 17-4 CLIPBRD1.DEF Module Definition File

```
NAME            clipbrd1
DESCRIPTION     'clipbrd1 application'
EXETYPE         WINDOWS
STUB            'WINSTUB.EXE'
CODE            PRELOAD MOVEABLE DISCARDABLE
DATA            PRELOAD MOVEABLE MULTIPLE
HEAPSIZE        1024
STACKSIZE       5120
EXPORTS         WndProc
```

Listing 17-5 Turbo C++ Project File for CLIPBRD1

```
clipbrd1.c
clipbrd1.def
clipbrd1.res
```

Listing 17-6 QuickC Project File for CLIPBRD1

```
clipbrd1.c
clipbrd1.def
clipbrd1.rc
```

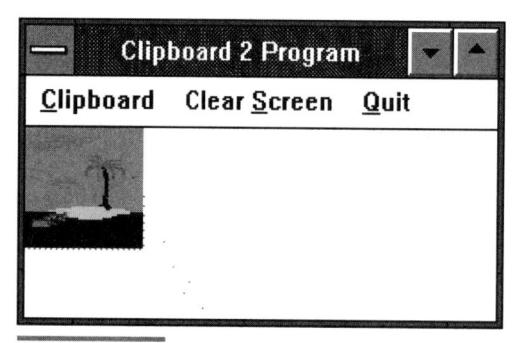

Figure 17-6 The CLIPBRD2 Program Displaying a Bitmap

Multiple Clipboard Formats

The next example program, CLIPBRD2, demonstrates saving multiple clipboard formats at the same time, and also creates a special clipboard format for saving numeric data. Figure 17-6 shows CLIPBRD2 running, displaying bitmap data that was obtained from the Clipboard. Figure 17-7 shows CLIPBRD2 after obtaining both CF_TEXT and a special numeric format from the Clipboard. CLIPBRD2 is an extreme example of Window's ability to handle multiple clipboard formats at the same time. Normally, the data passed to the Clipboard with different formats would represent different ways of saving the same basic data, such as different text formats. CLIPBRD2 manages to save three entirely different types of data in the Clipboard at the same time.

You can do a few experiments when CLIPBRD2 is running to demonstrate the impact of saving multiple clipboard formats at the same time.

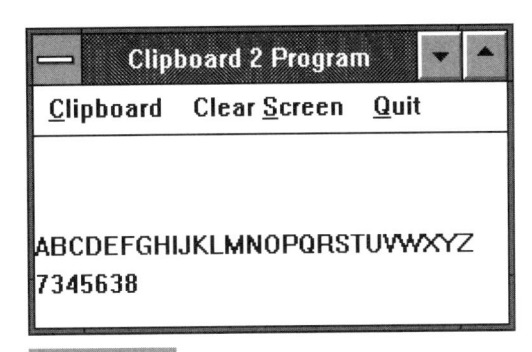

Figure 17-7 The CLIPBRD2 Program Displaying CF_TEXT and a Special Format

1. After CLIPBRD2 is running, and has been used to copy data to the Clipboard, start the Paintbrush application. If you select the "Paste" menu item in Paintbrush, the same bitmap shown in Figure 17-7 will appear in the Paintbrush client area. This is because Paintbrush reads and writes the CF_BITMAP clipboard format, which CLIPBRD2 uses to copy the bitmap to the Clipboard.

2. If you select "Paste" from within the Notepad application after CLIPBRD2 has copied data to the Clipboard, the text string (all the uppercase letters) will appear in the Notepad client area. This is because Notepad supports the CF_TEXT clipboard format. Notepad does not support the CF_BITMAP format, so the bitmap data is not copied from the Clipboard.

3. Some applications, such as Windows Write, support both the CF_TEXT and CF_BITMAP formats. If you select the "Paste" menu item, only the text string will be copied to the Windows Write client area. This is because Windows Write considers CF_TEXT to be a preferable format, compared to CF_BITMAP, if both formats are available. However, if you chose the "Paste Special" menu item, Windows Write will allow you to select either the bitmap or the text data in the Clipboard. Figure 17-8 shows Windows Write after both formats have been "pasted" from the Clipboard.

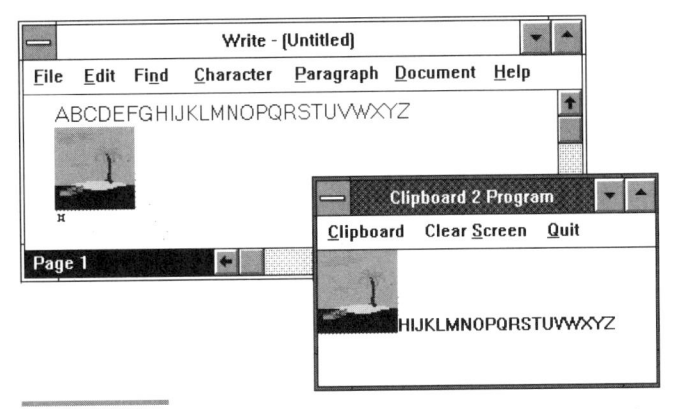

Figure 17-8 Windows Write Obtaining Data from CLIPBRD2 via the Clipboard

Chapter 17 • The Clipboard

An Example Using Multiple Clipboard Formats

The complete CLIPBRD2.C program is shown in Listing 17-7. This is a more complex example, so let's break it down into sections. CLIPBRD2 puts three different types of data in the Clipboard when the "Copy to Clipboard" menu item is selected. This requires that three separate global memory blocks be allocated. Each block is filled with the right type of data, and then passed to the Clipboard with SetClipboardData(). The text data in CLIPBRD2 is again just the uppercase letters A-Z, copied into a global memory block.

```
hGmem = GlobalAlloc (GHND, 32) ;
lpStr = GlobalLock (hGmem) ;
               /* copy 26 l etters to block */
for (i = 0 ; i < 26 ; i++)
    *lpStr++ = (char) ('A' + i) ;
GlobalUnlock (hGmem) ;
```

The bitmap image is stored in the program's resources with the name "IslandBMP." The island image was created with the image editor, and saved as a bitmap file. Figure 17-9 shows the ISLAND.BMP bitmap image.

Figure 17-9 The ISLAND.BMP Bitmap Image

```
IslandBMP    BITMAP island.bmp
```

With the bitmap stored in the program's resources, it is a simple matter to load the bitmap into a global memory block, using the LoadBitmap() function.

```
hInstance = GetWindowWord (hWnd, GWW_HINSTANCE) ;
hBitmap = LoadBitmap (hInstance, "IslandBMP") ;
```

This leaves one more clipboard format. CLIPBRD2 registers a new clipboard format called "DIGITS" with Windows. The returned value from the RegisterClipboardFormat() function is the WORD value for this special format.

```
wClipFormat = RegisterClipboardFormat ("DIGITS") ;
               /* put "DIGITS" data to clpbd */
hDigits = GlobalAlloc (GHND, 32) ;
lpStr = GlobalLock (hDigits) ;
               /* copy digits to block */
lstrcpy (lpStr, "7345638") ;
GlobalUnlock (hDigits) ;
```

At this point CLIPBRD2 has three memory blocks loaded with data and has registered the new clipboard format "DIGITS." The only step left is to pass these three memory blocks to the Clipboard using the SetClipboardData() function:

```
if (OpenClipboard (hWnd))
{              /* in clipboard at the same time */
    EmptyClipboard () ;
    SetClipboardData (CF_TEXT, hGmem) ;
    SetClipboardData (CF_BITMAP, hBitmap) ;
    SetClipboardData (wClipFormat, hDigits) ;
    CloseClipboard () ;
}
```

Note how the *wClipFormat* WORD value returned by RegisterClipboardFormat() is used just like the predefined CF_TEXT and CF_BITMAP formats to pass a format to the Windows Clipboard. The Clipboard now holds all three memory blocks. The remainder of the CLIPBRD2.C listing deals with retrieving the clipboard data so that it can be displayed. Getting the CF_TEXT data is done identically to the previous CLIPBRD1.C program, and is not repeated here. Displaying the bitmap is a little more involved. Here is the portion that displays the bitmap image retrieved from the Clipboard:

```
hDC = GetDC (hWnd) ;
if (OpenClipboard (hWnd))
{                              /* get handle to clipboard data */
    hClipMem = GetClipboardData (CF_BITMAP) ;
    if (hClipMem)   /* if there is CF_BITMAP data */
    {
        hMemDC = CreateCompatibleDC (hDC) ;
        SelectObject (hMemDC, hClipMem) ;
        GetObject (hClipMem, sizeof (BITMAP), (LPSTR) &bm) ;
        BitBlt (hDC, 0, 0, bm.bmWidth, bm.bmHeight, hMemDC,
            0, 0, SRCCOPY) ;
        DeleteDC (hMemDC) ;
    }
    CloseClipboard () ;
}
ReleaseDC (hWnd, hDC) ;
```

The handle of the memory block containing the bitmap in the Clipboard is retrieved with GetClipboardData(), and selected into a memory device context created with CreateCompatibleDC(). The only problem is figuring out how big the bitmap should be. CLIPBRD2.C uses the handy GetObject() function to read the beginning of the memory block and copy the data into a BITMAP structure. (Review Chapter 16, *Bitmaps*, if you do not remember the details of the BITMAP structure.) The *bmWidth* and *bmHeight* elements of the bitmap structure are then used to specify the correct width and height of the bitmap to display. BitBlt() copies the bitmap data to the window's client area.

Retrieving the special "DIGITS" clipboard format data is similar to retrieving CF_TEXT data. The GetClipboardData() function is called using the *wClipFormat* WORD value that was returned by RegisterClipboardFormat() when the new format was registered.

```
hDC = GetDC (hWnd) ;
if (OpenClipboard (hWnd))
{                              /* get handle to DIGITS data */
    hClipMem = GetClipboardData (wClipFormat) ;
    if (hClipMem)              /* if there is DIGITS data */
    {
        lpStr = GlobalLock (hClipMem) ;
        lstrcpy (cBuf, lpStr) ;
        GlobalUnlock (hClipMem) ;
        TextOut (hDC, 0, 70, cBuf, lstrlen (cBuf)) ;
    }
    CloseClipboard () ;
}
ReleaseDC (hWnd, hDC) ;
```

Note in these examples that the IsClipboardFormatAvailable() function is not used to determine if one of the three formats is available before attempting to read the data. The GetClipboardData() function will return NULL if the specified format is not available, even if a memory block with some other format is currently selected into the Clipboard. This stops applications from reading the wrong type of data by accident.

Listing 17-7 shows the complete CLIPBRD2.C program. The support files are shown in Listings 17-7 to 17-12. Figure 17-10 shows the program's icon.

Figure 17-10
CLIPBRD2.ICO
Icon Image

Listing 17-7 CLIPBRD2.C

```c
/* clipbrd2.c   multiple clipboard formats example */

#include <windows.h>
#include "clipbrd2.h"

int PASCAL WinMain (HANDLE hInstance, HANDLE hPrevInstance, LPSTR lpszCmdLine,
    int nCmdShow)
{
    HWND        hWnd ;      /* the window's "handle" */
    MSG         msg ;       /* a message structure */
    WNDCLASS    wndclass ;  /* window class structure */
    char        cBuf [128] ;

    if (!hPrevInstance)
    {
        wndclass.style          = CS_HREDRAW | CS_VREDRAW ;
        wndclass.lpfnWndProc    = WndProc ;
        wndclass.cbClsExtra     = 0 ;
        wndclass.cbWndExtra     = 0 ;
        wndclass.hInstance      = hInstance ;
        wndclass.hIcon          = LoadIcon (hInstance, "MyIcon") ;
        wndclass.hCursor        = LoadCursor (NULL, IDC_ARROW) ;
        wndclass.hbrBackground  = GetStockObject (WHITE_BRUSH) ;
        wndclass.lpszMenuName   = "MyMenu" ;
        wndclass.lpszClassName  = "MyClass" ;
                    /* register the window class */
        if (!RegisterClass (&wndclass))
            return 0 ;
    }
    LoadString (hInstance, S_PROGRAMCAPTION, cBuf, sizeof (cBuf)) ;

    hWnd = CreateWindow ("MyClass", cBuf, WS_OVERLAPPEDWINDOW,
        CW_USEDEFAULT, CW_USEDEFAULT, CW_USEDEFAULT, CW_USEDEFAULT,
        NULL, NULL, hInstance, NULL) ;
    ShowWindow (hWnd, nCmdShow) ;   /* display the window */

    while (GetMessage (&msg, NULL, NULL, NULL))     /* message loop */
    {
        TranslateMessage (&msg) ;   /* translate keyboard messages */
        DispatchMessage (&msg) ;    /* send message to WndProc() */
```

```
    }
    return (msg.wParam) ;
}

long FAR PASCAL WndProc (HWND hWnd, WORD wMessage, WORD wParam, LONG lParam)
{
    HDC         hDC, hMemDC ;
    HANDLE      hInstance, hGmem, hDigits, hClipMem ;
    HBITMAP     hBitmap ;
    LPSTR       lpStr, lpClip ;
    int         i ;
    BITMAP      bm ;
    static WORD wClipFormat ;
    char        cBuf [128] ;

    switch (wMessage)          /* process windows messages */
    {
        case WM_COMMAND:
            switch (wParam)
            {
                case IDM_SENDCLIP:  /* copy 3 types of data to clipboard */
                                    /* allocate global memory block */
                    hGmem = GlobalAlloc (GHND, 32) ;
                    lpStr = GlobalLock (hGmem) ;
                                    /* copy 26 letters to block */
                    for (i = 0 ; i < 26 ; i++)
                        *lpStr++ = (char) (_A + i) ;
                    GlobalUnlock (hGmem) ;

                                    /* load a bitmap into memory */
                    hInstance = GetWindowWord (hWnd, GWW_HINSTANCE) ;
                    hBitmap = LoadBitmap (hInstance, "IslandBMP") ;

                                    /* register a new clipboard format */
                    wClipFormat = RegisterClipboardFormat ("DIGITS") ;
                                    /* put "DIGITS" data to clpbd */
                    hDigits = GlobalAlloc (GHND, 32) ;
                    lpStr = GlobalLock (hDigits) ;
                                    /* copy 26 letters to block */
                    lstrcpy (lpStr, "7345638") ;
                    GlobalUnlock (hDigits) ;

                                    /* put all three types of data */
                    if (OpenClipboard (hWnd))
                    {               /* in clipboard at the same time */
                        EmptyClipboard () ;
                        SetClipboardData (CF_TEXT, hGmem) ;
                        SetClipboardData (CF_BITMAP, hBitmap) ;
                        SetClipboardData (wClipFormat, hDigits) ;
                        CloseClipboard () ;
                    }
                    break ;
                case IDM_GETTEXT:   /* read the CF_TEXT clipboard data */
                    hDC = GetDC (hWnd) ;
                    if (OpenClipboard (hWnd))
                    {               /* get handle to clipboard data */
                        hClipMem = GetClipboardData (CF_TEXT) ;
                        if (hClipMem)   /* if there is CF_TEXT data */
                        {               /* create 2nd block, sized for data */
```

```c
                            hGmem = GlobalAlloc (GHND, GlobalSize (hClipMem)) ;
                            if (hGmem)
                            {                   /* copy data from clipboard */
                                lpStr = GlobalLock (hGmem) ;
                                lpClip = GlobalLock (hClipMem) ;
                                lstrcpy (lpStr, lpClip) ;
                                TextOut (hDC, 0, 50, lpStr, lstrlen (lpStr)) ;
                                GlobalUnlock (hGmem) ;
                                GlobalUnlock (hClipMem) ;
                                GlobalFree (hGmem) ;
                            }
                        }
                        CloseClipboard () ;
                    }
                    ReleaseDC (hWnd, hDC) ;
                    break ;
                case IDM_GETBMP:        /* read and display bitmap from clipboard */
                    hDC = GetDC (hWnd) ;
                    if (OpenClipboard (hWnd))
                    {                       /* get handle to clipboard data */
                        hClipMem = GetClipboardData (CF_BITMAP) ;
                        if (hClipMem)   /* if there is CF_BITMAP data */
                        {
                            hMemDC = CreateCompatibleDC (hDC) ;
                            SelectObject (hMemDC, hClipMem) ;
                            GetObject (hClipMem, sizeof (BITMAP), (LPSTR) &bm) ;
                            BitBlt (hDC, 0, 0, bm.bmWidth, bm.bmHeight, hMemDC,
                                0, 0, SRCCOPY) ;
                            DeleteDC (hMemDC) ;
                        }
                        CloseClipboard () ;
                    }
                    ReleaseDC (hWnd, hDC) ;
                    break ;
                case IDM_GETSPECIAL:    /* get DIGITS clipboard data */
                    hDC = GetDC (hWnd) ;
                    if (OpenClipboard (hWnd))
                    {                       /* get handle to DIGITS data */
                        hClipMem = GetClipboardData (wClipFormat) ;
                        if (hClipMem)   /* if there is DIGITS data */
                        {
                            lpStr = GlobalLock (hClipMem) ;
                            lstrcpy (cBuf, lpStr) ;
                            GlobalUnlock (hClipMem) ;
                            TextOut (hDC, 0, 70, cBuf, lstrlen (cBuf)) ;
                        }
                        CloseClipboard () ;
                    }
                    ReleaseDC (hWnd, hDC) ;
                    break ;
                case IDM_CLEAR:                 /* clear the client area */
                    InvalidateRect (hWnd, NULL, TRUE) ;
                    break ;
                case IDM_QUIT:          /* Quit menu item */
                    DestroyWindow (hWnd) ;  /* destroy window, */
                    break ;         /* terminating application */
            }
            break ;
        case WM_DESTROY:            /* stop application */
```

```
                PostQuitMessage (0) ;
                break ;
            default:                /* default windows message processing */
                return (DefWindowProc (hWnd, wMessage, wParam, lParam)) ;
    }
    return (0L) ;
}
```

Listing 17-8 CLIPBRD2.H Header File

```
/* clipbrd2.h header file */

#define IDM_SENDCLIP       1    /* menu item ID numbers */
#define IDM_GETTEXT        2
#define IDM_GETBMP         3
#define IDM_GETSPECIAL     4
#define IDM_CLEAR          5
#define IDM_QUIT          10

#define S_PROGRAMCAPTION   1    /* string table ID numbers */

long FAR PASCAL WndProc (HWND, WORD, WORD, LONG) ;
```

Listing 17-9 CLIPBRD2.RC Resource Script File

```
/* clipbrd2.rc resource file */

#include "clipbrd2.h"

MyIcon     ICON     clipbrd2.ico
IslandBMP  BITMAP   island.bmp

MyMenu     MENU
BEGIN
    POPUP   "&Clipboard"
    BEGIN
        MENUITEM "&Copy to Clipboard",      IDM_SENDCLIP
        MENUITEM "Get clipboard &Text",     IDM_GETTEXT
        MENUITEM "Get clipboard &BMP",      IDM_GETBMP
        MENUITEM "Get &Special data",       IDM_GETSPECIAL
    END
    MENUITEM "Clear &Screen",               IDM_CLEAR
    MENUITEM "&Quit",                       IDM_QUIT
END

STRINGTABLE
BEGIN
    S_PROGRAMCAPTION     "Clipboard 2 Program"
END
```

Listing 17-10 CLIPBRD2.DEF Module Definition File

```
NAME          clipbrd2
DESCRIPTION   'clipbrd2 application'
EXETYPE       WINDOWS
```

```
STUB        'WINSTUB.EXE'
CODE        PRELOAD MOVEABLE DISCARDABLE
DATA        PRELOAD MOVEABLE MULTIPLE
HEAPSIZE    1024
STACKSIZE   5120
EXPORTS     WndProc
```

Listing 17-11 Turbo C++ Project File for CLIPBRD2

```
clipbrd2.c
clipbrd2.def
clipbrd2.res
```

Listing 17-12 QuickC Project File for CLIPBRD2

```
clipbrd2.c
clipbrd2.def
clipbrd2.rc
```

Delayed Rendering of Clipboard Data

Programs like Word for Windows that supply four or five clipboard formats at once could waste a lot of time and memory space if all five formats were copied to the Clipboard each time the "Copy" or "Cut" menu items are selected. It is unlikely that more than one of the Clipboard formats will be read at any one time. This leaves the other format's memory blocks unused.

Fortunately, Windows provides an intelligent alternative to simply copying all of the data to the Clipboard. An application sending data to the Clipboard can register the clipboard format without passing any data. This is done by passing null (zero) as the handle to the data block when SetClipboardData() is called. Here is an example that passes a null data handle for the CF_TEXT clipboard format:

```
OpenClipboard (hWnd) ;
EmptyClipboard () ;
SetClipboardData (CF_TEXT, 0) ;    /* delayed rendering of CF_TEXT data */
CloseClipboard () ;
```

The effect of passing a null handle with SetClipboardData() is illustrated in Figure 17-11. The Clipboard does not receive any data, but records that the window *hWnd* will supply CF_TEXT data on demand. Windows knows which window will supply the data because Windows records the window handle passed by the OpenClipboard() function.

When an application attempts to read CF_TEXT data from the Clipboard, several actions take place to supply the data. Figure 17-12 shows the sequence of events. The program requesting CF_TEXT data from the Clipboard calls the GetClipboardData() function. Windows recognizes that the CF_TEXT data needs to be loaded, and it sends a WM_RENDERFORMAT message to the window that called SetClipboardData() with

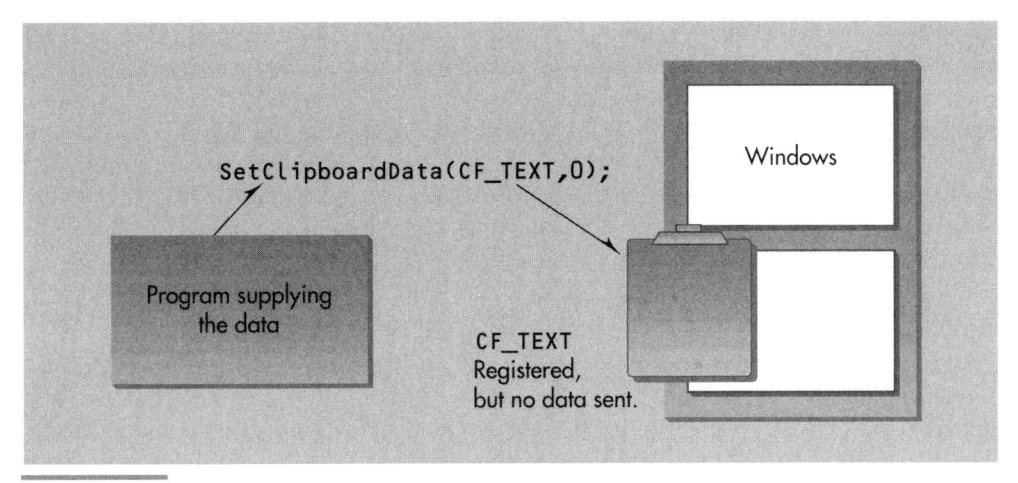

Figure 17-11 Preparing the Clipboard for Delayed Rendering

the null handle. That program calls SetClipboardData() again, but this time passes a handle to a memory block containing the data. Finally, Windows passes the handle to the data block to the program that requested the data.

One of the interesting aspects of delayed rendering is that the program requesting the data cannot tell the difference between getting data already in the Clipboard, and data

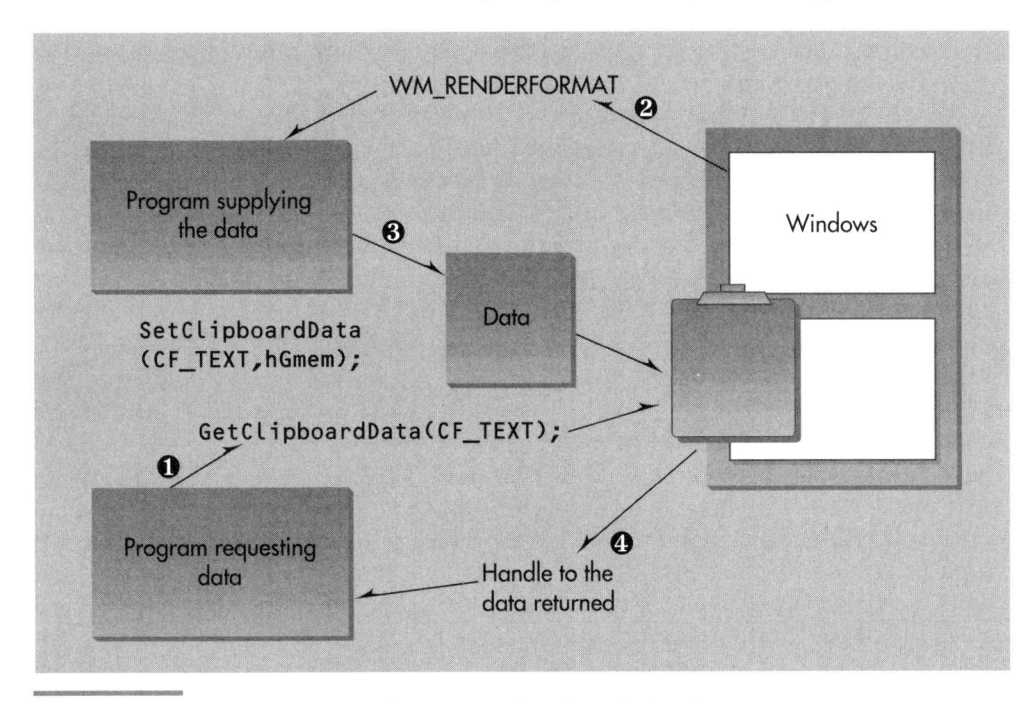

Figure 17-12 Retrieving Clipboard Data — Delayed Rendering Case

supplied later via delayed rendering. In either case, the requesting program receives a handle to the memory block containing the data when the GetClipboardData() function returns. In the delayed rendering case, the requesting program stops executing while it waits for the data block to be supplied by the supplying program. Windows passes execution to the supplying program by sending the WM_RENDERFORMAT message, and does not give control back to the requesting program until the handle to the clipboard data block is returned. All of these actions occur transparently. The user just sees the data being pasted as expected.

WM_RENDERALLFORMATS and WM_DESTROYCLIPBOARD

There are a couple of other situations that pop up when an application uses delayed rendering. One is that the program supplying data is terminated before the clipboard data is requested. A program that is not running cannot supply data, so some trickery is required. Windows gets around this problem by sending the supplying program a WM_RENDERALLFORMATS message before the program terminates. Programs that supply clipboard data are expected to send memory blocks containing data with all of the clipboard formats they support when a WM_RENDERALLFORMATS message is received. The result is that the data is put in the Clipboard before the program terminates, so it can still be obtained later by another program.

WM_RENDERALLFORMATS will only be sent to a program that has called SetClipboardData() with a null memory block handle, but has not yet supplied the data. The message is sent as the program terminates, after the program's window has been destroyed. Putting the appropriate data blocks back into the Clipboard is a "last gasp" effort the program makes before it dies.

Another message that program's supplying clipboard data will receive is WM_DESTROYCLIPBOARD. This message sounds serious, but all it means is that an application (usually another program) has called the EmptyClipboard() function. The idea is that the supplying program may be holding onto one or more memory blocks for delayed rendering. If another application calls EmptyClipboard(), the old clipboard data is no longer needed, so the supplying program can free any memory blocks that contain data. WM_DESTROYCLIPBOARD will be received only if the supplying program has called the SetClipboardData() using a null data handle for delayed rendering, but has not supplied the data.

A Delayed Rendering Example

The DELREND program was designed to demonstrate delayed clipboard rendering. When the "Copy to Clipboard" menu item is selected, DELREND passes the CF_TEXT clipboard format and a NULL data handle to the Clipboard. This tells Windows that DELREND will supply text data on demand. For example, if you then open the Notepad application and select "Edit/Paste," Notepad will attempt to read the clipboard data. Initially, there is no data in the Clipboard, so Windows sends DELREND a WM_RENDERFORMAT message for the CF_TEXT format. DELREND processes this message and passes a memory block containing the text data to the Clipboard. Windows then returns control back to Notepad, which reads the text data in the Clipboard and copies it to the Notepad client area. Figure 17-13 shows the DELREND program on top of the Notepad application after the "Edit/Paste" menu item has been selected in Notepad.

Listing 17-13 shows the complete DELREND.C program. When the "Copy to Clipboard" menu item is selected, DELREND calls the SetClipboardData() function, passing a null handle for delayed rendering of the CF_TEXT format.

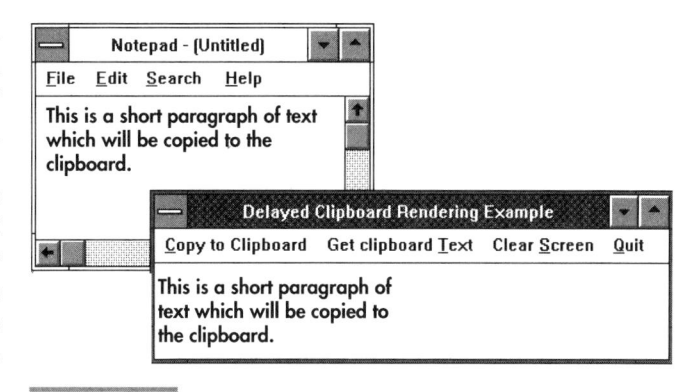

Figure 17-13 The Notepad and DELREND Programs

```
        case IDM_SENDCLIP:           /* set clipboard for */
          OpenClipboard (hWnd);      /* delayed rendering */
          EmptyClipboard ();         /* of only CF_TEXT data */
          SetClipboardData (CF_TEXT, 0);
          CloseClipboard ();
          break;
```

Nothing else happens unless an application tries to read the CF_TEXT data in the clipboard. Windows then sends the WM_RENDERFORMAT message to DELREND, and expects the program to supply a data block containing the text. The text is actually a custom resource, included in the program's resource script file and using the custom resource name "TEXT." The text data for the program is in a separate file PARAGRPH.TXT, which is included into the resource data with the following line in the resource script file DELREND.RC:

```
Paragraph   TEXT   paragrph.txt      /* custom resource file */
```

Resource data is read-only, so to give the text data to the Clipboard, the resource data must be copied into a global memory block. One additional requirement is that the text data is terminated with a null character before the block is sent to the Clipboard. The PARAGRPH.TXT file uses a tilde (~) to mark the end of the text data, making it easy to find the place to put the final null.

When a WM_RENDERFORMAT message is sent, the *wParam* parameter sent with the message is set equal to the clipboard format code. The program receiving WM_RENDERFORMAT must check to make sure that the requested format is one that the program supports. DELREND only supports the CF_TEXT format, so this is the only case considered.

```
        case WM_RENDERFORMAT:           /* request to render one format */
          if (wParam == CF_TEXT)        /* is the request for CF_TEXT? */
          {
            hInstance = GetWindowWord (hWnd, GWW_HINSTANCE);
            hRes = LoadResource (hInstance,
                FindResource (hInstance, "Paragraph", "TEXT"));
            if (hRes)
            {
```

Chapter 17 • The Clipboard

```
            lpStr = lpRes = LockResource (hRes) ;
            nResLong = 0 ;
            while (*lpStr++ != '~')           /* find end of string */
                nResLong++ ;                  /* = length of res. data */
            hGmem = GlobalAlloc (GHND, nResLong + 1) ;
            lpStr = GlobalLock (hGmem) ;
            for (i = 0 ; i < nResLong ; i++)
                *lpStr++ = *lpRes++ ;         /* copy res. data to block */
            *lpStr = 0 ;                      /* null terminate string */
            UnlockResource (hRes) ;
            GlobalUnlock (hGmem) ;
            SetClipboardData (CF_TEXT, hGmem) ;
        }
    }
    break ;
```

One important point in processing the WM_RENDERFORMAT message is that there is no call to OpenClipboard() or CloseClipboard(). This is because whatever application is requesting the data (it may be DELREND itself) has already opened the Clipboard. All DELREND must do is call the SetClipboardData() function to pass the data block to the clipboard.

Because DELREND only supports the CF_TEXT clipboard format, responding to the WM_RENDERALLFORMATS message is not very different from responding to a WM_RENDERFORMAT message for the CF_TEXT format. One important difference is that the Clipboard must be opened and closed when responding to WM_RENDERALLFORMATS. WM_RENDERALLFORMATS is sent when the program is terminating, not when another program has requested clipboard data. The Clipboard will not be open when the WM_RENDERALLFORMATS message is received.

```
    case WM_RENDERALLFORMATS:      /* request to render all formats */
        /* this application only renders the CF_TEXT format */
        hInstance = GetWindowWord (hWnd, GWW_HINSTANCE) ;
        hRes = LoadResource (hInstance,
            FindResource (hInstance, "Paragraph", "TEXT")) ;
        if (hRes)
        {
            lpStr = lpRes = LockResource (hRes) ;
            nResLong = 0 ;
            while (*lpStr++ != '~')           /* find end of string */
                nResLong++ ;                  /* = length of res. data */
            hGmem = GlobalAlloc (GHND, nResLong + 1) ;
            lpStr = GlobalLock (hGmem) ;
            for (i = 0 ; i < nResLong ; i++)
                *lpStr++ = *lpRes++ ;         /* copy res. data to block */
            *lpStr = 0 ;                      /* null terminate string */
            UnlockResource (hRes) ;
            GlobalUnlock (hGmem) ;
            if (OpenClipboard (hWnd))
            {                                 /* give clipboard data as CF_TEXT */
                EmptyClipboard () ;
                SetClipboardData (CF_TEXT, hGmem) ;
                CloseClipboard () ;
            }
        }
    break ;
```

The last clipboard-related message is WM_DESTROYCLIPBOARD. The only data in DELREND to be freed if the clipboard is emptied is the resource data. FreeResource() removes the resource data from memory.

```
case WM_DESTROYCLIPBOARD:      /* clipboard is being emptied */
     FreeResource (hRes) ;     /* not really necessary in this case */
     break ;                   /* as resource is discardable */
```

As you can see from these examples, using delayed rendering is a bit more complex than directly copying data to the Clipboard. However, delayed rendering is the best technique to use if large amounts of data are to be sent to the clipboard, or if more than one clipboard format is supported.

DELREND Listings

Listing 17-13 shows the complete DELREND.C program. The support files are shown in Listings 17-14 to 17-19. Figure 17-14 shows the program's icon.

Figure 17-14
DELREND.ICO
Icon Image

Listing 17-13 DELREND.C

```
/* delrend.c   delayed rendering of the clipboard example */

#include <windows.h>
#include "delrend.h"

int PASCAL WinMain (HANDLE hInstance, HANDLE hPrevInstance, LPSTR lpszCmdLine,
    int nCmdShow)
{
    HWND      hWnd ;         /* the window's "handle" */
    MSG       msg ;          /* a message structure */
    WNDCLASS  wndclass ;     /* window class structure */
    char      cBuf [128] ;

    if (!hPrevInstance)
    {
        wndclass.style          = CS_HREDRAW | CS_VREDRAW ;
        wndclass.lpfnWndProc    = WndProc ;
        wndclass.cbClsExtra     = 0 ;
        wndclass.cbWndExtra     = 0 ;
        wndclass.hInstance      = hInstance ;
        wndclass.hIcon          = LoadIcon (hInstance, "MyIcon") ;
        wndclass.hCursor        = LoadCursor (NULL, IDC_ARROW) ;
        wndclass.hbrBackground  = GetStockObject (WHITE_BRUSH) ;
        wndclass.lpszMenuName   = "MyMenu" ;
        wndclass.lpszClassName  = "MyClass" ;
                    /* register the window class */
        if (!RegisterClass (&wndclass))
            return 0 ;
    }
    LoadString (hInstance, S_PROGRAMCAPTION, cBuf, sizeof (cBuf)) ;
```

```
    hWnd = CreateWindow ("MyClass", cBuf, WS_OVERLAPPEDWINDOW,
        CW_USEDEFAULT, CW_USEDEFAULT, CW_USEDEFAULT, CW_USEDEFAULT,
        NULL, NULL, hInstance, NULL) ;
    ShowWindow (hWnd, nCmdShow) ;   /* display the window */

    while (GetMessage (&msg, NULL, NULL, NULL))    /* message loop */
    {
        TranslateMessage (&msg) ;   /* translate keyboard messages */
        DispatchMessage (&msg) ;    /* send message to WndProc() */
    }
    return (msg.wParam) ;
}

long FAR PASCAL WndProc (HWND hWnd, WORD wMessage, WORD wParam, LONG lParam)
{
    HDC             hDC ;
    HANDLE          hInstance, hClipMem, hGmem ;
    static HANDLE   hRes = NULL ;
    LPSTR           lpStr, lpRes ;
    int             i, nResLong ;
    RECT            rClient ;

    switch (wMessage)         /* process windows messages */
    {
        case WM_COMMAND:
            switch (wParam)
            {
                case IDM_SENDCLIP:          /* set clipboard for */
                    OpenClipboard (hWnd) ;  /* delayed rendering */
                    EmptyClipboard () ;     /* of only CF_TEXT data */
                    SetClipboardData (CF_TEXT, 0) ;
                    CloseClipboard () ;
                    break ;
                case IDM_GETCLIP:          /* read the clipboard data */
                    hDC = GetDC (hWnd) ;
                    if (OpenClipboard (hWnd))
                        {                  /* get handle to clipboard data */
                            hClipMem = GetClipboardData (CF_TEXT) ;
                            if (hClipMem)  /* if there is CF_TEXT data */
                            {
                                lpStr = GlobalLock (hClipMem) ;
                                GetClientRect (hWnd, &rClient) ;
                                DrawText (hDC, lpStr, lstrlen (lpStr), &rClient,
                                    DT_LEFT) ;
                                GlobalUnlock (hClipMem) ;
                            }
                            CloseClipboard () ;
                        }
                    ReleaseDC (hWnd, hDC) ;
                    break ;
                case IDM_CLEAR:     /* clear the client area */
                    InvalidateRect (hWnd, NULL, TRUE) ;
                    break ;
                case IDM_QUIT:                 /* Quit menu item */
                    DestroyWindow (hWnd) ;     /* destroy window, */
                    break ;       /* terminating application */
            }
            break ;
        case WM_RENDERALLFORMATS:    /* request to render all formats */
```

```c
            /* this application only renders the CF_TEXT format */
        hInstance = GetWindowWord (hWnd, GWW_HINSTANCE) ;
        hRes = LoadResource (hInstance,
            FindResource (hInstance, "Paragraph", "TEXT")) ;
        if (hRes)
        {
            lpStr = lpRes = LockResource (hRes) ;
            nResLong = 0 ;
            while (*lpStr++ != _~ )          /* find end of string */
                nResLong++ ;                 /* = length of res. data */
            hGmem = GlobalAlloc (GHND, nResLong + 1) ;
            lpStr = GlobalLock (hGmem) ;
            for (i = 0 ; i < nResLong ; i++)
                *lpStr++ = *lpRes++ ;        /* copy res. data to block */
            *lpStr = 0 ;                     /* null terminate string */
            UnlockResource (hRes) ;
            GlobalUnlock (hGmem) ;
            if (OpenClipboard (hWnd))
            {                   /* give clipboard data as CF_TEXT */
                EmptyClipboard () ;
                SetClipboardData (CF_TEXT, hGmem) ;
                CloseClipboard () ;
            }
        }
        break ;
    case WM_RENDERFORMAT:        /* request to render one format */
        if (wParam == CF_TEXT)   /* is the request for CF_TEXT? */
        {
            hInstance = GetWindowWord (hWnd, GWW_HINSTANCE) ;
            hRes = LoadResource (hInstance,
                FindResource (hInstance, "Paragraph", "TEXT")) ;
            if (hRes)
            {
                lpStr = lpRes = LockResource (hRes) ;
                nResLong = 0 ;
                while (*lpStr++ != _~ )          /* find end of string */
                    nResLong++ ;                 /* = length of res. data */
                hGmem = GlobalAlloc (GHND, nResLong + 1) ;
                lpStr = GlobalLock (hGmem) ;
                for (i = 0 ; i < nResLong ; i++)
                    *lpStr++ = *lpRes++ ;        /* copy res. data to block */
                *lpStr = 0 ;                     /* null terminate string */
                UnlockResource (hRes) ;
                GlobalUnlock (hGmem) ;
                SetClipboardData (CF_TEXT, hGmem) ;
            }
        }
        break ;
    case WM_DESTROYCLIPBOARD:    /* clipboard is being emptied */
        FreeResource (hRes) ;    /* not really necessary in this case */
        break ;                  /* as resource is discardable */
    case WM_DESTROY:   /* stop application */
        PostQuitMessage (0) ;
        break ;
    default:               /* default windows message processing */
        return (DefWindowProc (hWnd, wMessage, wParam, lParam)) ;
    }
    return (0L) ;
}
```

Listing 17-14 DELREND.H Header File

```
/* delrend.h header file */

#define IDM_SENDCLIP      1       /* menu item ID numbers */
#define IDM_GETCLIP       2
#define IDM_CLEAR         3
#define IDM_QUIT          10

#define S_PROGRAMCAPTION  1       /* string table ID numbers */

long FAR PASCAL WndProc (HWND, WORD, WORD, LONG);
```

Listing 17-15 DELREND.H Resource Script File

```
/* delrend.rc resource file */

#include "delrend.h"

MyIcon      ICON     delrend.ico
Paragraph   TEXT     paragrph.txt      /* custom resource file */

MyMenu      MENU
BEGIN
    MENUITEM "&Copy to Clipboard",    IDM_SENDCLIP
    MENUITEM "Get clipboard &Text",   IDM_GETCLIP
    MENUITEM "Clear &Screen",         IDM_CLEAR
    MENUITEM "&Quit",                 IDM_QUIT
END

STRINGTABLE
BEGIN
    S_PROGRAMCAPTION    "Delayed Clipboard Rendering Example"
END
```

Listing 17-16 DELREND.DEF Module Definition File

```
NAME            delrend
DESCRIPTION     'delrend application'
EXETYPE         WINDOWS
STUB            'WINSTUB.EXE'
CODE            PRELOAD MOVEABLE DISCARDABLE
DATA            PRELOAD MOVEABLE MULTIPLE
HEAPSIZE        1024
STACKSIZE       5120
EXPORTS         WndProc
```

Listing 17-17 Turbo C++ Project File for DELREND

```
delrend.c
delrend.def
delrend.res
```

Listing 17-18 QuickC Project File for DELREND

```
delrend.c
delrend.def
delrend.rc
```

Listing 17-19 PARAGRPH.TXT

```
This is a short paragraph of text
which will end up copied to the
clipboard.~
```

Using the Clipboard with an Edit Control

A number of the previous examples in this book have taken advantage of edit controls as a simple means of getting text input from the user. It turns out that Windows has built-in support of cut and paste operations for text selected within an edit control. Text is selected in an edit control by holding down the left mouse button and dragging the mouse cursor over a block of text. The selected text is highlighted in reverse video, as shown in Figure 17-15. You can also hold down the (Shift) key and select an area of text using the arrow keys.

Once a block of text has been highlighted, it can be copied to the Clipboard by sending the edit control a WM_COPY message. This is typically done in response to the user selecting the "Copy" menu item from the "Edit" menu. Essentially all Windows editors support this menu convention. Here is a typical call to SendMessage(), sending the WM_COPY message to the edit control:

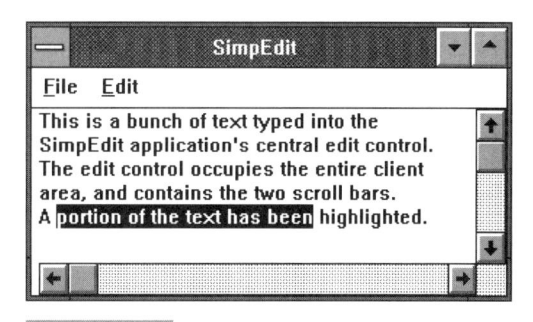

Figure 17-15 Text Highlighted in an Edit Control

```
case IDM_COPY:     /* copy menu item */
    SendMessage (hEditWindow, WM_COPY, 0, 0L) ;
    break ;
```

The WM_COPY message does not use the *wParam* and *lParam* parameters, so they are just set to zero. When the edit control receives the WM_COPY message, the selected text is automatically copied to the Clipboard using the CF_TEXT clipboard format. You can then paste the text elsewhere in the same edit control, or in a completely different application. Pasting text from the Clipboard into the edit control is just as simple. The WM_PASTE message does all of the work, assuming that there is CF_TEXT data in the Clipboard before the message is sent:

```
case IDM_PASTE:    /* paste menu item */
    SendMessage (hEditWindow, WM_PASTE, 0, 0L) ;
    break ;
```

Chapter 17 • The Clipboard

The pasted text ends up at the current insertion point in the edit control. The insertion point is where the blinking caret appears when the edit control has the input focus. You can also cut the selected text out of the edit control, so that the selected text ends up in the Clipboard, but vanishing from the edit control. The WM_CUT message does this magic.

```
case IDM_CUT:      /* cut menu item */
    SendMessage (hEditWindow, WM_CUT, 0, 0L) ;
    break ;
```

One last operation that you may want to implement is to allow deletion of the selected text in the edit control, without copying the data to the Clipboard. There is no specific message to do this, but it is easily done. Just cut the selected text to the Clipboard, and then empty the Clipboard.

```
case IDM_DELETE:   /* delete menu item */
    SendMessage (hEditWindow, WM_CUT, 0, 0L) ;
    if (OpenClipboard (hWnd))
    {            /* empty clipboard */
        EmptyClipboard () ;
        CloseClipboard () ;
    }
    break ;
```

Adding Clipboard Functionality to a Simple Editor

In Chapter 15, *Disk File Access*, the FILE2 program was created to demonstrate using the file selection dialog box. The last example in this chapter, SIMPEDIT, builds on FILE2 to create a fairly complete text editor. SIMPEDIT is shown in Figure 17-16, editing its own source code. (There is something wonderfully recursive about editing a program with itself.)

There is a little trick in SIMPEDIT to get around a bug in the Windows edit control logic. For some reason, Windows 3.0 and 3.1 will sometimes change the third byte in the edit control's memory buffer when a new memory buffer is attached to the control using the EM_SETHANDLE message. To get around this bug, the first four bytes are selected by sending the EM_SETSEL message, and then cut from the edit control using the WM_CUT message. The Clipboard must then be emptied to get rid of the four characters sent to it when the edit control receives the WM_CUT message.

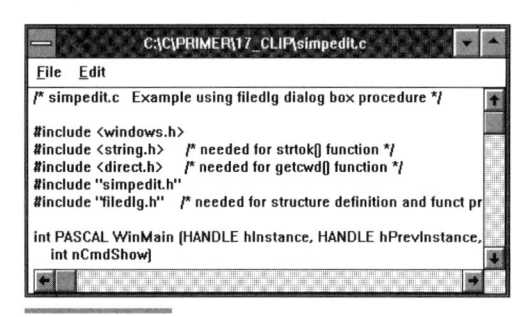

Figure 17-16 The SIMPEDIT Program

```
SendMessage (hEditWindow, EM_SETSEL, 0, MAKELONG (4, 0)) ;
SendMessage (hEditWindow, WM_CUT, 0, 0);
if (OpenClipboard (hWnd))
{
    EmptyClipboard () ;
    CloseClipboard () ;
}
```

The remainder of SIMPEDIT.C (Listing 17-20) is just like FILE2.C from Chapter 15, except that the cut, paste, copy, and delete operations have been added, exactly as shown in the previous section. SIMPEDIT also uses the FILEDLG procedures for displaying a file selection dialog box. These functions are exactly as described in Chapter 15 and are not shown again in this chapter. Note that keyboard accelerators have been added for the main menu selections, following the conventions used by Notepad, Windows Write, and many other Windows applications.

Listing 17-20 SIMPEDIT.C

```
/* simpedit.c   simple editor application - uses filedlg dlg box functions */

#include <windows.h>
#include <string.h>       /* needed for strtok() function */
#include <direct.h>       /* needed for getcwd() function */
#include "simpedit.h"
#include "filedlg.h"      /* needed for structure definition and funct prototype */

int PASCAL WinMain (HANDLE hInstance, HANDLE hPrevInstance, LPSTR lpszCmdLine,
    int nCmdShow)
{
    HWND        hWnd ;         /* the window's "handle" */
    MSG         msg ;          /* a message structure */
    WNDCLASS    wndclass ;     /* window class structure */
    char        cBuf [128] ;   /* character buffer */
    HANDLE      hAccel ;       /* keyboard accelerator handle */

    if (!hPrevInstance)
    {
        wndclass.style         = CS_HREDRAW | CS_VREDRAW ;
        wndclass.lpfnWndProc   = WndProc ;
        wndclass.cbClsExtra    = 0 ;
        wndclass.cbWndExtra    = 0 ;
        wndclass.hInstance     = hInstance ;
        wndclass.hIcon         = LoadIcon (hInstance, "MyIcon") ;
        wndclass.hCursor       = LoadCursor (NULL, IDC_ARROW) ;
        wndclass.hbrBackground = GetStockObject (WHITE_BRUSH) ;
        wndclass.lpszMenuName  = "MyMenu" ;
        wndclass.lpszClassName = "MyClass" ;
                    /* register the window class */
        if (!RegisterClass (&wndclass))
            return 0 ;
    }
    LoadString (hInstance, S_PROGRAMCAPTION, cBuf, sizeof (cBuf)) ;

    hWnd = CreateWindow ("MyClass", cBuf, WS_OVERLAPPEDWINDOW,
        CW_USEDEFAULT, CW_USEDEFAULT, CW_USEDEFAULT, CW_USEDEFAULT,
        NULL, NULL, hInstance, NULL) ;
    ShowWindow (hWnd, nCmdShow) ;   /* display the window */
                                    /* load the accelerator table */
    hAccel = LoadAccelerators (hInstance, "MyAccel") ;

    while (GetMessage (&msg, NULL, NULL, NULL))   /* message loop */
    {                                    /* translate accelerators */
        if (!TranslateAccelerator (hWnd, hAccel, &msg))
        {
            TranslateMessage (&msg) ;    /* translate keyboard messages */
```

```c
            DispatchMessage (&msg) ;    /* send message to WndProc() */
        }
    }
    return (msg.wParam) ;
}

long FAR PASCAL WndProc (HWND hWnd, WORD wMessage, WORD wParam, LONG lParam)
{
    static FILEOPENDATA   FOD ;       /* defined in filedlg.h */
    HANDLE                hInstance ;
    static HANDLE         hEditBuf ;
    FARPROC               lpfnDlgProc ;
    static HWND           hEditWindow ;
    BOOL                  bFileStatus ;
    int                   nFileHandle, nFileLong ;
    OFSTRUCT              of ;
    char                  cBuf [PATHNAMELONG], cBuf2 [128] ;
    PSTR                  pStr, pStr2 ;

    switch (wMessage)    /* process windows messages */
    {
        case WM_CREATE: /* create edit window, and link mem buffer */
            hInstance = GetWindowWord (hWnd, GWW_HINSTANCE) ;
            hEditWindow = CreateWindow ("EDIT", "",
                WS_CHILD | WS_VISIBLE | ES_AUTOVSCROLL | ES_MULTILINE |
                ES_LEFT | ES_NOHIDESEL | WS_VSCROLL| ES_AUTOHSCROLL |
                WS_HSCROLL, 0, 0, 1, 1, hWnd, NULL, hInstance, NULL) ;
                        /* get rid of default edit buffer */
            hEditBuf = (HANDLE) SendMessage (hEditWindow,
                EM_GETHANDLE, 0, 0L) ;
            if (hEditBuf)
                LocalFree (hEditBuf) ;
                        /* allocate a new edit buffer */
            hEditBuf = LocalAlloc (LMEM_MOVEABLE | LMEM_ZEROINIT, 100) ;
            PostMessage (hEditWindow, EM_SETHANDLE, hEditBuf, 0L) ;
            break ;
        case WM_SIZE:      /* keep edit control filling client area */
            MoveWindow (hEditWindow, 5, 0, LOWORD (lParam) - 5,
                HIWORD (lParam), TRUE) ;
            break ;
        case WM_COMMAND:
            switch (wParam)          /* menu items */
            {
                case IDM_OPEN:
                    hInstance = GetWindowWord (hWnd, GWW_HINSTANCE) ;
                    lpfnDlgProc = MakeProcInstance (FileOpenProc,
                        hInstance) ;
                    getcwd (cBuf, PATHNAMELONG) ;
                    lstrcpy (FOD.szPath, cBuf) ;
                    lstrcpy (FOD.szFile, "*.*") ;
                    LoadString (hInstance, S_FILEOPEN, cBuf,
                        sizeof (cBuf)) ;
                    lstrcpy (FOD.szCaption, cBuf) ;
                    bFileStatus = DialogBoxParam (hInstance, "FileOpenDlg",
                        hWnd, lpfnDlgProc, (DWORD)(LPSTR) &FOD) ;
                    FreeProcInstance (lpfnDlgProc) ;
                    if (bFileStatus)              /* if a file was opened */
                    {
                        CombinePathFile (cBuf, FOD.szPath, FOD.szFile) ;
```

```
            nFileHandle = OpenFile (cBuf, &of, OF_READ) ;
            if (nFileHandle == -1)
            {
                LoadString (hInstance, S_FILENOTOPEN, cBuf2,
                    sizeof (cBuf2)) ;
                MessageBox (hWnd, cBuf, cBuf2,
                    MB_OK | MB_ICONHAND) ;
            }
            else                /* file is open, so read it */
            {                   /* file name = window title */
                SetWindowText (hWnd, cBuf) ;
                                /* find the length of file */
                nFileLong = (int) _llseek (nFileHandle, 0L, 2) ;
                                /* go back to front of file */
                _llseek (nFileHandle, 0L, 0) ;
                                /* delete old edit buffer */
                LocalFree (hEditBuf) ;
                                /* allocate new block */
                hEditBuf = LocalAlloc (LMEM_MOVEABLE,
                    nFileLong + 6) ;
                if (hEditBuf)
                {
                    pStr = LocalLock (hEditBuf) ;
                                /* copy file data to block */
                                /* start 4 chars into buf */
                    _lread (nFileHandle, pStr + 4, nFileLong) ;
                    _lclose (nFileHandle) ;
                    pStr2 = pStr + nFileLong + 4 ;
                    *pStr2++ = 0 ;
                    *pStr2 = 0 ; /* append two nulls at end */
                    LocalUnlock ((HANDLE) pStr) ;
                                /* attach buffer to edit control */
                    SendMessage (hEditWindow, EM_SETHANDLE,
                        hEditBuf, 0L) ;
                            /* get around bug in edit control */
                            /* by deleting the first 4 chars */
                    SendMessage (hEditWindow, EM_SETSEL, 0,
                        MAKELONG (4, 0)) ;
                    SendMessage (hEditWindow, WM_CUT, 0, 0);
                    if (OpenClipboard (hWnd))
                    {
                        EmptyClipboard () ;
                        CloseClipboard () ;
                    }
                }
                else
                    StringTableMessageBox (hWnd, S_NOTALLOC,
                        S_MEMERROR, MB_OK | MB_ICONHAND) ;
            }
        }
        break ;
    case IDM_SAVE:
        hInstance = GetWindowWord (hWnd, GWW_HINSTANCE) ;
        lpfnDlgProc = MakeProcInstance (FileOpenProc,
            hInstance) ;
        getcwd (cBuf, PATHNAMELONG) ;
        lstrcpy (FOD.szPath, cBuf) ;
        lstrcpy (FOD.szFile, "*.*") ;
        LoadString (hInstance, S_FILEWRITE, cBuf,
```

Chapter 17 • The Clipboard

```
                sizeof (cBuf)) ;
            lstrcpy (FOD.szCaption, cBuf) ;
            bFileStatus = DialogBoxParam (hInstance, "FileOpenDlg",
                hWnd, lpfnDlgProc, (DWORD)(LPSTR) &FOD) ;
            FreeProcInstance (lpfnDlgProc) ;
            if (bFileStatus)              /* if a file was opened */
            {
                CombinePathFile (cBuf, FOD.szPath, FOD.szFile) ;
                nFileHandle = OpenFile (cBuf, &of, OF_CREATE) ;
                if (nFileHandle == -1)
                {
                    LoadString (hInstance, S_FILENOTCREATE, cBuf2,
                        sizeof (cBuf2)) ;
                    MessageBox (hWnd, cBuf, cBuf2,
                        MB_OK | MB_ICONHAND) ;
                }
                else
                {           /* file name = window title */
                    SetWindowText (hWnd, cBuf) ;
                            /* copy whole edit buffer to file */
                    nFileLong = FindEditSize (hEditBuf) ;
                    pStr = LocalLock (hEditBuf) ;
                    _lwrite (nFileHandle, pStr, nFileLong) ;
                    _lclose (nFileHandle) ;
                    LocalUnlock (hEditBuf) ;
                }
            }
            break ;
        case IDM_NEW:
            hEditBuf = (HANDLE) SendMessage (hEditWindow,
                EM_GETHANDLE, 0, 0L) ;
            if (hEditBuf)
                LocalFree (hEditBuf) ;
                    /* allocate a new edit buffer */
            hEditBuf = LocalAlloc (LMEM_MOVEABLE | LMEM_ZEROINIT, 100) ;
            PostMessage (hEditWindow, EM_SETHANDLE, hEditBuf, 0L) ;
            break ;
        case IDM_COPY:      /* copy menu item */
            SendMessage (hEditWindow, WM_COPY, 0, 0L) ;
            break ;
        case IDM_CUT:       /* cut menu item */
            SendMessage (hEditWindow, WM_CUT, 0, 0L) ;
            break ;
        case IDM_DELETE:    /* delete menu item */
            SendMessage (hEditWindow, WM_CUT, 0, 0L) ;
            if (OpenClipboard (hWnd))
            {       /* empty clipboard */
                EmptyClipboard () ;
                CloseClipboard () ;
            }
            break ;
        case IDM_PASTE:     /* paste menu item */
            SendMessage (hEditWindow, WM_PASTE, 0, 0L) ;
            break ;
        case IDM_ABOUT:
            StringTableMessageBox (hWnd, S_ABOUTTEXT, S_ABOUTCAPTION,
                MB_OK | MB_ICONINFORMATION) ;
            break ;
        case IDM_QUIT:                    /* "Quit" menu item */
```

```c
                    DestroyWindow (hWnd) ;     /* destroy window, */
                    break ;                    /* terminating application */
            }
            break ;
        case WM_DESTROY:                       /* stop application */
            LocalFree (hEditBuf) ;
            PostQuitMessage (0) ;
            break ;
        default:              /* default windows message processing */
            return (DefWindowProc (hWnd, wMessage, wParam, lParam)) ;
    }
    return (0L) ;
}

/* display a message box based on two string table entries */

int StringTableMessageBox (HWND hWnd, int nString, int nCaption, WORD
    wFlags)
{
    char    cBuf1 [128], cBuf2 [128] ;
      HANDLE  hInstance ;

    hInstance = GetWindowWord (hWnd, GWW_HINSTANCE) ;
    LoadString (hInstance, nString, cBuf1, sizeof (cBuf1)) ;
    LoadString (hInstance, nCaption, cBuf2, sizeof (cBuf2)) ;
    return (MessageBox (hWnd, cBuf1, cBuf2, wFlags)) ;
}

/* find the end of the edit buffer text by locating two null bytes */

WORD FindEditSize (HANDLE hEditBuf)
{
    int     i ;
    PSTR    pStr ;

    i = 0 ;
    pStr = LocalLock (hEditBuf) ;
    while (*pStr++ != 0)
        i++ ;

    LocalUnlock (hEditBuf) ;
    return (i) ;
}
```

Listings 17-21 to 17-25 show the support files for SIMPEDIT. The program's icon is shown in Figure 17-17.

Listing 17-21 SIMPEDIT.H Header File

```c
/* simpedit.h */

#define IDM_NEW      1       /* menu item ID numbers */
#define IDM_OPEN     2
#define IDM_SAVE     3
#define IDM_ABOUT    4
#define IDM_COPY     5
#define IDM_CUT      6
#define IDM_PASTE    7
#define IDM_DELETE   8
#define IDM_QUIT     10
```

Figure 17-17
SIMPEDIT.ICO
Icon Image

```
#define S_PROGRAMCAPTION   1       /* string table ID numbers */
#define S_FILENOTOPEN      2
#define S_NOTALLOC         3
#define S_MEMERROR         4
#define S_ABOUTTEXT        5
#define S_ABOUTCAPTION     6
#define S_FILENOTCREATE    7
#define S_FILEOPEN         8
#define S_FILEWRITE        9

long FAR PASCAL WndProc (HWND, WORD, WORD, LONG) ;
int StringTableMessageBox (HWND hWnd, int nString, int nCaption, WORD
    wFlags) ;
WORD FindEditSize (HANDLE hEditBuf) ;
```

Listing 17-22 SIMPEDIT.RC Resource Script File

```
/* simpedit.rc resource file */

#include <windows.h>
#include "simpedit.h"
#include "filedlg.h"
#include "filedlg.rc"     /* add the filedlg resources */

MyIcon      ICON    simpedit.ico

MyMenu      MENU
BEGIN
    POPUP   "&File"
    BEGIN
        MENUITEM    "&New",     IDM_NEW
        MENUITEM    "&Open File  F3",   IDM_OPEN
        MENUITEM    "&Save File  F2",   IDM_SAVE
        MENUITEM    SEPARATOR
        MENUITEM    "&About",           IDM_ABOUT
        MENUITEM    "E&xit      Alt-X", IDM_QUIT
    END
    POPUP   "&Edit"
    BEGIN
        MENUITEM    "Cu&t     Shift+Del" IDM_CUT
        MENUITEM    "&Copy    Cntl+Ins"  IDM_COPY
        MENUITEM    "&Paste   Shift+Ins" IDM_PASTE
        MENUITEM    "&Delete  Del"       IDM_DELETE
    END
END

MyAccel ACCELERATORS
BEGIN
    VK_DELETE,      IDM_DELETE,     VIRTKEY
    VK_DELETE,      IDM_CUT,        VIRTKEY,    CONTROL
    VK_INSERT,      IDM_COPY,       VIRTKEY,    CONTROL
    VK_INSERT,      IDM_PASTE,      VIRTKEY,    SHIFT
    VK_F2,          IDM_SAVE,       VIRTKEY
    VK_F3,          IDM_OPEN,       VIRTKEY
    "X",            IDM_QUIT,       VIRTKEY,    ALT
END

STRINGTABLE
BEGIN
```

```
    S_PROGRAMCAPTION      "SimpEdit"
    S_FILENOTOPEN         "Could Not Open File"
    S_NOTALLOC            "Could not allocate memory."
    S_MEMERROR            "Memory Error"
    S_ABOUTTEXT           "Simple Editor Application"
    S_ABOUTCAPTION        "File 2 Program"
    S_FILENOTCREATE       "Could not open or create file."
    S_FILEOPEN            "Open a file."
    S_FILEWRITE           "Write data to a file."
END
```

Listing 17-23 SIMPEDIT.DEF Module Definition File

```
NAME            simpedit
DESCRIPTION     'simpedit program'
EXETYPE         WINDOWS
STUB            'WINSTUB.EXE'
CODE            PRELOAD MOVEABLE DISCARDABLE
DATA            PRELOAD MOVEABLE MULTIPLE
HEAPSIZE        1024
STACKSIZE       5120
EXPORTS         WndProc
                FileOpenProc
```

Listing 17-24 Turbo C++ Project File for SIMPEDIT

```
simpedit.c
filedlg.c
simpedit.def
simpedit.res
```

Listing 17-25 QuickC Project File for SIMPEDIT

```
simpedit.c
filedlg.c
simpedit.def
simpedit.rc
```

Summary

Windows applications use the Clipboard to exchange information. Usually, the information is a block of text or a portion of a figure that has been selected, and "Cut" or "Copied" to the Clipboard. Once data has been sent to the Clipboard, any application can read the information. Clipboard data is owned by Windows, not by the program that created the data, so data in the Clipboard cannot be modified (read-only data).

Physically, clipboard data resides in a global memory block that has been sent to Windows. The application program sending information to the Clipboard must first allocate a global memory block, and copy data into the block. The Clipboard is then opened by calling the OpenClipboard() function. Only one program can have the Clipboard open at any one time. Usually, the EmptyClipboard() function is then called to free any memory blocks currently attached to the Clipboard. The SetClipboardData() function transfers the memory block from the program to Windows, making the block the property of Windows. Finally, CloseClipboard() closes the Clipboard, so that another application can open it and read the data.

To read data from the Clipboard, the Clipboard is first opened using OpenClipboard(). The handle of the global memory block in the Clipboard is obtained with GetClipboardData(). CloseClipboard() must again be used to close the Clipboard, allowing other programs to access the same data. The Clipboard can contain data in more than one format at one time. The common formats are given names like CF_TEXT and CF_BITMAP in WINDOWS.H. An application can also create a custom clipboard format using the RegisterClipboardFormat() function.

Windows also supports a more advanced technique for sending data to the Clipboard for cases where a program transmits large amounts of data to the Clipboard, or supports several clipboard formats at the same time. "Delayed rendering" of the Clipboard allows a program to register that one or more clipboard formats are available, but not send the data to the Clipboard unless an application requests it. To establish a clipboard format with delayed rendering, the SetClipboardData() function is called with null (zero) in place of the handle to the global memory block. If the clipboard data is requested, Windows will send the supplying program a WM_RENDERFORMAT message. The supplying program then transmits the data to the Clipboard using SetClipboardData(), passing a handle to a global memory block. Programs supporting delayed rendering should also process the WM_RENDERALLFORMATS message, which tells the program to copy any pending clipboard information to the Clipboard right before the application terminates. The WM_DESTROYCLIPBOARD message can also be processed, which alerts the program supplying clipboard data that EmptyClipboard() has been called, so any pending information for the Clipboard can be discarded.

Edit controls have built-in support of cut and paste operations using the Clipboard. Any text highlighted in the edit control can be copied to the Clipboard by sending the edit control a WM_COPY message. The WM_CUT message deletes the selected text from the edit control, and copies it to the Clipboard. Both messages use the CF_TEXT clipboard format. CF_TEXT data in the Clipboard can be pasted into an edit control by sending the control the WM_PASTE message.

QUESTIONS

1. Memory blocks sent to the Clipboard become the property of Windows, but another application can get read and/or write access to the memory block using the GetClipboardData() function. (True/False).
2. When the clipboard viewer program is operating, the clipboard viewer reads the clipboard data, which stops other applications from doing "Paste" operations. (True/False).
3. When one application has the Clipboard open, the only other applications that can open the clipboard are: a) Other applications reading data; b) Other applications writing data; c) No other application; d) a and b.
4. The type of memory block passed to the Clipboard is a: a) Global memory block; b) Local memory block; c) Global memory block allocated with a clipboard format flag such as CF_TEXT; d) None of the above.
5. The Clipboard can only hold one memory block at one time. (True/False)
6. The Clipboard can hold only one memory block of any one clipboard format at one time. (True/False)
7. To establish delayed rendering of a clipboard format, the handle to the memory block passed with SetClipboardData() should be _____ .
8. The WM_COPY message copies text to the Clipboard from an edit control. The text copied is: a) The entire edit control's contents; b) Text currently selected in the edit control; c) Text from the current insertion point to the end of the edit control; d) none of the above.
9. The difference between sending an edit control a WM_COPY and a WM_CUT message is: a) Only WM_COPY sends data to the Clipboard; b) WM_CUT also deletes the currently selected text; c) The two messages use different clipboard formats; d) none of the above.
10. To create a custom clipboard format, call the _____ function.

EXERCISES

1. Modify the CLIPBRD1.C program so that both the CF_TEXT and CF_OEMTEXT clipboard formats can be displayed when the "Get Clipboard Text" menu item is selected. Display the CF_TEXT format in preference to CF_OEMTEXT. Test your program by copying some data from an MS-DOS window to the Clipboard and displaying it in the window's client area.
2. Modify the DELREND.C program so that both CF_TEXT and CF_OEMTEXT clipboard formats are supported. You can use the same resource text data for both clipboard formats, as the characters in the PARAGRPH.TXT file are all common to both the ANSI and OEM character sets. Test your program by opening an MS-DOS window and pasting the OEM text into the DOS window.

ANSWERS TO QUESTIONS

1. False. Clipboard data is always read-only.
2. False. Any number of applications can read the clipboard data.
3. c.
4. a.
5. False. Mutiple clipboard formats can be sent to the Clipboard at one time, but no more than one memory block with any single clipboard format can be saved to the Clipboard at any one time.
6. True.
7. NULL or zero.
8. b.
9. b.
10. RegisterClipboardFormat().

SOLUTIONS TO EXERCISES

1. The only changes necessary are to look for both the CF_TEXT and CF_OEMTEXT clipboard formats, and to use an OEM font when displaying OEM text. Listing 17-26 shows the modified logic for displaying either of the two clipboard formats in the program's client area:

Listing 17-26 Modifications to CLIPBRD1.C for Exercise 1

```
hDC = GetDC (hWnd) ;
if (OpenClipboard (hWnd))
{           /* get handle to clipboard data */
    if (IsClipboardFormatAvailable (CF_TEXT))
        hClipMem = GetClipboardData (CF_TEXT) ;
    else if (IsClipboardFormatAvailable (CF_OEMTEXT))
    {
        hClipMem = GetClipboardData (CF_OEMTEXT) ;
        SelectObject (hDC,
            GetStockObject (OEM_FIXED_FONT)) ;
    }
    if (hClipMem)   /* if there is CF_TEXT data */
    {           /* create 2nd block, sized for data */
        hGmem = GlobalAlloc (GHND, GlobalSize (hClipMem)) ;
        if (hGmem)
        {           /* copy data from clipboard */
            lpStr = GlobalLock (hGmem) ;
            lpClip = GlobalLock (hClipMem) ;
            lstrcpy (lpStr, lpClip) ;
            TextOut (hDC, 0, 0, lpStr, lstrlen (lpStr)) ;
```

SOLUTIONS TO EXERCISES (cont'd)

```
                    GlobalUnlock (hGmem) ;
                    GlobalUnlock (hClipMem) ;
                    GlobalFree (hGmem) ;
                }
            }
            CloseClipboard () ;
        }
        ReleaseDC (hWnd, hDC) ;
        break ;
```

Note how the CF_TEXT format is selected if available. The CF_OEMTEXT format is only checked if the IsClipboardFormatAvailable() function does not find CF_TEXT data in the Clipboard. The complete solution to this exercise is under the file name C17EXER1 on the source code disks.

2. Both the WM_RENDERALLFORMATS and WM_RENDERFORMAT logic of the DELREND.C program must be modified to provide both CF_TEXT and CF_OEMTEXT clipboard data on demand. Listing 17-27 shows the changes to the WndProc() function of DELREND.C.

Listing 17-27 Changes to DELREND.C for Exercise 2

```
long FAR PASCAL WndProc (HWND hWnd, WORD wMessage, WORD wParam, LONG lParam)
{
  HDC            hDC ;
  HANDLE         hInstance, hClipMem, hGmem ;
  static HANDLE  hRes = NULL ;
  LPSTR          lpStr, lpRes ;
  int            i, nResLong ;
  RECT           rClient ;

  switch (wMessage)         /* process windows messages */
  {
      case WM_COMMAND:
          switch (wParam)
          {
              case IDM_SENDCLIP:              /* set clipboard for */
                  OpenClipboard (hWnd) ;      /* delayed rendering */
                  EmptyClipboard () ;         /* of data */
                  SetClipboardData (CF_TEXT, 0) ;
                  SetClipboardData (CF_OEMTEXT, 0) ;
                  CloseClipboard () ;
                  break ;
              case IDM_GETCLIP:               /* read the clipboard data */
                  hDC = GetDC (hWnd) ;
                  if (OpenClipboard (hWnd))
                  {                           /* get handle to clipboard data */
                      hClipMem = GetClipboardData (CF_TEXT) ;
                      if (hClipMem)           /* if there is CF_TEXT data */
                      {
```

SOLUTIONS TO EXERCISES (cont'd)

```
                    lpStr = GlobalLock (hClipMem) ;
                    GetClientRect (hWnd, &rClient) ;
                    DrawText (hDC, lpStr, lstrlen (lpStr), &rClient,
                        DT_LEFT) ;
                    GlobalUnlock (hClipMem) ;
                }
                CloseClipboard () ;
            }
            ReleaseDC (hWnd, hDC) ;
            break ;
        case IDM_CLEAR:                     /* clear the client area */
            InvalidateRect (hWnd, NULL, TRUE) ;
            break ;
        case IDM_QUIT:                      /* Quit menu item */
            DestroyWindow (hWnd) ;          /* destroy window, */
            break ;                         /* terminating application */
    }
    break ;
case WM_RENDERALLFORMATS:                   /* request to render all formats */
    /* this application only renders the CF_TEXT format */
    hInstance = GetWindowWord (hWnd, GWW_HINSTANCE) ;
    hRes = LoadResource (hInstance,
        FindResource (hInstance, "Paragraph", "TEXT")) ;
    if (hRes)
    {
        lpStr = lpRes = LockResource (hRes) ;
        nResLong = 0 ;
        while (*lpStr++ != '~')             /* find end of string */
            nResLong++ ;                    /* = length of res. data */
        hGmem = GlobalAlloc (GHND, nResLong + 1) ;
        lpStr = GlobalLock (hGmem) ;
        for (i = 0 ; i < nResLong ; i++)
            *lpStr++ = *lpRes++ ;           /* copy res. data to block */
        *lpStr = 0 ;                        /* null terminate string */
        UnlockResource (hRes) ;
        GlobalUnlock (hGmem) ;
        if (OpenClipboard (hWnd))
        {                                   /* give clipboard data as CF_TEXT */
            EmptyClipboard () ;
            SetClipboardData (CF_TEXT, hGmem) ;
            SetClipboardData (CF_OEMTEXT, hGmem) ;
            CloseClipboard () ;
        }
    }
    break ;
case WM_RENDERFORMAT:                       /* request to render one format */
    if (wParam == CF_TEXT || wParam == CF_OEMTEXT)
    {
        hInstance = GetWindowWord (hWnd, GWW_HINSTANCE) ;
        hRes = LoadResource (hInstance,
            FindResource (hInstance, "Paragraph", "TEXT")) ;
        if (hRes)
        {
            lpStr = lpRes = LockResource (hRes) ;
            nResLong = 0 ;
```

SOLUTIONS TO EXERCISES (cont'd)

```c
                    while (*lpStr++ != '~')     /* find end of string */
                        nResLong++ ;            /* = length of res. data */
                    hGmem = GlobalAlloc (GHND, nResLong + 1) ;
                    lpStr = GlobalLock (hGmem) ;
                    for (i = 0 ; i < nResLong ; i++)
                        *lpStr++ = *lpRes++ ;   /* copy res. data to block */
                    *lpStr = 0 ;                /* null terminate string */
                    UnlockResource (hRes) ;
                    GlobalUnlock (hGmem) ;
                    if (wParam == CF_TEXT)
                        SetClipboardData (CF_TEXT, hGmem) ;
                    else
                        SetClipboardData (CF_OEMTEXT, hGmem) ;
                }
            }
            break ;
        case WM_DESTROYCLIPBOARD:      /* clipboard is being emptied */
            FreeResource (hRes) ;      /* not really necessary in this case */
            break ;                    /* as resource is discardable */
        case WM_DESTROY:               /* stop application */
            PostQuitMessage (0) ;
            break ;
        default:        /* default windows message processing */
            return (DefWindowProc (hWnd, wMessage, wParam, lParam)) ;
    }
    return (0L) ;
}
```

The complete solution is under the file name C 17EXER2 on the optional source code disks.

CHAPTER 18

Dynamic Link Libraries

Dynamic Link Libraries, or "DLLs" for short, provide groups of functions for other Windows applications to use. One DLL can be accessed by any number of applications at the same time. DLLs are an efficient use of memory if the same functions are needed by several applications, because only one copy of the code is needed. For the programmer, DLLs provide the ultimate in reusable code. Once a DLL is compiled and debugged, it never needs to be compiled again or linked into another program. DLLs become an extension of the Windows environment, adding new functions to those already provided in Windows. Windows itself can be thought of as a collection of DLLs, as all of the code for functions (such as CreateWindow() and TextOut()) reside in DLLs (such as KERNEL and GDI).

Dynamic link libraries are simpler to create than complete Windows programs. However, there are a few unique aspects to programming DLLs that must be kept in mind to avoid problems. These unique properties stem from the fact that functions in one DLL can be called by any number of Windows application programs during the same Windows session. Compiling DLLs also takes slight changes to the compiler and linker settings to produce the right code in the finished program.

This chapter first creates a simple DLL, containing one string manipulation function. Three different methods for calling the function from another Windows program are demonstrated with this example. The chapter concludes by converting the file selection dialog box (created in Chapter 15, *Disk File Access*) to a DLL. This demonstrates a more complex DLL, which exports several functions for other applications to use, and which contains its own resource data as part of the DLL.

Concepts Covered

Runtime Libraries Versus DLLs

Separation of the Stack and Data Segments

Ordinal Numbers

Compiler/Linker Settings to Create a DLL

Exporting a Function

Importing a Function

Import Libraries

Resource Data in a DLL

Keywords Covered

WEP_FREE_DLL

WEP_SYSTEMEXIT

LIBRARY

EXPORTS

IMPORTS

SINGLE

Functions Covered

LibMain()

WEP()

UnlockData()

Compiler Runtime Libraries

The core C language is small, and lacks many basic features (such as the ability to output text). Instead of adding functions like printf() to the core language, C takes advantage of runtime libraries. During the development of a program, if you need a function like printf(), the linker extracts this code from one of the compiler's function libraries and adds it to your finished program. Figure 18-1 illustrates linking a pro-

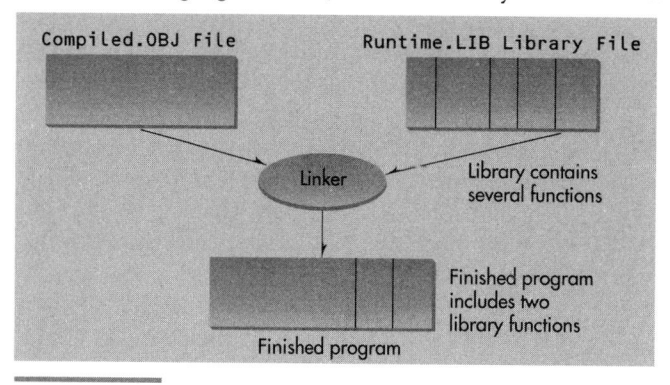

Figure 18-1 Adding Runtime Library Functions to a Program

gram that requires two functions from a runtime library. Only the functions needed by the program are extracted from the library. The code from the library file is physically added to your finished program, and acts just as if you had written the function in your own program's code. Runtime libraries are a huge time saver for C programmers, as they save you the time of needed to constantly retype code for basic functions like printf().

Runtime library files have the extension ".LIB" and are always associated with a header file that contains the function declarations for the functions in the library. Several of the example programs in this book used runtime library files for the functions that are not supported by Windows, such as getcwd() (get current working directory) and strtok() (string token). To use the strtok() function, the header file STRING.H is included at the top of the C program:

```
#include <string.h>
```

The angle brackets around the header file name tell the compiler to look in the compiler subdirectories for the file, rather than in the working directory. The header file includes the declaration of the strtok() function, so that the compiler knows what type of arguments the function should be passed. The compiler and linker extract the strtok() function's code from a runtime library and add the code to the finished program.

Runtime libraries are ideal for an environment like MS-DOS, where each program runs by itself. However, Windows allows many programs to run at the same time. Windows programs all need to access the screen, check the mouse and keyboard, allocate memory, and perform numerous other functions. Windows programs would be enormous if all of this logic had to be added to each program via runtime libraries. To be efficient, Windows programs need to be able to share common functions for screen access, mouse input, and so on, so that one copy of these functions can service every running application.

Dynamic Link Libraries

Dynamic Link Libraries are Windows' solution to the problem of sharing code between several running applications. DLLs are collections of functions that any Windows program can access, but which are maintained in separate files. Figure 18-2 shows a Windows application that accesses a function in a DLL. The application does not end up with a copy of the function added to its own code, as was the case with adding a runtime library function. Instead, the Windows application calls the function in a DLL. The DLL is a completely separate program and is not tied to the Windows application in any way.

Although Figure 18-2 only shows one Windows application calling a function in the DLL, there is no limit to how many applications can use the same DLL. All of the Windows functions that we have been calling, such as CreateWindow() and Rectangle(), reside in DLLs supplied by Windows. This is how Windows programs get their basic functionality. The DLLs for Windows are stored in the Windows system directory (C:\WINDOW\SYSTEM by default) and have names like USER.EXE and GDI.EXE. One confusing aspect of DLLs is that they can have the file extension ".EXE," ".DLL," or ".DRV." If you look in your computer's system directory, you will find all three types of files, all of which are DLLs.

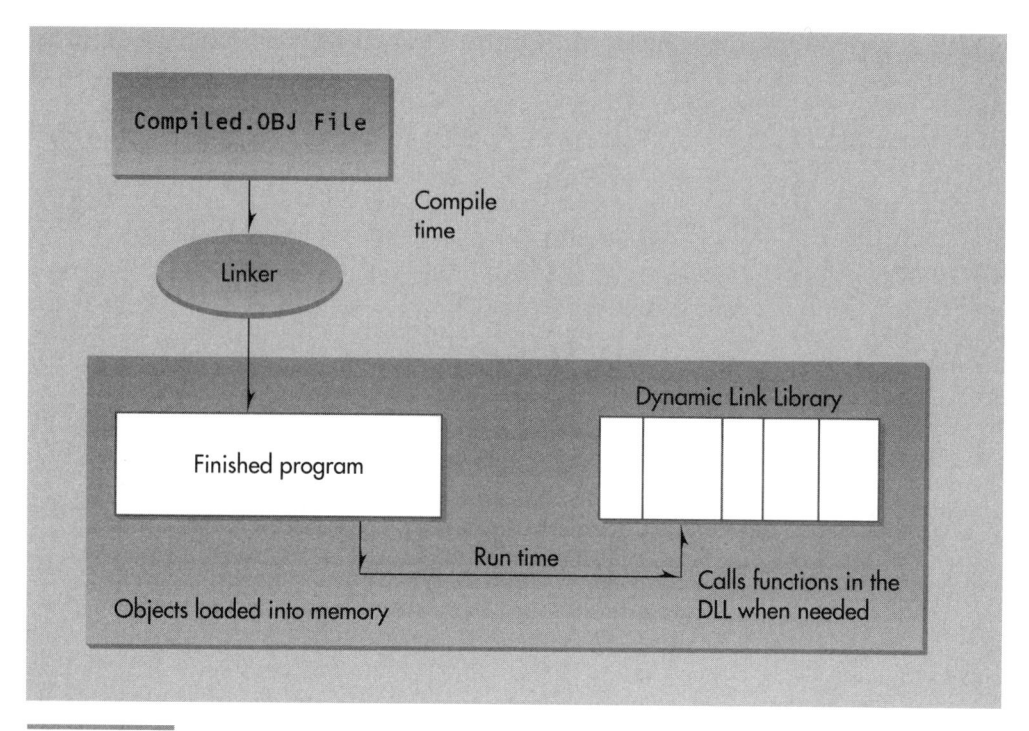

Figure 18-2 Windows Application Using a Function in a DLL

How DLLs Work

When you run a normal Windows program, its presence is made obvious by the appearance of the program's window on the screen. The physical program exists as a block of memory occupied by the program's code and data segments. DLLs generally consist of a series of functions that other programs use, and do not display a visible window. DLLs also have a slightly different structure in memory than regular Windows application programs, which is illustrated in Figure 18-3.

DLLs do not have their own stack, but instead use the stack of any program calling a function in the DLL. As you may recall from Chapter 1, *How Windows Works*, the stack is used for automatic variables (variables declared within a function, and without the "static" prefix). Having DLLs use the stack of the program calling a function in the DLL makes sense if you consider that one DLL could be accessed by hundreds of different Windows applications. Automatic variables declared within the DLL's functions end up spread around through all of the stacks of the calling programs, rather than piling up in a single stack of a DLL.

Problems with Static Variables in DLLs

As shown in Figure 18-3, DLLs have their own local heap for storing static variables. If you declare a character string in the DLL's code, such as:

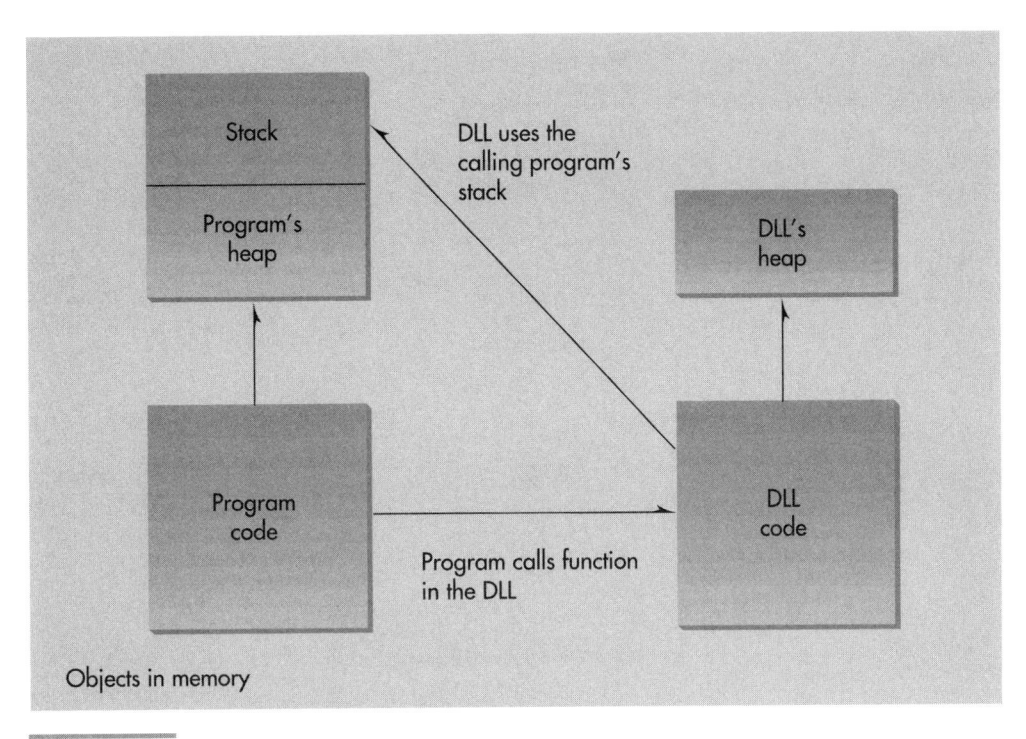

Figure 18-3 A DLL Loaded into Memory

```
char    cBuf [] = "This is static text." ;
```

the text will be stored in the DLL's local heap. Global variables declared in the DLL's code will also be stored in the DLL's heap. This leads to some interesting situations, when more than one Windows application is calling the same functions in a DLL. Imagine that the DLL stores an integer counter as a static variable, as shown in Figure 18-4. Any program that calls the DLL function results in the same static integer being incremented. This can foul things up in a hurry if each of the calling applications is not aware that other applications can change the value of the static variable.

Because there is only a single data heap for a DLL, static variables in DLLs are generally limited to things like text strings and variables that keep track of how many different programs are accessing the DLL. For a DLL to manage data for calling programs, the DLL will generally need to allocate separate memory blocks for each calling program's data. A common practice is to use the calling program's instance handle as a unique ID value to use to keep track of which data block belongs to which program. Figure 18-5 shows a typical DLL in memory, having allocated memory blocks for each of the programs currently accessing the DLL's functions.

Another interesting aspect of DLLs is that global memory blocks allocated within the DLL are "owned" by the program calling the DLL, not by the DLL itself. This means

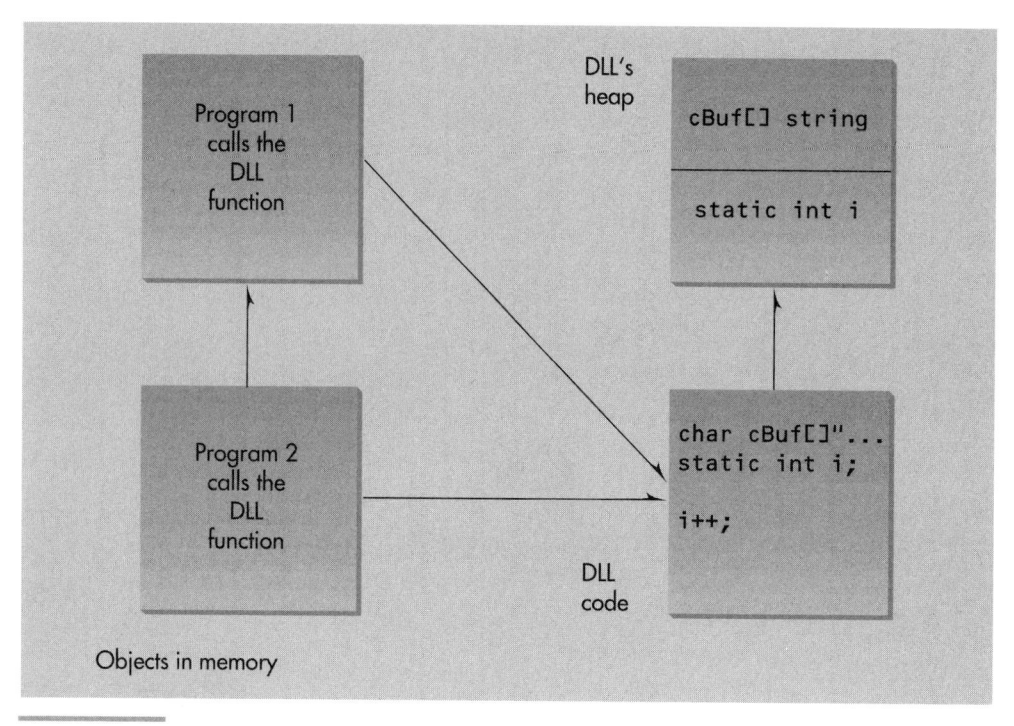

Figure 18-4 Problems with Static Variables in a DLL

that blocks allocated by Program 1 (see Figure 18-5) will be freed if Program 1 is terminated, even if the DLL is still in memory to serve Program 2. Normally, this is desirable behavior, but it can cause problems. There is an example later in the chapter demonstrating a programming error caused by assuming that a memory block allocated by the DLL is tied to the DLL itself.

Writing a DLL

The basic structure of any DLL is shown in Listing 18-1. There is one mandatory function that must be included: LibMain(). LibMain() is similar to the WinMain() function of a normal Windows application, in that this is the first function that is executed when the DLL is loaded into memory. LibMain() is where you will put any initialization code, such initializing static data. The other predefined function in a DLL is WEP() ("Windows Exit Procedure"), which is the function that Windows will call right before the DLL is removed from memory. WEP() is where you will put any final cleanup code, such as freeing memory blocks allocated by the DLL. Besides LibMain() and WEP(), there will be one or more functions which do whatever activities the DLL is expected to accomplish. Any function within the DLL that will be called by another program must be declared FAR (usually FAR PASCAL). Note that LibMain() and WEP() are also declared FAR PASCAL.

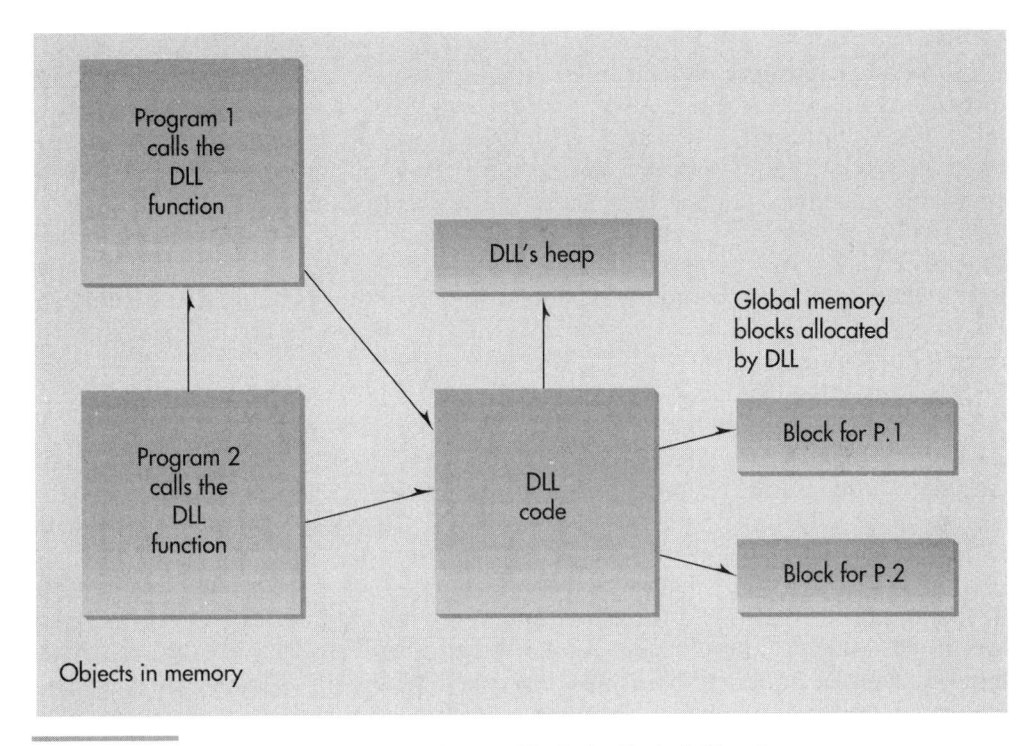

Figure 18-5 DLL Managing Separate Memory Blocks for Each Calling Program

Listing 18-1 Outline of a DLL

```
int FAR PASCAL LibMain (HANDLE hInstance, WORD wDataSeg,
    WORD wHeapSize, LPSTR lpszCmdLine)
{
    if (wHeapSize > 0)      /* unlock local data segment */
        UnlockData (0) ;
                            /* any initialization goes here */
    if (/* all OK */)
        return (1) ;        /* all OK, continue */
    else
        return (0) ;        /* initialization failed - quit */
}

void FAR PASCAL WEP (int nParameter) /* DLL terminator function */
{
    /* cleanup activities go here */
    return ;
}

int FAR PASCAL DoesSomething (...)
{
    /* one or more functions that do work */
}
```

Chapter 18 • Dynamic Link Libraries

Windows passes four parameters to the LibMain() function. *hInstance* is the DLL's instance handle, which you may want to save in a static variable if you will be calling functions within the DLL that require *hInstance* as a parameter. *wDataSeg* is the segment address of the DLL's local heap (the contents of the CPU's DS register if you are an assembly language programmer). *wHeapSize* is the size of the DLL's local heap. This value will be determined by the HEAPSIZE statement in the DLL's module definition statement. DLL's do not require a local heap if they do not use static variables. Finally, *lpszCmdLine* is a pointer to a command line string. Normally, command line strings are not passed to DLLs, although it is possible if the program using the DLL loads the DLL into memory using the LoadModule() function.

The only thing LibMain() must do is unlock the DLL's local data segment by calling the UnlockData() function, assuming that the DLL has a local heap. This logic is shown in Listing 18-1. LibMain() should return one if no problems were encountered (such as not being able to allocate memory), or zero if the DLL could not be properly started. Most DLLs only use the *hInstance* and *wHeapSize* parameters passed to LibMain() and ignore the *wDataSeg* and *lpszCmdLine* parameters.

The WEP() function is passed only one parameter, *nParameter*, which will either have the value of WEP_FREE_DLL if Windows is removing the DLL from memory, or WEP_SYSTEMEXIT if the Windows session is being terminated. WEP() is not strictly required if the DLL does not have any cleanup activities to do. However, the Microsoft documentation recommends including a WEP() function, perhaps for compatibility with future releases of Windows.

An Example DLL

The first example DLL in this chapter is named REVSTR.DLL. It provides a function named BlockRev() that reverses the order of the characters in a global memory block. BlockRev() will be used in another Windows program to print out a text string backwards. Any number of Windows programs can access the BlockRev() function in the same Windows session. Spelling things backwards is probably not something you do every day, but the REVSTR example has the advantage of demonstrating a number of features in a DLL, without a complex internal operation to confuse matters. This section examines the coding of the DLL's source code file. The next section will explain compiling the file to make a finished DLL, followed by an example Windows application that uses BlockRev().

Listing 18-2 shows the source code for the DLL. REVSTR.C includes the required LibMain() and WEP() functions. There is no initialization or cleanup to be done, so these two functions are fairly simple. The BlockRev() function reverses the order of the bytes in a global memory buffer. BlockRev() works by copying the contents of the input memory block into a temporary global memory block in reverse order, and then copies the contents of the temporary block back into the input block.

Listing 18-2 REVSTR.C Source Code for a DLL

```c
/* revstr.c  example of dll containing a string function */

#include <windows.h>
#include "revstr.h"


    /* dll initiator function */
int FAR PASCAL LibMain (HANDLE hInstance, WORD wDataSeg,
    WORD wHeapSize, LPSTR lpszCmdLine)
{
    if (wHeapSize > 0)     /* unlock local data segment */
        UnlockData (0) ;
    /* any initialization goes here */
        return (1) ;       /* all ok, continue */
}


    /* dll terminator function */
void FAR PASCAL WEP (int nParameter)
{
    /* any cleanup activities go here */
    return ;
}


/* The BlockRev() function reverses the order of the bytes in a */
/* global memory block.  The bytes are copied temporarily into */
/* the _hgMem block, and then copied back into the input block. */
/* Returns TRUE if all OK, FALSE on error. */

BOOL FAR PASCAL BlockRev (HANDLE hgInput, int nLong)
{
    int     i ;
    HANDLE  hgMem ;
    LPSTR   lpSource, lpDest, lps, lpd ;

        /* allocate temporary buffer, length + 1 for terminal null */
    hgMem = GlobalAlloc (GMEM_MOVEABLE | GMEM_DISCARDABLE,
        (LONG) (nLong + 1)) ;
    if (hgMem)
    {
        lpDest = GlobalLock (hgMem) ;       /* lock both blocks */
        lpSource = GlobalLock (hgInput) ;
        lpd = lpDest ;                      /* points to start of dest */
        lps = lpSource + nLong - 1 ;        /* points to end of source */

        for (i = 0 ; i < nLong ; i++)       /* reverse copy to dest */
            *lpd++ = *lpsñ ;

        for (i = 0 ; i < nLong ; i++)       /* copy back to source */
            *lpSource++ = *lpDest++ ;
```

```
            GlobalUnlock (hgInput) ;         /* leave input unlocked */
            GlobalFree (hgMem) ;             /* free temp buffer */
            return (TRUE) ;
        }
        return (FALSE) ;
    }
```

As you can see from Listing 18-3, there is nothing very unusual about the coding of the BlockRev() function. The main change compared with a function within a Windows application is to make sure that the function is declared FAR PASCAL, so that it can be exported. The DLL will reside in a different data segment than the application that calls the BlockRev() function, so far pointers are used in all cases (remember that "LPSTR" is equivalent to "char far *" in WINDOWS.H).

Module Definition File for a DLL

The module definition file for a DLL is a bit different than that for a Windows application. Listing 18-3 shows the REVSTR.DEF file, with the key changes highlighted. In place of the NAME statement, DLLs use the LIBRARY statement to name the file. Note that the DATA statement includes the key word SINGLE in place of the usual MULTIPLE. This is because the DLL will have a single data segment, and there will never be more than one instance of the DLL in memory at any one time.

A change that you might miss in Listing 18-3 is that there is no STACK statement. This is because the DLL will use the stack of any program calling the DLL's functions. The DLL does have a local data segment, which is sized with the HEAPSIZE statement.

Listing 18-3 REVSTR.DEF Module Definition File

```
LIBRARY        revstr
DESCRIPTION    'revstr application'
EXETYPE        WINDOWS
STUB           'WINSTUB.EXE'
CODE           PRELOAD MOVEABLE DISCARDABLE
DATA           PRELOAD MOVEABLE SINGLE
HEAPSIZE       1024
EXPORTS        BlockRev    @1
```

At the bottom of REVSTR.DEF is the EXPORTS statement. Only the function BlockRev() is exported, allowing other Windows programs (and other DLLs) to call this function. This is just like the EXPORTS statements used in Windows applications for the functions that are called by Windows, such as WndProc() and dialog box functions. Note that the function name is followed by an ampersand (&) and the digit one (1). This is called the function's "ordinal number." Using ordinal numbers is an alternative way to call a function in a DLL, which is demonstrated later in this chapter. If there are several exported functions in the same DLL, each will be given a different ordinal number:

```
EXPORTS        BlockRev    @1
               SecondFunc  @2
               ThirdFunc   @3
```

The information in the module definition file is used by the linker to correctly build the finished application.

Header File for a DLL

One last file that is needed to create the DLL is a header file. The REVSTR.H file (Listing 18-4) includes the function prototype for the exported function BlockRev(). This is used in the REVSTR.C program and will also be used later in the Windows program that calls the BlockRev() function.

Listing 18-4 REVSTR.H Header File

```
/* revstr.h */

BOOL FAR PASCAL BlockRev (HANDLE hgInput, int nLong) ;
```

Note that it is not necessary to declare the LibMain() and WEP() functions; they are declared in WINDOWS.H. Every exported function should be declared in the DLL's header file.

Compiling REVSTR to Make a DLL

Both compiler and linker settings need to be changed slightly when you are creating a DLL. The exact changes will depend on the compiler you are using.

Creating a DLL with Turbo C++

The REVSTR DLL is fairly simple, in that it does not have any resource data. You will not need to run the Resource Workshop application for this program. You will need to make the following selections from the Turbo C++ menus to correctly compile the DLL:

1. Select the "Project/Open Project" menu item and create a project file named REVSTR.PRJ.
2. Add the files REVSTR.C and REVSTR.DEF to the project file. REVSTR does not have any resource data, so there is no .RES file in the project list.
3. Select the "Options/Application..." menu item, and click the "Windows DLL" button. This tells the compiler that the output will be a dynamic link library.
4. Select the "Options/Compiler/Code generation..." menu item, and select the small memory model. This example is so small that the small memory model is ideal. Larger DLLs (over roughly 15K bytes) typically use the medium memory model.
5. Select the "Options/Compiler/Entry/Exit Code..." menu item, and select the "Windows DLL, explicit functions exported" option. This is important, as the exported function names are specified in the REVSTR.DEF file, and you do not want the compiler to generate a second set of duplicate function names for exported functions.

6. Select the "Options/Directories..." menu item, and verify that you have the correct subdirectory names for both the "Include Directories" and "Output Directory" names.

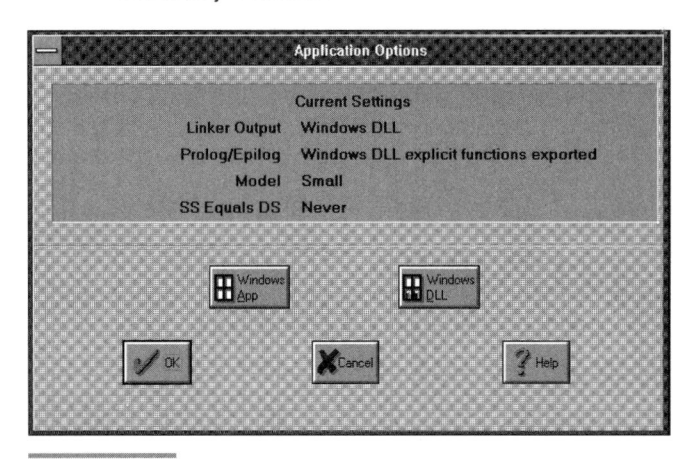

Figure 18-6 Correct Settings for Turbo C++ Creating a DLL

You can verify that the Turbo C++ is correctly set up by selecting the "Options/Application..." menu item again. The dialog box that appears should show the same settings as those shown in Figure 18-6. If your IDE dialog box shows different settings, go back and select the options shown above. The most common error is to forget to pick the "explicit functions exported" option, which will result in a series of errors when you compile due to having two attempts to export each function. Note that the Turbo C++ default "SS Equals DS - Never" is correct for DLLs, where the stack and local heap are always in different segments.

With the IDE properly set up, just select the "Compile/Build All" menu item, and watch the compiler and linker go to work. The compiler will issue four warning messages, reflecting the fact that four parameters passed to the LibMain() and WEP() functions were not used. You can disregard these messages, as the parameters were deliberately not used. The files REVSTR.OBJ and REVSTR.DLL will be created on the output subdirectory.

Because REVSTR.DLL is a dynamic link library, and not a Windows application, you cannot run it alone. In order to demonstrate that REVSTR.DLL actually works, you will need to create a short Windows program that calls the BlockRev() function, which is the next example program in this chapter.

Creating a DLL with QuickC

Creating a DLL from within QuickC is identical to creating a Windows application, except that you will select a different compiler option. Here are the steps to create REVSTR.DLL:

1. Open (create) the project file REVSTR.MAK. Add the files REVSTR.C and REVSTR.DEF to the project. REVSTR does not have any resource data, so there will be no resource script file in the project.

2. Select the "Options/Project..." menu item (a dialog box will appear) and select "Windows DLL." This tells QuickC that the project should produce a .DLL file, instead of the usual .EXE file.

3. From the same "Options/Project..." dialog box opened in the previous step, select the "Linker button." The "Customize Linker Options" dialog box will appear. Select the "Options" button, and enter the string "\NOD" in the edit control labeled "Custom Options\Global:." This avoids having the linker load a default WEP() function from a library file, which will result in a linker error if you have included your own WEP() function in the DLL source code. Select the "OK" button to save your selections.
4. Select the "Project/Build" menu item to compile the project. QuickC will create the files REVSTR.OBJ and REVSTR.DLL.

Unlike Turbo C++, the QuickC compiler will not issue warning messages for the parameters passed to LibMain() and WEP() that are not used.

Using the DLL

To put the REVSTR.DLL dynamic link library to work, you will need to write a Windows application that uses the only function that REVSTR.DLL exports: BlockRev(). The next example program, DLLCALL, will use the BlockRev() function to reverse the order of the characters in a character string. Figure 18-7 shows the DLLCALL program window, after the "Show Strings" menu item was selected.

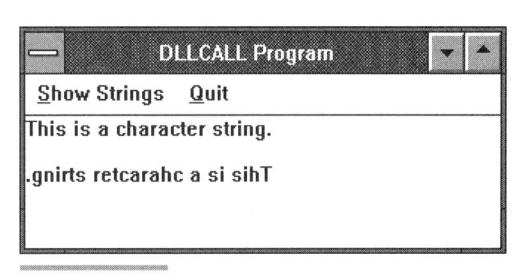

Figure 18-7 The DLLCALL Program

The first step in using a function in a DLL is to let your Windows program know where to find the function. This can be done in several ways. The most direct method is to add an IMPORTS section to the Windows application's module definition file. Listing 18-5 shows the DLLCALL.DEF file, with the IMPORTS section shown at the end. The IMPORTS statement tells the linker that the function named BlockRev() will be found in the DLL named REVSTR. A period is used to separate the DLL file name from the function name.

Listing 18-5 DLLCALL.DEF Module Definition File

```
NAME            dllcall
DESCRIPTION     'dllcall application'
EXETYPE         WINDOWS
STUB            'WINSTUB.EXE'
CODE            PRELOAD MOVEABLE
DATA            PRELOAD MOVEABLE MULTIPLE
HEAPSIZE        1024
STACKSIZE       5120
EXPORTS         WndProc
IMPORTS         REVSTR.BlockRev
```

Windows programs can import any number of functions from various DLLs. For example, the following IMPORT statement would allow the program to import three functions from two different DLLs.

```
IMPORTS       DLLONE.OneFunc
              DLLONE.TwoFunc
              DLLTWO.ThreeFunc
```

Once you have added the DLL/function names to the Windows application's module definition file, you can use the functions in the DLL just as if they were part of the application itself. Listing 18-6 shows the complete DLLCALL.C program, which uses the BlockRev() function to reverse the order of the characters in a character string. The portion of the code that outputs the character strings in normal and reverse order is shown here:

```
hDC = GetDC (hWnd) ;
hInstance = GetWindowWord (hWnd, GWW_HINSTANCE) ;
hgMem = GlobalAlloc (GHND, 128) ;
if (hgMem)
{
    lpStr = GlobalLock (hgMem) ;
    LoadString (hInstance, S_EXAMPLESTRING, lpStr, 128) ;
    nStringLong = lstrlen (lpStr) ;
    TextOut (hDC, 0, 0, lpStr, nStringLong) ;
    GlobalUnlock (hgMem) ;
    BlockRev (hgMem, nStringLong) ;
    lpStr = GlobalLock (hgMem) ;
    TextOut (hDC, 0, 30, lpStr, nStringLong) ;
    GlobalUnlock (hgMem) ;
}
ReleaseDC (hWnd, hDC) ;
```

The character string is loaded into a global memory block from the program's resource data using the LoadString() function. After the string is displayed once with the characters in the correct order, BlockRev() is called to reverse the characters. The string is then output again. One other important detail in the DLLCALL.C program file is that the header file REVSTR.H is included at the top of the listing. This header file (shown in Listing 18-4), includes the function declaration for the BlockRev() function. This lets the compiler know what parameters types will be passed to the BlockRev() function, even though the function resides in a DLL.

Listing 18-6 DLLCALL.C

```
/* dllcall.c    example calling function in a dll */

#include <windows.h>
#include "dllcall.h"     /* header file for this program */
#include "revstr.h"      /* header file for dll */
```

```c
int PASCAL WinMain (HANDLE hInstance, HANDLE hPrevInstance, LPSTR lpszCmdLine,
    int nCmdShow)
{
    HWND        hWnd ;      /* the window's "handle" */
    MSG         msg ;       /* a message structure */
    WNDCLASS    wndclass ;  /* window class structure */
    char        cBuf [128] ;

    if (!hPrevInstance)
    {
        wndclass.style          = CS_HREDRAW | CS_VREDRAW ;
        wndclass.lpfnWndProc    = WndProc ;
        wndclass.cbClsExtra     = 0 ;
        wndclass.cbWndExtra     = 0 ;
        wndclass.hInstance      = hInstance ;
        wndclass.hIcon          = LoadIcon (hInstance, "MyIcon") ;
        wndclass.hCursor        = LoadCursor (NULL, IDC_ARROW) ;
        wndclass.hbrBackground  = GetStockObject (WHITE_BRUSH) ;
        wndclass.lpszMenuName   = "MyMenu" ;
        wndclass.lpszClassName  = "MyClass" ;
                /* register the window class */
        if (!RegisterClass (&wndclass))
            return 0 ;
    }
    LoadString (hInstance, S_PROGRAMCAPTION, cBuf, sizeof (cBuf)) ;

    hWnd = CreateWindow ("MyClass", cBuf, WS_OVERLAPPEDWINDOW,
        CW_USEDEFAULT, CW_USEDEFAULT, CW_USEDEFAULT, CW_USEDEFAULT,
        NULL, NULL, hInstance, NULL) ;
    ShowWindow (hWnd, nCmdShow) ;       /* display the window */

    while (GetMessage (&msg, NULL, NULL, NULL))     /* message loop */
    {
        TranslateMessage (&msg) ;       /* translate keyboard messages */
        DispatchMessage (&msg) ;        /* send message to WndProc() */
    }
    return (msg.wParam) ;
}

long FAR PASCAL WndProc (HWND hWnd, WORD wMessage, WORD wParam, LONG lParam)
{
    HANDLE  hgMem, hInstance ;
    LPSTR   lpStr ;
    HDC     hDC ;
    int     nStringLong ;

    switch (wMessage)                   /* process windows messages */
    {
        case WM_COMMAND:
            switch (wParam)
            {
                case IDM_SHOW:
                    hDC = GetDC (hWnd) ;
                    hInstance = GetWindowWord (hWnd, GWW_HINSTANCE) ;
                    hgMem = GlobalAlloc (GHND, 128) ;
                    if (hgMem)
                    {
```

```
                    lpStr = GlobalLock (hgMem) ;
                    LoadString (hInstance, S_EXAMPLESTRING, lpStr, 128) ;
                    nStringLong = lstrlen (lpStr) ;
                    TextOut (hDC, 0, 0, lpStr, nStringLong) ;
                    GlobalUnlock (hgMem) ;
                    BlockRev (hgMem, nStringLong) ;
                    lpStr = GlobalLock (hgMem) ;
                    TextOut (hDC, 0, 30, lpStr, nStringLong) ;
                    GlobalUnlock (hgMem) ;
                    }
                    ReleaseDC (hWnd, hDC) ;
                    break ;
                case IDM_QUIT:                  /* Quit menu item */
                    DestroyWindow (hWnd) ;      /* destroy window, */
                    break ;        /* terminating application */
                }
            break ;
        case WM_DESTROY:            /* stop application */
            PostQuitMessage (0) ;
            break ;
        default:                    /* default windows message processing */
            return (DefWindowProc (hWnd, wMessage, wParam, lParam)) ;
    }
    return (0L) ;
}
```

The remaining support files for DLLCALL are shown in Listings 18-7 to 18-10. Figure 18-8 shows the program's icon.

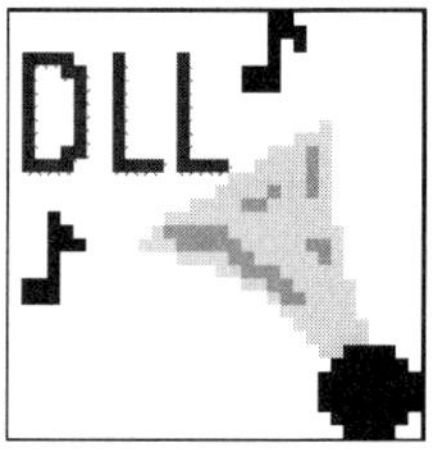

Listing 18-7 DLLCALL.H Header File

```
/* dllcall.h header file */

#define IDM_QUIT            1       /* menu item ID numbers */
#define IDM_SHOW            2

#define S_PROGRAMCAPTION    1       /* string table ID numbers */
#define S_EXAMPLESTRING     2

long FAR PASCAL WndProc (HWND, WORD, WORD, LONG) ;
```

Figure 18-8
DLLCALL.ICO
Icon Image

Listing 18-8 DLLCALL.RC Resource Script File

```
/* dllcall.rc resource file */

#include "dllcall.h"

MyIcon      ICON    dllcall.ico

MyMenu      MENU
BEGIN
    MENUITEM "&Show Strings",           IDM_SHOW
```

658 *Windows Programming Primer Plus®*

```
        MENUITEM "&Quit",              IDM_QUIT
END

STRINGTABLE
BEGIN
     S_PROGRAMCAPTION   "DLLCALL Program"
     S_EXAMPLESTRING    "This is a character string."
END
```

Listing 18-9 Turbo C++ Project File for DLLCALL

```
dllcall.c
dllcall.def
dllcall.res
```

Listing 18-10 QuickC Project File for DLLCALL

```
dllcall.c
dllcall.def
dllcall.rc
```

Alternate Ways to Reference DLL Functions

In the DLLCALL program, the linker was told the name of the DLL file containing the BlockRev() function by putting an IMPORTS statement in the DLLCALL.DEF module definition file. This is the standard way of importing functions from small DLLs. There is another shortcut method that you can use. Remember back in the module definition file for the DLL, the EXPORTS part of the REVSTR.DEF file included the "ordinal number" for the BlockRev() function as "@1." This is shown again in Listing 18-11.

Listing 18-11 REVSTR.DEF Module Definition File

```
LIBRARY           revstr
DESCRIPTION       'revstr application'
EXETYPE           WINDOWS
STUB              'WINSTUB.EXE'
CODE              PRELOAD MOVEABLE DISCARDABLE
DATA              PRELOAD MOVEABLE SINGLE
HEAPSIZE          1024
EXPORTS           BlockRev   @1
```

Ordinal numbers for exported functions in DLLs are optional, but they do allow you to refer to the exported function by its number, rather than the function's name. For example, the Windows application that uses the BlockRev() function could have a module definition file like the one shown in Listing 18-12. The name of the BlockRev() function has been replaced by the function's ordinal number.

Listing 18-12 DLLCALL.DEF Using the Ordinal Number for BlockRev()

```
NAME          dllcall3
DESCRIPTION   'dllcall3 application'
EXETYPE       WINDOWS
STUB          'WINSTUB.EXE'
CODE          PRELOAD MOVEABLE
DATA          PRELOAD MOVEABLE MULTIPLE
HEAPSIZE      1024
STACKSIZE     5120
EXPORTS       WndProc
IMPORTS       BlockRev = REVSTR.1
```

The advantage of using the ordinal number for a function is that it produces slightly smaller and faster code. The disadvantage is that it is easy to get the function numbers mixed up if the DLL contains a large number of exported functions. In general, using the ordinal numbers should only be done if the program's performance is critically important.

Import Libraries

If there are a number of exported functions, the best technique is to summarize all of the functions in an import library. Import libraries allow you to forget about adding function names or ordinal numbers to the IMPORTS section of the Windows application's .DEF file. Instead, you collect all of the names of the functions in the DLL

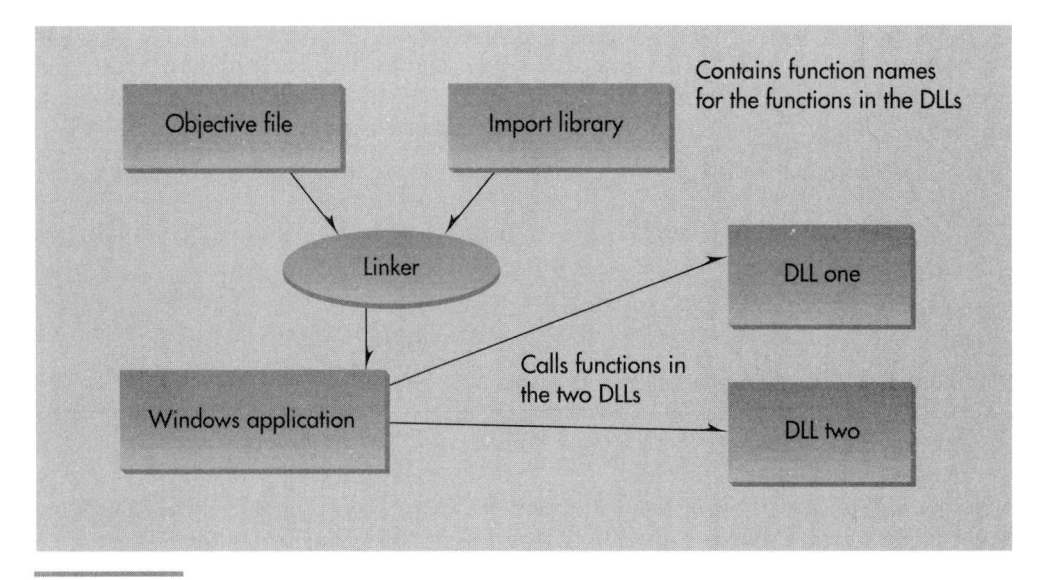

Figure 18-9 Using an Import Library

in a single library file, that can be included in the linking process. Figure 18-9 shows the effect of including an import library when creating a Windows application.

The import library tells the linker which DLLs contain the functions that the application needs. Unlike runtime libraries, import libraries do not add the functions from the DLL to the Windows application. Import libraries only contain the references to the locations of functions in DLLs. When the Windows application calls a function in a DLL, the DLL is loaded into memory (if it is not already loaded), and the function is executed within the DLL's code.

Creating an Import Library

Both the Turbo C++ and QuickC programming tools come with utilities for creating import libraries. Turbo C++'s is a Windows application called "Import Lib" (IMPLIBW.EXE), which is shown in Figure 18-10. All you need to do to create an import library for REVSTR.DLL is to select the "File/File Select..." menu item, and pick the REVSTR.DLL file. The Import Library application will read the DLL, and then will create the REVSTR.LIB file in the same directory. You can select more than one DLL, to create a library covering several DLLs.

Figure 18-10 The Borland Import Lib Application

QuickC comes with a DOS application named IMPLIB.EXE that creates an import library based on a module definition file. To create the REVSTR.LIB library, open a DOS window, move to the subdirectory containing your DLL and its DEF file, and type the following line:

```
implib revstr.lib revstr.def
```

This will work if the library containing IMPLIB.EXE is in your current DOS PATH. Otherwise, spell out the full path name for IMPLIB such as:

```
c:\qcwin\implib revstr.lib revstr.def
```

This is not as elegant as the Borland Windows application, but the results are identical. Check to make sure that the REVSTR.LIB file was created before trying the next section.

Using an Import Library

As mentioned previously, once you have created an import library, you do not need to list the imported function names in the IMPORTS section of the Windows application's module definition file. All you need to do is to add the import library file to the list of files that the linker uses to build the finished program. For example, the module definition file for the DLLCALL program is shown in Listing 18-13, modified by removing the IMPORTS section completely.

Chapter 18 • Dynamic Link Libraries   661

Listing 18-13 DLLCALL.DEF For Use with Import Library

```
NAME            dllcall
DESCRIPTION     'dllcall application'
EXETYPE         WINDOWS
STUB            'WINSTUB.EXE'
CODE            PRELOAD MOVEABLE
DATA            PRELOAD MOVEABLE MULTIPLE
HEAPSIZE        1024
STACKSIZE       5120
EXPORTS         WndProc
```

How you tell the linker about the import library name will depend on which development tools you are using.

Turbo C++ Import Libraries

With Turbo C++, simply add the REVSTR.LIB to the project file for an application that calls the BlockRev() function in REVSTR.DLL. For example, the project file for the DLLCALL program should contain the following file names:

```
dllcall.c
dllcall.def
dllcall.res
revstr.lib
```

Turbo C++ will include the information in the REVSTR.LIB import library during the creation of the DLLCALL.EXE program file. DLLCALL.EXE will call the BlockRev() function in REVSTR.DLL, just as if the function had been specified in the IMPORTS section of the DLLCALL.DEF module definition file.

QuickC Import Libraries

Like Turbo C++, QuickC just requires that you add the library file to the project list. For example, to compile DLLCALL using the REVSTR.LIB import library, use the following project file:

```
dllcall.c
dllcall.def
dllcall.rc
revstr.lib
```

The reference to the BlockRev() function in the REVSTR.DLL file will be extracted by QuickC from the REVSTR.LIB library file during the linking step.

The Big Picture on Import Libraries

As mentioned previously, the Windows functions like CreateWindow() and TextOut() all reside in DLLs. Every example program in this book calls functions in these DLLs. However, we have not needed to list all of the Windows functions in the IMPORTS section of each example's module definition file. Turbo C++ and QuickC take care of this for us by linking import libraries automatically. The import libraries contain function references for every Windows function, so that the example program knows where to call CreateWindow(), TextOut(), etc.

When you compile using Turbo C++ or QuickC, the various steps the compiler and linker go through to create the finished application are displayed in a small dialog box. The compilers are so fast that it is difficult to read the displayed messages and file names as they flash by. If you could, you would see that a number of files are included during the linking step to create the finished Windows application. Using Turbo C++ as an example, you may be able to pick out the names C0WS.LIB, CWS.LIB, and IMPORT.LIB during a compilation.

The C0WS.LIB and CWS.LIB files are regular runtime libraries. They contain startup code and other functions that are added into your Windows application to do low-level tasks, such as setting up the application's local heap when it is first loaded. You can think of these runtime libraries as containing the "secret functions" that your Windows application needs to get started and do a few low-level tasks. Microsoft provides documentation of these secret functions to developers of Windows programming tools (such as Borland), but most Windows programmers can take their existence for granted. For most of us, there are plenty of Windows functions to work with without worrying about the secret ones.

The IMPORT.LIB is an import library for the Windows DLLs that contains the locations of all of the built-in Windows functions like CreateWindow(), RegisterClass(), TextOut(), and so on. This is how your program finds where to call all of these Windows functions. One of the beauties of using DLLs to store Windows functions is that the functionality of Windows can be added to by simply adding more DLLs. For example, if you install a new printer, you end up copying a new DLL to the Windows system directory. The DLL (usually given the extension ".DRV") contains the functions needed to convert GDI graphics commands into the printer's own command set. Adding the printer driver basically extended Windows with this new information.

Programming Considerations for DLLs

When you write a DLL, there are a few things that you need to keep in mind that do not apply to Windows applications:

1. The DLL will be in a different segment from the application calling functions in the DLL. Declare all exported functions FAR (usually FAR PASCAL), and use FAR pointers for addresses.

2. The DLL will have its own static data, which will be common to all of the applications calling functions in the DLL. Don't store data for the calling applications in static variables that might cause an error if two or more applications are using the DLL at the same time. For example, do not store the current record number in a data base as a single static number if two or more application programs can change the record number.

3. The DLL will use the stack of the calling program(s), which will be in a separate segment from the DLL's static data on the local heap. This can cause problems,

particularly if you use runtime library functions that assume that the stack and static data are in the same segment. Any function that uses near pointers to data is highly suspect.

4. When you allocate global memory blocks from within a DLL, the memory blocks belong to the application calling the DLL, not to the DLL itself. This is how Windows gets around "sharing violations," where two different applications attempt to access the same block of memory. Memory blocks allocated by the DLL will be freed if the application that called the DLL is terminated.

An Example DLL That Fails

The fact the memory blocks allocated within a DLL belong to the application calling the DLL (not the DLL itself) can lead to some interesting bugs. As an example, look at the REVSTRF.C program in Listing 18-14. The only difference between REVSTRF.C and the REVSTR.C program in the last section is that the temporary memory buffer is allocated in the LibMain() function, rather than within the BlockRev() function. This looks at first glance like a good idea. The global block is allocated with the GMEM_DISCARDABLE flag set, so that it can be discarded if Windows runs out of memory. The block is reallocated within the BlockRev() function to match the size of the input data block. The block is freed from memory when the DLL is terminated and WEP() is called. If you use REVSTRF in place of REVSTR for the DLLCALL program, the example string gets reversed just as before. Where is the error?

Listing 18-14 REVSTRF.C An Incorrectly Coded DLL

```
/* revstrf.c  example of incorrectly written dll  */

#include <windows.h>
#include "revstrf.h"

HANDLE _hgMem ;              /* static data - handle of data */

/* dll initiator function */
int FAR PASCAL LibMain (HANDLE hInstance, WORD wDataSeg,
    WORD wHeapSize, LPSTR lpszCmdLine)
{
    if (wHeapSize > 0)       /* unlock local data segment */
        UnlockData (0) ;
                             /* any initialization goes here */
                             /* allocate a buffer here */
    hgMem = GlobalAlloc (GMEM_MOVEABLE | GMEM_DISCARDABLE, 1) ;
    if (_hgMem)
        return (1) ;         /* all ok, continue */
    else
        return (0) ;         /* initialization failed - quit */
}

/* dll terminator function */
void FAR PASCAL WEP (int nParameter)
{
```

```
        GlobalFree (_hgMem) ;    /* cleanup activities go here */
        return ;
}

/* The BlockRev() function reverses the order of the bytes in a */
/* global memory block.  The bytes are copied temporarily into */
/* the _hgMem block, and then copied back into the input block. */
/* Returns TRUE if all OK, FALSE on error. */

BOOL FAR PASCAL BlockRev (HANDLE hgInput, int nLong)
{
    int     i ;
    HANDLE  hInput ;
    LPSTR   lpSource, lpDest, lps, lpd ;
                        /* + 1 for terminal null */
    _hgMem = GlobalReAlloc (_hgMem, (LONG) (nLong + 1),
        GMEM_MOVEABLE | GMEM_DISCARDABLE) ;
    if (_hgMem)
    {
        lpDest = GlobalLock (_hgMem) ;      /* lock both blocks */
        lpSource = GlobalLock (hgInput) ;
        lpd = lpDest ;                      /* points to start of dest */
        lps = lpSource + nLong - 1 ;        /* points to end of source */

        for (i = 0 ; i < nLong ; i++)       /* reverse copy to dest */
            *lpd++ = *lpsñ ;

        for (i = 0 ; i < nLong ; i++)       /* copy back to source */
            *lpSource++ = *lpDest++ ;

        GlobalUnlock (_hgMem) ;             /* unlock both blocks */
        GlobalUnlock (hgInput) ;
        return (TRUE) ;
    }
    return (FALSE) ;
}
```

The problem with REVSTRF does not show up until you have more than one program using this DLL. The first program that uses the DLL causes the DLL to be loaded into memory. REVSTRF.DLL executes the LibMain() function, and allocates the memory block. However, the memory block belongs to the application that called the DLL, not to the DLL itself. Everything is fine in the beginning. You can start several programs that use the REVSTRF.DLL, and each will find that BlockRev() works fine.

Problems arise when you terminate the first application that caused REVSTRF.DLL to be loaded. The first application owns the memory block that REVSTRF.DLL allocated in the LibMain() function, so when the first application terminates, the temporary memory buffer is destroyed. Suddenly, BlockRev() does not work for the other applications.

You can prove to yourself that REVSTRF.C will not work properly by compiling this program in place of REVSTR.C, and using it with the DLLCALL application. Follow the following steps:

1. Start two instances of DLLCALL.
2. Verify that both instances work fine when the "Show Strings" menu item is selected. The second string will be reversed for both instances of DLLCALL.

3. Terminate the first instance of DLLCALL by selecting the "Quit" menu item.
4. Now try the "Show Strings" menu item on the remaining instance of DLLCALL. Both strings will be displayed with the characters in the normal sequence. This is because the BlockRev() function returns without any action when it cannot reallocate the memory block. This leaves the character string in its original state.

(If you have purchased the source code disks, the incorrectly designed DLL is demonstrated with the files DLLCALLF.EXE, which calls the REVSTRF.DLL.)

Avoiding Memory Problems in DLLs

The preceding section may have you concerned that DLLs are temperamental programs to write. Actually, the problems outlined above are seldom an issue. Having memory blocks allocated within the DLL belong to the application calling the DLL is almost always exactly what you want. Two general guidelines that will keep you out of trouble when allocating memory:

1. When there is a choice, allocate and free the memory blocks used by the DLL in the application program that calls the DLL, not in the DLL itself.
2. Avoid situations where the block is allocated in the DLL, but freed in the application program, or the opposite. It is too easy to forget to free the memory blocks when you are done.

A More Complete DLL Example

Back in Chapter 15, *Disk File Access*, a file selection dialog box was demonstrated in the FILEDLG.C program. This same code was used in Chapter 17, *The Clipboard*, to provide file selection features for the SIMPEDIT editor. This time the code will be modified to put the file selection dialog box functions in a DLL. This is a more complex DLL, including the following features:

1. Several exported functions in the same DLL.
2. The DLL contains an internal function used by the DLL, which is not exported.
3. The DLL contains resource data, including a dialog box definition.
4. More complex data is exchanged between the DLL and the application using the DLL's functions.

The DLL is called FILESEL.DLL for "file selection." To put the FILESEL.DLL to work, a Windows application program must also be created that calls the DLL. Figure 18-11 shows the FILETEST program running, with the file selection dialog box defined in the DLL visible over the FILETEST program window. All FILETEST does is call the dialog box function in the DLL, and display the full path/file name for the file selected from the dialog box.

Converting FILEDLG to a DLL

Converting the FILEDLG file selection program from Chapter 15 to the FILESEL.DLL requires only a few modifications:

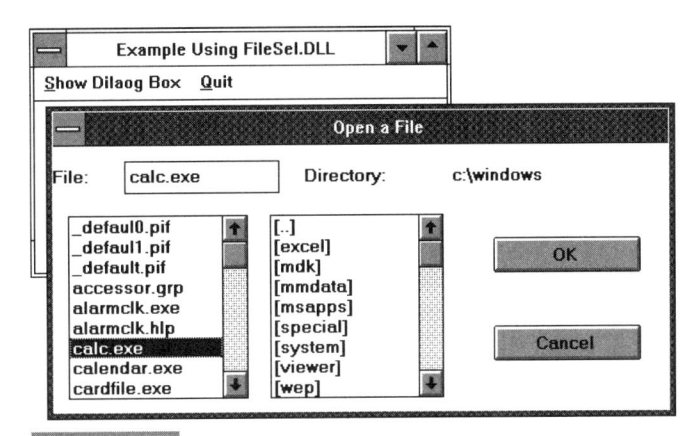

Figure 18-11 The FILETEST Program Demonstrating FILESEL.DLL

1. A LibMain() function must be added. WEP() is omitted from this example, as there is no data to clean up when the DLL terminates.
2. The functions are converted to the FAR PASCAL type.
3. Exported functions are added to the EXPORTS section of the module definition file.
4. Compiler runtime functions (such as getcwd() and strstr()) which may have built-in assumptions about the stack segment being equal to the data segment, are eliminated. (The versions of getcwd() and strstr() provided with the Microsoft C compiler do not cause problems in a DLL, but the Borland C++ version 3.0 functions do. Functions like strstr() which are declared with near pointers to strings should be avoided in writing DLLs.)
5. The compiler settings are changes to create a DLL.

As you can see, it does not take an enormous effort to make a DLL out of a set of Windows functions. If you find that several of your programs need the same functions, just collect the functions in a DLL so that they can be shared and reused in future projects.

Turbo C++ Bug

There is a minor and intermittent bug with the Turbo C++ 3.0 compiler that can cause problems with exported functions in a DLL. For some reason, the compiler will occasionally ignore the EXPORTS section of the program's module definition file. This will cause the exported functions to fail because the wrong entry and exit code is added to each exported function. There are two ways to get around this problem:

1. Turbo C++ and QuickC support the _export key word which can be included in the function declaration. This alerts the compiler that the function will be exported, regardless of whether or not the function is listed in the EXPORTS section of the module definition file. The FILESEL.C program (Listing 18-15) shows how the _export key word is used. _export must be placed immediately before the function name.

continued

> **Turbo C++ Bug (cont'd)**
>
> 2. Turbo C++ has a compiler option under the "Options\Compiler\Entry\exit code..." menu item that causes all functions to be exportable. If you use this option, be sure you do not include an EXPORTS section in the module definition file, as otherwise the compiler will detect two attempts to export the function.
>
> To get around the bug, the FILESEL.C program uses the _export key word in addition to showing the exported function names in the module definition file. This does not cause an error or duplicate code, and it compiles fine with both QuickC and Turbo C++. Compile the code with the "Options\Compiler\Entry\exit code...\Windows explicit functions exported" option under Turbo C++. No special considerations are required for QuickC. Using both the _export key word and an EXPORTS section in the module definition file is a "belt and suspenders" approach to exporting a function, but it keeps the Turbo C++ compiler happy.

Listing 18-15 shows the FILESEL.C program. Most of the logic for this program was explained in Chapter 15, *Disk File Access*, and will not be repeated here. However, there are a few points worth mentioning. Note that the DLL's instance handle is saved in a static variable within the LibMain() function. This is a common practice in DLLs, as there is no window handle to use with GetWindowWord() to retrieve the instance handle later. Another change is the addition of the short CallFileDlg() function, which creates the dialog box. CallFileDlg() saves steps for the calling program by collecting the MakeProcInstance(), DialogBoxParam(), and FreeProcInstance() functions all in one place.

Listing 18-15 FILESEL.C

```
/* filesel.c dll containing file selection dialog box functions */

#include <windows.h>
#include <string.h>     /* needed for strtok() function */
#include <direct.h>     /* needed for getcwd() function */
#include "filesel.h"

HANDLE ghInstance ;     /* static data */

    /* dll initiator function */
int FAR PASCAL LibMain (HANDLE hInstance, WORD wDataSeg,
    WORD wHeapSize, LPSTR lpszCmdLine)
{
    if (wHeapSize > 0)           /* unlock local data segment */
        UnlockData (0) ;
    ghInstance = hInstance ;     /* save instance handle */
    return (1) ;
}

/* the CallFileDlg() function calls the dialog box procedure, passing */
/* the names of the starting subdirectory, search path (like "*.*"), */
/* and the dialog box caption. CallFileDlg() returns a pointer to a */
/* FILEOPENDATA structure containing the selected path and file names. */
/* The calling program should check the bNotCancel variable in the */
```

```c
/* FILEOPENDATA to make sure that it is TRUE before proceeding.  FALSE */
/* value implies that the user did not select a file. */

BOOL FAR PASCAL _export CallFileDlg (HWND hWnd, HANDLE hFileOpenData)
{
    FARPROC             lpfnDlgProc ;
    BOOL                bRetStatus ;
    FILEOPENDATA FAR *  lpFOD ;

    lpFOD = (FILEOPENDATA FAR *) GlobalLock (hFileOpenData) ;
    if (lpFOD)
    {
        lpfnDlgProc = MakeProcInstance (FileOpenProc, ghInstance) ;
                                     /* call dialog box */
        bRetStatus = DialogBoxParam (ghInstance, "FileOpenDlg",
            hWnd, lpfnDlgProc, (DWORD)(LPSTR) lpFOD) ;
        FreeProcInstance (lpfnDlgProc) ;
        GlobalUnlock (hFileOpenData) ;
        return (bRetStatus) ;
    }
    return (FALSE) ;
}
/* FileOpenProc() function runs the FileDlg dialog box, defined in filesel.rc */
/* FileOpenProc() should be called using the DialogBoxParam() function, */
/* passing a pointer to a FILEOPENDATA structure containing the starting */
/* caption, path name and file search strings (like "c:\\", and "*.*"). */
/* The returned value is TRUE if a file was selected, FALSE if not */
/* No attempt is made to open the file within this procedure. */

BOOL FAR PASCAL _export FileOpenProc (HWND hDlg, WORD wMessage, WORD wParam, LONG
lParam)
{
    static FILEOPENDATA FAR * lpFOD ;
    static char FAR     szPathName [PATHNAMELONG], szFileName [FILENAMELONG] ;
    static char FAR     szPathFile [PATHNAMELONG] ;    /* working buffer */
    static BOOL         bMadeSel ;

    switch (wMessage)
    {
        case WM_INITDIALOG:
            lpFOD = (FILEOPENDATA FAR *) lParam ;       /* pointer to data */
            SetWindowText (hDlg, lpFOD->szCaption) ;
                                    /* initialize working buffer */
            CombinePathFile (szPathFile, lpFOD->szPath, lpFOD->szFile) ;
                                    /* fill both list boxes */
            DlgDirList (hDlg, szPathFile, DLI_FILELIST, DLI_EDIT, 0) ;
            DlgDirList (hDlg, szPathFile, DLI_DIRLIST, DLI_DIRECT, 0xC010) ;
            SetDlgItemText (hDlg, DLI_EDIT, lpFOD->szFile) ;
            bMadeSel = FALSE ; /* keep track of if file was selected */
            return (FALSE) ;
        case WM_COMMAND:
            switch (wParam)
            {
                case DLI_OK:                    /* OK button */
                    GetDlgItemText (hDlg, DLI_EDIT, lpFOD->szFile,
                        FILENAMELONG) ;
                    GetDlgItemText (hDlg, DLI_DIRECT, lpFOD->szPath,
                        PATHNAMELONG) ;
                    EndDialog (hDlg, bMadeSel) ;
```

```
                    break ;
                case DLI_CANCEL:                    /* cancel button */
                    EndDialog (hDlg, FALSE) ;
                    break ;
                case DLI_EDIT:                      /* the edit control */
                    if (HIWORD (lParam) == EN_CHANGE)
                        bMadeSel = TRUE ;           /* user entered file */
                    break ;
                case DLI_FILELIST:                  /* the file list box */
                    switch (HIWORD (lParam))
                    {
                        case LBN_SELCHANGE:         /* picked a file name */
                                                    /* get user's selection */
                            DlgDirSelect (hDlg, szPathFile, DLI_FILELIST) ;
                            SplitPathFile (szPathFile, szPathName,
                                szFileName) ;       /* display selected file */
                            SetDlgItemText (hDlg, DLI_EDIT, szFileName) ;
                            bMadeSel = TRUE ;
                            break ;
                        case LBN_DBLCLK:            /* double clicked file */
                            GetDlgItemText (hDlg, DLI_EDIT, lpFOD->szFile,
                                FILENAMELONG) ;
                            GetDlgItemText (hDlg, DLI_DIRECT, lpFOD->szPath,
                                PATHNAMELONG) ;
                            EndDialog (hDlg, bMadeSel) ;
                            break ;
                    }
                    break ;
                case DLI_DIRLIST:                   /* directory list box */
                    switch (HIWORD (lParam))
                    {
                        case LBN_SELCHANGE:         /* picked a dir name */
                                                    /* get user's selection */
                            DlgDirSelect (hDlg, szPathFile, DLI_DIRLIST) ;
                                                    /* refresh dir list */
                            DlgDirList (hDlg, szPathFile, DLI_DIRLIST,
                                DLI_DIRECT, 0xC010) ;
                                /* if directory name is just \.. */
                            if ((InStr (szPathFile, "..") != -1) ||
                                lstrlen (szPathFile) == 0)
                                lstrcpy (szPathFile, "*.*") ;
                                                    /* refresh file list */
                            DlgDirList (hDlg, szPathFile, DLI_FILELIST,
                                DLI_EDIT, 0) ;
                            SplitPathFile (szPathFile, szPathName,
                                szFileName) ;
                                                    /* show new file spec */
                            SetDlgItemText (hDlg, DLI_EDIT, szFileName) ;
                            bMadeSel = FALSE ;      /* reset file selection */
                            break ;
                    }
                    break ;
            }
            return (TRUE) ;
    }
    return (FALSE) ;
}

/* separate the directory and file name in lpSource into two strings */
```

```c
void FAR PASCAL _export SplitPathFile (LPSTR lpSource, LPSTR lpPath, LPSTR lpFile)
{
    LPSTR   lpChar ;

    lpChar = lpSource + (long) lstrlen (lpSource) ; /* point to end */
        /* move backwards through string looking for : or \ chars */
    while (*lpChar != ':' && *lpChar != '\\' && lpChar > lpSource)
        lpChar-- ;
    if (*lpChar != ':' && *lpChar != '\\')          /* none found ? */
    {
        lstrcpy (lpFile, lpChar) ;                  /* copy file name from end */
        *lpPath = 0 ;                               /* did not find subdirectory */
        return ;
    }
    else    /* found : or \, so can copy file and path names */
    {
        lstrcpy (lpFile, lpChar + 1) ;              /* copy file name from end */
        *(lpChar + 1) = 0 ;                         /* end path before file starts */
        lstrcpy (lpPath, lpSource) ;
    }
}

/* combine the szDir and szFile strings to make a complete dir/file name */

void FAR PASCAL _export CombinePathFile (LPSTR szFileName, LPSTR szDir, LPSTR
szFile)
{
    lstrcpy (szFileName, szDir) ;
    if (szFileName [lstrlen (szFileName) - 1] != '\\')
        lstrcat (szFileName, "\\") ;
    lstrcat (szFileName, szFile) ;
}

/* see if lpszCheck is in lpszString, return match pos, else ret -1 */
/* note: this is an internal function to the dll - not exported */

int InStr (LPSTR lpszString, LPSTR lpszCheck)
{
    LPSTR   lpCheck, lpString ;
    int     nMatch, nPos ;

    nPos = 0 ;
    do {
        lpCheck = lpszCheck ;
        lpString = lpszString ;
        nMatch = 0 ;
        do {
            if (*lpCheck == *lpString)
                nMatch++ ;
            else
                break ;
        } while (*lpCheck++ && *lpString++) ;
        if (nMatch == lstrlen (lpszCheck))
            return (nPos) ;
        else
            nPos++ ;
    } while (*lpszString++) ;
    return (-1) ;
}
```

The last function in FILESEL.C is InStr(). This function is used within the DLL to determine if one string is contained within another. Note that InStr() is not exported, so it does not need to be declared with the FAR PASCAL function type. If you want to use InStr() outside of the DLL, just make the function type int FAR PASCAL, and add the function name to the EXPORTS section of the module definition file.

Other Files for FILESEL.DLL

The key to communication between the calling program and the dialog box function is the FILEOPENDATA structure, which is defined in the FILESEL.H header file (Listing 18-16). The application using the FILESEL.DLL must allocate a global memory block to hold the FILEOPENDATA structure, and put the starting subdirectory name, file search string ("*.*"), and dialog box caption string into the data. The handle to this memory block is then passed to the CallFileDlg() function, which in turn passes the data on to the dialog box function FileOpenProc() by using the DialogBoxParam() function. The user's selections of subdirectory and file names are recorded back into the same memory block, so that the calling program can retrieve the selected file and directory name when the dialog box is destroyed.

Listing 18-16 FILESEL.H Header File

```
/* filesel.h header file for filesel.c */

#define DLI_EDIT            101        /* dialog box ID numbers */
#define DLI_DIRECT          102
#define DLI_OK              103
#define DLI_CANCEL          104
#define DLI_DIRLIST         105
#define DLI_FILELIST        106

#define FILENAMELONG        13         /* constants for string lengths */
#define PATHNAMELONG        128
#define FILEOPENCAPTIONLONG 32

typedef struct tagFILEOPENDATA          /* structure use to pass data */
{                                       /* to/from dialog box proc. */
        char    szPath [PATHNAMELONG] ;
        char    szFile [FILENAMELONG] ;
        char    szCaption [FILEOPENCAPTIONLONG] ;
} FILEOPENDATA ;

BOOL FAR PASCAL CallFileDlg (HWND hWnd, HANDLE hFileOpenData) ;
BOOL FAR PASCAL FileOpenProc (HWND hDlg, WORD wMessage, WORD wParam,
        LONG lParam) ;
void FAR PASCAL CombinePathFile (LPSTR szFileName, LPSTR szDir, LPSTR szFile) ;
void FAR PASCAL SplitPathFile (LPSTR lpSource, LPSTR lpPath, LPSTR lpFile) ;
```

Listing 18-17 shows the module definition file for the DLL. Note that four functions are exported. Each of the exported functions is given an ordinal number, although they will not be used in this example.

Listing 18-17 FILESEL.DEF Module Definition File

```
LIBRARY         filesel
DESCRIPTION     'file selection dll'
EXETYPE         WINDOWS
STUB            'WINSTUB.EXE'
CODE            PRELOAD MOVEABLE DISCARDABLE
DATA            PRELOAD MOVEABLE DISCARDABLE SINGLE
HEAPSIZE        1024
EXPORTS         CallFileDlg      @1
                FileOpenProc     @2
                SplitPathFile    @3
                CombinePathFile  @4
```

Unlike the previous DLL example, FILESEL.DLL contains resource data. Listing 18-18 shows FILESEL.RC, which is just a dialog box definition. DLLs can use resource data for string tables, bitmaps, dialog boxes, and any other static data that might be useful to the DLL. Resource data for a DLL will generally not include a menu or program icon, as DLLs normally do not have a visible window. The project files for FILESEL are shown on Listings 18-19 and 18-20

Listing 18-18 FILESEL.RC Resource Script File

```
/* filesel.rc */

#include <windows.h>
#include "filesel.h"

FileOpenDlg DIALOG 6, 18, 225, 106
STYLE DS_MODALFRAME | WS_POPUP | WS_VISIBLE | WS_CAPTION | WS_SYSMENU
CAPTION "Open File"
FONT 8, "Helv"
BEGIN
    EDITTEXT    DLI_EDIT, 26, 6, 56, 13, ES_AUTOHSCROLL
    LISTBOX     DLI_FILELIST, 6, 28, 64, 74, LBS_SORT | WS_VSCROLL |
                WS_TABSTOP
    PUSHBUTTON  "OK", DLI_OK, 160, 37, 54, 14
    PUSHBUTTON  "Cancel", DLI_CANCEL, 160, 72, 54, 14
    LTEXT       "File:", -1, 0, 8, 20, 12
    LTEXT       "Directory:", -1, 91, 8, 38, 11
    LTEXT       "", DLI_DIRECT, 145, 8, 76, 11
    LISTBOX     DLI_DIRLIST, 79, 28, 62, 74, LBS_SORT | WS_VSCROLL |
                WS_TABSTOP
END
```

Listing 18-19 FILESEL.PRJ Turbo C++ Project File Contents

```
filesel.c
filesel.def
filesel.res
```

Listing 18-20 FILESEL

```
filesel.c
filesel.def
filesel.rc
```

Using FILESEL.DLL

The FILETEST program is designed to provide a simple demonstration that the FILESEL.DLL library works. The complete FILETEST.C program is shown in Listing 18-21. FILETEST.C uses two of the exported functions from FILESEL.DLL, CallFileDlg() and CombinePathFile(). Before the CallFileDlg() function can be used to display the file selection dialog box, the starting subdirectory name, file search string ("*.*"), and dialog box caption string must be stored in a global memory block. When the block is locked in memory, the pointer to the block is cast to the data type FILEOPENDATA, to make it easier to put the strings in the correct locations. The FILEOPENDATA structure is defined in the FILESEL.H header file.

```
    getcwd (cBuf, 128) ;                 /* get current directory */
    hgMem = GlobalAlloc (GHND, sizeof (FILEOPENDATA)) ;
    lpFOD = (FILEOPENDATA FAR *) GlobalLock (hgMem) ;
    lstrcpy (lpFOD->szPath, cBuf) ; /* initialize */
    lstrcpy (lpFOD->szFile, "*.*") ;
    lstrcpy (lpFOD->szCaption, "Open a File") ;
    GlobalUnlock (hgMem) ;
                                         /* call dlg box in dll */
    bNotCancel = CallFileDlg (hWnd, hgMem) ;
```

The CallFileDlg() function resides in the FILESEL.DLL library. The dialog box takes control from the FILETEST program window while the file selection dialog box is on the screen. If the user selects a file while the dialog box is displayed, the file name and subdirectory name are copied back into the global memory block, and CallFileDlg() returns TRUE. When CallFileDlg() returns, control passes back to the FILETEST program. FILETEST can then extract the subdirectory and file name from the contents of the global memory block.

```
    if (bNotCancel)                      /* if a file was selected */
    {
        hDC = GetDC (hWnd) ;             /* show path & file */
        lpFOD = (FILEOPENDATA FAR *) GlobalLock (hgMem) ;
                                         /* combine path/file */
        CombinePathFile (cBuf, lpFOD->szPath,
            lpFOD->szFile) ;
        TextOut (hDC, 0, 0, cBuf, lstrlen (cBuf)) ;
        GlobalUnlock (hgMem) ;
        ReleaseDC (hWnd, hDC) ;
    }
    else
        MessageBox (hWnd, "No file was selected",
            "Message", MB_ICONINFORMATION | MB_OK) ;
    GlobalFree (hgMem) ;
```

The usual reason for obtaining a file name is to open or create a file. In either case, you will need to combine the subdirectory and file name to create the full path/file name

like "C:\WINDOWS\FILENAME.EXE." The CombinePathFile() function, which is also
exported from the FILESEL.DLL library, combines the subdirectory and file name.

Listing 18-21 FILETEST.C

```c
/* filetest.c   example calling function in a dll */

#include <windows.h>
#include <direct.h>        /* for getcwd() function */
#include "filetest.h"      /* header file for this program */
#include "filesel.h"       /* header file for dll */

int PASCAL WinMain (HANDLE hInstance, HANDLE hPrevInstance, LPSTR lpszCmdLine,
    int nCmdShow)
{
    HWND       hWnd ;         /* the window's "handle" */
    MSG        msg ;          /* a message structure */
    WNDCLASS   wndclass ;     /* window class structure */
    char       cBuf [128] ;

    if (!hPrevInstance)
    {
        wndclass.style          = CS_HREDRAW | CS_VREDRAW ;
        wndclass.lpfnWndProc    = WndProc ;
        wndclass.cbClsExtra     = 0 ;
        wndclass.cbWndExtra     = 0 ;
        wndclass.hInstance      = hInstance ;
        wndclass.hIcon          = LoadIcon (hInstance, "MyIcon") ;
        wndclass.hCursor        = LoadCursor (NULL, IDC_ARROW) ;
        wndclass.hbrBackground  = GetStockObject (WHITE_BRUSH) ;
        wndclass.lpszMenuName   = "MyMenu" ;
        wndclass.lpszClassName  = "MyClass" ;
                    /* register the window class */
        if (!RegisterClass (&wndclass))
            return 0 ;
    }
    LoadString (hInstance, S_PROGRAMCAPTION, cBuf, sizeof (cBuf)) ;

    hWnd = CreateWindow ("MyClass", cBuf, WS_OVERLAPPEDWINDOW,
        CW_USEDEFAULT, CW_USEDEFAULT, CW_USEDEFAULT, CW_USEDEFAULT,
        NULL, NULL, hInstance, NULL) ;
    ShowWindow (hWnd, nCmdShow) ;     /* display the window */

    while (GetMessage (&msg, NULL, NULL, NULL))    /* message loop */
    {
        TranslateMessage (&msg) ;     /* translate keyboard messages */
        DispatchMessage (&msg) ;      /* send message to WndProc() */
    }
    return (msg.wParam) ;
}
long FAR PASCAL WndProc (HWND hWnd, WORD wMessage, WORD wParam, LONG lParam)
{
    char              cBuf [256] ;
    FILEOPENDATA FAR *  lpFOD ;
    HANDLE            hgMem ;
    HDC               hDC ;
    BOOL              bNotCancel ;
```

```
    switch (wMessage)       /* process windows messages */
    {
        case WM_COMMAND:
            switch (wParam)
            {
                case IDM_SHOW:
                    getcwd (cBuf, 128) ;     /* get current directory */
                    hgMem = GlobalAlloc (GHND, sizeof (FILEOPENDATA)) ;
                    lpFOD = (FILEOPENDATA FAR *) GlobalLock (hgMem) ;
                    lstrcpy (lpFOD->szPath, cBuf) ;         /* initialize */
                    lstrcpy (lpFOD->szFile, "*.*") ;
                    lstrcpy (lpFOD->szCaption, "Open a File") ;
                    GlobalUnlock (hgMem) ;
                                             /* call dlg box in dll */
                    bNotCancel = CallFileDlg (hWnd, hgMem) ;
                    if (bNotCancel)          /* if a file was selected */
                    {
                        hDC = GetDC (hWnd) ; /* show path & file */
                        lpFOD = (FILEOPENDATA FAR *) GlobalLock (hgMem) ;
                                             /* combine path/file */
                        CombinePathFile (cBuf, lpFOD->szPath,
                            lpFOD->szFile) ;
                        TextOut (hDC, 0, 0, cBuf, lstrlen (cBuf)) ;
                        GlobalUnlock (hgMem) ;
                        ReleaseDC (hWnd, hDC) ;
                    }
                    else
                        MessageBox (hWnd, "No file was selected",
                            "Message", MB_ICONINFORMATION | MB_OK) ;
                    GlobalFree (hgMem) ;
                    break ;
                case IDM_QUIT:                  /* Quit menu item */
                    DestroyWindow (hWnd) ;   /* destroy window, */
                    break ;     /* terminating application */
            }
            break ;
        case WM_DESTROY:        /* stop application */
            PostQuitMessage (0) ;
            break ;
        default:                /* default windows message processing */
            return (DefWindowProc (hWnd, wMessage, wParam, lParam)) ;
    }
    return (0L) ;
}
```

The only preparation required to use the functions in FILESEL.DLL is to include the function names in the IMPORTS section of the program's module definition file (Listing 18-22).

Listing 18-22 FILETEST.DEF Module Definition File

```
NAME            filetest
DESCRIPTION     'filetest application'
EXETYPE         WINDOWS
```

```
STUB        'WINSTUB.EXE'
CODE        PRELOAD MOVEABLE
DATA        PRELOAD MOVEABLE MULTIPLE
HEAPSIZE    1024
STACKSIZE   5120
EXPORTS     WndProc
IMPORTS     CallFileDlg = FILESEL.CallFileDlg
            SplitPathFile = FILESEL.SplitPathFile
            CombinePathFile = FILESEL.CombinePathFile
```

The remaining support files for FILETEST are shown in Listings 18-23 to 18-26. Figure 18-12 shows the program's icon

Listing 18-23 FILETEST.H Header File

```
/* filetest.h header file */

#define IDM_QUIT          1       /* menu item ID numbers */
#define IDM_SHOW          2

#define S_PROGRAMCAPTION 1        /* string table ID numbers */

long FAR PASCAL WndProc (HWND, WORD, WORD, LONG) ;
```

Figure 18-12
FILETEST.ICO
Icon Image

Listing 18-24 FILETEST.RC Resource Script File

```
/* filetest.rc resource file */

#include "filetest.h"

MyIcon      ICON    filetest.ico

MyMenu      MENU
BEGIN
    MENUITEM "&Show Dialog Box",    IDM_SHOW
    MENUITEM "&Quit",               IDM_QUIT
END

STRINGTABLE
BEGIN
    S_PROGRAMCAPTION    "Example Using FILESEL.DLL"
END
```

Listing 18-25 FILETEST.PRJ Turbo C++ Project File for

```
filetest.c
filetest.def
filetest.res
```

Listing 18-26 FILETEST.NMK Microsoft C NMAKE File

```
filetest.c
filetest.def
filetest.rc
```

Summary

Dynamic link libraries are the basic building blocks of Windows. DLLs provide reusable code that can be shared by any number of applications at the same time. You can add to Windows by writing your own DLLs, as an efficient way to keep utility functions for your own use in future projects.

DLLs all have a LibMain() function, which is executed when the DLL is loaded into memory. LibMain() usually contains a call to the UnlockData() function, which unlocks the local data segment. LibMain() is also a good place to initialize static data. DLLs can also have a WEP() function, which is executed when the DLL is removed from memory. WEP() is a good place to do any cleanup activities, such as freeing memory blocks that were created by the DLL. The remainder of the DLL consists of one or more functions. Functions which are to be called by other Windows applications must be declared FAR (usually FAR PASCAL), and must be listed in the EXPORTS section of the DLL's module definition statement.

When a DLL is loaded into memory, it has its own data segment, but it uses the stack of any application that calls a function in the DLL. This separation of the segment containing the stack and data segment has several side effects. One is that DLLs will not behave properly if you attempt to use functions that assume that the stack and data segments are the same. This is a common fault of C compiler runtime library functions that use near pointers. Always use far pointers when writing DLLs, so that the complete segment and offset values are passed for addresses. Another effect is that the static data stored in the data segment is common to every application that calls functions in the DLL. Avoid situations where one application calling the DLL changes a value in a static variable, which then affects the next application calling the DLL.

Memory blocks allocated within the DLL are owned by the application calling the DLL, not by the DLL itself. This causes memory blocks allocated by the DLL to be freed when the application that loaded the DLL is terminated. This is normally desirable behavior, but it can cause problems if you allocate memory blocks in the LibMain() function, and then expect the blocks to continue to exist after the application that loaded the DLL has terminated.

There are several ways for a Windows application to reference functions in a DLL. One way is to list the function names in the IMPORTS section of the application's module definition statement. You can either reference the function by name, or by using the function's ordinal number. For large collections of functions, it is best to create an import library. Import libraries are included in the linking process to create a Windows application, and provide the linker with the DLL file name and function address for imported functions used by the application.

QUESTIONS

1. When you include a runtime library file in a C program, the entire contents of the runtime library are added to your program, even if you do not use all of the functions in the runtime library. (True/False).
2. Each DLL has its own stack to store automatic variables. (True/False)
3. Static data in the DLL's data segment can be accessed by any application calling the DLL. (True/False).
4. The _____ function is executed when the DLL is loaded into memory, and the _____ function is executed when the DLL is about to be removed from memory.
5. DLLs must have a LibMain() function, but they can do without a WEP() function. (True/False).
6. The LibMain() function should: a) Call UnlockData() to unlock the DLL's data segment; b) Return 1 if the library was correctly loaded; c) Return zero if the library encountered a serious error when executing LibMain(); d) a, b, and c.
7. The module definition file for a DLL uses the key word _____ in place of NAME.
8. The STACK statement in the module definition file for a DLL should be set to: a) 1024; b) 5120; c) The size should depend on the amount of data stored; d) There is no STACK statement in the .DEF file for a DLL.
9. The DATA statement for the module definition file of a DLL should contain the key word SINGLE in place of MULTIPLE. (True/False).
10. If a function in a DLL is declared FAR PASCAL, it does not need to be listed in the EXPORTS section of the module definition file to be called by another application. (True/False).

EXERCISES

1. Modify the DLLCALL program so that the BlockRev() function is imported from REVSTR.DLL using the ordinal number of the function.
2. Modify the DLLCALL program again, so that the BlockRev() function is imported from REVSTR.DLL using an import library.

ANSWERS TO QUESTIONS

1. False. Only the functions used by the program are loaded from the runtime library.
2. False. DLLs use the calling application(s) stack.
3. True.
4. LibMain(), WEP().
5. True. However, the Microsoft documentation recommends always including a WEP() function.
6. d.
7. LIBRARY.
8. d.
9. True.
10. False. Exported functions must be listed in the exports section of the DLL's module definition file.

SOLUTIONS TO EXERCISES

1. The only change to DLLCALL that is needed is to modify the module definition file, replacing the BlockRev() function name with its ordinal number (one). Listing 18-27 shows the modified module definition file that uses the ordinal number.

Listing 18-27 DLLCALL1.DEF Module Definition File

```
NAME         dllcall1
DESCRIPTION  'dllcall1 application'
EXETYPE      WINDOWS
STUB         'WINSTUB.EXE'
CODE         PRELOAD MOVEABLE
DATA         PRELOAD MOVEABLE MULTIPLE
HEAPSIZE     1024
STACKSIZE    5120
EXPORTS      WndProc
IMPORTS      BlockRev = REVSTR.1
```

The complete solution is given under the file name DLLCALL1 on the source code disks.

2. If an import library is used, the application's module definition file does not need to include the IMPORTS statement, as shown in Listing 18-28.

SOLUTIONS TO EXERCISES (cont'd)

Listing 18-28 Module Definition File

```
NAME         dllcall2
DESCRIPTION  'dllcall2 application'
EXETYPE      WINDOWS
STUB         'WINSTUB.EXE'
CODE         PRELOAD MOVEABLE
DATA         PRELOAD MOVEABLE MULTIPLE
HEAPSIZE     1024
STACKSIZE    5120
EXPORTS      WndProc
```

You will need to create an import library from the REVSTR.DLL library using either the Microsoft IMPLIB.EXE program, or the Borland Import Library Application. The import library will be named REVSTR.LIB, and will need to be included in the project file for program. The complete program is included under the file name DLLCALL2 on the optional source code disks.

Conclusion

If you have worked your way through this book, you can officially call yourself a Windows programmer. You now have the basic tools and understanding needed to create your own Windows applications. Like everything else in life, getting better at programming takes time and practice. The more programs you write, the easier the next one will be. Here are some suggestions for projects that you might want to try:

1. Add search and replace menu options to the SIMPEDIT program in Chapter 15. Also change the file access dialog box to use the FILESEL.DLL from Chapter 18. This will complete your basic text editor application.
2. Try your hand at a simple paint application or a game for the kids. These projects will give you experience processing mouse messages and using graphics functions.
3. Write a screen capture program that copies an area of the screen (outlined using the mouse) to the Clipboard as a bitmap.

Besides improving your skills by writing new Windows programs, you can expand your knowledge of Windows and C programming by reading other books on these subjects. The Bibliography includes a list of the books that you may find useful.

Good luck with your Windows projects!

Appendix A: Virtual Key Codes

These values are passed as the *wParam* parameter with WM_KEYDOWN and WM_KEYUP messages.

VIRTUAL KEY CODE	VALUE (HEX)	MEANING
A - Z	0x41 - 0x5A	The virtual key code for the letters is the same as the ANSI code. Use the uppercase letter in single quotes for the virtual key code ('A').
0-9 (at keyboard top)	0x30 - 0x39	The virtual key code for the digit keys at the top of the keyboard is the same as the ANSI code. Use the digit in single quotes for the virtual key code ('1').
VK_ACCEPT	0x1E	Kanji only (Japanese characters)
VK_ADD	0x6B	Plus key
VK_BACK	0x08	Backspace
VK_CANCEL	0x03	Control-Break
VK_CAPITAL	0x14	Shift lock
VK_CLEAR	0x0C	Clear key (Numeric keypad 5)
VK_CONTROL	0x11	Control (Ctrl) key
VK_CONVERT	0x1C	Kanji only (Japanese characters)
VK_DECIMAL	0x6E	Decimal point
VK_DELETE	0x2E	Delete
VK_DIVIDE	0x6F	Divide (/) key
VK_DOWN	0x28	Down arrow
VK_END	0x23	End
VK_ESCAPE	0x1B	Escape (Esc)
VK_EXECUTE	0x2B	Execute key (if any)
VK_F1	0x70	Function keys
VK_F2	0x71	
VK_F3	0x72	
VK_F4	0x73	
VK_F5	0x74	
VK_F6	0x75	

continued

Virtual Key Codes (cont'd)

VIRTUAL KEY CODE	VALUE (HEX)	MEANING
VK_F7	0x76	
VK_F8	0x77	
VK_F9	0x78	
VK_F10	0x79	
VK_F11	0x7A	Enhanced keyboard only
VK_F12	0x7B	Enhanced keyboard only
VK_F13	0x7C	Specialized keyboards only
VK_F14	0x7D	Specialized keyboards only
VK_F15	0x7E	Specialized keyboards only
VK_F16	0x7F	Specialized keyboards only
VK_HIRAGANA	0x18	Kanji only (Japanese characters)
VK_HOME	0x24	Home
VK_INSERT	0x2D	Insert
VK_KANA	0x15	Kanji only (Japanese characters)
VK_KANJI	0x19	Kanji only (Japanese characters)
VK_LBUTTON	0x01	Left mouse button
VK_LEFT	0x25	Left arrow
VK_MBUTTON	0x04	Middle mouse button
VK_MENU	0x12	Menu key (if any)
VK_MODECHANGE	0x1F	Kanji only (Japanese characters)
VK_MULTIPLY	0x6A	Multiply key
VK_NEXT	0x22	Next
VK_NONCONVERT	0x1D	Kanji only (Japanese characters)
VK_NUMPAD0	0x60	The numeric keypad keys
VK_NUMPAD1	0x61	
VK_NUMPAD2	0x62	
VK_NUMPAD3	0x63	
VK_NUMPAD4	0x64	
VK_NUMPAD5	0x65	
VK_NUMPAD6	0x66	
VK_NUMPAD7	0x67	
VK_NUMPAD8	0x68	

VIRTUAL KEY CODE	VALUE (HEX)	MEANING
VK_NUMPAD9	0x69	
VK_NUMLOCK	0x90	Num Lock
VK_PAUSE	0x13	Pause
VK_PRINT	0x2A	Print Screen (Windows versions below 3.0)
VK_PRIOR	0x21	Page Up
VK_RBUTTON	0x02	Right mouse button
VK_RETURN	0x0D	Return
VK_RIGHT	0x27	Right arrow
VK_ROMAJI	0x16	Kanji only (Japanese characters)
VK_SELECT	0x29	Select key (if any)
VK_SEPARATOR	0x6C	Separator key (if any)
VK_SHIFT	0x10	Shift
VK_SNAPSHOT	0x2C	Print Screen (Windows 3.0 and later)
VK_SPACE	0x20	Space bar
VK_SUBTRACT	0x6D	Subtraction key
VK_TAB	0x09	Tab key
VK_UP	0x26	Up arrow
VK_ZENKAKU	0x17	Kanji only (Japanese characters)

Virtual Key Codes

Appendix B: Using Command Line Compilers and the MAKE Utility

Because this book is designed to get you started programming in Windows with a minimum number of distractions, the new integrated development environments (IDEs) were used as example compilers. Both Turbo C++ for Windows and QuickC for Windows take care of many of the mundane details of compiling and linking a program for you. Windows-based IDEs are a fairly recent development, and many programmers still prefer to run the compiler and linker directly. Even if you decide to use an IDE for your own programming work, you are likely to run into examples in magazine articles on Windows programming that use the more conventional compiler techniques.

Both Microsoft and Borland offer advanced versions of their compilers, called Microsoft C++ and Borland C++. These tools include "command line" compilers. The term "command line" is used because the compilers are DOS programs and are executed from the DOS command line. When creating a Windows application, the command line compilers usually are run by opening up a DOS window from within Windows. One advantage of the command line compilers is that they allow more complete control over the compiler's code generation and optimization features than is available in the IDEs. These features are most important in large projects, and in cases where optimizing the speed or size of the program is critical.

MAKE Utilities

If you use the command line compilers, you must explicitly tell the compiler and linker how to build each file. Typing all of the commands is tiresome, so both compilers come with a "MAKE" utility that automates the compiling process. To use the MAKE utility, you must create a "MAKE file" that describes all of the operations that the compiler must perform. The MAKE utility has the ability to compare the creation date of files to determine if a file needs to be updated. For example, if you edit EXAMPLE.C and save the file, the date/time of EXAMPLE.C will be more recent than EXAMPLE.OBJ or EXAMPLE.EXE. The MAKE utility detects this and uses the MAKE file to determine which files need to be updated.

For example, Listing B-1 shows the Borland MAKE file used to create the MINIMAL4.EXE program. The top two lines are comments. Any text following a pound symbol (#) is treated as a comment and ignored by the MAKE program. The first line that does anything starts with MINIMAL4.EXE. This line (called the "dependence line") establishes that MINIMAL4.EXE should be updated if MINIMAL4.OBJ, MINIMAL4.DEF, or MINIMAL4.RES is newer than MINIMAL4.EXE. This makes sense because these three files are the ones that make up the program, and changing any one file requires rebuilding the .EXE file to incorporate the changed information.

Listing B-1 MINIMAL4.BMK Borland C++ MAKE File

```
# minimal4.bmk
# Borland C++ make file for minimal4.c

minimal4.exe: minimal4.obj minimal4.def minimal4.res
    tlink /Tw /v /n /c cOws minimal4, minimal4, ,cws import, minimal4
    rc minimal4.res

minimal4.obj : minimal4.c
    BCC -c -ms -v -H -W -wnod minimal4.c

minimal4.res : minimal4.rc
    rc -r minimal4.rc
```

A colon is used to separate the file name on the left that will be created (called the "target file") from the file names on the right (which are called "dependent files"). If MINIMAL4.EXE needs to be updated, the next two lines are executed from DOS. These lines run the TLINK linker and the RC resource compile, just as if you had typed the lines as commands at the DOS prompt.

Any indented lines following the dependence line are executed if the file to the left of the colon is older than the files to the right of the colon. Figure B-1 shows the top dependence line, and the TLINK and RC command lines that are executed if the target file needs to be updated. This is just one of the three comparisons made in MINIMAL4.BMK (Listing B-1). The other two run the BCC compiler if MINIMAL4.OBJ

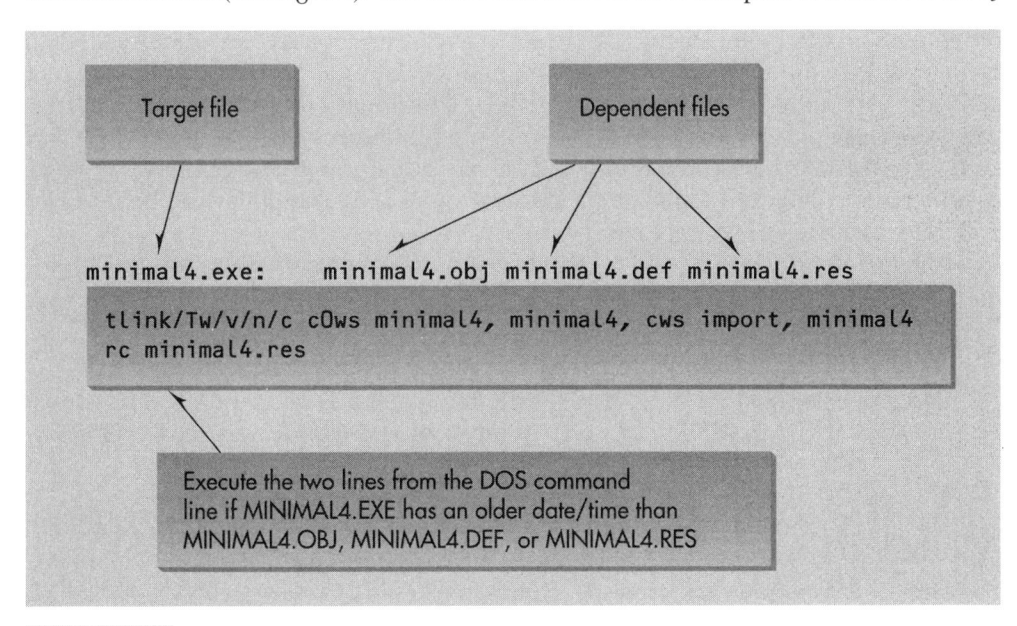

Figure B-1 Targets and Dependents in a MAKE File

is older than MINIMAL4.C, and the resource compiler RC if MINIMAL4.RES is older than MINIMAL4.RC.

Note that the order of the linker, compiler, and resource compiler dependence statements in the MAKE file is not important. The MAKE program figures out which files need to be updated first, regardless of their order in the MAKE file. For example, if the MAKE file is being used to create MINIMAL4.EXE for the first time, the BCC and RC compilers would be run before TLINK, even though the TLINK line comes first in the MAKE file. This is because the MAKE utility notices that BCC and RC must be run to create MINIMAL4.OBJ and MINIMAL4.RES files which are needed to run TLINK.

Compiler and Linker Switches

The compiler and linker require all sorts of command line options to compile a Windows program. These options are called "switches," as they switch various options on and off. The BCC compiler command line switches include "-c -ms -v -H -W -wnod." They tell the compiler to compile only (not link yet), to use the small memory model, to include debugging information, to use precompiled header files, to compile to create a Windows program, and not to search the default compiler directories for library files. They are typical compiler options during development of a small Windows program. Omit the "-v" switch for final compiles to eliminate debugging information from the final program.

The TLINK command line includes the switches "/Tw /v /n /c." These switches specify that the output will be a Windows program, to include debugging information, not to use the default library files, and that uppercase and lowercase symbols (variable names, etc.) are different. Omit the "/v" switch for the final compilation/linking of a debugged program to avoid including debugging information in the finished application. The C0WS, CWS, and IMPORT names are all library files that are included to build a finished Windows program. These files are supplied with the compiler. See your compiler documentation for a complete listing of all of the compiler and linker command line switches and library names.

To build the MINIMAL4.EXE program, type the following line from the DOS command line:

```
make -fminimal4.bmk
```

This starts the MAKE utility, passing the file name MINIMAL4.BMK. The source code disks include MAKE files for every example program and exercise. The Borland MAKE files all have the file extension ".BMK."

Microsoft Command Line Compiler and NMAKE

The Microsoft command line compiler comes with a similar utility called NMAKE.EXE (for New MAKE). It works the same way as the Borland MAKE utility, although the commands used to run the compiler and linker are different. Listing B-2 shows the MINIMAL4.NMK MAKE file needed to create MINIMAL4.EXE. This example uses the small memory model and has debugging options set on.

Listing B-2 Microsoft NMAKE File

```
# minimal4.nmk  Microsoft C NMAKE file for MINIMAL4.C
# the /co, -Zi and -Od flags are for debugging info

minimal4.exe : minimal4.obj minimal4.res minimal4.def
   link /NOD /co minimal4, , ,libw slibcew, minimal4
   rc minimal4

minimal4.obj : minimal4.c
   cl -c -Zi -Od -Gsw -W2 minimal4.c

minimal4.res : minimal4.rc
   rc -r minimal4.rc
```

To run the Microsoft NMAKE utility, type the following line from the DOS prompt:

`nmake minimal4.nmk`

This runs the NMAKE utility, passing the file name MININIMAL4.NMK. The source code disks include NMAKE files for every example program and exercise. The Microsoft NMAKE files all have the file extension ".NMK." See your compiler manual for a complete list of all of the compiler and linker options and the library names.

Appendix C: Glossary

Accelerators • Keyboard accelerators provide key combinations that will generate a WM_COMMAND message with a specified ID value for the keys depressed. This is a quick way to add keyboard functionality to a program.

Alignment • See Text Alignment.

Allocate • To set aside a block of memory for use by the program.

API • Application Programming Interface. The collection of functions and messages that Windows provides for the programmer to create new Windows applications using the built-in features of Windows.

Application • A program that can be executed (run) under Windows.

Automatic Variables • Variables that are declared within the body of a function, without the "static" prefix. Automatic variables use the program's stack, so the data is lost as soon as the function terminates.

Batch File • An ASCII text file with the file name extension ".BAT." A batch file is used to execute a series of MS-DOS commands in sequence.

Binary Flags • Coded on/off values that are stored together in a single variable. Each bit specifies a different on/off condition. The values are combined using binary operators such as |, &, and ^.

Bitmap • A picture image consisting of each dot (pixel) of the image. Windows supports two bitmap formats, the old device dependent bitmap (DDB) and the newer device independent bitmap (DIB).

Caption • The title area at the top of a parent, child, or popup window.

Child Window • A window that is created with the WS_CHILD style. Child windows are visible only inside the client area of their parent. Child windows can be the parents of other, lower-level child windows.

Class • See Window Class.

Client Area • The center part of a window. This area is where drawing activities take place. GetDC() and BeginPaint() return the device context of the client area.

Clipboard • A memory area maintained by Windows to allow different applications to exchange data. Usually the data is exchanged as part of cut and paste operations.

Compiler • A program that reads a text file containing the program statements and creates and object file (".OBJ" file extension). The object file contains the low-level computer instructions, but the memory addresses are not set until the object file is linked with a linker.

Cursor • The small image (usually an arrow) that moves on the screen when the mouse is moved.

DDB • Device dependent bitmap. This is the "old" bitmap format that encodes the color value of each pixel (dot) of an image. The color palette used to create the bitmap is not included with the data, so different colors may end up being displayed if the DDB is displayed on different devices.

DDE • Dynamic Data Exchange. Windows applications can exchange data in memory by sending each other messages. The DDE protocol describes a standard set of messages for data exchange.

Declaration • Functions are declared using a function prototype. The prototype informs the compiler of which data types are passed as parameters, and of the function's returned data type. This allows the compiler to check that the correct data types are passed to the function as parameters, and returned when the function returns a value.

Delayed Rendering • A Clipboard technique where the data is not loaded into the Clipboard unless an application requests the data.

Device Context • Windows program's output text and graphics data to a logical device, called the Device Context or DC. Windows then does the conversion from the DC to a real device, such as a video screen or printer.

Device Units • The physical system of units used by the device, such as pixels for a video screen or dots for a laser or dot matrix printer.

DIB • Device independent bitmap. This is a bitmap data format that encodes both the pixel data and the color palette used to create the picture.

DISCARDABLE • Program code or data that can be purged from memory when Windows needs more room. DISCARDABLE blocks are always moveable.

DLL • Dynamic Link Library. DLLs contain common functions that are used by more than one application program. The Windows functions reside in DLLs, and you can create your own DLLs to add other functions that can be called by any number of applications in the same Windows session.

Driver • A program (actually a DLL) that converts Windows function calls to machine instructions that a particular device will understand. Windows uses drivers to interpret information from the mouse, control the speaker or sound device, control printers, and so on.

Far address • An address that uses both the segment and offset value, suitable for specifying an address in the global heap, outside of the program's local memory heap.

Fixed • Code or data that cannot be moved in memory. Fixed blocks get in the way of Windows' ability to optimize memory, so moveable and DISCARDABLE blocks are used whenever possible.

Flags • See Binary Flags.

Focus • The window with the focus is highlighted and receives keyboard input. Normally, the user changes the window with the focus by clicking a window with the mouse. The SetFocus() function also can be used to change which window has the focus.

Font • A letter typeface. Font data defines the shape of each letter of a character set.

Global Heap • The memory area outside of any program's code or data. This is the free memory space that a program can access with GlobalAlloc(), and which requires far pointers to specify an address.

Global Variable • A variable declared outside of the body of any function. These variables can be referenced within any function following the declaration of the variable's type and name in the source code file.

GUI • Graphical User Interface. Windows' appearance to the user is based on GUI concepts. It is graphical, as all of the screen is drawn in graphics mode, not in a video character mode.

Heap • Memory available to the program. Under Windows, programs can access a local data segment, containing the "local heap," and unused memory outside of any program or data, called the "global heap."

Import Library • A file that contains the addresses of exported functions in one or more DLLs. Import libraries are included in the linking step when creating a program that calls functions in a DLL.

Input Focus • See Focus.

Instance • Windows allows several copies of the same application program to be run at the same time. Each running copy is given a unique ID value called the *program instance*.

Keyboard Accelerators • See Accelerators.

Linker • A program that reads both object files and runtime library files and creates an executable program.

LOADONCALL • Data or program code that is not loaded into memory when the program starts, but is loaded only when needed by the program.

Local Variable • A variable declared within the body of a function, and not preceded by the word "static." Local variables (sometimes called "automatic" variables) use the program's stack. The variable can be used only within the body of the function. The variable's value will not be saved after the function returns.

Locked Memory Block • A locked block cannot be moved in memory. Programs call LocalLock() and GlobalLock() to lock blocks before the data is accessed, and then unlock the blocks using LocalUnlock() and GlobalUnlock() when done, so that the blocks can be moved in memory again.

Logical Font • A font interpolated from existing font data to create a size or style that is not exactly specified in the font data. The CreateFont() function creates logical fonts.

Logical Units • The system of units used to specify a location on the screen or another device that uses a mapping mode other than MM_TEXT. Typical logical units are MM_LOMETRIC with each unit equal to 0.1 mm, and MM_LOENGLISH with each unit equal to 0.1 inch.

MAKE Program • A compiler utility that helps automate the running of the compiler and linker tools to create finished programs.

Mapping Mode • The system of units used by a device context to convert from a logical *X,Y* position to a physical location on the device.

Memory Device Context • A device context which is not tied to a physical device, such as the screen or printer. Memory device contexts are used to convert bitmap data to a format that can be displayed on a physical device.

Message • An 18-byte chunk of data sent from the Windows environment to an application program. Windows messages typically notify the application program of some action, such as the user pressing a key, or using the mouse. Different applications can also exchange messages — see DDE.

Module • An executable program in memory. This includes both application programs and DLLs.

Moveable • Code or data that can be moved in memory if Windows needs to make room for other objects. The opposite of moveable is fixed.

Near Address • An address within a single data segment. Data stored in the program's local data segment (such as static variables, variables on the stack (automatic variables), and blocks allocated with LocalAlloc()) all use near addresses.

Offset • The 80x86 family of microprocessors use what is known as "segmented" addressing. Each location in memory is defined by a combination of a segment and an offset. Locations within one segment can be specified with only the offset value. These locations are called "near" addresses. Locations that occupy more than one segment are called "far" memory addresses and require both the segment and offset to be specified.

OLE • Object Linking and Embedding. OLE documents allow the user to activate the editor that created a graph, text, or other image, by simply double clicking the portion to be edited. This "object-oriented" behavior is formalized in Microsoft's Windows 3.1 documentation.

Origin • The 0,0 point for a coordinate system. The default origin for a device context is the upper left corner.

Owned Window • A window that has the *hWndParent* parameter set to another window's handle when CreateWindow() is called to create the owned window. Owned windows are either child windows or popup windows. The owner of an owned window is the parent window.

Parent Window • A window that has one or more child windows. The child windows will be automatically redrawn if the parent is redrawn. Child windows are only visible if they are within the client area of their parent's window.

Pixel • One dot on an image. Pixel usually refers to a dot on a computer screen, although it can apply to any graphics device that has dot (raster) output.

Pointer • A variable that contains the address of another object in memory. For example, the declaration "char * cp" creates the pointer *cp* that will hold the address of another memory location that contains character data.

Popup Window • A window that is owned by the parent window and has the WS_POPUP flag set when CreateWindow() is called. Popup windows disappear when the top-level window that owns them is minimized or terminated. Otherwise, popup windows behave independently from the window that owns them and are visible outside of the owner's client area.

Preload • Data or program code that is loaded into memory when the program starts.

Printer Driver • See Driver.

Pseudocode • A technique of writing a program outline without using the details of a specific computer language. Pseudocoding is done during the design of a program to think through the overall structure of the program before any detailed coding is done.

Rendering • See Delayed Rendering.

Resource • Static data that is included with the application program. Resource data typically includes icons, menus, strings, and bitmaps. This data does not change as the program is executed.

Resource Compiler • A program that combines the resource data with the application program to make a finished Windows application.

SDK • The Microsoft Windows Software Development Kit. This kit contains the Windows resource compiler, CodeView for Windows debugger, other development tools, and full documentation of all Windows messages and functions. The SDK is now bundled with the Microsoft C++ 7.0 package.

Segment • The 80x86 family of microprocessors use what is known as "segmented" addressing. Each location in memory is defined by a combination of a segment and an offset. Locations within one segment can be specified with only the offset value. These locations are called "near" addresses. Locations that occupy more than one segment are called "far" memory addresses and require both the segment and offset to be specified.

Sibling Windows • If a parent has more than one child window, the child windows are siblings.

Static Data • Data in a program that does not change as the program is executed. Windows programs usually store static data as resource data.

Static Variable • A variable declared within the body of a function and preceded by the word "static." Static variables only have meaning within the body of a function, but retain their value between calls to the function. They are stored in the program's local heap, not on the program's stack. Static variables are typically used within functions to save variables that need to be "remembered" between calls to the function.

System • The running Windows environment. This includes all of the running application programs.

Termination • A program is terminated when the program finishes executing and returns control to the Windows environment. Windows removes the terminated program from memory.

Text Alignment • The location on the first text character of a character string that is used to specify the location of the string on the device context. The default alignment places text at a location based on the upper left corner of the first character of the string.

Top-level Window • The main application window for the program. Top-level windows are never children of other windows.

Viewport • The logical area on the screen or device for which a single device context operates.

Window Class • Before a window can be created, the window's class definition is registered with the Windows environment using the RegisterClass() function. This sets a number of basic parameters for all windows created from the class. Control classes such as BUTTON and LISTBOX are predefined, and do not need to be registered.

Window Function • The message processing function for a window. The window function that will receive messages for a window is specified in the window's class definition, created with RegisterClass(). Most programmers use the convention that main program windows call their window function "WndProc()."

Appendix D: Bibliography

Books on Windows
The Waite Group's Windows API Bible
Jim Conger
The Waite Group Press, 1992
   The Waite Group's Windows API Bible is a reference book for Windows programmers. The book is organized in subject order, with example code for every function and full descriptions of Windows messages.

Programming Windows
Charles Petzold
Microsoft Press, 1990
   Charles Petzold's book is an excellent intermediate-level guide to writing Windows applications. It covers all of the basic elements of Windows, and several more advanced topics such as DDE and MDI.

Windows 3.0 Power Programming Techniques
Peter Norton and Paul Yao
Bantam Books, 1990
   The Norton and Yao book is slower paced than Petzold's book, but it covers a bit less material. The discussions on memory management, the inner workings of dynamic linking, and the historical background on how Windows was developed are all interesting reading.

Windows 3: A Developer's Guide
Jeffrey M. Richter
M&T Books, 1991
   Jeffrey Richter's book covers advanced Windows programming techniques, including dynamic dialog boxes, custom controls, printer setup, and program installation.

Other Programming Reference Books
Systems Application Architecture,
Common User Access Advanced Interface Design Guide
International Business Machines, 1989
   The rules for programming the user interface for Windows and OS/2 applications are spelled out in an IBM document. Following these guidelines is strongly encouraged.

The C Programming Language, Second Edition

Brian W. Kerninghan and Dennis M. Ritchie
Prentice Hall, 1988

    The standard reference for the C language is the classic Kerninghan and Ritchie book on C.

The Waite Group's New C Primer Plus®
Mitchell Waite and Stephan Prata
SAMS, 1990

    If you need a more readable introduction to the C language.

Workout C
David Himmel
Waite Group Press, 1992
This hands-on, exercise-based C book comes with a complete C compiler.

The MS-DOS Encyclopedia
Ray Duncan, General Editor
Microsoft Press, 1988

    For a thorough understanding of the MS-DOS operating system that underlies Windows.

Articles

Adapt Your Program for Worldwide Use With Windows Internationalization Support, William S. Hall, Microsoft Systems Journal, November–December 1991, Vol. 6, No. 6.

Undocumented Functions in Windows, Part1, Part2, Andrew Schulman, PC Magazine, January 28, 1992, February 11, 1992.

Subclassing Applications, Mike Klein, Dr. Dobb's Journal, December 1991, No. 183.

Screen Capturing for Windows 3.0, Jim Conger, Dr. Dobb's Journal, February 1991, No. 173.

Index

Symbols
#else key word, 377
#endif key word, 377
#ifdef key word, 377
_lclose( ) function, 528-531, 534
_lcreate( ) function, 526
_llseek( ) function, 527-529, 531-534, 549
_lopen( ) function, 525-526
_lread( ) function, 527-528, 531, 549
_lread( )function, 534
_lwrite( ) function, 527-528, 531, 534, 550

A
Accelerator table
  FONT2.RC listing, 240
  Syntax listing, 241
Accelerators, 13
ACCELERATORS key word, 240, 241
Adding CS_DBLCLKS style to window class definition listing, 188
Adding cursor data to resource script file listing, 201
Adjusting child window sizes as parent processes listing, 268
alloc( ) function, 20
ALT key word, 241
AND (&) operator, 186-187
Animation, 583-590
ANISO program, 464-468
  ANISO.C listing, 465-466
  ANISO.DEF module definition file, 467
  ANISO.H header file, 467
  ANISO.RC resource script file, 467
  rectangles and ellipses, 464-465
ANSI character set, 213, 215-217
  converting to OEM character set, 216-217
  translating combination of keys, 223-224
AnsiLower( ) function, 216
AnsiLowerBuff( ) function, 216, 218
AnsiNext( ) function, 216
AnsiPrev( ) function, 216
AnsiToOem( ) function, 216
AnsiToOemBuff( ) function, 216
AnsiUpper( ) function, 216
AnsiUpperBuff( ) function, 216-218
ANSI_FIXED_FONT font, 106
ANSI_VAR_FONT character font, 99, 106
AppendMenu( ) function, 302-306, 312, 315

Applications, 3
  DOS vs. Windows, 4-5
  operation, 4-5
  running multiple simultaneously, 5-7
  windows, 6
Arc( ) function, 107-108
ASCII character set, 215
Automatic variables, 18-19
Automatic, Static, and Global Variables listing, 19

B
Background painting modes, TRANSPARENT and OPAQUE, 99
Backspace key, 225
BEGIN key word, 288-290
BeginPaint( ) function, 92, 101, 444, 447, 476, 500
Binary flags, 65
BitBlt( ) function, 564-570, 575, 583, 586, 613
BITMAP data format, 590-592
BITMAP.3DEF module definition file listing, 582
BITMAP1 program, 566-570
  BITMAP1.C listing, 568-569
  BITMAP1.DEF module definition file, 570
  BITMAP1.H header file, 569
  BITMAP1.RC resource script file, 567-568
BITMAP2 program, 571-574
  BITMAP2.C listing, 572-573
  BITMAP2.DEF module definition file, 574
  BITMAP2.H header file, 574
  BITMAP2.RC resource script file, 574
BITMAP3 program, 576-583
  BITMAP3.C listing, 579-581
  BITMAP3.H header file, 581-582
  BITMAP3.RC resource script file, 582
  brick bitmap, 577-578
BITMAP4 program
  animation, 584-590
  BITMAP4.C listing, 586-589
  BITMAP4.DEF module definition file, 590
  BITMAP4.H header file, 589
  BITMAP4.RC resource script file, 589-590
BITMAPFILEHEADER data structure, 593-594
BITMAPINFO data structure, 593
BITMAPINFOHEADER data structure, 592-593
bitmaps, 13, 304-305, 561-594
  animation, 583-590
  BITMAP data format, 590-592

Clipboard, 601
DIB data format, 591-594
displaying, 564-570
loading files, 563-564
manipulating images in memory, 591
memory, 583-590
raster operation codes, 575-583
storing images, 562-563
stretching and compressing, 570-574
BITMAPTALL constant, 585
BITMAPWIDE constant, 585
BLACKNESS raster operation code, 576
BlockRev( ) function, 650, 652, 654-656, 659, 662, 665
BMP file extension, 304, 563
BM_GETCHECK message, 146-147
BM_SETCHECK message, 145, 148, 346-347, 366
Borland C++, 25
Borland Resource Workshop, 26
    creating menus, 285
    menu program, 292-296
    vs QuickC, 73-74
Brushes, 106
BUTTON class, 125
Button control, 264-265
Button Handle Passed with WM_COMMAND listing, 148
BUTTON program, 140-148
    BUTTON.C listing, 141-143
    BUTTON.DEF module definition File, 144
    BUTTON.H header file, 144
    BUTTON.RC resource script file, 145
BUTTON window class, 52, 61, 125, 139
Button window controls, 139-149
    notification codes, 148-149
    processing messages, 145-147
    styles, 139-140

C

C language
    casting, 138-139
    function calling convention, 47
C0WS.LIB library, 663
C12EXER1.DEF listing, 439
C7EXER03.RC resource script file listing, 252
CallFileDlg( ) function, 668, 672, 674
Caret, 184, 203-204
    input focus, 203
Casting, 138-139, 156
CB_ADDSTRING message, 160
CB_SETCURSEL message, 160
Changes to DELREND.C for exercise 2 listing, 639-641

Changes to EDIT1.C listing, 181
Changes to header file listing, 281
Changes to LISTDLG.C listing, 372
Changes to LISTDLG.H listing, 371
Changes to Popup Window Definition listing, 281-282
Changes to resource script file listing, 280-281
Changes to TEXT1.C WndProc( ) Function Exercise 1 listing, 117-118
Changes to Windows Class Definition listing, 81
Changes to WinMain( ) of GRAPHIC2.C for Gray Background listing, 118-119
Changes to WndProc( ) function of DIALG3.C listing, 373
CHAR1 program, 217-221
    CHAR1.C listing, 219-220
    CHAR1.DEF module definition File, 221
    CHAR1.H header file, 220
    CHAR1.RC resource script file, 221
Character mode vs graphics mode, 84-85
Character sets
    converting between OEM and ANSI, 26
    functions, 216-221
Character strings, 376-377
    determining size, 247
    outputting, 226
    pointers, 404-405
    tables, 13
Characters
    dead, 224-225
    defining, 13
    logical units, 231
CHARARRAY data type, 350-351
Check box button, 140
CHECKED key word, 291, 296
CheckMenuItem( ) function, 300-301
Child windows, 135, 253
    button control, 264-265
    class, 255, 267
    creating, 254-259
    fixed, 266-272
    message processing function, 258
    messages, 267
    minimizing, 260-261
    movable, 260
    sending messages, 259-266
CHILD1 program, 254-259
    CHILD1.C listing, 256-258
    CHILD1.DEF module definition File, 258
    CHILD1.H header file, 259
CHILD2 program, 259-266
    CHILD2.C listing, 262-264
    CHILD2.DEF module definition file, 266

(continued)

699

CHILD2.H header file, 265
CHILD2.RC resource script file, 265
  parent window, 259-260
ChildProc() function, 255, 258, 262, 264-266
ChildProc1() function, 271
ChildProc2() function, 271
Chord() function, 107
Client area, 11
  invalid rectangle, 93
Clipboard, 599-635
  adding functionality to text editor, 628-635
  basic functions, 602-603
  bitmaps, 601
  CF_TEXT format, 603
  copying text into, 602-603
  delayed rendering of data, 618-627
  edit controls, 627-628
  formats, 603-605
  limitations, 605
  multiple formats, 610-618
  operation, 600-602
  text, 601
  user-defined formats, 604
  viewer application, 600
CLIPBRD.EXE file, 600
CLIPBRD1 program, 605-610
  CLIPBRD1.C listing, 607-609
  CLIPBRD1.DEF module definition file, 610
  CLIPBRD1.H header file, 609
  CLIPBRD1.RC resource script file, 609-610
CLIPBRD2 program, 610-618
  CLIPBRD2.C listing, 614-617
  CLIPBRD2.DEF module definition file, 617-618
  CLIPBRD2.H header file, 617
  CLIPBRD2.RC resource script file, 617
CloseClipboard() function, 602
CM_LBUTTONDBLCLK message, 189
CM_MBUTTONDBLCLK message, 189
CM_RBUTTONDBLCLK message, 189
Code, 12
  sharing with program instances, 13
Color, 98-99, 101
COLORREF data type, 98-99
CombinePathFile() function, 543, 545, 674-675
Combo Box window
  class, 126
  control, 156-161
COMBO program, 157-161
  COMBO.C listing, 158-160
  COMBO.DEF module definition file, 161
  COMBO.H header file, 160
  COMBO.RC resource script file, 160
COMBOBOX window class, 126, 156
Command line argument, 51, 77-78
Compilers, 24-25, 34
  changing subdirectory names, 40-41

FAR key word, 30-31
memory models, 29-30
NEAR key word, 30-31
runtime libraries, 644-645
switches, 688
Compiling programs, 14-15, 38-41
  problems, 38-41
  setup problems, 40-41
  typos in module definition file, 40
  typos in programs, 38-39
Complex menus, 296-302
Conditional compilation resources, 377-378
Constants, defining, 377
Contents of MINIMAL2.C project file listing, 56
CONTROL key word, 241
Copyright notices, embedding, 20
CountByTen() function, 18
CreateCaret() function, 203, 207
CreateCompatibleBitmap() function, 583, 585, 591
CreateCompatibleDC() function, 564-565, 613
CreateDC() function, 476-477, 485
CreateDialog() function, 358, 491
CreateDialogParam() function, 358, 362
CreateEllipticRgn() function, 101
CreateFont() function, 213, 231-234, 464
  parameters, 232-234
CreateHatchBrush() function, 104
CreateMenu() function, 302-303, 305
CreatePatternBrush() function, 100, 577, 579
CreatePen() function, 99-100, 103, 445
CreatePopupMenu() function, 302-303, 305
CreateRectRgn() function, 101
CreateSolidBrush() function, 100, 103, 267, 448
CreateWindow() function, 52-53, 64-66, 77, 125-126, 130, 134, 136,139-140, 144, 149-150, 162, 169, 172-174, 255-256, 273, 312, 315, 381, 548
  BS_PUSHBUTTON style parameter, 52
  dwStyle parameters, 129-130
  parameters, 127-128
  yntax listing, 126
Creating and Moving Caret listing, 203-204
Creating Child Window listing, 261
Creating Logical Font listing, 231
Creating MENU2 Program Menu listing, 305-306
Creating New Window Class in MINIMAL3.C listing, 64
Creating Red Pen Three Pixels Wide listing, 99
Creating Three Static Controls in STATIC.C listing, 135
Cursor, 13
  hot spot, 200
  IDC_ARROW, 202
  mouse, 184-185
  stock shapes, 202-203, 205

CURSOR reserved word, 200
CWS.LIB library, 41, 663

D

Data double word, 8
Data structures, 57-58
   DEVMODE, 507
   FILEOPENDATA, 541, 543-545, 549, 672
   MSG, 56, 58-60
   OFSTRUCT, 526
   PAINTSTRUCT, 92-93
   RECT, 93, 381, 390
   TEXTMETRIC, 234
   WNDCLASS, 255
Data types, 45
   CHARARRAY, 350-351
   COLORREF, 98-99
   DWORD, 58
   HANDLE, 45, 47-49
   HWND, 45, 58
   LONG, 58
   LPSTR, 47-49
   POINT, 58
   PSTR, 49
   WORD, 45, 58
Data word, 8
DDLCALL1.DEF module definition
   file listing, 680
Declaring and Initializating COLORREF Value
   listing, 98
DEF file extension, 14, 17
Definition of HANDLE and LPSTR in
   WINDOWS.H listing, 48
DEFPUSHBUTTON key word, 326
DefWindowProc( ) function, 60, 68, 70, 75, 90,
   134, 258, 313, 315, 339
DeleteDC( ) function, 447, 477, 479
DeleteMenu( ) function, 303, 306, 315
DeleteObject( ) function, 104, 304, 445,
   447, 449
Deleting Pen Using Stock Pen to Displace New
   Pen listing, 106
DELREND program, 620-627
   DELREND.C listing, 623-625
   DELREND.DEF module definition file, 626
   DELREND.H header file, 626
   DELREND.RC resource script, 626
DestroyCaret( ) function, 203
DestroyMenu( ) function, 303, 306
DestroyWindow( ) function, 76, 265, 359, 492
DEVCAP program, 499-504
   DEVCAP.C listing, 500-502
   DEVCAP.DEF module definition file
   listing, 503
   DEVCAP.H header file listing, 502-503
Development tools, 25

Device Context (DC), 83, 85, 89-90, 231, 443-468
   changing, 95, 96, 97, 98, 99
   default values, 90
   deleting objects, 105-106
   device units, 453
   forgetting to release, 90
   logical units, 453
   mapping mode, 101, 452-468
   memory, 564-565, 583
   printers, 476-504
   private, 444-452
   scaling, 101
   settings, 100-101
Device context handle (HDC), 89, 101
   Alternative listing, 93
Device independence, 83, 85
DeviceCapabilities( ) function, 498, 508-510, 512
   nIndex values, 509-510
   parameters, 508-509
devices
   calling functions in driver, 497-498
   getting information about, 497-504
DEVMODE data structure, 507
   listing, 507
DIAL1.DLG dialog box definition file, 331
DIALG.H header file for dialog box control ID
   listing, 328
DIALG1 program, 327-340
   DIALG1.C listing, 337-339
   DIALG1.DEF module definition file, 340
   DIALG1.DLG dialog box definition created
      by WRT, 334-335
   DIALG1.DLG dialog box template file, 326
   DIALG1.H header file, 335-336
   DIALG1.RC resource script file listing, 336
   DIALG1D.H header file for dialog box ID
      numbers listing, 335
DIALG2 program, 341-348
   DIALG2.C file listing, 343-346
   DIALG2.DEF module definition file, 347-348
   DIALG2.DLG dialog box definition file, 342
   DIALG2.H header file listing, 347
   DIALG2.RC resource script file, 348
   DIALG2D.H header file, 342
   dialog box template, 341-342
DIALG3 program, 349-357
   DIALG3.C program using the LISTDLG dialog
      box listing, 354-356
   DIALG3.H header file, 356
   DIALG3.RC resource script, 356-357
   DIALGD.H header file for dialog box control
      ID numbers, 332
Dialog base units, 327
Dialog boxes, 323-367
   buttons, 330
   compiling, 327

(continued)

controls in functions, 346-347
definitions, 13
designing, 327-335
dialog base units, 327
exchanging data, 341-357
file selection, 538-547
functions, 339
global variables, 341-349
icon control, 333-334
icons, 330
message proccessing, 346
modal, 357-359
modeless, 357-367, 491
operation, 325-327
pointers, 349-354
push button control, 334
saving definition, 331
setting box frame properties, 333
static text control, 333
system modal, 357-359
target, 329-330
template, 325-327
using, 335-340
Dialog Editor, 31
DialogBox() function, 325-337, 340, 343, 491, 541
DialogBoxParam() function, 349-351, 353, 362, 541, 543, 545, 549, 555, 668
function declaration listing, 349
DialogProc() function, 336, 339-340, 362, 366
DIB data format, 591-594
DISCARDABLE key word, 287-288, 377, 391-392
DISCARDABLE key words, 384
Discardable memory, 401
blocks, 418-427
compacting local heap, 421-422
verifying existance, 419
Disk caching, 530
Disk files. See also files
accessing, 523-556
names, 523
Windows accessing, 524-530
DispatchMessage() function, 62, 67-68, 109, 242, 358, 489, 584
Displaying string from string table listing, 379
Dithering, 99
DLG file extension, 325
DlgDirList() function, 539-540, 542-544
DlgDirSelect() function, 539-544
DLL file extension, 645
DLLCALL program, 655-659
DLLCALL.C listing, 656-658
DLLCALL.DEF for use with import library, 662
DLLCALL.DEF module definition file, 655
DLLCALL.DEF using ordinal number for BlockRev(), 660

DLLCALL.H header file, 658
DLLCALL.RC resource script file, 658-659
DrawBall() function, 109, 114
DrawBallBlt() function, 585-586
DrawBallGDI() function, 585
DrawMenuBar() function, 303, 306
DrawText() function, 381, 388, 390
DRIVINIT.H header file, 505, 508
DRV file extension, 474, 645
DSTINVERT raster operation code, 576-577
DWORD data type, 58, 138
Dynamic data, 12
Dynamic Data Exchange (DDE), 10
Dynamic link libraries (DLL), 504-506, 643-644, 651-678
alternate function referencing, 659-663
compiling, 653-655
converting FILEDLG program to DLL, 666-668
far functions, 648
global variables, 647-648
header files, 653
import libraries, 660-663
memory problems, 666
module definition files, 652
operation, 646
problems, 664-666
programming considerations, 663-664
static variable problems, 646-648
using, 655-659
writing, 648-650

E

Edit Control window class, 126
EDIT window class, 126, 173
Edit window controls, 172-177
Backspace key, 172
Delete key, 172
styles, 173
EDIT1 program, 173-177
EDIT1.C listing, 174-176
EDIT1.H header file, 176
EDIT1.H module definition File, 177
EDIT1.RC resource script file, 177
Ellipse() function, 104, 107-108, 114, 445, 448, 464-465, 484, 586
Ellipses, 464-465
EmptyClipboard() function, 602, 605, 620
EM_GETHANDLE message, 548
EM_GETLINECOUNT message, 174
EM_LINEINDEX message, 174
EM_LINELENGTH message, 174
EM_SETHANDLE message, 548, 550, 628
bug, 556
EM_SETSEL message, 628
EM_SETTABSTOPS message, 150
EnableMenuItem() function, 300, 312

EnableWindow() function, 491-492
END key word, 288-290
EndDialog() function, 325, 339-340, 353, 359, 544-545
EndPaint() function, 92, 102, 104, 447
Enhanced mode, 18
Enlarging Popup Window listing, 282
Error in MINIMAL1.DEF listing, 40
Error messages, 39-40
Escape() function, 477-478, 485, 489
Example module definition File (MINIMAL1.DEF) listing, 20
Example string tables listing, 378
Excerpt from FONT2.C Showing Caret Sizing and Positioning listing, 247
EXE file extension, 645
EXE files, unfinished, 14
Exit code, 47
ExitDeviceMode() function, 498
ExtDeviceMode() function, 505-507, 510, 512

F

FAR key word, 30-31
Far pointer, 48
FConvert program, 26
FILE1 program, 531-538
 displaying messages, 532
 FILE1.C listing, 534-536
 FILE1.DEF module definition file, 537
 FILE1.H header file, 536-537
 FILE1.RC resource script file, 537
FILE2 program, 547-556
 edit control, 548
 file selection dialog box, 549-550
 FILE2.C listing, 550-554
 FILE2.DEF module definition file, 556
 FILE2.H header file, 554-555
 FILE2.RC resource script file, 555
FILEDLG program, 540-547
 converting to DLL, 666-668
 FILEDLG.C listing, 545-547
 FILEDLG.H header file, 541-542
 FILEDLG.RC resource script file, 542
FILEOPENDATA data structure, 541, 543-545, 549, 672, 674
FileOpenProc() function, 543, 545, 555, 672
Files
 accessing, 523-556
 closing, 530
 current position, 529
 listing, 539-540
 module definition (DEF), 14, 17, 20-21
 names, 20
 object, 34
 opening, 525-527
 project, 33

reading and writing data, 527-529
resource data, 14
resource script, 17
selection dialog box, 538-547
source code, 35
unfinished EXE, 14
FILESEL.DLL program, 666-675
 FILESEL.C listing, 668-671
 FILESEL.DEF module definition file, 673
 FILESEL.H header file, 672
 FILESEL.RC resource script file, 673
 using, 674-678
FILETEST program, 674-678
 FILETEST.C listing, 675-676
 FILETEST.DEF module definition file, 676-677
 FILETEST.H header file, 677
 FILETEST.RC resource script file, 677
Filling List Box in LISTBOX.C listing, 154
FindResource() function, 386-387, 393
FIXCHILD program, 266-272
 FIXCHILD.C listing, 268-271
 FIXCHILD.DEF module definition file, 272
 FIXCHILD.H header file, 272
 FIXCHILD.RC resource script file, 272
Fixed child windows, 266-272
FIXED key word, 287-288, 391
fixed memory, 401
 blocks, 408-409
Fixed-pitch fonts, 230
FON file extension, 230
FONT keyword, 331
FONT1 program, 235-239
 FONT1.C listing, 236-238
 FONT1.DEF module definition file, 239
 FONT1.H header file, 238
 FONT1.RC resource script file, 239
FONT2 program, 242-248
 FONT2.C listing, 244-246
 FONT2.DEF module definition file, 248
 FONT2.H header file, 248
 FONT2.RC resource script file, 243
Fonts, 13, 100, 106, 213
 allowing user to choose, 235-239
 ANSI_FIXED_FONT, 106
 ANSI_VAR_FONT, 99, 106
 creating new, 231
 files, 230
 fixed-pitch, 230
 loading into memory, 231
 logical, 230-234
 stock, 229-230
 SYSTEM_FONT, 106
 text metrics, 234-235
 variable-pitch, 230
FOT file extension, 230
FreeLibrary() function, 506, 512

(continued)

FreeProcInstance() function, 337, 492, 668
FreeResource() function, 386, 389, 394, 623
Functions
    controls, 346-347
    device driver, 497-498
    global variables, 343
    memory allocation, 427
    passing addresses, 336-337
    passing handles, 407-408
    printer driver, 504-516
    tracking, 21

G

GDI.EXE file, 85
GetClipboardData() function, 602, 604, 607-608, 613-614, 618, 620
getcwd() function, 544, 549, 645, 667
GetDC() function, 89-90, 92, 101, 444-446, 447, 476, 505
GetDeviceCaps() function, 497-504
GetDlgItem() function, 346
GetKBCodePage() function, 221
GetMenu() function, 299
GetMenuState() function, 301-302
GetMenuString() function, 302
GetMessage() function, 54-55, 58-61, 67-68, 90, 108, 224, 358, 584-585
GetObject() function, 613
GetParent() function, 271
GetProcAddress() function, 506, 512
GetProfileString() function, 476
GetScrollPos() function, 163
GetScrollRange() function, 163
GetStockObject() function, 65, 106, 230, 236
GetSystemDirectory() function, 511
GetSystemMenu() function, 312
GetSystemMetrics() function, 196, 207, 247, 315
GetTextExtent() function, 100, 247, 483-484
GetTextMetrics() function, 234-235, 247, 502
Getting Handle to Previously Selected Pen listing, 105
GetWindowExt() function, 456, 463
GetWindowsDirectory() function, 511
GetWindowWord() function, 128, 201, 668
Global heap, 20, 402-404
Global memory
    allocation, 427-435
    blocks, 428-429
    flags, 428
    vs local, 402-404
Global variables, 18-19, 111
    exchanging dialog box data, 341-349
    DLLs, 647-648
    functions, 343
    problems, 348-349

GlobalAlloc() function, 427-428, 430
GlobalCompact() function, 427, 430
GlobalDiscard() function, 427
GlobalFlags() function, 427
GlobalFree() function, 427-429
GlobalLock() function, 427
GlobalLock() function, 428, 435-436
GlobalReAlloc() function, 427, 429-430
GlobalSize() function, 606
GlobalUnlock() function, 394, 427-428
Glossary, 690-695
GMEM1 program, 429-435
    GMEM1.C listing, 431-433
    GMEM1.DEF module definition file, 434
    GMEM1.RC resource script file, 434
GRAPHIC1 program, 102-106
    GRAPHIC1.C listing, 102-103
    GRAPHIC1.DEF module definition file, 104-105
    GRAPHIC1.H header file, 104
    GRAPHIC1.MAK QuickC project file, 105
    GRAPHIC1.PRJ Turbo C++ project file, 105
    GRAPHIC1.RC resource script file, 104
GRAPHIC2 program, 107-115
    GRAPHIC2.C listing, 111-114
    GRAPHIC2.DEF module definition file, 109
    GRAPHIC2.H header file, 110
    GRAPHIC2.MAK QuickC project file, 110
    GRAPHIC2.PRJ Turbo C++ project file, 110
    GRAPHIC2.RC listing, 110
    PeekMessage() loop, 108
Graphical environment, 3
Graphical User Interface (GUI), 3
Graphics
    animated, 107-115
    functions, 107
    NULL brush and NULL pen, 106
    output, 83, 101-107
    toggling, 110
Graphics Device Interface (GDI), 85-86
Graphics mode vs character mode, 84-85
GRAYED key word, 291, 296
Group boxes, 140

H

HAND.ICO cursor hot spot, 200
HANDLE data type, 45, 47-49
Handles, 49-50
    instance, 51
    NULL values, 51
    WNDCLASS data structure, 65
Hardware requirements, 24
Header file containing string table ID numbers, 378
Header files
    dynamic link libraries (DLL), 653
    Turbo C++ pre-compiled, 46

Heap, 18-20
HEAPSIZE key word, 425-426
HideCaret() function, 203
HIWORD() macro, 111, 185, 190
HOUSE.BMP file, 567-568
Hungarian Notation, 48-51
  used in declaring variable types listing, 49
HWND data type, 45, 58

I

ICON key word, 385
Icons, 13
  program, 71-72
  static, 135-136
Image Editor, 31
IMAGE.BMP file, 564
Import libraries, 26, 660
  creating, 661
  linking automatically, 662-663
  QuickC, 662
  Turbo C++, 662
  using, 661-662
IMPORT.LIB library, 663
IMPORTS key word, 659
Input focus, 193-194, 222
  caret, 203
InsertMenu() function, 302-303, 304
INSTALL program, Turbo C++ for Windows, 26
Instance handle, 51
InStr() function, 672
Instructions, 12
InvalidateRect() function, 169, 226, 422
IsAnsiPunc() function, 226, 228, 238
ischar() function, 216
IsCharAlpha() function, 216
IsCharAlphaNumeric() function, 226
IsCharAlphNumeric() function, 216
IsCharLower() function, 216
IsCharUpper() function, 216
IsClipboardFormatAvailable() function, 604, 614
IsDialogMessage() function, 358, 362, 491

K

KEYBD1 program, 225-229
  Backspace key, 225
  KEYBD1.C listing, 226-228
  KEYBD1.DEF module definition File listing, 229
  KEYBD1.H header file listing, 228-229
  KEYBD1.RC resource script file listing, 229
  static character buffer, 225-226
Keyboard, 214
  ANSI character set, 215-217
  dead characters, 224-225
  determining key pressed, 222
  interface, 225-229

international symbols, 215-216, 225
  keyboard accelerators, 213
  language installed, 221
  message processing, 221-223
  system key messages, 224-225
  translating combination of keys, 223-224
  translation table, 221
  virtual key codes, 222-223
Keyboard accelerators, 213, 240-243
  processing, 241-242
Keyboard shortcuts, 13, 72, 75
Keys
  specifying, 241
  virtual key code, 241
KillTimer() function, 313-315

L

LB_ADDSTRING message, 154, 351
LB_GETCURSEL message, 155
LB_GETTEXT message, 149, 155
LB_RESETCONTENT message, 154
LB_SETCOLUMNWIDTH message, 149
LIB file extension, 645
LibMain() function, 648, 650, 655, 665, 667-668
LIBRARY key word, 652
Lines, drawing, 101
LineTo() function, 107, 190, 458
Linker programs, 34
  switches, 688
List Box window class, 126
List Box window control, 149-156
  styles, 149-150
LISTBOX program, 150-156
  LISTBOX.C listing, 151-152
  LISTBOX.DEF module definition file, 153
  LISTBOX.H header file, 153
  LISTBOX.RC resource script file, 153
LISTBOX window class, 126, 149
ListDialogProc() function, 350-351, 353
LISTDLG.C listing, 352-353
LISTDLG.DLG dialog box template file listing, 354
LISTDLG.H header file listing, 350
LoadAccelerators() function, 241-243
LoadBitmap() function, 304-305, 564, 592, 612
LoadCursor() function, 65, 201-202, 205
LoadIcon() function, 65, 261
Loading and accessing TEXT custom resource OneLine listing, 386-387
Loading Icon Data from Program's Resource Data listing, 261
Loading Stock Cursor listing, 202
Loading Stock Icon listing, 261
LoadLibrary() function, 505, 512
LoadMenu() function, 302-303

(continued)

705

LoadModule( ) function, 650
LOADONCALL key word, 287-288, 377, 384, 391
LoadResource( ) function, 386-387, 393, 428, 592
LoadString( ) function, 378-379, 448, 656
Local heap, 19, 376, 402-404
   compacting, 421-422
   MEM3 program, 425-426
   setting size, 21
Local memory
   allocating, 410-413
   blocks, 405-409
   setting aside space, 408
   vs global, 402-404
Local variables, 111
LocalAlloc( ) function, 405-406, 409, 414, 419, 427, 533
   flags, 406
LocalCompact( ) function, 421-422, 427
LocalDiscard( ) function, 420, 427
LocalFlags( ) function, 419, 422, 427
LocalFree( ) function, 407, 409-410, 415, 420, 423, 427
LocalLock( ) function, 406-407, 409-410, 415, 427, 435
LocalReAlloc( ) function, 414-420, 422, 427
LocalUnlock( ) function, 406-407, 410, 420, 423, 427
LockResource( ) function, 386-387, 393, 428
Logical fonts, 230-234
LONG data type, 58, 138
LOWORD( ) macro, 111, 148, 164, 185, 190
LPSTR data type, 47-49
lstrcat( ) function, 217-218
lstrcmp( ) function, 217
lstrcompi( ) function, 217
lstrcpy( ) function, 217-218, 406
lstrlen( ) function, 217-218

M

main( ) function, 47
MAKE utilities, 686-688
MakeProcInstance( ) function, 337, 489, 492, 506, 668
MAPMODE program, 456-462
   MAPMODE.C listing, 458-461
   MAPMODE.H header file, 461
   MAPMODE.RC resource script file, 461-462
Mapping modes
   default, 453
   device context, 452-468
   moving origin, 455-462
   printers, 483-485
   scalable, 462-468
   text, 454-455

Masking, 187
MDIALG program, 359-367
   MDIALG.C listing, 363-366
   MDIALG.DEF header file, 367
   MDIALG.DLG dialog template file, 361
   MDIALG.H header file, 367
   MDIALG.RC resource script file, 361-362
MDIALGD.H header file, 360
Medium memory model, 30
MEM1 program, 410-413
   MEM1.C listing, 410-412
   MEM1.DEF module definition file, 413
   MEM1.H header file, 412
   MEM1.RC resource script file, 412-413
MEM2 program, 414-418
   MEM2.C listing, 415-417
   MEM2.DEF module definition file, 418
   MEM2.H header file, 417
   MEM2.RC resource script file, 418
MEM3 program, 420-427
   decimal handles and addresses, 420
   local heap, 425-426
   MEM3.C listing, 423-425
   MEM3.DEF module definition file, 426
   MEM3.H header file, 426
   MEM3.RC resource script file, 426-427
Memory
   addresses, 435
   allocating local, 410-413
   allocation functions, 427
   bitmaps, 583-590
   block lock count, 407
   color planes, 498
   controlling options, 20
   device context, 564-565, 583
   discardable, 17-18, 401, 418-427
   extra blocks, 65
   far addresses, 403
   fixed, 17-18, 401
   global, 427-435
   LOADONCALL option, 17
   local blocks, 405-409
   local vs global, 402-404, 429-430
   managing, 16-18, 401-437
   models, 29-31
   moveable, 17-18, 401
   moving objects, 16-17, 50
   MULTIPLE option, 18
   near addresses, 403
   options, 17-18
   passing handles to functions, 407-408
   pointers, 30-31
   PRELOAD option, 17
   requesting blocks, 19-20

resizing block, 414-418
resource management, 17
segments, 19, 30
SINGLE option, 18
system, 436
Windows, 435-437
Menu Definition listing, 72, 291
MENU1 program, 296-302
    MENU1.C listing, 297-299
    MENU1.DEF menu definition file, 301
    MENU1.H header file, 297
    MENU1.RC resource script file, 296
MENU2 program, 304-311
    MENU2.C listing, 307-310
    MENU2.DEF module definition file, 311
    MENU2.H header file, 310-311
    MENU2.RC resource script file, 305
MENUBARBREAK key word, 291, 297
MENUBREAK key word, 291
MENUITEM key word, 288, 290, 294, 297
MENUITEM SEPARATOR key word, 291
Menus, 13, 283-291, 303-319
    bitmaps, 305
    Borland Resource Workshop, 292-296
    check marks, 290
    checked/unchecked states, 300-301
    complex, 296-302
    creating, 285
    creating as program operates, 302-311
    defined as resource data, 285-287
    defining, 72, 285, 288
    determining item status, 301-302
    enabling/disabling items, 300
    functions, 299-301
    grayed items, 290-291
    handle, 299
    items, 288-291
    keyboard shortcuts, 72, 75
    loading options, 287-288
    memory options, 287-288
    multiline, 291
    popup, 204-205, 289-290, 296-299
    removing from menu, 303
    separators, 291
    system, 311-319
Message loop, 11, 68
    importance, 60-61
    program using modeless dialog box listing, 359
MessageBeep() function, 76, 87
MessageBox() function, 147, 299, 382
Messages, 7-10, 58-60
    Button window control, 145-147
    channeling, 9
    child windows, 259-267

data double word, 8
data word, 8
defining your own, 147
displaying, 532
ID, 7
keyboard processing, 221-223
MINIMAL1.C file, 54
mouse, 8, 194
nonclient mouse, 194-195
passing to programs, 7
processing, 62, 67-69
putting on-screen, 299
system key, 224-225
time, 8
window controls, 136-137
window ID, 7
Microsoft C++ Compiler version 7.0, 25
Microsoft command line compiler, 688, 689
Microsoft Dialog Box Editor (DBE), 328
    buttons, 330
    default style, 329-330
    saving definition, 331
Microsoft NMAKE file listing, 689
Microsoft QuickC for Windows, 25
    debugging, 32-33
    Dialog Editor, 31
    Image Editor, 31
    INSTALL program, 31
    installing, 31-33
    Options/Project menu item, 32
    QC/Win icon, 31
    QuickCase:W program generation tool, 31
    setup, 32-33
    small memory model, 33
    subdirectories, 31-32
    verifying setup, 32
    work subdirectory, 32
Microsoft Windows Software Development Kit (SDK), 25
MINIMAL.C file
    creating windows, 51-52
    message loop, 54-55
    MINIMAL.C listing, 35, 44-45
    MINIMAL.C revisited listing, 53
    MINIMAL.DEF file, 40
    MINIMAL.EXE file, 37-38
    MINIMAL.MAK file, 36-37
MINIMAL1 program, 33, 35-38, 43-45
    compiling and running, 37-38
    MINIMAL1.C file, 33, 35, 46-54
    MINIMAL1.C with typographical error, 39
    MINIMAL1.DEF file, 33, 35-36
    MINIMAL1.EXE file, 33
    MINIMAL1.MAK file, 33

(continued)

MINIMAL1.OBJ file, 33
MINIMAL1.PRJ file, 33, 36-37
MINIMAL2 program, 54-56, 58-61
  message loop, 59
  MINIMAL2.C listing, 55-56
MINIMAL3 program, 61-70
  compiling, 69-70
  EXPORTS statement, 66-67
  MINIMAL3.C listing, 62, 63
  MINIMAL3.DEF module definition file, 67
MINIMAL4 program, 70-78, 285
  compiling resources, 73-74
  defining menu, 72
  module definition file, 74
  passing command line argument, 77-78
  project files, 74, 75
  MINIMAL4.BMK file, 687
  MINIMAL4.C listing, 75-76
  MINIMAL4.DEF listing, 74
  MINIMAL4.H header file listing, 71
  MINIMAL4.ICO file, 71
  MINIMAL4.RC resource script file, 70, 286-287
MM_TEXT mapping mode, 453
Modal dialog boxes, 357-359
Modeless dialog boxes, 357-367, 491
  calling, 362
  defining, 360-361
Modifications to CLIPBRD1.C for Exercise 1 listing, 638-639
Modifications to MOUSE1.C listing, 211
Modifications to PRTDRIV.C listing, 520
Modifications to the DrawBall() Function listing, 120-121
Modified dialog box function listing, 370-371
Modified Printer Abort Procedure listing, 521
Module database table, 67
Module definition file (DEF), 14, 17, 20-21
  CODE statement, 20
  DESCRIPTION statement, 20
  dynamic link libraries (DLL), 652
  EXETYPE statement, 20
  EXPORT statement, 21, 28
  HEAPSIZE statement, 20-21
  MINIMAL4 program, 74
  MULTIPLE statement, 20
  NAME statement, 20
  STACKSIZE statement, 20-21
  STUB statement, 20
  Turbo C++ for Windows, 28
  typos in, 40
Module definition file listing, 681
Mouse, 183-203
  Button messages, 187-189
  capturing, 195-200
  Control key, 185-189
  cursor, 184-185

  messages, 194
  nonclient messages, 194-195
  position, 8
  reshaping cursor, 200-201, 203
  Shift key, 185-189
MOUSE.ICO cursor hot spot, 200
MOUSE1 program, 189-195
  ALT-C (Clear) keyboard shortcut, 193
  input focus, 193-194
  instances, 193
  MOUSE1.C listing, 190-192
  MOUSE1.DEF module definition file, 192
  MOUSE1.H header file, 192
  MOUSE1.RC resource script file, 192
  running with MOUSE2, 196
MOUSE2 program, 196-200
  capturing mouse, 195-200
  MOUSE2.C listing, 197-198
  MOUSE2.DEF module definition file, 199
  MOUSE2.H header file, 199
  MOUSE2.RC resource script file, 199
  running with MOUSE1, 196
MOUSE3 program, 200-208
  MOUSE3.C listing, 205-207
  MOUSE3.DEF module definition file, 208
  MOUSE3.H header file, 207-208
  MOUSE3.RC resource script file, 204
  popup menus, 204-205
  reshaping cursor, 200, 202-203
MOVEABLE key word, 287-288, 377, 383, 391-392
Moveable memory, 401
MoveTo() function, 107, 190, 454, 458
MoveWindow() function, 268, 313, 315
MSG data structure, 56, 58-60
  Definition in WINDOWS.H listing, 56

N

NEAR key word, 30-31
Near pointers, 404
NMAKE utility, 688-689
NMAKE.EXE, 688
NOINVERT key word, 241

O

OBJ file extension, 34
Object files, 34
ObjectC project file for RESOR1 listing, 391
Objects, 124-125
OEM character set, 215
  converting to ANSI character set, 216-217
OEMANSI.BIN file, 221
OemToAnsi() function, 216
OemToAnsiBuff() function, 216
OFSTRUCT data structure, 526
OpenClipboard() function, 602, 618

OpenFile( ) function, 217, 526, 531-532, 534, 549
    flag values, 527
OutDevCapValue( ) function, 499
Outline of DLL listing, 649
OutLocalText( ) function, 407-408
Output, limiting area displayed, 101
Output of Text in TEXT1.C listing, 89
OutputStuff( ) function, 479, 484
OutStringTable( ) function, 499
OWNDC program, 447-452
    OWNDC.C listing, 449-451
    OWNDC.DEF module definition file, 452
    OWNDC.H header file, 451
    OWNDC.RC resource script file, 452

P

PAINTSTRUCT data structure, 92-93
    definition in WINDOWS.H listing, 92
PARAGRPH.TXT file listing, 627
PASCAL function calling convention, 46-47
PASCAL key word, 46
Passing CHARARRAY data to dialog box
    function listing, 351
PatBlt( ) function, 577-578
PATCOPY raster operation code, 577
PATINVERT raster operation code, 576-577
PeekMessage( ) function, 55, 58, 61, 108-109,
    489, 491, 584-585
    Window Message Loop listing, 109
Pens, 106
PickDialogProc( ) function, 346-347
Pictures, 13
Pie( ) function, 107
Pixels, 53
POINT data type, 58
Pointers, 30-31
    character string, 404-405
    conventions, 404-405
    exchanging dialog box data, 349-354
    far, 48
    near, 404
Polygon( ) function, 107
Polygons, filling, 101
Polyline( ) function, 107
PolyPolygon( ) function, 107
POPUP key word, 288-290
Popup menus, 204-205, 289-290, 296-299
POPUP program, 273-277
    POPUP.C listing, 274-276
    POPUP.DEF module definition File, 277
    POPUP.H header file, 276
    POPUP.RC resource script file, 277
PopupProc( ) function, 273
Portion of STATIC.C that Changes the Static
    Text Control listing, 137
PostMessage( ) function, 137-138

PostQuitMessage( ) function, 68-69
PRELOAD key word, 287-288, 391-392
PRINT1 program, 478-483
    PRINT1.C listing, 479-481
    PRINT1.DEF module definition file, 482
    PRINT1.H header file, 481
    PRINT1.RC resource script file, 482
    problems, 482-483
PRINT2 program, 484-488
    PRINT2.C listing, 485-487
    PRINT2.DEF module definition file, 488
    PRINT2.H header file, 487
    PRINT2.RC resource script file, 488
PRINT3 program, 491-497
    PRINT3.C listing, 492-495
    PRINT3.DEF module definition file, 497
    PRINT3.DLG dialog box definition, 496-497
    PRINT3.H header file, 496
    PRINT3.RC resource script file, 496
Printers
    calling functions in driver, 504-516
    device context, 476-477, 497-504
    drivers, 474-475
    mapping modes, 483-485
    scaling output, 483-488
    sending special commands, 477-478
    support, 474-477
    WIN.INI file, 475-476
printf( ) function, 47, 644
Printing, 473-516
    print job interruption, 488-497
PrintStopDlg( ) function, 492
Private device context, 444-452
    using, 446-447
    window, 445-446
Processing of WM_COMMAND Messages in
    BUTTON.C listing, 146
Processing WM_KEYDOWN Messages listing,
    222-223
Processing wParam Flags Sent with
    WM_MOUSEMOVE listing, 186
Program instance, 13, 63
Program loop, 11
    DOS Application listing, 108
Program Manager, 436-437
Program module, 6
Programs
    code, 12
    command line arguments, 51
    compiling, 14-15, 38-41
    dynamic data, 12
    icons, 71-72
    instances, 193
    instructions, 12
    object oriented, 65
    passing message data, 7

(continued)

problems compiling, 38-41
requesting memory blocks, 19-20
resources, 12-13
running more than one copy, 13
segments, 17
sharing code, 645
static data, 12
structure, 10-12
terminating, 68-69, 76
typos in, 38-39
Windows version number, 14
Project file for MINIMAL3 listing, 69
Project files, 33
    QuickC and Turbo C++, 36-37
PRTDRIV program, 510-516
    PRTDRIV.C listing, 512-515
    PRTDRIV.DEF module definition file, 516
    PRTDRIV.H header file, 515
    PRTDRIV.RC resource script file, 515-516
Pseudocode Outline of Windows Program
    listing, 12
PSTR data type, 49
Push buttons, 140

Q

QuickC, 14-15, 25
    creating DLL file, 654-55
    FILESEL.PRJ project file, 674
    FILETEST.MAK project file, 678
    Image Editor, 71-72
    import libraries, 662
    vs Borland Resource Workshop, 73-74
QuickCase:W program generation tool, 31
QWIN.LIB file, 41

R

Radio buttons, 140
Raster
    device, 575
    operation codes, 575-583
RC file extension, 17
RCDATA program, 391-397
    RCDATA.C listing, 394-396
    RCDATA.DEF module definition file, 396
    RCDATA.H header file, 396
    RCDATA.RC script file, 392
RCDATA statement, 391-397
RECT data structure, 93, 381, 390
    Definition in WINDOWS.H listing, 93
Rectangle() function, 103, 107, 114, 443, 452-454,
    464-465, 473, 477, 479, 483
RegisterClass() function, 61-62, 64, 66, 125,
    127, 201, 255
RegisterClipboardFormat() function, 604,
    612-613
Registering First Child Window Class listing, 267

ReleaseCapture() function, 197
ReleaseDC() function, 89-90, 92, 102,
    445-446, 454
RES file extension, 14
RESOR1 program, 384, 386-391
    RESOR1.C listing, 388-389
    RESOR1.DEF module definition file, 390
    RESOR1.H header file, 390
    RESOR1.RC resource script file, 385
Resource data file (RES), 14, 70
Resource script file, 17, 70, 73-74
    for exercise 1 listing, 399
    string tables, 377
Resource Workshop Dialog Editor, 331-335
Resources, 12-13, 375, 384
    accelerators, 13
    bitmaps, 13
    compiling, 14, 73-74
    conditional compilation, 377-378
    cursors, 13
    custom data, 70-78
    dialog box definitions, 13
    fonts, 13
    icons, 13
    integer data storage, 392-393
    locating and loading custom, 386-387
    memory management, 17
    menus, 13, 285-287
    percent free, 436
    storing static data, 375
    string tables, 13, 376-384
    TEXT, 384-385
    user-defined, 13, 384-397
return() function, 69
REVSTR.DLL program, 650-653
    REVSTR.C listing, 651-652
    REVSTR.DEF module definition file, 652, 659
    REVSTR.H header file listing, 653
    REVSTR.LIB file, 662
REVSTRF.C listing, 664-665
RGB color model, 98-99
RGB() macro, 98-99
RGBQUAD data structure, 592-593
RoundRect() function, 107
Runtime libraries, 644-645

S

Safely Deleting Pen listing, 106
Scalable mapping modes, 462-468
SCRINVERT raster operation code, 576-577
Scroll Bar window
    class, 126
    controls, 161-172
SCROLL.H header file listing, 171
SCROLL1 program, 164-168
    SCROLL1.C listing, 165-167

SCROLL1.DEF module definition file, 168
SCROLL1.H header file, 167
SCROLL1.RC resource script file, 167
SCROLL2 program, 168-172
  SCROLL2.C listing, 169-171
  SCROLL2.DEF module definition file, 172
  SCROLL2.RC resource script file, 171
SCROLLBAR window class, 126, 162
Segmented memory model, 29-30
Segments, 17
Selction of List Box Item in LISTBOX.C listing, 155
Selection of List Box Item in LISTBOX.C listing, 156
SelectObject() function, 100, 105, 230, 236, 564-565
SelectPalette() function, 101
SendDlgItemMessage() function, 346-347, 366
SendMessage() function, 136-138, 143, 146-148, 154-156, 262, 271, 346, 627
SetBkColor() function, 99-100
SetBkMode() function, 100, 448
SetCapture() function, 196-197
SetCaretPos() function, 204
SetClipboardData() function, 602, 604, 606, 612, 618-622
SetClipRgn() function, 101
SetCursor() function, 201-202, 205
SetCursorButton() function, 366
SetDC() function, 484
SetFocus() function, 194, 492
SetHandleCount() function, 525
SetMapMode() function, 101, 454, 458
SetMenu() function, 302-303, 306
SetMkMode() function, 99
SetPolyFillMode() function, 101
SetRadioButtons() message, 347
SetRect() function, 381
SetROP2() function, 101
SetScrollPos() function, 163-165
SetScrollRange() function, 163-164
SetStretchBltMode() function, 572
SetTextAlign() function, 100, 458
SetTextCharacterExtra() function, 100
SetTextColor() function, 99-100, 226, 446, 448
SetTextJustification() function, 100
SetTimer() function, 313-314
Setting Mouse Cursor Shape listing, 201
SetViewportExt() function, 463, 465
SetViewportOrg() function, 101, 456, 458, 464
SetWindowExt() function, 463, 465
SetWindowOrg() function, 101, 456, 464
SetWindowText() function, 136-137, 165, 196, 461
SHIFT key word, 241
Shortcut keys. See keyboard accelerators
ShowCaret() function, 203
ShowScrollBar() function, 163, 169
ShowWindow() function, 51, 53, 255, 313, 315

SIMPEDIT program, 628-633
  SIMPEDIT.C listing, 629-633
  SIMPEDIT.DEF module definition file, 635
  SIMPEDIT.H header file, 633-34
  SIMPEDIT.RC resource script file, 634-635
SINGLE key word, 652
sizeof() function, 379, 408
SizeOfResource() function, 387
Small memory model, 30
SMARTDRV.SYS program, 530
Software requirements, 24
Solution to Chapter 15 exercise 2 listing, 560
Solution to exercise 2 listing, 440-441, 471-472
Solution to Exercise 8-1 listing, 280
Source code file, 35
Specifying Load and Memory Options listing, 288
SplitFilePath() function, 545
SplitPathFile() function, 544
SRCCOPY constant, 575-576
Stacks, 18-20
Static character buffer, 225-226
Static data, 12
  storing in resources, 375
Static icons, 135-136
STATIC program, 131-137
  STATIC.C listing, 131-133
  STATIC.DEV listing, 133
  STATIC.H header file, 133
  STATIC.RC resource script file, 134
Static Text window class, 125
Static variables, 18-19
  problems in DLLs, 646-648
STATIC window class, 125, 130
Static window controls, 130-137
  styles, 130-131
Stock
  cursor shapes, 202-203, 205
  fonts, 229-230
  objects, 106
StretchBlt() function, 570-575, 583
  parameters, 570-571
String tables, 13, 376-384
  defining, 377
  embedding unprintable characters, 379-380
  ID numbers, 378
  loading into memory, 378-379
  using data, 378-379
StringAtPoint() function, 578
Strings
  copying and comparing, 217
  copying formatted to character buffer, 147
  functions, 217
  length, 218
  outputting, 218-219
  printing backwards, 650-653
  upper- and lowercase, 218

(continued)

STRINGTABLE key word, 377
StringTableMessage( ) function, 380-382
StringTableMessageBox( ) function, 531-532
strok( ) function, 645
strstr( ) function, 667
STRTAB program, 379-384
    STRTAB.C listing, 382-383
    STRTAB.DEF module definition file, 383-384
    STRTAB.H header file, 380
    STRTAB.RC resource script file, 380
strtok( ) function, 476-477
strupr( ) function, 218
Subdirectories, listing, 539, 540
Syntax error message, 40
SYSMENU program, 313-319
    setting timer, 313-314
    spaceship icon, 313
    SYSMENU.C listing, 316-317
    SYSMENU.DEF module definition file, 318
    SYSMENU.H header file, 318
    SYSMENU.RC resource script file, 318
System
    compilers, 24-25
    development tools, 25
    hardware requirements, 24
    memory, 436
    setting up, 23-29
    software requirements, 24
    Windows 3.0 or 3.1, 24
System key messages, 224-225
System menu, 311-319
    item ID values, 312
System modal dialog boxes, 357-359
    template listing, 358
SYSTEM_FONT font, 106

T

TabbedTextOut( ) function, 381
Target dialog box, 329-330
Task Database table, 67
TCDEF.SYM file, 46
TCWIN\INCLUDE directory, 28
TCWIN\WORK directory, 28
TEST.H header file listing, 292
TEST.RC Created by WORKSHOP listing, 295
TESTTEXT.TXT file, 384-385
Text
    alignment, 100
    background, 100
    brush, 100
    Clipboard, 601
    color, 99-100
    displaying, 130
    editing, 172-173
    font, 100
    justification, 100
    mapping modes, 454-455
    origin, 101
    output, 83, 86-95
    pen, 100
    scalable mapping modes, 464
    spacing, 100
Text editor
    adding Clipboard functionality, 628-635
    creating, 547-556
Text files converting between OEM and ANSI character sets, 26
Text metrics, 234-235
TEXT resources, 384-385
TEXT1 program, 86-90
    module definition file, 87
    resource script file, 87
    text disappearing, 90
    TEXT1.C listing, 87-89
    TEXT1.DEF module definition file, 87
    TEXT1.H header file, 86
    TEXT1.RC resource script file, 87
TEXT2 program, 91-95
    invalid rectangle, 93
    TEXT2.C listing, 91-92
    TEXT2.DEF module definition file, 94
    TEXT2.H header file, 94
    TEXT2.RC resource script file, 94
TEXT3 program, 95-99
    TEXT3.C listing, 95-97
    TEXT3.DEF module definition file, 97
    TEXT3.H header file, 97
    TEXT3.RC resource script file, 97
TEXTMETRIC data structure, 234
TextOut( ) function, 89, 100, 218-219, 226, 236, 381, 394, 410, 423, 443, 448, 452-453, 455, 473, 477, 479, 483, 505, 532, 606
TEXTTEXT.TXT file listing, 385
time messages, 8
ToAscii( ) function, 216
tolower( ) function, 216
toupper( ) function, 216
TranslateAccelerator( ) function, 241-243
TranslateMessage( ) function, 75, 109, 223-225, 242, 288, 358, 489, 584
TransmitMessage( ) function, 90
Turbo C++, 14-15, 25
    _export key word, 667
    bug, 667, 668
    checking configuration, 28-29
    compiling and running MINIMAL1, 37-38
    creating DLL file, 653-654
    debugging on/off, 29
    directory names, 27-28
    FConvert program, 26
    import libraries, 26, 662
    installing, 26-29

module definition file (DEF), 28
parameters passed to functions, 38
pre-compiled header files, 46
Resource Workshop, 26, 71-72
setup options, 27-29
small memory model, 28
starting, 27
subdirectories, 26
Turbo Debugger for Windows (TDW), 26
work subdirectory, 26
Turbo C++ icon, 27y
Turbo Debugger for Windows (TDW), 26, 29
typedef statement, 45
Typical message loop with TranslateMessage() listing, 224

U

Undefined symbol error message, 39
UnlockData() function, 650
UnlockResource() function, 386
Unresolved external reference error message, 39
Unsigned long integer, 138
User-defined resources, 13, 384-397
    end of data, 387
    loading and locating, 386-387
    RCDATA statement, 391-397
Using GetTextMetrics() function to find line spacing listing, 235

V

Variable-pitch fonts, 230
Variables
    automatic, 18-19
    global, 18-19
    name prefix codes in Hungarian notation, 48-49
    static, 18-19
Vector device, 575
Virtual key codes, 222-223, 241, 683-685

W

WaitMessage() function, 54-55, 58
WEP() function, 648, 650, 655
WHITENESS raster operation code, 576
WIN.COM program, 3
WIN.INI file, printers, 475-476
Window controls, 123-137
    Button, 139-149
    casting, 156
    class types, 126
    Combo Box, 156-161
    Edit, 172-177
    List Box, 149-156
    Scroll Bar, 161-172
    sending messages, 136-137
    static, 130-137
    types, 125

Windows, 6, 124-278
    accessing disk files, 524-530
    advantages, 3
    automatic repainting, 90
    background color brush, 65
    BUTTON, 52, 61, 125, 139
    channeling messages, 9
    child, 135, 253-272
    classes, 52, 61-66
    client area, 11, 194, 456, 499
    Combo Box class, 126
    COMBOBOX class, 126, 156
    creating, 51-53
    cursor, 65
    default actions, 60
    defining, 2-3
    EDIT class, 126, 173
    Edit Control class, 126
    enhanced mode, 18
    exit code, 47
    file function names, 525
    GDI module, 436-437
    Graphical Environment, 3
    icon, 65
    ID, 7
    input focus, 193-194, 222
    KERNAL portion, 445
    List Box class, 126
    LISTBOX class, 126, 149
    memory, 16-18, 435-437
    menu name, 65
    MyClass class, 63-64
    nesting, 264-265
    new classes, 64
    nonclient area messages, 194-195
    operation, 1
    popup, 253, 273-277
    printer support, 474-477
    private device context, 445-446
    program module, 6
    program structure, 10-12
    resizing, 11
    Scroll Bar class, 126
    scroll bars, 168-172
    SCROLLBAR class, 126, 162
    setting caption, 196
    size and location, 53
    starting, 3
    STATIC class, 125, 130
    Static Text class, 125
    style information, 52
    USER module, 436-437, 445
    version 3.0 and 3.1, 24
    viewing/hiding, 53
    WS_OVERLAPPEDWINDOW style, 66
WINDOWS.H Excerpt listing, 45

(continued)

WINDOWS.H header file, 44-46
  binary flags, 65
  character string pointer notation, 404
  LPTR definition, 409
  raster operation codes, 578
WinMain function()
  hInstance parameter, 51
  hPrevInstance parameter, 51
  lpszCmdLin parameter, 51
  parameters, 50-51
WinMain() function, 38, 46-48, 56, 62-64,
    67, 69, 111, 188-189, 196, 205, 224, 241,
    243, 255, 261, 267, 273, 297, 306, 381,
    410, 448, 584
  lpszCmdLine parameter, 77, 78
WINSTUB.EXE program, 20
WM_CHAR message, 75, 223-225, 240
WM_CHARTTOITEM message, 150
WM_CLOSE message, 359
WM_COMMAND message, 76, 89, 128, 137,
    144-148, 150, 154-157, 174, 177, 195, 200,
    205, 240-243, 255, 265, 267, 271, 288-289,
    297, 299, 306-307, 339-340, 346-347, 353, 366
WM_COPY message, 627
WM_CREATE message, 111, 128, 134, 164, 235,
    264, 267, 271, 273, 304-305, 315, 410, 415,
    448, 510, 548
  title listing, 548
WM_CUT message, 628
WM_DEADCHAR message, 225
WM_DESTROY message, 68, 76, 315, 410, 415, 449
WM_DESTROYCLIPBOARD message, 620, 623
WM_FOCUS message, 207
WM_HSCROLL message, 164-165
WM_INITDIALOG message, 339, 346, 351,
    362, 366, 543
WM_KEYDOWN message, 54, 75, 222-226, 240
WM_KEYUP message, 222-225
WM_KILLFOCUS message, 194, 203, 246
WM_LBUTTONDOWN message, 54, 59-60, 188,
    194, 200, 204
WM_LBUTTONUP message, 188
WM_MBUTTONDOWN message, 188
WM_MBUTTONUP message, 188
WM_MOUSEMOVE message, 54, 184-185, 189,
    194-196, 200, 366
  notation codes, 185-187
WM_MOUSEMOVE() function, 190
WM_MOVE message, 315

WM_NCLBUTTONDBLCLK message, 195
WM_NCLBUTTONDOWN message, 195
WM_NCLBUTTONUP message, 195
WM_NCMBUTTONDBLCLK message, 195
WM_NCMBUTTONDOWN message, 195
WM_NCMBUTTONUP message, 195
WM_NCMOUSEMOVE message, 194
WM_NCRBUTTONDBLCLK message, 195
WM_NCRBUTTONDOWN message, 195
WM_NCRBUTTONUP message, 195
WM_PAINT message, 90, 92-93, 95, 103, 136,
    169, 218, 226, 236, 247, 258-259, 343, 354,
    393, 410, 422-423, 444, 446-448, 458, 465,
    500, 512, 572, 577
WM_PASTE message, 627
WM_QUERY OPEN message, 313
WM_QUIT message, 68, 108-109, 585
WM_RBUTTONDOWN message, 60, 188, 197
WM_RBUTTONUP message, 188
WM_RENDERALLFORMATS message, 622
WM_RENDERFORMAT message, 618, 620-621, 622
WM_SETCURSOR message, 201-202, 205, 307,
    362, 366
WM_SETFOCUS message, 194, 203, 246
WM_SETREDRAW message, 149
WM_SETTEXT message, 137-138, 271
WM_SIZE message, 54, 111, 267-268, 313, 315,
    390, 465, 548
WM_SYSCHAR message, 224-225
WM_SYSCOMMAND message, 313, 315
WM_SYSDEADCHAR message, 225
WM_SYSKEYDOWN message, 224-225
WM_SYSKEYUP message, 224-225
WM_TIMER message, 313-315
WM_USER message, 147, 260, 262, 274
WM_VKEYTOITEM message, 150
WM_VSCROLL message, 161
WNDCLASS data structure, 61-62, 64-65, 255
  definition from WINDOWS.H listing, 62
WndProc() function, 21, 62, 66-71, 76, 87, 89-90,
    102, 111, 131, 134, 144, 147, 164, 185-186,
    189-190, 196, 205, 224-226, 242-243, 246,
    255, 258, 264, 266, 268, 271, 273, 297,
    299, 315, 341, 343, 362, 410, 584
  for exercise 2 listing, 400
  MINIMAL3.C listing, 68
  Repositioning Buttons listing, 212
WORD data type, 45, 58, 45
wsprintf() function, 47, 147, 156, 218-219, 394

BUGGED BY DEBUGGING?

Order the Companion Disk for *Windows Programming Primer Plus*®, and avoid typing tedium and trouble.

COMPANION DISK

Not enough time in the day to slave over a hot keyboard? Don't sweat it! We've already done it for you. Thanks to compression technology, over 3.5 megabytes of files comprising the listings and programs in *Windows Programming Primer Plus*® are available on one high-density, 3.5-inch floppy disk.

Let us provide you with all of the source code files featured in this book. Save yourself time spent typing and debugging code, and concentrate on mastering Windows programming. You'll find all of the files organized into chapter directories and named to match the book's listings. Each program has been already pre-tested and debugged by the author, so all you need to do is load each listing into your compiler and run it. You can use the programs exactly as in the book, modify them, or build your own programs from these examples. The complete listings needed to compile the *Windows Programming Primer Plus*® example programs in Borland/Turbo C++ for Windows or QuickC are provided; you'll find code for all the menus, routines, and functions defined in this book. Also included are the resource script and compiled resource files as well as cursors, icons, and bitmaps.

Don't spend another minute typing this code, when you can get it for only $24.95, plus applicable taxes and shipping fees. To order this time-saving companion disk, fill out the order card in this book.

WAITE GROUP PRESS™

WINDOWS API BIBLE
The Definitive Programmer's Reference
Jim Conger

A single, comprehensive, easy-to-use reference with examples for the over-600 Windows Application Programming Interface (API) functions. Like all Waite Group bibles, API functions are organized into categories, preceded by lucid tutorials, and feature Windows version compatibility boxes. Contains the latest information on the new Windows Version 3.1.
**ISBN 1-878739-15-8, Trade paper, 1,158 pp., 7 3/8 x 9 1/4,
companion disk available, $39.95 US/$49.95 Canada**

WORKOUT C
Learn C Through Exercises
David Himmel

This C language training book and software package includes the popular Mix Power C compiler. With Power C you enter the examples into a text editor, compile the code on the spot, then watch your programs run. **Workout C** covers all topics and concepts of C programming from simple to complex and is the ideal companion to **Master C**, The Waite Group's interactive C programming tutorial.
**ISBN 1-878739-14-X, Trade paper, 2 5.25" disks, 825 pp., 7 x 9,
$39.95 US/$49.95 Canada**

C++ PRIMER PLUS
Teach Yourself Object-Oriented Programming
Stephen Prata

Teaches "generic" AT&T C++ 2.0, and 2.1, in the same style as the author's best-selling **New C Primer Plus** (Winner of the CPA's Best How-To Computer Book Award), over 400,000 copies sold. Gentle, step-by-step lessons teach the basics of OOP including classes, inheritance, information hiding, and polymorphism. No C programming experience needed. Perfect for UNIX and DOS. "Prata makes a relatively complex subject—professional programming—clear and enjoyable." — Computer Press Association.
**ISBN 1-878739-02-6, Trade paper, 744 pp., 7 x 9, companion disk available,
$26.95 US/$34.95 Canada**

Send for our unique catalog to get more information about these books, as well as our outstanding and award-winning titles, including:

Master C: Let the PC Teach You C and **Master C++:** Let the PC Teach You Object-Oriented Programming. Both are book/disk packages that turn your computer into an infinitely patient C and C++ professor.

Fractal Creations: Over 40,000 computer enthusiasts who've purchased this book/disk package are creating and exploring the fascinating world of fractals on their computers.

Image Lab: A complete IBM PC-based "digital darkroom" in a unique book/disk package that covers virtually all areas of graphic processing and manipulation, and comes with the finest graphics shareware available today.

Ray Tracing Creations: With the **Ray Tracing Creations** book/disk combination, you can immediately begin rendering perfect graphic objects like the ones in computer movies.

Virtual Reality Playhouse: Jack-in to the world of Virtual Reality with this playful new book/disk package.

Multimedia Creations: Contemplating the jump into multimedia? Do it with **Multimedia Creations** and its powerful bundled *GRASP* program.

Fractals For Windows: This is a perfect companion to **Fractal Creations**, but it probes deeper.

WAITE GROUP PRESS™

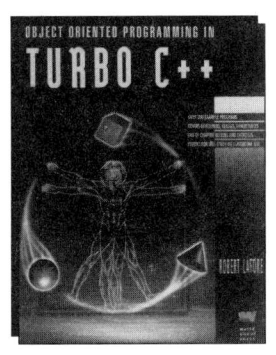

OBJECT-ORIENTED PROGRAMMING IN TURBO C++
Robert Lafore

Suitable for students, hackers, and enthusiasts, Lafore's practical, real-world lessons teach the basics of object-oriented programming, focucing on C++ as a separate language, distinct from C, and assuming no prior experience with C. Covers Turbo C++, Borland C++, and Borland BGI Graphics. Includes objects, classes, overloading, constructors, inheritance, and virtual functions. End of chapter quizzes, exercises, and answers.
ISBN 1-878739-06-9, Trade paper, 776 pp, 7 x 9, companion disk available,
$29.95 US/$38.95 Canada

OBJECT-ORIENTED PROGRAMMING IN MICROSOFT C++
Robert Lafore

A definitive and timely guide to the power of Microsoft's recently released version of the C++ language. Follow this best-selling author as he takes you from the basics of C and C++ to complete competency in C++ and object-oriented techniques. Covers graphics, fonts, animation, and uses both serious and fun programs to illustrate concepts.
ISBN 1-878739-08-5, Trade paper, 744 pp, 7 x 9, companion disk available,
$29.95 US/$38.95 Canada

TO ORDER TOLL FREE CALL 1-800-368-9369
TELEPHONE 415-924-2575 • FAX 415-924-2576
SEND ORDER FORM BELOW TO: WAITE GROUP PRESS, 200 TAMAL PLAZA, CORTE MADERA, CA 94925

Qty	Book	US/Can Price	Total
___	C++ Primer Plus	$26.95/34.95	___
___	Fractal Creations ❑ 3.5" ❑ 5.25" disk	$34.95/44.95	___
___	Fractals For Windows	$34.95/44.95	___
___	Master C ❑ 3.5" ❑ 5.25" disks	$44.95/56.95	___
___	Master C++ ❑ 3.5" ❑ 5.25" disks	$39.95/49.95	___
___	Multimedia Creations ❑ 3.5" ❑ 5.25"	$44.95/56.95	___
___	OOP in Microsoft C++	$29.95/38.95	___
___	OOP in Turbo C++	$29.95/38.95	___
___	Ray Tracing Creations ❑ 3.5" ❑ 5.25" disk	$39.95/49.95	___
___	Virtual Reality Playhouse ❑ 3.5" ❑ 5.25" disk	$22.95/29.95	___
___	Windows API Bible	$39.95/49.95	___
___	Workout C ❑ 3.5" ❑ 5.25" disks	$39.95/49.95	___

Calif. residents add 7.25% Sales Tax ___

Shipping
UPS ($5 first book/$1 each add'l) ___
UPS Two Day ($10/$2) ___
Canada ($10/$4) ___

TOTAL ___

Ship to
Name _____
Company _____
Address _____
City, State, Zip _____
Phone _____

Payment Method
❑ Check Enclosed   ❑ VISA   ❑ MasterCard

Card# _____ Exp. Date _____

Signature _____

SATISFACTION GUARANTEED OR YOUR MONEY BACK. NO QUESTIONS ASKED.

ENVIRONMENTAL AWARENESS

Books have a substantial influence on the destruction of the forests of the Earth. For example, it takes 17 trees to produce one ton of paper. A first printing of 30,000 copies of a typical 480 page book consumes 108,000 pounds of paper which will require 918 trees!

Waite Group Press™ is against the clear-cutting of forests and supports reforestation of the Pacific Northwest of the United States and Canada, where most of this paper comes from. As a publisher with several hundred thousand books sold each year, we feel an obligation to give back to the planet. We will therefore support and contribute a percentage of our proceeds to organizations which seek to preserve the forests of planet Earth.

BREAK into Windows Programming

Subscribe to **Windows Tech Journal**,
the new magazine of tools and techniques for
Windows programmers.

(see other side for more information)

Plan for a programming breakthrough.

To get your free issue and start your no-risk subscription, simply fill out this form and send it to **Windows Tech Journal**, PO Box 70087, Eugene OR 97401-0143 or you can FAX it to 503-746-0071.
You'll get a full year—12 issues in all—of Windows tools and techniques for only **$29.95.**
If you're not completely satisfied write "no thanks" on the subscription bill.
The free issue is yours to keep and you owe nothing.

Windows Tech Journal

NAME

COMPANY

ADDRESS

CITY　　　　　　　　　　　　　　　STATE　　　ZIP

PHONE

For fastest service call **800-234-0386** or FAX this card to **503-746-0071.**

49204

We're breaking Windows programming wide open with **Windows Tech Journal,** the only magazine devoted exclusively to tools and techniques for Windows programmers.

Windows programming demands new skills, new knowledge, and new tools. That's why we've packed **Windows Tech Journal** with authoritative reviews, enlightening articles, and insightful commentary by top Windows experts. **All the Windows information you need in one place.**

Inside every issue, you'll find feature articles on innovative Windows techniques, with complete source code. Our detailed reviews of new products will help you choose the best tool for the job. Columns will keep you up-to-date on C and the SDK, C++ and class libraries, database engines, OOP languages like Actor, Pascal, and Smalltalk, and tools like Visual Basic. A "first look" section will give you advance information on the latest products. We'll tell you which books to add to your Windows library and keep you informed on industry developments.

Plan for a programming breakthrough. For a **FREE ISSUE,** call **800-234-0386** or FAX your name and address to **503-746-0071.** We'll send you a free issue and start your **no-risk** subscription. You'll get a full year—12 issues in all—of Windows tools and techniques for just **$29.95.** If you're not completely satisfied, simply write "cancel" on the invoice. The free issue is yours to keep, and you owe nothing.

Whether you're just getting started with Windows or have been developing for years, **Windows Tech Journal** is for you.

Windows Tech
JOURNAL

NOTES

NOTES

NOTES

NOTES

SATISFACTION REPORT CARD

Please fill out this card if you wish to know of future updates to *Windows Programming Primer Plus*, or to receive our catalog.

WAITE GROUP PRESS™

Company Name: _____

Division/Department: _____ Mail Stop: _____

Last Name: _____ First Name: _____ Middle Initial: _____

Street Address: _____

City: _____ State: _____ Zip: _____

Daytime telephone: (____) _____

Date product was acquired: Month _____ Day _____ Year _____ Your Occupation: _____

Overall, how would you rate *Windows Programming Primer Plus*?
- ☐ Excellent   ☐ Very Good   ☐ Good
- ☐ Fair   ☐ Below Average   ☐ Poor

What did you like MOST about this book? _____
_____
_____

What did you like LEAST about this book? _____
_____
_____

How did you use this book (problem-solver, tutorial, reference...)?
_____

How did you find the pace of this book? _____
_____

What programming tools do you use to write Windows applications?
- ☐ Borland/Turbo C++   ☐ MS-C++   ☐ Windows Software Dev. Kit
- ☐ MS-QuickC   ☐ Other _____

What is your level of computer expertise?
- ☐ New   ☐ Dabbler   ☐ Hacker
- ☐ Power User ☐ Programmer ☐ Experienced Professional

What computer languages are you familiar with? _____
_____

Please describe your computer hardware:
Computer _____   Hard disk _____
5.25" disk drives _____   3.5" disk drives _____
Video card _____   Monitor _____
Printer _____   Peripherals _____

Where did you buy this book?
- ☐ Bookstore (name): _____)
- ☐ Discount store (name): _____)
- ☐ Computer store (name): _____)
- ☐ Catalog (name): _____)
- ☐ Direct from WGP   ☐ Other _____

What price did you pay for this book? _____

What influenced your purchase of this book?
- ☐ Recommendation   ☐ Advertisement
- ☐ Magazine review   ☐ Store display
- ☐ Mailing   ☐ Book's format
- ☐ Reputation of Waite Group Press   ☐ Other _____

How many computer books do you buy each year? _____

How many other Waite Group books do you own? _____

What is your favorite Waite Group book? _____
_____

Is there any program or subject you would like to see Waite Group Press cover in a similar approach? _____
_____

Additional comments? _____
_____
_____

☐ Check here for a free Waite Group catalog

Windows Programming Primer Plus

NO POSTAGE
NECESSARY
IF MAILED
IN THE
UNITED STATES

BUSINESS REPLY MAIL
FIRST CLASS MAIL   PERMIT NO. 9   CORTE MADERA, CA

POSTAGE WILL BE PAID BY ADDRESSEE

Waite Group Press, Inc.
Attention: *Windows Programming Primer Plus*
200 Tamal Plaza
Corte Madera, CA 94925

FOLD HERE

Companion Disk Order Form

Filling out this order form may change your life, help you impress your friends, and perhaps even influence people. The companion disk for *Windows Programming Primer Plus* includes all the program listings contained in this book, organized by chapter, and pre-tested and debugged.

The 3.5-inch, 1.44MB companion disk ensures that you spend more time programming, and less time debugging.

To order by phone call 800-368-9369 or 415-924-2576 (FAX)
or send to Waite Group Press, 200 Tamal Plaza, Corte Madera, CA 94925

Name

Company

Address Street Address Only, No P.O. Box

City   **State**   **ZIP**

Daytime Phone

Quantity and Type

Name	Item #	Quantity	Price	
The Waite Group's *Windows Programming Primer Plus* companion disk	sw004		x $24.95	

Sales Tax—California addresses add 7.25% sales tax.

Shipping—Add $5 USA, $10 Canada, or $30 Foreign for shipping and handling. Standard shipping is UPS Ground. Allow 3 to 4 weeks. Prices subject to change. Purchase orders subject to credit approval, and verbal purchase orders will not be accepted.

Sales Tax

Shipping

Total Due

Disk Type: ☐ 5.25-inch   ☐ 3.5-inch

Method of Payment

Checks or money orders, payable to The Waite Group. To pay by credit card, complete the following:

☐ Visa   ☐ MasterCard   **Card Number**

Cardholder's Name _____   **Exp. Date**

Cardholder's Signature _____

Phone Number _____

©1992 The Waite Group, Inc. All rights reserved. The Waite Group is a registered trademark of The Waite Group, Inc.

**NO POSTAGE
NECESSARY
IF MAILED
IN THE
UNITED STATES**

BUSINESS REPLY MAIL
FIRST CLASS MAIL   PERMIT NO. 9   CORTE MADERA, CA

POSTAGE WILL BE PAID BY ADDRESSEE

Waite Group Press, Inc.
Attention: *Windows Programming Primer Plus*
200 Tamal Plaza
Corte Madera, CA 94925

FOLD HERE